Y0-CCR-696

THE DEVELOPMENT OF MODERN EDUCATION

The Old and the New Methods of Education: Rousseau's Monument at Geneva.

THE DEVELOPMENT OF MODERN EDUCATION

In Theory, Organization, and Practice

Frederick Eby
Professor of the History and Philosophy of Education
The University of Texas

Second Edition

PRENTICE-HALL, INC.
Englewood Cliffs, N. J.

L. C. Cat. Card No.: 52-11504

First printing....................October, 1952
Second printing...............November, 1953
Third printing.......................May, 1955
Fourth printing..............September, 1957
Fifth printing.................January, 1959
Sixth printing................February, 1960
Seventh printing................August, 1961

PRINTED IN THE UNITED STATES OF AMERICA

20762

DEDICATED

IN GRATEFUL MEMORY

TO

ALBERT HENRY NEWMAN

PREFACE

When *The Development of Modern Education* was first written, the reaction against the professional study of the history of education had not yet spent its force. During the years that followed its publication, the gratifying reception accorded this effort to rehabilitate the subject is, perhaps, evidence that a change has set in, and the historical approach to educational understanding has been accepted with more favor. This change of view has for some time called for a revision of the text to keep abreast of the new materials in the field. In the interval, it has become somewhat clearer that, as a professional preparation, history can be most helpful if pursued on the upper and graduate level.

In the new edition, material is condensed, emphasis has been shifted, and several new lines of value have been added. A determined effort has been made to trace causal connections in the various school movements. Most significant in this connection has been the light that Kant's idealistic philosophy and, more particularly, Schiller's aesthetic discussion shed on the revolution of thought at the beginning of the 19th century. For many years the author was unable to account satisfactorily for the sudden change from the utilitarianism of Locke, Rousseau, and Pestalozzi, in the first phase of his educational efforts, to the idealistic position. A closer study of Schiller and the German theorists led to the discovery of the source in aesthetic idealism.

Another major revision has been the attempt to acquaint students with the tremendous developments in the first half of the present century. One must, necessarily, be apologetic for the number, character, and consequence of educational innovations during this period which obviously cannot be adequately treated in a few pages.

The author expresses hearty appreciation for the efficient assistance of Mrs. H. W. Newman in suggesting improvements and correcting the manuscript.

Cordial acknowledgment is also extended to the following publishers, who have consented to the reprinting of excerpts from their works: American Book Company, New York; D. Appleton & Company, New York; Edward Arnold Publishers, London; Bardeen School Supplies, Inc., Syracuse; A. & C. Black, Ltd., London; Cambridge University Press, Cambridge, England; University of Chicago Press, Chicago; Columbia University Press, New York; Concordia Publishing House, St. Louis; Constable & Company, London; F. G. Cottasche Buchhandlung Nachfolger, Stuttgart, Germany; Thomas Y. Crowell Company, New York; De Wolfe, Fiske, & Co., Boston; Harper & Brothers, New York; D. C. Heath & Company, Boston; Dr. Felix E. Held, Ohio State University, Columbus; Hispanic Society of America, New York; Houghton Mifflin Company, Boston; University of Michigan Press, Ann Arbor; Kegan Paul, Trench, Trübner & Co., Ltd., London; Little, Brown & Company, Boston; Longmans, Green & Company, New York; Macmillan Company, New York; McGraw-Hill Book Company, Inc., New York; Moravian Book Shop, Bethlehem, Pa.; National Education Association, Washington; Preserved Smith, Ithaca, New York; Progressive Education Association, Washington; Charles Scribner's Sons, New York; Paul Siebeck, Tübingen, Germany; Teachers College, Bureau of Publications, Columbia University, New York; University Tutorial Press, Ltd., Cambridge, England; Veit & Company, Leipzig, Germany; The American Psychological Association.

FREDERICK EBY

Austin, Texas

TABLE OF CONTENTS

THE DEVELOPMENT OF MODERN EDUCATION

Chapter 1

CONDITIONS THAT CAUSED THE NORTHERN REVOLT AND REFORMATION

A MANY-SIDED transformation. The revolution of the 16th century, usually termed the *Reformation,* was the most far-reaching and profound awakening in the history of western civilization. To think of it merely as a reform of church organization or moral practices and doctrine is to misinterpret its broader significance for human progress. No aspect of human life was untouched, for it involved political, economic, religious, moral, philosophical, literary, and institutional changes of the most sweeping character; it was, in fact, a Nordic revolt and reconstruction.

For a thousand years the Teutonic peoples had been dominated by the Roman world. They had received their religious practices, arts, books, the language of learning and their laws—in fact, all the conventionalities of civilization—from the south. Whatever indigenous contributions may have sprung from their own genius had been transformed and consecrated by an ever-watchful mother church. Now this tutelage was drawing to an end.

These northern peoples found in the free spirit of the Renaissance the stimulus they needed for their independent development.

Discovery and invention. That the busy mind of man was embarking on a vast renovation of ideas and institutions is evidenced by the startling discoveries and inventions which distinguished the period just prior to the 16th century. Successive explorers had pushed back the limits of the geographical environment, and enormously increased man's knowledge of the world. Columbus landed in America, Magellan circumnavigated the globe. Not only did man begin to realize that many of his cherished concepts were discredited, he experienced the re-awakening of his imagination and the challenging of his powers to highest achievement. He began to suspect that his information concerning other fields of knowledge, with their presuppositions, prejudices, and dogmatic assumptions, might be equally erroneous. The shell of medievalism, which had long enclosed and encumbered the human mind, was cracking; soon it was to be completely shattered, and a modern civilization was to emerge.

Of greatest consequence for human culture were the process of making paper, discovered in the 13th century, and the perfection of movable type, by Gutenberg in Mainz about 1438. For centuries, vellum and parchment had been used for records, but these materials were very expensive, and the supply was uncertain. Paper made from rags was cheaper, and it was also fairly easy to secure. The invention of printing vastly increased the supply of books and pamphlets, and greatly assisted, not only in bringing about a profound mental awakening, but also in imparting a powerful desire for learning. Soon presses were set up in Holland, France (at the Sorbonne), Italy, and England. Germany and Switzerland, however, became the most active centers of publishing. Mainz had five printing establishments; Ulm, six; Basle, 16; Augsburg, 20; Cologne, 21; and Nuremberg, 25. In Italy and France publishers were interested particularly in printing the works of ancient classical authors; in Germany books of piety and the Scriptures were the chief works.

The most revolutionizing discovery of the age was still to be made. About the middle of the 16th century, Copernicus gave to the world his astounding theory of heliocentricity, the doctrine that the earth revolves about the sun and is not the center of the universe. The human mind had never been confronted with an idea more incredible or subversive. The effects of this theory in discrediting conceptions of the past cannot be overemphasized. As J. A. Symonds said: [1]

> It is not necessary to add anything to the plain statement; for, in contact with facts of such momentous import, to avoid what seems like commonplace reflection would be difficult.

---

[1] Symonds, J. A., *The Renaissance in Italy; The Revival of Learning,* p. 15. New York: Henry Holt & Company, 1883.

The same year in which Copernicus finally published his revolutionizing theory, 1543, also brought forth another work of far-reaching importance. This was *On the Structure of the Human Body,* by Andreas Vesalius (1514-1564), an anatomist born and educated in the Netherlands. Two years after the publication of these significant works, Jerome Cardan, an Italian professor of mathematics, published the first scientific work on algebra, which he entitled *The Great Art.* This book helped to bring about the synthesis of mathematical knowledge and astronomy that was to produce the most profound changes in human thinking.

Ethics, law, and government. Human relationships have, from earliest times, formed the chief subject of man's reflection and education. In this general field are found the study of morals, and of law and government, and in each of these important changes were taking place which affected the fundamental basis of the schools of Europe during this era.

The moral degradation of western Europe reached its apex during the Renaissance in Italy. So far as the formal study of ethics was concerned, Aristotle's text was taught in the universities and accepted everywhere as authority. Luther rejected this work because it represented a pagan view of life, and was not in accord with the ideals set forth in the Scriptures. Little change was made, however, in the study of the subject in the universities.

In connection with law, highly significant developments took place. During the Middle Ages, two distinct systems of law were in vogue: the civil law of the secular states; and the canon law of the church. The two were actually in conflict in many ways. It will be recalled that the church exercised temporal authority over large portions of Europe. Within these territories, canon law was the accepted law for civilians as well as for the clergy. In all the secular states, priests and other members of religious orders were subject only to canon law and, consequently, could not be tried in the civil courts. Moreover, in many cases, laymen elected to be tried by ecclesiastical courts, in order thus to evade the severer penalties of the civil courts. At first both civil and canon law were studied by the clergy, but in 1254 Pope Innocent IV prohibited the clergy from teaching the civil law. As a consequence, civilians became masters of the civil statutes, and the two types of law grew apart.

In theory, civil law applied to crimes, and canon law to sins; in the eyes of the church, however, all crimes were likewise sins and could, accordingly, be judged by the church courts. Canon law became a powerful instrument in the hands of the unscrupulous. It was employed frequently to advance the policies and interests of the church, to favor the priesthood, and to collect funds from the ignorant masses.

Civil law, too, was often administered in a tyrannical fashion to further the interests of the ruling class. By this means the common people were cheated and oppressed. At the beginning of the 16th century, lawyers were greatly disliked because of their sharp and oppressive practices. The recovery of the Justinian Code, and its substitution for canon law during the Reformation period, constituted one of the most momentous changes. In England, where both forms of jurisdiction were decidedly oppressive, Henry VIII established at the universities professorships of Roman law, and forbade the teaching of canon law. The same changes occurred in the German institutions. Such modifications deprived the church of all jurisdiction over civil issues in Protestant lands, and subjected priests and members of religious orders to the civil courts.

Civilization thus took one of its longest strides, for it now safeguarded the individual against oppression from the priesthood, and made for greater freedom. The Nordic revolt resulted in the establishment of secular government as the supreme power in every Protestant country and made all courts subject to civil control. The suppression of canon law effected the transition from an ecclesiastical, or clerical, to a secular civilization. The translation of the law into vernacular languages was a powerful influence for emphasis on the rights and dignity of the common individual.

Social and institutional changes. The opening of the 16th century marked the termination of one social era and the beginning of another. Never has so short a space of time witnessed such rapid and extensive institutional changes. Many outmoded institutions and customs ceased entirely; and others were altered in varying degrees.

Medieval thought divided the world into the spiritual and the temporal, the sacred and the secular, the realm of grace and the realm of nature. Individuals belonged either to the religious or to the secular, the one being looked upon as more holy than the other. In each division a number of strata, or classes—tier upon tier and rather sharply marked off from each other—formed human society. At the top were the nobility: the Pope and the princes of the church, in the one order; the rulers and the secular princes, in the other. The religious classes ranged from prelates, bishops, and abbots to parish priests and ordinary monks. The laity likewise ranked from the imperial family, electoral princes, minor nobility, knights, and citizens of the free cities to the peasants and serfs.

The passing of knighthood. The knightly class formed a highly active and important element of medieval society. The free knights within the empire owed allegiance directly to the emperor, and formed a fighting force which could be readily mobilized for their incessant wars. They nursed a special grievance against the free cities, the growth of which appeared to them as a degeneration from the "good old times," the golden age of chivalry. The knights generally became free lances, attaching themselves as occasion offered to any cause; they plundered the peasantry of their produce, and took toll of commerce as it moved along the highways of trade.

The invention of gunpowder was the chief cause of the passing of knight errantry. The arrogant knight in coat of mail was no match for even the despised peasant armed with a gun; his moated castle was no defense when his enemy could employ a cannon to batter down his stronghold. Thus the knight witnessed the passing of his order, even as a fighting force. Armed with guns, the common soldiers organized into infantry were much more effective.

At the beginning of the Reformation, Götz von Berlichingen, Franz von Sickingen, and Ulrich von Hutten endeavored by private wars to arrest the decline of the knightly order. The latter two joined in a scheme to overthrow the ecclesiastic princes. They valiantly came to the rescue of the humanist, John Reuchlin, against the obscurantist attack of the Dominicans, and offered shelter to the religious reformers. But all their efforts were in vain, for the feudal order was passing, and a new social structure was taking its place.

Monasteries. This is another of the important institutions of the Middle Ages which was doomed to extinction so far as the Protestant world was concerned. Beginning in the 4th century, monasticism did not reach its climax until the 9th. By that time it had made its most vital contribution to western civilization; and as the centuries passed, it became less and less a true expression of the aspirations of men.

The enormous wealth of the monasteries, as well as the livelihood they provided, still attracted many aspirants. The destruction of these institutions at the time of the Reformation created a great disturbance in society, especially because it affected large numbers of children who would otherwise have entered those institutions for their education and livelihood. This condition involved all of the northern portion of Europe where the monasteries were overthrown and their property and wealth seized by secular princes and barons or transferred to the Protestant churches and the schools.

Ecclesiastical estates and the priestly class. As mentioned previously, the church had large territories over which its beneficiaries were appointed or elected rulers. These ecclesiastical principalities were now abolished in Protestant countries, and became secular states. Similarly, the great foundations by which numerous priests were supported passed into other hands. The civil power of the priesthood, from parish priest to cardinal, was overthrown.

Mendicancy and charity. "Go sell all that thou hast and give to the poor, and thou shalt have treasure in heaven," was an injunction which received a literal interpretation by medieval Christianity. Charity was a means of grace highly exalted by the church; the esteem in which it was held gave rise to mendicant orders, but it likewise so encouraged general begging that Europe was overrun and impoverished by beggars of all kinds. Relief from mendicancy became a pressing problem. Among the reforms demanded by Luther was "the urgent necessity of abolishing all begging in Christendom." Moreover, he placed poor relief under civil, rather than ecclesiastical, authority.

It was the people of the Netherlands, however, who first reached a practical scheme for the suppression of mendicancy. They saw that it was cheaper to prevent pauperism by means of the school than to support it by charity. In 1525 the Council of Ypres formulated with perfect clarity the fundamental principles of public assistance. The council centralized in a common treasury the revenues for all local charitable institutions. Public begging was forbidden. A committee collected all alms, held regular weekly conferences and visited the poor in their homes. The council finally stipulated that the children assisted should be either sent to school or placed in apprenticeship. In 1531 a law was made extending the most important features of this system to all the towns and villages of the Netherlands. Municipalities were required to open schools in which poor children could be taught to care for themselves, and trained for some manual vocation or for domestic service. The subject of poor relief found its most representative discussion in the work of the educational reformer Juan Luis Vives, *On the Support of the Poor* (*De Subventione Pauperum*), published at Bruges in 1526. This book was widely read throughout northern Europe and exerted a powerful influence.

Free towns as centers of progress. The many free towns of northern Europe must be looked upon as the true nurseries of progress; they were, furthermore, the chief factor in the creation of popular schools. The first of these towns grew up where conditions afforded a sheltered harbor either on the sea or on a navigable river. Following the Crusades, manufacturing and commerce greatly increased the population in these ports. Among the seaports which arose in this way were Bruges, Antwerp, and Ghent, in the Netherlands; and Hamburg and Lübeck, in Germany. On the navigable rivers were Paris, London, Cologne, Mainz, and Strassburg.

The cities of the Netherlands throbbed with energy and became models for other towns to emulate. With their manufacturing and trade, these cities rapidly amassed great wealth and far outstripped other places. Bruges, Antwerp, and Ghent had more wealth than either Paris or London, and the Low Countries shared with Italy the greatest opulence. A virtual monopoly of woolen, silk, and linen manufacturing belonged to their weaving guilds. Their tapestries, brocades, and cloths of all kinds became famous everywhere. Porcelain, iron, steel, agricultural products, furs, and fish formed industrial sources of increasing wealth. Moreover, the extraordinary manual skill of these peoples, combined with a genius for invention, produced many new articles which were soon to become the common essentials of civilization.

About the beginning of the 16th century there were in the Netherlands approximately 3,500,000 persons, about the same number as in England; but in wealth, technical skill, and culture, the Netherlands were much in advance of neighboring lands. Concerning their social and industrial condition, we are informed: [2]

> In the sixteenth century, the common people of the Netherlands, owing to their great mechanical, agricultural, and nautical skill, their intelligence and their diversified industries, were the best fed, the best clothed, the best educated, and the most religious in the world.

The primary cause for this extraordinary prosperity must unquestionably be sought in the large measure of liberty and autonomy which was enjoyed by these towns. An indomitable spirit of individualism charac-

---

[2] Griffis, William E., *The Influence of the Netherlands in the Making of the English Commonwealth and the American Republic,* pp. 4-5. Boston: DeWolfe, Fiske & Co., 1891.

terized their inhabitants. Following the example of the Italian cities, these towns early broke away from their overlords, and obtained important rights and privileges. Their security, independence, and power were greatly enhanced by the Hanseatic League, organized to protect commerce against pirates on the sea, and marauding barons and knights on the land.

Some provinces had never submitted to any oppressor, for special circumstances favored the growth of an independent spirit. First, it will be noted that monastic life and ecclesiastical organization had never become so dominant in the Netherlands as in neighboring territories. Again, by virtue of knowledge and skillful seamanship, these peoples had never been subjected to the same degree of feudal servitude that blighted early development elsewhere. Rights and privileges which could not be otherwise obtained were often readily obtainable for gold. Thus, liberty provided a favorable environment for the creative powers and intelligence of these peoples.

Growth of fine art and industry. The restless energies of these centers of the crafts and trades soon turned attention to the higher arts. Not only was there close intercourse with the Italian cities, where culture was revived to the highest degree, but also large numbers of Italian artisans and men of culture settled in the cities of the Netherlands. During the 14th and 15th centuries the peoples of these lands developed architecture, goldsmithing, weaving of artistic tapestries, wood carving, and other fine arts. If the earliest printing from movable type did not take place in the Netherlands, at least the use of wooden blocks which led to printing was first practiced there. Moreover, printing found favorable quarters and a high development in these centers.

Of supreme significance was the sudden and surprising development of painting in Flanders and Holland. Their best painters rivaled those of Italy. The Flemish school of painting was founded by Jan van Eyck (*c.* 1385-1441), who was the first artist to use oil. It has been said that his "imitation of reality has never been surpassed." To the same school belong, at a later period, Rubens (1577-1640) and Van Dyck (1599-1641). The Dutch school also furnished such remarkable figures as Lucas van Leyden (1494-1533), Frans Hals (1581-1666), and Rembrandt (1606-1669).

It would indeed seem strange if this high achievement in arts and crafts could be attained unaccompanied by an advancement in learning. Commerce, the trades and crafts, and even self-government, necessitated the diffusion of writing, reading, and calculation. The towns consequently radiated learning in all directions.

The political and economic factor in the revolution. In large measure the Nordic revolution came about because of oppressive political and economic conditions. From the time when civilization began in northern lands, three main factors tended to unify the scattered social elements which constituted, at first, the tribal and, later, the feudal system.

(1) First of all was the papal church, which had exercised universal sway in all matters of religion and culture. But not only in the spiritual sphere did the church govern; as the centuries passed, in accordance with its unswerving policy the papacy had enormously increased the areas over which it exercised sovereignty. Furthermore, as previously mentioned, it had extended its jurisdiction over the civil and personal affairs of every individual.

At the time of the Reformation, more than one-fourth of the total area of Germany had come under the temporal sovereignty of the church. These ecclesiastical states were ruled by the princes of the church, who were either elected or appointed to their positions and who ranked in power with the hereditary nobility.

(2) Secondly, in the political sphere the Holy Roman Empire constituted the most extensive sovereignty in existence. For a time it was all-powerful; but as centuries passed, the power of the imperial throne gradually diminished until only a shadow of authority remained. Nevertheless it continued to influence civilization in many ways.

(3) The third factor in the political evolution of this period was the process by which the feudal system concentrated more and more power in the hands of the princely houses. By inheritance, intermarriage, warfare, and other means the numerous petty estates had been combined into a comparatively small number of principalities, and, by combining these, the kingdoms of western Europe were gradually formed.

Owing to the greater extent of territory involved and the stabilizing power of the imperial throne, this process of political integration had not gone so far in Germany as it had in France, England, and the Scandinavian lands. At the beginning of the 16th century, the Teutonic people were still divided into more than a hundred petty dukedoms, principalities, and electoral states, each asserting more or less self-determination within the limits of imperial sovereignty. Scattered among these hereditary holdings were over 100 free imperial cities, which jealously guarded their rights and exerted a strong influence in all political and economic affairs. Furthermore, a large number of ecclesiastical states existed alongside the domains of the secular princes. As a consequence of the distribution of power, successive popes, cardinals, emperors, electoral princes, ecclesiastical princes, and the various orders of lesser nobility engaged in interminable intrigues, alliances, rivalries, and armed conflicts, in which each struggled to wrest greater power, wealth, and territory for himself.

These developments paved the way for the great northern revolt. The Church of Rome had come to be looked upon not only as a tyrannical, but, what was worse in the eyes of the people, as a foreign power. Had it not been for the protection and active sympathy which some of the princes, free cities, and the minor nobility extended to Luther, he would probably have fared no better than other noted heretics before him: he would have been burned at the stake, and his doctrines stamped out.

Similar causes paved the way for revolt in other countries. Because of conditions in England, Henry VIII was able to overthrow the Roman Church largely by his own power. In Scotland, John Knox was successful in his reform movement because of the support of the barons. In Scandinavia, it was the reigning sovereigns who put down Catholicism and accepted the Lutheran faith. In Switzerland and the Netherlands, the people themselves were more actively concerned in the revolt, but even in these lands the revolution was a political and economic as well as a spiritual upheaval. Everywhere the civil powers became active in destroying the monasteries, abolishing the temporal sovereignty of the Roman Curia, and in suppressing canon law and the ecclesiastical courts.

The economic revolt. Economic dissatisfaction played a decisive part in the revolution. Gradually through the centuries, wealth had been accumulating into the control of the churches, the monasteries, and other ecclesiastical foundations. The conditions that caused this concentration of wealth were, in large measure, peculiar to the social and religious life of the age. The doctrines that salvation is due to charitable works, that absolution for sins can be purchased, and that purgatory can be shortened by endowing a living for a priest to celebrate mass, were some of the most prominent causes. Thus, gifts, endowments, indulgence money, and tithes had increased the treasuries of the churches, the monasteries, and other institutions, until two-thirds of the entire wealth of Germany had passed into the hands of these ecclesiastical foundations. Added to this was the yearly economic drain that went directly to the papal court at Rome. As Beard says, Germany was "the milch cow of the Papacy, which it at once despised and drained dry." [3]

Similar, or even worse, conditions were to be found elsewhere. In Scandinavian lands, it is calculated that two-thirds of Sweden was in the hands of the church, and the remaining one-third belonged almost entirely to the secular nobility. This state of affairs largely explains the rapid conquest of Sweden by Lutheranism. In the Netherlands, as in other parts of Europe, the Church of Rome held vast estates amounting, it has been estimated, to one-fifth of the entire property of the country.

Everywhere in these northern lands an irresistible patriotic response arose to the outcry of the reformers against the exactions of the church, which had come to be looked upon as a malevolent power. Financial corruption and crass materialism abounded. Much of the funds received from the people of northern Europe went directly to Rome to increase the glory of the papal court, and to aid in oppressing the very people from whom it had been obtained.

The economic situation was aggravated because, a short time before, money had been introduced to replace bartering, a change which added greatly to the increasing cost of living. Moreover, interest rates were so high that they amounted to usury. These desperate economic conditions, together with the widespread moral degeneracy of the day, aroused the righteous disgust and wrath of the northern peoples.

Condition of the peasants. Everywhere outside the cities and towns during the later Middle Ages, the lot of the peasantry had grown deplorable. This was especially the case in Germany, England, and France. The common man was oppressed by overlords and plundered by the knights; and because of dense ignorance and gross superstition, he fell an easy prey to the extortions of the priesthood.

In central Europe, local revolts frequently took place, but since the peasants were unaccustomed to unity of action and lacked leadership, their uprisings were quickly suppressed. The romantic success of the Swiss peasantry in defeating their tyrannical oppressors instilled fresh hope in the hearts of the German peasants. Here and there zealous but ignorant preachers aroused a burning desire for social justice. Moreover, the spread of a knowledge of the Scriptures led to a general belief that the millennium was close at hand and that universal Christian brother-

---

[3] Beard, Charles, *Martin Luther and the Reformation in Germany*, p. 33. London: K. Paul, Trench & Co., 1889.

hood and goodwill would shortly ensue. Some even looked for the coming of a Messiah to rescue them from oppression. Luther's doctrine of individual Christian liberty also greatly exalted their hopes.

In consequence of these provocative conditions, the long-smouldering fire broke into the Peasants' War of 1524-1525. An alliance among the nobility quickly put an end to the revolt, and as a result the lot of the peasants in Germany sank to a condition of virtual serfdom, and their emancipation was delayed at least two centuries.

RELIGIOUS AND ECCLESIASTICAL CONDITIONS

Pre-Reformation reformers. The religious revolution was by no means sudden. Following the Crusades, not a few raised their voices in protest against the growing domination of the papal hierarchy, the increasing corruption within the church, and the laxity of spiritual life. They were generally treated as heretics and subjected to persecution by Roman Catholic authorities. From century to century the number grew, until they finally developed into many sects, with different names according to the part of Europe in which they lived. In Italy and elsewhere were the Cathari (the pure), and the Arnoldists, followers of Arnold of Brescia; and in Lombardy the Waldenses, so called after Peter Waldo. In France were the Petrobrusians, named after Peter of Bruys, and the Albigenses; in Germany and the Netherlands were the Beghards, who begged bread on the streets for the poor. In England were Wycliffe and the Lollards; and in Bohemia, the Hussites and Taborites.

Not much unity existed among these sects, although a number of them on the continent used the same catechism. They all, however, vigorously opposed the evils which stained the church, and on occasion their protests flamed out with fanatical zeal. Persecution, torture, and even martyrdom tended to intensify rather than diminish the bitterness of their opposition to the Roman hierarchy.

The evils of which these sects complained were not unrecognized by the church itself. In the official message to the Diet of Worms at the trial of Luther, Pope Adrian VI with astounding frankness confessed the corruption of the church from the Papal seat down. Speaking of Luther's attack, he wrote,

> We confess that God permits this persecution to fall upon His Church on account of sins, especially the sins of priests and prelates. We know that for some years many abominations have been done in this holy

> chair; and that all things have been changed to evil. It is astonishing that the disease has proceeded from the head to the members, from the Pope to the prelates. We have all gone astray from the good road, and for a long time there is none of us, no not one, who has done anything good. The disease is chronic! [4]

Numerous efforts were made by church councils and other authorities to effect reform. However, the degeneracy was too firmly entrenched to respond to half measures. Only a cataclysmic change that would engulf the entire civilization, destroy outgrown institutions, and reorganize European life in harmony with new ideals could bring about success.

The Brethren of the Common Life. By far the most consequential factor in pre-Reformation religion and education in northern Europe was the work of the Brethren of the Common Life. The rise, character, and far-reaching effects of this group deserve more attention than they have received. It succeeded in tying together a resurgent Christianity and the various social developments which already have been set forth.

Conditions that brought about the Brotherhood. Nowhere north of the Alps were conditions so favorable for the emergence of a free civic life as in the Netherlands. All the background causes which have been set forth were active in the Netherlands. Thriving cities had arisen and the population had amassed wealth. All the routes of travel and commerce of northern Europe converged upon this region; and no other people were so closely associated with the progressive life of Spain and Italy. These conditions enabled the more intelligent to center their attention upon art, literature, and science, as well as on religion.

Groote (1340-1384). The one who first discerned the most effective remedy for the ills of that era was Gerhard Groote, a native of Holland who graduated from the University of Paris. After some years of loose living he experienced a yearning to know the sublime mystery of the universe, and to serve others. He saw the need for Christian charity not as a means to enslave the recipient, but to help him to self-dependence; the need for knowledge of the Holy Scriptures; for science other than formal Scholasticism; and a more effective command of Latin and Dutch. Finally he saw that these various interests could be most effectively advanced when men live and work in Communities or Brotherhoods.

Groote was a man of intelligence and learning. Inspired by the teaching of St. Augustine and the mysticism of his friend, Ruysbroecht, an

---

[4] Raynaldus, Annales, XXXI § 70.

Augustinian monk, he took his message of reform to the people in the cities of the lower Rhine. He rebuked the monks, the Friars, and the priests for their sins. His efforts had phenomenal success for he called laymen and women as well as priests and monks to a new devotion. His main conviction was that "all should imitate the Apostolic life." Mysticism, communism, learning, and industry were blended with a phenomenal compassion for the poor and the distressed, and a special zeal for the education of boys. Gradually a brotherhood formed. They took no vows and practiced no rule, but their mysticism led them to seek unity with God. They refused steadfastly to follow the custom of the Friars in begging, but each member was required to earn his own living.

The Brethren lived in communities, or what they called "houses," all levels of society together, nobles, scholars, students, artisans, and common laborers. About 20 brothers occupied a house, pooling their earnings. Usually four were priests and the rest were laymen. The clerics employed their time in preaching and ministering to the poor; others taught in the schools. Their fundamental goal was to recreate primitive Christianity by living and working in the outside world.

About 100 "houses" were established as this revival of Apostolic life spread into the surrounding countries. Their simplicity, sincerity of purpose, and love for underprivileged humanity were infectious. Their ideal of practical Christianity produced one of the most remarkable books ever written, the *Imitatio Christi* which, next to the Bible, has been the Catholic world's most used book of spiritual devotion. Its originator, Thomas à Kempis, was educated by the Brethren and lived all his days in one of their houses.

Ever since the time of Charlemagne the priests had been supposed to preach to the people in their mother tongue. But their messages retained the Latin form, and the substance was scholastic doctrine, neither of which was understood. Groote introduced a simple and direct mode of preaching and no buildings could accommodate the crowds that attended. Moreover, many great preachers were trained by the Brethren. These laid the emphasis upon practical Christian living and they spoke with power and feeling.

The most far reaching reform introduced by Groote and the Brethren was the employment of the mother tongue in preaching and teaching. For the first time Christianity, in something like its original intent and purity, was brought home to the heart of the people of northern Europe.

The Italian Renaissance represented largely a return to the values of ancient paganism; this Hieronymian Renaissance was an attempt to reinstate Apostolic Christianity. The two movements were contemporary and spontaneous expressions of life in two widely separated parts of Europe. They expressed the interests and aspirations of peoples of different cultural backgrounds.

Evaluation. The Brotherhood originated the only abiding reforms of the 15th century. They corrected the *Vulgate,* translated much of the Scriptures into the vernacular, circulated thousands of portions of the Bible and of other religious works, reformed education and textbooks, comforted the afflicted, fed the indigent, housed poor but deserving students, and inspired the writing of some of the best literature of the period.

None of the pre-Reformation groups equalled the Brethren of the Common Life in the extent of their reforms. They were outspoken in denouncing the evils that infested the Roman Church. By the revival of preaching and return to the simplicity and goodwill of Apostolic days they pointed the way religious reform must always take. Their encouragement of the study of Latin and Greek paved the way for increased scholarship. But of greatest consequence was the reinvigoration of Christian education. Despite the opposition of the Brethren to separation from the Mother Church and the express approval of the papacy, their reform measures contributed to the Protestant revolt. Their services to the new learning and to education will be touched upon later in this chapter.

The Wycliffe movement in England. Next in importance to the resurgence of primitive Christianity in the Netherlands was the religious awakening by John Wycliffe in England. It began about the same time and in general it had the same causes and followed something of the same pattern. Wycliffe was profoundly shocked at the brazen immoralities and venality of the papacy, and the slothfulness and lack of spirituality of monks and priests. On one point he was confronted by a situation that Groote did not face, the growing friction between the Papacy and the rising authority of the Crown and aristocracy of England. Revolt against the interference of the Popes in temporal, civil affairs took definite form in England.

For some time Wycliffe confined his efforts to preaching reform at Oxford. In 1378 he took a more radical step and publicly opposed the Roman policies; he asserted that the supreme authority in the Christian religion did not rest in the Pope or the Roman hierarchy but in the Holy Scriptures. This was no longer reform but revolution, for it denied the rock-bottom claim of the Roman Church to be the vicar of Christ, the sole agency of the Holy Spirit to administer divine Grace on earth. Wycliffe was far more radical than Gerhard Groote ever dared to be. He now began to take two new measures to effect a change: he began to preach to the masses of the people, and he undertook to translate the *Vulgate* into English.

Doctrinal controversy. Most of the profound doctrines of the Christian faith were involved in the controversies of the Protestant Reformation. Among the chief issues were: the doctrine of salvation, the worship of images, and the ultimate authority in religion. The Roman Church taught the doctrine of salvation by good works; Luther and other Protestants believed that salvation comes by faith and the Grace of God in Christ. The Roman Church contended that the final authority was the Roman Curia, and based its doctrines upon the Scriptures as interpreted by the Pope and the rulings of the church councils. Luther and Calvin lodged ultimate authority in the Old and New Testaments; the Anabaptists maintained that the New Testament alone is supreme together with the Christian conscience illumined by the Holy Spirit through the new birth. The Roman Church claimed that the priest is the mediator between God and man, and has the power to forgive sins. The Protestants contended that the only mediator is Christ himself and that every man has direct and immediate access to God. The Lord's Supper and the form of worship were further subjects of profound and prolonged, as well as bitter, controversy. These controversies helped to intensify the aversion which determined the Nordic peoples to seek a purer Christianity and a more independent political status.

PRINTING SPREAD KNOWLEDGE AND REVOLT

The printing of the Scriptures and religious literature. Undoubtedly printing was the most powerful assistance to the religious reformers, and the chief means of intellectual awakening. It is significant that the Latin Bible, known generally as the *Vulgate,* was the first complete book that issued from the press. Four years were required to accomplish the task, which was completed in 1456. Before the year 1500 no less than 92 editions of this version were published, while during the following century the astounding number of 438 editions came from the presses of Europe. Between 1457 and 1517 over 400 editions of the Bible, or parts of it, were printed in France alone.

Of still greater importance, however, was the publication of the Scriptures in the vernacular in Holland, Germany, France, and Bohemia. Gerhard Groote, the founder of the Brethren of the Common Life, translated portions of the Scriptures before 1384 into Dutch and as early as 1477 the Bible as a whole was widely read in the vernacular; no other people were so saturated with Scriptural knowledge. Prior to 1518, no less than 14 editions were printed in High-German dialects, and at least three in Low-German. Between 1513 and 1531, as many as 25 translations of the Bible or the New Testament appeared in Dutch, Flemish, and French. Nor was this the whole story: many portions of the Scriptures were published separately. Before 1509 there had appeared 22 editions of the Psalter; and 25 editions of the Gospels and the Epistles, before 1518. A large number of books of devotion also figured among the publications at this time.

Interior of a Sixteenth-Century Printing Establishment.

The printing of the Bible in English. William Tyndale (1492-1536) translated and published (1526) the first edition of the New Testament in English. This version had to be printed in Germany, for the reading and sale of the Scriptures were prohibited in the realm.

Copies were, however, smuggled in and widely read. The entire text was likewise issued on the continent and smuggled into England in 1535. It was not until 1538 that the Bible as a whole was allowed to be printed in the vernacular in England. In the translating of the Scriptures into English and in printing the complete text the English were, however, behind the continental peoples.

Along with the other reform measures which Gerhard Groote began out of his profound spirit of goodwill, he insisted that the farmers and burghers should read the Bible for themselves, and seeing that they did not know Latin, he determined that the Scriptures be furnished in the vernacular tongue. Cele, rector of the School at Zwolle, was of the same mind: "The Bible should be studied," he said, "by everyone in order to regain the image of God in which man was made."

Gerhart Zerbolt, another member of the Brethren, wrote a treatise upon the *Utility of Reading the Bible in the Mother Tongue* [5] in which he gave fifteen reasons for such reading. He showed by cogent arguments from the Scriptures and the Church Fathers that laymen are admonished to read. But if they are to read intelligently it must be in their own tongue. Despite the fact that reading of the Scriptures in the vernacular was prohibited by the Catholic authorities, it continued to increase rapidly. No other single movement meant so much to the intellectual awakening of the people of Europe as the use of the vernacular in religious life.

It is notable that France, Spain, Italy, and Bohemia, as well as Holland possessed the Bible in the vernacular before 1500. Many portions were translated by Groote and others and were copied in great numbers in the houses of the Brethren.

The Bible was read by persons of every rank in society and its words and ideas became the common possession and spiritual standard of the people generally. The facts about early publication point to the universal interest in the reading of the Scriptures at that time. Lindsay declares: [6] "The 'common man,' especially the artisan of the towns, knew a great deal about the Bible. It was the one book he read, re-read and pondered over." Green writes: [7]

---

[5] Zerbolt, Gerhart, *De libris teutonialibus.*

[6] Lindsay, Thomas M., *A History of the Reformation,* Vol. II, p. 439. New York: Charles Scribner's Sons, 1906-1907.

[7] Green, J. R., *Short History of the English People,* pp. 460-461. New York: American Book Company, 1916.

England became the people of a book and that book was the Bible. It was the one English book familiar to every Englishman; it was read at churches and read at home, and everywhere its words, as they fell on ears which custom had not deadened, kindled a startling enthusiasm.... Sunday after Sunday, day after day, the crowds that gathered round Bonner's Bible in the nave of St. Paul's, or the family group that hung on the words of the Geneva Bible in the devotional exercises at home, were leavened with a new literature.

Other publications. Next to the Scriptures must be placed the works of St. Augustine, the Church Father of the 5th century. No other writings exerted so powerful an influence in medieval theology; no other, except Holy Writ itself, caused such spiritual renewal. They influenced the Brethren of the Common Life and, still more profoundly, Luther and Calvin. Whenever and wherever the works of St. Augustine were studied, there began a movement for a deepening piety and a reform of education. As to their publication,

Between the year 1467 and the end of the fifteenth century, no fewer than twenty editions were called for, that is to say, a fresh edition every eighteen months.[8]

The effect of printing on the Reformation can be inferred from the fact that by 1525 no less than 2,000 printings of Luther's writings appeared.[9]

SCHOOLS BEFORE THE REFORMATION

Three grades of schools. Three grades of schools were prevalent: first, elementary vernacular schools; second Latin Grammar schools; and third, the universities. Many different kinds of school were in existence, especially for boys. Girls were not so well provided for. Just what school, if any, a boy would attend depended upon the circumstances of birth, parentage, class in society, intelligence, native country, and his aim in life. The following types of schools were pretty generally found throughout northern Europe:

Monastic or cloister schools. Although the monastic movement

---

[8] Schaff, Philip, *A Select Library of the Nicene and Post-Nicene Fathers of the Christian Church,* Vol. II. Translator's Preface by Rev. Marcus Dods, p. xiii. New York: Charles Scribner's Sons, 1907.

[9] Seligman, E. R. A., *Encyclopaedia of the Social Sciences,* p. 522. New York The Macmillan Co., 1930-35.

had passed its climax centuries before, it was still vigorous and the numerous orders of monks recruited their ranks by receiving young lads whom they trained to take the vows and spend their lives under monastic rule. These institutions had grown immensely wealthy and, in consequence, offered their inmates a more peaceful and permanent living than could be found in any secular calling. Such monastic establishments were found everywhere throughout Christendom, though in some countries they were not so rich, powerful, and extensive as in others.

Cathedral schools. These schools, located in the centers of population, had been growing for some centuries. They originally trained the priests, but later also prepared boys who looked forward to high positions in church or state or in commercial activities. Every cathedral provided such a school.

Collegiate church schools. This was not a different kind of school, but merely a school in a church in the parish under the Bishop and other than the Cathedral. As cities grew in population and new towns arose in the parishes it was not customary to create new parishes but to build other churches. Many of these churches had livings for a number of priests who led a common life and conducted Latin grammar schools. The organization and instruction were the same as in the cathedral school. It is estimated that in England at the time of the Reformation over 200 of such schools were in existence. Many of them were endowed by benevolent patrons.

Chantry schools. Similar in character to the elementary work in the Cathedral and Collegiate church schools, Chantry schools were taught by priests whose living was provided by endowments for the celebration of mass for the souls of the donors and for the instruction of poor boys.

Song schools. Music was an abiding interest of the church, particularly after Gregory the Great introduced the Gregorian chant in the 6th century. Charlemagne took a deep interest in religious music in the 9th century, and introduced Roman music teachers into the churches of Gaul. The services of the church everywhere needed a choir composed of men and boys. The chanting of the Psalms and the hymns not only required some knowledge of music, but of Latin as well, for all songs and services were in this tongue. It was essential that the choristers know how to read and as a consequence all churches from the Cathedral down to the parish chapel had song schools. In the Cathedral and Collegiate churches this instruction was not connected with that of the grammar school. In the smaller churches a grammar school was not needed, but the song teacher would sometimes teach the elements of grammar as well as singing.

Burgh schools. Next in order may be listed the *burgh* Latin grammar schools and the vernacular schools under the management of the towns. A fuller explanation of these schools is necessary for an understanding of the evolution in the next era. In fact, it may be quite positively asserted that the most vital and significant feature of education during the 15th and 16th centuries was the establishment of schools fostered by the Hanseatic towns of northwestern Europe.

Civil control of schools. In the Hanseatic towns of northern Europe, schools were established under municipal auspices, and in most such places the church authorities opposed this movement vigorously. Nowhere did the schools appear earlier than in the busy towns of the Netherlands, and nowhere was there less opposition to their establishment. As already explained, these towns enjoyed a greater measure of autonomy than those in other lands. The church was largely overshadowed, and the nobility were favorable to the schools, especially when education assisted the commercial activities in which they were interested. According to Douma,[10]

> In the fourteenth century the town was already in control of education, and would never again surrender it. The civil authorities appointed the teachers, paid their salaries and provided for the building and all the furnishings. . . . Instruction was a monopoly of the municipal authorities.

In most instances, the schools were supported in part by tuition fees, which were collected by the town authorities. In some cases, the schools were actually free and all children were welcomed.

The following Netherland towns established public schools in the 14th century: Gravesande in 1322; Leyden in 1324; Rotterdam in 1328; Schiedam in 1336; Delft in 1342; Hoorn in 1358; Haarlem in 1389; Alkmaar in 1390.[11]

Large numbers of such schools were established in the cities of Germany and England. A fee was generally required for instruction so that education was not usually available for the poor.

In the vernacular schools, reading and writing were taught. Because

---

[10] Douma, H., *Geschiedenis van het Lager Onderwijs en de Schoolopvoeding in Nederland,* pp. 34-35. Purmerend: J. Muusses, 1900.

[11] Ulmann, C., *Reformers before the Reformation,* p. 58. Edinburgh: T. & T. Clark, 1855. Also, Delprat, H. M., *Brüderschaft des Germeinsamen Lebens,* p. 113.

these institutions were established for the artisans and business people, arithmetic was also an important subject of instruction. As early as the 13th century, French likewise was taught in many of the schools, for this language was well-nigh indispensable in business. Frenchmen were often employed to teach bookkeeping. French was the language of the court, of the official class, and of business and even in the small schools of the towns the children of the common people were taught to read and write this language.

These elementary schools were looked down upon as purely practical in character, while the Latin schools were considered purely cultural. They were especially designed to meet the needs of the higher commercial classes and of all who sought to enter professional life.

Hospital, almonry, and endowed schools. Throughout the middle ages the church encouraged charity as a means of salvation, and in consequence funds were donated or devised to support benevolent projects. Indigent children and orphans received considerable attention. Provision was frequently made for orphanages and hospital schools to furnish a modicum of instruction for poor children.

The universities. To complete this list it remains to add the universities, which obviously were the most important of all. None of the others quite so completely represented the expanded intellectual interests of the age or the power of learning. By the end of the 15th century, 79 universities were recognized in western Europe. Almost all had the blessings of the Pope, even if they did not owe their initiation to papal decree. Italy had the most, but even the smaller lands each contained at least one, which was usually the result of the interest of King or Emperor. The most renowned, such as Paris, Bologna, Pavia, and Prague, exercised an influence throughout Christendom, and not along academic lines alone, but on the course of social and political affairs. Students flocked from all nations to these because their standards and degrees were universally credited. Institutions were accorded the status of universities or *studia generalia* not because they taught universal knowledge but because their graduates were empowered to practice the art of instruction everywhere in Christendom.

Some four points must be kept firmly in mind in regard to the universities of the pre-Reformation era:

1. The division between the preparatory and higher instruction had not as yet been sharply drawn, so that the student-bodies contained a large proportion of adolescent youth, as well as men of all ages.

2. The normal set-up of a university contained four faculties: (a) The philosophical which included mathematics, natural science, logic, ethics, and metaphysics, all comprehended in the system of thought known as Scholasticism; (b) Law, which embraced both civil law and canon or ecclesiastical law, which was highly important; (c) medicine; and (d) theology, the queen of all the sciences. Some institutions became more notable for one of these studies than others.

3. In many instances the universities had grown out of the existing cathedral schools whose primary function had been to train for the priesthood. The universities superseded the cathedral school as theological seminaries and for three centuries the priests were trained in these institutions where there was little or no discipline.

4. Although the universities received the full approval of the church, and were accounted to all intents and purposes to be truly religious, they gradually became more secular. Most of the students were laymen, and secular subjects such as law, medicine, and the sciences dominated their interest. The life of the students was often corrupt.

THE REFORM OF EDUCATION BY THE BRETHREN OF THE COMMON LIFE

Groote's interest in education. Gerhard Groote, who founded the Brethren of the Common Life, never taught. However, he launched with a minimum of fanfare one of the most consequential movements in educational history. While temporarily prohibited from preaching, he turned his attention to assisting boys and young men to get an education. He saw the need of better education for all classes but most especially for the clergy. As he stated it, "How are these to instruct the masses, if they have no knowledge to give, their brains being empty and void of all sound learning?" He entertained boys in his home and conversed with them about their studies. His interest in boys led him to see in education the means of training a new generation. Accordingly he encouraged his followers, who had the capacity, to teach in the schools for the good they could accomplish. As a consequence, teaching became the most effective instrument for realizing the purposes of the Brethren and the chief reason for their fame.

John Cele. The first of the Brethren to become a teacher was John Cele, a bosom friend of Gerhard Groote. "These two," we are told, "were as one heart and one soul." He desired to become a monk but Groote persuaded him to accept the rectorship of the town school at Zwolle, a post he held from 1374 or 1375 until his death in 1417. He was a native of Zwolle, and had obtained a M. A. degree, probably at Prague. He made the school at Zwolle the most noted institution of its kind in pre-Reformation days and the model for many others. Among those which it influenced were Schlettstadt under Dringenberg, Deventer under Hegius, Strassburg under Sturm, Geneva under Calvin and the system of colleges established by the Jesuit order. Pupils flocked to Zwolle from many countries and as far away as Poland; at one time 1,200 were enrolled. Among his pupils was John Busch, who spent his life reforming the monasteries.

Cele improved the curriculum in many ways. He pruned canon law, medicine, astronomy, and formal disputation, for he saw that these had little meaning for the adolescent boy. He retained grammar, rhetoric, logic, ethics, and philosophy. The change was not so much in the list of subjects, but rather in the definite practical aim which he set forth for teaching these branches. He believed the future priests and even laymen could make use of this information.

In rhetoric he had his pupils write down those points of his discourses which seemed most useful. He also required everyone to copy in a notebook select sayings and passages of Scripture which he dictated. In this way the points were not only given emphasis but were more readily memorized. His greatest innovation however, was in the field of religious education.

Cele shared the desire of Groote and all the Brethren to make imitators of Christ. Religious education up to that day consisted in learning the Lord's Prayer, the Ten Commandments and the Apostles' Creed. Everyone was required to attend the ritualistic services of formal worship. Pupils engaged also in singing. All these efforts were in the Latin language. Cele introduced the teaching of the Bible, not only on Sunday but also on week-days and holidays. He substituted the teaching of the New Testament for that of scholastic formalism. In the morning he used the Epistles, in the afternoon the Gospels, and in the evening other books. Three times a day he expounded the Scriptures. He dictated to his pupils prayers both in Latin and Dutch. As a devout imitator of Christ, Cele taught by example as well as by instruction. His maxim was, "The Kingdom of heaven consisteth not in knowledge and speech but in work and virtue." Good behavior and saintly living were the goal to be realized. The supreme objective was practical Christianity.

The school was divided into eight classes, which was another innovation he made. The two highest classes were taught by specialists in each subject. The consequence was that his pupils were well trained and were enabled to excel in their studies when they entered the universities. In an age when there was practically no way of obtaining control, and discipline and punishment were barbarous, the methods of the Brethren were gloriously successful.

Alexander Hegius (1433-1498). "The greatest educator of Transalpine Europe," says Albert Hyma. Hegius attended the town school at Zwolle, and taught for eight years at Emmerich, where he had an enrollment of 1,500 pupils. In 1483 he was appointed rector of St. Lebuin's Church school at Deventer, where the attendance reached 2,200. Among his pupils here was the young Erasmus, who attended for nine years. From Hegius and his assistant, John Sintheim, Erasmus derived that love of letters which was the dominant passion of his life.

Hegius had very definite leanings toward classical humanism, and had not only a gift for poetry but an unmistakable sense of taste. In one of his few writings he declared that the diction of Cicero, Virgil, and Sallust should be followed and the style of the Italian humanists imitated. When along in years he learned Greek from the humanistic scholar, Agricola, and strongly favored the study of Greek authors. It could not have been a mere accident that during his lifetime a great number of books were published at Deventer, many, if not most of them, Latin and Greek classics. But Hegius never diverged from the pietistic purpose of the Brethren. Writing to Wessel he stated, "You wish more particular information respecting my method of education. I have followed your advice. All learning is pernicious if acquired at the expense of piety."

Helping poor boys get an education. It was a general custom during the later middle ages for poor boys and also university students to get a bare subsistence by begging. The Brethren, following Groote's example, stoutly opposed this practice and sought new ways to help needy students. To secure lodging for boys who had no place to live, they persuaded benevolent widows to take them into their homes and to treat them as their own. They also made provision for many in the "Houses" of the Brethren, and in some instances they constructed dormitories in connection with schools but under the control of the Brotherhood. They provided many boys with books and other necessities, and also with employment.

The business of copying. The passion for reading reached flood stage in the 14th and 15th centuries. Commercial life, curiosity, a deepened religious interest, and, above all else, the dearth of textbooks, served to increase the need. The demand for books was never so great, the supply never so inadequate. During the middle ages the monasteries instituted the practice of copying books in their *scriptoria*. But for centuries monastic copying had declined.

A Monastic Scriptorium.

The multiplication of books was imperative to supply the Houses of the Brethren, the students with texts, and the people with religious reading matter. Discerning this crying need, these practical Dutchmen, by setting up *scriptoria* in their Houses, expanded the copying of manuscripts into a business. They employed school boys, students, anyone and everyone. Under their management copying grew into a fine art, illuminated writing adorned the texts, and pictures and drawings were not slow in appearing.

When the art of printing was introduced, the Brethren were quick to replace the *scriptoria* with printing presses. "In 1490, there were no less than 60 different printing establishments carried on under the supervision of the Brethren."[12] The celebrated schoolmaster, John Sturm, after studying for some years in the Liége School of the Brethren, attended the University of Louvain, where he set up a press. Later in Paris he issued many editions of Latin authors. More than 450 works were printed before 1500 at Deventer alone. But despite their industry the Brethren could not compete with the renowned printers of Basle, Venice, and Paris, and consequently their work of publication declined.

The general character of the works published by the Brethren was predominantly religious; the materials included the Scriptures, books of devotion, and Latin and Greek classics used as texts in the schools and universities. While the Brethren did not give these publications away, as did the monks, the books were sold at very low prices so that even the poor might possess them. Many of their works were printed in the vernacular tongues.

The Brethren strove earnestly to encourage their students to unite learning and practical Christianity. The curriculum was selected with this objective clearly in view. Up to this time all learning had been in the Latin language; knightly training required French, and commercial life led to the teaching of the vernacular. The Brethren now began the teaching of religion in the vernacular which proved in the course of events to be the greatest innovation of all.

The schools of the Brethren. In many places such as Deventer, Zwolle, and Münster they found church and city schools already in existence which could be reformed under their influence. In some places they were invited to establish new schools, namely at Utrecht, Groningen,

---

[12] Putnam, George Haven, *Books and Their Makers During the Middle Ages*, Vol. 1, p. 400. New York: G. P. Putnam's Sons, 1896-1897.

Liége, and farther afield in Rostock, Cassel, Ghent, and Nijmegen. One of their number, Louis Dringenberg, a former pupil at Deventer, was invited to take charge of the newly founded school at Schlettstadt, Alsace, in 1450. In 1517, under his successor, it had 900 pupils. A good description of this famous school has been left us. Among its students were many who became famous; from the standpoint of education, John Sturm was the most important. The school at Hertzogenbush was likewise founded by the Brethren; Erasmus attended there three years after being at Deventer. Its enrollment ran to 1,200.

Before the Reformation, all northwest Europe was permeated with the influence of these men. One of their leaders, Busch, listed fifty schools under their charge by 1470. Later, as many more were added; moreover, through the scholars they trained, the influence of the Brethren penetrated everywhere. From their original center in Deventer, their school activity spread down the Rhine to Switzerland, then into Germany on the one side, and to Belgium on the other. Their schools furnished the models for the reorganization and reform of all the large institutions of western Germany. Most of the great scholars of this period were the direct products of the schools of the Brethren. John Wessel was said to be the "second founder" of the University of Paris and "the light of the world"; Erasmus, though far from enthusiastic about the efficiency of their schools, owed to them the inspiration and training that made him the leading humanist of his day. The school of John Sturm, at Strassburg, was a continuation of their work, and even the Jesuits owed much to their practices.

Instruction among the evangelical sects. The educational activities of the many evangelical sects scattered throughout central Europe have uniformly been ignored by educational historians. The importance of their contribution to the evolution of popular culture can no longer be overlooked. According to a recent German authority, literacy was widespread among them: [13]

> All children could read and write; important passages of Scriptures were given as copy for writing, and also learned by rote. Portions of the Gospels were possessed not merely by their preachers, but also by the well-to-do and the more zealous. Every member was taught the Gospels especially, so that their inquisitors and the priests were amazed.

---

[13] Thudichum, Friedrich, *Papsttum und Reformation im Mittelalter,* p. 11. Leipzig: Eduard Schmidt, 1903.

Not only men, but women too, frequently learned the Gospels by heart, and in one instance a common countryman could repeat from memory the entire book of Job. The meeting places of these peoples were sometimes called schools (*scholae*). It was notorious that even the less learned among them knew the Scriptures more thoroughly than the scholarly doctors. The catechism of the Waldensians was used extensively among many of these sects. The training of the leaders of the evangelicals was generally confined to the vernacular, though individuals were often familiar with the Greek and Latin classics, as well as the writings of Church Fathers. Before Luther's Reformation, the Hussites had printed the Scriptures in the vernacular, and they possessed a good system of schools and a celebrated university.

The point of greatest significance in all the efforts of the evangelical Catholics, like the Brethren of the Common Life, and of the heretical sects, lies in their interest in diffusing a knowledge of reading so that every individual might know the Scriptures for himself.

Extent of cultural opportunity in the Netherlands. All authorities agree that learning was more widely diffused in the Netherlands than in any other country. Guicciardini, an Italian historian, testified that "even the peasants in Holland could read and write well." [14] Motley, the chief historian of the Netherlands, paints a glowing picture of the learning and culture of these peoples. He tells us: [15]

> It was a land where every child went to school, where almost every individual inhabitant could read and write, where even the middle classes were proficients in mathematics and the classics, and could speak two or more modern languages. . . .
>
> An excellent reason why the people were so well governed, so productive, and so enterprising, was the simple fact that they were an educated people. There was hardly a Netherlander—man, woman, or child—that could not read and write. The school was the common property of the people, paid for among the municipal expenses. In the cities, as well as in the rural districts, there were not only common schools but classical schools.
>
> In the burgher families it was rare to find boys who had not been taught Latin, or girls unacquainted with French. Capacity to write and

---

[14] Davies, C. M., *History of Holland and the Dutch People,* Vol. I, p. 487. Quoted by Campbell, Douglas, *The Puritan in Holland, England, and America,* Vol. II, p. 340. New York: Harper & Brothers, 1893.

[15] Motley, John Lothrop, *The United Netherlands,* Vol. IV, p. 432, and pp. 566-567. New York: Harper & Brothers, 1867.

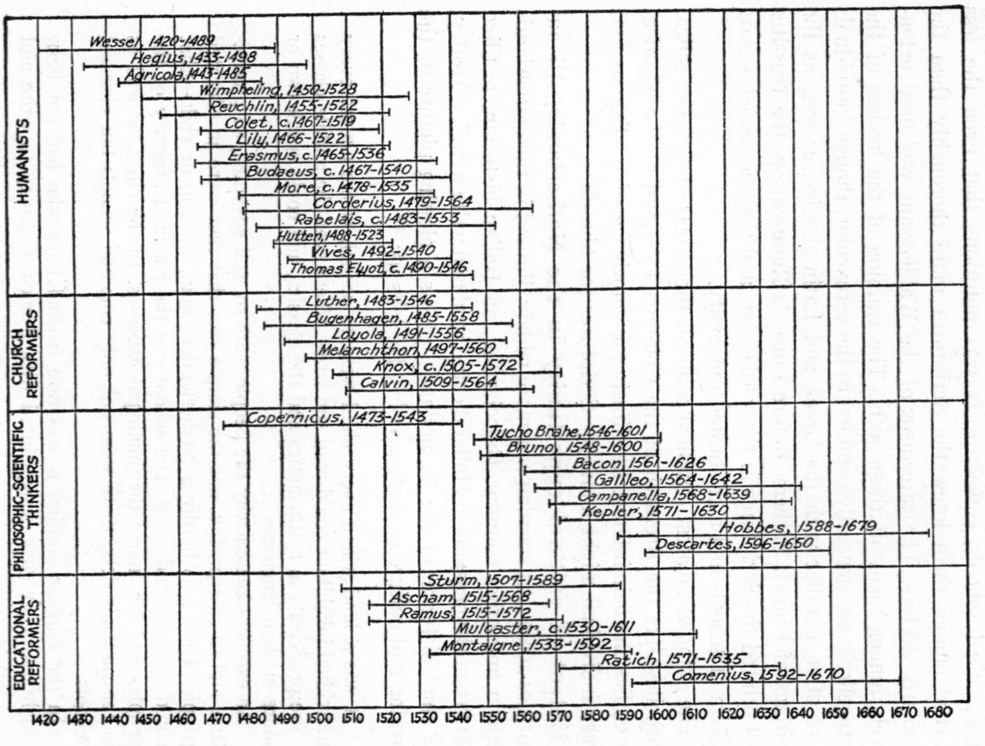

Chronological Chart, 1400–1700.

speak several modern languages was very common, and there were many individuals who had made remarkable progress in science and classical literature.

Undoubtedly the inhabitants of the Netherlands were among the most highly educated and progressive people in the world at that time. They were also the wealthiest.

The culture of the Netherlands spread along the Rhine and over into Germany. As Janssen states: [16]

> One is guilty of no historical inaccuracy in inferring, roundly, that from the fourteenth century onward every market town, or, at any rate, every bigger town in the Upper Palatinate had its own school.

Frankfort on the Main had three collegiate schools, which in 1478 totaled 318 pupils. Brunswick had two municipal Latin schools. In 1490, Zwickau had, in a two-story building, a school of four classes with 900 students. This school was supported by an endowment. In 1491, Görlitz had six teachers employed and from 500 to 600 pupils. Emmerich, on the lower Rhine, in 1503 had a school of six classes; in 1510 there were 450 pupils; and 11 years later the number had risen to 1,500. Schlettstadt, in Alsace, in 1517 had 900 pupils. Nuremberg, one of the wealthiest and most aggressive commercial towns, had four Latin schools.

---

[16] Janssen, Johannes, *History of the German People at the Close of the Middle Ages*, Vol. XIII, p. 30, note 1. London: Kegan Paul, Trench, Trübner & Co., 1905.

Chapter 2

THE NORTHERN RESPONSE TO THE ITALIAN RENAISSANCE

THE significance of the Renaissance. So extraordinary was this epoch of history named "the rebirth" that no student can understand the emergence of modern civilization without reliving its dramatic scenes and events. Most authorities contend that this transcendent renewal was the rightful beginning of modern education and to this point of view there can be no genuine objection. It was, chiefly for purposes of convenience, considered wisest to treat the Italian phase of the movement as the conclusion of ancient and medieval education; [1] and to reserve the transfer of "The New Learning" to northern lands as the opening of the modern period. Students who wish to appreciate fully this historic transition will review the early phase of the Italian background.

The transplanting of classical Humanism. The introduction of "The New Learning" into northern Europe took place in the Netherlands. It must be credited primarily to the Brethren of the Common Life. Starting with John Wessel and Alexander Hegius, the Brethren took an increasing interest in the revival of classical Latin and the study of New Testament and Patristic Greek. It was, therefore, not at all accidental that the most scholarly disciples of Humanism in the north were products of their instruction. Inspired by these devout leaders of the Low Countries, Rudolph Agricola and John Reuchlin transplanted the new enthusiasm to Western Germany.

Agricola (1443-1485) was born near Groningen, Holland, where he attended the town school. He graduated from Erfurt and Louvain. In

---

[1] A discussion of the Italian Renaissance can be found in Eby & Arrowood, *History and Philosophy of Education.* New York: Prentice-Hall, Inc., 1940.

1468 he went to Italy to study law, but switched to Greek under Battista Guarino and Theodore Gaza. Returning home he refused a teaching position, but as an itinerant humanist, he quickly spread a love of The New Learning in Holland and Germany.

Next in humanistic leadership was John Reuchlin (1455-1522), a German born at Pforzheim. He studied Greek privately at Paris, and in 1481 went to Italy and studied at Florence.

Invited to Heidelberg University, he became the center of an enthusiastic group of young humanists, who called themselves the "Rhenish Society." But like many of the humanists he was a restless spirit, and like a wandering knight of letters he soon returned to Italy to pursue the study of Hebrew and became the leading scholar in northern Europe in this language. Reuchlin's chief contribution to the rebirth of culture lay in making Hebrew one of the languages of learning. The object of his interest was of course primarily the Old Testament, but a secondary reason lay in the Mohammedan threat to Europe and the resulting interest in languages cognate to Hebrew.

Reuchlin acquired another practice of the humanistic movement, and that was dependence upon the patronage of princely houses. The Italian Renaissance was largely a product of the aristrocracy of the courts. This same interest began to show itself north of the Alps. Because of his command of languages he was employed by Count Eberhard of Stuttgart as private secretary and for a time he was professor at the University of Tübingen, which the Count founded in 1476. The bastions of ignorance and Scholasticism and the immoralities of the Middle Ages were in the monasteries and the universities. The University of Cologne in Germany, Louvain in Belgium, and most of all, Paris, were strongholds of scholastic doctrines. The humanists, so far as they had any headquarters, were centered in Erfurt and Heidelberg in Germany. The monks directed their bitterness against the revival of classical Latin and more particularly of Greek; they picked out John Reuchlin as their chief victim, for he was the most scholarly linguist of the day in Latin, Greek, and Hebrew. He inspired Ulrich von Hutten and Franz von Sickingen to form a humanistic society, and when he became the central figure of attack by the Dominicans and other reactionaries these two literary knights came to his rescue and won the victory for The New Learning. After the rise of the Lutheran Reformation opposition to Humanism ceased.

The transition from the early spirit of the Brethren to its full amalgamation with classicism can be seen in a comparison of the programs of John Wessel, who represented the highest integration of the mystic spirit with classical learning, and that of Goswin of Halen. Wessel spent many years at Paris and in Italy where he learned Greek from Bessarion and other scholars. Somewhere along the line he also acquired some knowledge of Hebrew. Wessel's point of view may be seen in the following quotation from his writings: [2]

> Knowledge is not our highest aim, for he who only knows how to know, is a fool; for he has no taste of the fruit of knowledge, nor does he understand how to order his knowledge with wisdom. The knowledge of truth is its own glorious fruit, when it meets with a wise husbandman; for by this truth he may, out of his clear knowledge, come to God, and become God's friend; since through knowledge he unites himself to God, and progresses step by step in this union, until he tastes how gracious the Lord is, and through this taste becomes more desirous, yea, burns with desire, and amid this glow God loves him and lives in him, until he becomes wholly one with God. This is the true, pure, earnest fruit of an earnest knowledge, which in very truth all men by nature do rather desire to possess than mere memory, that is to say, than knowledge, in and for itself. For, as unsettled and wavering opinions are empty without knowledge, so knowledge is unfruitful without love.

From this passage it is clear that Wessel during his sojourn at Paris had come under the influence of the mystics of St. Victor. Moreover, his studies in Italy were directed to the acquisition of Greek, not for the study of the philosophy and literature of Greece, but of the New Testament.

The following passage from Goswin reveals how the intellectual horizon had changed:

> You may read Ovid and writers of that stamp through, once; but Virgil, Horace, and Terence are to be studied with more attention, and oftener, because in our profession we need to bestow especial study upon the poets. But, above all, I will that you read the Bible constantly. And, since one ought not to remain in ignorance of history, I counsel you to take up Josephus, and for church history to read the *Tripartita*. Of the profane writers, Plutarch, Sallust, Thucydides, Herodotus, and Justin, will especially profit you. Then it will do you no harm to go through with the writings of Plato and Aristotle. But with Cicero we must remain longer, in order that we may acquire a truly Roman style. Next to our Bible it is well to give thorough and earnest study to Augustine. Him

---

[2] Barnard, Henry, *German Educational Reformers*, pp. 57-58. Hartford: Brown & Cross, 1878.

you may follow up by Jerome, Ambrose, Chrysostom, Gregory, Bernard, and Hugo St. Victor, a man full of rich instruction.[3]

The circle of reading prescribed by Groote was narrowly religious, that of Wessel still pietistic, that of Goswin took in all ancient literature. Now no important author, either profane or religious, was overlooked. Although early Christianity continued to be the inspiration of life and education, a profound transition had taken place from the narrow-mindedness of the religious extremist to the far-seeing Christian.

Beginning of the classical Renaissance in England. The dawning of the Renaissance in England came at the end of the 14th century. A number of prominent Englishmen visited Italy in the 14th and 15th centuries. Manuel Chrysoloras, the celebrated teacher of Greek, and Poggio, the great Italian humanist, made brief visits to England. Among the first Englishmen to visit Italy and become acquainted with the Italian Renaissance were Chaucer and Henry Beaufort. About this same time Humphrey, Duke of Gloucester, son of Henry IV, employed Italians to teach him classical Latin and Italian poetry. He was educated at Balliol College, Oxford University, and despite his wild character was an indefatigable reader. He studied the Latin poets and orators and Latin versions of Plato and Aristotle. Of modern authors he read Dante, Petrarch, and Boccaccio. He was a liberal patron of learned men and collected a number of manuscripts which he presented to the library of Oxford. A few other men had first hand contact with The New Learning in Italy, but none of them had more than a passing interest in the great awakening. It was not until the study of Greek became prevalent that the revival took genuine hold on English scholars.[4]

William Grey was the first Englishman to pursue The New Learning in Italy. He spent some time in Florence and Padua, but more at Ferrara where he studied under Guarino, the celebrated educator, around the middle of the 15th century. He became somewhat proficient in Greek. Like most scholars of that day he felt the urge to collect manuscripts and to have classical works copied; he presented 200 of these to Balliol College at Oxford. As Bishop of Ely he exercised a strong influence.

---

[3] *Ibid.,* p. 58.

[4] For a succinct account of the introduction of the new learning into England consult: Sandys, J. E., *A History of Classical Scholarship,* Vol. II, Chapter XV. Cambridge: The Cambridge University Press, 1908.

The next Englishman to study Greek was William of Selling. Haunted by a passion for learning, he studied three years (1464-1467) at Padua, Bologna, and Rome. He collected many manuscripts, which he presented to Christ Church, Canterbury, where he was Prior for many years.

Thomas Linacre. In the school of Christ Church, Canterbury, William of Selling inspired his nephew, Linacre, with a desire to acquire The New Learning. After attending Oxford, where he was a fellow, he went with his uncle on an embassy to the Pope in 1485-1486. He visited Florence at length to study Latin with Politian and Greek with Chalcondyles. He then proceeded to Padua where he graduated with great distinction in medicine in 1492. He was an all-around scholar, for he served not only as physician to Henry VIII, but as tutor to Princess Mary in Latin (along with Vives) and taught Greek and medicine and translated Galen's writings into Latin. His work in this field led to the revival of the ancient medical sciences of anatomy and botany. He wrote a Latin grammar [5] and founded the college of medicine. Like the other English scholars of this period he was more interested in the practical side of The New Learning than in the aesthetic or stylistic.

William Grocyn (about 1446-1519). Grocyn was educated at Winchester and Oxford where he was tutor. He spent the years 1488 to 1491 visiting Florence, Rome, and Padua where he studied Latin and Greek under Politian and Chalcondyles, both renowned humanists. On returning to England he was the first man to teach Greek at Oxford. It is possible he had already studied Greek under Cornetius Vitelli, who visited Oxford about 1475, and this experience led him to visit Italy. He was highly esteemed by the renowned band of scholars who introduced The New Learning into England, Linacre, Latimer, Colet, More, and Lily. It was this same group which welcomed Erasmus to England. While a man of genuine scholarship, Grocyn, like so many others, did not become a creative thinker.

John Colet (about 1461-1519). Colet stands out as the chief figure in the group of men who brought The New Learning to England. The eldest son of the lord mayor of London, Colet graduated from Oxford in 1490. Evidently he was not content with the knowledge he received

---

[5] His Latin Grammar was too elaborate for use by the boys of St. Paul's. The last part of the work is devoted to Greek constructions and may be considered the first published Greek work in England.

at Oxford, for in 1493 he proceeded to Paris to study canon and civil law, the Church Fathers, and the rudiments of Greek. Here he became acquainted with Budaeus and Erasmus and was inspired to go to Italy, the fountainhead of learning. After three years he returned to England and lectured at Oxford on the Epistles of Paul. In this he aided the reform movement by emphasizing the significance of the Greek language and the direct method of interpreting the New Testament rather than the allegorical method used by Scholasticism. Furthermore, he promoted a clearer understanding of original Christianity.

Colet's great opportunity to promote The New Learning came when he was made Dean of St. Paul's Cathedral Church in the heart of London. Here he preached church reform and lectured on the Scriptures. He re-established the grammar school and made it the foremost in England in humanistic learning. He endowed the school with the wealth he inherited from his father.

William Lily (about 1468-1522). Among the group of reformers Lily was the most practical educator; as headmaster of St. Paul's school during its first years from 1510 to 1522, he formulated the curriculum and methods of the lower school for The New Learning. His preparation for this position was the best. In 1486 he entered Oxford, where Grocyn was lecturing, and after graduation went on a pilgrimage to Jerusalem. He spent some time at Rhodes where he came into contact with Greek refugees. At Rome he attended lectures in Latin and Greek so as to become thoroughly proficient in these languages. From experience as an instructor at St. Paul's, Lily felt it necessary to have a Latin grammar more in line with The New Learning. The text he wrote was the most outstanding in the English world.

The condition of education in England. English schools did not conform in all particulars to the continental patterns. The ecclesiastical system of schools was in large measure the same, but the aristocracy exerted a stronger influence than it did on the continent. An account of education must begin with the two celebrated universities, Oxford and Cambridge. Each consisted of a large number of colleges founded by different agencies for different purposes. Each college had its own endowment, buildings, teaching staff, and body of students. The colleges were bound together by the overall control of the church and the authority of the university, which alone could grant degrees. Unlike the continental universities, Oxford and Cambridge consisted of groups of arts colleges, rather than the four faculties of philosophy, medicine, law, and theology. They continued to give the bachelor's degree, while the master's remained for a few who desired more specialization.

"The Great Public Schools." During the later Middle Ages, probably following the practice of chivalric training, the aristocracy sent their younger sons away from home to be trained for future service in church and state. Boarding or hospital schools were endowed partly for this purpose, and partly to give opportunity for poor but worthy pupils. The local town schools and all the regular church schools had in view only training for the services of the church.

A departure from the uniformity of medieval English schools was made when William of Wykeham established New College at Oxford in 1379 and connected with it a preparatory school in the town of Winchester for the education of needy students. Preparatory schools had been attached to several colleges before this; but the new factor was that the school was placed in a different town and was entitled "Grammar School of the College of the Blessed Mary of Winchester." An elementary school had already existed in the church at Winchester for seven centuries. In 1378 a papal bull authorized Wykeham to appropriate a church for the support of a college "for 70 poor scholars who should live college-wise and study grammatically." The point of greatest moment was that Winchester College was the first collegiate church school that conceived education in a broader way. Instead of training the youth for the services of the church, it prepared them to go to the university. It had become essential that preparation for college be a more definite objective of training and that special schools be organized for this purpose.

Eton, the most renowned of the Great Public Schools of England, was founded and endowed by Henry VI in 1440. It had in view the education of poor and needy boys for the church, but like Winchester was connected with a college, this time at Cambridge University.

Under the inspiration of The New Learning, John Colet in 1510 reinterpreted the function of the education of youth, and St. Paul's school, as already discussed, was established with a humanistic curriculum in line with the new ideals. Just as in the case of Winchester, an earlier church school was reformed for the purpose.

The good intentions of the founders of schools are frequently sidetracked by circumstances over which they have no control, and their purposes frustrated. Wykeham desired to aid poor boys, but in his final arrangements for Winchester he permitted 10 "sons of noble or powerful persons, special friends of the said college, to be instructed and taught grammar without charge to the college." In time the aristocrats came to dominate the institution as they did Eton and St. Paul's.

These three schools set the pattern. Others, as we shall see, followed their example in consequence of the Reformation, all together comprising the nine "Great Public Schools" of England. But they were not "public" in the American sense; they were distinguished from the private schools on the one hand, and from the local or town schools on the other, because they trained students with a view to public office, that is, for service in church or state.

Beginning of lay control and support in England and Scotland. During the early Middle Ages the church exercised control over all schools. In 1511 the control of St. Paul's was transferred by Colet to the Trade Company of Mercers, members of which became its trustees and governors. This act must be attributed to the influence of the Renaissance, which was a secular movement. It thus became the first school in England under lay control. Soon many religious, craft, and merchant guilds were chartered to support and control schools; a famous example of this type of guild school was the grammar school of Stratford-on-Avon, owned and controlled by the Guild of the Holy Cross. In some cases, laymen endowed schools and placed them under the control of chartered bodies of laymen. Many schools supported by the towns were taken under full municipal control before the end of the 15th century. In Scotland many such burgh (town) schools were established.

Courses of study and textbooks. The curriculum of the 16th century was in transition so far as the principal subjects of study were concerned. Catechism, manners, and morals, together with reading and writing, constituted the course of instruction in elementary vernacular schools. In learning to read, the pupil studied the hornbook first; then, an ABC book; and next, a primer. Latin grammar continued to be the chief primary study, but it was pursued in a new spirit, as literature superseded scholastic theology. Logic, the chief interest of the faculty of arts in the medieval university, was studied in English grammar schools until late in the 17th century, and in the dissenting academies until much later. However, there was a sharp reaction against medieval dialectic. Peter Ramus simplified the subject, and his logic was imitated by a number of writers.

Many important textbooks were produced during the 16th century. The most famous of these were the Latin grammars of Linacre and Lily;

an ABC book and a primer, which were published by royal authority; the catechisms of Colet, Erasmus, and Nowell, one of the outstanding educators of England; the *Colloquies* of Corderius, Erasmus, and Vives; and a great number of word-lists, dictionaries, and phrase-books. Lily's Grammar was most popular in the English-speaking world. Lily gets the credit, but Colet evidently had a hand in the writing of the famous text; and Erasmus probably added suggestions. First published in 1515, it continued at Eton College as late as 1868. Care was taken to maintain uniformity in the teaching of grammar. In his effort to make everybody adopt the same religion, Henry VIII commanded that no other grammar could be used in England so that there would be "one absolute and uniform sort of learning." The early Greek grammars came from the Continent. Editions of the Latin and Greek classics were prepared for the schools and after the middle of the century, the Bible was used as a schoolbook. Other texts widely used were Cato's *Disticha de Moribus,* Aesop's fables, Cicero's orations and letters, and selections from Terence, Ovid, Livy, Sallust, Quintus Curtius, Virgil, and Horace.

The relation of Humanism and the Reformation. Humanistic culture had scarcely been introduced into the schools of the Netherlands, Germany, and England when the Reformation began; henceforth the two movements became closely associated. Among the most significant points of agreement were the following:

(1) Both Humanism and the Reformation opposed Scholasticism and the scholastic method. They agreed in their contempt for the formalism and futility of Aristotelian logic, and for the degeneracy of monastic life.

(2) Both believed in the emancipation of the individual from the limitations of institutionalism, uniformity, and conventionality. Humanism tended to stimulate the expression of individuality in literary and artistic creation and even in intellectual activity. The Reformation cut more deeply and liberated the individual conscience from the bondage of traditionalism and ritualistic formalism.

(3) Humanism and the Reformation were interested alike in the classical languages and antagonistic to medieval Latin. For the one, Latin and Greek were the gateways to the classical literatures of Rome and Greece, the most sublime treasures of human thought, knowledge, and beauty of expression. For the other, these same languages unlocked the treasures of the original Scriptures and the writings of the Fathers of the early Christian church.

(4) The New Learning revealed a lofty state of culture not only transcending that of the time, but antedating the very existence of Christianity. Such learning tended to free the mind from the narrow ecclesiastical ideas of the Middle Ages. Humanistic scholars read Aristotle in the original Greek and found that he actually contradicted many statements which the Mohammedan texts attributed to him. The religious reformers, on the other hand, found that the original church of the New Testament was quite different from the Roman Church that they knew.

(5) The New Learning, as well as the Reformation, profited by critical scholarship. Grammars and dictionaries of the Hebrew, Greek, and Latin languages, as well as critical editions of the Scriptures, enabled Luther, Melanchthon, Tyndale, Coverdale, Calvin, and Beza to do their work. Erasmus edited the New Testament in Greek and he desired, as had the Brethren of the Common Life before him, to place the Scriptures in the hands of every person. Then, again, knowledge of Greek and classical Latin enabled the Reformers to profit by the extensive writings of the Church Fathers.

But there were likewise great differences separating the two movements:

(1) They were unlike in origin. Humanism had its beginning in Italy; the Reformation not only was northern in origin but it continued to be confined to Germanic lands.

(2) Italian Humanism was patrician, fostered especially by the rich, the princes of state and church, and by men of superior intellectual power and artistic sensibilities. It widened the breach between the lower and higher classes. The Reformation originated in the lower strata of society and appealed more particularly to the masses. To be sure many of its leaders were university trained, but they were of humble station.

(3) Humanism was predominantly intellectual, aesthetic and literary; the Reformation, on the other hand, was emotional, moral and religious. The former emphasized human or worldly interests; the latter, the spiritual.

(4) So far as the schools were concerned, the two movements worked in harmony. Humanism largely dictated the aim of learned and patrician education, together with the general curriculum and the methods which were to be employed. Protestantism dominated the religion of the schools, furnished their spirit, and added to the curriculum catechetical

instruction, the reading of the Scriptures, and church music. Moreover, Protestantism was interested in popular instruction while Humanism was not.

Four groups of educational reformers. The first half of the 16th century was an era of intense discussion of educational theory. The rediscovery during the previous century of the pedagogical writings of Plato, Plutarch, Quintilian, Cicero, and others aroused extraordinary interest. Moreover, the new educational views that were proposed were instrumental in forming a new order of schools which was to endure down to our own day. The reformers were fully united in their contempt for medievalism in all its forms, but by no means did they see eye to eye in their plans for reorganization. In general it is virtually impossible, as well as misleading, to classify educational thinkers. There are, nevertheless, certain points of common agreement which may be observed among the thinkers of that individualistic age. The lines that divided them into groups, strange to say, had little to do with the great religious schism.

The leading thinkers of the day may be roughly divided into four groups: (1) moralistic humanists; (2) realistic humanists; (3) religious reformers; and (4) stylists. These will be discussed in this and the following chapters.

(1) Moralistic Humanists. This was an extensive group, including such scholars as Colet, Lily, and More, in England; the Brethren of the Common Life in the Netherlands; Agricola, Reuchlin, Melanchthon, and Bucer in Germany; and Budeaus and Ramus in France. The greatest of all was Erasmus. These men subscribed to the current slogan, *Res et verba;* but *res* (things or realities) signified to their minds truth as it is in the moral life. They looked upon classical literature as the source of moral power in the formation of character, a storehouse of knowledge, especially knowledge of man and of the art of living the best life. Humanistic scholars could point to numerous examples of wild young men who, caught by a powerful enthusiasm for classical literature, had become noble scholars.

Erasmus. It may be doubted whether any scholar was ever more worshipped by his contemporaries. Born in Rotterdam (1465) and educated chiefly under Hegius at Deventer, Erasmus might be considered the most celebrated product of Dutch humanistic culture. He did not, however, enjoy his early schooling under the Brethren, and in later years criticized their methods.

For higher training he went to the University of Paris, which was still the foremost center of learning outside of Italy. The university was at this time taking on The New Learning. Here Erasmus taught Latin and took up the study of Greek. He made several visits to England, where he lectured at Oxford and later at Cambridge, but where he mainly engaged in learned intercourse with Colet, More, and others who were introducing The New Learning. By nature rather timid and averse to conflict, he declined to join the Protestant cause. Nevertheless, he deplored as deeply as anyone the degeneracy of the Roman Church, and labored to reinstate Christianity in its original purity and simplicity. He held that reform could be more effectively brought about from within the church than it could by schismatic and revolutionary measures.

The aims of his life were to refine taste, to purify morals, to promote the unity and peace of Europe, to reform ecclesiastic abuses, and to correct theological errors. The means by which this program was to be effected was exact scholarship. The knowledge needed was contained in the Scriptures, in patristic literature, in the classical authors, and in the interpretations of the church. Erasmus hoped to make Latin the universal language.

Erasmus spoke and wrote Latin with meticulous purity and beauty and among scholars of northern Europe he had the best command of Greek. More than any other man he edited accurate texts of classical authors. His New Testament was a work of highest scholarship which had no little effect upon the religious revival of the time. No man in northern Europe contributed so much to the restoration of the exact languages of the ancient Roman and Greek worlds.

While medieval training was rapidly being replaced by The New Learning, questions of education necessarily demanded attention. The principles and methods of humanistic pedagogy had to be worked out. The aims of Humanism had also to be determined.

There was general agreement that education begins with the mastery of speaking and writing Latin, together with a thorough knowledge of Greek, but there was no agreement in regard to details. Should Latin be taught by the grammatical method, or the conversational? Should grammar be a series of rules or a study of usage as found in the best authors? Educators disagreed on which authors should be read.

The question of the best kind of school arose. Should it be private tutoring in the home, together with a selected number of students, or should the child be sent to a private school, or was the public town-school the best? These, as well as numerous other problems, were discussed by Erasmus.[6]

The educational views of Erasmus consisted of principles culled from ancient writers and of shrewd observations from his own experience as pupil and teacher. The main sources were Quintilian and Plutarch. The aim of education was the "good man," refined and informed by the study of classical literature. Latin was not an end in itself, as advocated by the stylistic Humanists. This extreme Erasmus satirized in the *Ciceronianus,* which severely criticized the imitation of Cicero.

To accomplish his purposes, Erasmus wrote a number of textbooks that were printed in every country of Europe and continued to be used for several centuries. Several of these contain short sentences embodying proverbs, maxims, witty utterances, or pithy sayings of ancient times. *The Colloquies* (1519) was the most popular text of the time. In this work Erasmus made an effort to teach boys to speak Latin by talking about the common objects of life.

Other texts were as follows: The *Adagia,* containing 800 proverbs, was issued in 1500; *De Copia Verborum et Rerum* (1511) was a storehouse of rhetorical phrases to assist students in ready and correct Latin composition. Sixty editions of this were printed in his lifetime. It was prescribed at St. Paul's in 1518.

Attack upon monastic life, Scholasticism, and the schools. The attack upon traditional culture assumed varied aspects. They included: (1) ridicule for the barbarous Latin used by the monks and university scholars; (2) scorn for scholastic doctrines and for Aristotle, whose works furnished the foundation of the system; (3) contempt for monastic life; and (4) criticism of the methods of instruction employed in the universities and lower schools.

Everywhere revered as the greatest scholar of the age and the master of purest Latin, Erasmus attacked medieval culture in a biting satire,

---

[6] The chief writings of Erasmus on education are as follows:

1. *De Ratione Studii:* a treatise on the right method of instruction. 1511.
2. *Dialogus Ciceronianus:* a dialogue on the best style of speaking. 1528.
3. *De Pueris statim ac Liberaliter Instituendis:* a work dealing with the constant and liberal instruction of youth. 1529.
4. *De Civilitate Morum Puerilium Libellus:* a book of good manners for children.

Several of these are translated in Woodward, W. H., *Desiderius Erasmus.* Cambridge: Cambridge University Press, 1904.

The Praise of Folly (*Moriae Encomium*), published in 1509. In this work he ridiculed all the abuses of the church and Scholasticism. He lambasted the insatiable greed of the popes and of the monks and clergy, their intolerance, immorality, and hypocrisy, pilgrimages to the tombs of saints, pretended miracles, and the use of indulgences. Scholastic methods were boldly ridiculed: vulgar Latin, the bombastic and silly disputations of the school men, and the allegorical interpretations of the Scriptures. His boldness and vigorous, clear style captured the attention of all classes.

Even more effective was the work, *Letters of Obscure Men* (*Epistolae Obscurorum Virorum*), written from 1515 to 1519. In these letters, which, for bitter sarcasm and stinging wit, are unequalled in all literature, the monkish culture was held up to scorn and ridicule until it became a universal laughing stock. These letters were written by a small group of which Ulrich von Hutten, the brilliant knight and humanistic scholar, was the leader. Satirizing the barbarities of medieval Latin and scholastic learning with their own crude terms, this untranslatable lampoon caused all European students to jeer at medievalism. No work was more effective in making the monks and scholastics ashamed of their uncouth and barbarous learning.

The struggle against medievalism was without a full measure of success so long as the real stronghold remained intact; that bulwark was the logic and philosophy of Aristotle. The history of Aristotelianism was, for more than three centuries, the story of human thought. Someone has suggested that God created man, but left it to Aristotle to make him rational.

During the first part of the Middle Ages, western scholars knew nothing of Aristotle's work except several chapters from his *Logic*. Arabic translations of his treatises on ethics, physics, metaphysics, and other subjects were made at an earlier date, not directly from his original works but from the Syrian translations of the Nestorian Christians, and brought into Spain by the Mohammedans during the first half of the 13th century. At first the Church of Rome was hostile and burned some of these treatises in public condemnation of their heresy. Later its attitude was completely reversed, and the Stagirite was exalted as the official philosopher of the Christian religion. He was made the *Predecessor of Christ in the Realm of Nature, just as John the Baptist was in the Realm of Grace* (*Precursor Christi in rebus naturalibus, sicut Joannes Baptista in rebus gratuitis*). Thomas Aquinas was the master mind who brought about this great change by integrating the philosophy of Aristotle and Christian theology.

Thus Aristotle became the infallible and authoritative source of all scientific truth, and his logic was the supreme method of thought. Upon his philosophy and logic the entire structure of scholastic theology and science was constructed. But, unfortunately, this foundation was itself all too fragile.

At the close of the 15th century, Theodore of Gaza and John of Trebizond, both ardent Peripatetics, translated a number of the works of Aristotle from the original Greek. It was then discovered that this genuine Aristotle differed essentially from the Aristotle of the Schoolmen, especially upon points vital to Christian doctrine. In fact, the true Aristotle sharply contradicted not only the theology of the church but the new discoveries of science as well. Luther looked upon him as a "damnable heathen," yet hesitated to reject all of his writings. Peter Ramus, graduating (1536) from the University of Paris, defended as his thesis the proposition: "All that Aristotle has said is false." Nothing could have been more audacious, for every university of Europe, as well as the church, looked upon Aristotelianism as the repository of all truth in philosophy and science. The logic of Ramus was based upon actual experience and usage. It attained a widespread influence, and aided materially in bringing in the realistic era of the 17th century. The downfall of Aristotelianism carried with it the immediate decline of the scholastic method and doctrine.

The power of the Roman Church, scholastic theology, and the existing practices in the schools were all so closely bound together that one could not be destroyed without affecting another. The struggle against medieval methods of instruction and training was led by Luther, in Germany; Erasmus and Vives, in the Netherlands and England; and Rabelais and Ramus, in France.

Rabelais ridicules the old education. Satire is frequently a more successful instrument in discrediting outworn forms and institutions than is censure. This means had been effectively used by Erasmus in *The Praise of Folly,* and also by the Humanists in *Letters of Obscure Men.* Rabelais, a French monk and physician, in a grotesque and ribald allegory made Frenchmen laugh at the old education. He portrayed a giant youth, Gargantua,[7] brought up according to the medieval custom.

[7] Rabelais, F., *The Works of Rabelais,* pp. 33-34. London: Chatto and Windus.

In the first place, he was taught by a wonderful master of Sophism, Holofernes,

> ... who taught him his A. B. C.'s so well, that he could say it by heart backwards; and this took him five years and three months. Then he read to him *Donat, le Facet, Theodolet,* and *Alanus in Parabolis.*[8] These took him thirteen years, six months and two weeks. But you must remember that in the meantime he did learn to write in Gothic characters, and that he wrote all his books; for the art of printing was not then in use....[9] After that was read unto him *De Modis Significandi* and ... a rabble of others; and herein he spent more than eighteen years and eleven months, and was so well versed therein that in school disputes with his fellow-students, he would recite it by heart, backwards; and he did sometimes prove on his fingers' ends to his mother that *De Modis Significandi* was not scientific. Then was read to him the *Compost* on which he spent sixteen years and two months.[10] And at that very time, his preceptor died of the pox.
>
> There was then placed over him an old cougher who read to him ... [a number of treatises] [11] by the reading whereof he became as wise as any we ever since baked in an oven.

Thus Rabelais ridiculed the length of time taken in teaching the young and the utter foolishness of what was taught. In the end, Gargantua, placed alongside a young fellow trained in the new education for "only two years," appeared to be nothing but "a fool, a sot, a dolt, and blockhead."

Vives, the most scientific student of education in that day, criticized the methods of instruction. He was the first to point out the function of sense impressions, and to insist upon inductive thinking as opposed to the memoriter and authoritarian teaching. He also opposed the use of disputation. Of this he said: [12]

> When a boy is brought to school, on the very first day, immediately he is taught to wrangle, though as yet unable to talk. The same practice is

[8] Donatus, a Roman rhetorician, wrote his *Ars Grammatica* in the 4th century; the text was in universal use for over a thousand years, probably the most successful textbook ever written. The author's name came to be used as a synonym for grammar. *Le Facet* was a work on morals. *Theodolet* was an allegory against paganism. *Alanus in Parabolis* comprised the writings of Alain de Lille.

[9] This remark indicates how slowly old methods of education yield to progress. The art of printing had been known 80 years when this satire was written.

[10] *De Modis Significandi* involved methods of interpretation. The *Compost* was a treatise on calculating the calendar.

[11] Rabelais mentions the treatises in detail.

[12] Watson, Foster, *Luis Vives,* pp. 18-19. Oxford: Oxford University Press, 1922.

> followed in grammar, in the poets, in history, in dialectic and rhetoric, in every subject. Nothing is so clear that some bit of a question cannot be raised about it, and even as a wind, be stirred into action. Beginners are accustomed never to be silent, lest at any time they should seem to have ceased speaking. At breakfast they wrangle; after breakfast they wrangle; at supper they wrangle; after supper they wrangle. At meals, at the bath, in the sweating room, in the temple, in the city, in the country, in public, in private, in every place, at every time, they are wrangling.

This method of disputation had some good effects upon older students but had sadly degenerated into a contest of wits and bombast. Instead of leading the young to the love of truth and to more accurate methods of research, it had become so overemphasized that it was having precisely the opposite effect. Moreover, this exaggerated use of disputation was turning many against the university system.

The humanistic forerunners of Realism. At the very hour when the literary Humanists were sweeping aside the rubbish of Scholasticism, the forerunners of a still later era were announcing ideas of the greatest consequence. The chief of these far-seeing thinkers were Vives, Rabelais, Ramus, Montaigne, and the English schoolmaster Richard Mulcaster. These men were alike in that they used classical literature, not for its own sake, but rather for the scientific and historical information which it contained. They were not interested in style or in mere words, as were Sturm and his followers; nor yet were they interested primarily in religious and moral precepts and guidance, as were Erasmus and Melanchthon. Furthermore, they did not revere the ancients as infallible authorities and as the only source of knowledge, but they boldly asserted their right to use their own eyes, and to observe nature for themselves.

Not merely was Vives a prophet of Realism; he must also be regarded as the first great modern student of educational theory. He was a Spaniard, born at Valencia. Of noble birth, he was well reared and carefully guided in his education by his gifted mother. As a young man with strict scholastic training and traditional views, he entered the University of Paris, where for the first time he came into contact with humanistic learning. He then went to Bruges, the seat of a large Spanish colony in the Netherlands; here he established his headquarters and married. For a time he studied and taught at Louvain, where he enjoyed the friendship of Erasmus, who, though much older, acknowledged his superior intellectual ability. From this time he was recognized as one of the leading humanistic scholars of Europe.

In 1522, when he visited London, Vives associated with Sir Thomas More and other English leaders. The queen, Catherine of Aragon, at once befriended him and brought about an appointment at Oxford to a readership in humanities. In 1523, after he had published several works on the education of women, he was appointed supervisor of the education of Princess Mary. His attachment to the queen led him to oppose the divorce of Henry VIII; in consequence, he lost the royal support and returned to Bruges, where he taught, engaged in business, and wrote. Vives died comparatively young. In the midst of the Protestant movement, he remained Catholic, but in many ways his sympathies were Protestant.

Vives was the most extensive and progressive Catholic writer on education during the 16th century. In 1523, he wrote *On a Plan of Studies for Youth* (*De Ratione Studii Puerilis*) for the son of Lord Mountjoy, and a similar plan for the education of Princess Mary. These were followed by a larger work, *On the Instruction of a Christian Woman* (*De Institutione Feminae Christianae*), the most outstanding work on the education of women. As poverty had everywhere become a pressing problem, Vives wrote (1526) *On Poor Relief* (*De Subventione Pauperum*). This was the first scientific work on civil charity, and one that exerted a powerful influence in western Europe. The Netherlands, where he was living, advanced beyond other peoples in civil government, and especially in the care of the indigent.

In 1531, Vives published twelve books entitled *Concerning the Teaching of the Arts* (*De Tradendis Disciplinis*). This has justly been termed "the most thorough-going educational book of the Renascence." [13] In addition to this he wrote a number of textbooks which were widely used. His last writing, *Concerning the Mind* (*De Anima*), was a work on psychology of great significance for philosophy and education.

Vives applied himself to psychology, with a view to making the principles of the mind's operations the basis of teaching practice. He may be called a precursor of empirical psychology. Concerning himself with how the mind acts, not with the problem of its essence or substance, he

---

[13] Watson, Foster, *Luis Vives*, p. 100. Oxford: Oxford University Press, 1922.

rejected the subservience of philosophy to theology; he insisted upon reading Aristotle for himself, and positively declared: [14]

> It is our rightful claim to employ these our powers [of observation and thought], in the examination of all facts and all truths, comparing and ordering them one with the other, and surveying the whole universe as it were our own domain: even though we may wander ignorantly therein and fail to view it with right apprehension.

No other man had such a clear conception of the function of sense perception, and of the natural growth of knowledge in the individual mind. Vives drew upon earlier theorists of the Renaissance, as well as upon their masters, Quintilian, Plutarch, and Aristotle. He criticized the current method of teaching the arts, and drew up a comprehensive plan of education, adapted to the needs of his day. He also made suggestions respecting school buildings and school organization.

The education of children is the concern of both parents: the father will oversee everything, and the mother may well be the child's first teacher. At seven years of age, boys are to be placed in public day schools; the pupils continue, however, to live with relatives or with friends, not in dormitories. If it is necessary to have a child taught by a tutor, one companion at least will be brought in. Sports, entertainments, presentation of Latin plays, and physical exercise have a place in education. Schoolmasters must be men of sound scholarship. The individual education of pupils should be planned by masters who study each student individually, and who adapt the course each one is to pursue to his particular ability. Vives suggested that boys enter the school a month or two in advance, in order that their capacities may be thoroughly studied by the instructors. Four times a year the teachers will hold conferences at which they exchange their observations regarding the progress of the pupils. Slow wits are preferred, and only those students who are really capable are given higher training. The stipend of the masters is a public charge, and no master receives money directly from his pupils for tuition, meals, or lodging. Great care must be exercised in choosing the site of school buildings, as well as in their planning, construction, and equipment.

Concerning the use of the vernacular Vives wrote: [15] "It is the duty of

---

[14] Woodward, W. H., *Studies in Education During the Age of the Renaissance*, p. 188. Cambridge: Cambridge University Press, 1906.

[15] *Ibid.*, p. 197.

the parent and of the master to take pains that children speak the mother tongue correctly." That this suggestion should have been made by a Spaniard from Valencia is not surprising. In the year of Vives' birth, Antonio de Lebrija wrote a Castilian grammar, *Grammatica Castillana,* for use in the education of young women of the Spanish Court.[16] Spanish scholars recognized in their native speech a medium adequate to the demands of literature and scholarship. Furthermore, Vives believed that, to teach ancient languages effectively, schoolmasters must be able to use fluently and correctly the language of their pupils, and that it was not beneath the dignity of even a learned scholar to purify and enrich his national speech. In advocating the use of the vernacular as an introduction to Latin, Vives was a century ahead of his day. Moreover, in insisting upon the use of the direct method in teaching languages, he was far in advance of his age.

Vives was by no means a foe to the teaching of ancient languages. He felt that Latin, as a universal language, served in promoting intercourse between scholars, the wide distribution of books, and the diffusion of the Catholic religion. He rejected the absurd adulation of Cicero, the dialectical grammars of the Middle Ages, and the view that antiquity had supplied all the information and wisdom needed. He advised the study of such *utility* grammars as Melanchthon's, based on current usage; history, and also geography, he felt, should find a place in the curriculum. In the study of literature, he considered form secondary to sense and good taste; the goal of this study was to be the development of character. Logic was to be studied for mental discipline. *Physics,* by which he meant mathematics and natural sciences, was to be added to the curriculum when methods and materials suited to the school could be provided. His was the most urgent appeal made in this century for the study of nature; he claimed that nature is the best book: "Whatever is in the arts was in Nature first, just as pearls are in shells, and gems in the sand." [17] The adult studies were the technical and professional subjects such as theology, law, medicine, architecture, political science, and war. Morals and the Catholic faith formed the crowning course of general education.

The program of women's education advocated by Vives included careful training in vernacular speech, Latin, religion, moral maxims and

---

[16] Watson, Foster, *op. cit.,* p. 5.
[17] *Ibid.,* p. 5.

conduct, the care and education of children, and household management. He neglected music, dancing, and drawing, which usually held a prominent place in the education of women. Mathematics, science, politics, and much of history were likewise omitted.

Education should develop personality, render a man competent in business, and, above all else, make him a true Christian. In furtherance of this ideal, Vives wrote: [18]

> This must be the first rule of any study of Nature in school: not to push research into causes and principles, which are beyond our reach, but to order all our enquiry with reference to the practical needs of life, to some definite advantage of mind or body, or to the end of personal piety.

In another connection, he wrote: [19]

> This is the fruit of all our studies, this is the goal. Having acquired our knowledge, *we must turn it to usefulness,* and employ it for the common good.

Vives was the most democratic and humanitarian of the great Humanists. He advocated the education of defectives, rejected almsgiving as a means of aiding the poor, and suggested methods of relief similar to those employed at the present time. In his attitude toward the masses, Vives is quite different from the typical Renaissance scholar. He wrote: "We [scholars] must transfer our solicitude to the people." [20] In another passage Vives declared that, if the language of the disputants of the university was translated into the speech of the people, the workmen, "with hissing and clamour and the clanging of tools, would hoot the dialecticians out of Paris." [21] Vives had faith in democracy. Sensing the Nordic revolt against Scholasticism and the Roman hierarchy, he predicted: [22]

> I see from the depths a change is coming. Amongst all the nations men are springing up, of clear, excellent and free intellects, impatient of servitude, determined to thrust off the yoke of this tyranny from their necks. They are calling their fellow-citizens to liberty.

Although Vives was favorable to Humanism, his whole system moved in the realm of Realism.

---

[18] Woodward, W. H., *op. cit.,* p. 203.
[19] Watson, Foster, *op. cit.,* p. 60.
[20] *Ibid.,* p. 32.
[21] *Ibid.,* p. 32.
[22] *Ibid.,* p. 32.

François Rabelais. The chief significance of this lovable buffoon lies in the fact that he stripped education of its superficial, external circumstances, and directed attention to the very heart of the matter. Little indeed is known about him; even the exact date of his birth, guessed variously from 1483 to 1500, is unknown. His birthplace was Chinon, in Touraine. He became a monk, first, of one order and, later, of another, and then left monastic life entirely. It is known that he studied medicine, a fact which sheds much light on the character of his mind. He employed humor, satire, and buffoonery to express his criticisms of the evils of the day, and to suggest in a subtle way the reforms needed. He attacked the church and its abuses, but he did so without evoking the wrath of its authorities. His ideas exercised a powerful influence on the greatest of men, such as Montaigne, Locke, and Rousseau.

In 1533 appeared the strange story of Gargantua, a mythical young superman. His education followed the plan of the Middle Ages.[23] When it was discovered, from a comparison with a young gentleman educated by the method of the Renaissance, how crude and ignorant he was despite his fifty years of application to medieval learning, Gargantua was subjected to a pedagogical purgative that "made him forget all he had learned under his ancient preceptors." There was then placed over him a new instructor whose method introduced a new era in educational thinking. First, as the story goes: [24]

> They brought him [Gargantua] into the company of learned men, which stirred in him an emulation and desire to whet his wit and improve his parts and to bend his study another way, so as that the world might have a value for him. And afterwards he put himself into such a road, that he lost not any one hour in the day, but employed all his time in learning and honest knowledge. Gargantua awaked about four o'clock in the morning. Whilst they were in rubbing of him, there was read unto him some chapter of the Holy Scriptures.... According to the purpose and argument of that lesson, he oftentimes gave himself to worship, adore, pray... to that good God, whose word did show his majesty and marvelous judgment.... They considered the face of the sky, if it were such as they had observed it the night before.... This done he was apparalled, combed, curled, trimmed, and perfumed, during which time they repeated to him the lessons of the day before. He himself said them by heart, and upon them would ground some practical cases concerning

---

[23] See page 47 of this text.

[24] Rabelais, F., *Gargantua,* Book I, Chap. XXIII. London: Chatto and Windus, *n.d.*

> the estate of man, which he would prosecute sometimes two or three hours.... Then for three good hours he had a lecture read unto him.

There followed tennis or other games, as long as they pleased, "exercising their bodies as they had done their minds," and then "were they very well wiped and rubbed."

> In the meantime Master Appetite came, and then very orderly sat they down at table.... There was read some pleasant history of the warlike actions of former times.... Then, if they thought good, they continued reading, or began to discourse merrily together; speaking first of the virtue, propriety, efficacy, and nature of all that was served in at the table; of bread, of wine, of water, of salt, of fleshes, fishes, fruits, herbs, roots, and of their dressing....

Reference books were often brought to assist their discussions. After the meal a new form of lessons was introduced thus:

> They brought in cards, not to play, but to learn a thousand pretty tricks and new inventions, which were all grounded upon arithmetic. By this means he fell in love with that numerical science, and every day after dinner and supper he passed his time in it as pleasantly as he was wont to do at cards and dice.... And not only in that, but in the other mathematical sciences, as geometry, astronomy, and music.

He learned to sing and

> ... to play upon the lute, the virginals, the harp, the flute with nine holes, the viol, and the sackbut. This hour thus spent, and digestion finished... then betook himself to his principal study for three hours together, or more, as well to repeat his morning lectures.

Then followed expert horsemanship, in complete coat of mail and arms, and later, swordmanship, hunting, wrestling, jumping, and swimming.

> Coming out of the water, he ran furiously up against a hill, and with the same alacrity and swiftness ran down again. He climbed up trees like a cat, and leaped from the one to the other like a squirrel.

Finally supper came. As at dinner, lessons were read and discussion engaged in. Before retiring,

> ... they went unto the most open place of the house, to see the face of the sky.... Then with his master did he briefly recapitulate, after the manner of the Pythagoreans, that which he had read, seen, learned, done and understood in the whole course of that day. Then prayed they unto God the Creator, ... which being done, they went to bed.

This exhausting program was varied in rainy weather, when they studied painting, wood carving, and other arts.[25] They visited all the establishments for manufacturing, such as the metal workers, goldsmiths, cutters of gems, alchemists, money-coiners, upholsterers, weavers, printers, organists, and so on,

> ... and everywhere did learn and consider the industry and invention of the trades. They went also to hear the public lectures, the solemn commencements, ... the pleadings of the lawyers, and sermons of evangelical preachers. ... They visited the shops of druggists, herbalists, and apothecaries, and diligently considered the fruits, roots, leaves, gums, seeds. ...
>
> Thus was Gargantua governed, and kept on in this course of education ... which, although at the beginning seemed difficult, became a little after so sweet, so easy, and so delightful, that it seemed rather the recreation of a king than the study of a scholar.

In due time Gargantua had a son as gigantic as himself. He wrote to him, while the boy was a student at Paris, what subjects he should pursue:[26]

> I intend, and will have it so, that thou learn the languages perfectly; first of all, the Greek, as Quintilian will have it; secondly, the Latin; and then the Hebrew, for the Holy Scripture-sake; and then the Chaldee and Arabic likewise. And that thou frame thy style in Greek, in imitation of Plato; and for the Latin, after Cicero. Let there be no history which thou shalt not have ready in thy memory; and to help thee therein the books of cosmography will be very conducible. Of the liberal arts of geometry, arithmetic, and music, I gave thee some taste when thou wert yet little, and not above five or six years old; proceed further in them, and learn the remainder if thou canst. As for astronomy, study all the rules thereof; let pass, nevertheless, the divining and judicial astrology, and the art of Lullius, as being nothing else but plain cheats and vanities. As for the civil law, of that I would have thee to know the texts by heart, and then to compare them with philosophy.
>
> Now, in matter of the knowledge of the works of nature, I would have thee to study that exactly; so that there be no sea, river, or fountain, of which thou dost not know the fishes; all the fowls of the air; all the several kinds of shrubs and trees, whether in forest or orchards; all the sorts of herbs and flowers that grow upon the ground; all the various metals that are hid within the bowels of the earth; together with all the diversity of precious stones, that are to be seen in the orient and south parts of the world. Let nothing of all these be hidden from thee. Then

---

[25] *Ibid.*, Book I, Chap. XXIV.
[26] *Ibid.*, Book II, Chap. VIII.

> fail not most carefully to peruse the books of the Greek, Arabian, and Latin physicians, not despising the Talmudists and Cabalists; and by frequent anatomies get thee the perfect knowledge of the microcosm, which is man. And at some of the hours of the day apply thy mind to the study of the Holy Scriptures; first in Greek, the New Testament, with the Epistles of the Apostles; and then the Old Testament in Hebrew. In brief, let me see thee an abyss and bottomless pit of knowledge: for from henceforward, as thou growest great and becomest a man, thou must part from this tranquillity and rest of study, thou must learn chivalry, warfare, and the exercise of the field, the better thereby to defend my house and our friends, and to succour and protect them at all their needs, against the invasion and assaults of evil-doers.

In this jesting fashion, Rabelais points forward to an age of individual liberty, when men will rely upon a sense of honor to guide them in proper conduct. Even coeducation is suggested in the Abbey of Thélème, where boys between twelve and eighteen and girls from ten to fifteen live in free association and leave the institution when they mate—the true end and purpose of the institution.

In Rabelais one finds the educational process for the first time completely stripped of all its externalities and non-essentials of space, time, and people. He exhibits childhood and youth expressing their natural, exuberant activities spontaneously in play, pursuing their native interest in gathering knowledge; and at the same time, responding to the influence of those who have already tasted the delights of liberal learning. Spontaneity and interest are substituted for formalism and authority; the world of nature and everyday life, for the cloister and the classroom; observation and direct contact, for textbooks; and reasoning, for rote memorization. Learning truly becomes, not the drudgery of imprisoned schoolboys, but "the sport of kings."

The revival of learning and the sciences. The students of science, as well as the men of literary taste and the theologians, journeyed to Italy, attracted by the great enthusiasm for ancient Latin and Greek writers. Copernicus, graduate of the University of Cracow, went to Bologna to study canon law but became infected with a passion for astronomy.

In the field of anatomy, Vesalius, a native of Brussels, went to Italy to pursue his investigations at Padua, Bologna, and Pisa. The author of the first comprehensive and systematic work on anatomy, he surpassed his contemporaries because he not only studied the ancients but engaged in researches of his own.

THE EXPANSION OF SCIENTIFIC KNOWLEDGE

Importance. We are accustomed to pride ourselves on living in the supreme age of scientific discovery. The progress of scientific knowledge and the consequent control over the forces of nature are the boast of our times. We fail to appreciate that some of the commonplace things of today were the great discoveries of yesterday, and that many of them aroused as great a thrill as any of the wonderful inventions of the present. At the beginning of the 17th century, Campanella closed his utopia, *The City of the Sun,*[27] with this highly modern boast: [28] "Our age has in it more history within a hundred years than all the world had in four thousand years before."

The theological furor and the political turmoil of the 17th century have so dominated the attention of historians generally that consideration has been distracted from more significant events. During the later 16th century and the early part of the 17th, the foundations for modern science were laid. There are no monuments erected to the inventors of "o" (zero), and "*x, y, z,*" or any of the other mathematical signs; but, as a matter of cold fact, these men actually conferred greater benefits upon civilization than did most of the heroes who adorn the pages of history. Even the histories of education have too frequently treated with silent indifference this progress of science. Moreover, while great honor has always been bestowed upon Bacon, who was not a creative scientist, too little credit has been accorded the men who actually advanced scientific knowledge.

The progress of mathematics. The outstanding events of modern mathematical science may be summed up in the following five major points:

Through all the early centuries, the conquest of numbers was well-nigh impossible because of cumbersome symbols. The change effected by the adoption of the Arabic notation made calculation of large numbers so vastly easier that the study could be transferred from the senior year of college to the grades. By the end of the 13th century, the *Arabic notation* had been introduced into Europe; by 1500, the symbols employed were practically the same as those now in use. The popularizing of the new notation took place outside the schools. The chief

---

[27] See page 153 of this text.

[28] Morley, Henry, *Ideal Commonwealths,* p. 263. London: G. Routledge and Sons, 1887.

means of spreading the new notation was its use in trade, in keeping accounts, and in the making of almanacs and calendars. The calendar was particularly important because of its relation to religious feast days.

The second step in facilitating the use of numbers was made possible by the invention of the idea and symbol of zero. The use of decimal fractions, begining in 1585, was the invention of Simon Stevin, a Dutch mathematician and physicist.

The new art of algebra immediately came to be of the greatest service in promoting the advancement of science. One may call it a universal or abstract arithmetic. Cardan, an Italian mathematician, made the most important advance when, in 1545, he published *The Great Art* (*Ars Magna*), a treatise on algebra. Between this date and the year 1600, the present symbols used in algebra were found. Recorde added the sign of equality; Descartes introduced the common use of *a, b, c,* and *x, y, z,* as symbols to express abstract numbers. It was the lack of such handy symbols which hindered the ancients from making progress in this field of thought.

The discovery of logarithms was due to Sir John Napier, a Scotch mathematician, who originated the system and published his work in 1614. This development made possible the elaborate and lengthy calculations required in astronomy and other sciences.

Important developments in geometry and trigonometry followed. Gradually the signs and symbols employed in these sciences were elaborated, and then accepted by all. The establishment of chairs of mathematics in the various universities of Europe at this time did much to increase a knowledge of the subject. Furthermore, mathematical thinking soon led to the invention of numerous instruments for exact measurement and for demonstrating scientific facts.

The part printing played in the advancement of mathematical, as well as other science, is stated by Ball: [29]

> The invention of printing rendered . . . the dissemination of discoveries comparatively easy. . . . We are perhaps apt to forget that when a mediaeval writer "published" a work, the results were known to only a few of his contemporaries. . . . There was no common center through which men of science could communicate with one another, and to this cause the slow and fitful development of mediaeval mathematics may be partly ascribed.

---

[29] Ball, W. W. Rouse, *A Short Account of the History of Mathematics,* pp. 199-200. London: Macmillan and Company, Ltd., 1922.

The first printed arithmetic appeared at Treviso, near Venice, in 1478; and a few years later the first book in arithmetic and algebra combined was published. Soon other arithmetics were issued in northern Europe; the first in the English language was written by Robert Recorde, in 1540.[30]

> By the beginning of the seventeenth century we may say that the fundamental principles of arithmetic, algebra, theory of equations, and trigonometry had been laid down, and the outlines of the subjects as we know them had been traced. It must be, however, remembered that there were no good elementary text-books on these subjects.... Though much of the modern algebraical and trigonometrical notation had been introduced, it was not familiar to mathematicians, nor was it even universally accepted; and it was not until the end of the seventeenth century that the language of these subjects was definitely fixed.

Astronomy and astrology. Aside from the direct attention from the starry heavens, which springs spontaneously from sheer wonder and curiosity, men became interested in astronomy for several quite practical reasons. First, and most necessary, was the desire for strict accuracy in calculating the calendar. Accuracy was of extraordinary concern not only for agricultural and other seasonal operations, but especially for dating religious celebrations. Throughout the Middle Ages, a controversy raged over the proper time for celebrating the Easter Mass. The Greek Catholic Church and the Celtic Church in Britain celebrated Easter at one time; the Roman Church, at another. This sharp disagreement resulted in raising astronomy to a place of foremost importance, not only for scholars, but also for popular attention.

Quite a different interest took precedence over scientific astronomy during the later medieval period. This was the pseudo-science of astrology, which was the product of superstitions. Absurd as the practice may now seem, one must remember that astrology was accepted and practiced in all good faith by many of the most intelligent mathematicians and physicians even down to the 18th century. Bacon accepted it. Kepler, the astronomer, made his living for a while by telling fortunes and casting horoscopes; for, said he, "Nature has designed astrology as an adjunct and ally to astronomy." Cardan "at one time did nothing but rave on astrology." The same was true of Regiomontanus. Moreover, astrologers were regularly attached to the universities. This wide-

---

[30] *Ibid.*, pp. 258-259.

spread belief in astrology began to decline only after the 17th century.

Interest in the cure of disease and the forecasting of future events combined to place this study among the branches of medical science. Chairs of astrology were established at some of the chief universities. Casting the horoscope, to foretell future events in the fortune of an individual, required not only great astuteness, but equally great skill in making calculations. With the final triumph of the Copernican theory, the reign of astrology came to an end so far as intelligent men were concerned. Nevertheless its prolonged hold upon human credulity must not blind one to its actual service in spite of its absurd claims. For a long time astrology kept alive the interest in astronomy and, by the casting of horoscopes, contributed vitally to the application of mathematical principles to astronomical study.

In 1543, Copernicus published the final statement of the heliocentric theory. At first, because of its incredible character, the theory was greeted with derision. Later, powerful opposition sought to crush it. Among the theologians, Luther, Calvin, and Melanchthon took issue with Copernicus on the ground that his theory was contradictory to the Scriptures. The Roman Curia, through the Congregation of the Index, condemned the new theory, forced a recantation from Galileo in 1633, and proscribed all books which taught the theory.

Many of the most learned scientists were as strongly opposed to the Copernican theory as were the theologians. Tycho Brahe, the astronomer, Cardan, the algebraist and astrologist, Jean Bodin, the French scientist, Montaigne, the celebrated French savant, and Bacon and Harvey, the leading thinkers of England—all discredited the strange idea. Nevertheless, the new view gradually became dominant. By 1596, Kepler could boast that all famous astronomers were Copernicans, and by the middle of the following century, the new theory had triumphed everywhere. Mathematics, as an *a priori* science applied to the objective universe, had revealed knowledge which, for daring, sweep, and positiveness, far transcended everything the ancients had discovered, the supreme triumph attained by human knowledge. Furthermore, all later thinkers must henceforth measure their results by this sublime achievement. Copernicus made the greatest advance by his bold hypothesis that the sun, and not the earth, is the center of the universe.

In summary, the period of deepest significance may be said to have begun in 1543 and to have ended in 1687, a little less than a century and a half later, with the publication of Newton's *Principles of Natural*

Philosophy. The initial events took place in the fields of astronomy, mathematics, and medicine.[31]

> Suddenly, within two years, appeared three of the most momentous works of science that the world has ever seen, Copernicus, *On the Revolutions of the Heavenly Orbs* (1543), Vesalius, *On the Structure of the Human Body* (1543), and Cardan's *The Great Art* (a treatise on algebra, 1545).

---

[31] Smith, Preserved, *A History of Modern Culture,* Vol. I, p. 18. New York: Henry Holt, 1930.

Chapter 3

PROTESTANT EDUCATIONAL REFORMERS

MARTIN LUTHER. In Germany the irresistible demand for a religious and moral reformation was chiefly due to the intense conviction, the contagious faith, and elemental courage of Martin Luther. He did more than any other individual to provoke the storm and to unite and direct its energies.

Luther was born at Eisleben, Saxony, in 1483, and spent his childhood at Mansfield, where his father was a poor miner. In spite of poverty, the boy secured the usual elementary education. Later he attended the University of Erfurt, just when it was becoming interested in the humanistic movement. After his course Luther became an Augustinian monk and was called to the faculty of the newly formed University of Wittenberg. Here, through reading the Scriptures, he reached the conviction that salvation comes by faith and not as a result of good works. Henceforth this conviction became the master motive of everything he did. In 1517, when he nailed his ninety-five theses to the door of the university chapel, he took the first step in his career as a reformer. The further steps and final rift with Rome quickly followed.

Luther approached education, not as a Humanist nor yet as a practical schoolmaster, but rather as a religious reformer. He dealt chiefly with broad general principles; the details he left for others to work out. His educational reforms grew out of his contacts with the rapidly changing conditions that characterized the decade from 1520 to 1530. During these years he frequently discussed education, especially in his addresses, sermons, table talks, letters, commentaries, and other writings.

In 1520, Luther published in rapid succession three of his most powerful and epochal works. The first was the *Address to the Christian*

Nobility, in which he pleaded with the German princes to undertake the reform of the church.

The second treatise was *The Freedom of a Christian Man.* In this dynamic work Luther gave expression to the growing sense of individual independence which was springing up among the Northern peoples. The treatise added vitally to the self-respect of the lower classes, and encouraged the peasantry to question the galling tyranny of their petty feudal overlords and to lay claim to the most ordinary rights of common humanity.

The third treatise, which issued red-hot from Luther's soul, was *On the Babylonish Captivity of the Church.* This scathing denunciation of the doctrines and practices of the papacy marked his complete break with the Roman hierarchy.

These three publications threw the German world into a state of religious bewilderment and educational chaos. The following year Luther was cited before the judgment seat of the papal church and condemned as a heretic. But this condemnation could not turn the mounting tide of revolution. Luther violently assailed the schools, the subjects taught, and the texts used. Oftentimes in criticizing the objects of his dislike, he was not overparticular as to nicety of language. He termed the schools "hells, purgatories where a boy was forever tormented with cases and tenses, and where he learned nothing, by reason of ceaseless flogging, trembling, woe and anguish." In the same spirit he continued: [1]

> Was it not a burning shame that formerly a boy must needs study twenty years or longer only to learn a jargon of bad Latin, and then to turn priest and say mass? And he, who finally arrived at this pinnacle of his hopes, was accounted happy. . . . But, for all this, he remained a poor illiterate man all his days, and was neither good to cluck nor to lay eggs. Such are the teachers and guides that we have had to put up with, who knew nothing themselves, and accordingly were unable to teach anything that was either good or true.

Downfall of medieval schools. The new wine of Humanism and Protestantism could no longer be contained in the old schools of Catholic medievalism. None of the other institutions of the time showed a more immediate and decisive reaction to the reform movement. The greatest effect upon the schools was felt in Germany, and followed Luther's attack upon the abuses of the church. The new doctrines circulated every-

---

[1] Barnard, Henry, *German Teachers and Educators,* p. 149. Hartford: Brown & Gross, 1878.

where with incredible speed, and aroused the highest pitch of popular enthusiasm. The downfall of the monasteries and cloisters put an end to the educational work which they had fostered. The cathedral and other church schools went down before the same attack. A similar fate overtook the town Latin schools, and also the German reading and writing schools.

The universities were affected as seriously as were the lower schools. The University of Cologne, which had 370 students in 1516, 8 years later matriculated only 54. Erfurt, the foremost seat of humanistic learning in Germany, enrolled 311 during the year 1520-1521, and by 1527 the number had declined as low as 14.[2] The celebrated University of Vienna enrolled 661 new matriculants in 1519; by 1532 only 12 students were enrolled. Rostock, the leading educational center in northern Germany, which had usually enjoyed an attendance of about 300, matriculated, in 1525, 15; the next year, only 5; and in 1529, none.[3] In 1521 Leipzig had enrolled 340; and in 1526, only 81.

Wittenberg, where Luther, Melanchthon, and Bugenhagen were teaching—the arsenal of the Lutheran revolt—experienced a peculiar fortune. For several years the number of students rose to phenomenal heights; then suddenly the enrollment fell to such a condition of depletion that Luther despaired and felt obliged to appeal to the Elector John Frederick of Saxony to rescue the institution. According to Janssen, who is not an unfair critic, there were 245 students in 1521, and only 73 in 1527. In Heidelberg there were as many professors as students. The same disheartening decline took place among the Swiss universities. From Basle, the flourishing center of printing, the wail arose in 1524: "The University is as though dead and buried. Empty are the chairs of the teachers, and empty the benches of the learners." In 1522 only 29 new students were matriculated and four years later only 5.[4] Several institutions—among them, Erfurt—never recovered from their disastrous experience.

What were the reasons for this wholesale desertion of both the higher and the lower schools at a time when Europe was seething with new intellectual energy? Erasmus placed the blame squarely upon Luther: "Wherever Lutheranism prevails, there learning disappears," he charged.

---

[2] Janssen, Johannes, *op. cit.*, Vol. XIII, p. 258.

[3] Paulsen, F., *Geschichte des gelehrten Unterrichts,* Vol. I, pp. 184-195. Leipzig: Veit & Co., 1896.

[4] Janssen, Johannes, *op. cit.*, Vol. III, pp. 359-360.

Even earlier than this, Luther had himself become profoundly distressed at the desertion of the schools. He blamed, in turn, the town authorities, the parents of the children, and the Devil. In 1529 he wrote: [5]

> The members of town councils, and nearly all the municipal authorities let the schools go to ruin, as though they had had absolution from all responsibilities. Nobody seems to think that God earnestly wills that the children He sends us should be brought up to his praise and for His service; but everybody nowadays is in a hurry and scurry for his children to be earning temporal sustenance.

The first cause for this decline was the violent denunciation by humanistic scholars, especially Luther himself. He termed the universities "great gates of Hell"; he condemned the monasteries; and he called Aristotle a "damnable heathen," and human reason the "Devil's mistress." But it must not be overlooked that even before this time the monasteries and ecclesiastical schools had come into disrepute and popular aversion.

Another cause lay in the attitude of the common people toward the products of the schools. Through the years people generally had conceived an intense hatred of all higher learning and learned men. They felt that the priests had duped and led them astray from the simple truth of the Gospel, and that the lawyers were using their knowledge to deceive and cheat them out of their rights. They believed that worldly learning and dissoluteness, intellectual pride and chicanery were inherently associated. Now that they had the Scriptures in the vernacular to teach them how to live good lives, they saw no need of the learning of the schools.

A third cause for the decline lay in the relation which education bears to the securing of a livelihood. Parents had sent their children to school to prepare them for positions which would afford a living. Up to this time the largest number of the most desirable livings were in the gift of the church. Prebends, abbacies, benefices, bishoprics, cardinalates, curacies, bursaries, chancellorships, endowed priesthoods, and various other clerical positions abounded. Generally speaking, the poor entered the monasteries. The rich and ambitious entered the secular services of the church because of numerous preferments. Any boy might rise to a position of great power, wealth, and celebrity. "A butcher's son might become

[5] Janssen, Johannes, *op. cit.*, Vol. XIII, p. 18.

a cardinal; a fisherman's boy fill the chair of Saint Peter."[6] Girls had two choices: first, to marry and have a home; or second, to enter a convent, where a living was assured.

The vast number of ecclesiastical livings can be guessed from a single example. In the city of Lübeck there were five parishes, each with its large church and numerous chapels. The city itself had a population between 30,000 and 50,000 people. At the time of the Reformation, the cathedral supported 66 priests and another church had 68, while the total number of priests in the city was about 800. This meant a priest for every 10 or 12 families in the town. In addition to these offices, monasteries and convents, as well as brotherhoods, existed in abundance.[7]

Before the Reformation, education had trained the young directly for the kind of living and type of work expected of the individual.

The overthrow of the Roman Church, together with all the monasteries and ecclesiastical foundations, threw Germanic civilization into wild disorder. All the offices, livings, and appointments within the gift of the ecclesiastical order were threatened with extinction. Futhermore, for some centuries there had been no more admirable feature of medieval civilization than the phenomenal flow of charity which furnished support to poor students. Among the innovations which the Reformation introduced was the doctrine that good works are not essential to salvation. As a result, the new movement dried up at its source the stream of charity which had nourished countless institutions and organizations of Christian benevolence, and had furnished livings for numberless scholars.

As a consequence of the changed order of things, with no certainty of future appointments to offices and livings, parents lost all incentive to educate their children. Luther belabored the mercenary attitude of those parents who preferred rather to train their children for manual and commercial vocations than to send them to the school to become pastors, teachers, and civil servants. A new civilization was being born, involving a new order of vocational life. Until these new livings could be established, and new schools could be organized that would train for the new posts, parents did not know what training to give their children.

---

[6] Beard, Charles, *Martin Luther and the Reformation in Germany,* p. 14. London: K. Paul, Trench, Trübner, and Company, 1889.

[7] Ruccius, Walter M., *John Bugenhagen Pomeranus,* p. 75. Philadelphia, United Lutheran Publishing House, 1924.

Finally, the process of readjustment was delayed by the intense and interminable theological wrangling and struggle which ensued. Throughout the 16th century, religious bigotry and bitterness hampered the schools; only when toleration became the general practice did progress become possible.

Contradictory views of Luther's services. Luther's educational services have been extolled in superlative terms by some, and as greatly berated by others. One controversy centers about his relation to the rise of the state common school; another finds its focal point in his attitude toward higher learning, particularly humanistic culture.

A sharp conflict as to Luther's significance for popular education divides educational historians. Dr. F. V. N. Painter characterizes the *Letter to the Mayors and Aldermen* as "the most important educational treatise ever written." He concludes his study by declaring: [8] "Luther deserves henceforth to be recognized as the greatest, not only of religious, but of educational reformers." Bruce, an American writer, adopts the same point of view: [9] "Luther, therefore, stands forth as the greatest educator of his age, and in the very front rank of the world's greatest educators." Dr. T. M. Lindsay, Scotch historian of the Reformation, reaches a similar conclusion: [10]

> It is to Luther that Germany owes its splendid educational system in its roots and in its conception. For he was the first to plead for a universal education—for an education of the whole people, without regard to class or special lifework.

Many other writers of general history, church history, and educational history have expressed the same high appraisal of Luther's contribution to popular education.

On the opposite side range numerous Catholic and a few non-sectarian authorities. Janssen, in his voluminous *History of the German People,*[11] is especially critical of Luther and the effects of his new doctrines upon

---

[8] Painter, F. V. N., *Luther on Education,* p. 168. St. Louis, Mo.: Concordia Publishing House, 1928.

[9] Bruce, G. M., *Luther as an Educator,* p. 299. Minneapolis: Augsberg Publishing House, 1928.

[10] Lindsay, T. M., *Luther and the German Reformation,* p. 238. New York: Scribner and Sons, 1900.

[11] Janssen, Johannes, *History of the German People at the Close of the Middle Ages,* Vols. I, III, and XIII. London: Kegan Paul, Trench, Trübner, and Company, 1905.

the schools. Paulsen, the German philosopher and educational historian, treats the question with more discrimination but does not credit the origin of popular education to the "Great Reformer." [12]

This extreme diversity of views is due not so much to bigotry or prejudice as to more inherent causes. The contradictory attitudes which Luther himself expressed at different periods of his experience are chiefly responsible. A change occurred in Luther's attitude toward the common people during the period from 1525 to 1530, when three experiences profoundly affected his judgment and altered his views. These events were the Peasants' War, the church-school survey, and the spread of the Anabaptist doctrines. To appreciate both Luther's contribution to education and his change of view, it is essential to reconstruct, in part, the drama of his life from 1520 to 1530.

Among the serious problems which confronted Luther was that of finding pastors for the churches. In former times the innumerable benefices, prebends, and similar livings had taken care of poor boys and young men who were studying for the priesthood and for other professions. But these livings were swept away in the general welter. Moreover, when once appointed, a priest had formerly been assured a permanent living; under the new order there was as yet no certainty that the pastoral office would provide a livelihood. Parents refused to have their sons study for a vocation so uncertain. As a result of these conditions the universities were deserted, and Germany faced the utter collapse of all culture and learning.

What made matters still worse was the attitude of the common people toward the study of the learned languages. Having obtained the Scriptures in German, the people saw no reason why their sons should spend years in the study of the forgotten tongues in which they were originally written. As Luther rather savagely puts it: [13]

> But, you say again, if we shall and must have schools, what is the use to teach Latin, Greek, Hebrew, and the other liberal arts? Is it not enough to teach the Scriptures, which are necessary to salvation, in the mother tongue? To which I answer: I know, alas! that we Germans must always remain irrational brutes, as we are deservedly called by surrounding nations.

---

[12] Paulsen, F., *German Education, Past and Present,* pp. 76-77. London: T. F. Unwin, 1908.

[13] Painter, F. V. N., *op. cit.,* p. 183. See also Eby, Frederick, *Early Protestant Educators,* p. 57. New York: McGraw-Hill, 1931.

He regarded such a point of view as a "malicious trick of Satan"; for he believed the revival of the classical languages had been of most vital service to mankind. The greatest services of the Renaissance had been (1) the recovery of the Scriptures through a knowledge of the Greek and Hebrew languages; (2) the unmasking of the false claims and evils of the papacy; and (3) the return of the learning of the ancient world.

Furthermore, Luther foresaw that in the mighty struggle with the Roman Catholic hierarchy Protestant pastors would need to know Latin, Greek, and Hebrew. This view has been well stated by Dr. E. Nohle: [14]

> As the reformatory movement, at least among the leaders, had started from a scientific dispute over the foundations of church doctrines, so the future existence of the new church was dependent upon the possession of scientific weapons in the battle for the right creed, and for this purpose knowledge of the three ancient languages was absolutely necessary.

Luther felt so strongly about the matter that he called the neglect of languages "a disgrace and a sin." For, as he declared, "we cannot preserve the Gospel without the ancient languages. They are the sheath wherein is contained the sword of the spirit: they are the shrine that holds the jewel."

Confronted with the sudden decline of educational interest, Luther took immediate and energetic measures to bring about reorganization. He issued a stirring appeal to the *Mayors and Aldermen of the Cities of Germany* to revive their municipal schools. There were well over 100 wealthy and powerful municipalities which were free and independent members of the Holy Roman Empire. For several centuries towns had conducted Latin schools and also vernacular reading and writing schools. Now that Luther had definitely decided to overthrow the authority of the Roman Church, the first and most natural step was to urge the city authorities to promote schools in harmony with the Protestant view. Luther appealed to these towns for the following reasons: (1) They had for several centuries been asserting the right to establish schools independent of the Roman Church. (2) These free towns were less directly controlled by the papal influence than were the princes. (3) At this time the people of the towns were generally in enthusiastic accord with Luther's break with the Roman authority. (4) The towns had it

[14] Nohle, E., "History of the German School System," in *Report of the United States Commissioner of Education* (1897-1898), Vol. I, p. 30.

within their power to utilize the wealth of the churches and of the cloisters for the support of schools.

Of far-reaching significance was Luther's appeal for a church-school survey of the principalities of Germany, in order to secure exact information in regard to conditions. In 1527, Luther himself took part in one of the first of these inspection tours, and he was profoundly moved by the dense ignorance and indifference, gross immorality and spiritual destitution which prevailed everywhere. This intensified his zeal as is shown in his famous *Sermon on the Duty of Sending Children to School* in 1530.

Causes of Luther's reaction. Meanwhile two other experiences provoked his deepest and bitterest antagonism. The first of these was the Peasants' War and the second was the Anabaptist movement.

It is an error to believe, as some critics do, that Luther's emphasis upon the doctrine of individual competency in spiritual matters, caused the revolt of the peasants. Popular discontent had been accumulating for a long time. There can be no doubt, however, that Luther's writings, so avidly devoured by the leaders of the lower classes in Germany, gave them renewed hope and confidence. Their long smouldering grievances burst into a bloody war in 1524. The demands of the peasants were modest indeed, and they were couched in such terms of Christian humility that even Luther was inclined to grant the justice of their claims. But the resort to armed conflict touched another spring of deep passion in the reformer, his immeasurable respect for civil authority. Passing by chance directly through the scene of conflict, he was aroused to the highest pitch of indignation and at once denounced the peasants in the fiercest manner.

Then another terror began to receive his censorious attention; this was the rise and rapid spread of Anabaptist doctrines. In Luther's eyes this heresy was even more wicked, and less to be tolerated, than the Roman Church. The more interesting is the whole situation when one recalls that these people merely carried to their logical conclusion the principles of religious liberty and the right of everyone to interpret the Scriptures for himself which Luther had espoused so enthusiastically a few years before.

These experiences evidently produced a crisis in Luther's views. He now turned quite positively to a confessional, or institutional, religion, and away from a simple reliance upon that experimental faith which had made him the courageous reformer of a few years earlier. Some very positive alterations in his educational views likewise arose out of this crisis:

(1) In his earlier period Luther had proclaimed the thesis: "A Christian man is the most free lord of all, and subject to none." He had looked upon the church as an independent organism, separate from the state and founded upon the Scriptures. Hereafter the church was more and more completely subordinated to the civil power. Luther came to regard civil rulers as divinely commissioned to rule, not only in temporal, but in ecclesiastical affairs as well. Later he adopted the view that every child must be taught the Lutheran confession only, and at least outwardly every man must profess the religion of his prince. *Whose territory, his religion* (*Cujus regio, ejus religio*) was the future policy. Though Luther was more tolerant than most reformers and Catholics in that bloodthirsty era, he never reached an attitude of genuine religious liberty.

(2) Another alteration may be seen in his attitude toward the vernacular tongue. Before the change, Luther had advocated the use of German, as well as of Latin, Greek and Hebrew. After this period he restricted the use of German to home reading and to religious instruction. In the school plan of Saxony, written in 1528, the schools were specifically limited to teaching only in the Latin language. German and Greek were prohibited in no uncertain terms. Having assisted in its writing, Luther evidently approved this plan. In his last educational tractate, *On the Duty of Sending Children to School* (1530), he severely rebuked parents for sending their boys to the vernacular rather than to the classical schools, charging them with low, materialistic motives.

(3) Formerly he had demanded the free use of the Scriptures by everyone, young and old. Henceforth, Luther confined the religious instruction of the common people and of children to the catechisms. Moreover, they were to be taught precept upon precept, line upon line, without the liberty of individual interpretation.

(4) Formerly Luther had desired every child to receive an education. Later his chief aim came to be to select the children of ability who might become leaders in church and state. All children were to receive religious instruction, but only the brighter ones were to go to the Latin schools where they would get the foundation for the study of law, civil service, medicine, and especially theology.

State control and support of the schools. Luther's most significant innovation lay in placing both the schools and the church under the guardianship of the state, and in holding the civil authorities responsible for their establishment and support. Having reached the conclusion that the papal church was a usurper of power, Luther's profound reverence for authority led him to invest civil officers with all the sacred prerogatives and jurisdictions of divine sovereignty. In beginning the task of reforming the great abuses in the church, he had appealed to the princes and electors of Germany; it was their protection that saved him from repeating the tragedies of the earlier reformers, who had been sent to the stake because of their faith. He appealed to the princes on the ground that they derived their power and authority from God and were His representatives on earth. Furthermore, he held that they were as much responsible for the preservation of spiritual and cultural values as they were for the maintenance of order and the security of life and property within their kingdoms. But his appeal involved the surrender of the ancient independence of the church and its subjection to civil authority. He thus debased religion to a subordinate position, and the pastors to the status of civil servants. Statecraft superseded priestcraft in the management of man, and the vast estates of church and monastery passed to the control of the secular princes.

Since the towns were more directly interested in the promotion of schools, they early began reorganization. The principalities, however, had to await a deeper sense of responsibility on the part of the princes. In any case, Luther's action in giving the civil authorities the control of the schools was one of the momentous steps toward modern society. In doing so, he laid the foundation of national control of education and religion throughout Germany.

Compulsory school attendance. Luther must be recognized as the first modern reformer to advocate compulsory education. This idea he owed partly to the Old Testament and partly to the practice of the Turks. He insisted that it was the duty of municipal authorities and princes to establish and support schools; and he went so far as to demand that, for the sake of the state, the city, and the church, parents should be compelled to send their children to school.

He reached the first conclusion as early as 1526, as the following letter to the Elector John of Saxony shows: [15]

---

[15] Smith, Preserved, and Jacobs, Charles M., *Luther's Correspondence and Other Contemporary Letters,* Vol. II, p. 384. Philadelphia: The Lutheran Publication Society, 1918. See also Eby, Frederick, *op. cit.*, p. 85.

> If there is a town or a village which can do it, your Grace has the power to compel it to support schools, preaching places, and parishes. If they are unwilling to do this or to consider it for their own salvation's sake, then your Grace is the supreme guardian of the youth and of all who need your guardianship, and ought to hold them to it by force, so that they must do it. It is just like compelling them by force to contribute and to work for the building of bridges and roads, or any other of the country's needs.

Similarly, in the *Sermon* (1530), he was emphatically in favor of compulsory education:[16]

> I maintain that the civil authorities are under obligation to compel the people to send their children to school, especially such as are promising. ... If the government can compel such citizens as are fit for military service to bear spear and rifle, to mount ramparts, and perform other martial duties in time of war; how much more has it a right to compel the people to send their children to school, because in this case we are warring with the Devil.... The Turk does differently, and takes every third child in his Empire to educate for whatever he pleases.

This demand for compulsory education was based upon the public welfare. Educated people make better civil servants, judges, doctors, pastors, and more obedient subjects. Naturally Luther did not have in view the modern concept of enlightened voters; nor was attendance to be universal. Yet, in holding up the ideal of the commonweal, he was leading the way to important future developments.

Home discipline. Luther got his views of education, as well as his views of doctrine, chiefly from the Scriptures. He considered the Commandment, "Honor thy father and thy mother," as the foundation of all social order. He held that home training and obedience produced sound family life, and that good households are the foundation of good government in city, principality, and empire. In vigorous language he censured laxity in parental control and faulty methods of training. On the other hand, he frowned upon undue severity. In his childhood home he had suffered from the cruelty of his parents, yet, he held them in the highest veneration through all his days. He loved his own children tenderly, and a more natural, happy family relationship can scarcely be imagined. There was nothing of the aloofness and frigidity of the Calvinistic home, nor the practice of home supervision by the church

---

[16] Painter, F. V. N., *op. cit.*, pp. 269-270; also Eby, Frederick, *op. cit.*, pp. 149-150.

authorities, which Calvin instituted. Nevertheless, he regarded home discipline as the foundation of all institutional and social existence.

Vocational training. In his letter to the authorities of the cities, Luther wrote of trade and vocational training,[17] "My idea is that boys should spend an hour or two a day in school, and the rest of the time work at home, learn some trade, and do whatever is desired." Some writers find in this statement the origin of industrial training. A careful study of its significance does not warrant such a conclusion. All through the Middle Ages, children learned trades and crafts in the fashion that Luther advocated here. The class of people who had formerly sent their children to school to fit them to secure their livings in religious vocations now turned their attention to practical arts and means of livelihood. It was notorious how few wished their sons to look forward to the uncertainties of life as pastors, teachers, or professional men. Of this, Luther wrote: [18]

> Because selfish parents see that they can no longer place their children upon the bounty of monasteries and cathedrals, they refuse to educate them. "Why should we educate our children," they say, "if they are not to become priests, monks, and nuns, and thus earn a support?"

This was written in 1524. Six years later he grew still more vehement. He declared: "the common people are placing themselves in opposition to the schools, and wish to bring up their children without instruction other than that pertaining to their bodily wants." He thundered against these parents as "worshippers of Mammon," and as "Idolators," and charged that Satan was deluding them in order to keep people in ignorance.

In his statement on learning a trade, Luther merely tried to show that school work need not necessarily interfere with practical training in the home. There is no evidence that he was looking to the introduction of arts and handicrafts into the schools, as in the movement which was just beginning in some of the progressive schools of the Netherlands. Luther naturally accepted industrial training at home, but objected when it interfered with sending boys to the Latin school.

Schools for girls. Luther strongly encouraged the education of girls along religious lines. In 1520 he declared: [19] "Would to God each town

---

[17] Painter, F. V. N., *op. cit.*, p. 199.

[18] *Ibid.*, p. 171.

[19] Eby, Frederick, *op. cit.*, p. 41.

had also a girls' school, in which girls might be taught the Gospel for an hour daily, either in German or Latin!" Similarly, in 1524 he wrote:[20] "In like manner, a girl has time to go to school an hour a day, and yet attend to her work at home; for she sleeps, dances, and plays away more than that." It is easy to presume that in this suggestion Luther was far beyond his contemporaries. Such, however, was not the case. Education of girls of the upper classes had long been in vogue. Moreover, schools for girls had long been in operation in the larger towns.

Subjects of instruction. What was to be taught in the elementary schools that Luther desired to establish? Primarily, religion, but a number of other subjects as well. His elementary curriculum is summed up in the following sentence: [21]

> I would have them learn not only the languages and history, but also singing, instrumental music, and the whole course of mathematics.

At first Luther was emphatic in a demand for the use of the Scriptures themselves, as his *Address to the Nobility* (1520) declares: [22]

> Above all, in schools of all kinds the chief and most common lesson should be the Scriptures, and for young boys the Gospels. . . . Should not every Christian be expected by his ninth or tenth year to know all the Holy Gospels, containing as they do his very name and life?
>
> Where the Holy Scriptures are not the rule, I advise no one to send his child. Everything must perish where God's Word is not studied unceasingly.

Again, four years later he wrote: [23] "It behooves Christians at all times to use the Bible as their only book." But his insistence upon the Scriptures did not continue. After his contact with the Peasants' War and the Anabaptist movement, he came to believe that the circulation of the Scriptures among the common people was a dangerous practice. He concluded that the masses were not capable of arriving at truth by the light of the Scriptures alone. Religious instruction must be definitely controlled. To this end he wrote, in 1528-1529, the *Short Catechism* and the *Longer Catechism,* and required their use in place of the Scriptures. "The Catechism," he now declared, "is the right Bible of the laity; wherein is contained the whole sum of Christian doctrine neces-

---

[20] *Ibid.,* p. 71.
[21] Painter, F. V. N., *op. cit.,* p. 198.
[22] Eby, Frederick, *op. cit.,* pp. 41-43.
[23] *Ibid.,* p. 65.

sary to be known of every Christian to salvation."[24] For moral instruction he translated Aesop's fables, which he considered next to the Scriptures in importance.

What type of schools did Luther urge the towns to set up? The new schools were to be Latin grammar schools which would lay the foundation for professional study; first, to train for the ministry; second, to train for the other learned professions; and third, to train for the various civil positions in town and state. The schools must give the boys a thorough knowledge of Latin, Greek, and Hebrew, with which they might clearly understand the Scriptures and the writings of the Church Fathers. Whether or not the students would become pastors did not matter greatly, for the study of these languages would help them to be better men.

It was natural in this age, when men had rediscovered the ancient world with its literary and other treasures, that the study of history should be emphasized. To the Protestant reformers, history was of great significance in combatting the claims of the Roman hierarchy; but it was as a means of understanding human nature, morals, and institutions that Luther recognized its greatest value. "Historians," he declared, "are the most useful of men, and the best teachers." "How I regret that I did not read more poetry and history and that no one taught me in these branches."

No educator since Plato had ascribed a higher educational value to music. Before the Reformation all church music was in Latin. One of Luther's first movements for reform was the creation of a vernacular hymnology, so that the people might participate in the service of the church in a language they could understand. He wrote a number of hymns in German and urged his friends who had poetic talent to do likewise. The first German hymnal was printed under his direction in 1524. Religious music henceforth became one of the chief interests of all German schools; and for several centuries the school provided the choir for all church services. In his exalted love of music and his desire for its inclusion in the school curriculum, Luther was superior to the other reformers.

Reform of higher instruction. Luther has been severely condemned by some as an obscurantist opposed to the highest culture, but he has

---

[24] *Ibid.*, p. 97.

been as greatly extolled by others as an advocate of learning. Erasmus made the charge: "Wherever Lutheranism prevails, culture and learning perish." Many later authorities, both Catholic and Protestant, have taken the same attitude.[25] Among the more recent, Janssen elaborates the charge at length. Luther denounced the universities as "dens of murderers," "temples of Moloch," and "synagogues of corruption." In a sermon preached in the year 1521 he declared: [26] "The Univerities were only worthy of being reduced to dust; nothing more hellish or devilish had ever appeared on the earth from the beginning of things, or ever would appear." Never have higher institutions of learning been so reviled. Luther went even further and attacked the rational nature of man which produced the need for universities. No words were too scathing to denounce natural reason and its representatives, Aristotle and the Scholastics who had cruelly duped and misled the people to their spiritual ruin.

Luther's extreme bitterness against rationalism may be readily explained. For years he had sought peace of soul by the study of rationalistic theology and scholastic science, but all was in vain. Finally, through reading the Scriptures, he reached a sense of divine forgiveness. Here, then, was his first great grievance: Reason had been a false guide. Again, the employment of reason by certain sects in their interpretation of the Scriptures intensified his distrust. Hence he called reason, "the Devil's bride or harlot," who "should be trampled underfoot or have dirt thrown in her face to make her the more hateful."

Though he regarded the universities as "Schools of Satan," he did not agree with the large body of common people who wished to abolish them entirely. On the contrary, Luther exerted every effort to reform their discipline and courses of study; for, in spite of his violent denunciation, he realized that the universities had an indispensable service to perform for the welfare of society.

To the higher schools he would send "only the aptest pupils." Here, scholars were to "train men of good understanding in the Scriptures, who wish to become bishops and priests, and to stand at our head against heretics and the Devil and all the world."

---

[25] Among such critics may be cited: John I. von Döllinger, *Die Reformation,* Vol. I, p. 422. Regensburg: Manz, 1851; and F. Paulsen, *Geschichte des gelehrten Unterrichts,* Vol. I, pp. 182-184. Leipzig: Veit and Company, 1896-1897.

[26] Janssen, Johannes, *op. cit.,* Vol. III, p. 355.

As in other matters, so in his attitude toward the various learned studies, Luther was dogmatic and expressed his views in vigorous terms. Most of the works of Aristotle and those on scholastic philosophy he vehemently rejected as "Satanic filth." He was tolerant only of Aristotle's logic, rhetoric, and poetry. He denounced canon law and called for its complete abolition. He concluded that civil law should be reformed and theological courses drastically changed. At one time he said: "Teach the Scriptures and nothing else." He never expressed an interest in humanistic literature, and, even as a student at Erfurt, the German center of the movement, he did not belong to the circle of The New Learning. Nevertheless he strongly advocated the study of the ancient languages, Latin, Greek, and Hebrew; but only for the aid they contribute to an understanding of the Scriptures. Like all the reformers, he believed that these languages were indispensable for the exposition of the Scriptures. No one who could not read the Scriptures in the original tongues could qualify for the pastoral office.

After his attack upon the papal hierarchy Luther soon found the churches without pastors and teachers, and few students preparing for the duties of civil life. To train people for these positions was his supreme aim for the Latin schools and the universities. On the whole he was not a scholarly influence so far as secular culture and science were concerned.

Popular vernacular education. A critical investigation reveals little evidence that Luther desired popular elementary education as one understands the term today. In all his arguments for education his chief point was the necessity of the Latin school as *the* institution of learning. He called upon the civil authorities to suppress vernacular private schools. He subscribed to the Saxon school ordinance of 1528, which prohibited the teaching of German and Greek. He pleaded that all boys be compelled to attend the Latin schools, in order that Germany might be provided with a sufficient supply of learned men. Even the boys who proved less promising were to learn at least to read and write Latin. For this he gave a rather lame excuse: [27]

> If such a boy who has learned Latin afterwards works at a trade, you will have him in reserve, to labor as a pastor in case of need; and such knowledge will not interfere with his gaining a livelihood and will enable him to govern his house all the better.

---

[27] Painter, F. V. N., *op. cit.*, p. 235; also Eby, Frederick, *op. cit.*, p. 122.

Luther proposed that gifted youth be selected for public service. In writing to the Margrave George of Brandenburg, he suggested: [28]

> It is well that in all towns and villages good primary schools should be established out of which could be picked and chosen those who are more fit for the universities, out of which the men can then be taken who are to serve your land and people.

Subsequent events were in line with Luther's proposals. In later decades the vernacular school was often suppressed, on the contention that it took boys away from the Latin schools. Sometimes it was tolerated, but it always remained strictly subordinate to the classical school. Had Luther been a strong advocate of popular education, one is constrained to believe conditions would have developed quite differently in Germany.

Summary of Luther's educational contributions. Summarizing Luther's services, the following points are to be noted: (1) He included all children in his plans for vernacular religious instruction, although he had in view chiefly a formulated system of instruction embodied in the catechisms. (2) When the Elector Frederick sheltered him in Wartburg Castle, to save him from his enemies, Luther translated the Scriptures into the High German dialect. No other thing which Luther ever did contributed so profoundly to the real education of the German people. His was the first translation in which not merely the sense, but something of the beauty and force of the original Scriptures was transferred to the German. By this work he raised High German from a mere dialect into a permanent language of power and classical beauty, and gave the German peoples a unifying bond. (3) Furthermore, his translation of Aesop's fables had a remarkable influence. But next to his translation of the Scriptures, nothing had so profound an influence on German education as his catechisms. (4) In his break with Rome he had assumed a stand which favored popular emancipation and enlightenment. Even in his reactionary role he could not dam the tide that, as a liberal reformer, he had set in motion; and this flood was soon beyond his control. The liberalizing forces found other advocates, and, though driven to shelter temporarily, they were to emerge in later decades and under more favorable circumstances. (5) Another contribution which Luther made which is incapable of exact measurement was that of music. All German teachers had to play the violin and teach the children to sing.

---

[28] Smith, Preserved, and Jacobs, Charles M., *op. cit.*, Vol. II, p. 487.

Johannes Bugenhagen. Bugenhagen was at once town preacher and university professor at Wittenberg. He came from northern Germany, and it was in the northern towns and principalities that he exerted greatest influence. He is honored as the practical reformer of the Lutheran Church, possessing, as he did, a larger capacity for organization than his more renowned colleagues, Luther and Melanchthon. In 1528 he formulated the church and school ordinance for the town of Brunswick; this was followed by similar ordinances for Hamburg, Lübeck, Bremen, and also for the leading principalities of northern Germany and the Kingdom of Denmark.

The opening words of this Brunswick school ordinance indicate Bugenhagen's deep interest in education: [29]

> Above all, three things are deemed necessary. First, to establish good schools for children. Second, to engage preachers who will proclaim God's Word in its purity and who are able to lecture and explain the Scriptures in Latin. Third, to organize charity.

The educational provisions of these ordinances emphasized the Latin schools and religious instruction; some of them, however, also made provision for public libraries and courses of public lectures. Bugenhagen went further than his colleagues in placing great stress upon elementary reading and writing schools in the vernacular tongue. Moreover, his plans of organization always included separate schools for girls.

Bugenhagen's schools were in reality only reorganizations of the reading and writing schools which had been set up in the Hanseatic towns long before this. Down to this time they had been schools of a purely practical character, designed to furnish boys of the commercial class with the tools of learning. Formerly the church had exercised authority over them, in the employment of teachers. They were now reëstablished by the town councils, and the teachers were appointed by the councils which controlled them. These schools were to be supported from fees paid by the parents. The new feature of great importance, however, was that the teachers were to receive, from the municipal treasury, a bonus for teaching catechism, religion, and church music. In this manner the old town school was now linked up with religious instruction, and was

---

[29] Ruccius, Walter M., *John Bugenhagen Pomeranus*, pp. 61-62. Philadelphia: The United Lutheran Publication House, 1916.

on its way as the elementary school of the common people. However, everywhere throughout Germany, and especially by most of the Reformation leaders, it was considered a makeshift, wholly inferior to the Latin school. One must look elsewhere for the influences which were finally to elevate this school to the state common school system of the present day. Yet, despite the attitude of his contemporaries, Bugenhagen deserves the credit for taking one of the most significant steps in this evolution of the vernacular school.

Philip Melanchthon. Melanchthon (1497-1560) was the ranking scholar of the German Reformation. In breadth of erudition he was second only to Erasmus. His vast attainments and profound influence on German culture won for him the immortal title, *Praeceptor Germaniae.*

Melanchthon was born at Bretten, near Pforzheim. John Reuchlin, the renowned Hebrew scholar, was his maternal uncle. Philip was extremely precocious, taking his bachelor's degree at Heidelberg at fifteen. After a period at Tübingen, he became a professor at Wittenberg, where Luther was just beginning his reform of the church. The two became intimate friends and labored together for the reform of church and school until Luther's death.

In command of languages and in knowledge of theology and of school curriculum and organization, Melanchthon surpassed the Great Reformer; he was lacking, however, in Luther's originality, profound conviction, indomitable courage, and capacity for leadership. Melanchthon was the erudite, retiring scholar, with a strong tendency toward pedantry. His fame rests upon the many outstanding contributions which he made to the reconstruction of Protestant education.

Melanchthon took a foremost part in the church-school survey during 1527-1528, in Thuringia and Saxony. As a result he wrote the Saxon church-school ordinance, which was the first of many such codes adopted in German cities and states throughout the 16th century. The plan, revised and approved by Luther, was also published with his works. According to this plan, the obligation to establish and maintain schools was squarely placed upon the civil authorities.

As stated by this ordinance, the chief purpose of the schools was to prepare men for ecclesiastical and civil offices. Melanchthon felt nothing but contempt for the popular vernacular schools. He regarded Latin as the only language suitable for elementary learning; German was expressly forbidden. Greek, too, was excluded, though it was to be studied in the university. The ordinance states emphatically: [30] "Schoolmasters shall look to it diligently that children learn only Latin, and not German, Greek, or Hebrew. So many languages at once are not merely useless but detrimental."

According to the plan schools were to be established in every town and would consist of three groups of pupils. The first group was for beginners, who were to learn to read Latin. Their first instruction consisted of the alphabet, then followed *Donatus,* a simple grammar, and later, Cato's *Disticha de Moribus,* a collection of wise sayings. The teacher read one or two verses from this book daily and explained in Latin the meaning of the words. The pupils were required to memorize lists of words and sentences, in order to secure a large vocabulary as quickly as possible. This method of teaching he considered very superior. In addition to such grammatical and moral instruction, religion also was taught in Latin and learned by heart. Singing in Latin by the entire group formed a most important part of the daily program. Religion and music were continued throughout the entire course.

In the second group, which like the first was planned to extend over several years, Latin grammar was exhaustively studied. Aesop's fables, *The Colloquies* of Erasmus, the comedies of Terence and Plautus, and similar works were read and explained in minute grammatical detail, and practically all were memorized.

The third group took up more advanced linguistic studies. By this time the boy was expected to be able to speak, read, and write Latin. Now he was to acquire a classical vocabulary and become thoroughly versed in the Latin tongue and literature. Virgil, Ovid, and Cicero were the chief authors, and they were to be acquired in detail. Exercises in rhetoric, in addition to some study of logic, were also required.

This Saxon plan of elementary instruction was generally adopted because of the great influence of Melanchthon.

Melanchthon was frequently called upon by town authorities for advice in the reorganization of their schools. Nuremberg called him to become rector of its new Gymnasium, a position which he declined. Two

---

[30] Melanchton was particularly fond of Greek, and the Greek grammar which he wrote when only 16 years of age was long used. His exclusion of all languages except Latin was probably due to the lack of success in teaching all these languages in the Gymnasium at Nuremberg, with the founding of which he had most to do. For the text of the Saxon school ordinance, consult: Barnard, Henry, *German Teachers and Educators,* pp. 169-171. Hartford: Brown and Gross, 1878.

men whom he recommended were appointed. In other instances also, when he declined important educational appointments, he helped institutions to find teachers. In the early period of Protestant reconstruction, no man was so much sought after as Melanchthon to guide the founding of the municipal Latin schools.

While still a boy, Melanchthon wrote a Greek grammar for other boys. He wrote a Latin grammar which, during the following ten years, was printed 53 times, and was adopted in Catholic as well as in Protestant schools. In 1519 he wrote a text on rhetoric, and in 1520, one on logic, both of which were widely used. He wrote not only on these subjects, which composed the trivium of the Middle Ages, but also, though not so exhaustively, on the quadrivium, arithmetic, geometry, astronomy, and music. The great merit of these various texts was not the originality of their materials, but rather their better order and treatment. Melanchthon was preëminently a schoolmaster whose singular clarity of mind enabled him to bring these subjects down to the comprehension of young boys.

Influence on higher education. Melanchthon labored most of his life at Wittenberg, where at one time or another he was called upon to teach almost every subject. His extensive learning made him the leader in the transition from Scholasticism to the newer methods and curriculum of Protestantism. While the most extensive changes took place in the field of theological study, it is well to remember that law and philosophy also underwent profound alterations. The universities of Germany were all more or less transformed by this quiet scholar.

Influence of his scholarship. The influence of Melanchthon was spread throughout Germany by the students whom he taught. He was extremely popular as a lecturer, and deeply beloved. The most illustrious of his pupils were Michael Neander (1525-1595), who conducted the famous cloister school at Ilfeld, in Thuringia, for 45 years, and Valentin Trotzendorf (1490-1556), who for 23 years was rector of the school at Goldberg, in Silesia.

Paulsen sums up the greatness of Melanchthon's services to Germany in the following statement: [31]

> When Melanchthon died there was probably not a city in Protestant Germany in which some grateful student did not mourn the loss of the

[31] Paulsen, F., *The German Universities,* p. 33. Translated by Frank Thilly and William W. Elwang. New York: Scribner's Sons, 1906.

Praeceptor Germaniae. And long after his death he controlled, through his method and text-books, the instruction in the Protestant schools and Universities. It was primarily due to him that the Protestant half of Germany won the ascendency over Catholicism in the realm of education and culture. There can be no doubt whatever about the final outcome: German philosophy and science, German literature and culture grew up in the soil of Protestantism.

PROTESTANT EDUCATIONAL REORGANIZATION IN GERMANY

Early reorganization of the municipal schools. The first efforts at reconstruction came in response to Luther's appeal to the mayors and aldermen of the cities in 1524. In that very year Magdeburg consolidated several parish schools into a new Protestant institution. Several other cities at once took similar action. A decided advance was effected by the publication of the Saxon school plan in 1528.

The cities reorganized by Bugenhagen followed in most details the Saxon school plan of 1528. There were, however, important differences. (1) The curriculum was not restricted to Latin, for the elements of Greek and Hebrew were to be learned after the students had acquired some proficiency in Latin. (2) Furthermore, in all these towns, German reading and writing schools for boys were established, but the private schools were suppressed. Similarly, vernacular schools for girls were now to be conducted. (3) Another interesting feature was the *lectorium*, a sort of preliminary or popular university course where lectures on theology, law, and medicine were given free to everybody who desired to attend.

Municipal support and control of schools. The foremost fact about the early Protestant schools was that they were established and controlled by municipal authority. In the accomplishment of this purpose, in many instances the city councils took over the property of the church. In this way buildings were provided and, to some extent, means of support were furnished. Such action became general throughout the towns of Saxony. The teachers in the Latin schools were paid out of the city treasury. Generally, a small fee for tuition was charged and collected by the city officers. Special efforts were made, however, to provide free instruction, and often the entire living was supplied for poor boys who had exceptional ability. Nothing was more admirable throughout the history of early Protestant education than the insistent emphasis upon the discovery of gifted youths, and provision for their free education.

Protestant leaders of western Germany were likewise interested in the reorganization of education. In 1524, Martin Bucer, the noted reformer of Strassburg, approached the magistrates with a plan for a system of free schools. The money for their support was to be derived from the revenues of the former religious orders, for Bucer believed that by right these revenues should be used for the aid and education of the poor and not for the expenditures of the town government. Several Latin schools were organized, as well as elementary schools in which reading and writing of German, catechism, and music were taught.

Vernacular town schools. In some towns higher fees were charged in the new German reading and writing schools. The teachers were not paid a regular salary by the council; but in addition to the fees which they received, they were given a bonus from the council in return for which they obligated themselves to teach the catechism, Christian doctrine, and religious music. This alliance of practical studies with religious instruction, under the town council, must be considered the origin of the German *Volksschule*.

This type of school was, however, not regarded throughout the 16th century as an important institution; it was tolerated but not encouraged, for it was considered inferior to the Latin school. As a matter of fact, the preference shown the German *Volksschulen* over the Latin was considered injurious to scholarship "because they drew scholars from the Latin schools, and also because Latin pupils would write Latin with German script and read with German accent." [32]

State school control. The first of the princely domains to project schools was Saxony in its church school order of 1528. This plan, it will be recalled, came as the result of the survey which had been made the previous year. Schleswig-Holstein, on the border between Germany and Denmark, followed.

By the fifth decade of the century, Protestantism had become so securely established that the nobility felt sufficiently confident to form state-churches and schools. It is to be noted especially that the tem-

---

[32] Nohle, E., "History of the German School System," in *Report of the U. S. Commissioner of Education* (1897-1898), Vol. I, p. 36.

poral rulers had secured control over the wealth of the church foundations and monasteries, and that the general willingness of the rulers of the German states to utilize these endowments and buildings for the educational purpose for which they were established gave Germany a superior advantage over several other European countries. In many places the monasteries or cloisters were converted into state schools.

Church program of religious instruction. In Germany the Reformation did not so much foster a deep interest in popular education; it sought rather to improve the character of religious training.

From the earliest Christian centuries, the church had utilized catechetical instruction for the indoctrination of the young. During the later Middle Ages, the sexton of the parish church taught the Lord's Prayer, the Ave Maria, the rosary, the Ten Commandments, and the Apostles' Creed. As Protestant sects emerged, each in turn composed a catechism which expressed its fundamental religious tenets. The Waldensians had such a work, which was very widely used by other dissentient sects. The Bohemian Brethren published a catechism in 1505. Luther required the use of the short and the longer catechisms, which he wrote in 1529. Similarly, Calvin wrote a catechism which was used extensively. The Heidelberg catechism, published in 1563, became the most widely used among the Reformed Churches.

These catechisms have played a significant role in Protestant religious instruction down to our own day. In 1527, all pastors were required by the Saxon Church Inspection Board to instruct their people, especially the children of the parishes, on Sunday afternoon in religious doctrine and church music. As it was quite impossible for the pastors to find time for this work, the duty of teaching the young was imposed upon the church sextons. In 1533, the church ordinance of Meissen required the pastors in the villages to give such instruction, not alone on Sunday, but on one afternoon also during the week. The church ordinance of the principality of Lippe in 1538 stated: [33]

> The sexton in the villages, where there are no schools, at noon on Sunday shall assemble the children and youth who are capable of instruction, and read to them slowly and constantly the smaller catechism of Luther so that the youth not be neglected.

---

[33] Weber, Adalbert, *Geschichte der Volksschulpädagogik und der Kleinkindererziehung,* p. 59. Eisenbach: J. Bachmeister, 1877.

The general church ordinance of Saxony in 1557 demanded: [34]

> The Sacristans of the villages are obliged every Sunday at noon and on a particular day in the week diligently and clearly to teach the children the catechism and Christian hymns in German and later to review and to examine them on these materials.

Almost everywhere the evangelical church-school ordinances during the 16th century required the teaching of the catechism. Similarly, in western Germany where Calvinism had a powerful grip, the Synod of Heidelberg passed an order "that only such clergy were to be appointed as were capable of teaching the catechism to the children."

German Protestantism was not long content with purely religious instruction. There soon came the feeling that, in order to preserve itself, it was imperative for the new religious movement to provide for the teaching of reading and writing. Furthermore, the state, which had attained a new position of dignity, power, and responsibility, took an interest in education for its own preservation. Accordingly, in 1559 Duke Christopher of Würtemberg, in his Grand Ecclesiastical Ordinance, broadened the scope of the German schools. The sexton was still the teacher; but, in addition to the catechism and church music, reading and writing in the German language were added. The teachers were required to pass an examination and were subject to supervision. Of greatest consequence, however, was the provision punishing parents for the absence of their children from *catechism school.* During the next two decades similar laws were passed in other states.

The Protestant revolt and the universities. The revolt of the 16th century had its origin, in large measure, in the universities. This was particularly true of Germany, where the leaders of The New Learning and of church reform were all, directly or indirectly, connected with the higher institutions.

Every religious movement must sooner or later face the issue of its future growth, and must undertake to insure its perpetuity by the founding of higher institutions of learning. For this reason a number of new Protestant universities were now established, and the existing institutions were reformed, in accordance with Protestant views. Hence, wherever Protestantism gained a dominant hold, it set about in a determined manner to transform higher education for its own ends.

Among the older universities which were reformed along Protestant

[34] *Ibid.*, p. 59.

lines were: in central Germany, Wittenberg, the home of the German Reformation, 1533; Tübingen, in Würtemberg, 1535; Leipzig, in Saxony, 1539 to 1559; Frankfort on the Oder, 1538; and in northern Germany, Greifswald, 1539, and Rostock, 1563. Heidelberg, which had come under Calvinistic influence, was reformed during this same period.

The first of the new foundations was the University of Marburg, 1527. It was planned by Melanchthon and established by the Landgrave Philip of Hesse, one of the first ardent supporters of the Reformation. The university was designed to teach everything according to the pure word of God: theology, law, medicine, the liberal arts, and languages. It had the slogan, "Let him be accursed, whoever teaches anything contrary to the Scriptures." Under similar circumstances, the University of Königsberg, in East Prussia, was established in 1544; Jena, in Saxony, 1558; and Helmstedt, in north Germany, 1576. During the next century some six other institutions were founded in Germany; the most important of them were: Giessen, 1607; and Strassburg, which grew out of the college founded by Sturm, 1621.

German universities invariably included four departments: theology, law, medicine, and philosophy. The faculties of theology were the first to reform their courses, by repudiating scholastic theology and offering Biblical exegesis in its place. Because of their training of pastors, the theological faculties now took the place of first importance. They were responsible for the orthodoxy of evangelical doctrine, the adjudication of all theological controversies, and the training and examining of candidates for the ministry.

The other faculties were more or less deeply affected by the reform spirit. The abandonment of canon law and the ecclesiastical courts gave a new impetus to the pursuit of civil jurisprudence. The study of the ancient languages, Latin, Greek, and Hebrew, was pursued with intense interest because of their relation to the original Scriptures. Moreover, increasing interest was manifested in philosophical and scientific studies, which naturally found expression in higher education.

Chapter 4

HUMANISM AND CHURCH AND SCHOOL REFORM

NATIONAL, class, and sectarian differences. During the Middle Ages, education was substantially the same everywhere and for everyone in western Europe. With the Nordic revolt and Humanism, sectarian as well as class and national differences appeared. The interests of Humanism and Protestantism were by no means identical, and consequently in the reconstruction the two did not blend into a uniform educational policy. In some situations Humanism was dominant and Protestantism an appendix; in other cases Protestantism was dominant and classicism a mere means.

The schools of the Netherlands did not suffer any violent transition, for they had long been under the control of the city authorities and the change to Protestantism was readily effected. In Germany, on the other hand, when the old system of schools, controlled entirely by the church, suddenly declined, a radical reconstruction was necessary through the initiative of the city and state governments. In England, Henry VIII took the initiative in educational reform, and progress was humanistic in its trend. The Scottish Church, in accordance with its Calvinistic policies, early set in motion plans for the reorganization of schools, but for some time it did not have the full cooperation of Parliament. France (except for the Calvinistic Huguenots) and other Catholic lands came under the control of the newly established Society of Jesus.

THE PROGRESS OF HUMANISM

John Sturm: Founder of the Classical Gymnasium. Sturm (1507-1589) was the organizing genius of Humanism in northern Europe; he visualized most clearly the precise aim of classical instruction, firmly grasped its methods and curriculum and understood the form of organization which gave promise of achieving the results desired by the new age. Of all the schoolmasters beyond the Alps, Sturm was most infatuated with the Ciceronian eloquence which dominated Italian scholarship at this time. More than any other of the educational reformers, he established the standard for the new classical gymnasium.

Life and training. John Sturm came to life at Schleiden, a village near Cologne. His father was steward to Count Manderscheid, and Sturm's early training was received in the home with the sons of the count. For several years he attended the famous school of the Brethren of the Common Life at Liége, Belgium. It was this institution which furnished the principles and organization that he later embodied in his gymnasium at Strassburg. Leaving Liége, he studied at the Trilingual College, established by Erasmus in Louvain. Through the inspiration he received from the professor of Latin here Sturm acquired the ideal of Latin eloquence which was the dominant feature of his educational program. Here, too, he taught Latin for some time and, following the practice of the Brethen, set up a printing press from which Latin and Greek texts issued for the students in the university.

Sturm went to the University of Paris about the time the French King was establishing the College of France for the promotion of classic Latin and Greek. Among his pupils was young Peter Ramus, who years later declared: [1]

> It was in the lessons of this great master that I first learned the use of logic and then taught it to the youth in quite a different spirit from the sophists, relegating to them their furor for disputation.

Having embraced Protestantism through his friendship with Martin Bucer, who combined in a rare manner evangelical fervor and humanistic culture, Sturm was led to accept a call to Strassburg in 1537. The following year he was made rector of the newly founded gymnasium. Here, for over forty years, he was the most renowned schoolmaster of the time.

Aim of education. No educator has conceived a more clear-cut aim for education than that set up by Sturm and none has excelled him in skillful adaptation of the means for the realization of his purpose. A man of iron will, he knew exactly what he wanted and the way to get it. He stated his objective in these terms: [2]

---

[1] Graves, F. P., *Peter Ramus and the Educational Reformation of the Sixteenth Century,* p. 17. New York: The Macmillan Co., 1912.

[2] Barnard, Henry, *op. cit.,* p. 195.

> Knowledge and purity and elegance of diction, should become the aim of scholarship, and toward its attainment both teachers and pupils should sedulously bend their every effort.

So far as piety is concerned, that should belong to every man; but eloquence should be the distinguishing acquirement of the cultured man. True eloquence, furthermore, is possible only in the Latin tongue and must accord with the Ciceronian manner, verbiage and phraseology. Sturm was deeply grieved that children did not learn Latin as their mother tongue, and he bewailed the handicap which was thus placed on them. He bitterly lamented the situation in these terms: [3]

> Cicero was but twenty years old when he delivered his speeches in behalf of P. Quintius and Sextius Roscius; but, in these latter days, where is the man, of fourscore even, who could bequeath to the world such masterpieces of eloquence? And yet, there are books enough, and there is intellect enough. What, then, do we need further? I reply, the Latin language, and a correct method of teaching. Both these we must have, before we can arrive at the summit of eloquence.

To supply these two deficiencies, Sturm used every resource and all the industry at his command. He became the leading "stylist" educator north of the Alps. This name has been given to all those schoolmen who received their inspiration from the Italian Renaissance in that final period when Ciceromania had become dominant. The entire course of study from childhood on had as its objective the attainment of Ciceronian eloquence.

The gymnasium.[4] The town council of Strassburg maintained in the different sections of the town three inefficient Latin schools, with 140, 80, and 56 pupils, respectively. Sturm recommended that these be united. Up to this time German schools had followed the ineffectual plan proposed by Melanchthon. Pupils had been divided into three groups, with a teacher for each; and every individual within the group was permitted to advance at his own pace. Sturm substituted the plan of Liége, where each class had its own teacher and instruction was carefully graded.

Ten classes were projected. There followed a college or university course of five years. Boys entered the school usually in their sixth year;

---

[3] *Ibid.*, p. 197.

[4] The use of this term for the classical school did not originate with Sturm; it had been in vogue in Italy and the Netherlands long before this time, but the dominating influence of Sturm's school stamped its use permanently upon German education.

but if they were exceptionally bright, they could enter a year earlier. Each class had a definite objective, and the work to be accomplished during the year was set down with absolute detail. Similarly, the instructional methods and devices to be followed were definitely formulated for each teacher. Sturm discussed in a masterly way the management of the school, and wrote texts for some of the classes.

Curriculum. The course of study for the gymnasium was as narrow as his aim was definite. It included religion, the Greek and Latin languages and literatures, and logic; but all these subjects were in one way or another merely contributory to the supreme end, which was the acquisition of genuine Latin eloquence.

The elementary classes were to learn Luther's catechisms by rote. This was the sole recognition of the vernacular tongue. In the middle grades, the catechisms were translated into Latin, and some works of piety were read. In the upper classes, the Epistles of Paul were read and explained in Greek and Latin, and then translated from the one language into the other. All this instruction was confined to Saturdays and Sundays; throughout the week singing of the psalms in Latin or Greek was the only recognition of religion. One must conclude from these facts that religion was not Sturm's supreme concern, but was utilized chiefly as a help to the study of Latin.

In evaluating this curriculum, it is essential to note what it omitted. There was little or no mathematics, geography, history, natural philosophy, or astronomy. German was employed slightly in the earlier grades, but no systematic instruction whatever was given; nor was any other modern language studied. Attention was never focused upon what was said, but only upon the manner of saying it. Greek, religion, the dramatization of plays, and the entire round of school work were utilized for the realization of one supreme end, the acquisition of pure, fluent Ciceronian eloquence.

Sturm's historical importance. The success of Sturm's school was phenomenal. Its enrollment reached several thousand students, for all northern Europe sent boys for him to train. The nobility were amply represented. At one time, 200 noblemen, 24 counts and barons, and three princes were enrolled. But the historical importance of Sturm's efforts were even more striking. His advice on the reorganization of schools was widely sought. Princes and kings as well as celebrated scholars paid him honor. His former pupils were among the "men of mark" throughout northern Europe. They carried his ideas far and wide; one of them drew up the Würtemberg school ordinance of 1559, and this was copied in Saxony and elsewhere. The English schoolmaster Ascham corresponded regularly with him, and paid a high tribute to him in *The Schoolmaster*. For several years John Calvin lectured in the Strassburg college, and considerable similarity can be found between Calvin's gymnasium, established in Geneva in 1559, and Sturm's institution. Because of the great similarity of organization and curriculum, it has been held that the Jesuits borrowed their school plans from this Protestant fellow-humanist. It is more probable, however, that both drew from the same source, the schools of Liége and Louvain.

HUMANISM AND THE REFORMATION IN ENGLAND

Comparison with other countries. The ecclesiastical revolt in England was basically the same as in continental lands; but some important differences were present. Attention has already been called to the stirring effects of Wycliffe and the Lollards. This evangelical movement was connected with similar awakenings on the continent, for all these peoples had similar cultures. Then, too, there was the same repugnance against the abuses of the medieval church. Englishmen were just as ripe for a break as were their fellow Nordics.

However, in two significant respects the situation in England was different. First, England had received its earliest knowledge of doctrines and practices of Christianity from the East by way of southern France, prior to the ascendancy of the Roman bishopric. Consequently the Church of England had a tradition of Apostolic origin independent of the Roman hierarchy. Even more significant at the moment was the fact that Henry VIII possessed far more control over political and social affairs than any continental sovereign. His divorce was not so much the cause of the schism but only the final straw that gave the will of the English people occasion to assert itself and to declare their independence of Rome. The gathering opposition united the evangelical and the formalist parties into a solid front of dissent. But in the doctrines and practices of the Church of England little difference appeared. The main point was that Henry, a layman and sovereign, replaced the Pope as "head of the Church" and "defender of the Faith." The resulting consolidation of church and state remains to this day.

The actual split with Rome and the movement for reform were brought about by various acts of parliament. The first and most important of these was the Act of Supremacy passed in 1534, which declared the King as the "only supreme head in earth of the Church of England," and gave him all authority to reform abuses and control the possessions of the church. The Treasons Act enabled the King to move against every one who should oppose the measures for reform. The new Church of England, unlike the Roman Church, encouraged the reading of the Bible. It was not only freely printed but copies were required by law to be placed in the churches.

The Act of Uniformity of 1552 required conformity to the Established Church. All clergy who refused were to be dismissed from their churches. Schoolmasters were required to profess faith and attend the services of the church. Catholics and dissenting Protestants had to conform or suffer punishment; many were put to death for non-compliance. The completion of the work of reformation and the re-establishment of educational institutions took many years.

The progress of Humanism in England. The advent of Henry VIII was hailed with rejoicing by humanistic scholars. Henry was himself not only an enthusiastic Humanist, versed in Latin, French, Italian, and Spanish, but he exercised sound judgment in the choice of scholars upon whom to bestow his royal bounty. Opponents of The New Learning were silenced. Henry long remained the patron of Vives, Erasmus, and Elyot; and under his royal favor, Humanism spread with astonishing rapidity. Among other things, he established a chair of Greek at Corpus Christi College, Oxford.

For Englishmen the Renaissance signified one thing supremely, a clear ideal of the all-around cultured man. He must be sportsman, gentleman, and scholar, equally ready to serve in church or state; reserved, self-contained, self-confident, imperturbable, and snobbish withal, but always in a genteel way. This ideal was embodied in the ruling prince upon whose leadership the national welfare depends. All classes of society were united in loyalty to the knightly leader, strong in body, brave, magnanimous, wise, and of an awe-inspiring dignity. He was head, leader, protector, and judge of the people. Humanistic training was the means to produce this paragon of culture. English theory of education at that time had one dominant aim, to serve the aristocracy of birth and position by teaching classical humanism. To these worshippers of precedent, tradition, and class, "good form" or "taste" was the only fixed article in the constitution of state and society.

The aristocratic ideal of the Italian Renaissance was set forth in England by Sir Thomas Elyot in connection with the Tudor doctrine of royal supremacy. The son of an attorney of high position, he was educated at home, chiefly by his own efforts. He mastered Latin and Greek and translated a number of important works, among them Plutarch's treatise, *On the Education of Children.* Elyot was a Humanist of the early Italian pattern when The New Learning was promoted by rulers to enhance their power and prestige.

In addition to *The Boke Named the Governour,* Elyot compiled a Latin-English dictionary; translated the works of Cyprian, Isocrates, and Plutarch; and wrote essays on practical conduct and devotional life.

The Governour (1531) was the first work on education written and printed in English and it set the main pattern of English culture for four centuries. The fact that it passed through ten editions during the 16th century is evidence of its power and popularity. It deals with the training of the rulers of the state in virtue and manners. The first section of the book discusses "the public weal," and was conceived from the standpoint of Plato's Republic, except that Elyot was a confirmed monarchist. He believed that rulers who govern with intelligence would be most efficient in promoting the common good. He believed that stable government, security, and peace are dependent upon the existence of differences in social classes, hierarchies in the church, and superior and inferior ranks in the nation. The "public weal" can have but "one capital and sovereign governour." Under the sovereign are inferior "governours," who have their authority from him and govern in his name.

The men most qualified to assist in governing are to be from among persons of "that estate of men called worshipful"—that is to say, they are the aristocracy of birth and estate who are accustomed to exercise authority, are acceptable as magistrates to the people; and, because of their wealth, are least liable to venality. Other men "of the base estate of the commonality" who are possessed of "excellent virtue and learning" may in some cases be advanced to official position.

The Boke Named the Governour then proceeds to elaborate a system of education for the future public leader. His nurse must be selected with the greatest care. The education of the youngster should be the chief concern of the father. Parents, tutors, and servants, all who surround the child, must speak Latin elegantly, for this is the mark of a gentleman. After seven years of age the boy should be placed under a tutor and begin his education in music, not for acquiring skill but for recreation. Drawing, painting, and carving were to be added. Greek would then receive chief emphasis although he would be using Latin as a "familiar language." For Greek, *Aesop* would be the primer and would be followed by Lucian, Homer, and Hesiod; for Latin, Virgil, Horace, and other poets would be read.

Learning must never be made difficult. For that reason the natural method of learning languages must be followed rather than the memorizing of grammar. Despite his emphasis on Greek and Latin, Elyot must be credited with being the first to advocate the use of English to explain ethics, law, philosophy, and other learned subjects. He did much to make it an effective medium to express these subjects.

After the poets had been read, logic, rhetoric, and oratory would be studied, especially to train the rational faculties, for Elyot was a rationalist after the Platonic model. Demosthenes, for Greek, and Cicero, for Latin, naturally came first. These would be followed after the age of 17 by Aristotle, Cicero and, most of all, Plato, to form the student's views of philosophy and ethics. "Lorde God," Elyot wrote, "what incomparable sweetness of words and mater shall he find in the workes of Plato and Cicero." Those who were to have the Commonwealth under their charge, who were to be Governours, must of necessity know the laws. Accordingly the study of law would occupy their attention after 21.

So much for learning and mind-forming which takes up 10 sections, or about 50 pages. Next comes physical training, which consumes about 45 pages; and finally character education to which over 180 pages are devoted.

Attention to the physical, which was suppressed during the Middle Ages, found two weighty supports during the Renaissance; first, the knightly arts, and second, the revival of knowledge of ancient Greek and Roman gymnastics. Elyot advocated wrestling, running, swimming, handling of weapons (sword and battle ax), riding, and hunting. Hawking was approved but only with reservations. The two outstanding exercises according to Elyot are dancing and archery which he discussed at length. Archery he praised as the "principal of all other exercises," for it is the best all-around coordinator of the muscles of the arms and other parts of the body. It is useful in hunting.[5]

---

[5] "Footeballe" called forth his utmost disapproval "wherein is nothing but beastly furie and extreme violence; whereof procedeth hurte, and consequently rancour and malice do remaine with them that be wounded; wherefore it is to be put in perpetual silence." As to the English classics, cricket was not yet much of a sport, nor were horse racing, boat racing, and fox hunting.

Elyot was a typical Renaissance scholar who diligently studied ancient authorities, and assembled all information on any point he discussed. Unless one knows this fact he will be puzzled at the peculiarity of Elyot's ideas of dancing. Next to archery, dancing was the best exercise; but it is not its physical, but its moral values that make it important. Elyot has in view Plato's conception of dancing as a representative or symbolic art rather than our conception of social recreation. It was an introduction to the first moral virtue, "prudence," and from its movements or gestures arose what Plato called "images of virtue." From prudence arises honor to God. Out of honor come fear, love, and "Maturitee (the mean between extremes)," providence and industry, circumspection, experience, and modesty. Dancing would begin at 20 years.

Since Elyot's day the term "gentleman" has had a distinctive meaning in the British Empire. He must be born to the manor and educated to the proper form. The son of a tradesman may be brilliant and have the same education but he can never qualify. A recent newspaper correspondent tells that in an office two Englishmen worked for forty years and yet they were not on speaking terms, because one was a graduate of Eton and the other came from an ordinary school. Sir Thomas Elyot and others believed that children of good birth, station, and wealth are pedigreed, and in addition are privileged to become the true aristocracy of character and wisdom. They are not so much snobs but models of virtue, whose conduct must be governed by *noblesse oblige.*

Works describing the ideal prince and courtier had been fairly common, at least eight having appeared in the 15th century. Topping all was the Italian work of Baldasarre Castiglione, *Il Cortegiano,* written about 1516 and published by Aldus in 1528 when it immediately became the best seller in Europe. Woodward rightly appraised it, "If one (book) rather than another is to be taken for an abstract or epitome of the chief moral and social ideas of the age, that one must be the Courtier." [6] English educators seized upon this concept of ideal manhood as the aim of the schools.

Summary of English education in the 16th century. The chief changes which took place in the schools and in the two universities of

---

[6] Woodward, W. H., *Studies in Education during the Age of the Renaissance,* p. 251. Other works that show that this ideal was common are: Leo Battista Alberti, *Trattaro della Cura Famiglio,* 1532-1533; Matteo Palmieri, *La Vita Civile,* 1435; Aeneus Sylvius (Pius II), *Letter upon the Right Education of a Prince,* 1445; Guillaume Budé, *De l'Institution du Prince,* 1515-1516.

England during the Reformation may be listed as follows: (1) Song schools in the parish churches were abolished, as were the monastery schools. (2) Schools at the courts of abbots, bishops, and noblemen, and even the palace school disappeared. (3) Catechisms and primers in the English tongue were generally introduced. (4) As a result of the suppression of monasteries, nunneries, and the shrine and chantry foundations, the enormous wealth that had belonged to these foundations was diverted to the new grammar schools and the colleges of Oxford and Cambridge. The precedent, set by his predecessors, of endowing schools by royal funds, was followed by Henry VIII and continued by his successors. (5) Humanism replaced Scholasticism as the course of study of secondary schools and the universities. Grammar and literature took precedence over dialectic. (6) Many schools were placed under lay corporations. (7) The appointment of bishops and the licensing of clergymen and teachers and the issuance of schoolbooks were now subject to state authority and approval. Every person taking orders in the church and everyone admitted to any degree at the universities was required to take an oath acknowledging the supremacy of the crown. During the last part of Elizabeth's reign strict supervision was exercised over schoolmasters in their conformity to the established religion and their loyalty to the crown. Schools were fined for employing masters not properly accredited. (8) Boarding and day schools were patronized increasingly by some noblemen and wealthy commoners. Tutors were employed at most great houses. The Latin schools were regarded as agencies for the training of boys for public life. It is certain that there were grammar schools in all English towns of any considerable size during the reign of Queen Elizabeth.

EDUCATION AMONG SMALL PROTESTANT SECTS

Bohemian Brethren. A high degree of culture existed in Bohemia long before the awakening took place in Germany, and the first university in that part of Europe was established at Prague as early as 1348. Here John Huss studied, taught, and disseminated the radical doctrines which led to his martyrdom, but nevertheless established the Protestant group.

The Bohemian Brethren had schools and publications prior to the Lutheran Reformation. At the beginning of the 16th century, they boasted three printing establishments and, among other works, published a catechism and a hymnal. A Bible in the Bohemian language was issued in Venice. Between 1500 and 1510, some 60 new publications appeared in Europe, and 50 of them were published by the Brethren.

At the beginning of the 17th century, schools began to flourish in an unprecedented way. De Schweinitz, in his history of the Moravian church, draws a rather flattering picture of educational conditions: [7]

> There was not a market town without at least one school, while larger towns had several. In Prague there were sixteen, besides two gymnasia. It was claimed these Bohemian schools were the best schools in Europe. There were parish schools, each in charge commonly of two teachers, sometimes five or six. No one was employed as an instructor unless he had attained to the degree of a Bachelor of Arts; in a majority of cases the teachers had reached the degree of Masters.
>
> This was the golden age for Bohemian learning and literature. Prague could boast of celebrities like Tycho Brahe, the astronomer; John Kepler, the mathematician and John Jessen, the physiologist and anatomist.

Other small sects. Among the other small groups which developed an indigenous culture at that time and which were to make important contributions to education were the Waldensians in southern France and the Piedmont, the Anabaptists and Zwinglians in Switzerland, and the Mennonites in Holland. Up to 1553 the Mennonites grew rapidly and became the most numerous and influential of the evangelizing parties in the Rhine valley. Doubtless they found a soil well prepared by the Brethren of the Common Life. But their doctrines of quietism and separation of church and state forestalled any dominant development in that era when it was essential to wage war and control government to survive.

PROGRESS OF HUMANISM IN FRANCE

The Renaissance in France. The French came under the influence of the Renaissance much later than other people, although, because of its close relation to Italy, southern France responded to The New Learning earlier than did Paris. The University of Orleans became its first seat. Here Budaeus (1467-1540), a native of Paris, first came into contact with the movement and carried his enthusiasm back to Paris, but as neither the University nor the Church were interested, he turned for encouragement to the nobles, especially young Francis I. To induce

[7] De Schweinitz, Edmund, *The History of the Church, The Unitas Fratrum,* p. 468. Bethlehem, Pa.: Moravian Publishing Office, 1885.

Francis to promote The New Learning, he wrote *De l'Institution du Prince* in 1516. Influenced by Budaeus, Francis founded in 1530 the *Collegium Trilingue,* which afterwards became the College de France where Latin, Greek, and Hebrew were taught, and freedom of thought was permitted. He also set up the national library, and when the Sorbonne (1533) urged that printing be prohibited he declined to follow its advice. Paris soon wrested from Italy the first place in the pursuit of Greek literature and philosophy, for the Italians were unwilling to subordinate their devotion to the Latin language.

The Renaissance movement was still further advanced in France by the invective hurled by Rabelais against the scholastic system and his praise of common sense realism.

Not only was the introduction of The New Learning delayed, but it must also be recalled that the Reformation played but a minor role in France and feudalism, monasticism, and scholasticism continued for two more centuries. In spirit, method, and curriculum, education remained what it had been. During the second half of the 16th century two men were interested in reform measures, one from the inside as an educator, the other from the outside as an observer.

Peter Ramus (1515-1572). The most persistent and comprehensive effort to effect a reform of the schools of France was made by this scion of a noble but impoverished family whose father was a charcoal burner. Ramus made his way through the College of Navarre in Paris, working as a servant. By sheer force of ability he rose to be the foremost educator of France in his day and attained international leadership as a reformer. His master's thesis defended the sweeping proposition: "All that Aristotle said is false." In as much as Aristotelianism was the foundation of Scholastic philosophy, science, and theology and had the special blessing of the Roman Catholic Church, the proposition was the ultimate in audacity. After securing his degree he began teaching at the University of Paris and writing books on the reform of education. Three times the king prohibited his works and forbade him to lecture. Reinstated on the accession of Henry II (1546), he was given a chair in the College of France in 1551, and began to reform all education. Soon he became a Protestant. He held his post, however, until he was murdered in his study on the third day of the massacre of St. Bartholomew.

The reform of subject matter. Ramus was a prolific writer and a sweeping reformer of the liberal arts. He published revised grammars for Latin, Greek, and even the French language. Rhetoric and logic likewise he desired taught in a more practical and natural way. He defined grammar as the art of speaking correctly; rhetoric as the art of speaking effectively; and logic as the art of thinking clearly.

The underlying principle of approach to these subjects was changed. In place of learning abstract precepts and definitions, the knowledge of these subjects, he contended, should come from examining the usage of the writers. Logic should be learned by observing the actual reasoning processes as shown in the classical writers. Cicero, for example, was not to be memorized for the beauty of his vocabulary and phrases, but examined for the logical correctness of his thought. Upon this basis there should be training in the use and practice of language by the pupil. "Few precepts and much use" was his slogan. He believed that true logic finds its materials in literature, and that the study of literature is best approached through logic. Scholastic logic must be abandoned, and a new logic, based on a study of the working of the human mind, especially as revealed in the greatest books, should be developed. This logic would have none of the puerile verbal distinctions and speculative digressions that had marred medieval logic. The new logic would consist of two parts: analysis and genesis, that is to say, a critical part and a creative part. Ramus recognized that no learning process is completed until a student has applied what he has learned. Not only did he publish works on grammar, rhetoric, and logic, but also on Cicero, Quintilian, Virgil, and Caesar.

In the quadrivium Ramus singled out arithmetic and geometry for special treatment. He also added the new subject of algebra. The pragmatic or utilitarian attitude of Ramus' mind came out again in regard to geometry, which he looked upon as a practical rather than a pure science. He was one of the earliest adherents to the Copernican system, but neither astronomy nor physics played an important role in his thinking. His translations of ancient works on mathematics and his revision of arithmetic and geometry texts gave such impetus to mathematical studies that he may be regarded as one of the truly important figures in the teaching of mathematics.

In 1562 he recommended that the University of Paris be reorganized. All fees, he contended, should be abolished, along with the traditional practice of allowing all who had been granted the master's degree to lecture. He recommended that only a few professors be employed and that they be paid by the state. He further recommended that secondary and higher education be separated, a step of the greatest consequence.

Ramus based all his educational reform on three ideas, (1) *nature,* (2) *system,* and (3) *practice.* (1) Nature, he taught, should be the guide. By this he meant that the materials of a field of study should be drawn by observation of nature, or, in modern terminology, from experience. Grammar, for example, is determined by usage, not by the application of formal canons. Logic is not a normative science but an art, and its content is to be determined by observing the mental processes of those who have thought most clearly. Students of physics are to avoid metaphysical problems and build up their subject by using their senses in observing the physical world.

(2) "System" meant the organization of knowledge or facts and principles. This comprised three parts: the "law of truth," the "law of justice," and the "law of wisdom." The "law of truth" is simply that, if a thing is once true, it is true always. The "law of justice" demands that boundaries between fields of knowledge must be maintained and nothing that is not germane to a discussion may be introduced into it. For example, the concepts of rhetoric should not be introduced in a lesson on grammar. The "law of wisdom" demands that general principles be stated first, and that particulars be then introduced to illustrate the general principles. In a word, Ramus here advocated a deductive approach to teaching.

(3) The principle of "practice" has to do with teaching methods. By this principle Ramus meant that pupils should use, in creative work, what they have read or been told.

Abiding effects of Ramism. The Ramian reforms were widely accepted, more particularly by Calvinistic thinkers. His logic was favored at Leyden, at the universities of Scotland, and at Cambridge, England, where Digby, tutor of Bacon, gave it vogue. A century after his death, John Milton published an abridgment of this work. In France it exerted a powerful influence upon the thinking of Descartes and the ideas and work of the Port Royalists. The chairs of philosophy at most German universities for some time were held by Ramists. Through Alsted, one of the most encyclopaedic minds of the day, it exerted an influence upon Comenius.

Michael Eyguem, Lord of Montaigne (1533-1592). This essayist and critic of education did much to prepare for a revolution. It was not what he did but what he wrote that counted. In general, his life is not significant, but his own education was, for it formed the basis of most of the reforms he suggested. Anxious to give his son the best, the father inquired of the wisest what to do. At their suggestion he committed Michael to a German who knew no French but would speak only Latin to him. The father, mother, and all the servants, likewise, studied Latin, so that young Michael heard no other tongue up to six years of age. "I had learned to speak as pure Latin as my master himself without art, book, grammar or precept, whipping or a single tear." The chief thing, however, that the father desired was "affability of manner and a good disposition." Discipline was gentle but firm. That life might be without irritation Michael was always awakened by the playing of some musical instrument. During early years he was kept in a country village, "and was brought up in the meanest and most common way."

From six he attended the college of Guinne where he received quite the opposite of his earlier training. He conceived a bitter, lifelong hatred for the ferocity of the teachers and their stupid pedantry. At the conclusion of his college course at 13, immature though he was, he began the study of law.

Looking at his education as a whole it must be acknowledged that it was none too good. He spoke Latin well, but of Greek he had only a smattering. He had little interest in books, and acquired no passion for science, literature, theology, or art. His chief intellectual interest was history, but this was more for its ethical content than its value for the evolution of society.

Educational writings. Montaigne's contribution to education consists of chapters in his essays, entitled, *Of Pedantry, Of the Education of Children, Of the Affection of Fathers to their Children;* also a number of short excerpts on various topics. The importance of these writings does not spring so much from their intrinsic impact, but from their effect on great minds of a later day.

The foremost significance of Montaigne came from his denial that speaking and writing classical Latin was the main objective of education. This pet ideal of both the church reformers and the Renaissance scholars was thus repudiated by the man who learned to speak Latin as though it were his mother tongue. In another respect did the Lord of Montaigne jolt the educational fashion of his day; he declined to worship the conventional courtier and gentleman-scholar as the ideal of manhood.

Montaigne agreed with Aristotle and Plutarch that education depends on habit. For this reason he stressed early impressions; "Our principal education depends upon the nurse." Again, in the same vein, "Upon the choice of a tutor you shall provide for your son, depends the whole success of his education and bringing up."

In sharp contrast to the English, Montaigne has little to say about the sports that form the body of a gentleman. Here again he got his ideas from his own experience. He had a delicate constitution; he desired a rugged one that could stand hardship. This suggestion of ruggedness and the hardening process found great favor with Locke and Rousseau.

The cruel beatings given by schoolmasters to force boys to learn what had no interest for them were universally reprobated by the educators of the Renaissance. Montaigne cried out in indignation against the colleges: [8]

> They are mere jails, where youths are corrupted by being punished before they have done any wrong. Go into one of these institutions during lesson hours, and you hear nothing but the outcries of boys being punished and the thundering of pedagogues drunk with fury. A pretty way it is to tempt these tender and timorous souls to love their books—a furious countenance, rod in hand. O wicked and pernicious manner of teaching!

Montaigne observed that love of learning requires alluring the appetite and affection. "I condemn all violence in the education of a gentle soul that is designed for honor and liberty." He advocated play, travel, and books easy to read, requirements that are pleasant.

The second half of the 16th century brought great emphasis upon the value of nature. This had its origin in the study of Plato, Aristotle, and Plutarch. Plato had emphasized the innate capacities, and Aristotle emphasized nature and habit as the chief factors in education. Montaigne made it central and spelled it with a capital letter. The concept of nature does not refer to the outer, physical world but to what is natural to man. It was inevitable that this idea should become increasingly consequential during the next two centuries.

Criticisms of the curriculum. Montaigne severely arraigned the education received in the schools. He charged that it stuffed the memory but neglected moral training and left "the conscience and understanding empty." It made pedants, men affected in dress and manners and given to sophistical subtleties, but not men of prudence and good judgment.

---

[8] Rector, L. E., *Montaigne, The Education of Children,* p. 62. New York: D. Appleton and Company, 1899.

The existing colleges spent 15 to 16 years in teaching the young to speak Latin. Montaigne preferred the private tutor to the schools and colleges.

Luther revolted against reason but not against learning and knowledge; Montaigne revolted against learning and knowledge, but not against judgment. He decried mere memory: "To know by heart only is not to know at all; it is simply to keep what one has committed to his memory." He glorified peoples who are least learned, preferring Sparta to Athens. He found the manners and language of country people better suited to true philosophy than those of the philosophers themselves. He disparaged formal logic and regarded "all knowledge that exceeds the natural as well nigh superfluous."

He insisted that only the useful should be taught. "Most of the subjects now taught are of no use to us; and even in those that are useful, there are many points it would be better to leave alone, and following Socrates' direction, limit our studies to those of real utility." Only after he has become wise and good is it advisable for the boy to learn logic, physics, geometry, and rhetoric. Only the philosophy that teaches the boy how to live should be communicated to him. The truth of the matter is that Montaigne had all the marks of the 20th century utilitarian pragmatists. He insisted on things before words, action rather than books, and living before learning. "A boy," he stated, "should not so much memorize his lesson as practice it. Let him repeat it in his action." "We need little learning to show us how to live at ease." Like the pragmatists he relied upon nature and experience; "the more simply a man commits himself to nature, the more wisely."

Montaigne held the functional theory of mind and knowledge: to make the mind perform its "true function we must cultivate and prepare it." No learning is of use but what we make our own; "for though we may become learned by other men's reading, a man can never be wise but by his own wisdom." Again, he held that learning is merely ornament and instrument.

Montaigne quotes Xenophon and Plato on Persian education with approval, and he commended the reform of Spartan education by Lycurgus. Instead of the arts and sciences the Spartans were instructed in contempt of fear, valor, prowess, temperance, prudence, and justice. He added also that honesty, integrity, good judgment, and reflection are the qualities to be sought. The part of philosophy that interested him most was ethics, or man and his duties.

Method. Montaigne commended likewise the method of the Spartans who thought best to initiate their children to a knowledge of cause and effect, and to instruct them not by hearsay and rote, but by experience and action; forming and moulding them not by words and precepts, but by deeds and examples. In this way knowledge is not only in the mind but in the will. The child is taught to use his eyes to see objects and actions, not to look at books. He is to be inquisitive about everything. "Mother Nature" is the book the young gentleman will study with most industry. Montaigne made it abundantly clear that he feared books and desired to divorce them from learning.

When one gets down to the issue it is not difficult to place Montaigne and to calculate the power of his influence among the stars of education. He may be more accurately classed as the first utilitarian pragmatist. It is true he drew his inspiration from Plato, but it was Plato in his reactionary days. He preferred the sober, practical life of the Spartan with its simplicity and severity rather than the intellectual and artistic brilliance of the Athenian. The words that stand out in his thinking are Nature, experience, action, good judgment, common sense, prudence, and virtue. He favored a rigorous hardening process of physical education, but an easy-going regimen for the mind. He paid lip service to the gentleman and scholar, the courtier, religion, humanism, history, family-life, the education of woman, and knowledge. He reprobated book learning, pedantry, and mental discipline. Only that knowledge was to be sought which could be put into action.

For the solution of the great problems of the day he had no contribution. What languages should be taught and the method of teaching them were outside his interest; also, what to do about mathematics and the expanding fields of natural science. He failed to influence the course of education in his own day; but his suspicion of teaching and some of his ideas of discipline reappear in the writings of John Locke and more powerfully in Rousseau.

REFORM WITHIN THE ROMAN CATHOLIC CHURCH

Conditions necessitating reform. Many of the conditions which provoked the Nordic revolt were operative in southern countries as well, and compelled reform within the Church of Rome itself. Feudalism was everywhere outmoded and had to give way to a new social and political order. During the Renaissance, interest in ancient civilization and literature had absorbed attention to the extent of sidetracking or even neglecting Christianity, and a return to conservative moral action was inevitable. The situation was further aggravated by the expansion of knowledge along new lines which required that Scholasticism be compromised. The medieval cosmology was absurd in the face of the discovery of America and the Copernican theory. Moreover the doctrines of the Roman Catholic Church had never been finally formulated and many theological differences now pressed for settlement. In addition, many licentious practices which grew out of the Middle Ages had to be dealt with by the church authorities.

Most of these problems revolved about education as carried on in the schools. For some centuries the priests generally had received their training in the universities which were not directly under the control of the church. Intellectual pride and wordly philosophy had displaced faith in vital Christianity. Scholastic disputation had ruined the spirit of conformity. Most important of all, the lack of discipline at the universities was the major cause of the dissolute behavior of the priests.

Reform measures. Five main methods of reform were put into operation by the Roman hierarchy, some of them beginning even before the Protestant revolt. These were as follows: measures to correct the licentiousness of the clergy and the abuses of the church, the setting-up of the Spanish Inquisition, the repression of heresy by the Index Expurgatorius, the Council of Trent, and the founding of the Jesuit and other new orders. Cardinal Ximenes began by instituting strong measures against abuses in Spain. Urban VI, who was educated to strict moral ideals by the Brethren of the Common Life and later served at the Spanish Court, took stern measures to combat the profligacy and licentiousness of the papal court. The Inquisition and Index operated to repress all expression of heretical ideas and doctrines harmful to the church.

The Council of Trent. Luther and the German Princes before revolting had demanded that a *General Council,* free from papal control, be called to reform abuses and to make the Scriptures the criterion of doctrine and practice. After the Protestant schism, Emperor Charles V promised that a Council would be called. The papacy finally agreed to hold a council at Trent near the Italian border in 1545. Although it came too late to heal the Protestant break, it did effect many reforms. It set forth precisely what the Catholic Church taught and what errors it could not tolerate. It did much to cleanse the church of its abuses and the clergy of licentiousness, and it demanded a reform of the education for the priesthood.

It now remained to launch a new movement of education within the frame of the church. This took place in accordance with the method already traditional with the church, the organization of new orders. By far the most consequential was the Society of Jesus, commonly known as the Jesuit Order. The Ursuline Order was founded at Brescia in 1535 and approved by Paul III for the education of girls and the care of the sick.[9]

The Catholic Reformation and education. The inevitable conflict of the conservative force with liberalism showed itself on two fronts, the bloody field of war and the quiet field of educational, diplomatic, governmental, and missionary activity. The Jesuits were the chief leaders on this latter front.

The struggle for control between the Roman Church and the Protestant world took place in the various theaters at different times. It came first in the Netherlands in the efforts of the Emperor, Philip II, to stamp out the Protestant faction. The Duke of Alva was the leader and the war was exceedingly cruel and bloody. It was fought between 1567 and 1609 and resulted in a victory for liberty and Protestantism in Holland, but also in the severance of Belgium, which remained Catholic.

The struggle in Germany did not come until the Thirty Years' War from 1618 to 1648. The theater of conflict was primarily in Moravia. The clash of forces in Britain came between the Stuarts and the Puritans.

France was saved for the Catholic Church by the work of the Jesuits, which led to the elimination of the Huguenots as a contending power. But this only postponed their own fall to the end of the 18th century.

The Society of Jesus the new Catholic educational force. This organization, usually called the Jesuit Order, was founded in 1534 by Ignatius of Loyola (1491-1556), a Spanish soldier of noble lineage. At around the age of thirty, Ignatius was seriously wounded in battle, and languished many months convalescing. Aware that he could no longer be a soldier, he turned his attention to reading two religious books, and a work entitled *Spiritual Exercises,* the precepts of which he

---

[9] Marique, P. J., *A History of Christian Education,* Vol. II, pp. 128-129. New York: Fordham University Press, 1926. This work gives a list of the new orders and a sketch of the more prominent.

began to practice. After an inner struggle, he decided to devote the remainder of his life to being a spiritual soldier or crusader for the church. His first impulse led him to Jerusalem to convert the Mohammedans. Meeting difficulties arising from his lack of knowledge, he became convinced that to accomplish his purpose he needed more education. He thereupon made his way to Paris in 1528 where he attended lectures on humanities for two years at the Collège de Montaigu, which had a reputation for piety.

Ignatius' plans matured slowly. In 1534 he and six companions of like purpose took a solemn vow in the Church of Montmartre dedicating themselves to missionary work at Jerusalem and, if that failed, placing themselves at the command of the Pope for any service. Their general purpose was to act as a militant body of men absolutely dedicated tc crushing out heresy by every means and to converting the heathen world to the Catholic faith. This, they fervently believed, was the will of God, which they symbolized by the leters O.A.M.D.G., which stood for the phrase, *Omnia ad majorem Dei gloriam* (All for the greater glory of God).

Contemplative and subject to visions though he was, nevertheless Ignatius was a man of action and had no thought of withdrawing from the world in pious seclusion. He believed the church to be at war with evil, a situation which demanded crusading action of the most aggressive character. The organization of the Order was devised with all possible sagacity and precision. Five lines of action were gradually seen to be necessary for the accomplishment of their design: preaching, missions, charity and care of the sick, influencing all those who exercised public authority or diplomacy, and education.

Organization of the Society. The members of the Society have always been regular priests who live under rules and who have taken the vows of absolute obedience, poverty, and chastity. The head of the Order was the *general,* elected for life, whose only superior was the pope. The world was divided into provinces; over each province was a *provincial,* appointed by the *general.* Jesuit colleges have always been presided over by *rectors* appointed by the general of the Order. Each rector reports to the provincial of the province in which his college is situated.

The Jesuit system of education. Education was not at first intended to be the chief means of operation, although the last vow of the

Order contained the words, "I vow according to obedience a special concern for the education of boys"; and a section of the constitution set forth the educational policy of the Society.

Not many years passed before the Order came to see the school as the most effective instrument for the long-range achievement of its objectives. The celebrated *Ratio Studiorum* (Plan of Studies) was begun in 1594 but was chiefly and finally formulated under Aquaviva, fifth general of the Order and its outstanding genius in 1599. It set forth in strict detail the educational practices adopted by the Order, the course of studies, the administration of colleges, methods of teaching and of discipline, and the system for training teachers. Never has a plan of education been more perfectly worked out to attain the end in view. Except for some minor alterations in 1832 the *Ratio* remains as originally adopted.

The educational aim. University life was wild and dissolute and led young men, the future clergy among them, into licentious living. Renaissance learning increased these evil tendencies by glorifying the ancient civilizations of Rome and Greece, and by throwing contempt upon the austerity and simplicity of the Christian way of life. The problem of reform that faced Loyola and his followers was to assimilate The New Learning in such an adroit fashion that it would not antagonize their ideal of perfect obedience to the will of God. Above every other result the Renaissance had let loose upon the world a rampant individualism. But as the Jesuits conceived it, individualism conflicts directly with obedience and submission to Christ and His Church. How to teach classical Latin and Greek without glamorizing ancient paganism and without emancipating the free speculative capacity was a delicate problem. The kind of men the Order desired to produce was clear and definite: identifying the Kingdom of God with the Roman Catholic Church, the Society required abject submission to the Church; as one Father put it, "To renounce one's own wishes is more meritorious than to raise the dead."

Growth of the Society. With great rapidity the Order increased in numbers and power, and, despite its infancy, played an important part in shaping the decisions of the Council of Trent. Jesuit colleges quickly rivaled the schools and universities of Protestant countries, and for two centuries dominated secondary and higher education in Catholic lands. By 1615, the Order conducted 572 colleges, and by 1705, the number had grown to 769. Many of these were very large; in 1627 the fourteen Jesuit colleges of the province of Paris enrolled more than 13,000 students.

Because of the inordinate aggressiveness of its members and its questionable activities, the Order soon came into violent conflict with civil authorities, universities, members of the secular clergy, and some of the other Catholic orders. Numerous charges were preferred against the Order in the papal court. So bitterly was the Order detested that by the middle of the 18th century, it was expelled from Spain, Portugal, France, and all other European countries except two, and in 1773 it was suppressed by the Pope.

Jesuit colleges. The educational work of the Jesuits has been exclusively on the secondary and higher levels. Only in a few instances where primary schools were not available has the Order reluctantly supplied instruction. Obviously the Order did not credit the old slogan: *Give me a child until he is seven and I do not care who has him after that,* for elementary education was never regarded as an indispensable part of its program. Jesuit colleges did not admit boys under ten.

Two types of colleges were conducted by the Order, the lower, which covered five or six years, and the higher, of regular university rank. The course of study of the lower colleges was divided into three grammar classes, followed by a fourth, called humanities, and a class called rhetoric. In the universities, philosophy, including mathematics and natural science, was pursued for three years. From the beginning, colleges were established only when endowment funds sufficient to support the number of teachers required to conduct the institution adequately were provided. Instruction was free, but the practice of accepting presents took the place of fees.

As a rule only Jesuits trained for the work were trusted to give instruction. At the head of each college was a rector, assisted by two prefects, "the prefect of studies" and "the prefect of discipline." The rector and the prefects exercised sleepless surveillance over all teaching, examination, and discipline, as well as over the conduct of the students. Each college underwent an annual inspection by the provincial, who interviewed teachers individually.

The curriculum and texts. The Latin language was held to be "the indispensable vehicle of all learning." The curriculum of the colleges was an astute combination of the seven liberal arts and the study of selected classical Latin authors. The use of the mother tongue was suppressed just as far as possible, and the Greek language and learning given a subordinate role. The subject matter of each year and the texts were prescribed, and variation was not permitted. The works of pagan authors were expurgated; and where it was deemed necessary to adapt the text for use by Christian youth, notes were supplied.

In the universities, mathematics, the sciences, and scholastic theology were pursued.

The methods of discipline and motivation. The discipline and methods of motivation were the best of that day and of the past skillfully combined. Like all educators of that time, the Jesuits faced the problem of teaching young boys a course of study that was little adapted to their mental interests. It was nevertheless held as a fixed principle that learning must be made easy, gradual, thorough, and definite. Nothing must be left to chance, and the youth must be cut off from outside influences that would distract attention.

The Society developed an invariable technique and its teachers, without any exceptions, have been trained to follow in the beaten path. As to method of instruction the whole reliance was upon memorizing word for word the material to be acquired. The mind had to be stored with just that knowledge and information that pertained to the central purpose in view. The ancient slogan, *repetitio mater studiorium* (repetition is the mother of learning) was never more adroitly practiced by any group of teachers. First the lesson for next day was carefully explained to the pupils; then they learned it by heart; and then by systematic reviews daily, weekly, monthly, and annually, it was indelibly stamped upon the memory until it became an integral part of the mind itself.

The entire battery of natural motivations for learning were skillfully applied, such as abject respect for instructors, the sense of duty, love of parents, desire for praise, fear of disgrace, rewards and punishments (never too severe), prizes, badges of honor, positions of leadership, and, above all, the use of rivalry.

The greatest educational artistry of the Jesuits was exemplified in their use of rivalry. This motivation was traditional. Students familiar with Greek life and pedagogy will recall that this was basic to all their best accomplishment in art, literature, philosophy, and government. It received the approval of every ancient writer and was revived in full by Renaissance educators. But that the Jesuits should use it is surprising;

for it is an incontrovertible fact that rivalry naturally promotes the development of an exaggerated individualism. Now individualism was precisely the one quality which Jesuit education was designed to curb. As sailors know how to tack against the wind, the teachers of the Order employed emulation so adroitly that, although it stimulates individualism, it served to restrain the youth from behavior that did not meet the approval of the authorities. Each class was divided into rival groups, called "Romans" and "Carthaginians." Moreover, each pupil in the classes was paired against a fellow pupil. Colleges were divided into contending "camps," membership in which distinguished a pupil.

The training of teachers. While Mulcaster in England was suggesting that a department be established at the University for the training of teachers, the Jesuit Order put plans into operation so that its teachers received the most perfect training possible to fit them for their task. Methods of instruction had to be absolutely uniform for every teacher; variations from the set pattern would wreck their entire system. In order to secure efficiency in this changeless system the teachers had to be trained with utmost precision. The Jesuit Order must be credited with introducing the practice of teacher training, and their methods of preparation may well be studied for application in all teacher training institutions.

The candidate for admission to the Society was usually accepted for training upon completion of the lower college. He then spent two years as a novice undergoing moral and spiritual discipline, in order to acquire ability to control himself. After completing his novitiate, the candidate reentered school for a period of from one to three years, depending upon the quality and extent of his earlier training, during which time he reviewed the subjects he was to teach. Throughout the early stage of this training, he observed the methods employed by the best instructors. This period, known as the *juniorate,* was followed by three years of study of mathematics, science, and philosophy in the university.

The period of training completed, the novice began teaching in a lower college. He was always under surveillance by his superiors, and received correction and encouragement. After three or four years of teaching, the candidate entered the *house of studies* of his province, where for four years he studied theology. After this was successfully completed, he was approved for ordination.

Appraisal of Jesuit education. Much has been written in acid criticism[10] of the aim, methods, curriculum, and results of Jesuit education. These are intensely interesting and important issues, because of the efforts of the Society in checking the Protestant movement and in reformation of the Catholic Church. Much of the opposition to the Jesuits came from other Catholics and from brilliant men who were themselves trained in Jesuit colleges, but who later reacted against the education they had received.

While the Jesuit system was unquestionably the most perfect ever devised and practiced to control the human personality by indoctrination, and while it was a widespread factor in the education of Catholic countries and to some extent in Protestant as well, it can only be regarded as the ultra conservative element in the evolution of modern education. The Society had no message for the feminine half of the species. For some reasons, warmly debated, it confined itself to the education of boys above ten years of age. This disregard for primary and elementary education came at a time when both Protestant and Catholic philosophy believed that the attitudes of the child were determined before seven years of age. Again the Jesuit philosophy rigidly required exclusive control over the training of the boy and would not share it with the influence of the home or any other agencies. More significantly still, the Order had no program for the education of the masses. Even the church, which it was organized to serve with an absolute devotion unparalleled in all human history, did not approve of its work. Much less did it fit into the irresistible trend for the enlightenment of all humanity.

The Society must be credited with initiating the training of teachers and assisting in missionizing heathen lands and establishing colleges in Latin America and other countries.

Since its reestablishment in 1814, it has flourished and now conducts numerous colleges and universities all around the world; some of them of the highest rank. Their contributions in some scientific lines are notable. In the past half-century Jesuit educators have published many works on the philosophy of education.

---

[10] For the Jesuit reply to these criticisms, consult the article *Educational Work of the Society of Jesus* by Robert Schwickerath, S. J., St. Louis, Mo.: B. Harder, 1903.

Chapter 5

EDUCATIONAL PROGRESS DURING THE SECOND HALF OF THE 16TH CENTURY

THE general situation. The overall condition of European civilization during the latter part of the 16th century may well occupy some of our attention. The initial impact of the Renaissance and of the Protestant revolt having subsided, the various forces began to readjust. The first point to be noted is that European civilization no longer retained its unity as in the middle ages. National rivalries intensified and the race for worldwide imperialism began. But the greatest cause of conflict was the determination of the Roman Church to regain the hegemony it had lost. This resulted in the Catholic Reformation, in various efforts at the reestablishment of religious unity, and in a century of bloody warfare.

A period of major educational readjustment. The last half of the 16th century was a time when earlier movements were reaching maturity and new developments exerted their weight. By this time Calvinism began to spread through northwestern lands. The Jesuit Order, on its part, became the aggressive force in the Roman Church and spread both in Catholic and Protestant countries. Meanwhile, Dutch and English leaders of education seized the initiative in solving the new problems and setting new trends.

CALVINISM THE NEW PROTESTANT EDUCATIONAL FORCE

The nature of Calvinism. Calvinism was not an economic, or national, or cultural revolt, but a mental and spiritual revolution. Geneva was a tiny canton with no sovereign or political power. Yet Calvinism was more than a theology; it was a leaven, an ideology which respected no state boundaries or traditions. It appealed to people of strong wills, powerful individual conviction and rational insight.

John Calvin. According to Philip Schaff, "No name in church history . . . has been so much loved and hated, admired and abhorred, praised and blamed, blessed and cursed, as that of John Calvin."

This remarkable man was the son of the secretary to the Bishop of Noyon in Picardy, France. Here Calvin was born in 1509. The father decided to make him a priest and, to this end, provided him every educational advantage by procuring for him several remunerative appointments. Needless to say, he was precocious. In his 10th year he was sent to Paris to attend the *Collège de la Marche,* where he came under the instruction of Mathurin Corderius, an excellent scholar and teacher and his life-long friend. Soon prepared to go higher, Calvin transferred to the famous *Collège de Montaigu,* where he began the study of theology. By the peculiarity of fate, only a brief time after this young man, who was to become the rigorous Protestant reformer, withdrew, the future founder of the Jesuit Order, Ignatius of Loyola, sat on the same benches and was taught by the same masters.

Not long before he died, Calvin's father incurred the displeasure of the Roman Church and, as a consequence, advised his son to turn his attention from the clerical to the legal profession. With this new purpose in view young Calvin attended the universities of Orleans and Bruges. However, his heart was not in the study of law, though no one would be so rash as to accuse him of lacking a legalistic mind. It was rather The New Learning which captured his interest. At 22, his father having died, Calvin felt free to follow his own inclination. He thereupon returned to Paris and devoted his attention to classical literature. However, late in the year 1532, he took a step which was of momentous significance: he suddenly broke with the Catholic faith and became intensely absorbed in theology. Finding France hostile to Protestantism, Calvin betook himself to Geneva, where he became a city pastor. At 26, he wrote the first edition of the *Institutes of the Christian Religion,* which, at a stroke, marked him as the master theologian of the day. Driven from Geneva by a reactionary element, he sought refuge for a short period in the liberal city of Strassburg. Here he was pastor of a church for French Protestants and lectured on theology at the local college. In close association with this college was the celebrated classical gymnasium, recently founded by John Sturm.

Recalled to Geneva (1541), Calvin, by his inflexible will power, transformed the city into the "Rome of Protestantism." From this center his doctrines dominated church reform in France, eastern Germany, Holland, England, Scotland, and a large part of Switzerland. He died in 1564, the most creative theologian of his day, and an important figure in education.

The Academy of Geneva. For many years Calvin held steadily in view the establishment of a school which would be the capstone of the ecclesiastical organization of the city of Geneva, for the moral and spiritual discipline of all the people. Because of numerous difficulties, he was unable fully to realize his plans until 1559, when he reorganized several weak Latin schools into a consolidated gymnasium and academy. The gymnasium, a conventional preparatory Latin school, had seven classes and was under the supervision of the city but was supported by tuition fees. The curriculum was thoroughly humanistic, and resembled that of Sturm's gymnasium at Strassburg. The academy was a higher institution which gave instruction in Greek, Hebrew, ethics, logic, rhetoric, oratory, poetry, physics, and mathematics. Ten professors assisted Calvin; among them Mathurin Corderius, Calvin's former teacher in Paris, who was long rector of the institution.

No other school of that day paid stricter attention to religious training. Classes began each morning with prayers, and ended with the recitation of the Lord's Prayer and the offering of thanks. The hour from 11 to 12 was devoted to singing psalms. At four in the afternoon the assembly was given over to reciting of the Lord's Prayer, the confession of faith, and the Ten Commandments. On Wednesday morning, students and faculty listened to a sermon; Saturday afternoon, all studied the catechism. On Sunday, the students attended religious worship, and then spent the rest of the day in meditation on the sermon.

The success of the school and academy was amazing. During the first year 900 young men enrolled from all the nations of Europe. The institution was immediately recognized as the nursery of Protestant preachers and teachers for France and other lands. It was taken as the model for the organization of the University of Leyden in Holland, Edinburgh in Scotland, and Emmanuel College at Cambridge University, England, which in turn influenced the founding of Harvard in Massachusetts. Wherever the Calvinistic faith was carried, it aroused an extraordinary zeal for education.

Calvin and the common school. Many have attributed the origin of the common school to Calvin. The historian George Bancroft asserted: "Calvin was the father of popular education, the inventor of the system of free schools." [1] The facts scarcely warrant this claim any more than do similar facts in the case of Luther. Calvin had no interest in elementary vernacular education. He complained to the council of Geneva that there were too many small schools, and the number was then reduced to four—one for each quarter of the city. He required that only those boys who were unable to learn Latin should be allowed to attend these schools. No provision was made for the education of girls, nor for compulsory training, except in the home. On the other hand, it must be admitted that his catechism furnished a small measure of religious instruction to everybody. So far as the vernacular language was concerned, it must be admitted that Calvin required the pupils in the gymnasium "to read French fluently."

Moral pessimism. Educational theories and practices are determined in large measure by one's basic ethical conceptions. From St. Augustine, Calvin acquired that moral pessimism which was the fundamental motive in all his religious doctrines and plans for education. To his way of thinking, the child is inherently bad; his depravity is total; all elements of his nature, emotions, reason, and will are alike perverted; all his natural childish inclinations, appetites, and interests lead him astray. In the interest of moral and religious life, they all must be suppressed, and in their place must be engrafted good habits and pious thoughts.

This point of view explains Calvin's anxiety to organize all the institutions of society into one harmonious environment so as to subject the youth to the impact of a single regimen, carefully supervised by an institutional conscience. The doctrine of total depravity played a prominent role in the theories of 16th-century education, and finally led, in the philosophy of the 18th century, to a reaction which favored the declaration of the original goodness of man.

View of government and civic life. One can secure an adequate conception of Calvin's educational program only by understanding his view of government and Christian life. His genius led to the welding of church, state, and family into one combined institution for the instruc-

---

[1] Schaff, Philip, *History of the Christian Church,* Vol. VII, p. 522, New York: Charles Scribner's Sons, 1903.

tion, discipline, training, and control of the entire citizenship. These institutions were the individual organs of a unified organism, with a single objective, which was to realize the Will of God on earth. Calvin visualized a theocracy, conceived in accordance with the Old Testament and under the dominance of the pastors of Geneva.

In the home the parents were obliged to teach the children the catechism and Christian living. This work, as well as the daily conduct of parents, was strictly supervised by the *consistorium*. Every home was inspected at least once a year to see that the regulations were carried out. The church was used not only for worship, but likewise as a place of instruction in the catechism for both old and young. The state existed to make laws in accordance with the puritanic ideas of the pastors, to organize and support schools, and to see that the ecclesiastical regimen was carried out.

Effect of Calvin's discipline on Geneva. The effect of this regimen can be seen from the following statements: John Knox declared, Geneva "is the most perfect school of Christ that ever was in the earth since the days of the apostles." There is also the judgment of the Lutheran pastor Johann Valentin Andreä, who visited Geneva in 1610 and reported as follows: [2]

> When I was in Geneva, I made a notable discovery, the remembrance of which and longing for which will die only with my life. Not alone is there in existence an absolutely free commonwealth, but as an especial object of pride (*ornamentum*), a censorship of morals (*disciplina*), in accordance with which investigations are made each week into the morals and even into the slightest transgressions of the citizens, first by the supervisors of the wards, then by the aldermen, and finally by the magistrate, according as the case demands. As a result, all cursing, gambling, luxury, quarreling, hatred, conceit, deceit, extravagance, and the like, to say nothing of greater sins, are prevented. What a glorious adornment—such purity of morals—for the Christian religion! With our bitterest tears we must lament that this is lacking and almost neglected with us.

THE SPREAD OF CALVINISM

An international religious reformation. It is important for the student of history and of education to understand that whereas the Lutheran Reformation was allied with national governments, Calvinism

---

[2] Held, Felix Emil, *Johann Valentin Andreä's Christianopolis,* p. 27. Urbana: University of Illinois Press, 1914.

gave birth to the Reformed Church which knew no state boundaries. It exerted great influence in Switzerland and France, but took root in a broader way along the river Rhine in Germany, with Heidelberg University as its center, and was especially strong in Holland. For several decades the Mennonites had been the most numerous and influential evangelizing party in this sector. Then to escape the persecution of "Bloody Mary" from 1553 to 1558, thousands of Calvinists from England sought refuge in Holland and helped to increase the trend toward the dominance of the Reformed Church.

THE REFORMATION IN SCOTLAND

Calvinism introduced. The Reformation reached Scotland later than other lands, and it owed its victory to the fervent preaching of John Knox, who had come under the influence of Calvin and his school at Geneva. Knox induced the Scottish parliament (1560) to adopt a new confession of faith with this decisive resolution, "the bishops of Rome have no jurisdiction nor authority in this Realme." By this act Scotland abolished Romanism and accepted the Calvinistic system.

In the *First Book of Discipline* Knox proposed an autonomous church after the pattern of Geneva, with control over morals and religion, both public and private, including education. The young and ignorant were to be instructed in a graded system of schools; every church was to have an elementary school, every town a secondary school, and every city a university. The crucial provision proposed by the *Book of Discipline* was that the wealth of the monasteries and churches and all tithes be devoted to the support of the churches, schools, universities, and the poor. This was asking more than the rapacious lords of Scotland could tolerate. Moreover, while they were willing to grant the church oversight of elementary schools, they demanded that the towns should not be disturbed in their control of secondary schools. As a result of all this opposition nothing of consequence was done for many years.

THE NETHERLANDS

General developments. In the transition to Protestantism, the Netherlands experienced the fiendishness of a fanatical religious war with their Spanish overlords. Thousands of people were martyred, others died in the war, and tens of thousands crossed the channel into the eastern counties of England. As a consequence of the conflict, the southern provinces were saved for Catholicism, but the northern provinces became intensely Protestant and, in the end, set up the Dutch Republic.

In spite of these withering experiences, the culture of the Netherlands continued to flourish, and Holland shortly attained the leading role in European civilization. In commerce, manufacturing, exploration, and invention, the Dutch had no rivals. In painting and smithing her craftsmen likewise set the pace. As early as 1576 the Prince of Orange proclaimed toleration of all religions, even for Catholics and Anabaptists, and soon Holland became an asylum for religious refugees from every land.

The University of Leyden, established in 1575 as a reward for the heroic defense against the Spaniards, became the most progressive center of learning in northern Europe, and the city of Amsterdam became a rendezvous and refuge for learned men from every country. Most of the teachers became Protestant; especially was this true of the Brethren of the Common Life, who had long been inclined toward evangelical faith. Almost every man, woman, and child had learned to read in the pre-Reformation public schools. As the schools were already in the hands of the town authorities, the transfer to the new order was effected without much opposition. With the general acceptance of Protestantism, the city councils forbade the teaching of Catholic prayers and religious practices, and required the substitution of the reformed catechism and doctrines.

School endowments. Another great advantage for the Netherlands was the ease with which the revenues and property of the old church were now diverted to the support of the public schools. In 1580 the state of Utrecht set apart its ecclesiastical property for the maintenance of schoolmasters. Three years later Zealand passed a similiar law, on the ground that education "is the foundation of the commonwealth." In 1603 the revenues of the old church were turned over to the support of common schools in Friesland.

The Dutch Reformed Church, in accordance with its Calvinistic doctrine of theocratic government, cooperated with the state authorities to advance the interests of education. In 1574 the Synod of Dort passed an ordinance directing "the servants of the Church" to obtain from the magistrates in every locality permission for the appointment of schoolmasters, and an order for their compensation as in the past. In 1582 the province of Friesland decreed that the inhabitants of the towns and villages should, within the space of six weeks, provide good and able reformed schoolmasters. If they neglected this order, teachers would be appointed for them. The Synod of Nimeguen in 1606 voluntarily requested the civil authorities to make education compulsory. So far as jurisdiction over schools outside the towns was concerned, the authority lay in the hands of the states-general or the legislature.

The attitude of the rulers is shown in the following letter, which Count John of Nassau wrote to his sons and nephews, among them Lewis William, Stadtholder of Friesland, urging "the necessity of establishing a system of common schools in the United Provinces." [3]

> You must urge upon the States-General that they, according to the example of the Pope and the Jesuits, should establish free schools where children of quality as well as of poor families, for a very small sum, could be well and christianly educated and brought up. This would be the greatest and most useful work, and the highest service that you could ever accomplish for God and Christianity, and especially for the Netherlands themselves.... *Churches and schools, good libraries, books and printing-presses, are better than all armies, arsenals, armouries, munitions, alliances, and treaties that can be had or imagined in the world.*

Three levels of schools. There were three grades of schools fostered: common schools for the masses; classical schools for boys who expected to enter professional life; and the universities.

The common school systems of Europe and America owe their origin, in large measure, to the town schools of the Netherlands. These schools were the outcome of three factors, the first of which was the demand made by commercial life. For several centuries before the Reformation, reading and writing had been taught in town, as well as in private, schools. Davies asserts: [4]

> We have the testimony of the Italian Guicciardini to the fact that before the outbreak of the war with Spain even the peasants in Holland could read and write well.

The second factor was the virtual democracy of the government. The third factor was the Reformation.

During the Reformation in Holland the Calvinist doctrines con-

---

[3] Quoted from Motley, John Lothrop, *History of the United Netherlands,* Vol. III, p. 119. New York: Harper & Brothers, 1867.

[4] Davies, C. M., *History of Holland and the Dutch People,* Vol. 1, p. 487. London: G Willis, 1851.

tributed to the demand for popular education. The aims of the church required: (1) learning of the creed and chief dogmas as found in the catechism; (2) training in moral habits and attendance upon the services of the church; (3) reading the Scriptures; and (4) the singing of the Psalms. This much of religious instruction was to be universal. Girls as well as boys were admitted to the elementary schools.

A Dutch School of the Sixteenth Century.

The organic unity of church and state implied, moreover, the ideas of compulsory training, service to the commonwealth, state support and control of the schools, and gratuitous instruction. In spite of its establishment as the official religion of the state, the Reformed Church did not have complete control of education in the provinces. Large numbers were Catholics, Arminians, and Mennonites. These peoples thwarted the ambition of the Calvinists for full authority. In consequence of this division, the secular authorities kept control over all educational affairs. All these factors assisted in realizing a fairly effective system of public schools in Holland long before it was found elsewhere.

Grammar schools were widely distributed, and were under the control of the municipal authorities. Latin and Greek were usually taught; but many schools expanded their curricula beyond the narrow course of Sturm. French, mathematics, and philosophy were frequently included in the courses of study.

The progressive culture of the Dutch people is well exemplified in their universities. The following institutions were established: Leyden, in 1575; Franeker, in Friesland, 1585; Groningen, 1614. Leyden attained greatest celebrity. It was founded to commemorate the heroic resistance of the town against the siege of the Spaniards. Offered a choice of immunity from taxation or the establishment of a university, the inhabitants of Leyden chose a "free school and university." The new institution immediately became a rendezvous for French and English Protestants, as well as students from their own people. Over 2,000 students of English nationality matriculated in Leyden during the 17th century. Among the celebrated scholars connected with Leyden were Joseph Scaliger, Grotius, Arminius, Stevin, and Boerhaave.

Influence of Dutch education. Historians have devoted too little attention to the influence of the Dutch. Their advanced ideas of school organization, curricula, and methods radiated in every direction.

It has been estimated that about 10,000 Englishmen took up residence in Holland during the stay of the Pilgrims; many of them attended the universities, and their children were taught in the schools. Among these were Robinson and Brewer, who played so conspicuous a role in the emigration to the New World. In 1609 when the Pilgrim Fathers took up their residence in Leyden, the school had already become the property of all the people: [5]

> It was a land where every child went to school, where almost every individual could read and write, where even the middle classes were proficient in mathematics and the classics, and could speak two or more modern languages.
>
> There was hardly a Netherlander—man, women, or child that could not read and write. The school was the common property of the people, paid for among the municipal expenses. In the cities, as well as in the rural districts, there were not only common schools but classical schools. In the burgher families it was rare to find boys who had not been taught Latin, or girls unacquainted with French.

According to Griffis,[6] the leaders of the Pilgrims in Holland "became citizens, paid their taxes, and took advantage of the common schools."

---

[5] Motley, John Lothrop, *op. cit.*, Vol. IV, p. 432.

[6] Griffis, W. Elliot, *The Influence of the Netherlands in the Making of the English Commonwealth and the American Republic*, p. 17. Boston: De Wolfe, Fisk & Co., 1891.

Griffis also states that between 80,000 and 100,000 persons emigrated from the Netherlands into England.[7]

> The direct influence of these refugees on the English people was seen in this—that each foreign workman was compelled by law to take and train one English apprentice. The law sent, probably, fifty thousand English boys and young men to school, not only in industry, but in republican ideas and liberal notions.

Again, we must not overlook the influence of Dutch education upon colonial America, which will be discussed later.

THE ADVANCE OF EDUCATION IN ENGLAND

Educational reformers. The chief developments of education in England were in the field of humanistic theory and the reorganization of the schools under the monarchy. The chief thinkers were Roger Ascham and Richard Mulcaster.

Roger Ascham (1515-1568). The educational historian is constantly obliged to face the problem of evaluating materials. The *Encyclopaedia Britannica* (11th Ed.) allots Ascham a page and a half, but entirely ignores Mulcaster. From the standpoint of 16th century English opinion Mulcaster was only an unimportant schoolmaster; Ascham a highly successful courtier, twice teacher of Princess Elizabeth and one-time secretary of Queen Mary. From the standpoint of any lasting improvement to English education he contributed nothing but the exaggeration of the value of archery as a form of exercise for the typical gentleman of the age, and the method of teaching Latin by means of a double translation. In the context of European education he must be located as a follower of Sturm of Strassburg.

Ascham is credited with two books, *Toxophilus* (1544) on archery; and *The Schoolmaster,* published two years after his death. Like all the scholars of that era he diligently searched what the ancients had written on education, and he accepted the familiar pattern of the "gentleman" already set forth as the educational ideal. The real reason attention was centered on the education of the aristocracy was that the lower classes aped the manners and standard of life set by the higher. The social pattern of culture or style was determined by the aristocracy.

---

[7] *Ibid.,* p. 10. See also De Vries, Tieman, ***Dutch History, Art and Literature for Americans,*** p. 37 *et seq.* Grand Rapids: Eerdmans-Sevensma Co., 1912.

For some time educational complexity had increased everywhere. First the English language was undergoing rapid changes. No attention, however, was given to teaching it, though it could no longer be ignored. Again, the medieval jargon of Latin was not so much in evidence as it had been. Third, classical Latin had to be learned in the schools. Imagine small boys five and six years of age trying to learn to speak Latin by memorizing the rules of Latin grammar! Most teachers had neither method nor sound learning themselves, but they knew how to beat the child without mercy. To correct this inhuman method of motivation, Ascham proposed "a plaine and perfite way of teachyng children to understand, write and speake in Latin tong." Ascham, like all reformers for several centuries, pleaded for gentleness and persuasion.

The men of the Reformation as well as those of the Renaissance were in full agreement that, for the right education of the youth, speaking and writing of classical Latin was absolutely essential. Ascham rightly stated, "All men covet to have their children speak Latin." This objective clearly visualized, the method of realizing it was the supreme problem of the educator. Unfortunately, in his eagerness to make sound Latin scholars, Ascham discounted the value of learning music, arithmetic, and geometry.

Ascham proposed to teach a small amount of grammar first of all and then tackle Sturm's *Select Letters of Cicero* in Latin. By learning to read the text slowly and memorizing the words, the boy gradually acquired a vocabulary, and a more accurate knowledge of the construction of the language. He was taught to translate the text into English and then to turn about and put his translation back into Latin. This accomplished, the tutor compared his Latin with the original. After much practice of this double translation, the pupil wrote essays in English and then translated them into Latin.

Richard Mulcaster (c. 1530-1611). Unquestionably the most astute educational mind of his day and perhaps the equal of any of any day, Richard Mulcaster merits extensive treatment. His *Positions* was printed in 1581 and then consigned to oblivion for three centuries. The *Elementarie* was printed twice in 1582 and never again until 1925. The *Positions* is one of the most creative educational works ever produced in England; the *Elementarie* was the first and most comprehensive treatise on primary education down to the 19th century. Why did Englishmen consign these two works to the dust and give great popularity to Ascham's *Schoolmaster?* Because of the peculiarity of Mulcaster's English, say his recent discoverers. A better explanation was that his position in regard to popular training did not meet the approval of the upper crust; it was out of line with the trend of English social thinking. Mulcaster aimed to educate an aristocracy of brains and social capacities selected according to the plan of Plato from all ranks, and not from inherited stations.

If Mulcaster's influence upon English education had been commensurate with his insight, many pages would have been needed to sketch it adequately. But why treat of ideas dead three centuries? Chiefly because of the acceptance of his insights on the continent by minds more progressive.

Mulcaster's profound insight into education can be explained as follows: first, like Elyot, Ascham and Montaigne he had weighed what the best ancient and contemporary writers had to say on the bringing up of children. Second, years of keen observation as headmaster of the Merchant Taylors' School gave him a rich fund of experience. None of the previous writers on education had such opportunity to observe the processes of education by dealing directly with young boys from various social strata.

The third main point was Plato's conception of the state and of education in relation to it. The Platonic influence was dominant in most of Renaissance education. To serve the state was accepted as the prime purpose in the training of the "gentleman-scholar." None, however, followed Plato so closely as Mulcaster in the selection of those who were to be advanced to a complete education.

The facts in the biography of Mulcaster that have genuine significance are not numerous. The family was of some standing; Richard was sent to Eton, and then to King's College, Cambridge. For some unknown reason he transferred to Oxford where he was elected to a studentship in 1555. Three years later he became a schoolmaster in London, where his reputation as a scholar and teacher led to his appointment as Head Master of the Merchant Taylors' School, just founded (1561). The new institution had as its purpose "the better education and bringing up of children in good manners and literature." This was strictly in accord with the English tradition of aristocratic education. The Merchant Taylors' School differed from other "great public schools" only in that it was a "day school," and for the common run of boys. Here Mulcaster served efficiently and thoughtfully, for 25 years. After an interval of 10 years, when otherwise engaged, he was appointed Head of St. Paul's, one of the oldest of the "Great Public Schools." Meanwhile he published his two chief works on education. Mulcaster was conversant with the educational theories and practices of the past. The treatises of Elyot, Ascham, and others were rehashes of what the ancients had written; but not so with Mulcaster's. He discusses the vital educational issues of his day, and not merely what Plutarch or Quintilian held 15 centuries earlier.

The educational problems that faced England during the second half of the 16th century were clearly set forth in the writings of Mulcaster and were intelligently faced.

The middle class was growing in wealth and naturally sought for its sons the same education that was given to the sons of the aristocracy. The founding of the Merchant Taylors' School was strictly in line with this trend. The danger then arose that too many people would receive a classical education, for only a limited number could be employed in state service. Mulcaster was very insistent upon this point.

Educational training in foreign languages had increased greatly in complexity. For centuries western Europe was bilingual; religion and learning were carried on in a jargon of medieval Latin, and only vulgar activities utilized the vernacular tongues. Then classical Latin and Greek came in as requirements for a learned man. Hebrew too was considered by many scholars as a rival of Greek. Finally, religious life had switched to the vernacular in all Protestant lands, and the church, along with business interests, demanded that it be made a subject of school training. The problem of learning all these languages complicated the curriculum of the schools.

Again, Mulcaster and others of his day had become poignantly aware that Latin grammar, which was the first subject taught, could not be understood by children of five and six for they were not mentally ready for it. Their faculties had first to be developed by a preparatory course of training.

How did Mulcaster react to this complex situation? He was living in a society passionately devoted to monarchy and completely convinced of the superiority of an aristocracy, and he unreservedly subscribed to this attitude. At the same time he shared with Elyot, Ascham, and others of his day a profound reverence for Plato's conceptions of society and government. It will be recalled, furthermore, that he was teaching boys of the upper middle class in English society who looked to the crown for advancement to high station in life. Plato did not admit in his scheme an hereditary monarch or ruling caste of aristocrats to the manor born. The rulers of Plato's state were the aristocracy of character and brains who won their right to rule because they were the most virtuous, intelligent, and wise citizens. This principle of selecting the best for superior education was uppermost in Mulcaster's thought. He was an ardent supporter of monarchy and he was patriotic in the extreme.

The goal of education, as Mulcaster phrased it, was to bring up "the young fry" so "that they may prove good in the end and serve well in that place, whereinto they shall be allotted for the benefit of their country when they come to maturity." Despite his subserviency to aristocracy, the benefit of the commonweal was always in his mind.

Who are to be educated? Mulcaster is credited by some with favoring universal literacy. He did so in a very grudging fashion, but let him speak for himself: "Sure all children may not be set to schole, may not, though private circumstances say yea. And therefore scholes may not be set up for all." But for the purpose of religion and necessary affairs they might learn to read and write provided they would not go further. The parish priest could help children to acquire these primary arts. That is as far as Mulcaster went in his plans for universal literacy. It was literacy but not enlightenment.

In his conception education had only one purpose, that is, service to the commonweal, and he feared greatly that too many would be educated beyond the actual needs of the state. In other words, the pupil to be chosen is the child most likely to become a cultured gentleman, who is devoted to the interest of his sovereign and superiors, is well liked by his fellows, and will be able to govern his inferiors agreeably. The children who showed the sharpest intellect and the best morals were to be selected and advanced to the higher levels of training. Here again Mulcaster availed himself of Plato's suggestion. The conclusion from Plato's *Republic* that impressed Mulcaster and all others in his day was this: each individual should be put to the use of the state in the position for which nature designed him. These men took this to mean that children are to be trained not for the life station of the father, but for the place for which their capacities fit them.

Service to the Commonwealth. On what basis should selection be made of those who are to receive the highest education? It would depend on two things: First, on the capacity and desire of the child to acquire learning; and, second, on the need society has for learned men to serve in the offices of the church and government and in the various professions. One physician can serve many people, so the number of physicians will depend on the need of society. So it will be in all other services.

Learning or knowledge is a social good and must not be turned to private profit. Education is not for the advantage of the individual but for the benefit of society. "In the end they [educators] consider whether he that is learned do live privately for himself or publically for others."

Whether an individual would serve society well when he had been educated would depend on his zeal for moral virtue and the good of society regardless of profit to himself.

Mulcaster, perhaps motivated by sad experience, was intent upon limiting educational opportunity. He did not wish to encourage too many to climb to a higher social level. Accepting Aristotle's division of governments into monarchy, democracy, and oligarchy he chose the first. Only those children are selected for continued training to the highest level whose capacities are best fitted to advance the interests of the monarchy. He then proceeded to define the qualities of "the child that is like to prove so fit a subject for a monarchie in matters of learning." "The monarchical learner," as he calls the good candidate, must have these qualities in high degree, "obedience to superiors and superiorite, friendliness and fellowship toward companions, and equalles; substance to deserve well and winne it, desire to avoide ill and flee it."

The education of girls. A number of writers of the 16th century had favored the education of girls and some excellent books were written on the subject. Chivalry, the Renaissance, and the fact that women were accepted as queens and occupied other high positions convinced men that girls, especially of the aristocracy, must receive a liberal education. Mulcaster was for them, "toothe and naile." Summing up his reasons in a burst of burning eloquence he wrote: [8]

> Our countrey doth allow it, our duetie doth enforce it, their aptnesse calls for it, their excellencie commandes it: and dare private conceit, once seeme to withstand, where so great, and so rare circumstances do so earnestly commende?

An added reason for his acceptance of the full participation of girls in education was that it enjoyed the full endorsement of Plato.

Before one becomes too enthusiastic, however, over Mulcaster's demand for the education of "young maidens," it is well to take a closer look. They are to be taught reading, writing, drawing, music (singing and playing), and needlework. They remain in the elementary school until they are 13 or 14. Mathematics is considered beyond them as are

[8] Mulcaster, R., *Positions,* p. 167. London: Longmans, Green and Company, 1887

all professional and learned subjects. An exception is made of women of the nobility who, because of the station they must occupy, must be trained in learned and modern languages.

The use of the vernacular. Mulcaster was as great an advocate and as determined a protagonist of English as any language ever had. In the *Peroration* to his *Elementarie* he ardently exclaimed: [9]

> I love *Rome,* but *London* better. I favor *Italie,* but *England* more. I honor the Latin, but I worship the English . . . I do not think that anie language, be it whatsoever, is better able to utter all arguments, either with more pith, or great explainnese, than our English tongue is.

The *Elementarie* is the fullest discussion of training in the elements of English until recent times.

Principles of method. Mulcaster accepted Plato's notion that "all our learning" is innate, the soul having it in itself naturally. From this doctrine he concluded that there are in the child "natural abilities which nature planteth in our mindes and bodies, prepared by himself for us to use." But these natural capacities are to be perfected by ourselves. Nature is the foundation on which we must build.[10]

> The end of education and training is to help nature unto her perfection which is, when all her abilities be perfected in their habit.

"Education is an art that assists nature to attain an artificial perfection." The teacher must not force learning or good moral behavior, but wait for the signs that the child's capacities are ripe. Mulcaster has much to say about "ripeness," just as primary workers look for "reading readiness" in their pupils today.

Man transcends the beast because "divine qualities" arise out of the natural abilities as the best fruit arises out of the first blossom. We detect here the early, if not the first, theory of natural development. The education of the young gentleman is to be mild and pleasant. Its end is not learning for learning's sake.

Training of young most important. The most important part of all education was to get the right start, to lay a sound foundation. Elementary training accordingly received extensive treatment by Mulcaster. No one until Pestalozzi placed so much emphasis upon elementary training.

---

[9] Mulcaster, *Elementarie,* pp. 269-274. Oxford: Oxford University Press, 1925.
[10] *Ibid.,* p. 31.

The curriculum. Having once determined who is to be educated and how and to what end, the next question has to do with the course of study. Elementary education should, he believed, consist of reading, writing, drawing, painting, music (singing and instrumental), dancing, and playing. This, it is readily seen, is the traditional Renaissance humanistic course. But there is one startling change. Latin is not mentioned. For the first time a man in one of the most noted school positions proposes a curriculum leading to the highest learning that begins with the vernacular and not with Latin. Moreover, it did not begin with grammar. Elementary education for some years must precede and prepare for the study of Latin grammar; that was the most radical and eventful suggestion to come from any man at this juncture.

In the learned school, Mulcaster provided for Latin, Greek, and Hebrew; these were to be preparatory for the university.

Physical education. English educators have always looked with special favor upon physical exercise not because humanism required it, but because, like the ancient Greeks, they love strenuous action in the open. Mulcaster devoted much space to discussing the educative values of dancing, wrestling, fencing, tops, walking, running, leaping, skipping, swimming, riding, hunting, shooting, handball, and football. Consideration was given to qualities, time, place, preventive medicine, and other aspects of the subject.

Other suggestions. Among the numerous valuable insights for the advancement of education in the fertile experience of Richard Mulcaster, the following must be mentioned: he disapproved of education by private tutors, preferring public schools. He urged that care should be taken to afford plenty of light and air in schoolhouses, and that playgrounds be provided for all schools. A complete reorganization of university education was advocated so as to set up separate colleges for each profession, and among them Mulcaster urged an institution for the training of teachers, which, he claimed, "is comparable to the greatest professions." This is the earliest suggestion of the professional training of teachers.

Mulcaster urges that conferences be held between all those who have interest in children "to see them well brought up." He suggests conferences between parents, neighbors, and teachers. The home, community, and church must coöperate in giving children certainty and constancy as to behavior.

Influence. Despite the disregard of the reforms advocated by Mulcaster by his own countrymen, they were not devoid of fruit. Ratich, and perhaps Comenius, were awakened to the importance of these measures and made them the basis of their reforms in the next generation.

Institutional changes. Some few changes took place in English education at this time.

Before the Reformation in England only three of the nine so-called "Great Public Schools" had been founded: Winchester, Eton, and St. Paul's. As a result of the Reformation, the remaining six were established within about sixty years. In 1540, Henry VIII changed the monastery at Westminster into a college with two masters and forty scholars. Twenty years later it was refounded by Queen Elizabeth. Pupils had to be eight years of age and have a knowledge of writing and elementary grammar to enter. Seven forms or classes constituted the curriculum. Shrewsbury was founded in 1551 by Edward VI. The Merchant Taylors' School (1560-61) was the child of the Merchant Taylors' Gild or Company. The enrollment was limited to 250. The next to follow was Rugby, founded in 1567 by private endowment. It was not opened until 1574, but became with Eton and Harrow one of the most famous of these schools. Charterhouse was founded by a wealthy merchant in 1611. The last of these Great Public Schools was Harrow, founded in 1615. Although not so old and venerable, in general fame it ranked among the first because of the wealth of its patrons and the number of prominent men, especially great statesmen, who received their training there.

These institutions were the English equivalent of the schools of the Italian nobles, and the Knightly Academies of Germany. Their purpose was to train boys of the higher class to fill the offices of church and state. Boys of the nobility were sent to them as a matter of course; some of the lower class were selected because of special intellectual ability and given an opportunity through the patronage of some person of commanding influence. These schools took the boys of six to eight and prepared them to speak, read, and write Latin so that they were ready to enter one of the colleges of Oxford or Cambridge. It was customary for the founders of these public schools to make provisions for scholarships for the graduates in some college at Oxford or at Cambridge. These schools were, therefore, the chief preparatory schools of England.

During the Middle Ages the seven liberal arts were divided into the trivium or lower course which consisted of grammar, rhetoric, and dialectic or logic; and the quadrivium which consisted of arithmetic, geometry, astronomy, and the theory of music. These were preparatory to professional subjects, law (civil and canon), medicine, philosophy, natural science, moral science or ethics and metaphysics, and the queen of the sciences, theology. For a long time there was no separation of the two levels of work. Then the tendency arose to separate the trivial from the quadrivial and the higher studies.

The Latin grammar schools gave the elementary training. The colleges or the universities then carried the educatee through the secondary and higher studies.

Until the Renaissance university students learned all the professional subjects. The expansion of knowledge by the rediscovery of the ancient Roman, Greek, and Hebrew civilizations and the advancement of the sciences rendered the acquisition of all branches of knowledge impossible, and as a consequence, specialization on the professional level gradually arose.

The economic chaos that followed the breakdown of feudalism, the transition in England from agriculture to sheepraising with the consequent shifting of population from the country to the cities precipitated a crisis which Parliament was obliged to deal with. To ameliorate these conditions the Statute of Apprentices was passed in 1562. This act had had several far reaching effects: (1) It divided the English people into two classes, the rich or property owners, and the poor. (2) By requiring that no one can practice a "trade or mystery" without serving an apprenticeship of seven years, it stabilized industry and the gilds. (3) It likewise acted to train the youth in agriculture, animal husbandry, and industrial arts. No child under nine could be bound as a parish apprentice and the master was required to teach the apprentice not only his trade but also reading and writing.

The Poor Law of 1601. Confronted with widespread poverty, unemployment, and the necessity of controlling the lower class, Parliament enacted the famous Poor Law. This act provided for the relief of poverty out of local taxes and for a measure of supervision of the poor by a board of overseers in each parish. This board was given authority to levy taxes, build working-houses, and put the poor to work. It also was authorized to place poor children in work-houses and to bind them out as apprentices. The most harmful result of this measure was that it stamped public education as a charity extended by the state or community and not a natural right of the child as a preparation for his future participation in the social structure. The rich made provision for the education of their children as a family function; the state stepped in to do it for the indigent. Public education was henceforth considered a public charity.

SPECIAL ASPECTS OF EDUCATIONAL PROGRESS

Review of accomplishments. If one compares the condition of culture and education at the close of the 16th century with that before the Protestant revolution he is enabled to evaluate more definitely the development which had taken place.

This era produced new ideals of personal worth and, consequently, new aims for the schools. The Germanic peoples had slowly risen to a consciousness of power, and now asserted intellectual and moral self-determination. They rejected the old Catholic ideal as too narrow, and set up others which more truly expressed their own inner strivings. Asceticism—that is, the renunciation of all desires as the means of happiness—was foreign to the Germanic culture. Moreover, it must be noted that this old ideal of the Christian life had not been wholly consistent. It upheld one standard of ethics for the religious, but quite another for secular life.

Protestantism replaced the authority of the church with the authority of the Scriptures and direct obedience of the individual to the will of God. Ritualism gave way to inner piety; good works, to goodwill; blind obedience, to faith. Holiness was no longer self-renunciation or world renunciation, but rather the benevolent spirit which lives the normal life of the human being in social relations, without yielding to sensuality or selfish interest.

The educational aim of the Protestant world attempted to combine the best ideals of the past with the new sense of personal worth. From the ancient Greek and Roman worlds, it borrowed the ideals of elegant expression and of rational inquiry, and the concept of public service. From chivalry, it took a deepened appreciation of refined manners. From Christianity, it acquired the new ideal of personal piety. The three elements, knowledge, virtue, and piety, were not valued equally by all educators, nor were they fully attained by any; but some integration was generally attempted wherever the new Protestant culture was established.

Outside of the universities there was no teaching profession before the 16th century. Teaching had been merely a temporary apprenticeship leading to the priesthood, and not a lifetime vocation. The Reformation brought about a marked change so far as the teaching office was concerned. The wandering bacchants were suppressed. A new spirit was stirring in the schoolroom, and teaching was accorded a new dignity. The great reformers ascribed an exalted significance to it. Gradually teachers were employed for a longer tenure of office. Cities searched for suitable rectors and assistant teachers, and their appointment was often an event. They married and settled down for lifetime service. Signal honors were often conferred upon them, even by kings and princes. Few centuries have produced a list of more celebrated teachers; the roll included Melanchthon, Sturm, Neander, Trotzendorf, Wolf, Corderius, Colet, and Lily.

The disintegration of medieval institutions, which had molded human life for a thousand years, challenged the intelligence of European scholars. As a consequence, for the first time since ancient days the study of education demanded attention. Just as the great reformers went to ancient literature for their theology, rhetoric, and philosophy, so they sought information on pedagogy from the same sources. Nor was their search in vain. Among the ancient works which had been rescued from the dust of centuries were such priceless treasures as Cicero's *De Oratore*, Quintilian's *De Institutione Oratoria*, and Plutarch's *Education of Children*, not to mention the works of Plato and Aristotle. As the scholars of the Renaissance had found in the ancient civilization culture, eloquence, beauty, philosophy, wisdom, and piety, so the new leaders felt that the education which had produced these grand products of the human spirit ought to be for all time the true pedagogy. In this educational literature they discovered, clearly discussed, the chief principles of school organization, method and curriculum. Quintilian and Plutarch flourished once more in Erasmus, Sturm, Mulcaster, Ascham, Melanchthon, Elyot, and others. To be sure, these Reformation teachers borrowed too much; but their models were good. Nevertheless a few epochal works were written, such as those of Erasmus, Luther, Vives, Rabelais, and Mulcaster.

Many of the aspects of modern education which are today of great importance had their origin in the Protestant reconstruction. The church-school inspection undertaken in Saxony by Luther and his associates in 1527 was the first school survey. Many similar surveys were made in the other cities and principalities throughout Germany. Reports of the conditions were recorded. The recommendations usually took the form of church or school ordinances, of which there are several hundred. The results of one of these surveys, in Strassburg, led to the establishment of Sturm's famous gymnasium. The same was true of Calvin's academy in Geneva.

Supervision of instruction likewise began at this time. The most peculiar effort of this kind was the supervision of family life and teaching which Calvin instituted in Geneva, and which was practiced by his followers generally. Such inspection was prescribed by the Reformed Church at the Synod of Dort in 1619, by the Scottish Church, and the Puritans of New England in the law of 1642.

Not only was home instruction inspected, but likewise the teaching in all the schools. This supervision was conducted by the ministers and elders. The original purpose of inspection was not concerned so much with the effectiveness of the instruction; of chief moment was the desire to check any heretical doctrines which might be imparted to the children. It was, therefore, not so much supervision as censorship.

In Germany the schools were regularly inspected by the church officials: first, by the local pastor; then, by the superintendent (an officer of the Lutheran Church who took the place of the bishop); and lastly, by the state consistory. The first concern of all inspectors was to watch the observance of school regulation; their duties included publishing the rules and reforming the schools. Inspection was by no means so rigorous among the Lutherans as among the Calvinists.

Attention was now directed, also, to the examination of teachers. This was provided for in many of the school ordinances of Germany, as well as in the Calvinistic regulations.

It has frequently been assumed that the education of girls began with the Lutheran Reformation; but this view is far from true. Excluding, because of its special character, the education given girls in monastic institutions, one finds that, under chivalry, the training of girls was of great importance. Although it was confined to a small and aristocratic circle and provided less for intellectual emancipation and more for external embellishment and training in domestic arts and management, nevertheless it was a good beginning. Long before the Reformation, moreover, girls in the cities of the Netherlands, even in the lower classes of society, were given some education. Schools of a public character were provided, and it was not uncommon for girls to read not only the vernacular but also Latin and French. The advanced position of female education in the Netherlands prompted the discussion of the subject by Erasmus, Vives, and others; the Netherlands were far in advance of

Germany, France, and England in this matter of general female education. But in all these countries, schools for girls were to be found in the larger centers of population; and, so far as the wealthy and privileged classes were concerned, private tutors were generally employed to give instruction at home.

Although the Reformation did not originate education for girls, it gave the movement a fresh and vigorous impetus. In Holland, coeducation sprang up in the elementary vernacular schools. Luther appealed for instruction of girls "an hour or two a day," and made no sex discrimination so far as religious instruction was concerned. Bugenhagen, in his Brunswick ordinance in 1528, provided for schools for girls in every quarter of the city. On the other hand, the more conservative Melanchthon made no mention of girls. Though many of the school ordinances did make provision for female education, except for the aristocracy, a higher education was not generally provided for young women.

The relation of church, state, and school. This period was marked by significant developments in civil government and its relation to schools. For the first time in centuries, theories of government were formulated and put into operation. Previously, national concerns had been subordinate to ecclesiastical interests; and, although the church and the empire did not always live in harmonious relationship, no one seriously called in question their vital connection or the preeminence of the papal hierarchy in religion and education. The church was centuries old when national governments arose, and emperors and kings acknowledged its overlordship. Under this medieval form of organization education was purely a function of the church.

In a general way, the most important fact of Protestant school reorganization was the emergence of the state as the agent for the establishment and maintenance of schools. All through the Middle Ages the church had taken the initiative and jealously guarded its prerogative of teaching. In northern cities, Latin and vernacular schools had gradually been founded by the municipal authorities, but with the consent of the church. In the Netherlands, however, the towns subordinated the church to their authority. Elsewhere the church held undisputed sway.

Theories of relation of church and state. With the separation from the Roman Church, the question of the relation of church and state became a matter of gravest controversy. Four main positions as to the relation which should obtain between these institutions were held.

(1) The Catholic position remained as it had always been, the church claiming, as Christ's Vicar, universal authority over all civil powers, and the exclusive right of teaching.

(2) In his break with Rome, Luther sought refuge under the civil power as the supreme authority, which he taught was divinely instituted to govern in all earthly affairs. He, therefore, subordinated the church and the school to the power of the princes and municipal authorities. Church buildings became the property of the state; pastors became civil servants. Moreover, the church became a mere agency of the state. At his baptism every infant became a member of the church and a subject of the state. The school likewise became a civil institution, established and controlled by the state and municipalities, though still closely identified with the cultural and instructional interests of the church.

(3) Calvin, the reformer of Geneva, reached quite a different conclusion. It may be stated that he was one of the first in modern times to formulate a clear-cut theory of the functions of civil government which he based upon the theocracy of the ancient Hebrews. Owing to the situation in Geneva, he had the opportunity, as no other man, to put his ideas into actual practice. According to his view, the two institutions, church and state, are separate but have one and the same ultimate purpose, to realize the will of God on earth, yet they function in different fields. The church alone can interpret what God's will is, and, therefore, it has the right to determine the moral standard and the duty of the state. The office of the state is to carry out the divine will in all matters pertaining to the moral and spiritual welfare of the people. Church and state function as two separate organs, but together they form a united organism.

According to this Calvinistic theory, church and state cooperate to discipline, train, and instruct the people. Church and state, therefore, constitute one comprehensive educational agency, combining family, church, state, and school into one functional organization. In the operation of this organic plan, the school is supported by the state, but its aim, methods, curriculum, regimen, and teachers are controlled by the church. While this theory recognized the educative function of the family, it gave the church-state the right to supervise its activities. This plan proved highly effective because of the power exercised by the clergy. But like the other plans it was lacking in genuine democracy, though it professed to be the rule of the people.

(4) There arose at this time a fourth point of view, which was destined to become the policy of the New World. This was the doctrine of the Anabaptists, who held that church and state must be entirely separate. They contended that religion is no business of the state, but is purely a private and individual concern. At a stroke, this principle does away with all religious intolerance. However, since every European state of that day clung tenaciously to a particular established faith, there was no possibility of putting this doctrine into practice. Having no connection with the schools established under joint state-church action, these religionists did not flourish in any country except Holland, where education was controlled by the state. Scattered in small societies or groups, they united in an intense opposition to any and every form of union of church and state. They declined to bear arms, to pay taxes for war, to hold civil office, to swear by oath, and to go to law. They also refused to persecute anyone for his religious beliefs. These peoples advanced the cause of religious freedom, and later played an important part in bringing about the complete separation of church and state in America.

THE NEW LANGUAGE PROBLEM

How the language problem arose. The educational situation of the 16th century became more involved because of the increased study of languages. During the Middle Ages men of learning were obliged to be bilingual. They had to speak the vernacular for ordinary affairs and Latin for religion and scholarly life. With the coming of the Renaissance classical Latin, Greek, and, to some extent, Hebrew were added. This greatly increased the curriculum. The Reformation required the vernacular in religious life. Education for most boys became a grind on languages; and because the only introduction was grammar the situation became intolerable. The sharpest educational problem was how to teach Latin to young boys whose native tongue had no kinship with that language. It was naturally easier for young French, Spanish, or Italian boys to grasp Latin than it was for the Teutonic peoples.

Educators, moreover, had reached two conclusions: first, that learning by sheer memorization was not an intelligent method; nor was pounding Latin grammar into unwilling minds. The best pedagogical brains of the day directed their attention to this problem.

Rise of vernacular tongues. During the Middle Ages Latin was everywhere the language of all higher interests, of religion, literature, philosophy, diplomacy and, to a large extent, even of commerce. The only way to worship or pray was in Latin. The inumerable dialects of the barbarian tribes did not possess the breadth of vocabulary necessary to express other than the most common ideas of practical life. However, the later period saw a profound change. From the creative genius of these various peoples there sprang spontaneously a wealth of literary materials—legends, popular romances, fairy stories, heroic tales, and poetry. For a time these were not written, nor were they composed to be read; rather, they were memorized and either recited or sung by wandering minstrels, troubadours, and minnesingers. Princely courts, baronial manors, and the castles of the knights offered the stage and setting for the expression of these gentler arts.

The growth of commerce and of the reading and writing schools further added to the increasing use of the native tongues. Of course, no single condition was so potent in the growing popularity and importance of these languages as the invention of printing. The outburst of the great religious conflict, as well as the translation of the Scriptures into the vernacular dialects, added tremendously to the dignity of these tongues. But the most powerful impetus of all came from the use of the vernacular in popular worship, in preaching, in church music, and in drama. The Council of Trent in 1562 required that preaching be in the vernacular. Added to this was the practice of all Protestant communions of teaching the catechism and the Scriptures in translation.

By the end of the 16th century the two important realms of human interest, religion and commerce, had turned completely to the use of the vernacular. Latin still dominated the schools, philosophy, and diplomacy, but these, too, began to capitulate.

Use of Italian. In spite of the grip of Latin upon chuch and school in Catholic lands, the vernacular was rapidly growing more powerful. The Italian was the first modern language to develop literary form. Dante did not think it beneath the dignity of his theme to write *The Divine Comedy* in Italian. Petrarch, in lyric poetry, and Boccaccio, in prose, followed his example.

In the 16th and early 17th centuries, hundreds of "literary academies" were established in Italy for the purification of the language. The most celebrated of these was the *Accademia della Crusca,* formed in 1587.

Use of Spanish. The conflict with the Moors in Spain tended to advance the Castilian dialect into an instrument of national expression. Court rulings were rendered at Valencia in the native tongue. As early as 1492 Antonio de Lebrija wrote a Spanish grammar for the ladies of the court of Queen Isabella. Soon the Castilians created a literature which added to their pride in their country and language.

Use of Dutch. Long before the Reformation not only the vernacular but French also was commonly taught in Dutch schools. The early translation of the Scriptures into Low Dutch, and the "houses of rhetoric" were highly effective in strengthening the vernacular as a means of learning.

Use of French. That rollicking humorist, Rabelais, master of more tongues than any other man of his day, not only wrote in French but urged the use of the vernacular for learning. The leaders of Protestant education, especially Corderius and Calvin, greatly assisted the progress of the vernacular. Corderius wrote a text to teach children morals, in "pure French." Calvin advanced the cause by translating his *Institutes of Christianity* from Latin into French (1541) and by having this language taught in his gymnasium. So rapidly had the French language evolved that, as early as 1550, Mestre could boast: [11]

> Our language is today so enriched by the study and practice of Greek and Latin that there is no science so difficult or subtile, not even high theology, that it cannot handle fully and elegantly.

A quarter of a century later, Louis Le Roy, professor at the *Collège royal,* which had been founded expressly for the cultivation of the classical languages, explained the speeches of Demosthenes in French. As early as 1629, the *Académie française* was established by Cardinal Richelieu as an agency to guard the purity of the French language.

Descartes, father of modern philosophy, wrote his chief work, *Discours de la Méthode* (1637), in French so that a larger number would be able to understand it. French soon replaced Latin as the language of international affairs.

The English language. During the latter half of the 16th century, the vernacular found strong backing in England. Elyot not only wrote *The Boke Named the Governour* (1531), but advocated the use of English along with Latin for daily living, religion, and for the exposition of learned subjects. He also published an English Dictionary in 1538.

---

[11] Kandel, I. L., *History of Secondary Education,* p. 153. Boston: Houghton Mifflin, 1930.

Mulcaster wrote his treatises purposely in English, and urged that the mother tongue be used in the schools before teaching Latin. In the next decades, John Brinsley advocated the use of English in connection with the teaching of Latin. He pointed out: (1) that English is the language of all sorts and conditions of men; (2) that few go on to a learned education; and (3) that the English language is the glory of the English people. Even in far-off Virginia, the colonial court was interested in his *Consolation for our Grammar Schools,* which was written "for the more speedie attaining of our English tongue" that all may speak one and the same language in such rude countries as Ireland, Wales, Virginia, and the Summer Islands.

But far more important than these advocates of English were the King James version of the Bible (1611) and the works of Shakespeare, Milton, and others. These celebrated authors won imperishable glory for the English language before the French and the Germans had produced their great literary products. Within half a century of Milton's death, English literature was introduced into the dissenting academies, and a little later, into the colleges.

The defeat of Spain by the British launched the British Empire and gave the English language its start toward universality. Not until after the middle of the 18th century, however, was English used in university lectures at Glasgow by Adam Smith; and for instruction in the nonconformist academies by Philip Doddridge.

The development of German. The greatest single events which made for the progress of the German language were the invention of printing and Luther's translation of the Bible into High German. The great simplicity and beauty of this translation made High German the standard language for all Germany. The movement for the use of the vernacular was further stimulated by the organization of special societies for this purpose. In 1617 there was formed at Weimar the *Fruitbearing Society* (*Fruchtbringende Gesellschaft*), to promote the use of German and to purify it of foreign words.

In spite of these efforts students went to the universities unable to write their native language with any degree of accuracy. The reason for this deficiency is indicated by Francke, at the end of the 17th century: [12]

---

[12] Barnard, Henry, *German Teachers and Educators,* p. 415. Hartford: Brown and Gross, 1878.

> I find that there are few theological students who can write a German letter correctly spelled. They violate orthography almost in every line. I even know of many examples where, after they have entered upon the university, and have had occasion to have something printed, it has been necessary to have their manuscript first corrected almost in every line. ... The reason for this defect is usually in the schools, where only the Latin translation of their exercises is corrected, but not the German; so that they learn nothing of spelling.

It was a scandalous innovation of learned propriety when Thomasius announced that he would lecture in German. This bold step occurred at the University of Leipzig in 1687. To make his act still more revolutionary, he chose to expound a modern philosophic book. About the same time, his colleague, Christian Wolff, published his own philosophic work in German. Both of these men, because of their iconoclastic tendencies, soon found it necessary to transfer to the more liberal atmosphere of the University of Halle.

By the beginning of the 18th century the vernacular tongues had become the medium of communication everywhere except in the secondary and higher schools. But even here they had begun to find greater favor; it was not long before pupils in the classical gymnasiums were beginning Latin at nine years of age rather than at six.

EVALUATION OF 16TH CENTURY EDUCATION

Its weaknesses and advances. Despite its reforms and significant accomplishments, education during this eventful era had many weaknesses which became more and more apparent as time wore on. Many of these were due to the humanistic ideal and the lack of understanding of the educational process; others were due to outer circumstances over which education had little direct control.

(1) A high degree of progress was rendered impossible by the interminable and irascible religious conflicts which occurred. Quarrels over theological questions, many of them trivial and nearly all impossible of final settlement, divided the Protestants and sapped their energies.

(2) From the glowing generalizations of educational historians, one is led frequently to assume that elementary schools became well-nigh universal during this age. Such a conclusion is, however, quite erroneous. In Germany, even down to the close of the century, the schools were for the most part confined to the cities and larger towns. Most of the villages and country places were quite destitute. There were numer-

ous reports of the wretched conditions which generally prevailed in the smaller parishes, where the duty of instruction was imposed upon the sexton of the church. In 1556 there were only seven schools in all the villages of lower Saxony. In Nassau it was found: [13] "all the sextons, with but one exception, were unable to read and this one had no inclination to hold school; in only three places did the pastors show a willingness to assume the burden of giving instruction to the children." In the Palatinate, a report of a survey in 1556 stated: [14] "The people are undisciplined and wild; they live from day to day like unreasoning cattle." Similar conditions existed at that time in Lippe: [15]

Such conditions of abysmal ignorance were found not only in Germany but in other countries as well. Sporadic efforts were made to establish schools in the villages and country places, but the prime requisites for educational work were absent; the people had little incentive to seek instruction for their children, for the condition of the peasantry was no better than serfdom. Moreover, buildings and funds for the support of schools were lacking. Even if these materials had been secured, there was still the difficulty of finding teachers, since, as yet, no one was being prepared for the teaching office.

(3) But all was not going well even in the town Latin schools. Grave weaknesses became more and more apparent. The high promises of humanistic culture were not being realized. First, too much was expected from the study of classical literature. Its effects upon character forming were greatly exaggerated.

(4) An extreme form of *Ciceronianism* seized the schools. The teachers strained every nerve and used every artifice to teach young Germans, Frenchmen, and Englishmen to speak Latin with the fluency and elegance of Cicero. They had to employ his vocabulary, his phrases, and his manner of delivery. The most absurd results appeared in this effort to confine speech to the Ciceronian diction. God, the Father, had to be called Jupiter Optimus Maximus; Jesus, the Son, Apollo; the Virgin Mary, Diana. When the pupil mentioned the *church,* he had to say the *sacred assembly,* or the *republic.* Criticism was fruitless, and the schools

---

[13] Robbins, Charles L., *Teachers in Germany in the Sixteenth Century,* p. 25. New York: Teachers College, Columbia University, 1912.

[14] Janssen, Johannes, *History of the German People at the Close of the Middle Ages,* Vol. XIII, pp. 40-41. Tr. by A. M. Christie. London: Kegan Paul, Trench, Trübner & Co., 1909.

[15] *Ibid.,* p. 39.

directed every effort to produce young Ciceroes even though there was no genuine need for Latin eloquence. The language was no longer employed in the courts of law, nor in diplomacy, preaching, popular assemblies, or in the conduct of business. The only occasions on which Latin was used were embassies to Rome. To be sure, Latin continued to be employed in the universities as the language of learning, but a vocabulary and mode of address very different from those of Ciceronian eloquence were needed for such scholastic purposes. At no time has an ideal, sought by the schools with such infinite toil, been more purely artificial and extraneous to the vital interests of the age. The absolute futility of stylistic Humanism became more and more apparent as time passed.

(5) The supreme difficulty with the education of the 16th century lay in its narrowness and opposition to the free development of thought and life. Both Humanism and the Reformation began with the fairest promises of liberty and enlightenment. The one soon capitulated to the blighting influences of Ciceronianism; the other, to a new scholasticism which arose out of the confessionalism imposed by Luther and Calvin. In their original principles, these leaders had asserted the right of the individual to follow his own religious views and to interpret the Scriptures for himself; but in the interest of regularity, the dread of heresy, and the alliance of church and state, both men, in the end, largely denied these very principles on which they had justified their break with Rome. They defended the persecution of all who differed from them in belief or in practice. They substituted their catechisms and a rigid confessionalism for the unrestricted use of the Scriptures and the free development of religious life. They gave no aid to the infant efforts of scientific thought, particularly when the conclusions of the scientists appeared to conflict with the teachings of the Scriptures. They narrowed the school curriculum to those subjects which favored their point of view.

Was the Reformation, then, from the standpoint of enlightenment and freedom, a failure? This is only partially true. Once having envisioned liberty of conscience, free speech, academic freedom, and political liberty, it was impossible for rockbound churchmen forever to stop the progress of intelligence.

Chapter 6

BACONIAN REALISM, CARTESIANISM, AND CALVINISM

LIBERATION from Roman and Spanish domination. The 17th century opened with the greatest promise for advancement in northern Europe. Spanish supremacy was thoroughly defeated; first, by the English in the destruction of the Invincible Armada in 1588; second, by the Dutch both on land and sea in their prolonged conflict. Its domination of the seas and consequently over colonization in the Orient and America was terminated. Henceforth Spanish sovereigns devoted their attention to the promotion of their cultural interests at home and in their colonies under the guidance of the Roman Catholic Church.

The effort of Catholicism to crush the Protestant schism had, however, just made a beginning. Henceforth the struggle became more localized in three theaters of war. In Germany it was the clash of Catholics and Lutherans in the devastating Thirty Years' War (1618-1648); in England it was the prolonged conflict between the Puritans and the Stuarts; in France it was the onslaught of the Catholic monarchy upon the Huguenots.

It will be recalled that the revolt against the Latins was not merely political and religious, it extended to the field of thought as well. For some unknown reason during the first half of the 17th century northern Europe was provided with a quality of brains and genius unequaled in creative power by the Latin world. Bacon, Shakespeare, Milton, William Gilbert, Oliver Cromwell, Pascal, Descartes, Gustavus Adolphus, Grotius, Oxenstierna, and Comenius are but a few who adorned the roster of celebrities engaged in action in their various fields. Whether men of genius cause great eras to arise or great problems evoke men of genius we must leave to others to resolve. In any case, history must record that situations of the greatest moment were matched by men of commensurate capacity.

CURRENT THOUGHT PATTERNS AND MOVEMENTS

Preliminary survey. By the beginning of the 17th century the different educational patterns of western Europe became more definitely organized and were projected into the future. These may be differentiated as follows:

1. The humanistic gentleman-scholar tradition had been accepted as the ideal by the English gentry, and to a lesser extent by the French and the German aristocracies.

2. The Lutheran system of culture dominated most of Germany and the Scandinavian countries and had scattered groups of adherents in other lands.

3. The new realistic movement started by some of the humanists was now taken over by the Baconian realists.

4. The Calvinistic ideology and practice, which were accepted fully in Geneva and Scotland, were embraced by the dominant party in Holland, the Hugenots in France, the Puritans in England, and groups of zealous followers in other lands, especially in the Palatinate.

5. The educational pattern and practices of the Society of Jesus and several other orders which grew out of the Counter Reformation formed the new educational force of the Roman Catholic Church.

6. The educational activities of minority groups such as the Moravian Brethren, the Anabaptists and the Mennonites were of minor interest in Europe, but were to become important in America.

7. The new rationalism of Descartes dominated philosophy, and its educational implications were put into practice by the Port Royalists and others.

GROWTH OF SCIENTIFIC KNOWLEDGE

The expansion of knowledge. The 16th century got the bulk of its information from books written by ancient scholars two thousand years before. The 17th century now called much of this knowledge of the ancients into question and improved upon it. Not only did the various sciences advance, but the whole question of the method of science emerged for discussion. The most important lines of advancement will be noted first.

Mathematics. Descartes invented analytic geometry and gave the final exposition of it in 1637. This and the calculus of Leibnitz in 1675, "completely revolutionalized . . . the subject, and have proved the most powerful instruments of modern progress," says W. W. R. Ball, in his *Short Account of the History of Mathematics.* The chief difference between the ancient geometry and that of Descartes lies in that the one required a procedure for every particular problem while the other applied a general rule for all problems of the same kind. Another consequential step in mathematics at this time was the introduction of the decimal system.

Astronomy. This important science was greatly advanced during the 17th century, first by Galileo, and later by Newton. Galileo early accepted the Copernican theory and laid the basis for its proof. He improved the telescope which had just been invented and was the first to employ it to study the stars; this initiated a new era in astronomical science. In 1615, he attempted to convert the papal court to the new astronomy by upholding that the sun is immovable in the center of the universe, and that the earth revolves daily on its axis. But he was condemned for heresy. In 1687, Newton put the capstone on modern astronomy by his celebrated work, *The Celestial Mechanics.*

The physical sciences. Progress was far less rapid in the physical sciences. Stevin was the first since Archimedes to advance the study of mechanics. Moreover, not only mechanics, but dynamics, statics, hydrostatics, and other forms of physical science were developed. About 1600 Galileo demonstrated from the leaning tower of Pisa that Aristotle's statement that bodies fall with velocities proportional to their weights was false. William Gilbert published (1600) his epochal work on magnetism, which made possible the later study of electrical phenomena. An appreciative estimate [1] states: "His work is one of the finest examples of inductive philosophy that has ever been presented to the world." The prodigious advance in scientific knowledge during the 17th century must be credited to the change from mere philosophizing about nature to careful experimentation. Harvey, Torricelli, Boyle, and numerous others engaged in genuine inductive research.

As further aids in the progress of scientific knowledge came the invention of the various instruments for exact measurement. The ther-

---

[1] Sedgwick, W. T., and Tyler, H. W., *A Short History of Science,* p. 229. New York: The Macmillan Company, 1917.

mometer dates from 1597. During the first half of the 17th century came the telescope, compound microscope, micrometer, thermoscope, barometer, air pump, the pendulum clock, and numerous other inventions. Without these the sciences would never have been able to make progress. What signs and symbols did for the advancement of mathematics, the so-called "philosophic apparatus" did for the various physical sciences.

Geography. In the advancement of civilization during the 17th century, the importance of geographical knowledge must not be overlooked. Its development correlates with that of astronomy and history. A globe made by a German mariner in 1492 shows the world round, but he possessed as yet no knowledge of the existence of the American Continents or the Pacific Ocean. A century later, Mercator (Gerhard Kremer) devoted his attention to mathematical geography. He made maps, globes, and astronomical instruments. In 1595, his son published the first atlas, which greatly increased popular interest in geography and led to the inclusion of modern geography in the course of study in the schools.

Medicine and the biological sciences. For well over a thousand years no perceptible progress had been made in medical science. In fact, down to the 16th century, Hippocrates and Galen continued to be the only authorities. Vesalius, in the early half of the 16th century, was the first to publish drawings of his dissections of the human body. Great interest was taken in this subject in Italy, where substantial progress resulted. Anatomy, medicine, geometry, art, and mathematics were closely related. In 1616 Harvey, the English physician, discovered the circulation of the blood. About the same time botany became a recognized part of medical science. Much progress was soon made in the classification of plants and in a knowledge of their properties.

A most notable forward step was taken in the 17th century, when medicine, replacing magic, mysticism, and astrology, began to search for purely material causes of diseases. But no really significant progress was effected until the more accurate knowledge of anatomy and physiology, brought about by the use of the microscope, opened the way.

Interrelation of mathematics, the physical sciences, and the arts. Mathematics and the sciences did not develop apart from one another. Each helped the other and, in turn, was stimulated in its own growth. Pure mathematics, applied mathematics, medicine, astrology, astronomy, geography, architecture, and even art advanced together.

During the later Middle Ages men confined their mathematical interests to the simple requirements of trade, keeping accounts, making the calendar, the constructions of the architect and military engineer, and the calculations of astrologers and navigators. It was, of course, purely accidental that Copernicus' great work on astronomy and Vesalius' work on anatomy appeared in the same year, and Cardan's algebra only two years later. But accidental though this synchronization may have been, the deeper fact was that these sciences were interdependent in their progress. The mathematics assisted in expanding knowledge of the physical world, and its language soon became, by the work of Descartes, the precise method of scientific thought.

What really contributed most vitally to the growth of higher mathematics was its relation to astrology and medicine. Many great mathematicians—such as Cardan, Recorde, Regiomontanus, and even Copernicus—were also students of medicine. It was generally believed at the time that "a physician without astrology was no better than an eye which did not see." He had to know how to cast the horoscope, and be familiar with the elements of astrology, in order, by observing the conjunction of the planets, to determine the critical days in the course of diseases.

The application of mathematics to astronomy, which revealed clearly the true nature of the physical universe, found expression in Newton's *Principia* (1687). It must not escape notice that, in the vast amount of new information poured upon the human mind during this era, the mathematical sciences took the foremost place. As a matter of fact, mathematics displaced, not only philosophy, but even theology, the erstwhile queen of the sciences. Scientific investigators were quick to discern that mathematics furnished a magic instrument for the uncovering of natural phenomena. The integration of mathematical thinking with sense observation, in the fields of astronomy and physics, was the most significant triumph of the human mind. Newton's view of celestial mechanics gave to mankind its most profound revelation of the nature of the physical universe until our day. It set the standard by which the success of all scientific achievements was henceforth to be measured; moreover, it imparted to all the sciences a new impulse to realize an ideal of accuracy and excellence which was to dominate the following century.

In this new scientific movement there was one aspect of peculiar significance. The new science had an authority and positiveness that neither the ancient writings nor scholastic philosophy had ever possessed. Even Aristotle, formerly the veritable deity of the natural world, was time and again shown to be in error, and was more and more discredited. A higher degree of certainty came into human experience—a feeling of certainty based not upon the personal experience of an individual, but upon the rational deductions of inevitable and universal laws. Leonardo da Vinci (1452-1519), universal genius, painter, sculptor, engineer, architect, physicist, biologist, and philosopher, was one of the first modern minds to understand the new method of science. He declared [2]

> ... that mathematics, arithmetic, and geometry give absolute certitude within their own realm; they are concerned with ideal mental concepts of universal validity. True science, he held, began with observation; if mathematical reasoning could then be applied, greater certitude might be reached, but, those sciences are vain and full of errors which are not born from experiment, the mother of all certainty, and which do not end with one clear experiment. Science gives certainty, and science gives power.

Establishment of scientific societies. The progress of science was greatly facilitated by the formation of the many learned academies and societies during this epoch. For a long time men interested in the promotion of knowledge were handicapped because they did not learn, until many years had passed, what others were doing in the same or related fields. Publication assisted much to overcome this difficulty, but was wholly inadequate to perform the task. The scientific academies founded to meet the need came into existence as follows:

1560, *Academia Secretarum Naturae,* founded in Naples, by Della Porta.
1603, *Academia dei Lincei* (of the Lynx), founded at Rome.
1660, The Royal Society of London, chartered 1662.
1660, *Académie des Sciences.* Descartes and Pascal were members of this society and Newton was a foreign correspondent.
1700, The Berlin Academy.

It is worthy of special note that the Royal Society of London became the most important agency for the promotion of scientific advancement in the English-speaking world. As a consequence of its activities, practically all the great leaders of scientific progress in England did their

---

[2] Dampier-Whetham, W. C. D., *A History of Science and its Relations with Philosophy,* p. 115. Cambridge: Cambridge University Press, 1929.

work outside the universities; in fact, until recently, the English universities did not engage in much research. The opposite was true of Germany. Practically all the immense erudition of German scientists and scholars has come from their universities; for the professors were primarily agents of research and only in a secondary way faculties for the transmission of knowledge by instruction.

SOCIAL UTOPIAS BASED ON SCIENCE AND EDUCATION

Science forecasts social progress. Civilization in the Middle Ages was relatively static. The best minds of the time complacently assumed that all knowledge had been already discovered, and that human nature and society were unalterable. In the epoch of invention and discovery which followed, enlightenment fired the imagination to attempt great achievements. In the 16th century, and even more so in the first half of the 17th century, utopian schemes were numerous, all of them expressing profound faith in the possibility of reconstructing human society,[3] particularly through the power of education.

> A new epoch of culture seemed about to open and an exotic impulse seized the imagination. Unbelievable things were about to happen; nothing was to be impossible any more. The telescope unlocked the mysteries of the heavens, and the forces of the earth began to obey the investigator. Science would be the leader of the human spirit in its triumphant course through nature. Through her discoveries human life would be transformed.

A century earlier, the Englishman, Sir Thomas More, had written his *Utopia,* in which he gave expression to faith in the improvement of man's lot through social and political measures. Most of the utopias written in the 17th century, however, looked on education as the essential means of bettering the individual and society.

Campanella (1568-1639). Early in the century, Campanella, an Italian scholar and scientist, wrote *The City of the Sun* (*Civitas Solis*), in which he described an ideal commonwealth. He tracked Plato in many ways, especially in devoting great attention to education. "They have but one book," he said of the citizens of this ideal community, "and in it all the sciences are written." This book is read to all the

---

[3] Windelband, W., *Lehrbuch der Geschichte der Philosophie*, p. 325. Tübingen: J. C. B. Mohr (Paul Siebeck), 1928.

people, and furnishes them a knowledge which is encyclopedic in range though fixed in content. An even more ingenious means of instruction is Campanella's use of pictures. Taking his cue from ancient practices, he has the walls of the city, inside and outside, and the great buildings, also, painted with the finest pictures, maps, charts, and diagrams, to represent all the arts, sciences, mathematical figures, minerals, metals, forms of biological specimens, mechanical crafts, and even the laws and customs of mankind. Drawing and painting are highly cultivated; but, for some strange reason, music is confined to women. The shops of artisans are visited in order to discover the individual interests of the children. The home is completely abandoned in favor of Plato's system of breeding and state training.

Johann Valentin Andreä (1586-1654). The next great educational utopia is the *Christian City* (*Christianopolis*), written in 1619 by Andreä, a German savant and pastor. As the name of the work implies, Andreä conceived the ideal city as ruled by the principles of Christ. None of the other utopian schemes discussed education so extensively, and none was so completely motivated by the Christian spirit.

This gifted Christian author and educator was a native of Würtemberg, where he spent practically all his life in ecclesiastical office. As an ardent student at the University of Tübingen, he mastered many languages; then he traveled widely in France, Switzerland, and Italy. He was deeply interested in mathematics and the new scientific developments of the day. A visit to Geneva profoundly affected him; although decidedly opposed to Calvinistic theology, he had unbounded admiration for the ecclesiastical discipline carried out in the city. As a Lutheran Church superintendent for many years in Würtemberg, he did much to reestablish the schools under his charge, for they had suffered a setback because of the Thirty Years' War. His chief service to the cause of education lay in his influence on Comenius, who regarded him most highly and borrowed many of his ideas.

Andreä's Utopia has no aristocracy of wealth or of birth. Honor and position only are the reward of virtue and service. No one possesses property, for the government is a Christian communism. As all citizens are on an equality, everyone must receive an education; this requirement holds for both sexes, and the youth are looked upon as "the most valuable asset of the republic." The greatest emphasis is placed upon sense impressions, a practice which even Comenius and Pestalozzi did not stress more completely. Just as in Campanella's *City of the Sun*, paintings, pictures, and diagrams adorn the walls; but it must be added that *things* also are used for direct instruction.

Education is compulsory and is carried on in public schools, which are "a common charge for all the citizens." The aim of education may be inferred from the following: [4]

> Their first and highest exertion is to worship God with a pure and faithful soul; the second, to strive toward the best and most chaste morals; the third, to cultivate the mental powers.

The curriculum proposed by Andreä was encyclopedic, embracing all learning; chief emphasis, however, was given to mathematics and history.

Bacon's New Atlantis. The best known of all the utopias of this period was *The New Atlantis,* written by Francis Bacon but left unfinished and only published in 1629. He pictured an island on which exists an ideal commonwealth, in which men live happily on a high level of civilization. The inhabitants set themselves to investigate systematically the secrets of nature, and for this purpose organized a scientific society, called "Solomon's House." In this suggestion Bacon foreshadowed the establishing of laboratories for the promotion of scientific research and invention.

The writing of utopias had been a favorite means of advancing social and educational progress since the days of Isaiah and Plato. Bacon's *New Atlantis* influenced the founding of the Royal Society (1660), the Scientific Academies, and the new trends of education in the 17th century.

Other Utopias. In 1641, Samuel Hartlib published *Description of the Famous Kingdom of Mascaria, wherein the Inhabitants live in great Prosperity, Health and Happiness; The King obeyed, the Nobles honored and all good men respected; Vice punished and Virtue rewarded.* The secret of this impeccable condition was the right education of children. About eight years later Samuel Gott wrote *Nova Solyma,* the story of an ideal government. He, also, based his conception upon the proper education of the young. One of the least brilliant of the utopias of the time was *The Commonwealth of Oceana,* by James Harrington, published in 1656. This work treated of government and social and economic affairs, and, like other utopian dreams, it was interested in education. Although a born aristocrat, Harrington advocated free schools and compulsory training for all boys.

---

[4] Held, Felix Emil, *Johann Valentin Andreä's Christianopolis,* p. 209. Urbana: University of Illinois Press, 1914.

TWO THEORIES OF SCIENTIFIC METHOD

The question of scientific method. The Renaissance had begun to extricate the mind of man from the shackles of scholastic modes of thought, when a formalized Humanism and a reactionary ecclesiasticism again placed youthful science in bondage to ancient authorities. The situation of the 17th century was somewhat different, however, and definitely temporary. First, the theologians of the Protestant churches came to entertain an intense hatred for Aristotle. Luther called him an "accursed heathen," and bitterly arraigned most of his writings. Later theology took much the same attitude when they discovered the many points in which Aristotle contradicted the Scriptures. For example, Aristotle did not definitely teach the immortality of the individual soul, the resurrection of the dead, the triune nature of God, the creation of the world by fiat, and many other of the most sacred and fundamental tenets of the Christian faith. Peter Ramus, the French scholar and educator, astounded the scholastic Brahmans of Europe by maintaining, as his graduating thesis, that everything Aristotle had taught was false. Later, he wrote a new logic, which was based upon the concrete data of experience.

From a different angle, the phenomenal growth of scientific knowledge awakened suspicions of Aristotle's infallibility in regard to nature. Furthermore, thinkers began to question the authority of all the ancient writers. The sphericity of the earth, heliocentricity, the density of water, the pressure of the atmosphere, and many other newly discovered facts squarely contradicted what the ancients had stated as facts.

In the field of science, the downfall of authoritarianism raised the question as to what method would give assurance of certainty and truth. The two outstanding leaders in the search for a new scientific methodology were Francis Bacon, the celebrated Lord Chancellor of England, and René Descartes, the French thinker and the father of modern philosophy. The views of these two men in regard to the best method for the advancement of science were radically divergent; they originated two lines of philosophical thought which, in the succeeding centuries, produced startling results.

Francis Bacon (1561-1626). Although not primarily a scientist and certainly not an investigator, Francis Bacon saw, more clearly than any other man of his day, the far-reaching implications of the inductive method. He made himself the chief publicity agent and literary advocate of the scientific method and the direct study of nature. So convincingly did he set forth the new method and predict its promise for the future, that he has ever since been given more credit and honor than even those men who, at the time, were patiently wresting from nature its innermost secrets.

In regard to education and the best method of instruction, Bacon had nothing better to suggest than the practices of the Jesuits, but his efforts in behalf of the advancement of learning, the inductive method, and the practical application of science, were so consequential that he must be accorded a substantial place in the history of education.

Philosophy, Bacon contended, had applied itself to the discovery of final causes, whereas it should have sought only formal or efficient causes; it had neglected the study of nature for the study of morals and religion. Bacon began the movement for a critical scrutiny of the human mind, to measure its capacity for attaining truth and accuracy. Introspection was not at this time a common instrument of psychological use, and Bacon had little skill in employing it. He did, however, perceive some of the outstanding obstacles looming in the way of the advancement of knowledge. He presented these as "idols" (*idola*), which hinder the mind in its efforts to attain truth. These he classified as: "idols of the tribe," "idols of the den," "idols of the theater," and "idols of the market place." The "idols of the tribe" are the limitations of human capacities simply because human beings are finite. The senses of sight and hearing are restricted in range and environment, and the faculties of the mind cannot comprehend the infinite. The "idols of the den" are the limitations peculiar to the individual. The "idols of the market place," or the place of exchange, are caused by the difficulties encountered in reaching precision and exact knowledge, and are due primarily to the limitations of language. The "idols of the theater," or show place, are the particular limitations arising from dogmas of philosophy or of religion which the individual accepts and which blind him from seeing truth in other theories.

Bacon was not interested in the discovery of nature from pure curiosity or for the sake of knowledge as an end in itself, but rather to utilize the forces of nature for the welfare of mankind. He does not belong with the scientists who are interested primarily in understanding the nature of the world and man and who seek to accumulate knowledge for its own sake. Bacon belongs with the practical scientists, who utilize the secrets of nature to make inventions for the benefit of man. The function of knowledge for them is to relieve suffering and contrive means to decrease drudgery. In his Aphorisms, he declared: [5]

I

Man, being the servant and interpreter of Nature, can do and understand so much and so much only as he has observed in fact or in thought of the course of Nature: beyond this he neither knows anything nor can do anything.

II

Neither the naked hand nor the understanding left to itself can effect much. It is by instruments and helps that the work is done, which are as much wanted for the understanding as for the hand. And as the instruments of the hand either give motion or guide it, so the instruments of the mind supply either suggestions for the understanding or cautions.

III

Human knowledge and human power meet in one; for where the cause is not known the effect cannot be produced. Nature to be commanded must be obeyed.

Yet, strangely enough, Bacon was ignorant of all that was being accomplished, by the mathematicians of his day, to discover the secrets of nature. He even raised special objection to studying astronomy by mathematical methods. In such conclusions he showed himself not altogether competent to judge the true method of science, even in its practical aspects, which could have done so much to advance human welfare.

One of the most penetrating intellects of all times, whose vaulting ambition as a courtier led to perfidy and an ignominious downfall, Bacon was born to the purple in York House, London, a representative of the English spirit at its best and worst. Information as to his early education is lacking. At twelve he entered Trinity College, Cambridge, where he spent three years. It is evident that the humanistic side of the curriculum did not interest him, and we know that he conceived an abiding contempt for the Aristotelianism that dominated the curriculum.

Philosophy was for Bacon a sideline in which he had deep interest and fair capacity, but his involvements and duties as courtier and high public servant prevented him from giving it the time necessary for highest achievement. It is a profound error to class him among the great

[5] McClure, M. T., *Bacon Selections,* pp. 279-280. New York: Scribner's Sons, 1928.

constructive philosophers or as the lone discoverer of modern science. He was too busy with his other concerns to inform himself properly as to the progress of science in his own day and his knowledge of education was quite lacking.

Bacon made no contribution to science and no important discovery can be traced to the application of his rules. His method was logically defective. He opposed the Copernican theory and had no understanding of the work of William Gilbert, and he had no interest in mathematics, which is the greatest instrument of pure science. Why, it may be asked, was he accepted as the leader of what has been called the "Bacon philosophy"?

Through the latter half of his stormy career, though harassed by adversities of the gravest kind, and elevated to the highest positions, he wrote his *Essays* and from time to time worked on a grandiose scheme which he termed *Instauratio Magna,* the "Great Renewal." He proposed to revolutionize learning, turn it about, and set it on a new path. Five parts were originally planned; only two were realized. The first part was the publication in 1605 of the celebrated work *Advancement of Learning*. The second part was the *Novum Organum* (1620) (the new instrument) which was to replace Aristotle's *Organon,* that is, his traditional Deductive Logic. The other parts were never finished but during his last days he wrote *New Atlantis,* which was never completed but was published three years after his death.

Bacon did many things that were of the utmost importance in quickening the thoughts of men. Moreover, the time was far riper than he was aware for a change in direction. First, he pointed out the futility of the new disputation of theology which engulfed the Christian world because of theological disputes between Protestant sects, and between Protestants and Catholics. Scholasticism was arid enough, but the new theology was even more given to controversy. Second, Bacon assailed The New Learning of Humanism. The wing headed by Sturm and Ascham emphasized the stylistic aspects; the other, led by Vives and Rabelais, had stressed the use of ancient literature to gain a knowledge of nature. Bacon condemned both as fruitless. He was not unique in discerning that Scholasticism and the Humanism which replaced it were equally futile so far as the advancement of learning was concerned. The impotency of these movements was widely felt, but no one saw clearly the new path to progress.

On the positive side Bacon's chief contributions were the demand for the observation of nature, the use of experimentation, and inductive reasoning. The inductive method had always been employed in thinking, but no analysis of the inductive process had as yet been attempted comparable to the treatment of deduction in the logic of Aristotle. For this reason, deductive logic was regarded as the only instrument which gave men infallible truth. The great weakness of the deductive method was that it did not lead to the advancement of learning in the very field which was now, more and more, occupying the thoughts of men, the field of nature. This failure of the traditional logic, that is, of the *organon*, or "instrument," of Aristotle, to advance knowledge led Bacon to write the *New Organon* (*Novum Organum*), in order to remedy the defect. This "new method" was merely the inductive process which was used to good effect by the scientists. It was based upon the idea that observations of the phenomena of the external world by the senses combined with experiment are the source of true knowledge. Experimentation, as a process, is not different from observation, but involves merely the expert control of conditions, so as to facilitate or simplify observation.

The greatest contribution that Bacon made was to call upon men to give attention to the study of nature. Scholasticism was an integrated system with the emphasis upon rationality. The Italian Renaissance reinstated the ancient interest in esthetics and literature. The Protestant Reformation placed morality and religion in the forepart of human interest. In all these movements the attitude was one of receptivity from the past; it was deductive. Nature had been subordinated to more pressing considerations.

René Descartes (1596-1650). Like Bacon, Descartes does not figure directly in the history of education; yet one is compelled to agree with the judgment of another Frenchman, Compayré, when he declared: "There is no thinker who has exercised a more decided influence on the destinies of education." [6] The truth is that Descartes began the movement in philosophy and education which resulted in the most profound and prolonged conflict in modern thought.

Descartes was born of a distinguished family, in Touraine, France, and received his education in the Jesuit school at La Flèche. His course of training, while thorough in a way, was narrowly linguistic, and consequently superficial in content. Dissatisfied with what he learned, Descartes engaged in military service in the Netherlands. Here he came

---

[6] Compayré, G., *The History of Pedagogy*, p. 188. Boston: D. C. Heath, 1901.

under the scholarly influence of Beeckman, who awakened in him an absorbing passion for science and mathematics.

At the time when his heart was filled with bitter disappointment because he had not been able to discover any certainty in knowledge, he began to devote himself to mathematics. In his meditations he noticed that this was the only field of human thought in which there were no disputes. Here alone was to be found that indubitable certainty, that absolute clearness which his intellect demanded. He thereupon devoted his whole attention to the study of geometry and was able to make permanent contributions to the world's knowledge of this subject. He then became aware of the remarkable services of mathematics in placing beyond dispute the observations of astronomy and physics. The thought occurred to him that perhaps the same method which produced such infallible truth both in mathematics and the natural sciences could be applied with equally good results in other fields. Concerning this experience he wrote: [7]

> I was delighted especially with the mathematics on account of the certainty and evidence of their demonstrations; but I had not as yet found out their true use, and although I supposed that they were of service only in the mechanical arts, I was surprised that upon foundations so solid and stable no loftier structure had been raised.

With this illuminating idea of utilizing the geometrical method in other fields, Descartes began to construct a new philosophy. What interests the student of education is, not so much his philosophic results, as the criteria which he set up for scientific knowledge. Working with an inflexible determination to lay an indubitable foundation for knowledge, Descartes adopted several rules to guide his thinking: [8]

> The first was, never to accept anything for true which I did not clearly know to be such . . . what was presented to my mind so clearly and distinctly as to exclude all ground of doubt.

The second rule was to divide every problem into its component parts. The third was to begin with the simple and proceed systematically to the more complex and difficult.

---

[7] Descartes, René, *Oeuvres de Descartes*, published by Victor Cousin, Vol. I, p. 128. Paris: Levrault, 1824. Also *A Discourse on Method,* in the HARVARD CLASSICS, Vol. 34, p. 9.

[8] *Ibid.*, p. 17.

But Descartes' chief contribution to education has not yet been stated, for it lies in the philosophical implication rather than in the application of his mathematical method. This implication was his assumption that the fundamental postulates of all knowledge are inherent in the nature of the mind itself. He assumed this to be true, not only of the axioms of mathematics, but equally of the fundamental principles of all fields of human thought. He believed that all primary ideas are innate, and that the growth of knowledge consists merely in drawing out their implications. The true method of science, therefore, is deductive in its procedure. The fundamental process of learning is rational, constructive thinking.

Nothing whatever is to be accepted as true unless it is as certain and clear to the rational judgment as the propositions of Euclidean geometry. If truth can be found only by the exercise of the rational judgment, then human reason must be accorded a dignity that it had not enjoyed since the ancient Greeks. Here, for the first time, human reason, so long humiliated in the interest of theological authoritarianism, found a new and dauntless champion.

The implications of this view for educational science were speedily drawn. Humanistic culture was frankly linguistic; it exercised memory, esthetic sensibility, association, and imagination; but it did not teach children to reason. The Oratorians and the Port Royalists in France endeavored to revise education in accordance with the Cartesian philosophy. After this time all the great educational reformers demanded that knowledge must possess those qualities of certainty, clearness, and positiveness which characterize rational thinking.

Even more significant than this change of attitude, however, was the radical antagonism between the Cartesian theory of innate ideas and the principle of sense perception as the origin of knowledge. This deep-seated difficulty was to appear later as the dominant problem of both philosophy and education.

NEW EDUCATIONAL PROBLEMS AND DEVELOPMENTS

New educational problems. Among the most pressing problems that confronted the educators of Northern Europe at the beginning of the 17th century were the following:

1. How far shall the privileges of education be extended? Up to this time English theorists feared that too many would become learned, and in consequence they advocated the limiting of opportunity to boys of the

upper class and those few poor who showed outstanding capacity and had the good fortune to find benevolent patrons. The only training considered suitable for the masses was apprenticeship to industry. The "Poor Law Act" of 1601 made the apprenticing of pauper children by local authorities compulsory. Education was the sacred prerogative of parents, but where the state or voluntary agencies supplied schooling it was henceforth stigmatized as "charity."

2. A second problem had to do with the curriculum. The main issue here was the use of the vernacular in place of Latin as the means of instruction. Catholics and learned men generally favored the teaching of the Latin tongue exclusively as in the past. Another division of opinion took place over the question of whether the curriculum should remain humanistic or should become realistic.

3. The question of method of instruction came to the front in a new and demanding way. Especially were those who controlled the schools interested in new methods of teaching boys to read and speak Latin.

4. The profoundest of all problems, that of the origin of knowledge or of the method of scientific advancement, came to the front at this time. For a long time a naïve psychological empiricism had been developed, especially among those thinkers who favored realism. As we have seen, a powerful reaction had arisen against the formal logic of Aristotle and against scholastic modes of thought. Bacon presented the new logic of investigation. The rationalistic point of view was presented in a new and striking way by Descartes.

5. The education of girls, especially of the better class of people, now emerged as a problem of much importance.

WOLFGANG RATICH AND PROGRESS OF EDUCATION IN GERMANY

Life and work. The first and most influential of the didactic reformers was Wolfgang Ratke (1571-1635), now generally called Ratich. He was born in the town of Wilster, in Holstein. He received his education at the gymnasium in Hamburg, and then took up theology at the University of Rostock, long a center of progressive learning. He was an ardent Lutheran, profoundly religious, but a defect in speech turned him from the pulpit and pastorate. The idea of reforming education came to him suddenly, and he went to England where he became acquainted with Bacon's early ideas of the advancement of learning. He soon settled in

Amsterdam, Holland, the most advanced center of liberal and scientific learning, where he studied Hebrew and cognate languages and mathematics, and taught school for eight years. His attention now centered upon the improvement of the teaching of languages, which was one of the chief needs of the day.

Returning to Germany, Ratich traveled from place to place seeking a favorable opportunity to demonstrate his new method of instruction. He was determined, however, to keep his ideas a profound secret to be disclosed only to those who paid him well. In 1612, upon the insistence of friends, he went to Frankfurt at the time of the election and coronation of Mathias as emperor. Here he gained the opportunity to place before the assembled body of electors a memorial in which he proposed:[9]

> With the help of God to give directions for the service and welfare of all Christendom:
>
> 1. How the Hebrew, Greek, Latin, and other tongues may be learned both by young and old, more easily and in very much shorter time.
> 2. How, not only in High German, but, also, in all other tongues a school may be established, in which all arts and sciences may be thoroughly learned and propagated.
> 3. How, in the whole Empire one and the same speech, one and the same government, and finally one and the same religion, may be pleasantly introduced and peacefully maintained.

He followed the memorial, within a few hours, with a further explanation in which he offered:

> 1. A much better method of teaching foreign languages than had hitherto been used.
> 2. To produce German text-books in all sciences, to organize schools, preparatory for the *Gelehrtenschulen* [learned schools] in which the foreign languages would be taught.
> 3. In the schools for the learned (*Gelehrtenschulen*) everyone would learn first German, then Hebrew and Greek in order to be able to read the Holy Scriptures pure and unfalsified, so that in the whole Empire, "Lutheran Speech" might prevail.

Great interest in the memorial was expressed, for many of the leaders were aware of the need of reform in methods of instruction. Landgrave Ludwig von Darmstadt appointed Professors Helwig and Jung, of the University of Giessen, to investigate the new method. About the same

---

[9] Schmid, K. A., *Geschichte der Erziehung*, Vol. III, Part II, pp. 6-7. Stuttgart: J. G. Cotta, 1892.

time the Duchess Dorothea Maria of Weimar became the devoted supporter of Ratich, and at her suggestion, four professors of the University of Jena were commissioned to report on his method. Both of these investigations highly praised Ratich's new method of teaching languages.[10] The Duchess Dorothea was so delighted with Ratich that she called him to Weimar to instruct herself, her sons, and her sister, the Princess Anna Sophia of Anhalt, in the Latin tongue. The two sisters remained the warmest friends that Ratich ever had, and it was through them that opportunity came for him to test his ideas.

At this point Ratich was given the most promising opportunity ever offered to set up a demonstration school. Prince Ludwig von Anhalt-Köthen had first met Ratich in Weimar with his sisters, Dorothea and Anna Sophia. At their urgent request, Ratich was invited to Köthen, where Prince Ludwig furnished him buildings, a printing press to supply books, type for six languages, assistants to help him, and all the other equipment necessary for the success of his plans. Nor was this all! To insure a school full of children, the prince resorted to compulsory attendance, enrolling by this method 231 boys and 202 girls. The purpose of the school was admirable: that of so instructing and training teachers that they should be able

> ... to impart to their pupils a thorough, good, and fluent knowledge of any language, especially of Hebrew, Greek, and Latin, in less time, not to exceed half as much, than could be done by any other method usual in Germany, and also with much less pains.[11]

The school was divided into six classes. In the lowest three, the mother tongue was taught; in the fourth, Latin was begun; and in the sixth, Greek. In addition to training in the languages, instruction was given in arithmetic, singing, and religion.

Numerous reasons have been suggested to account for the speedy failure of this school. Prince Ludwig was deeply chagrined and, in a spirit of revenge, threw Ratich into prison for nine months, releasing him only after he had signed a statement in which he acknowledged that he "had claimed and promised more than he knew or could bring to pass." Thus comedy mingles with tragedy in the educational history of this warring age.

---

[10] Barnard, Henry, *German Teachers and Educators,* pp. 341-342, gives summaries of both reports. Hartford: Brown and Gross, 1878.

[11] Quoted by Barnard, Henry, *op. cit.,* p. 321.

The motive which animated Ratich's endeavors must be fully stated. First of all, he was an intense partisan of Lutheran theology and could never refrain from showing his hostility toward all other faiths, especially the Calvinistic. Again, he had a carping, selfish spirit. Repeatedly refusing to give his ideas to the public, he declared that he would sell his discoveries only to a prince, at a high rate and upon the condition that the men of learning to whom he would communicate them should promise to conceal them. He quarreled incessantly with his superiors, into whose service he entered, and was always suspicious of his subordinates, who were chosen to demonstrate the advantages of his plans. He persisted in promising to reveal some wonder-working principles, but he was always afraid to trust anyone to carry them out. In modern education Ratich was the first to originate the idea of systematic instruction; however, he was too crabbed and mean to accomplish any great reform. And yet, through the efforts of his followers, his principles formed the beginning of a remarkable new development.

The method of nature. In the study of the Realism of the early 17th century, it is well to remember that attention was not concentrated entirely upon the observation of the outer world. Here and there, leaders were beginning to observe the inner processes of their own minds and to see that the operations of the mental life were also a part of nature. As a result of such observations, Ratich and Comenius criticized the crude methods employed in the schools, and initiated the search for the *method of nature,* which has since dominated modern pedagogy.

Ratich's principles of teaching. Ratich was the first man who really sought to discover the natural order in which the mind of the child learns. He then undertook to reorganize methods and the curriculum in harmony with the following principles: [12]

(1) *Everything in its order; or the course of nature.* Although this principle was somewhat indefinite, in general it signified that regard must be had for the natural order which the mind of the child follows in learning.

(2) *Only one thing at a time.* One book or one language or one topic only must be learned at a time, and it must be thoroughly mastered before the next is attempted.

(3) *Each thing should be often repeated.* This principle was practiced

[12] The headings are quoted from Barnard, Henry, *op. cit.*, pp. 334-339.

in the interests of thorough understanding. Ratich had the children read Terence three times in German, and then six times in Latin.

(4) *Everything first in the mother tongue.* Children should first learn German well, before they are taught Latin or any other language. The universal practice in the schools of that day was to plunge boys of five and six years of age into Latin grammar as soon as they knew the alphabet. Ratich reversed this order. His pupils learned first to read Terence in German. Then, knowing what the author was saying, they read the work in Latin. Rules and constructions were not studied from a textbook on grammar; they were learned from the usage of the author by the inductive method, a plan advocated also by Ramus. While this procedure was not a great step toward Realism, it was, nevertheless, an important one in that general direction. Even such a change was strongly opposed by some people, because they imagined that this study of grammar, in and by the usage of the author, was somehow an attack upon the Lutheran religion.

(5) *Everything without compulsion.* Ratich's statement is that [13] "Boys cannot be whipped into learning or wishing to learn. By compulsion and blows youth are disgusted with their studies, so that study becomes hateful to them."

(6) *Nothing must be learned by rote.* Experience had demonstrated that rote learning weakened the development of the understanding and judgment. Moreover, there was a far better way of learning than sheer memorization without understanding of what was learned.

(7) *Mutual conformity in all things.* This principle signified that similar subjects—for example, Latin and Greek grammar—should be taught in the same way.

(8) *First a thing by itself, and afterwards the explanation of the thing.* For illustration, rules must not be taught before the materials demonstrating them are presented.

(9) *Everything by experience, and investigation of parts.* This principle may be better stated: Everything through induction and experimentation; languages must proceed from things to names.

So far as the curriculum was concerned, Ratich was chiefly interested in the acquisition of the Latin, Greek, and Hebrew languages. He was fully aware of the failure of Humanism to give the youth a thorough and working knowledge of these tongues. He believed his method could

---

[13] Barnard, Henry, *op. cit.*, p. 336.

accomplish this end more speedily and effectively for both the old and the young. He further believed that, in a year at the most, anyone could learn any language better than his mother tongue; and, with industry, in half a year, if he applied himself to the study for three or four hours a day.

Influence of Ratich. Ratich's efforts exercised a widespread influence. Reyher and Evenius put them into practice in the reformed school system of the principality of Gotha, under Duke Ernst the Pious. The most important effects of his ideas, however, were found in the influence exerted over the great Comenius.

CALVINISTS FORM THEIR SYSTEM OF EDUCATION

The Synod of Dort. From 1618 to 1619 there was held at Dordrecht, Holland, the most consequential council of Reformed Churches. It was composed of 100 members from many lands and the number of sessions reached 154. The deep interest of these people in religious education found expression in a general system of training. The plan comprehended religious instruction in the home and the church, and the establishment of schools by the civil authorities. Particularly did the council urge the extension of schools to the villages and country places. But the chief concern of the Synod, as shown in the following resolutions adopted by the body, was the promotion of religious instruction: [14]

> In order that the Christian youth may be diligently instructed in the principles of religion, and be trained in piety, three modes of catechising should be employed. I. *In the house, by parents.* II. *In the schools, by schoolmasters.* III. *In the churches, by ministers, elders and catechists especially appointed for the purpose.* That these may diligently employ their trust, the Christian magistrates shall be requested to promote, by their authority, so sacred and necessary a work; and all who have the oversight of churches and schools shall be required to pay special attention to this matter.
>
> I. The office of parents is diligently to instruct their children and their whole household in the principles of the Christian religion, in a manner adapted to their respective capacities; earnestly and carefully to admonish them to the cultivation of true piety; to engage their punctual attendance on family worship, and take them with them to the hearing of the Word

[14] Dunshee, Henry W., *History of the School of the Collegiate Reformed Dutch Church,* pp. 3-4. New York: Aldine Press, 1883.

of God. . . . Parents who profess religion, and are negligent in this work, shall be faithfully admonished by the ministers; and, if the case requires it, they shall be censured by the Consistory, that they may be brought to the discharge of their duty.

II. Schools, in which the young shall be properly instructed in the principles of Christian doctrine, shall be instituted not only in cities, but also in towns and country places where heretofore none have existed. The Christian magistracy shall be requested that well-qualified persons may be employed and enabled to devote themselves to the service; and especially that the children of the poor may be gratuitously instructed, and not be excluded from the benefit of the schools. In this office none shall be employed but such as are members of the Reformed Church, having certificates of an upright faith and pious life, and of being well versed in the truths of the Catechism. They are to sign a document, professing their belief in the Confession of Faith and the Heidelberg Catechism, and promising that they will give catechetical instruction to the youth in the principles of Christian truth according to the same. . . .

III. In order that due knowledge may be obtained of the diligence of the schoolmasters, and the improvement of the youth, it shall be the duty of the ministers, with an elder, and, if necessary, with a magistrate, to visit all the schools, private as well as public, frequently, in order to excite the teachers to earnest diligence, to encourage and counsel them in the duty of catechising, and to furnish an example by questioning them, addressing them in a friendly and affectionate manner, and exciting them to early piety and diligence. If any of the schoolmasters should be found neglectful or perverse, they shall be earnestly admonished by the ministers, and, if necessary, by the Consistory, in relation to their office.

This statement of policy by the general Synod became the standard for Calvinistic education in all countries so far as local conditions permitted. It gave educational leadership to the people of Holland, but it likewise inspired progressive action among Calvinists in Scotland, England, France, and America. The reform measures of the Germans, including those of Evenius, Ratich, and Kromayer, were definitely inspired by the Calvinists; and the same was true of the innovations of Comenius.

Progress in the Netherlands. The first half of the 17th century was the golden age for the Dutch Republic; rapid progress was made in all lines and Amsterdam was the virtual capital of the world so far as progress and trade were concerned. The Dutch navy was the most formidable, having defeated that of Spain, and Dutch traders sailed unrestricted in every sea and brought great profit to the Republic. The East India Company, chartered in 1602, established a chain of trading posts from the Cape of Good Hope to Japan and virtually monopolized

Oriental trade. Colonies were established in the New World, including New Amsterdam.

So far as education was concerned, the Dutch schools retained the lead. The Calvinists were not in a position to control all education in Holland, but their enthusiasm for a full program had great weight everywhere. Instruction in the home (in the Heidelberg Catechism), elementary vernacular schools, Latin Grammar Schools, and university or college training promoted by the civil authorities constituted their complete program. The school order of Drente introduced compulsory education in 1638. In addition to the Universities of Leyden, Franeker, and Groningen founded earlier, three others were now established, Amsterdam, 1630; Utrecht, 1638; and Harderwijk, 1648. In all, Holland boasted 14 higher institutions of note, but Leyden remained the most influential. It had come under the domination of the Calvinistic party. Despite the high achievements of the Dutch, their period of leadership was short-lived. Internal dissension among the religious bodies, and among the provinces and political parties weakened national life and prevented the continuance of independent action.

Weimar reform. The most important effort at educational reform just after the beginning of the Thirty Years' War took place in Weimar, a small principality in central Germany. The initiative was taken by the Duchess Dorothea Maria, who had been profoundly interested in educational methods from the time she learned Latin from Ratich. At her request the court preacher, Kromayer, drew up a new school order for the schools of the duchy in 1619. He was well acquainted with the principles of Ratich and had written a number of textbooks in accordance with the new method. Among other requirements, this school order obliged pastors and schoolmasters to keep a "careful list" of all boys and girls from the sixth year to the twelfth; this was probably the first scholastic census. School attendance was made compulsory "through the power of the civil authorities." This provision is notable, for not only was it the first compulsory education law promulgated in a German state, but an effort was actually made to put it into effect. Another important point was that, in accordance with the trend of events, children were taught the vernacular before they learned the Latin tongue.

Devastations of the Thirty Years' War. It has been asserted that religious wars are the most ruthless and savage of all. Certainly the Thirty Years' War, between Catholics and Protestants in northern Europe, may well be cited as an illustration of this contention. The entire country was devastated, and the population of Germany decreased by one-half. In many places the people were reduced to savagery. In the villages there was often not a wagon nor a draft animal to be seen; many a peasant was forced to harness himself or his wife and dog to the plow. A number of the free cities never recovered their ruined trade and industries. The Moravians who inhabited the central theater of the conflict were well-nigh exterminated.

Religion, morals, and the arts of civilization were practically forgotten. The bestiality and licentiousness of the soldiers were incredible. Pastors and teachers having nothing to sustain them at their labors ceased their ministrations. The people lapsed into barbarity, ignorance, superstition, and crime. Except in the largest centers of population, every trace of schools was destroyed. Church and school buildings were requisitioned as hospitals or barracks for soldiers, or even as stables for their horses. It was under such horrible circumstances that the reform of education was attempted by several of the princes of Germany even before the termination of the conflict.

Duke Ernst and school reform in Gotha. By far the most epochal action for the advancement of education in the early part of the 17th century was taken by Duke Ernst, called "the Pious." He was known as the prince among the pedagogues, and the pedagogue among the princes. Generally credited with the founding of the German school system, Duke Ernst came by his enthusiasm for education honestly; his mother was the Duchess Dorothea Maria of Weimar, who had called Ratich to assist in the education of her sons and who had later employed Kromayer to reform the schools of the duchy. The reforms instituted by Duke Ernst, as well as those effected by his mother, had this highly significant feature: they definitely marked the passing of the initiative in school reform from church authorities to the civil power. Not that there was any lack of coöperation between church and state, but henceforth the leadership rested primarily with the magistracy.

Duke Ernst took over his small domain of Gotha in 1640. The condition of the territory at the time was pitiable because of the war. Many churches and schools were in ruins; others were used by the soldiers as hospitals and stables. Towns and villages were impoverished and depopulated, and the remaining inhabitants had largely reverted to savagery. In most communities, even religious instruction had ceased. Duke Ernst began a general survey of conditions in all churches and schools, but he did not wait to initiate reform. He issued an imperative order to the civil officers to look after the discipline of children, and to the pastors to give their attention to religious instruction, particularly of pre-school children.

Duke Ernst's chief reforms had to do with the schools. In most villages either no schools existed or they had been destroyed by the ravages of war. He first sought to improve the condition of the teachers: a minimum income was assured them, and a knowledge of the elements of learning and good character were required before appointment. His next step in carrying out his far-reaching program was to issue a school law.

School organization. Duke Ernst called to his assistance Andreas Reyher, a thoroughgoing schoolman, the rector of the Gotha gymnasium. Reyher was well acquainted with the principles of Ratich and Comenius, and was himself a man of some originality. His first task was to write a new plan of school organization, which was then amended by Duke Ernst. It was adopted in 1642, but was later subjected to numerous revisions and entitled *School-Method* (*Schulmethodus*). In this he set forth the organization and aims of the schools; methods of instruction; means of education and discipline; duties of children, parents, teachers, and supervisors; in short, everything that was essential for the establishment of a school system. The new code required that schools be established everywhere, in the villages as well as in the towns. This was, in fact, the first time in any German state, that an effort was made to establish vernacular elementary schools for all children. Among the many and comprehensive provisions the following may be noted as the most progressive:

(1) *Schoolmasters* must live respectable lives, and observe punctiliously the rules laid down in the school ordinance; otherwise they will be summarily dismissed. Inhumane punishments will not be tolerated.

(2) The *school term* shall continue throughout the entire year, except that, during the four weeks of harvest time, full weekly attendance is not necessary.

(3) *Compulsory attendance* is required. Every year after the harvest all children who have passed their fifth year of life shall report at school, and must attend until their twelfth year. On Sundays and holidays they must attend church. The daily lessons shall be three hours in the morning, and three in the afternoon in the villages. Saturday afternoon is free; also, Wednesday afternoon is free in the towns.

(4) The daily schedule of lessons is laid down as follows: religion and reading, in the morning; writing, singing, and reckoning, in the after-

noon. In the villages the children are grouped into two classes for purposes of instruction. In the lower class, the alphabet and syllables are learned; in the other, reading, writing, singing, reckoning, catechism, psalms, proverbs, and the Gospels.

Reyher prepared textbooks for each class in the various subjects, in which, also, detailed directions were given the teachers as to how each subject was to be taught.

Realistic studies. For the first time in German schools, realistic studies received considerable attention, for Duke Ernst and Reyher tracked closely the plans of Comenius. A special text on *The Things of Nature* was written with the following divisions: (1) Of the things of nature; (2) Of some useful sciences; (3) Of religious and civil arrangements; and (4) Of domestic regulations. Directions in teaching these branches were likewise given. It was required that every school be provided with apparatus: a rule, a circle, a plummet, two or more balls of twine, a compass, and six weights. The children were given instruction about climate, natural phenomena, geology, botany, and natural history, and about man's body and soul. The practical affairs of life were kept constantly in view.

In the directions to the teachers, stress was laid upon direct sense perception of things, models, or pictures, and on the stimulation of interest through self-activity and observation of nature and life. Geometry and political affairs were taught to boys only. Parents were required to train their sons in some honorable handicraft or in farming; and their daughters, in sewing, spinning, and housekeeping.

Supervision. The supervision of the country and village schools was placed in the hands of the clergy. It was their duty to keep the school roll, to correct the weaknesses of the teachers, to admonish and warn them when necessary, and to make reports to the superintendent. Likewise the superintendent had to admonish and to warn parents, and, in case they did not observe the school regulations regarding their children, to apply punishment. In the towns, the civil authorities and judges had the oversight of the schools. The church superintendent and the consistorium, at the head of the entire system, were responsible for the schools but were subject to the approval of Duke Ernst. An annual examination of each school was instituted for the inspection of the work and the promotion of the pupils. Duke Ernst in company with his court preacher often visited the schools in person and observed the attitude of those in charge.

Summary. The following points of progress in the Gotha school system are especially noteworthy: (1) compulsory attendance; (2) control of the period of attendance; (3) extension of the term over the entire year; (4) supervision by the state and in the interests of the state; (5) humane discipline; (6) reform of instruction according to the principles of Ratich and Comenius; (7) introduction of realistic instruction; and (8) insistence upon the class system.

Duke Ernst not only improved the condition of the teachers, but promoted the construction of buildings and founded some twenty new schools. His efforts put life into the little state of Gotha and made it the most prosperous and progressive. His reforms had a far-reaching influence and marked a new epoch in German education.

It was said that the peasants of Gotha were better instructed than the nobles and city folk elsewhere. At his death no one in the duchy was unable to read and write.

Knightly Academies. During the 16th century the education of the aristocracy continued to occupy attention and was highly elaborated in Italy, France, and England. The theory that the princes and nobility needed education to be competent rulers of their domains had existed for a long time. In France, several academies were set up to serve this end. Furthermore the brilliancy of the French court became the model for all others in Europe. In England, young nobles were trained at home by private tutors, and then sent to the great public schools and universities and on tours to the Continent to complete their training.

During the 16th century, young German princes attended the better gymnasiums and studied the usual classical programs.

After the middle of the 17th century the German princes established *knightly academies* (*Ritteracademien*) in which to train their boys. The nobility attended these institutions in preference to the gymnasiums and the universities. The objectives of these new institutions were: (1) to train in courtly manners; (2) to prepare for military service; and (3) to prepare for statecraft and administrative work. In addition to courtly manners, French, poetry, dancing, drawing, painting, and music were taught. As a preparation for military service, riding, fencing, ball play, hunting, military activities, and physical culture were practiced. Attention was given also to many of the realistic studies: geography, history, technology (especially in relation to fortifications and war), genealogy, and heraldry. Greek and Hebrew were abandoned, and the amount of Latin was decreased. After the development of the modern gymnasiums, these academies ceased to exist. However, they had served a purpose for the time being, and had assisted in the transition from the old classical gymnasiums to the more realistic type.

ADVANCE IN ENGLISH THEORY AND PRACTICE

English educational theory and practice. Four influences played upon the educational reformers in England in the 17th century: (1) devotion to the traditional Protestant humanistic program; (2) the new emphasis upon the vernacular; (3) Baconian realism; and (4) the program of Calvinistic education adopted at the Synod of Dort in 1618.

John Brinsley (dates unknown) was a life-long Puritan schoolmaster devoted to the task of finding the best methods to help his pupils. He wrote two important books. The first was entitled *Ludus Literarius* [15] or *The Grammar Schools,* published in 1612 and again in 1627. This gives some account of the methods, curriculum, organization, and conduct of Latin Grammar Schools at this time. The course consisted of Latin, Greek, and Hebrew, and the authors and texts were those familiar since the Reformation took up The New Learning. The main objective of all Protestant scholarship was to acquire a ready command of both Latin and English and a reading knowledge of New Testament Greek and of Hebrew. The problem was how to induce young boys to learn Latin and Greek. Brinsley gave great attention to this task as did Ascham, the Jesuits, Ratich, and Comenius.

Ascham had made history by using double translation from Latin to English and then turning the English into Latin and comparing with the original. The two most noteworthy innovations which Brinsley added were to explain to the pupils in English what the Latin passage was about, and to arrange the Latin words in the order in which they are translated into English. The order of words in the mind of the Latin author, Brinsley held, was artificial and adopted for oratorical effect. The English mind would think them quite differently. Brinsley got this device from Martin Crucius, a German professor of Latin and Greek. The German language is notorious for having a part of the verb shifted to the end of the sentence and it was natural for a German to see this difficulty. The change of order would certainly assist the pupil to get the meaning

---

[15] The term *ludus* connotes a playground where children take pleasure in learning the elements of literary culture.

PRISCIANUS NASCENS

OR

A Key to the Grammar School.

Serving much to the Expoſition of the Grammatical Rules of *Lilly*, and the more eaſie and certain Tranſlating of Engliſh into Latine.

To the no ſmall eaſe of the Maſter in Teaching and the Scholar in Learning.

Filiole; huc adsis; & quam tibi porrigo Clavem.
Accipe; quâ nostros poteris reserare Penates.

GRAMATICA

Priscian Nascens

LUDUS LITERARIUS

(i.e.) *My Son approach; I give thee here a Key*
To all my Treasures that Shall cleare ẏ Way

The Reader may for his fuller ſatisfaction peruſe the Preface to this book; in which the Reaſons and Uſe of it is unfolded.

LONDON, Printed for *William Garret*, and are to be ſold by *Timothy Garthwait*, 1660.

Title Page of a Grammar Textbook.

of the Latin text. Brinsley was alert to all the new and clever devices of teaching.

In 1622 Brinsley published a second work whose lengthy title fully explains its purpose and contents:

> *A Consolation for our Grammar Schooles: or a faithful and most comfortable incouragement for laying a sure foundation of all good learning in our Schooles, and for prosperous building thereon. More especially for all those of the inferiour sort, and all ruder countries and places, namely for Ireland, Wales, Virginia with the Summer Islands, and for their most speedie attaining of our English tongue by the same labour, that all may speak one and the same language. And withall, for the helping of all such as are desirous speedily to recover that which they had formerly got in the Grammar Schooles, and to proceed aright therein, for the perpetual benefit of these our Nations and of the Churches of Christ.*

One is justified in assuming that this work, coming just four years after the Calvinistic educational program of the Synod of Dort was formulated, was fully in accord with that program. The broad geographical scope, the concern for universal training, for one tongue, and for the welfare of both church and state are all marks of the Calvinistic spirit. His desire to make English the universal tongue is also noteworthy.

Chapter 7

COMENIUS, PROPHET OF MODERN PRINCIPLES AND METHODS

CHILDHOOD and education. None of the great educators is so deservedly admired and so little criticized today as this erudite, wise, and benevolent bishop of an exterminated people. In the works of Comenius, one feels that a prophet is speaking; he was indeed a colossal figure, but only in recent years have his ideas received the respect they merit.

Comenius, or, as the name was originally spelled, Komensky, was born at Nivnitz, a Moravian village, in 1592. His people were Slavs, and Brethren who were followers of John Huss. Doctrinally, they were related to the Wycliffites of England and the Waldensians of central Europe; their religious faith was marked by simplicity, warm-hearted love, evangelical zeal, deep personal piety, self-sacrifice, and humility. Interest in education was an outstanding characteristic of these people. They made Prague the earliest and most aggressive university in northern Europe; they established elementary and secondary schools, and taught catechism in their homes long before Luther entered upon reforming the church in Germany. Comenius was the product and the chief representative of this Moravian spirit for the enlightenment and uplift of the common people.

Both parents died when Comenius was a child. Although his father had been a well-to-do miller, his guardians misappropriated his inheritance; as a consequence, Comenius received, at the village school, only a meager education in reading, writing, catechism, hymn singing, and arithmetic. Not until he was 16 did he enter a school which taught

Latin in preparation for a scholarly career. There may have been a great advantage in this circumstance, for he was able to perceive the serious defects in the method of teaching Latin to his fellow victims, who were at least ten years younger than himself.

Having the minstry in view, at 20 years Comenius went to the College of Herborn, in Nassau. This institution had been established to promote Reformed Church doctrine, which was more akin to the Moravian faith than the Lutheran theology which dominated most of the German universities. At Herborn, Comenius came under the influence of John Henry Alsted, a Calvinistic theologian who was deeply interested in educational reform. Alsted introduced him to the principles advocated by Ratich and, what was even more important, to the advanced system of education in operation in the adjacent provinces of the Dutch Republic. Profoundly attracted by the new movements, Comenius spent some time studying in Amsterdam, which, at the time, was the most enlightened and progressive center of culture in Europe.

Work as an educator. The period of training over, Comenius returned to his people in Moravia and entered upon a life of alternate tragedies and successes, during which he taught school and wrote many books. As the chief bishop of the Moravian Brethren, he endeavored to succor his people in their horrible persecution and dispersion. At the same time he corresponded with practically all the great scholars of his day. More than any other man, he focused the attention of the peoples of northern Europe upon education as the supreme means of human progress.

Driven from Moravia by the fiendish persecution and having lost all his property, he settled in Lissa, Poland, where he became rector of the gymnasium. Here he wrote his *Great Didactic,* and his *Gate of Tongues Unlocked* (*Janua Linguarum Reserata*), an introduction to the Latin language. These works were followed by *The Vestibule* (*Vestibulum*), which was still more elementary. In 1641, at the solicitation of Samuel Hartlib, the noted English philanthropist, the English Parliament invited Comenius to lay before it his plans for a college. Unfortunately, an Irish revolt put an end to the whole matter.

An invitation from Ludevic de Geer, a native of Holland then living in Sweden, induced Comenius to go to that country to lead in reforming the instruction in the schools. In the expectation that its military power would reestablish the Brethren and give him an opportunity to set up his *pansophic* college, Comenius sold his services to Sweden. These hopes were sadly disappointed. In Stockholm he was directed by the famous, but all too practical, Swedish Chancellor Oxenstierna and John Skyte, of the University of Upsala, to write textbooks for their Latin schools. To accomplish this, Comenius retired to the town of Elbing, on the Baltic Sea, and for six years labored on textbooks, grammars, and lexicons.

At the completion of this work, in 1650, Comenius accepted an invitation to establish a school at Sárospatak, in Hungary. He had expected to realize here a life-long dream of a reformed institution but, in the end, suffered another disappointment. From 1654 to the end of his life, in 1670, he made his home in Amsterdam, where he devoted his days to writing and to the care of his scattered fellow religionists.

Pansophia. Throughout his whole life Comenius was obsessed by a grandiose scheme for the correlation and advancement of science, which he grandiloquently called by the intriguing name *Pansophia,* that is, "Universal Wisdom." The plan included three aspects: (1) In the first place, it comprehended the publishing of an encyclopedia of universal learning. This idea may have come to him from Alsted. Among his 120 volumes, this prolific scholar had produced an encyclopedia. Comenius, however, planned a new encyclopedia, to which all European scientists would contribute. Working independently of each other, as they were, and without a clearing house, these men were often ignorant of what was being accomplished elsewhere even in their own fields. An exhaustive statement of all science, Comenius believed, would coördinate and assist its progress. (2) Again, from Bacon, Comenius had received the idea of promoting scientific discovery by establishing a college in which not only laboratories for scientific research but all the other necessary conditions would be available. (3) Finally, in his planning he went further than others. He saw that teaching and research were interdependent. In consequence of this insight, he came to the problem of finding a new method of instruction by which every individual, to the limit of his capacity, might avail himself of the benefits of knowledge in all fields of learning.

The pansophic plan of education. Comenius' plan of pansophic education comprehended the art of teaching everyone everything. Considering the present expansion of knowledge along every line, the suggestion is wholly preposterous; but in the 17th century it was not so quixotic. Nevertheless, Comenius had an exaggerated conception of the intellectual capacity of the masses of people. The ideal which inspired the amiable bishop in all his efforts was the noble vision of so educating every child that he might share, to the full extent of his capacities, in all knowledge and social life.

Practically all theologians of that era accepted the doctrine of human depravity; in the case of Comenius, however, this belief was merely incidental. He believed that the forces making for goodness are stronger than those leading toward evil, that man still retained, though greatly marred, the image of his Creator; and that this original goodness showed itself in man's desire to return to his former state of perfection. Like all great educators, Comenius possessed a sublime confidence in the improvability of the race. He repeatedly affirmed that the "seeds of knowledge, virtue and piety" are found in all normal individuals, and are susceptible of unlimited cultivation. No educator has had a stronger faith in the power of education to save mankind and thus to bring it back to its original divinity.

Democracy in education. Another fundamental quality of Comenius was his profound sympathy for the common man. No great champion of the education of the masses had yet risen into prominence in educational history. In his early years as a reformer, Martin Luther approached this lofty ideal but in the end fell far short of achieving it. Even the provisions of the Synod of Dort, which required the establishment of village schools, had not emphasized complete democracy in education. The emphatic declaration of Comenius must have been shocking in an age moving rapidly toward political absolutism.[1]

> The education that I propose includes all that is proper for a man, and is one in which all men who are born into this world should share. All, therefore, as far as is possible, should be educated together, that they may stimulate and urge on one another.

Children are not born human, according to Comenius, but all are born with the capacity to become human; and they can only become human by proper training in society. Not to educate them is to act contrary to God's purpose. He visualized the reforming of society on a Christian basis and he employed the term "Christian Republic" to designate the new organization. This was truly an astounding point of view at the beginning of the 17th century, the anticipation of the principle of equality of all men that emerged a century and a half later.

---

[1] Keatinge, M. W., *The Great Didactic of John Amos Comenius,* p. 418. London: Adam and Charles Black, 1896.

All the Protestant reformers had established elementary schools to train a learned class in the Latin language. Comenius declared emphatically, "From this view my whole didactic system forces me to dissent." He demanded that admission to the Latin school should not "be reserved for the sons of rich men, nobles and magistrates."

> We wish all men to be trained in all the virtues, especially in modesty, sociability, and politeness, and it is therefore undesirable to create class distinctions at such an early age, or to give some children the opportunity of considering their own lot with satisfaction and that of others with scorn.

What explanation can be given for this thoroughly democratic attitude? It would be decidedly an error to assign it wholly to the originality and initiation of Comenius. His breadth of sympathy and universality of educational thinking generally expressed the profound spirituality of the Moravian Brethren. Their spirit of democracy can be gauged from their attitude toward the nobility, whom they excluded from church fellowship until they relinquished their titles. Interpreting the principles of Christianity as found in the New Testament literally, they believed that in the "Christian Republic" all are indeed brethren and without distinction of rank.

In Comenius, for the first time in the history of culture, one finds a truly great representative of those evangelical, nonconformist groups of people who were the doctrinal descendants of the early Waldensian movement. Broadminded as were the Calvinists, none of their varied branches approached the genuine liberalism and democracy of Comenius, who proclaimed: [2] "We are now seeking a way by which the common people may be led to understand and take an interest in the liberal arts and sciences." Such a wholehearted espousal of democracy in an age when the aristocracy of birth and position closed the door of opportunity for the lower class pointed backward to primitive Christianity and forward to a new era of social justice.

PLANS FOR EDUCATIONAL ORGANIZATION

Aim of education. The purpose of the *"school of universal wisdom"* (*Schola Pansophica*), may be taken as Comenius' aim for all education: [3]

---

[2] *Ibid.*, pp. 423-424.

[3] Laurie, S. S., *John Amos Comenius,* p. 200. Syracuse: C. W. Bardeen, 1892.

> They will learn, not for the school, but for life, so that the youths shall go forth energetic, ready for everything, apt, industrious, and worthy of being intrusted with any of the duties of life, and this all the more if they have added to virtue a sweet conversation, and have crowned all with the fear and love of God. They will go forth capable of expression and eloquence.

Three words summarize his aim: knowledge, virtue, and piety. Comenius deduced these from man's capacity to know and to do, and from his relation to God. It is instructive to compare this statement of the aim of education with that of Sturm, which, it will be recalled, gave priority to eloquence rather than to piety. Comenius, on the other hand, made piety the supreme purpose of education. Of this he said: [4] "Our schools, therefore, will then at length be Christian schools when they make us as like to Christ as is possible. How wretched is the teaching that does not lead to virtue and to piety." The aim of education is to teach all men everything. "Charity bids us not niggardly to withhold from mankind what God has intended for the use of all, but to throw it open to the whole world." Comenius had a sublime confidence in the power of education to regenerate human life; he was convinced that "there is no more certain way under the sun for raising sunken humanity than the proper education of the young." [5]

Function of the school. To attain his educational objective, Comenius asserted that three things were essential: good textbooks, good teachers, and good methods. The school is *ludus literarius*—that is to say, an institution where children live and work together under conditions which resemble the activities of the playground. The school must provide opportunity for movement, spontaneity, social relations, rivalry, good order, and, finally, pleasurable exercises in learning.

Comenius held the conviction that education is the indispensable process by which the young are made human. He cited several cases in which infants deprived of all human association and care grew up as animals. From this he concluded that education is an absolutely essential process in order to develop children into human beings; moreover, this process must begin at birth and not merely when the children enter school. Led by this view of education as an indispensable need, he envisaged the school as "a forging-place or manufactory of humanity"

---

[4] Keatinge, M. W., *op. cit.*, p. 226.

[5] *Ibid.*, p. 166.

(*Officina Humanitatis*). Comenius did not intend by this term to stress training as a mechanical process; he desired merely to emphasize the necessity of training. Inadequate psychological knowledge frequently led him to overdo the use of analogies. The conception of the school as a garden in which children grow as plants, would have expressed his general conceptions just as well; in fact, this idea was frequently in his mind when he was considering the processes of development. However, the transformation from the animal to the human level is so much more significant than the development from childhood to manhood that he chose the analogy of the forging-place.

In projecting his school, Comenius held clearly in view the glaring defects and failures of the schools of his time. Both the humanistic Protestant schools and the Catholic institutions, as fostered by the Jesuits, had succeeded only in furnishing the memory of students with choice Latin verbiage and rhetorical phraseology. The ability of students to observe with their own eyes, or to think with their own minds, had not been exercised.[6]

> The result is that most men possess no information but the quotations, sentences, and opinions that they have collected by rummaging about in various authors, and thus piece their knowledge together like a patchwork quilt.

In such fervent language Comenius pleaded for independent thinking: to see with one's own eyes, and to become wise by using one's own mind.

Organization of the school system. Comenius' generous concepts regarding the functions of education were to be realized in a clear-cut system of schools. Anticipating the present-day point of view, he took as his guiding principle in the grouping of the grades the stages in the growth of the child to maturity. His school system is divided into four levels of six years each.[7]

I. For infancy	the	The mother's knee (Schola materna).
II. For childhood	school	The Vernacular-School (Schola vernacula).
III. For boyhood	should	The Latin-School (Schola Latina).
IV. For youth	be	The University and travel.

> A Mother-School should exist in every house, a Vernacular-School in every hamlet and village, a Gymnasium in every city, and a University in every kingdom or in every province.

---

[6] *Ibid.*, p. 300.
[7] *Ibid.*, p. 408.

All schools shall begin at a uniform date, and children shall be admitted at no other time. A daily and yearly schedule of work shall be followed: [8]

> The subjects of instruction are to be so divided that each year, each month, each week, each day, and even each hour may have a definite task appointed for it.

A separate room with a special teacher shall be appointed for each class.

The practical schoolmaster is further seen in the daily schedule that Comenius prepared. He objected to the rigorous practice of forcing young children to study six or eight hours a day. For younger children, he specified four hours of school work a day; for older ones, six. No home work shall be required, as it is apt to be done badly; this is a strange prophecy of a similar attitude in American schools of today. A half hour of relaxation shall follow each class, and holidays shall be frequent but not prolonged. The morning hours shall be devoted to work which taxes the intellect and memory; the afternoon, to handwork, music, and practical activities. These provisions are examples of how strikingly Comenius anticipated modern innovations, in this case, the science of school hygiene.

Simultaneous or class instruction; textbooks. Until the time of Comenius, although pupils were graded in a general way into large groups, they were not taught in classes. Instruction was not given to all the pupils in a class at the same time; each individual was taught separately. This greatly hampered the progress of instruction. Comenius undertook to show how a single teacher could "teach a number of boys, no matter how great, at one time." Thus he anticipated, by over half a century, the practice of simultaneous instruction adopted by the Brothers of the Christian Schools; and, by almost two centuries, the similar practice of Pestalozzi, who finally introduced simultaneous instruction into permanent school practice.

Another great drawback was the lack of satisfactory textbooks. Books were still scarce because they were expensive. Boys took to school whatever texts they had most readily at hand, and used them to learn Latin. The medieval custom of copying the text from the dictation of the teachers, as Comenius pointed out, was a waste of time. He wanted each pupil to have his own copy of the common text, and, furthermore, each class to have a text containing everything to be taught in that particular class.

---

[8] *Ibid.*, p. 326.

I. School of infancy. Education begins at birth; the home is, therefore, the first school. Comenius was the first to appreciate the full significance of these facts. In this he anticipated the thinkers of later centuries, and gave the world a sketch of pre-school training astonishing in its completeness. His *The School of Infancy* is filled with information and suggestions that testify to extraordinary insight into the nature and needs of young children. One is amazed at his detailed observations of the activities and capabilities of pre-school children. Unlike most treatises of this kind, it is not a compilation of broad generalizations. Comenius stated in detail what should be done for children at each successive year of life. Nor is the book confined to a few phases of child training; it comprehends every aspect of education: physical, mental, expressional, manual, moral, social, and religious.

Comenius set out to teach each child at this stage the fundamental facts of all the sciences. The foundations of encyclopedic knowledge are laid in the observations made by the children themselves. The school of infancy has as its special functions the exercise of the external senses, early social training, and instruction in religion. But in all these functions Comenius did not propose any activity beyond the scope of the real, spontaneous interests of normal children. Moreover, he was an enthusiastic advocate of fairy tales, Mother Goose rhymes, and stories, play, manual constructivity, music, and even of humor.

II. Vernacular school. The suggestion of this school constituted one of the most radical departures ever urged in the reorganization of education. Comenius demanded a well-rounded elementary education for every child, poor or rich, high-born or low, boy or girl. All children were to be instructed together in the same schools—an unheard-of innovation in an age reeking with aristocratic aloofness. Nor was this all. It was obligatory that every child attend the vernacular school, for it was to furnish the elementary training necessary for life and, at the same time, to give preparatory training to those who were to enter the Latin school and prepare for the learned professions. European peoples have always provided a different type of institution for the lower classes of society than for the learned classes and the nobility; but not so Comenius.

The most striking characteristic, however, was the requirement that pupils spend six years in the study and use of the vernacular tongue before they take up Latin. As we have already seen, the vernacular tongues had made great strides in their development in all western countries. The Protestant Reformation greatly stimulated their growth and use in worship and instruction in the catechism. The use of the vernacular had been urged by Vives as an introduction to Latin; but it was most probably the position of Mulcaster that six years of instruction be given in the mother tongue prior to the study of Latin that caused Ratich and Comenius to accept this innovation.

According to the program of Comenius, the vernacular school should train "the internal senses, the imagination and memory in combination with their cognate organs." The course of study includes reading, writing, practical arithmetic, singing, religion, morals, economics and politics, general history, cosmography, and the mechanical arts. It is an institution where all children are trained in all the arts of humanity. To this time no reformer had so comprehensive a system of education for all children.

III. Latin school or gymnasium. According to Comenius, the Latin school was not a special educational route which only the learned or higher classes may travel. The Schola Latina was designed as the institution for development in the adolescent age. All boys "who aspire higher than the work shop" were to receive this training. Comenius was not in the least afraid that large numbers would be trained above their station in life; he had confidence that knowledge and training would be beneficial to the student, even if his lot in life were a humble one.

Psychologically, the purpose of the Latin school is to train the pupil "to understand and pass judgment on the information collected by the senses" in the former period. The means to this end are logic, grammar, rhetoric, and the sciences and arts "that are based on principles of causation." In other words, in this school the higher faculties of the mind are to be exercised. Four languages are to be learned: the vernacular, Latin, Greek, and Hebrew, though the vernacular and Latin are to receive the chief emphasis. For the introduction to Latin, Comenius prescribed his own texts.

The Latin school is divided into six classes, or years, called after the subjects, grammar, natural philosophy, mathematics, ethics, dialectic, and rhetoric. Finally, it must be added, Comenius provided that such a Latin school shall be found in every city and town, where all who wish may attend.

IV. University and travel. The university course and travel form the highest level of education. A university is to be established in every province or kingdom. Comenius expected only brightest students, who were also of high moral character, to attend the universities. The selection was to be made by a public examination of the students who completed the Latin school.

It is curious that Comenius believed the special mental faculty calling for development at this stage to be the will. He evidently had in view the student's interest in professional training for vocational life. Of this he wrote:[9] "To the University belong those subjects that have special relation to the will."

In addition to preparing candidates for the ministry, medicine, and law, Comenius recognized the duty of the university to train teachers and leaders for the state. He believed that "the curriculum should be really universal, provision being made for the study of every branch of human knowledge." He fully recognized that research is also a function of the universities; a function, however, which he hardly expected them to perform. He believed that the progress of the sciences could be more successfully brought about by the voluntary coöperation of scientists throughout all countries. Furthermore, like other educators of his day, Comenius believed in the advantages of travel in furnishing direct information concerning human nature and institutions. He felt that such experience should follow the university career, after moral habits were fully formed.

Educational psychology. Among his numerous treatises Comenius did not include a special discussion of psychology; yet all of his principles and methods of instruction were based upon a fairly well-formed theory of the mental life and the growth of children. He possessed a remarkably acute capacity for observation of phenomena in many fields: he observed carefully the development of plants and animals, the operation of the manual arts and crafts, and the spontaneous activities and interests of children.

Another strong trait, but one which frequently led him into vagaries of imagination, was his life-long tendency to reason from analogy. Because of this he sought the basis for his principles of method in the analogies of external nature and of the mechanical arts. He understood clearly, however, the idea that the true basis of educational science must be the natural growth of the child. Among his numerous statements of this genetic principle is the following:[10]

---

[9] *Ibid.*, p. 409.
[10] *Ibid.*, p. 409.

> Let our maxim be to follow the lead of nature in all things, to observe how the faculties develop one after the other, and to base our method on this principle of succession.

He was firmly convinced that "the exact order of instruction must be borrowed from nature." However, he did not clearly distinguish external nature and its processes from the inner conduct of the mind.

The greatest weakness of Comenius' ideas arose from the want of a deep and accurate knowledge of the mental life. Lacking something better, he utilized the psychological conceptions that had come down from Aristotle, and also those of Vives. A belief in "faculties" was generally accepted, and Comenius did not possess knowledge enough to dissent from this point of view. In spite of this lack of correct knowledge, however, one is amazed at the profound wisdom of Comenius' principles. His conceptions of the mind, far more than those of any other thinker of his time, accord in a general way with the functional view of the present day.

Knowledge through the senses. Concerning the source of knowledge, Comenius left no doubt as to his point of view. The five senses are "the gateways to man's soul." He accepted the old common-sense doctrine "There is nothing in the intellect which was not previously in the senses" (*Nihil in intellectu quod non prius in sensu*). This doctrine formed the basis of the principles of method which he applied in the school of infancy and in the vernacular school.

Imagination. This faculty is the inner sense, just as seeing and hearing are the outer senses. It develops from sensibility and is indispensable for the further development of the child's knowledge and spiritual being.

Memory and formal discipline. Memory is important in the education of the young; but teachers had relied upon it too much and, as a result, instruction had become a mere cramming process. Comenius clung to the popular fallacy that the memory can be developed and strengthened through practice. On this point he quoted Vives:[11]

> The memory should be exercised in early youth, since practice develops it, and we should therefore take care to practice it as much as possible. Now, in youth, the labor is not felt, and thus the memory develops without any trouble and becomes very retentive.

In this connection, it must be said, Comenius believed firmly in formal discipline. But he had the wisdom to discern that, before anything is

[11] *Ibid.*, p. 304.

committed to memory, there must be a "clear, firm, and true impression on the senses"; and again, that nothing must be memorized which has not previously been fully discussed and clearly understood. Writing, pictures, and repetition fix impressions more permanently in memory and are constantly to be employed. For this purpose he advised the greater use of blackboards, diagrams, and other similar means. Finally, it must be stated that only the most important things were to be memorized.

Reason or understanding. This faculty, according to the psychological views of Comenius, "measures and determines, what, where, and how far anything should be sought after or avoided." He does not assign to reason a function so high as is usually given to it; yet he valued it more than did the schools of his day. The faculty of judgment has as its function to utilize the materials brought to the mind through the senses and the imagination. Judgment emerges especially during the adolescent years of life when reflection and reasoning are the nascent developments.

Emotions and will. Comenius was greatly in advance of his time in recognizing the prime importance of the emotions of children and in diagnosing their relation to the process of education. This aspect of child nature had never before received sympathetic consideration. In his insisttence upon interest, attention, and sense of need in connection with everything to be learned, he anticipated present-day theories. He would foster the native curiosity, or "desire to see, hear, or handle everything new." He recognized that in these emotional tendencies nature provides the inner striving after knowledge. Every study must be pursued in such a manner as to produce a real liking for it, and should continue to be pleasant and desirable. Good methods of instruction are the only means necessary to incite the desire to learn; the true teacher need not resort to artificial incentives. The desires or affections influence the will and determine the character. Thus Comenius assigned the foremost place in human experience to the will and moral nature, which form the capstone in the process of development.

Individual differences. Educational theorists from time immemorial, recognizing that all children are not alike, had insisted that they should not be treated in precisely the same manner. In spite of these numerous admonitions, schoolmasters had not learned to adapt their methods to individual differences, largely because of a lack of clear perception of the nature of the differences which characterize children, and, also, because of ignorance as to methods of dealing with them. Comenius pointed out some of the chief differences and discussed how to deal with them wisely.

Adaptation to stage of development. The principle of fitting instruction to the comprehension of the child was one of Comenius' chief contributions to educational science. He possessed extraordinary insight as to what children at each stage of development could comprehend, and what would interest them. Such information had long been known in a vague sort of way, but was still largely disregarded in school practice and textbooks. For the course of instruction that he recommended, Comenius proposed a text covering each year of school life; in each of these texts he set down, in graded order, everything suitable to the comprehension and interest of the child. He believed that development is not merely a gradual and uniform unfolding, but rather that each stage has its own dominant and nascent tendencies:[12]

> To attempt to cultivate the will before the intellect (or the intellect before the imagination, or the imagination before the faculty of sense perception), is mere waste of time. But this is what those do who teach boys logic, poetry, rhetoric, and ethics before they are thoroughly acquainted with the objects that surround them. It would be equally sensible to teach boys of two years old to dance, though they can scarcely walk.

In his conception of the stages of development, Comenius attempted, in the 17th century, to give education the scientific foundation which it has scarcely adopted at the middle of the 20th.

Learning by doing. Comenius' theory of learning is expressed very clearly in *The Great Didactic.* He believed that the increase of power comes through the exercise of particular and not of general functions. On this point he agreed with Aristotle and the modern pragmatic view:[13]

> What has to be done must be learned by practice. Artisans do not detain their apprentices with theories, but set them to do practical work at an early stage; thus they learn to forge by forging, to carve by carving, to paint by painting, and to dance by dancing. In schools, therefore, let the students learn to write by writing, to talk by talking, to sing by singing, and to reason by reasoning.

It is clear, however, that he would not agree with the pragmatic or the progressive philosophy in all respects.

---

[12] *Ibid.,* p. 409.
[13] *Ibid.,* p. 347.

THE CURRICULUM

Pansophic curriculum. The curriculum proposed by Comenius is encyclopedic in scope. Everyone is "to know all things, to do all things, and to say all things." Every subject appears in the course of study of each level of the schools.[14]

> There is nothing in Heaven or Earth, or in the Waters, nothing in the Abyss under the earth, nothing in the Human body, nothing in the Soul, nothing in Holy Writ, nothing in the Arts, nothing in Economy, nothing in Polity, nothing in the Church of which the little candidates of Wisdom shall be wholly ignorant.

In the 20th century nobody in his right senses would hazard such a suggestion, and even three hundred years ago it was a palpable exaggeration. However, modifications render the suggestion somewhat more reasonable. First of all, Comenius did not intend that the details of each subject should be fully mastered, but merely that the outlines, or principal ideas, should be learned. Furthermore, by a careful grading of the materials and by the application of better methods of instruction, he confidently expected to advance the pupils far beyond what the schools were teaching.

Although it is not necessary to list all the subjects of study which he advocated, a few of his more revolutionary suggestions may well be mentioned. So far as languages are concerned, he urged less attention to Latin, Greek, and Hebrew than was the custom, but exalted the vernacular, and, what is particularly worthy of note, he advocated the study of modern foreign languages "for the sake of holding intercourse with neighbors."

The charge has been made that Comenius was in reality not a Latin scholar. He freely admitted the justification of this criticism. The fact is, Comenius was in no sense a genuine Humanist, though he wrote texts to facilitate the learning of the Latin tongue. He did not thrill to the charm of Ciceronian eloquence and did not reverence classical literature. For a memory well-stocked with the brilliant phrases of classical orators, he had only contempt. Furthermore, he flatly denied the supreme claim of Humanism, the moral value of pagan literature. The truth is that he wished to boot the entire pack of classical writers out of the schoolroom, and he desired to do this in the interest of the moral and spiritual wel-

---

[14] Laurie, S. S., *op. cit.*, pp. 199-200.

fare of the pupils. Regarding the classical writers he declared: [15] "If we wish our schools to be truly Christian schools, the crowd of Pagan writers must be removed from them." Again, he said: [16]

> Some one else may object: "They are not all lascivious writers. Cicero, Virgil, Horace, and others are serious and earnest." I answer: None the less, they are blind pagans, and turn the minds of their readers from the true God to other gods and goddesses.

Finally relenting to a slight degree, Comenius admitted that such moralists as Seneca, Epictetus, Plato, and even the other writers, may be read by Christians who are sufficiently established in faith so that their morals will not be corrupted. As a matter of fact, Ratich, Alsted, Andreä, and Comenius agreed that all sciences must be in harmony with the Holy Scriptures.

The Latin language as well as the vernacular was to be employed in learning the trivial and quadrivial subjects: grammar, rhetoric, dialectic, arithmetic, geometry, astronomy, and music. In addition, Comenius included physics, geography, chronology, history, morals, and religion. For history he had extraordinary regard: [17]

> An acquaintance with history is the most important element in a man's education, and is, as it were, the eye of his whole life. This subject, therefore, should be taught in each of the six classes, that our pupils may be ignorant of no event which has happened from ancient times to the present day.

Comenius insisted upon the manual arts and industry in connection with the vernacular school. In the interests of happiness and health, Comenius advocated plenty of physical activity and play.

The kindly bishop looked upon children not only with a discerning but also with an indulgent eye. He was wholly free from that carping spirit, so common among puritanic theologians who believed the sports, games, and plays of childhood were due to the presence of human depravity. He was the first to understand that the play-life of the child is nature's method of building a healthy, vigorous body and a normal, keen mind.

Comenius revealed his most unique insight when he urged the development of the sense of humor or wit as a means of education. No other

---

[15] Keatinge, M. W., *op. cit.*, p. 383.
[16] *Ibid.*, p. 395.
[17] *Ibid.*, p. 432.

educator has gone quite so far in his declaration that children "ought to be taught, and that thoroughly, to understand what is said in a joke." Moreover, humor is not to be indulged merely for idle fun, but it should be employed "for the purpose of sharpening their intellects." [18]

Useful knowledge only. The Baconian principle of utility dominated the progressive thinking of the 17th century. Comenius too, in spite of his encyclopedic interests and his theological conceptions, demanded only useful knowledge.[19]

> Nothing should be learned solely for its value at school, but for its use in life.... Whatever is taught should be taught as being of practical application in every-day life and of some definite use. That is to say, the pupil should understand that what he learns is not taken out of some Utopia or borrowed from Platonic Ideas, but is one of the facts which surround us, and that a fitting acquaintance with it will be of great service in life.

Although such quotations emphasizing the principle of usefulness are abundant in the writings of Comenius and of his contemporaries, it must not be concluded that he was, therefore, a low utilitarian. The "useful," or "practical," has a broad interpretation in his thinking; the term comprehends everything "of undoubted use in this world and in the world to come." Nature produces nothing that is useless. Consequently, all facts are of value, but, in teaching it is essential that the instructor should show the pupil wherein they are of use.

Method. "Comenius is to be regarded as the true founder of modern method," says Professor Laurie.[20] A few years ago an American educational publisher wrote of *The Great Didactic:*[21]

> I do not believe a more practically helpful treatise on method was ever published; certainly there is no other at once so broad and sound and suggestive.

Comenius' interest in method was born of bitterest grief over the memory of his own wasted years, which, he testified, had "wrung sighs from my breast, drawn tears from my eyes, and filled my heart with sorrow." [22]

---

[18] Monroe, Will S., *Comenius' School of Infancy*, p. 41. Boston: D. C. Heath, 1896.

[19] Keatinge, M. W., *op. cit.*, p. 341.

[20] Laurie, S. S., *op. cit.*, p. 222.

[21] Bardeen, C. W., Preface to Laurie's *John Amos Comenius.*

[22] Keatinge, M. W., *op. cit.*, p. 232.

He described the methods used in the schools of his boyhood as follows:[23]

> The method used . . . has generally been so severe that schools have been looked on as terrors for boys and slaughter-houses of minds in which the great number of the students have contracted a dislike for learning. For five, ten, or more years they detained the mind over matters that could be mastered in one. What could have been gently instilled into the intellect, was violently impressed upon it, nay, rather stuffed and flogged into it.

The great purpose of Comenius so far as method was concerned was to find how instruction might be imparted (1) "surely and thoroughly," (2) "certainly and clearly," and (3) "easily and pleasantly." These same terms had been used by Andreä and remind one of the criteria of knowledge set up by Descartes.

In his observations of nature, Comenius saw many operations that by analogy suggested principles of instruction. He used such analogical material in great profusion. A few examples may be given:

(*a*) *Nature observes a suitable time.* The birds hatch their eggs in the spring, and the gardener plants his seeds at that season. From this, Comenius drew the principle that "the education of men should be commenced in the Spring time of life."

(*b*) *Nature prepares the material before she begins to give it form.* In the schools the study of form should precede the learning of subject matter. For illustration, languages are taught before the sciences, which is to teach expression before the child has knowledge to express. The method of nature proceeds differently; it teaches things and language together.

(*c*) *In all the operations of nature, development is from within.* A subject should be thoroughly understood by the child before he is called upon to memorize any definitions. Grammar is the most striking example of the application of this new method.

(*d*) *Nature, in its formative processes, begins with the universal and ends with the particular.* In instruction, the large, simple, general elements come first; details follow.

(*e*) *Nature makes no leaps, but proceeds step by step.* A chicken develops slowly and without sudden changes. So all studies should be carefully graded by minute steps.

---

[23] *Ibid.*, pp. 229-230.

(*f*) *Nature compels nothing to advance that is not driven forward by its own mature strength.* "Nothing should be taught to the young, unless it is not only permitted but actually demanded by their age and mental strength."

There are many more such analogical principles. It is clear that they have little if any value for modern educational thought. Comenius was unfortunate in having an inadequate understanding of psychology.

Everything through the senses. This is one of the fundamental principles which Comenius frequently repeated. He was the first thoroughly consistent Sense-Realist. Vives, as indicated in an earlier chapter, preceded him in the statement of this principle, and Comenius frankly avowed his indebtedness. But he is even more emphatic than Vives. Comenius referred to Aristotle's comparison of the mind of man to a blank tablet, and he compared "the brain, the workshop of thought, to wax," which receives impressions made upon it. The sense organs are the means through which impressions of things are made upon the mind.[24]

> Whatever makes an impression on my organs of sight, hearing, smell, taste or touch, stands to me in relation of a seal by which the image of the object is impressed upon my brain.

He would not countenance the employment of substitutes for things:[25]

> Those things, therefore, that are placed before the intelligence of the young, must be real things, and not the shadows of things. I repeat, they must be *things;* and by the term I mean determinate, real, and useful things that can make an impression on the senses and on the imagination. . . .
>
> From this a golden rule for teachers may be derived. Everything should, as far as is possible, be placed before the senses. . . . The commencement of knowledge must always come from the senses (for the understanding possesses nothing that it has not first derived from the senses).

If the thing is not available, representations may be used. The walls of the room should be hung with pictures, and books should be full of them. Charts, maps, drawings, diagrams, models, engravings, and other apparatus should be freely employed. It is astonishing that a principle

[24] *Ibid.*, p. 197.
[25] *Ibid.*, pp. 336-337.

so fully expounded in the 17th century should have remained unheeded for almost two hundred years. Visual instruction really began with this doctrine of Comenius.

Grading of subject matter. So far as subject matter is concerned, Comenius was the first to apply a system of grading on the basis of psychological ability. The failure of teachers to understand the minds of children led them to foist upon their pupils the rules and principles of grammar, rhetoric, logic, and other subjects which they could memorize but were incapable of comprehending. Comenius discerned the trouble and he complained:[26]

> No fixed landmarks were set up, which might serve as goals to be reached by the scholars at the end of each year, month, or day, and there was a complete lack of system.

The method of nature must be followed, for she makes no sudden leaps, but proceeds step by step: all studies should, therefore, be graduated in such a way that those coming first may prepare the way for and throw light upon those that follow. The laws which govern grading are as follows: nature advances from the whole to its parts, from what is easy to what is more difficult, from the simple to the complex, and from the concrete to the abstract.

Everything without compulsion. The common use of the rod to force children to learn is clear evidence of the unfortunate lack of true educational insight in that day. Against this crude and cruel method Comenius threw the full weight of his power:[27]

> No blows should be given for lack of readiness to learn; for if the pupil does not learn readily, this is the fault of no one but the teacher, who either does not know how to make his pupil receptive of knowledge, or does not take the trouble to do so.

This was an entirely new attitude, which schoolmasters were quite incapable of appreciating. Comenius would not require anything by force. To induce the child to learn he relied implicitly upon the propulsion of inner desires, interests, and the instinctive curiosity of the pupil. Nature, he believed, had implanted the seeds of knowledge, virtue, and piety in the child, and these potentialities are compelled by inner force to develop just as an acorn under the proper conditions will burgeon into

---

[26] *Ibid.*, p. 313.
[27] *Ibid.*, p. 291.

an oak. Those who drive boys to studies do them great injury.[28] "A rational creature should be led, not by shouts, imprisonment and blows, but by reason. Any other method is an insult to God, in whose image all men are made." The school should be a pleasant and happy place. The intellect should be forced to nothing for which it does not have a natural bent. Learning should always be made attractive.

Socialization. In many of his principles Comenius was in advance not only of his own day but of the present time also. Thus he advocated the advantage of encouraging pupils to tell others what they have learned. He was well aware that teaching others is an excellent means of clarifying and fixing what one is learning. Of this practice he said: "Whatever has been learned should be communicated by one pupil to the other that no knowledge may remain unused." Again he quoted Fortius to the effect that, if a student wishes to make progress, he should arrange to give lessons daily in the subject which he is studying, even if it is necessary to hire the pupil. In this principle Comenius recognized knowledge and expression as coördinates which must always proceed together, for knowledge is a social commodity, and is most readily acquired when a need is felt to communicate it to others.

He approved the plan of forming classes and the school as a whole into "a republic, its senate and proctor, which will hold sessions occasionally, and pronounce judgment on conduct."[29] In this manner he would train the individual for self-government and social life. His Latin school at Sárospatak was organized as a Latin republic.

Integration or correlation. Another fundamental principle which Comenius recognized is that of properly combining, or integrating the materials that are learned. It was customary in the elementary schools to teach children to read, but they were not taught to write until many months later. In the Latin schools of Comenius' day, boys had always spent years learning words without knowing their meanings. Moreover, grammar was pursued for a long time as the major study with no relation to literature.

Comenius was of the opinion that no sense or faculty should be brought into action by itself; rather, he charged: "Let every sense be engaged in the perception" of the object.[30]

---

[28] *Ibid.*, p. 208.
[29] Laurie, S. S., *op. cit.*, p. 204.
[30] Keatinge, M. W., *op. cit.*, p. 291.

> The sense of hearing should always be conjoined with that of sight, and the tongue should be trained in combination with the hand. The subjects that are taught should not merely be taught orally, and thus appeal to the ear alone, but should be pictorially illustrated and thus develop the imagination by the help of the eye. . . . It is desirable to represent pictorially on the walls of the classroom everything that is treated of in the class, by putting up either precepts and rules or pictures and diagrams illustrative of the subject taught.

"The senses (hearing, and seeing), the tongue and the hand; or the senses, the memory, the imagination, and the understanding," should be "daily exercised in conjunction." Words and things, style and thought should likewise be correlated.

From the known to the unknown. It is hard nowadays to realize how much children at that time had to learn by rote without any understanding of the meaning of what they memorized. This fault was particularly true of the instruction in Latin. The little fellows were made to learn words and long passages which were just so many nonsense syllables to them. It was not until the 17th century that men like Ratich and Comenius pointed out the supreme folly of this procedure. The latter declared it was wrong "to teach the unknown through the medium of that which is equally unknown."

Avoiding confusion in the child's mind. Comenius was afraid that the methods pursued were producing confusion in the child's mental growth. To avoid this danger, he recommended a number of principles. One, and only one, text is to be used in a subject. Many texts for young children lead to distraction of mind. One, and only one, teacher is to be in charge of a class. The whole class is to have the same exercises. All languages are to be taught by the same method.

Textbooks and other writings. As a writer of books and pamphlets, Comenius was indefatigable in his efforts and most versatile in subject matter. His works may be classified under three heads: (1) those which treat of educational principles; (2) textbooks and other helps for schoolroom instruction; and (3) miscellaneous works. This third class included religious works, such as sermons, church histories, devotional books, commentaries, hymnals, catechisms, translations, and works of prophecy. These productions reveal exalted devoutness of motive, but some of them indicate mental aberrations, induced probably by belief in the revelations and prophecies of fanatic religionists who artfully duped him.

Comenius' most important contribution to educational thought was *The Great Didactic* (*Didactica Magna*). It was originally written in the Czech language, and later translated into Latin and published in Amsterdam in 1657. The other works of greatest historic merit were *The School of Infancy* (*Schola Infantiae*) and the *World in Pictures* (*Orbis Pictus*).

In many respects *The Great Didactic* is the most remarkable treasury of pedagogical wisdom ever written. Its complete title is: [31]

THE GREAT DIDACTIC

Setting forth
The Whole Art of Teaching all
Things to all Men

or

A certain Inducement to found such Schools in all the Parishes, Towns, and Villages of every Christian Kingdom, that the entire Youth of both Sexes,
None being excepted, shall,

Quickly, Pleasantly, Thoroughly

Become learned in the Sciences, pure in Morals,
Trained in Piety, and in this manner Instructed in all things necessary
for the present and for
the future life.

> Let the main object of this, our *Didactic,* be as follows: To seek and to find a method of instruction, by which teachers may teach less, but learners may learn more, by which schools may be the scene of less noise, aversion, and useless labour, but of more leisure, enjoyment, and solid progress; and through which the Christian community may have less darkness, perplexity, and dissension, but on the other hand, more light, orderliness, peace, and rest.

Comenius diligently searched every author, and quizzed every educational reformer, for fruitful ideas. But not only did he borrow from other men; he was a restless and resourceful observer and a creative thinker himself. He took a profound interest in nature in all its varied operations. Most important of all, he caught the genetic point of view, and thus anticipated many ideas of the later centuries. Down to his day no one had been so observant of the growth, ideas, activities, and developments

---

[31] *Ibid.*, pp. 156-157.

of childhood. His shrewd insight repeatedly amazes the reader. All of his principles find analogy in the processes of nature, such as the growth of trees, plants, and the human body; and then again, in the operations of printers, builders, watchmakers, and artists.

The School of Infancy shows remarkable insight into the education of children from birth to six years of age. Comenius goes into quite minute details.

Strange to say, these wonderful treatises on education mouldered unknown in the dust for two centuries. As Keatinge says:[32] "For all the result they might as well have perished in the flames at Lissa." The textbooks, on the contrary, "frequently reprinted, were thumbed for years to come by boys in every corner of Europe."

Comenius' textbook productions included several introductory texts in Latin, lexicons, grammars, and readers. The age demanded a new method by which young boys could learn the Latin language in shorter time and with greater ease. Ratich and many others had attempted to meet this universal need, but with more boasting than genuine success. Comenius was aware of these attempts and, in 1631, printed the *Gate of Tongues Unlocked* (*Janua Linguarum Reserata*), in which he skillfully arranged all the principal words of the Latin language in twelve hundred sentences. Each important word was used only once. Because this work did not suit him, several years later he brought out the *Vestibule to the Gate of Tongues Unlocked* (*Januae Linguarum Reseratae Vestibulum*). In this work he aimed to simplify and grade the instruction in Latin: to teach words through things, and then to teach things through words. This text enjoyed great success and was translated into many languages; but, successful as it proved to be, he made another attempt to secure a more scientific introduction to the Latin tongue. This work was his celebrated *Orbis Pictus,* or *World in Pictures.*

The special interest attaching to this text lies in the fact that Comenius, having worked out a concise Latin vocabulary, used pictures together with the words to impress the memory of the child, and to give him a knowledge of Latin in the quickest possible way. The use of pictures in textbooks and other works was not absolutely new, as some historians have thought. It had, moreover, been urged by such men as Andreä and Lubinus. However, as a psychological instrument for learning Latin words more easily, it was a striking innovation.

---

[32] *Ibid.,* p. 98.

(3)

Cornix cornicatur, The *Crow* crieth.	à à	A a
Agnus balat, The *Lamb* blaiteth.	b è è è	B b
Cicàda stridet, The *Grasshopper* chirpeth.	cì cì	C c
Upupa dicit, The *Whooppoo* saith.	du du	D d
Infans ejulat, The *Infant* crieth.	è è è	E e
Ventus flat, The *Wind* bloweth.	fi fi	F f
Anser gingrit, The *Goose* gagleth.	ga ga	G g
Os halat, The *Mouth* breatheth out.	hà'h hà'h	H h
Mus mintrit, The *Mouse* chirpeth.	ì ì ì	I i
Anas tetrinnit, The *Duck* quaketh.	kha, kha	K k
Lupus ululat, The *Wolf* howleth.	lu ulu	L
Ursus murmurat, The *Bear* grumbleth.	[mum mum-	M

ORBIS PICTUS, PAGE 3.
(English Version)

(79)

The Carpenter. **LXIV.** **Faber lignarius.**

We have seen Man's food	Hominis victum & ami-
and clothing: now his	ctum, vidimus: sequitur
Dwelling followeth.	nunc Domicilium ejus.
At first they dwelt	Primò habitabant
in *Caves*, 1. then in	in *Specubus*, 1. deinde in
Booths or *Huts*, 2.	*Tabernaculis* vel *Tuguriis*, 2.
and then again in *Tents*, 3.	tum etiam in *Tentoriis*, 3.
at the last in *Houses*.	demum in *Domibus*.
The *Woodman*	*Lignator*
felleth and heweth down	sternit & truncat
Trees, 5. with an *Ax*, 4.	*Arbores*, 5. *Securi*, 4.
the *Boughs*, 6. remaining.	remanentibus *Sarmentis*, 6.
He cleaveth *Knotty Wood*	Findit *Nodosum*,
with a *Wedge*, 7.	*Lignum Cuneo*, 7.
which he forceth in	quem adigit
with a *Beetle*, 8.	*Tudite*, 8.
and maketh *Wood-stacks*, 9.	& componit *Strues*, 9.
The *Carpenter*	*Faber Lignarius*
squareth *Timber*	ascit *Ascia*, 10.
with a *Chip-Ax*, 10.	*Materiem*,

ORBIS PICTUS, PAGE 79.

The success and failure of Comenius. Two authorities have summed up the effect of the ideas and works of Comenius, and both of them are highly sympathetic in their judgments. Keatinge, an English scholar, says:[33]

> The man whom we unhesitatingly affirm to be the broadest-minded, the most far-seeing, the most comprehensive, and withal the most practical of all the writers who have put pen to paper on the subject of education, Comenius, we say, the prince of schoolmasters, produced practically no effect on the school organization and educational development of the following century.

Laurie, a Scotch educator, states:[34]

> When we consider, then, that Comenius first formally and fully developed educational method, that he introduced important reforms into the teaching of languages, that he introduced into the schools the study of Nature, that he advocated with intelligence, and not on purely sentimental grounds, a milder discipline, we are justified in assigning to him a high, if not the highest, place among modern educational writers.

From these statements it is clear that Comenius furnishes the educational historian a strange enigma. His textbooks, which embodied his principles of method, attained extraordinary popularity. His curricular recommendations, though somewhat extravagant and grandiose, were nevertheless in harmony with the new trend of reform in subject matter. But his general scheme of reform met only with the coldest reception and was speedily consigned to oblivion.

What were the reasons for this striking success on the one hand, and the stark failure on the other? To say that Comenius was ahead of his age, as many do, is to beg the question. Most writers are content to blame the horrors of the Thirty Years' War. To be sure, this tragedy, which practically wiped out civilization in large areas of Germany, played its part; but it must be remembered that wars are invariably followed by changes in education, and that many changes actually took place after this war. Keatinge offers a different and more plausible explanation. Comenius was subject to a fanatical belief in prophetic revelations. His credulity was childish, and he permitted himself to be duped by several utterly irresponsible creatures. He not only accepted

---

[33] *Ibid.*, p. 98.
[34] Laurie, S. S., *op. cit.*, p. 224.

as divinely revealed their prophecies but even induced his coreligionists to act upon them. Then, Keatinge adds:[35]

> Imagine the effect produced, when eight months after Comenius' death, Drabik formally retracted all the prophecies and went over to the Roman Catholic faith. The reaction was terrible.

Undoubtedly this reaction was discrediting. But we have not yet penetrated to the chief reason for the failure of his age to evaluate Comenius' noble conceptions of education. He represented a despised sect, persecuted and dispossessed of land and exiled from country. For a long time this sect resisted all government authority, practiced Christian communism, and was strongly opposed to aristocracy. They declined to admit into their fellowship any of the nobility until they renounced their titles and power. Comenius' program of education was democratic to an extreme and urged the wiping out of class distinctions. In an age that believed in the divine right of kings and gave them autocratic power, such a school system was anathema. This is sufficient explanation to account for the consigning of his ideas to the grave. As the first major prophet of the modern age he suffered the usual fate that befalls men of farflung vision.

---

[35] Keatinge, M. W., *op. cit.*, pp. 98-99.

Chapter 8

EDUCATIONAL PROGRESS IN THE FIRST HALF OF THE 17TH CENTURY

THE spirit of the 17th century. Behind the fanatical religious and civil wars that raged in the chief theaters of western Europe, three spirits were contending to replace the traditional Humanism in the minds of men: Baconian realism, Calvinism, and Cartesian rationalism. These integrated in various degrees with the interest in the ancient literatures. The most encyclopedic mind of the age was the Moravian Bishop, John Amos Comenius, who combined evangelicism, realism, and linguistic traditionalism with a background of Christian socialism. The English Puritans combined Calvinism with something of realism and a strong interest in languages. The new Catholic education integrated the Augustinian theology with the rationalism of Descartes.

ENGLISH REFORMERS

The educational reformers. During this period several writers combined the realistic tendencies of Bacon with the educational ideas of Comenius. The dynamic center of the groups was Samuel Hartlib and the most notable of the collaborators were John Dury and Sir William Petty. They pursued a common policy which included universal literacy, teaching of practical subjects, scientific research, engineering, and industrial training. They believed that education is the supreme means for improving humanity, and held that it is the duty of the state directly to provide schools.

Samuel Hartlib (1600-1670). Son of a rich Polish merchant and an English mother, Hartlib settled in England in 1628, where he was to exercise an extraordinary influence for the advancement of educational theory, and, in his zeal, bankrupt himself. He was the go-between who brought Comenius to the attention of the English people and induced Parliament to invite him to come to London to reform education. The project failed because of trouble in Ireland. Hartlib's services, however, were so meritorious that Parliament under Cromwell rewarded him with a generous pension.

Despite the fact that he was engaged in a business enterprise, Hartlib became a prolific writer and promoter. He wrote and translated a number of books and pamphlets, published works others had written, and induced still others to write on education. In connection with his proposal to establish an Academy for the Gentry, John Milton wrote his tractate *Of Education* (1644). Among other works written at his suggestion were Dury's *Reformed Schools,* Petty's proposals for the advancement of education, and two progressive pamphlets by Hezekiah Woodward. His boundless admiration for Comenius led to the publication of a number of treatises and translations to spread a knowledge of the ideas of the great Czech educator. His most memorable production was *A Description of the Famous Kingdom of Macaria,* a plan for a utopian state.

The reforms which Hartlib discussed touched the crucial issues of his day. He proposed to procure "ecclesiastical peace among Protestants" for he saw that religious antagonism was the greatest barrier to progress. His greatest proposal for the advancement of prosperity was the establishment by Parliament of what he termed "Office of Address." This was a government bureau which was to perform many functions. It was to be a bureau of labor, an employment agency for the poor, a bureau of information, an office for promoting better relations among religious bodies, an agency for the advancement of learning in accordance with the proposals of Bacon, an office for the dissemination of information about inventions, and an office of international relations to keep scholars informed as to the progress of inventions and scientific discoveries and improvements in other countries. Finally, it was to be the agency of public education.

Hartlib was profoundly interested in horticulture, agriculture, and animal husbandry, on each of which he published a treatise.

He was indefatigable in pushing measures for educational reform, and insisted that the state be responsible for teaching every child. In 1647 he published *Considerations Tending to the Happy Accomplishment of England's Reformation in Church and State.* In this he insisted that it was the duty of the magistrates "to see schools opened, provided with teachers, endowed with maintenance, regulated with constitutions." He warned that "Without the reform of schools no other work of Reformation will be effectual." He was interested in better methods of teaching languages and in 1656 published *A True and Ready Way to Learn the Latin Tongue.*

It is doubtful whether England ever harbored anyone who had her interests more at heart or expended himself more disinterestedly for her educational welfare. But a state supported, public controlled system of education was contrary to the English tradition of education as a family matter. Again, he advocated schools for "all ages and qualities of scholars" and this conflicted with her society of classes.

Hezekiah Woodward (1590-1675). No Puritan schoolmaster excelled Woodward in enthusiasm for Comenius and realistic methods of instruction. He was a friend of Hartlib to whom he dedicated a pamphlet, *A Light to Grammar and all other Arts and Sciences* (1641). Another pamphlet was *A Gate to Science.* Woodward was a thoroughgoing sense realist. He contended "Teachers should make their words as legible to children as pictures are, for next to Nature, pictures are the most intelligible books that children can look upon."

He believed all of grammar could be taught children by this realistic method. If it goes into the child at "the gates of the senses, all sciences will follow by the same light and at the same doors." He was also interested in discovering the nature of the mind of the child. Teachers, he charged, had thought only of subject matter. He undertook to bring learning down to the level of the child. Language and grammar should be taught by the direct method with plenty of illustrations and explanations.

John Dury (1596-1680). Dury was a Puritan clergyman, who, like Ratich, Comenius, and Hartlib, wanted to abate sectarian antagonism and unite all Protestants in Europe into one body. At the request of Hartlib, he wrote a pamphlet entitled *Reformed Schools* (1650) in which he combined the Puritan ideal of godliness with the practicality of Bacon and the pedagogical principles of Comenius. He undertook to subordinate the learning of languages to the practical arts and sciences. He believed that there are three sources of knowledge: sense, tradition, and reason, but everything must begin with sense perception. Teaching must be adapted to the mental capacity of the child. Formal education should not begin before nine years of age. The curriculum of the elementary school is to be enriched, and to become encyclopedic in the more advanced work. Common schools and training for industry, business, public service, and the professions must be at public expense.

John Milton (1608-1674). Urged by his friend, Samuel Hartlib, Milton, the great English poet, wrote a celebrated tractate entitled *Of Education,* published in 1644. He was a strict Humanist of the old type, and one of the most erudite men of his day. He was educated at St. Paul's and Christ College, Cambridge; and, as was the custom, completed his education by a tour of the Continent. He is further identifiable as a Puritan and a member of Parliament. He taught a private school for boys in London for some years. What went on in this home-school has unfortunately not been recorded.

Three contributions of the greatest consequence to education and life generally must be credited to Milton's honor. First, he advocated in his tractate the establishing of a system of academies which were to supplant training given in the existing Latin grammar schools and universities. One, at least, of these institutions was to be conducted in each city. He succeeded in persuading the Puritans to establish these academies, which became the chief seminaries of learning in England for more than a century.

Second, in the field of religion and government, Milton made a contribution of greatest consequence to modern society in defense of toleration, human liberty, and freedom of speech. But a third contribution of enormous importance to the enrichment of life came from his pen. Although he did not appreciate fully the cultural possibilities of the teaching of English literature, he greatly promoted its study by writing masterpieces which are among the classical literature of western civilization.

Milton's heart and will were with Geneva and no one has stated the Calvinistic educational aim with greater clarity and precision. His tie with Genevan theology was quite direct, and not merely through the mediation of secondary sources. In two glowing sentences, he etched on the page of history the Puritan educational ideal:[1]

> The end then of learning is to repair the ruins of our first parents by regaining to know God aright, and out of that knowledge to love him, to imitate him, to be like him, as we may the nearest by possessing our souls of true virtue, which being united to the heavenly grace of faith makes up the highest perfection....
>
> I call, therefore, a complete and generous education, that which fits a

---

[1] Milton, John, *Of Education,* pp. 97, 102. London: Thomas Dring, 1673.

man to perform justly, skillfully, and magnanimously all the offices, both private and public, of peace and war.

Milton's mind, however, was with the realists. He taught the sons of Hartlib and held his ideas in such esteem that he dedicated the tractate *Of Education* to him. Moreover, his choice of curriculum was broadly realistic. Latin and Greek were to be the languages taught, but the curriculum he proposed was encyclopedic in scope. Milton was a humanistic realist who used the ancient authors to teach science and morality. From the ancient classics boys were to learn agriculture, geography, history, physiology, politics, ethics, education, law, government, medicine, and architecture. They were in addition to master riding, fencing, wrestling, sailing, music, and military arts and science (tactics and fortification). All ancient and modern authors were to be utilized along each line.

The earliest form of training from 12 years of age onward embraced grammar, arithmetic, geometry, and religion in Latin; all designed to inspire the youth with a lofty ambition to excel and to give themselves ardently to study. The advanced course included agriculture, history, geography, Greek, astronomy, physics, trigonometry, fortification, architecture, engineering, navigation, and medicine.

Authorities in all practical fields were to assist by relating their experiences in these fields. The ancient poets were to be studied, followed by concentration on the writers on morals and on Scriptures until the students are "perfect in the knowledge of personal duty." Greek, Latin, and Italian tragedies were to be studied with great industry. Politics was to be learned from the ancient writers and on down to English law. Theology was to be studied on Sundays and every evening; and Italian was to be sandwiched in along the years "at any odd hour."

Only a genius would set up a curriculum as comprehensive as this: and only for minds of the highest order. All students were to go on excursions to various points in England to learn facts of use in national defense, government, and commerce. But mature young men alone were to complete their education by a tour of the Continent.

What limitations are found in Milton's comprehensive coverage of human interests and knowledge? In subject matter slight attention is accorded metaphysics, and logic is not stressed. Only education from 12 to 21 got his attention; the elementary field, and the enlightenment of the masses were not within Milton's interest.

Sir William Petty (1623-1687). Petty had eminent talents, practiced between 15 and 20 professions in his 64 years, and was knighted for his great contributions. One would not call him a school man, but he influenced schools in several important ways; and he assisted in forming the Royal Society.

Petty's chief work on education, *Advice of W. P. to Mr. Samuel Hartlib for the Advancement of Some Particular Parts of Learning* (1647-1648), proposed three kinds of school. First, the "Literary workhouse" (*Ergastulum Literarium*), or common school, to be attended by all children, who were to learn to read, write, and practice some trade. A trade would help one to make a living and to be industrious, and would give healthful recreation and understanding of how to deal with artisans. Second, a higher "Colledge of Tradesmen" (*Gymnasium Mechanicum*) for the advancement of all the mechanical arts and manufactures. The history of arts, design, invention, and research were the chief lines of instruction. In this way workmen were to be assisted so that they could perfect their craftmanship. Third, an Academy for all knowledge (*Nosocomium Academicum*) which, like a modern university, was to include museums of every kind, an observatory, a library, an aquarium, art galleries, and laboratories. It was to be "an Abstract of the whole world." Petty, like Dury, was an ardent supporter of Hartlib's "Office of Public Address."

One can see the kind of education he advised for the aristocratic class from the directions for his son's education. He prescribed arithmetic (he was himself an expert statistician), geometry and drawing for surveying, geography, writing good Latin, history, logic, literature, law, sports, and polite accomplishments. The fact is that Petty was the typical English self-made man who achieved great success and pointed the way to others.

Charles Hoole (1610-1667). After Brinsley, Hoole was the leading school reformer and "the most important writer on contemporary school practice of the seventeenth century." He was thoroughly acquainted with the writings of Mulcaster, Ascham, Brinsley, and at least the Latin texts of Comenius, which he recommended and used. For some years Hoole taught a town grammar school, and later a private school in London. He was profoundly interested in improving methods of instruction and in the organization of schools. The problem of how to teach Latin held a particular fascination for him. For a teacher he was a prolific writer and translator, leaving in all some 24 contributions to pedagogical literature.

Among his translations were the *Colloquies of Corderius, Aesop's Fables,* and Comenius' *Orbis Pictus.* He wrote a Latin grammar and children's stories, and compiled an English-Latin vocabulary. His greatest book was *A New Discovery of the Old Art of Teaching School,* written some 23 years before it was published in 1659. This work was the product, as he stated, of his experiences as a teacher. In it he discussed the condition of the schools and methods of instruction and how he would reform them.

Hoole advocated two grades of schools: the Petty school and the grammar school; and he set forth in considerable detail the method and studies to be used in both. The practices of the Dame schools in which elderly women earned a pittance by teaching young children the alphabet and simple reading called forth his utter disapproval. Hoole was interested in how children could be educated in groups as large as five or six hundred. Children, he advised, should begin to learn the alphabet between three and four years of age, by the phonetic method. The method of teaching spelling and of reading English perfectly he admirably discussed. This task, he thought, would take two or three years. A division was most reluctantly recommended at seven or eight years of age between those who were not to receive a classical education and those who were. Hoole would have all proceed to the Latin grammar school; but if parents declined to send them, he recommended they be sent to a writing school where they would continue to learn reading, writing, arithmetic, and other arts to fit them for any ordinary calling.

A further difficulty now arose. The best Latin grammar schools generally required that boys should have a knowledge of *Accidents* (i. e., the elements of Latin grammar) before they were admitted. This preliminary training was wretchedly taught in the ordinary schools. Hoole recommended that "Petty" (i.e. for little ones) schools be endowed and that teachers with some knowledge of Latin be employed. They were, however, to teach only a few of the children the elements of Latin. This Petty school was to be divided into four forms or classes. In method Hoole accepted the new ideas of the time; he was a convinced sense realist, believed in making educational practical, in universal literacy, in the postponement of Latin to a later age, and in the use of the vernacular as a means of education. A master should teach only 40 boys. But there should be one for every form or grade.

A master would preside over the grammar school, but most of the instruction would be given by the ushers. The chief problem at this level was how to teach Latin to boys of seven and eight. The ushers taught the three forms or grades so that boys read Latin well and knew the grammar. The fourth form studied grammar to become more perfect, and began rhetoric. Ascham's method of double translation was employed. Greek was to be begun in the fifth form, and Hebrew in the sixth.

Fluctuations in governmental policy. Throughout the 17th century the English government was in an unstable condition and its educational policy vacillated. When in control of Parliament the Puritans undertook to reform education in harmony with their well-established principles. In 1641, a proposal was made to have Parliament appoint a commission to invite Comenius to England to reform education. Comenius journeyed to London, but whether he went by invitation of Parliament is not known. The plan of Hartlib and others interested in the reform of education was to set up a realistic, encyclopedic college. But conditions were too unsettled and Comenius went to Sweden. In 1649, the Commonwealth Parliament provided for the support and regulation of schools in Wales; another measure passed the same year provided for the support of ministers and schoolmasters in England and Wales out of the national revenues. When it is recalled that the first public money to be granted for the promotion of schools in England came 184 years after this law, it is realized that those who sponsored the measure were motivated by a very different philosophy of government and education than was representative of English policy.

Suppressive policy of the Stuarts. Freedom of all men to teach was upheld by the court of common pleas in England as early as 1450. But under a new law in 1603 no one was permitted to teach without a license from the bishop. This policy of control over the dissemination of ideas was vigorously resisted by dissenters. The struggle led to civil war and the execution of the King, Charles I, and the establishment of the Commonwealth government.

With the Restoration of Charles II, Parliament in a reactionary state of mind set about to crush every vestige of nonconformacy. The first measure was the Act of Uniformity (1662) which expelled all clergymen from their benefices and all teachers from their schools who refused to conform to the established church. The Five-Mile Act which followed (1665) had for its purpose the extinction of all nonconformist teaching by forbidding all dissenting pastors to teach within five miles of their pulpits.

These drastic measures affected both the established church with its monopoly of instruction, and the stubborn dissenters at whom they were aimed. Secure, as they now felt themselves to be, the Church of England clergy relaxed their efforts. The majority of them were fox-hunting squires who had interest only in their livings, despised learning, and cared nothing for religion, which was merely part of the conventional formalism of civic life. University tutors spent their time imitating the fast society of London. Lord Chesterfield wrote his son in 1749 that Cambridge "is sunk into the lowest obscurity and the existence of Oxford would not be known if it were not for the treasonable spirit publicly avowed and often excited there."

The suppression of academic freedom strangled English education for over two centuries. De Montmorency has correctely evaluated the blighting consequences upon English culture: "A more benighted and heart breaking policy was never conceived.... The schoolmaster was forbidden by law to think for himself and indeed the possibility of thought was extinguished."

CALVINISM IN SCOTLAND

Slow educational progress. Scotland, it will be recalled, became strongly Calvinistic and, following the views of John Knox, favored popular education. The General Assembly of the Scottish church petitioned Parliament in 1639 to establish schools. In 1641, the General Assembly sent to Parliament a petition asking that "every parish have a reader and a school, wherein children are to be bred in reading, writing, and the grounds of religion. . . . And where grammar schools may be had, as in burghs and other considerable places."

This overture, which was in accord with the resolution of the Synod of Dort, had no immediate effect. In 1646, the General Assembly petitioned again, and Parliament promptly passed an "act" which required that a school be set up and a schoolmaster appointed in every parish. The schools were to be supported by taxation of property, and were to be under the supervision of the Presbyteries. Scarcely had this legislation been enacted when Scotland became involved in the quarrel which led to the war with Cromwell, and the law was never put into effect. After the Restoration, all legislation between 1633 and 1660 was annulled and domination by the English was imposed. Every minister, schoolmaster, and private tutor was required to have a license from an Episcopal bishop.

The Scottish people supported the Revolution of 1688, and in 1696, the Parliament enacted legislation similar to that of 1646. A national system of schools was set up.

NEW DEVELOPMENTS IN CATHOLIC EDUCATION

New educational agencies. Education in France remained in the hands of the Catholic Church, and schools were conducted by various orders and groups of both men and women. On the Protestant side academies and colleges arose after the Genevan model but were wiped out at the Revocation in 1685. During the 16th century the University of Paris practically controlled secondary education, but in the next century the teaching orders dominated. Religious reform within the Catholic Church was still of great interest but the new force in the realm of ideas was the rationalism of Descartes.

THE ORATORY OF FRANCE

Its origin and aim. The Oratory was the first of the new teaching orders that was notable for the innovations introduced into the course of study and methods of instruction. Cardinal de Bérulle became deeply concerned at the ignorance of the parish priests and was led to organize the Oratory to conduct retreats and seminaries, and to improve the discipline and learning of the clergy. He disagreed sharply with the military type of organization adopted by the Jesuits. Because of the piety and efficiency of their instruction the order rapidly increased in numbers and influence. By the middle of the century it had colleges in all parts of France, the most noted being Juilly College, founded in 1638 for the training of French nobles.

Behind every educational movement of consequence will be found some new emphasis in philosophy. The Oratory was no exception, and in this case the philosophy was that of Descartes.

The aim remained strictly Catholic; and though secular authors were used, they were for aid to religion. Father Thomassin, the most eminent humanist of the order, endeavored to prove that Christian truth was foreshadowed in the writers of ancient Greece and Rome. Malebranche, one of the leading followers of Descartes, worked out a thoroughly orthodox philosophical system.

The educational ideas of the Oratorians were in accord with the new trends in the early part of the 17th century. The vernacular tongue was used in the first four years, and to the end of the course for lessons in history. Discipline was gentle but firm. They believed that a caress, praise, a mere threat, the promise of reward, or the fear of humiliation had greater power to motivate learning than whips.

The curriculum. The curriculum was broad, for their spirit was liberal. French, Latin, Italian, and Spanish were taught to some, if not all, pupils; and nowhere were ancient writers more loved than in the Schools of the Oratory. Latin, however, was preferred to Greek. Grammar and rhetoric were taught by realistic methods, and by the aid of the vernacular. Oral expression was more emphasized than written essays. The teaching of history was an innovation in French education; geography accompanied history, and was taught by using maps.

The Oratorians encouraged scientific curiosity. They believed in sense perception and promoted the study of physics, chemistry and anatomy, all by the aid of laboratories. Knowing their admiration for Descartes, one is not surprised that Père Lamy wrote, "I know of nothing of greater use than algebra and arithmetic." The College of Juilly as a school for young noblemen naturally offered ornamental arts, horsemanship, music, and dancing.

The Oratory conducted many schools and colleges in France, and some in Spain and the Netherlands. Their writings on education were of a high and progressive character. An honest attempt was made to integrate liberal ideas, refinement, advancing science, and Humanism within the framework of religion.

THE LITTLE SCHOOLS OF PORT ROYAL

Origin of the Port Royal movement. It is not at all difficult to analyze the dynamic interests that motivated the remarkable group known sometimes as Jansenists and sometimes as "the Solitaires of Port Royal." They were unfortunately the center of a fanatical catastrophe, but in a brief space of time they left such an abiding deposit of spiritual power that Compayré was moved to say that "Through their works, [they] have remained perhaps the best authorized exponents of French education." When it is recalled that their schools lasted less than 20 years, that their doctrines and practices were detested more violently than Protestantism, and that they were treated with far less pity and humanity than beasts, it is astonishing that they should merit mention anywhere except as an educational monstrosity.

1. The first fact to note was that two young men, Cornelius Jansen (1585-1638) and Du Vergier de Hauranne attended the University of Louvain at the beginning of the 17th century and became fast friends. At that time, a violent struggle raged between the Jesuits, who stood staunchily for Scholasticism, and the followers of the theology of St. Augustine. These two young fellows became zealous Augustinians, accepting the doctrines of human depravity, regeneration by the Holy Spirit, and predestination. Augustinianism has always acted as a powerful stimulant to all who accept it. Jansen became Bishop of Ypres, and father of an evangelical revival in the Catholic Church; Du Vergier became Abbot of Saint Cyran, and "director of consciences" especially for the solitaires of Port Royal.

2. Moral and spiritual reform within the Roman Catholic Church was the basic goal of these men, for they had come into contact with the Huguenots and desired to reform the Church; to do so they rivalled the Calvinists in denouncing the evils of the clergy. Their zeal for reform excited the opposition of the Jesuits, who sought a monopoly in directing the Roman Catholic hierarchy. They hated the Jesuits for their political machinations, their rigorous suppression of individuality, and their totalitarianism. They were as evangelical as the Calvinists but resolute to beat them with their own weapons, the doctrines of Augustine.

3. These two men and their followers accepted the logic of Ramus and the new system of philosophy of René Descartes. They became ardent admirers of Plato, and this naturally set their minds against Aristotle and the scholastic system based upon his ideas. The desire of Descartes for clear concepts was basic for all their pedagogical innovations and reforms.

4. The central burden of these reformers was their infinite zeal for the education of the young. "I wish," cried Saint Cyran, "you might read in my heart the affection I feel for children." It amounted to a consuming passion and was infectious. Nothing else so fully explains their outpouring of texts and books on education, and their devotion to their schools. Like their arch foes, the Jesuits, a century before them, and indeed all reformers of mankind, they saw in education the only instrument of abiding improvement among men.

5. Finally, they did not look to the past for their principles of character, organization, and instruction. Jansen was from Holland, the chief center of educational progress, and abreast of the times in ideas of education.

The Solitaires of Port Royal. Port Royal, located near Paris, which gave the group its name, was from the early 13th century the site of an important convent. At this time it was under the supervision of a strenuous reformer, Jacqueline Arnould, sister of the noted Jansenist theologian. Saint Cyran became father confessor of the convent. In addition to this work he drew around him a number of brilliant men who accepted the views of the Augustinian theology he shared with Jansen. They were laymen who lived a life of strictest piety, and gave their attention to teaching and writing.

Next to Saint Cyran, Antoine Arnould, a layman, was the most important of the followers of Jansenism. He was an ardent theologian and, although he never taught, he influenced education through his writings, which included, among others, *Logic, General Grammar,* and *Regulation of Studies in the Humanities.* Nicole was preëminently a moralist and author of *Port Royal Logic,* and the *Education of a Prince* (1670). Lancelot was primarily a grammarian, and his *Methods,* which treated of the teaching of Latin, Greek, Italian, and Spanish, was deservedly popular. Coustel wrote *Rules for the Education of Children;* Varet, *Christian Education;* and Jacqueline Pascal, *Regimen for Children.* De Sacy and Guyot distinguished themselves by publishing a large number of translations of classical works. Fertile as French brains have been in setting forth ideas on education, no other such group can compare with these devout and dour men, the Catholic Puritans of France.

The Little Schools of Port Royal. Saint Cyran regarded right education as "the one thing needful," for if that be attended to, he felt, most problems would be solved. While in prison because of his theological views, he encouraged the formation of the famous *Little Schools of Port Royal,* which began in 1646 and were closed by royal decree in 1661. These were Latin schools for training leaders for church and state. They were called "Little Schools" because they took but few pupils, usually about 25, and there were never in residence in one institution more than 50.

Their educational aim. The aim of Port Royal education was determined by the Augustinian doctrine that human nature is totally depraved from birth. The function of education was to transform this corrupt nature into one which was pure and holy. The aim of higher schooling was to develop strong Christian leaders who would be able to employ, in the saving of souls, all the resources of literature, science, and eloquence. The moral and spiritual welfare of pupils was uppermost. De Sacy, one of their chief teachers, wrote: "The chief end of education should be to save them [the pupils] and ourselves [the teachers] with them." Saint Cyran warned children against study for purposes of selfish advancement, and urged them to study only to be obedient and to fit themselves for the service of God.

Certain objectives of education were sought that are secondary to the supreme religious aim. The individual who is to be useful in God's service must be fully developed; his ability to speak, to think, and to act must, therefore, be cultivated. Hence, Port Royal education made use of science and literature.

The intellectual objective of the Port Royalists was not to make first class Latin or French scholars, but to call into function judgment and reflection. Books were chosen and methods used to fortify the morals rather than to improve the scholarship of the boys.

Instruction in science was but a means of training the judgment; as Nicole stated it: "The sciences should be employed only as an instrument for perfecting the reason." There was no disinterested devotion to knowledge as such; literature, history, and scientific knowledge were not pursued for their own sake. Their value lay in their use in developing just and judicious men. As followers of Descartes they desired clarity, but not profundity. They were more interested in warding off evil than in developing the capacities for knowledge. They sought prudence rather than erudition or elegance of expression.

The school organization. The moral pessimism of the Port Royalists determined the organization of their schools. Believing human nature to be inherently bad, they considered it necessary to build a wall of isolation about each individual, so that the evil nature within could have no opportunity for expression and growth, and to keep others from leading the individual into still further evil. The number of pupils was kept small purposely so that the boys might never, day or night, be without the supervision of the tutor. They demanded complete control of pupils committed to their charge, and permitted them a minimum of communication with the outside world, even with their own parents. No more than six boys were assigned to a master, and these slept in his room and were never out of his sight during the day.

Discipline. The discipline of the Little Schools was gentle; teachers controlled by persuasion, by example, and by kind compulsion. Saint Cyran exhorted his teachers in their dealings with pupils to "speak little, bear with much, and pray more." The maxim of the Port Royalists was summed up in the phrase, "Pray rather than scold." The belief that human nature was so completely corrupt moved these teachers not to severity but to profound compassion. In controlling the boys the rod was used sparingly and in extreme cases only. Pupils who exercised a bad influence were dismissed.

The Port Royal curriculum. Two ideas dominated the choice of materials of instruction. First, they must bear on the religious life; and, second, they must be clear, exact, and readily comprehended by the child. Religious books and ancient Latin works, carefully chosen, formed the staples of the Port Royal curriculum. Sound judgment and clear ideas were next in importance to sound moral practices.

The vernacular must precede Latin because children can comprehend it. The traditional procedure was well satirized by Saint Beuve: "It is to compel unfortunate children to deal with the unintelligible in order to proceed toward the unknown." They felt that mere words and obscure principles do not furnish insight into things. Pupils were thoroughly grounded in French translations of the classics. For the first time the French language was made the object of careful study. Pupils were drilled in writing French letters and narratives from their own experiences.

After learning French the pupils were taught to read Latin and Greek with understanding, and to write and speak French and Latin correctly. All useless verbiage, memory exercises, and sterile and artificial erudition were eliminated. They had no use for esthetic Humanism and Latin poetry. In the advanced work more emphasis was placed upon translation of Latin and Greek into French than upon correct Latin or Greek. The writing of Latin verses was discontinued as a school exercise; but oral exercises, reading aloud and discussing of the style and content of ancient authors were much used. There was much reading of history, both ancient and modern; and emphasis was placed upon correlating geography with it. Grammars of the French and Spanish languages were prepared by Lancelot. The Port Royalists' textbook in logic represented an advance upon the work of Ramus; it reflected clearly the method of Descartes. Nicole's discussion of the reasons for fallacious judgments resembled Bacon's treatment of the same topic. Mathematics and the sciences found places in the course of study.

The Port Royal method. Although they added little of new content to the course of study, they affected it profoundly by the methods which they introduced. They employed but few rules, and these were illustrated by a great number of examples. The Port Royalist teachers were careful to proceed from the known to the unknown; and they attempted to employ materials interesting to children. Felix Cadet stated, "The greatest merit of Port Royal is to have introduced Cartesianism into teaching."

The new pedagogy was based upon a clearer understanding of the nature of the child's mind. By the beginning of the 17th century educators knew that the intelligence of children is dependent on their senses, and that all instruction must appeal to the eye as well as the ear. The teachers of Port Royal, like Ratich and Comenius, used pictures. In geography maps and pictures of the largest cities were used. Nicole recommended the use of pictures that represent the arms, dress, and machines of the ancients, and the portraits of kings and illustrious people.

The Cartesian love of exactness and clearness led to teaching children only things they could comprehend. No word was allowed to pass without being understood. The instruction of the past had been in a tongue unknown to the child, and ideas were conveyed which were far beyond his discernment. The result was mental confusion. The grammars of Port Royal were in French; its rules were observed in the authors read and put into practice in speaking and writing. In this way grammar was simplified and a live interest was maintained.

Lancelot discussed the importance of impressing upon children the correct sound and component parts of words, before any effort was made to have pupils recognize or pronounce them. The Port Royalists saw that much of the difficulty of teaching children to read and spell arose from teaching the names of the letters rather than how they are sounded in words. It was therefore proposed "to teach children to know the letters only by the names of their real pronunciation, to name them only by natural sounds." Then, having laid through the senses a sure foundation of knowledge, the teacher must exercise the greatest care to see that children understand all they do and say. He must take precautions to make explanations full and lucid; he must question pupils, to assure himself that they understand what they have been told, and he is to encourage questions from them. Students were to exercise their reasoning powers in discussing the content and style of the authors studied.

Extinction. The reforming zeal of the Jansenists, their evangelical spirit, and especially their educational work excited furious opposition from the Jesuits, who hated all the things for which they stood. The Society induced the Pope and the French Government to condemn Jansenism in 1661, to close their schools, and to disperse the Solitaires of Port Royal. So vindictive and relentless were they that they sought in their vengeance to destroy every vestige pointing to the existence of these men.

The contributions of Port Royal. In the development of French education, the Port Royalists have an importance that is out of all proportion to the size of their order and the length of time their schools operated. Their abiding significance is due to the improvements which they effected in the teaching of languages and of logic. They made French the medium of instruction in elementary and secondary schools, and they applied Cartesian principles of thought in the organization of the course of study and in methods. Within less than half a century after the close of the Little Schools, these reforms were widely embodied in French educational practice.

CATHOLIC EFFORTS TO EDUCATE THE POOR

Charity school movement in Catholic lands. Popular education was generally neglected in Catholic Europe during the 16th and 17th centuries. Stipends and scholarships still kept open, for a limited number of poor boys, the road for advancement in the church, and occasionally prelates and other persons of wealth supported poor boys of promise at school or university. Such opportunities, however, made no real impression upon the illiteracy and ignorance of the masses; they were open, for the most part, only to poor members of influential families. There was no education to supply the needs of the laboring classes.

The motives which led, in the 17th century, to a movement that would refine the manners, tastes, and morals of the poor, and render them more competent, were charitable and religious. It was not until the late 18th century that political democracy and the study of society were to become factors for the development of popular schools.

There were in France in the 17th century many parochial schools and isolated charity schools of elementary grade poorly supported and badly taught. No provision for training teachers existed. Efforts to improve the quality of instruction in the elementary schools were, however, not altogether lacking. In 1655, there appeared a manual, *The Parish School, or the Manner of Properly Instructing Children in the Little Schools.*[2]

---

[2] Here the phrase *Little Schools* refers to elementary schools.

Father Démia, a priest of Lyons, founded, in 1666, the *Congregation of St. Charles,* an order devoted to the education of poor children in his city. This order received the special approbation of the ecclesiastical authorities, and also the support of the merchants of Lyons. Démia followed, in the main, the Catholic practice of his time, but introduced one significant innovation, the establishment of a sort of seminary for the training of teachers.

Brothers of the Christian Schools. In 1684, St. Jean-Baptiste de La Salle, Canon of Rheims, organized the *Institute of the Brothers of the Christian Schools,* the first effort of the Catholic Church to establish a common school system. The Brothers were not priests, but after 1694 they took perpetual vows. Although the order has conducted some higher institutions, its special service has been the gratuitous instruction of the poor on the elementary level.

The course of study included reading, writing, arithmetic, manners, morals, catechism, and religious observances. In the early history of the order discipline was severe, but later it became mild and gentle. Although the methods of school management and instruction of the Brothers in the 18th century had little in common with those of modern schools, they did anticipate several features of later practice. Pupils were divided into weakest, mediocre, and most capable groups; and teaching of children in classes was practiced. Writing lessons of a very practical sort were devised; pupils were required to compose letters, bills, and receipts. Monitors taught the younger pupils; and a course of study for elementary schools was created. In 1685 the Brothers established, at Rheims, the first normal school for the training of teachers.

The order gradually extended its work. Permanent organization was effected in 1717, and seven years later received full papal approval. Abolished by the French Assembly in 1792, the order was kept alive at Rome and, in 1802, resumed its work in France. It has greatly expanded its scope to include secondary and higher education, and teacher-training institutions. Its chief service is in Europe, but it has spread all over the world and gives instruction to hundreds of thousands of pupils.

CATHOLIC EDUCATION OF GIRLS

The close of the 17th century witnessed a deepening interest among Catholics in France in women's education. New teaching orders of women were founded, and there were parish schools as well. Elementary schools for girls, however, were not as numerous nor as well conducted as those for boys. Most girls of the wealthy and the aristocracy were taught at home by governesses or tutors. The chief institutions for the higher instruction of girls of the upper and middle classes were the convents, which trained both those who aspired to enter a religious order, and those who were to become wives and mothers.

In general the women of France were woefully ignorant. The Abbe Fleury stated the case as follows: [3]

> This, doubtless, will be a great paradox, that women ought to learn anything else than their catechism, sewing and different pieces of work, singing, dancing, and dressing in the fashion, and to make a fine courtesy. As things now go, this constitutes all their education.

Girls sent to convents at a tender age were so isolated from the world that they had no inkling of the facts of life. The functions of women were confined to bearing children, training them in manners and morals, and the management of the home. By the end of the 17th century a change in the status of women was apparent, especially among those of the wealthy and aristocratic classes. Some brilliant women had exhibited great learning in ancient, others in modern languages; and a few had shown creative ability of a high order. They had proved, despite the universal notion that women were lacking in intelligence and perhaps even without souls, that they had wit and a capacity to learn and to reason equal to men.

Many women became widows at an early age and were confronted not only with the problem of bringing up the family, but of managing large estates. Discerning men, seeing this situation, concluded that the feminine sex, at least of the higher class, should be enlightened so that they could perform these broader functions. Others went so far as to advise that women be enlightened on every subject. Some of these efforts to liberalize the education of women in France are so important that they must receive further attention.

Ursulines. This Order, founded by Angela Merici at Brescia in 1535, had its chief influence in France during the following century, and may be considered a good example of the modern teaching order. The Ursulines conducted numerous schools in both hemispheres. The school at Quebec was founded as early as 1639, and that at New Orleans in 1727.

---

[3] Compayré, Gabriel, *The History of Pedagogy*. Tr. by W. H. Payne, p. 214. Boston: D. C. Heath and Company, 1901.

Their aims have always been to train those girls who expect to enter an order, and to fit others for lives as wives and mothers.[4] Discipline was at once firm and gentle but intellectual training was somewhat neglected.

Port Royalist education of girls. If the men of this famous group brought about a more enlightening training for boys, the same cannot be said about the women and girls. Quite the contrary was the case, as the treatise by Jacqueline Pascal, *Regulations for the Pupils of Port Royal* (1665), shows. Discipline was not merely extreme, but unnatural. Both teachers and pupils were sequestered. Allowed to speak as little as possible and then only in a whisper, never talking to companions but only to nuns, always compelled to walk between two nuns, one in front and one behind, hands forever kept busy to prevent the mind from wandering, opposing all the natural inclinations—such was the grim remedy to counteract the total depravity of human nature, even in tender girlhood.

Fénelon. The most popular French treatise on education during the 17th century was Fénelon's *On the Education of Girls.* He was Archbishop of Cambrai and tutor to the Duke of Burgundy, heir apparent to the throne of France. For his royal pupils, he wrote *Fables,* a series of moral tales; *Dialogues of the Dead,* in which history is explained by imaginary conversations between the persons who made it; and *Télémaque,* a novel on civics designed to teach the Duke that kings exist for the good of their subjects, and not the subjects for the benefit of the kings. *Télémaque* has been one of the most popular novels, not only in France, but in French-language classes in English and American schools.

On the Education of Girls, written in 1680 for the guidance of the Duchess de Beauvillier in educating her children, was first published seven years later. The education of both women and men, Fénelon contended in this work, should be a preparation for their careers, and the proper career of a woman is motherhood. Home making is of great public importance, and girls should be trained for it as boys are educated for professions. Fénelon was opposed to the notion, fashionable at the time, that the less a woman knows the better. Girls should learn to read and write, and should study ancient and modern history to extend their knowledge and insight. Women of wealth and station should learn to manage their estates. This included training in law, in the keeping of

---

[4] Barnard, H. C., *The French Tradition in Education,* p. 64. Cambridge: Cambridge University Press, 1922.

accounts, in the manufacture of articles used in the house and on the estate, in buying and marketing agricultural products, in the management of servants, and in the performance of household tasks. Fénelon did not favor teaching girls foreign languages, though he was willing to have them study Latin.

Fénelon emphasized the importance of education in earliest childhood. The health, strength, and emotions of the young should be carefully guarded. Children should not be suppressed, but should be allowed to grow freely. Their manners should be simple, modest, direct, affectionate, and honest. Teaching that is indirect is more effective than that which is direct; instruction should not be formal. "Teach with animation: that is best learned which is learned with pleasure." Fénelon favored the home rather than the convent for the training of girls. In convents, they were kept ignorant of the world and the facts of life.

Fénelon's ideas of female education exercised an extraordinary influence. For more than a century after his death, most educated people believed that the feminine mind is different from the male and requires a different cultivation. People now accepted the idea that girls should be educated, but not in the same way as boys.

Saint Cyr. Madame de Maintenon, second wife of Louis XIV, and governess to his children, founded (1686) a school to care for 250 girls of noble birth. Saint Cyr was a boarding school, not a convent. She became so devoted to the institution that she visited it daily and directed every phase of its life.

The aim of Saint Cyr was to train girls for a woman's career as mother of a family. For some half dozen years the program of the school was unusually broad and liberal, and discipline was lax. Madame de Maintenon wrote: "I wished the girls to be witty, high spirited, and trained to think." [5] She succeeded even better than she desired and then came to reproach herself most bitterly for her blunder.

Accordingly, after six years, she transformed Saint Cyr into a sort of convent and founded the Order of Saint Augustine to take charge of it. Henceforth nothing, in the view of Madame de Maintenon, was more detestable than a "learned lady." Saint Cyr remained a boarding school, but was stripped of all those liberal features which made it different. It continued, until the Revolution, to be the most prominent school for girls in France.

---

[5] Compayré, Gabriel, *The History of Pedagogy,* p. 220. Translated by W. H. Payne. Boston: D. C. Heath, 1905.

EDUCATIONAL BEGINNINGS IN THE NEW WORLD

Colonization. It is unfortunate that American Education has been considered apart from developments in Europe, for this approach misses the point of chief importance, the continuity of cultural causes and effects. It was natural that the colonizers of the New World should desire to set up in the colonies the kind of education they considered best in the old. It is fitting, therefore, to begin the study of American education at this point and to follow each succeeding movement of reform as it passed from Europe to the New World until the systems of the colonies became independent.

Spanish education in the Americas. The first attitude of the Spanish government toward the natives was one of exploitation and cruelty with no thought of permanent colonization by their own people nor of "civilizing" the natives. But after Bishop Las Casas had protested against this barbarous policy, Cardinal Ximines, as regent, decreed that all Indians be treated as freemen and steps be taken for their civilization and conversion to Christianity. They were to be gathered into settlements where churches and schools could be established for their welfare.

Various Catholic orders, particularly the Franciscan, began the task of teaching the aborigines the Spanish language, the Christian religion, and the practical arts of European civilization. Most significant was the emphasis upon the teaching of music, which was essential for religious services. The Padres imported organs from Europe, trained choirs and established schools and colleges. As the result of the urging of various parties, Charles V (1551) ordered that there be "founded in the city of Lima, of the Kingdom of Peru, and in the city of Mexico, of New Spain, a University or center of general studies in each respectively." A small fund from the royal treasury was granted for these institutions. The opening of the University of Mexico was delayed until 1553.

Subsequent developments gradually made the Latin American civilization what it is today. From the Rio Grande south to Cape Horn Catholic culture has prevailed. The means utilized first was the Mission system; later, as culture advanced, came the establishment of towns with parish churches and schools. Within the confines of what later became the United States, Missions and schools were established at St. Augustine, Florida; New Orleans, Louisiana; Laredo, Texas; and in New Mexico and California.

French education in the New World. It must not be forgotten that France vied with Spain and Britain for the conquest of America. Her chief hold was upon Canada and to this day the French life, language, and religion prevail in the Province of Quebec; and from there, because of the fecundity of the population, the French Canadians have filtered into the other provinces of the Dominion and also into New England.

British North American Colonies. During the 17th century, permanent settlements were established in 12 of the 13 colonies which made up the original states of the Union, leaving Georgia to be organized early in the 18th century. The region of the Hudson River and northern New Jersey was first settled by Dutch colonists from Holland; but late in the 17th century, England took over this portion of the country, and British settlers soon outnumbered the Dutch. The Swedes early established a successful settlement on the Delaware River; but this region also was soon acquired by Great Britain, and the Swedes, who mingled freely with the British, were assimilated.

The growth of the colonies was slow during the 17th century. Virginia, although first colonized in 1607, had in 1625 a population of only about 1,200. Plymouth, Massachusetts, had but 180 settlers in 1624, and 300 in 1630. The next decade was one of heavy immigration of English nonconformists, and in 1642 the population had grown to about 3,000. The Massachusetts Bay colony grew rapidly from the first. In 1664, when England seized New Amsterdam, it had a population of 1,500. At the close of the 17th century there were about 270,000 persons in all the colonies. Of these, 105,000 were in New England; 55,000 in the middle colonies; and 110,000 in Maryland, Virginia, and the Carolinas. Boston, the largest city in the colonies, had a population of 7,000; Philadelphia had 4,000.

About the beginning of the 18th century there was a large Scotch-Irish immigration, which continued until the American Revolution. Germans, Swiss, and Moravians, fleeing from religious persecution and economic distress brought on by wars and bad trade conditions, furnished thousands of immigrants. These groups were most numerous in New Jersey, Pennsylvania, Virginia, North Carolina, and Georgia. French Protestants (Huguenots) escaping from their country after the revocation of the Edict of Nantes, made up another important group that formed settlements in a number of states. These Huguenots adopted the English language, and soon entered into the social and religious life of their fellow Americans. From them have come many of the social, political, religious, and scientific leaders of the United States. The Germans, the Swiss, and the Moravians, on the other hand, clung to their ancestral languages and customs, and for a long time remained as distinct peoples.

Before Plymouth was settled, African Negroes were brought to Virginia and sold into slavery; their children, unlike the children of European indentured servants, were born to a life of servitude. Negro slaves proved to be valuable property; consequently, in the 18th century, traders both in England and New England and planters in southern colonies were enriched by the traffic in slaves, as well as by their labor.

Social and political background. The majority of the settlers in North America between 1607 and 1745 were British. Each of the colonies had a handful of "gentry" who were descended from the ruling class in England and who were chiefly engaged in government service and agriculture, together with artisans and small traders, and numerous laborers and servants. The people imported as servants fell into four classes: First, there were the Negroes from Africa. Next were the criminals transported to the colonies, where they were obliged to serve a term at labor before they were released. A third class was made up of political offenders, who were treated much as were the criminals. Fourth, there were great numbers of poor people who, in order to secure a passage to this land, voluntarily entered into contracts to work in the colonies for a given number of years.

In Virginia and the other Southern colonies the plantation system favored the employment of cheap labor. While it did not prove profitable to work skilled artisans as slaves, until the Industrial Revolution free labor was unable to compete with slaves in raising crops, building roads, and in other unskilled work. When the government of Virginia recognized that large-scale production of tobacco would yield quick profits and result in the rapid colonization of the country, a policy of large holdings of land was adopted. Officials of the colony and capitalists who imported laborers were granted large tracts to encourage production.

Colonists in all parts of America were accustomed to class distinctions; the plantation system tended to perpetuate this practice. The class system dominated the economic life of the South until the Civil War and determined the educational provisions of this region.

In New England throughout the Colonial Period, lumbering and shipbuilding, trade with the Indians, and fisheries furnished the chief basis for commerce. The land which was owned by the towns was distributed in small tracts to individuals, a policy quite different from that followed in Virginia. There was little chance for these people to amass wealth for their farms were small and the soil not too fertile, and their products were locally consumed. Another great distinction between the New England colonies and Virginia lay in the fact that the government of New England towns was highly democratic, for each freeholder had a voice in directing its affairs. This and other circumstances produced in New England a very different form of social life and institutions from that in the Southern colonies.

In Virginia the Church of England, established by law, was as rabidly intolerant as in the Motherland. In Massachusetts, New Hampshire and Connecticut, the Congregational Church, made up of English Puritans, exercised full authority and for bigotry and intolerance it was as guilty as other bodies. In Rhode Island, however, Roger Williams set up the first government in all history which separated church and state and did not require religious conformity nor the support of the church as a requirement for the exercise of citizenship.

Colonial forms of government. Virginia created in 1619 the House of Burgesses as a representative assembly. The colony was then divided into counties and in each county a court was formed. The members of the House of Burgesses were elected by the citizens of counties and incorporated towns.

Massachusetts also set up a representative body called the General Court, which shared with the governor and the council the conduct of affairs. The town was the organ of local government, and it exercised important functions in the development of education.

In all these early colonies suffrage was restricted to owners of property. The qualifications prescribed for voters differed in the various colonies; in some, religious tests were added to property qualifications. Differences in voters' qualifications and in economic conditions caused great divergence in the proportion of persons participating in the government of the various colonies. About four-fifths of the men of Massachusetts were eligible to vote. In Pennsylvania and Virginia the privilege of the ballot was limited to a very few.

In New England all local affairs were handled by the towns, which were governed by qualified voters and by officers whom the voters elected. Voters met at town meetings, where public affairs were discussed, officers elected, and matters of administration and management settled by action of the voters. Schools and roads were made the special charge of the towns. Local churches exercised almost complete autonomy in the conduct of their affairs. A large measure of uniformity was introduced into religious faith and practice by the law, which established the church in the colonies and organized all the congregations into an association.

The autonomy allowed to towns and to congregations discouraged the crushing of dissent. In some localities, fierce outbreaks of persecution took place; but even though the law against nonconformity was strict, toleration was practiced in most towns.

In Virginia, New York, and five of the other colonies, the Church of England was established by law. In Virginia a commissioner represented the Bishop of London. In the colonies in which the Church of England was established, various attempts were made to require schoolmasters to have a license from the Bishop or other authority. However, the law was everywhere a dead letter as it was in England. A few instances of persecution for religious belief took place; but after the Revolution of 1688 dissenters were generally tolerated.

COLONIAL SCHOOLS

Virginia. Efforts began by 1618 to establish an educational system in Virginia, although there were only a few children. The King of England, the Virginia Company, and some benevolent individuals interested themselves in plans for the training of both English and Indian children, and contributions of land and money were made for the undertaking. Steps had actually begun for education when an Indian massacre in 1622 and the revocation of the Virginia Company's charter in 1624 ended these early efforts.

In 1634 Benjamin Symms willed 200 acres of land and eight cows as an endowment for a free school in Elizabeth County. The bequest of Symms was the first of many contributions made in Virginia for the founding of schools; such endowments were principally in land, livestock, and slaves. Records of county courts and parishes furnish evidence that the parish schools were regarded as agencies of the established Church and, consequently, they were subject to the control of parish, county, and colonial officials. In 1805 the Symms endowment and one by Thomas Eaton (1690) were combined to form Hampton Academy.

This method of providing for schools and their control was in accord with the practice in England for many centuries past.

The courses of study in the schools varied. Most schools offered elementary instruction only in reading, writing, and, particularly, in catechism. It was, however, a common practice for learned clergymen to teach small groups of more advanced scholars Latin, Greek, and sometimes French in order to prepare them for college. In certain parish schools there was no tuition; in others, fees were charged, but children of parents who were unable to pay were admitted free.

Apprenticeship. Until the 19th century, the apprenticeship system remained one of the most important agencies of training both in England and the colonies. Following English precedent the Assembly of Virginia advanced an elaborate plan of industrial training in 1646. All the colonies had laws on apprenticeship which included girls as well as boys.

Apprenticeship served two levels of vocation. Boys of the higher economic group were apprenticed to the more skilled trades and also to the professions. The period of apprenticeship on this level began after the boys had already received considerable training. By contacting members of the trade or profession these apprentices not only acquired the specialized information which belonged to their profession, but became familiar with its techniques and usages. Chemists, physicians, architects, carpenters, shipbuilders, ship officers, lawyers, and members of other professions received a part, at least, of their vocational and professional training in this way.

Apprenticeship served, too, as a means of providing education for the lower economic level. Poor boys were usually apprenticed to unskilled vocations so that they could support themselves as early as possible.

All through the Colonial Period, the colonies attracted from England college graduates, schoolmasters, rectors, parish clerks, and teachers of elementary schools; many of these came as indentured servants. Wealthy Virginians generally sent their sons to Britain for instruction at English schools and universities, and to the Inns of Court where they studied law.

The philosophy and plan of colonial school organization. The policy of the Dutch and Puritan colonists in establishing schools is not difficult to ascertain. The complete pattern of education was formulated, in part from the schools which they had known in Holland or in England, and in large part from the instructions of the Synod of Dort for all Calvinists. The primary motivation was a profound religious conviction, theocratic and authoritarian in character. They conceived that the aim of education was service to the church and the state, an idea which was repeated constantly in their literature. Religion, it was asserted, must be taught in the family, and in the churches and the schools, both of which were state-supported. Because reading was considered essential to intelligent living the elementary school had to be set up, and it was felt that every fifty families should support such a school.

As soon as the colonists had time to reflect upon their situation, they discovered that the pastors who had led them to the New World could no longer supply the needs of the churches. Furthermore, the New Englanders could not send their young men back to Europe for training as did wealthy Virginians and the Dutch of New Amsterdam. First, the journey was hazardous; second, they could not afford the expense; and finally, there were no colleges in England where Puritan doctrines were taught. They were, therefore, obliged to set up a college to train their own ministry. But as college education required a preliminary training in the Latin language, a grammar school was also needed.

Dutch colonial schools. It was the custom of the Dutch Government to require a pastor and schoolmaster to accompany each group of colonists departing for America. The schoolmaster had to be a member of the Reformed Church of Holland and qualified by piety and education to take charge of the instruction of the young; and to conduct divine services during the absence of the pastor. The Dutch Church followed the Calvinistic faith and its educational policy as formulated at the Synod of Dort.

The West India Company, conducting the settlement of New Netherlands, bound itself "to maintain good and fit preachers, schoolmasters and comforters of the sick." The establishment of schools and the appointment of schoolmasters rested jointly upon the Company and the church authorities in Amsterdam, but the supervision and the management of the schools were in the hands of the deacons of the local church. These were elementary, vernacular schools. The schoolmaster of a public school served also as clerk, chorister, and visitor of the sick. The first schoolmaster of New Amsterdam was Adam Rolandsen, who conducted the town school from its founding in 1633 until 1639. This school of the Collegiate Dutch Church was a regular parish school, where reading, writing, arithmetic, and religion were taught. It is still in operation.

When the census of 1656 showed that New Amsterdam had 120 houses and 1000 people, the colonists felt the need of higher instruction, and steps were taken to secure an academy or classical school. It was accordingly established by the West India Company and the city authorities, and continued until closed by the English in 1673.

Under the Dutch regime, "schools existed in almost every town and village" in New Netherlands. Furthermore, "the whole system was but a counterpart of that to which the settlers had been accustomed" in Holland. These were public schools dispensing the elements of learning gratuitously, the teachers receiving their appointment and remuneration from the constituted authorities. Private elementary and Latin schools were also conducted.

THE BOSTON LATIN GRAMMAR SCHOOL IN EZEKIEL CHEEVER'S DAY.

The founding of schools in New England. Boston was founded in 1630 and was soon chosen as the seat of government for the entire colony. The town meeting of Boston five years after its founding voted "to entreat Philemon Pormort to become scholemaster for the teaching and nurturing of children." The moving spirit in this event was John Cotton, "The Patriarch of New England." It is not certain whether the school was opened by Pormort. But the next year at a meeting "of the richer inhabitants" a subscription was taken toward the maintenance of a free schoolmaster, and Daniel Maud was elected the teacher. This was a Latin grammar school, and it effected the preparation of boys for college. It became prosperous before long and was granted 1,000 acres of land by the colonial government. The most renowned master was Ezekiel Cheever, who was educated at Emmanuel College, Cambridge University, England, but for some reason did not graduate. He went to Boston in 1637, but began teaching in a private school at New Haven, Connecticut, in 1638. He transferred to Ipswich in 1650, and to Charlestown eleven years later. In 1670 he took charge of the Boston Latin Grammar School and held this position for 35 years. This was the only school in Boston for nearly half a century, and the most famous in New England.

The second public school began at Charlestown in 1636. The following year another was organized at Salem. It owed its existence to Rev. John Fisk, a wealthy settler who taught the school himself and on his own land.

In 1633 Dorchester made history by initiating the town meeting form of government. Six years later it placed a rental of £20 on Thompson's Island and this fund was "paid to such a schoolmaster who shall undertake to teach English, Latin, and other tongues and also write." This entitles Dorchester to be called "the first school in America supported by direct taxation." Moreover, it set up the first school board to govern the school. Cambridge had a school to prepare students for Harvard, but when it began is not known. In 1643 Elijah Corlett received commendation for his teaching and he continued teaching until he died in 1686.

Recognizing "how necessary the education of their children in literature will be, to fit them for public service, both in church and commonwealth" (note the familiar Puritan phrase), Roxbury opened its Latin grammar school in 1645. This same year Braintree put forth an effort, but the results are not known.

The curricula of these colonial New England schools were the same as those in England of the same day. Ezekiel Cheever took boys first through Latin grammar; then, through the *Colloquies* of Erasmus and Corderius; and finally, set them to translating the classics and to writing Latin prose and verse. The purpose was to prepare boys to enter college. In the earliest days, New England schools were managed through town meetings, though frequently temporary committees were appointed to look after them.

Ministers took the leadership in school affairs, first because they had most learning, but second and chiefly because they were charged by the church to be the watchdogs of right doctrine. A Massachusetts law of the late 17th century required "the grammar master must be approved by the minister of the town, and of two next adjacent towns or two of them." [6] As time went on, this practice was changed and the control of the school was placed in charge of a board or committee and this became later the universal practice.

THE TOWN SCHOOL AND WATCH HOUSE AT DEDHAM.

Early Massachusetts Schools

Towns	*Year Established*	*First Teacher*
Boston	1635	Philemon Pormont
Charlestown	1636	William Witherell
Salem	1637	John Fiske
Dorchester	1639	
Newbury	1639	Anthony Somerby
Ipswich	1641	
Cambridge	c1642	
Roxbury	1645	
Braintree	1645	
Dedham	c1645	

First Massachusetts school ordinances. Between 1637 and 1660, the colonies were permitted to manage their own affairs with little or no

[6] Martin, G. H., *Evolution of the Massachusetts Public School System,* p. 78. New York: D. Appleton, 1904. See also Small, W. H., *op. cit.,* p. 321.

interference from the English government; as a consequence, the Puritans seized the opportunity to promote education, precisely as did the Puritan party in England and Scotland. The first of these ordinances, passed by the General Court in 1642, reads, in part, as follows: [7]

> This court, taking into consideration the great neglect of many parents and masters in training up their children in learning and labor, and other employments which may be profitable to the commonwealth do hereupon order and decree that in every town the chosen men appointed for managing the prudential affairs of the same shall henceforth stand charged with the care of the redress of this evil, so as they shall be sufficiently punished by fines for the neglect thereof.

The ordinance directed the selectmen to take account of children's "ability to read and understand the principles of religion and the capital laws of this country, to fine parents and masters who fail to teach their children or to put them to work, and to apprentice the children of such parents as they find not able and fit to employ and bring them up"; and they "shall have the power to take account from time to time of all parents and masters and of their children." This Massachusetts ordinance clearly reflected the Calvinistic doctrine that the moral and religious welfare of the theocratic state takes precedence over the individual and the family. It reflected also the Poor Act of 1601, which expressed the permanent policy of the English in regard to the education of the children of the lower class.

Five years later, the General Court passed another ordinance which marked the establishment of common school education. This ordinance, which has been dubbed "the old deluder Satan act," was, like that of 1642, strictly in accord with the spirit of the Synod of Dort. It declared: [8]

> It being one of the chief projects of that old deluder Satan to keep men from the knowledge of the Scriptures, as in former times by keeping them in an unknown tongue, that so in these latter times by persuading from the use of tongues, so at least the true sense and meaning of the original might be clouded by false gloss of saint-seeming deceivers, that learning may not be buried in the grave of our fathers in the church and commonwealth, the Lord assisting our endeavors:

---

[7] Hinsdale, A. B., "Documents Illustrative of American Educational History" in *Report of the United States Commissioner of Education* (1892-1893), Vol. II, p. 123. See also *Massachusetts Colonial Records,* Vol. II, pp. 6-9.

[8] Hinsdale, A. B., *op. cit.,* p. 123. See also *Massachusetts Colonial Records,* Vol. II, p. 203.

> *It is therefore ordered,* That every township in this jurisdiction, after the Lord hath increased them to the number of fifty householders, shall then henceforth appoint one within their town to teach such children as shall resort to him to write and read, whose wages shall be paid either by the parents or masters of such children, or by the inhabitants in general, by way of supply, as the major part of those that order the prudentials of the town shall appoint: *Provided,* Those that send their children be not oppressed by paying much more than they can have them taught for in other towns; and
>
> *It is further ordered,* That where any town shall increase to the number of one hundred families or householders; they shall set up a grammar school, the master thereof being able to instruct youth, so far as they may be fitted, for the university: *Provided,* That if any town neglect the performance hereof above one year, that every such town shall pay five pounds to the next school until they shall perform this order.

Most towns obeyed this ordinance, though so many neglected to set up schools that it was later found necessary to increase the penalty.

The Connecticut school law of 1650 combined these laws of 1642 and 1647 and was perhaps stronger in its authoritarian attitude.

Reading and writing schools. Overshadowed by the Latin grammar school and the colleges, these others have received far too little attention. Reading and writing are so completely fused in our thinking that it is difficult nowadays to imagine ourselves in the time when they were separate arts, taught by different masters in different schools. Writing received greatest emphasis during the later Middle Ages when it became essential to the conduct of business and commerce. *Schrift* schools were taught by private teachers. Quite a different point of view arose when printing came in and the reading of the Scriptures became the passion of the middle class. This required a new kind of school. The unification of the teaching of writing and the teaching of reading took place much later.

Both reading and writing were prerequisites for entrance to the Latin grammar school. Reading was acquired in the homes in connection with religion, or in the Dame schools which became common in New England towns. Men sometimes taught reading in private schools. "Before 1684," Seybolt assures us, "some of the grammar school students, who had not learned to write, attended private schools from eleven to twelve o'clock in the mornings, and from five to six in the afternoons, for instruction in that subject."

By 1682 the citizens of Boston felt the need for more effective training for business. At the town meeting the selectmen were instructed "to consider of & pvide [provide] one or more Free Schools for the teaching of children to write & cypher within this towne." A few months later it was voted "that two schools shall be pvided [provided]." One of these was opened in 1684 and the other later. In addition to writing, arithmetic was included in the course of study along with, as a matter of custom, religious training. In 1719 the selectmen, among other directions, voted "that proper seasons be stated & sett apart for encouraging of good spelling." One can readily see that it was needed.

From 1636 the Records of Boston always referred to its first institution as "The Schoole" or "The Free Schoole"; but after the public writing schools opened (1684) it was known as "The Latine School" or "The Free Grammar School"; the others were designated "The Free Writing Schools."

HARVARD COLLEGE IN 1739.

New England colleges. Virginia was settled by all levels of English society. New England, on the contrary, was colonized by a homogeneous group from the middle class and the number of graduates of Oxford and Cambridge among them was out of all proportion to the size of the group. Furthermore, the spirit of self-determination in government was strong among them.

Harvard. The pioneers soon found they had to face the problem of the replacement of men in the pulpit and in public offices of all kinds; the supply of ministers, teachers, and leaders in public affairs did not keep pace with the expanding needs. The literature of the times dwells upon this difficulty, showing that they were particularly conscious of it. Not enough new men came from England to care for the situation, and many of those who came did not fit into the pioneering and straight-laced Puritan demands.

Among the founders of Harvard were 100 college men, 70 of whom had been students in the colleges of Cambridge, and 30 in the colleges of Oxford.

From its beginning Harvard was to all intents and purposes an English college: it might easily have nestled among the various foundations of Cambridge University. Doubtless these would have treated it with proper academic disdain as a newcomer; but its family likeness they would have quickly recognized. The purpose of Harvard was set down in *New England's First Fruits,* a pamphlet published in London in 1643 as follows: [9]

> After God had carried us safe to *New England,* and wee had builded our houses, provided necessaries for our livelihood, reared convenient places for God's worship, and setled the Civill Government: One of the next things we longed for, and looked after was to advance *Learning,* and perpetuate it to Posterity; dreading to leave an illiterate Ministery to the Churches, when our present Ministers shall lie in the Dust.

In consequence of these conditions the leaders of Massachusetts early felt the need for an institution of higher learning. In 1636, the General Court voted £400, and because of the large number of her graduates in the colony, they called the town Cambridge after the English University of that name. John Harvard bequeathed one-half of his estate and his library, and that determined the name of the new institution. For two years, beginning in 1638, only grammar school instruction was given. Henry Dunster was then appointed president and he gave the institution real college status. He held office 14 years.

Yale College. By the end of the 17th century liberal theology had begun to rise in England and the American colonies. Moreover, the rigorous religious bigotry of the past was abating. Science, philosophy, and even immoral conduct had come to weaken the faith and Harvard

---

[9] Shelley, Henry C, *John Harvard and His Times,* p. 150. Boston: Little, Brown and Company, 1907.

College showed signs of these trends. Conservative theologians like Cotton Mather led in the establishment of a new college to bulwark the faith, and as a result the General Court of Connecticut chartered a new "Collegiate Institute" in 1701. The college was organized to instruct youth "who may be fitted for public employment both in Church and Civil State." To safeguard the institution the governing body consisted of eleven clergymen.

WILLIAM AND MARY COLLEGE IN 1874.

Elihu Yale, a native of New Haven, who had made his home in England after accumulating a fortune in the service of the East India Company, made liberal gifts to the college, which therefore took his name in 1745. Bishop Berkeley, the renowned philosopher, associated himself with the institution in its early days.

The College of William and Mary (1693). By the last decade of the 17th century the necessity for a college was strongly felt in Virginia. Before this, wealthy planters sent their sons to England or to Harvard for higher training. But such methods were too drastic and expensive for most people. Moreover, ministers were needed for the churches, and public leaders for local and general service as lawyers, physicians, surveyors, and men of intelligence to direct new enterprises of all sorts. James Blair, a graduate of Edinburgh University and missionary representative of the Bishop of London began the movement for the establishment of a college. Planters subscribed £2,500 and Blair was sent to England to obtain a charter for a "Free School and College, wherein shall be taught the Latin, Greek, and Hebrew Tongues, together with philosophy, mathematics and Divinity." The attorney-general for the king was irritated by Blair's request for funds and told him they were needed for other and better purposes. Blair urged that "the people had souls to be saved." "Souls! Damn your souls! Make to-bacco!" shouted the angered custodian. But the king and queen consented and gave their name and £2,000. Others, both in England and Virginia, gave handsome gifts and the Assembly added valuable grants; the college became wealthy, but was nevertheless not without great hardships.

YALE COLLEGE IN 1786.

Its purpose, as stated in the charter was:

> "that the Church of Virginia may be furnished with a seminary of Ministers of the Gospel, and that the youth may be properly educated in good manners, and that the Christian faith may be propagated among the Western Indians to the glory of Almighty God; to make, found and establish a place of universal study or perpetual college of divinity, philosophy, languages, and other good arts and science."

William and Mary had the best endowment in the colonies, and was the only institution with a full faculty. When the organization was completed in 1729, there were six professorships: two of divinity, one of Greek and Latin, one of physics, mathematics, and metaphysics; one of rhetoric, logic, and ethics (including law) and the professorship of the school for the Indians. The curriculum was that of the English Universities. As a center of learning and political discussion this institution was by far the most progressive in the 18th century. Led by George Wythe, it laid the foundation for the long succession of Virginia champions of constitutional government. Thomas Jefferson, James Monroe. Peyton Randolph, John Marshall, and John Tyler are a few of its illustrious alumni.

Original character of the American college. The early American colleges were distinctly English in origin and character. This is the first fact to be considered in the effort to understand the development of our higher education. It is difficult today to realize how perfectly they once reproduced the English model. Why this was the case may be readily grasped when we recall that all the early institutions were fully scrutinized by British officials before their charters were granted; and furthermore, that for the most part they looked to English sympathy for financial assistance. Moreover, they drew most of their organizers and teachers from the colleges of Oxford and Cambridge.

The entrance requirement, form of government, religious discipline, course of study, and requirements, for degrees of the colonial colleges were the same as in the English colleges of that day. To enter the college, students were required to read Cicero, "speak true Latin in verse and prose," and to recite perfectly the paradigms of nouns and verbs in the Greek tongue. The college course of study was a combination of the seven liberal arts, the languages of Renaissance education, and the moral and religious training of the Calvinistic Reformation. It embraced grammar, rhetoric or composition (prose and verse), good style, continuous disputations, and logic. The more advanced work included Latin literature, Greek and Hebrew, arithmetic, and astronomy; to which were added ethics (including politics or law), history, botany, physics, and to cap it all, the Scriptures and theology.

All students were obliged to live in the college dormitory and to submit to its exacting regimen. Daily worship, the supervision of study, and the inculcation of certain habits of morals and manners were the means of forming character. The college still clung to the medieval mode of instruction—the tutorial method—by which each instructor carried half a dozen or more students through their entire course of study. It was a highly organized system of apprenticeship in the fine art of gentlemanly living.

Chapter 9

GERMAN PIETISM AND THE NEW CHRISTIAN EDUCATION

PREVIEW of changes. The latter part of the 17th century and first half of the 18th marked the beginning of the transition to the era of present-day society and education. The world had grown weary of the deadening routine of Humanism and of dogmatic theology. Moreover, political turmoil and clashing religious interests had greatly retarded the progress of culture. Four outstanding movements challenged the best thinkers of the time and produced bitter controversies: (1) religious toleration versus uniformitarianism; (2) political democracy versus autocracy; (3) the emergence of a new spirit of philanthropy; and (4) the advance of realism. In Germany the new movement took the form of Pietism, and in England it was the rise of nonconformist education. At the same time the empirical philosophy of John Locke was projected into the general confusion of the day. All of these movements had consequences of the greatest moment not only on contemporary life and the reorganization of schools, but more remotely upon the philosophy of the 18th century.

Religious toleration the only resort. The inhuman wars of the 17th century bled the peoples of northern Europe to exhaustion, and practically put an end to the progress of all culture. Finding it impossible to annihilate each other completely, Catholic and Protestant settled down to a truce in which each was to have exclusive jurisdiction in his own domain. After the revocation of the Edict of Nantes in 1685, the Huguenots were well-nigh exterminated, and France remained Catholic. French education continued in the hands of the Jesuits and of such minor orders as met with their approval. Germany, where the religious struggle had reached the utmost degree of barbarity, was still divided;

Protestantism was dominant in the northern principalities, and Catholicism, in the southern. The Netherlands separated sharply: Holland was composed of Calvinists, Mennonites, and some Lutherans; Belgium remained Catholic. Scotland became Presbyterian, while England remained divided among Anglicans, Puritans, Presbyterians, and several minor sects. By the Act of Toleration (1689) the Anglican Church was kept as the established church but religious freedom was granted to all Christians except Unitarians and Catholics. Even these were no longer seriously interfered with in the practice of their views. The principle of toleration, though not of complete religious liberty, was making progress in Holland and England, where religious life was most diversified.

Origin of Pietism. Pietism was the name given to a devout religious movement which began in western Germany toward the middle of the 17th century. It exerted a profound influence on German life, literature, philosophy, and education. On the religious side, the originator of the movement was Philip Jacob Spener (1635-1705), pastor at Strassburg, and later court preacher at Dresden and Berlin. The educational and missionary head of the movement was August Hermann Francke.

Causes of the Pietistic movement. Pietism resulted from a variety of causes inherent in the spiritual and economic conditions of the time. Exhausted by the Thirty Years' War, Catholics and Protestants found it necessary to suspend further bloodshed and destruction. The Lutheran Church was ruled from without by the civil authorities and from within by autocratic theologians, all of whom disagreed among themselves. The prolonged struggle over the precise statement of orthodoxy produced religious formalism and sterility. The clergy assumed that the mere profession of sound doctrine would insure salvation. Luther had held the heart to be the seat of religion and faith the all-sufficient means of grace; but the striving for credal orthodoxy had made religion a matter of hair-splitting, intellectual discrimination, and the church services creed-bound ritualism. Pietism was the reaction against all this cold, deadening, rancorous system, in consequence of which there arose throughout Germany a deep longing for freedom from the odious tendency of the ruling theology. Moreover, the war had destroyed the moral habits and standards of the people, and produced a pagan bestiality. The pastors were no longer interested in the practice of Christian living, or in teaching the Christian virtues.

On its positive side, Pietism was no new phenomenon, but just another of the ever recurrent revivals of the benevolent, evangelical spirit which always reappears as a reaction to an era of formalism. Throughout the history of the church, periods of formalism and rationalism have invariably been followed by the reassertion of the more emotional, sacrificial, and mystical expression of the Christian consciousness. Moreover, periods of moral laxity and pagan licentiousness have usually been followed by times of puritanic rigor.

Pietism represented a reaction to the grim distress of war: the more disconsolate and disappointing the present lot in this world, the greater the tendency to transcend the present and look toward a brighter and happier future in the world to come. Pietism placed a new emphasis upon self-examination, study of the Scriptures, and reliance upon God. It strove for a knowledge of Christ as an inner light, a sense of peace and forgiveness. This experience expressed itself in love and sacrifice for others. It required the separation of the individual from the world and the avoidance of the ordinary pleasures of life, which it regarded as sinful. Pietists opposed dancing, children's play, theatergoing, overdressing, joking, and the reading of romances and even of newspapers. They united Luther's insistence upon the study of the Scriptures, prayer, and faith, with the Calvinistic insistence upon puritanism in conduct. But they went further than either of these in emphasizing the experience of the new birth, inner light, and a certain degree of mysticism.

The Pietism of Spener and Francke was not separatist in character but remained within the bounds of Lutheran Christianity. The movement was, in fact, in harmony with Luther's early evangelical point of view. It was, however, more irenic in tendency and readily coöperated with the Church of England, the Reformed Church, and the persecuted sects of Germany. Several of the older sects, such as the Moravian Brethren and the Salzbergers, were revived through contact with Pietism.

The emergence of Pietism about the same time as scientific Realism was no mere coincidence. As a matter of fact, Pietism in its main character was the religious aspect of the realistic movement. As the one drew its strength from direct individual experience of the objects of the external world, the other emphasized the indispensable need of religious experience and practice. As Realism was a reaction against authority in the sphere of science, the insistence upon a change of heart, inner light, and religious feeling was in opposition to externalism and authoritarianism.

Pietistic criticism of the schools. Spener was severely critical of contemporary religious life and education. Neither the Lutheran nor the Jesuit schools had given real emphasis to the development of Christian virtues and practical piety. He was strongly influenced by Andreä and the Christian idealism of the Calvinists of Geneva. Because of their lack of genuine religious training for the young, he made the following criticisms of the schools: (1) They provide for secular knowledge, which is of service only in this life, but they do nothing to cultivate the feelings which produce a living Christian faith and the fruits thereof. Teachers must have regard to the godly living of their students as well as to the acquisition of knowledge. (2) Most of the time is devoted to learning Latin, the language of the learned class, and very little time is left for Greek and Hebrew, the languages of the Scriptures. (3) Too little attention is given to the Holy Scriptures, and too much to memorizing dogmatic doctrines. (4) In the course of study the heathen ethics of Aristotle takes the place of practical Christian morals.

August Hermann Francke (1663-1727). He was the noblest example of the practical Christian educator of Germany. It may well be doubted if there ever has been in the history of education a more efficient representative of the Christian spirit. He was born at Lübeck, but his father was appointed privy councilor and justice by Duke Ernst the Pious of Gotha. The father died when the boy was only seven. August Hermann was given a good education, under private instruction, until he was prepared to enter the advanced class of the gymnasium. Extremely intelligent, he was able to complete in one year the gymnasium course in preparation for the university. Still only in his 14th year, he was given several years of further private instruction before he entered the University of Erfurt.

Intending him for clerical office, his guardian placed him under private scholars, who trained him in special lines. Francke's studies took a wide range, including Greek and Hebrew; philosophy, with special emphasis upon metaphysics and ethics; general history and church history; physics and natural history; theology; and rhetoric. Transferring to the University of Leipzig, he took his degree and became an instructor. Well started on his way to success as a scholarly leader, Francke went to Lüneburg, in order to contact the noted theologian, Sandhägen. Here he had the experience which completely transformed his heart and life. From early years Francke had shown a pious spirit, but nevertheless he was possessed with powerful instincts leading to a self-centered and ambitious life. Assailed by doubts of the truth of the Christian religion and the Scriptures, he found himself, while at Lüneburg, obliged to preach on a special evangelical text. Praying earnestly for light, he experienced a sudden conversion. Shortly after this he became acquainted with Spener who had already begun to give a new impetus to evangelical religion in Germany. Henceforth these two were of one mind and spirit.

Driven from the University of Leipzig, and later from a pastorate at Erfurt, by enemies of the Piestistic spirit, Francke was appointed, through the efforts of Spener, to the chair of oriental languages and religion at the University of Halle. This institution had just been founded (1694) by the Prussian King, to counteract the hostility of Leipzig and Erfurt to progress in science and theology. To provide for his living, Francke was made pastor in the suburban village of Glauchau. Here he established an astonishing number of institutions and radiated an influence which penetrated throughout Germany and had a very definite effect on American education.

Francke's preparation as an educator. Francke's interest in education was no sudden awakening. Gotha, where he was reared from the time he was three to the age of 16, was the center of the educational reforms of Duke Ernst. The progressive atmosphere of Gotha must have entered deeply into his inner life. While an instructor at Leipzig, he delivered a course of lectures under the title *The Education of Boys and Pubescents,* which showed profound interest in educational problems.

But the real motivation of Francke's life came with his conversion, when a boundless reservoir of love for God and for his fellow men filled his heart. He came to believe that the reason for human degeneration and unhappiness lay in the neglect of genuine Christian training in childhood. To demonstrate the power of true Christian education in the home and school was henceforth his supreme ambition.

Francke was brought to a clearer understanding of his mission by a visit to Johannes Winckler, the leading pastor of Hamburg, an adherent of the Pietistic group who was deeply interested in schools for poor children. Francke spent some months in Pastor Winckler's home teaching an infant school. He declared frequently that this was the basis of all that God afterwards accomplished through him. From this experience there arose a powerful conviction that the betterment of mankind depended "upon the education of children to piety and Christian wisdom."

An understanding of the spirit and devotion of the man can be ascertained from his attitude toward his many great achievements, which he humbly attributed directly to God and not to himself. He stated: [1]

> The world ascribes these works which have gone through my hands to my activity.... The foolish world alone gives no honor to God but ascribes everything to the power of man.... I have been in all matters always *passive,* have sat quiet, and have not gone a step farther, than I had the finger of God before me. When I saw what the hand of God had in store, I went at it like a slave and realized it without care or trouble. Accordingly, what has not turned out a success for others with all their intelligence, craft and wisdom, has come about for me without effort.

Principles of Christian education. Francke did not get his educational ideas from reading the works of others. According to him, the supreme aim of life is to honor God, and all conduct and thought must conform to this end. No subsidiary aim, such as a particular vocation or profession, must be set before the children to arouse their ambition. Obedience and industry are to be awakened in them through the desire to honor God. All else is an appeal to the cupidity, the selfishness, and natural jealousy of the human heart.

This main objective has two elements, godliness and wisdom (*Klugheit*). The most essential means for training in godliness are good example and a living knowledge of Christ. Examples of piety, avoidance of evil, the catechism, prayer, and daily study of the Scriptures for light and guidance in practical living—these are the means of Christian education. But he went still further, and insisted upon the development of the evangelical spirit. For him, godliness is not merely a matter of good conduct, nor of ceremony, nor of knowledge; it is an attitude of heart and will and comes from faith.[2]

> One dram of living faith is more to be valued than one hundred weight of mere historic knowledge; and one drop of true love, than a whole sea of learning in all mysteries.

Francke and the other Pietists were not obscurantists, nor even ordinary conservatives. They endeavored to integrate knowledge and piety; but felt that learning must always be subordinate to practical Christian living. "All learning and knowledge is folly if it does not have as its

---

1 Kramer, D. G., *A. H. Francke's pädagogische Schriften,* p. liv. Langensalza: H. Beyer & Söhne, 1885.

2 Barnard, Henry, *German Teachers and Educators,* p. 413. Hartford: Brown & Gross, 1878.

foundation true and pure love toward God and Man." Not only is knowledge to be utilized for the advancement of the honor of God, but, in a way, the Pietists came to believe that knowledge originates from divine illumination. Earnest study is essential, but the discernment of truth is due to inspiration. According to Spener:

> The Christian student prays as earnestly for divine illumination as if he had no need of his own industry, and studies with as much zeal as if he must do everything by his own unassisted labor.

The Pietists had come to realize that intellectual assent to theological doctrines does not make for Christian living; that goodness is more a matter of the heart than of the head. Others had expressed this basic fact before, but their voices could not be heard above the clash and din of theological controversy. The horrors and sufferings of the Thirty Years' War made men realize the utter futility of coercive methods in fostering Christian piety. The first one to find the true way, as we have seen, was Philip Jacob Spener, the father of the pietistic movement, but it was Francke who applied the idea to the education of children.

The sprouting of Francke's institutions. The institutions which Francke established may most fittingly be described as "sprouting" from insignificant beginnings. All of them were the result of the same spirit. They arose from his eager desire to grasp every opportunity that presented itself to help the needy, most especially poor and ignorant children.

While he was pastor at Glauchau, poor children customarily came for bread every Thursday afternoon. He called them into his study and questioned them on the catechism and Christian faith. He at once discovered their abysmal ignorance. His next step was that of providing funds for the tuition fees of some children by foregoing his supper each evening. But he quickly discovered they took the money but did not go to school. Next, he placed a box in his home for the depositing of alms for the poor. Finding therein a gift of seven gulden, he declared: "This is a handsome capital. I must do something important with it. I will establish a poor school." He bought 27 books, which he gave to poor children, and employed a university student to teach them two hours a day. The children sold all but four books, and did not return. Francke purchased more books, but, instead of giving them to the children, he collected them at the close of each period. Such was the origin of his poor school.

So successful did it quickly become that some well-to-do citizens requested that their children be permitted to attend the classes for pay. The number of such pupils grew so rapidly that Francke separated the groups into two schools: the one for the poor, and the other for the children of burghers.

MEMORIAL TO AUGUST HERMANN FRANCKE.

In 1695, Frau von Geusau of Sandersheim requested Francke to select a tutor for her children. Having none to recommend, he suggested that she and others send their children to him at Halle. The first to come were three boys, who were given instruction by university students under the oversight of a director. This small beginning grew into the *Pädagogium,* a school for the youth of the nobility. It was later recognized by the Prussian King and placed under royal patronage.

The same year a friend presented him with 500 thalers, with which he began his famous orphanages: one for boys, the other for girls. This was the beginning of the movement for the establishment of orphanages in Protestant Germany; quite a large number were later founded after the model set by Francke.

In 1697, another school was organized for the boys of the well-to-do middle class who were preparing for higher training. This was first known as a Latin school, but was later recognized as an approved gymnasium.

About the same time Francke began to operate a free table for poor university students. In return for their meals these students were to give instruction in the schools. Some ten years later this group developed into the *Teachers' Seminar* (*Seminarium Praeceptorum*), a training class for common school teachers, and the *Select Seminar* (*Seminarium Selectum*), for teachers in the Latin schools. In these classes Francke initiated teacher training in Germany.

Other institutions. These various institutions do not complete the list. Discovering a demand for a new literature to satisfy the pietistic spirit, he set up the *Canstein Bible Institute,* which printed and sold tracts, sermons and copies of the Scriptures. This brought a steady income for the institutions. Again, having secured some popular prescriptions, he established an apothecary shop, which furnished medicines free to the needy but which, by its sales to others, brought in considerable income.

Institutions established. The colossal character of his achievements can be measured by taking a cross-section survey of his various institutions at the time of his death in 1727:

FRANCKE'S INSTITUTIONS

	Boys	*Girls*	*Total*
Orphanages	100	34	134
German School			1725
Latin School	400		400
Pädagogium	82		82
	Men	*Women*	
Teachers in the schools	167	8	175
Ordinary free table for students teaching in his schools			155
Extraordinary free table for students teaching in his schools			100
Poor children fed at noon			148
Poor children fed at night			212

These institutions, still flourishing in Halle, are an admirable monument of Christian philanthropy, especially when it is considered that they were established at the end of an age noted for religious intolerance, bitterness, and bloodshed.

Curricula. In the courses of study in his schools the emphasis was placed upon the religious, the useful, and the realistic; all the sciences were viewed in relation to the honor of God and love to fellow man.

Religion was the central feature of the course of study in every school; all other subjects were of secondary importance, their value being determined by what they could contribute to religious life. Every means was employed to keep children from evil influences and to implant piety. Religious music, catechism, and the Scriptures were compulsory studies, and attendance upon church services was required. But Francke was not content with formal religious inculcation. He aimed to make religion a living enthusiasm in the life of every child. Accordingly, he set forth in detail a technique by which the spiritual life would be fostered, even in its most personal aspects; prayer and worship were to be taught children, not as mere formal habits, but as vital experiences.

Francke's attitude toward Humanism was about the same as that of Comenius. His aim in teaching Latin was its value in an understanding of the culture of the day; he placed little emphasis upon Latin eloquence and rhetoric. There was no special opposition to classical authors as such, though some of them were manifestly obnoxious to the pietistic spirit. But he placed much greater emphasis upon Greek and Hebrew, because they were the keys to unlock the sacred pages of Scripture. The charge has been made, and it was undoubtedly true, that classic Greek was neglected for the reading of the New Testament.

Realistic studies as extra-curricular activities. The relation of Francke to the development of Realism in the schools requires special explanation. In his Latin school, in addition to religion and the ancient languages, he included mathematics, history, geography, physics, botany, anatomy, painting, and music. For some reason he did not offer French. In the *Pädagogium,* which was a school for young nobles, were found these subjects, together with French, mineralogy, and astronomy. Francke also provided equipment for courses in mechanics, glass blowing, copper engraving, wood carving, and health guidance; a natural history museum and dissecting apparatus; an herbarium; and physical and chemical laboratories. Observation trips were made to shops of hand workers and artists. But all these activities were extra-curricular, confined to free periods and employed for the purpose of relaxation. There was evidently no intention of utilizing these experiences for vocational preparation, except in the broader sense of the term. Practical knowledge and handicrafts found no place even in the regular course of Francke's German school, but were introduced as extra-curricular activities. In the free periods, children were taken for walks, during which the objects of nature and the industries of man were explained to them. The free periods in the orphanages were occupied by the girls with spinning, knitting, sewing, and housework; by the boys with knitting and darning.

Summing up the situation, one finds that the tendency of Francke's educational philosophy was distinctly empirical and practical. If empiricism is experience as such and an emphasis upon the useful aspects of knowledge, Francke was decidedly empirical. In religious life he appealed directly to experience: he felt that religion must be a living reality, a genuine experience of the heart and will. In the *Pädagogium* the use of French and the various sciences leaned in the direction of the pragmatic.

Francke's influence on Prussian education. Of special importance was the influence of Francke and his institutions exerted on the progress of education in Prussia. Frederick William I, King of Prussia, visited The Halle Foundation and became its avowed patron. He later established the Prussian elementary school system on the principles of Francke. Of wider, deeper, and weightier influence, however, was the work of Johann Julius Hecker.

Numerous orphanages after the model of Francke's institutions were established throughout Germany. Moreover, men who were trained in his schools were in demand everywhere as pastors, teachers, and supervisors in orphanages and schools, and as missionaries.

Francke's work extended beyond the confines of Germany. The King of Denmark became interested in Christian missionary work in East India, and Francke was called upon to make the selection of the missionaries from among his students. He was a corresponding member of the English Society for the Propagation of the Gospel and the Society for the Propagation of Christian Knowledge; and his students established churches, schools, and orphanages in several of the American colonies.

Hecker and the realistic movement. Our chief interest in the amiable German pastor-educator, Hecker (1707-1768), lies in the fact that he advanced the most important contributions of the pietistic movement. In youth he came under the influence of Francke directly when he attended the University of Halle, and after graduation, taught in the *Pädagogium* for several years.

In 1739, Hecker became pastor of Trinity Church, Berlin, a position which presented an excellent opportunity to engage in educational reform under advantageous circumstances. The King of Prussia followed Hecker's efforts with closest attention, and supported his institutions with royal bounty. Hecker began his reforms by improving the instruction of poor children. In almost every street, well appointed and supervised schools were established.

In 1747, Hecker opened the first permanent school of realistic studies under the name *Oekonomisch-Mathematische Realschule.* This institution was designed particularly for boys who were not to receive a finished education; but students in the Latin school were likewise permitted to pursue the various realistic lines of instruction at their option. The curriculum was comprehensive, including: [3]

> ...arithmetic, geometry, mechanics, architecture, drawing, and the knowledge of nature. A knowledge of the human body was especially taught, then plants and minerals, and instruction was given in the cultivation of mulberry trees and silk-worms, and the scholars were taught by being taken to workshops. Among the classes were a manufacturing class, an architectural class, an agricultural class, a bookkeeping class, and a mining class.

For some years J. F. Hälm was the teacher of the *Realschule* and he put into practice the object-lesson method. In regard to this, we are told: [4]

> A large collection of real objects was used, among which were models of buildings, ships, chests, plows, churns, columns of the different orders, pictorial representations of an entire Roman triumphal procession, collections of merchandise, a miniature shop, a pharmacological collection, specimens of leather and other things. There was also a botanical garden.

In subject-matter and in method of instruction, this school followed in the wake of Comenius and Semler, and anticipated the application of the object-lesson principle by Basedow and Pestalozzi. Hecker's

---

[3] Barnard, Henry, *German Teachers and Educators,* p. 437. Hartford: Brown and Gross, 1878.

[4] *Ibid.*, pp. 437-438.

efforts largely failed to accomplish his full purpose because he was overpractical. He made the school a workshop for trade training. Not until later did it become clear to German educators that the *Realschule* must develop intelligence as to fundamental processes, and avoid the mechanical training of the trade school.

Teacher training. Another movement which Hecker carried forward according to the example set by Francke was the training of teachers. He established a teachers' seminar in connection with his elementary schools. In this undertaking, also, he enjoyed the assistance of Frederick the Great, who went so far as to require that all teachers to be employed in the schools located on his private domains must be educated in this institution.

Hecker's influence reached its climax when Frederick directed him to prepare the general school regulations of 1763. This law established the elementary school system of Prussia on a new and permanent basis.

Francke's influence in America. The spirit and the institutions of Francke directly affected education in Georgia and Pennsylvania. This influence was exerted through his followers, a considerable number of whom came to America. During the early part of the 18th century, numerous sects migrated to the New World for the purpose of securing religious liberty. Small colonies of Salzburgers and Moravians settled in Georgia. These were highly evangelical in religion, and in both groups the pastors and leaders had been trained under the influence of Francke's institutions. Bishop Spangenberg, the chief agent of the Moravians, had been a Halle professor and an inspector of the Latin school in Francke's orphanages. The Georgia colonists established orphanages and schools which exercised considerable influence. Similarly, the Moravians and large bodies of Lutherans founded new homes in Pennsylvania, where their leaders established orphanages, churches, and schools after the models of Francke. In all, several scores of Francke's followers, a number of whom had served as instructors or as supervisors in his schools, came over to Pennsylvania. The most prominent of these leaders were Count Zinzendorf, Henry Melchior Muhlenberg, and John Christopher Kunze.

Count Zinzendorf, a Saxon nobleman of great celebrity, lived in Francke's home and under his personal care for six years while a student in the *Pädagogium*. He was a man of like religious convictions and nature. He gathered the remnants of the Moravian Brethren and set up on his estate a religious community known as *Herrnhut*, that is, the

"Lodge of the Lord." He united in his religious life the faith of the old Moravian Brethren, the piety and missionary zeal of the Pietists, the credal views of the Lutherans, and the strict discipline of the Reformed Church. Imitating the example of Francke, he established a number of orphanages and schools. Among these were a girls' orphanage at *Herrnhut,* a school for girls of the nobility, a home for noble ladies, a *Pädagogium,* and a Latin school.

The most important work of Zinzendorf, however, was the establishment of Moravian colonies and schools in Pennsylvania. Such colonies were begun in Bethlehem, Nazareth, Lititz, and elsewhere. These colonies were semi-communistic in character, and their schools were not merely places of instruction but institutions in which to live a well-ordered life. They had nurseries for young children, boarding schools for boys and girls, and secondary boarding schools for adolescents. In addition to religion and the regular subjects the children were given vocational training. Several of the institutions have become noted. All show the influence of Francke.

It was likewise through the followers of Francke, especially Henry Melchior Muhlenberg, that a system of schools was organized among the Lutherans of Pennsylvania. Muhlenberg had been an instructor in the Halle orphanage, and later rose to an inspectorship. Selected by the son of Francke, who succeeded his father, he was appointed to take charge of the Lutheran Churches about Philadelphia. When he arrived in 1742, there were approximately 50,000 Germans in Pennsylvania. By 1750 the number had increased to 90,000, and there was great religious and cultural need among them.

Following the practice in Germany, each congregation in Pennsylvania established a parish school alongside the church. The teachers usually were German immigrant schoolmasters. The importance of Muhlenberg's work lay in the fact that he created a uniform system of parochial schools. He secured schoolmasters, admonished the people to support them, visited the schools, and examined pupils and teachers. Because of lack of steady support, Muhlenberg coöperated with the movement of Benjamin Franklin and Dr. William Smith, of the Academy and Charity School of Philadelphia, to establish charity schools. Funds were supplied by the S. P. G. in London and by similar organizations on the Continent. As a result of these efforts, a number of German-English schools were conducted. The movement had the coöperation of the Church of England, the Lutherans, and the Reformed Church, but was vigorously attacked by the quietist groups and came to an end after about ten years. The Reverend Michael Schlatter was the officially designated *superintendent* of the system.

Some 24 pastors and teachers from Francke's schools assisted Muhlenberg. The chief of these was John Christopher Kunze. While pastor in Philadelphia, he established a Latin school in 1773, with a view to giving a better secondary training to future pastors and teachers. He served on the faculty of the University of Pennsylvania, into which institution he introduced the German language, literature, and philosophy. Removing to a pastorate in New York City, he performed the same service for Columbia College.

The revitalizing of the German universities. The universities of Germany experienced no new impulses for more than a century after the death of Melanchthon. Their intellectual vigor, absorbed and wasted in sterile theological controversies, exhibited few signs of healthy vitality and none of genuine progress. But a new era was at hand, and it was to raise them to the greatest renown as centers of research and progress. The adaptation of the advancement of knowledge as the main function of university scholarship, dates from the last decades of the 17th century. It was the outcome of the Pietistic movement, on the one hand, and the realistic-rationalistic movement on the other.

The first important result of the Pietistic movement in the field of higher education was the establishment of the University of Halle by the Elector Frederick of Brandenburg. The only university that he had at this time in his scattered domains was the far-distant one at Königsberg, in East Prussia. The Universities of Saxony, Erfurt, and Leipzig showed themselves so hostile to progressive educational movements, and especially to Pietism, that Frederick, who strongly approved this doctrine, felt obliged to establish an institution to teach the new point of view. As a result, Halle, founded in 1694, may justly claim to be the first modern university. Here, the new religious spirit combined with the yearning for free inquiry put an end to formalism, traditionalism, and subservience to authority, so far as German universities were concerned.

Among the first and most celebrated members of the faculty were: Christian Thomasius, disciple of Grotius and Pufendorf, and professor of law; Christian Wolff, disciple of Leibnitz, and professor of philosophy and mathematics; and August Hermann Francke, professor of oriental languages and religion. Halle opened with 700 students, and soon overshadowed its more conservative rivals. Supported by Leibnitz, the greatest German scholar of the age, the institution boldly assailed the traditional methods, aims, and materials of university instruction. The first far-reaching innovation was the use of the German language. Thomasius and Wolff contended that the lack of progress in science and philosophy was due to the pedantic adherence to Latin as the medium of expression. Still more radical was their disregard of the ancient authorities. When all other university professors throughout Europe were still the slaves of Aristotelianism, the professors of Halle refused to bow the knee. Wolff contended that all sound knowledge is based upon exact sciences, not on theology.

One perceives that here began the warfare, so far as the universities were concerned, between the principle of authoritative teaching, which had hitherto controlled both subject matter and method of instruction, and the new principle of free investigation. According to the old view, it is the task of the academic teacher to hand on the tradition of an inherited and absolute truth; according to the new view, his task is to seek the truth through his own investigations, and to lead his students to do the same. Independent thought is the right and duty of every member of the university. The new principle was well expressed in a memorial address delivered at Halle by Professor Gundling in 1711, when he discussed the question, "What is the task of the university?" Gundling answered: "To lead to wisdom, *i. e.*, to the ability to distinguish the true and the false; but this is impossible, if there be any limits imposed upon research." He then proceeded to discuss this question: "Has a man the right to compel another by threat of punishment to accept an opinion which he himself holds to be true?" Gundling denied it. By natural right and expediency, coercion must be rejected. There is nothing so practical as freedom of teaching and writing. Through these, all intellectual powers are called forth; all sciences come to their fruitage; and art, riches, and population increase. However, someone might object, freedom is indeed good, but not license. Gundling replied:

> Has ever anything new been sought, without the reproach of subjectiveness and of licentiousness being brought against it? . . . Therefore, in these things coercion is above all else an evil; instruct, admonish, request; if they hear, it is well; if not, learn to bear it.

Thomasius, following Grotius and Pufendorf, based law upon the nature of man; Wolff sought the foundations of philosophy in reason; and Francke relied on the inner light for religious life. They all agreed in abandoning the old policy of teaching authoritative texts, and began to offer courses along the new lines. Halle quickly rose to fame, and other universities in Germany gradually accepted the new order.

The general results of Pietism. Pietism exerted highly important effects upon the culture of the age. These may be briefly summarized as follows: (1) It placed a new value upon feeling or emotion. This emphasis upon the role of feeling in religion paved the way for the emphasis upon feeling in all other aspects of life. (2) It emphasized the study of the Scriptures in relation to practical piety rather than the catechism and dogmatic theology for doctrinal orthodoxy. (3) It vindicated the right of laymen to participate in church services. (4) It gave a new impetus to hymnology. (5) It brought forth a powerful new interest in philanthropy and missionary work. (6) Its chief significance, however, lay in the reorganization of education as a synthesis of Christian culture, realistic knowledge, and training for practical life. (7) Another great contribution lay in directing attention to the need for education of all children, the poor as well as the rich. (8) The effects upon university methods and academic freedom were likewise consequential.

The efforts of the Pietists have not received due credit in the history of education. Furthermore, their results would have been even greater had it not been for several inherent weaknesses. At its best, Pietism was somewhat narrow and one-sided, and it contained a tendency toward fanaticism. The evangelical spirit is not universal; consequently rationalistic and conventional minds could not share its zeal.

Chapter 10

NONCONFORMIST EDUCATION AND CHARITY SCHOOL MOVEMENTS

THE rise of Nonconformist Education in Great Britain. The effect of the suppressive measures of the established church and the crown upon the strongwilled Presbyterians and Puritans was not what these enemies intended. Prevented from carrying out in England the usual program of education and indoctrination adopted wherever the Calvinists controlled the government, and threatened with stern penalties, these dissenters chose to organize instruction in a less conspicuous way. But it had the same well-known features, home instruction, elementary and higher instruction, all of them profoundly religious and intellectual, not to say rationalistic in tendency.

A number of background factors tended to popularize the nonconformist educational movement: (1) The clergy of the Church of England failed to institute parish schools after the Reformation as did the Lutheran pastors in Germany and the Calvinists in other lands; the consequence was a lack of elementary instruction in England. (2) The Revolution of 1688 brought a new spirit of religious toleration, and, as a consequence, the intense bitterness against the Puritans began to abate, and opposition to their schools was surprisingly slight. (3) The interest in Latin as the sole means of attaining culture declined. No longer a commonly spoken tongue, it retreated to the classrooms of the grammar schools and to the colleges of Oxford and Cambridge. As a consequence the Latin grammar schools no longer satisfied the cultural needs and ideals of the people. (4) From 1670 onward a number of dissenters who had no license from the bishop to teach were prosecuted in the law courts. But the courts, which leaned to the side of liberty, ruled that the law required the bishop's license only for those who taught in the Latin grammar school. In 1700 in "the Cox suit" the decision rendered was still more favorable to the dissenting schoolmen. It declared: "There was not and has never been an ecclesiastical control over any other than grammar schools." Again in 1714 the court ruled that teaching an elementary school without a bishop's license was not a civil offense. (5) The nonconformist schools adopted up-to-date methods and broadened the curriculum by adding realistic studies.

In these ways it came about that, despite the stringent laws that were intended to restrict teaching to the established doctrine, nonconformists set up schools and academies superior to the orthodox system. It will be noted, however, that neither the Church of England nor the Parliament took a positive stand in favor of universal literacy, enlightenment, and a national system of schools. England as a whole was quite averse to the conception that literacy is indispensable for social, political, and economic progress. The leaders of England never conceived that the poor needed any other education than agriculture, factory work, and unskilled labor.

The interest in home instruction. The stressing of morals, manners, and religion by the Calvinists awakened interest in home education. However, not only Calvinists but the aristocracy of England regarded the home as the best school for young children. A multitude of books was published to assist parents in their task. There comes first to mind Comenius' *School of Infancy;* William Gouge's work, *Of Domestical Duties* (third edition, 1634); and the most popular of all, Defoe's *The Family Instructor* (1715), and *The New Family Instructor,* which had phenomenal sales, as a guide to parents in the instruction of their children. There was also a flood of new catechisms.

Elementary schools. In place of a state-supported system of elementary schools, the dissenters had to content themselves with private institutions which would not openly flout the law. Despite the various measures of the church and the crown, so obviously intended to destroy utterly all nonconformist indoctrination, many schools sprang up. The dissenting pastors offered instruction so that their boys would not need to go to the schools where they would be required to swear to conform to the articles of faith of the Church of England; that they might themselves make a living by their profession, and might carry on their work of religious indoctrination. It is known that between 1660 and 1730 about 1000 elementary schools were endowed most of which lasted until the middle of the 19th century. It may also be inferred that many nonconformist institutions were conducted that did not survive so long.

The exact extent of nonconformist instruction at this time is not known. The information on these schools is so scanty that one feels completely befogged. When it is recalled that all teaching except by those licensed by the bishop was illegal and punishable with severity, it is obvious that for a long time the education of the nonconformists was on a "black market" basis. Only when these nonconformist groups were assured by action of the courts that their work was not to be banned did they begin to teach openly.

The Academy movement. By far the most consequential development from the Restoration onward was the instituting of Academies by the various dissenting groups. Scholarly Puritan and Presbyterian pastors and university men, dispossessed of their pulpits or college positions because of the intolerance of church and crown, saw the necessity of schools of secondary and college rank. John Milton had advised the supplanting of the universities by academies; moreover, this was the means which Calvin had used so effectively in Geneva to train the young men who carried his reforming doctrines to other lands.

The first academies were small, each taught by a master in his home. The number of students varied up to 40 or 50 in the more popular institutions. Some had a four year course of college level, others, because of poor preparation of their students, added two years of elementary training in Latin. The age of admission ranged from 12 to 14 years. The curriculum followed the pattern set by the grammar schools and colleges but varied from school to school. In addition to the Latin and Greek languages, the main subjects were mathematics, natural philosophy (physics), astronomy, logic, rhetoric, geography, ethics, and metaphysics. In some schools, Hebrew, anatomy, and even "politics," as a science, were offered as extras.

After the Act of Toleration (1689) the restrictions against nonconformist teaching were slightly relaxed, and the elusive academies entered upon a new period of development. They were now more public in character, some of them had boards to direct them, and the number of students increased three or four times. A head master now added assistants to help carry the work of instruction.

The academies now became more distinctly training schools for professional life and vocations. From the first they were largely seminaries for the preparation of ministers; now they prepared young men to study law, medicine, and other vocations, and to become merchants, military and naval experts, squires, and civil servants. Their services were expanded far beyond those of the colleges in Oxford and Cambridge which were practically dead so far as learning was concerned. The best families of the established church, as well as nonconformists, sent their sons to these schools because of the efficiency of their moral discipline and instruction.

Some of the academies had an encyclopedic curriculum such as that advocated by Comenius and Milton. The academy at Kibworth, in a four year course, included geometry, algebra, trigonometry, conic sections, physics, mechanics, hydrostatics, geography, natural history, astronomy, celestial mechanics, chronology, Latin (used for all lectures), Greek, Hebrew, French, logic, disputations, rhetoric, oratory, civil history, ethics, pneumatology (psychology), metaphysics, theological disputations, Christian evidences, architecture, and military sciences. Such was the course to train men for service in church and state.

Defoe (1659 or 1660-1731). After Locke the first Englishman to make any worthwhile contribution to educational theory was Daniel Defoe. In 1697 he published *Essay upon Projects* in which he advocated the establishing of academies. The first was to be a national society "to polish and refine the English Tongue." The common habit of swearing especially excited Defoe's censure and he called for an organization to combat it. The second was to be "A Royal Academy for Military Sciences"; the third an academy for the education of women; and another academy for music. This book deeply affected Benjamin Franklin and led to the founding of the Academy and Charity School of Philadelphia, which ripened into the University of Pennsylvania. This was the beginning of the academy movement in America.

Defoe's chief claim to celebrity, however, rests on *Robinson Crusoe* (1719) which deserves acclaim not only as one of the greatest books in children's literature, but also as an educational work of importance because of the power it exercised on Rousseau's theory of natural education.

Phillip Doddridge was a student at Kibworth academy and later became head of the most famous of all academies at Northampton, where for twenty-seven years he made educational history. He discontinued lecturing in Latin, trained men for many different professions and vocations, and raised the academy movement to such a high position of esteem that persecution of nonconformists virtually ceased. He made realistic training the new type of education in England.

McLachlan, in his exhaustive history of the academies, lists some 72 established from 1662 to 1799.[1] If they appear few in number, it must be remembered that they were competitors of the colleges of Oxford and Cambridge, not mere secondary schools. Many of the leading men of England received their training in these institutions.

Scotland. In this land of Calvinism education was in a flourishing condition from the primary level through the universities. According to Adam Smith, the noted economist who recommended parish schools for England, "In Scotland the establishment of such parish schools has taught almost the whole common people to read, and a very great portion of them to write and account."

New religious awakenings. The most phenomenal quality of the Christian religion is its capacity for reviving its original apostolic fervor. Founded upon the emotional response of the individual to the spirit of justice and goodwill in the universe, it is forever breaking the encrustations of custom and circumstance and expressing itself anew in living acts of concern for others. Times of extremity and suffering are particularly apt to arouse the elemental feeling of compassion which is basic to the Messianic spirit.

Nothing could be more obvious than the failure of both the Protestant and Catholic confessions to satisfy the spiritual instincts of the people just before and during the early part of the 18th century. Interest in religion had reached a low level. The fury of the prolonged struggle of Anglicans, Puritans, and Catholics had spent itself and a working accord was reached. But the cold ritualism and the dry doctrinal and moralistic sermons of the established clergy held no strong appeal for the masses. Church services languished, and gross immorality, drunkenness, and ignorance abounded. Samuel Wesley (father of John and Charles) in 1701 reported that, for the "7000 souls" in his parish, he had set up monthly sacraments but had only 20 communicants; 'That there are no Papists nor Presbyterians in his Parish. That there are about 40 Quakers, and above 70 Anabaptists that insult him everywhere, and about 100 of little or no Religion.' It must be further stated that the dissenting

---

[1] McLachlan, H., *English Education Under the Test Acts, being the History of the Nonconformist Academies, 1662-1820.* Manchester: Manchester University Press, 1931.

churches were just as lacking in spiritual fervor as those of the Establishment.

At this time both in England and America, the revival of religious enthusiasm broke out. In the established church, where it began, it took the form of a new interest in the improvement of manners and morals and the founding of missions and charity schools for underprivileged children; it reached out to America in an earnest effort to furnish religious services to the colonists on the plantations and to convert the Negroes and Indians. A number of Religious Societies were formed in the Anglican churches by Dr. Anthony Horneck, a German, who became the most popular and zealous preacher in England, and by Dr. Thomas Bray, who was especially interested in missions. Under the leadership of Dr. Bray, and with the loyal support of Queen Anne, two benevolent groups flourished, "The Society for Promoting Christian Knowledge" (The S.P.C.K.) in 1698 and "The Society for the Propagation of the Gospel in Foreign Parts" (The S.P.G.) chartered in 1701.

The second phase of the religious movement in England was the revival, begun in the 1730's, which resulted in Methodism. It started in a student club at Oxford under the leadership of John Wesley. The fervent preaching of John and Charles Wesley and the still more impassioned evangelism of George Whitfield in England and America were exceedingly disgusting to the Anglicans who despised earnestness of any kind and branded enthusiasm "as a folly or a crime." Contemporary with the new enthusiasm of Methodism in England and the colonies was the "Great Awakening" under Jonathan Edwards in Massachusetts. All these revival movements belong to the field of church history, though they had inevitable and far reaching consequences for education.

Kinds of schools in England. The English Parliament had no interest in establishing a system of schools, for education was considered a voluntary concern. Parents, local interests, and charitable societies looked after the training of children as best they could. The following plans were followed in the first part of the 17th century:

1. *Home instruction.* Family instruction was the policy of both Puritans and Anglicans. The aristocracy of wealth and title employed nurses who spoke French to their charges, and private tutors who taught the older children.

2. *Dame schools.* Parents in the cities, who wished to do so and could afford it, sent their young children to Dame Schools. This was the practice as early as the 15th and 16th century. In the 18th century

such schools became fairly common in the towns and cities and they continued until near the close of the 19th century, when they were superseded by publicly aided elementary schools. A Dame School was a combination nursery and primary school conducted by a mistress who divided her time between teaching and domestic tasks.

A Hornbook, from the Time of Charles II.

The course of study included learning the Lord's Prayer, the Apostles' Creed, and the alphabet, and reading easy words. Many of the dames could themselves scarcely read or write. The hornbook was the common text. The children were often too young to learn anything other than a little discipline; in any case expert methods of educating young children were not yet developed. The compensation was such a mere pittance that no capable woman could afford to undertake this work. Some such schools were carried on in the growing towns of the American colonies.

3. *The Latin Grammar school.* The ideas of John Brinsley affected the elementary and Latin schools of England. While the course of study remained much the same, its character underwent a change, especially in that Latin ceased to be the only object of scholarship, culture, and literary merit. It had declined to such an extent by the middle of the 17th century that the Latin secretary to the king was dispensed with at the Restoration. However, because it was no longer a spoken language, the problem of learning to read it was rendered more difficult. The grammar school came under a barrage of criticism because of its continuous grind on Latin grammar. Men like Elyot and Montaigne had advocated the direct method of learning Latin and urged the employment of nurses and tutors who would speak it to the children. Obviously this could only be possible for the rich. Milton and Locke criticized the method used. The realistic group of reformers insisted upon putting more concreteness into methods of learning the languages and resorted not only to pictures but to things to give children a Latin vocabulary. Latin grammar schools were still conducted in the towns, but the opposition to the learning of Latin had caused a loss of interest and even a decline in these schools, for by this time Latin was a spoken language only in university circles.

4. *The great public schools.* These institutions were utilized for higher elementary and secondary education by the aristocratic class.

5. *Universities.* The two universities, Oxford and Cambridge, changed little during this period. The thing of greatest significance was the work of Newton in mathematics at Cambridge. This was not only significant in itself as a contribution to science, but it was all the more conspicuous because English universities did not look upon the advancement of knowledge as one of their functions. At this time they occupied a low place in the national life and were severely criticized by men of letters.

The Charity School Movement. The medieval custom of instructing children in religion in parish churches was neglected in England after the Reformation. By the end of the 17th century the poverty, squalor, debauchery, and ignorance were appalling. According to Samuel Wesley, reporting on his parish of Epworth, "The People are so extremely ignorant, that not one in 20 can say the Lord's Prayer right, nor one in 30 the Belief." Conditions were just as bad elsewhere.

Human depravity as applied to young children is a gloomy doctrine, yet it profoundly affected the educational thinking of the 17th century. One may claim that the most aggressive school movements of the time got their impetus from this belief. Its program of education was paramount in Holland where hyper-Calvinism flourished, and from there it radiated in all directions. Comenius became the fountainhead of the new theory of education and his ideas and plans were motivated by a desire to raise "sunken humanity." Not only was this same influence in the saddle in Scotland; but, notwithstanding the opposition of the established church, it gave England its greatest educators and schools in the late 17th and early 18th centuries. The doctrine of human depravity dominated the educational views of all the leaders such as Comenius, John Milton, Hoole, Woodward, Defoe, and Doddridge.

In France the Port Royalist educators were also under the influence of this doctrine. That it was an impelling motive in other cases is borne out by the testimony of many writers. Woodward was emphatic in regard to it: "We have filled our children's bones with sin. It is our engagement to do all we can to root that sin out, which we have been a means to root so fast in. . . . We see what an engagement it is—*the greatest and strongest that can be thought of*." The sense of responsibility to undo the ravages of innate depravity led to increased emphasis upon education.

Thomas Gouge (1609-1681), a dissenting minister, set up a catechetical class in his church in London, and also employed the poor in spinning flax and hemp. Driven from his church by the Act of Uniformity (1662) he went to Wales, which was quite destitute of knowledge and religion. Here he set up churches and schools, 300 of them by his death in 1681. His efforts were thereafter carried on by philanthropic friends.

The movement to establish charity schools was due in part to a wave of compassion for the poor, but even more to a revulsion of feeling against the gross "immorality," "profanity," "barbarous ignorance," and "vile practices" of the masses which prevailed during the last half of the 17th century.

The charity movement in England was linked with German Pietism and there are substantial reasons to believe causal relations obtained between the two. First, Dr. Anthony Horneck, German-born and educated, the outstanding preacher in the established church in London, organized various charitable societies which preceded the establishment of the S.P.C.K. and its affiliate, *The Society for Propagating the Gospel* (S.P.G.). Second, Francke was a corresponding member of these societies, and helped to supply them with workers from his training schools. Third, the instruction given in the charity schools and the other methods of work of the societies resembled that of the Pietists. Fourth, the two societies had the zealous support of Queen Anne and her husband, a scion of the Royal family of Denmark, whose King worked in close harmony with Francke.

The S.P.C.K. was founded for the express purpose of promoting Christian education at home and abroad. Its scope included providing libraries for clergymen and mission workers in England and in the plantations of the Colonies; catechetical free schools for the instruction of poor children in reading and writing, and more especially in the principles of the Christian religion; and promoting legislation in England requiring the teaching of reading and the catechism by all those employing or apprenticing children in their workhouses.

The Society for the Propagation of the Gospel in Foreign Parts (S.P.G.), founded by Royal Charter in 1701, patterned its work after that of the S.P.C.K. The two Societies divided the territory; the S.P.C.K. worked in England, and the S.P.G. in the American colonies, European countries, India, and other places. During the 18th century it had over 300 members.

Working through their missionaries, the S.P.C.K. and the S.P.G. offered instruction in catechism, reading, writing, elementary mathematics, navigation, gardening, farming, and household arts such as spinning, sewing, and knitting. The societies also promoted a few grammar schools. The S.P.C.K. apprenticed some boys, and, for those who displayed special ability, places were provided in the higher schools and universities. It conducted 89 charity schools in England in 1704. The charity schools provided not only instruction but, in many cases, free clothing, board and lodging.

"In 1712 manual labour, such as spinning, sewing, knitting, gardening, ploughing, and harrowing," was recommended for the charity schools. In some places "navigation and mathematics" were taught, and the trustees looked out for talented pupils, "who might be advanced to posts of credit and trust." The Bible and prayer books were circulated. The S.P.C.K. was opposed to the Wesleyan movement and no Methodist schools were assisted. Samuel Wesley had been a member of the society but neither John nor Charles were. Work was carried on by the society in England, Ireland, European countries, and East India. A similar society was established to work in Scotland.

Children were taught "to read truly and distinctly," and "to write a plain and legible hand," arithmetic was an added subject. The object was preparation for a vocation, but most important was the desire to train them to be moral and religious. To accomplish this they were taught to read the Scriptures "and other pious and useful books," to learn the church catechism, to hear prayers in school and at home, and to attend church services.

Textbooks and methods. An era as mercurial as the 17th century was bound to see significant changes in the textbooks. Most of the old texts were revised or discarded, and many new ones published. The hornbook was more used than ever as the teaching of reading increased.

The use of catechisms increased, particularly as Calvinistic synods required that it be taught in all families, churches, and schools. One of the oldest, and certainly the most attractive, of all the Reformation texts was the Heidelberg Catechism, published first in 1563. It was officially endorsed by the Synod of Dort (1618) and was used by Calvinists everywhere. It shared popularity with Bunyan's immortal *Pilgrim's Progress* (1678). A flood of new catechisms now flowed from the presses.

Edmund Coote wrote the most popular textbook of the 17th century, printing it first in 1596. It was designed for beginners and had the title: *The English Schole-Maister, Teaching all his Scholars of What age soever the most easie, short and perfect order of distinct Reading and true Writing our English tongue, that hath ever been known or published by any.* This work contained the alphabet, spelling lessons, short catechism, some psalms, chronology, and a few pages of arithmetic. Tailors, weavers, shop-keepers, and seamsters were advised that they could "sit on thy shopboard, at thy books, or thy needle and never hinder any work to hear thy scholars." This work received the approval of Brinsley and Hoole and sold 39 editions.

Many changes took place in grammar texts as the methods of teaching Latin changed. For the first time in the history of textbooks, Comenius used pictures to teach children the Latin and vernacular words together. This device made a strong impression and was widely copied. Slowly the teaching of Latin grammar was changed, and by 1700 the best texts used explanations in English even for the teaching of Latin. Lily's *Latin Grammar,* still the prime favorite, was translated into English. In English grammar, the texts were at first written in Latin. Greenwood's *Grammatica Anglica* (1694) was famous. Brightland marked a new era in 1712 by the publication of *A Grammar of the English Tongue....*

making a compleat System of an English Education for the Use of the Schools of Great Britain and Ireland. This work marks the independence of English culture. Although he did not deny its indebtedness to Latin, he pointed out a greater debt owed to a number of other languages.

Arithmetic, also, because of its use in trade and the arts, acquired a number of texts. Robert Recorde had published the first in 1540, called *The Grounds of Arts.* His text on geometry followed. Some years later he published in the English language the second part with the peculiar title *The Whetstone of Witte,* the first work on algebra in English. Hodder's *Arithmetic* in 1661 became the outstanding text in its field and was imitated by later works.

The use of Colloquies. The heart of humanistic education was the inculcation of manners and morals so as to produce the gentleman-scholar. This remained the unaltered goal of English education for the aristocracy, and people of the middle class who followed the pattern set by their social superiors. To effect this objective the most valuable texts were *The Colloquies* of Erasmus, Vives, and Corderius. After Latin grammar was mastered the leading texts used to help young boys to speak Latin were Cicero's *Select Letters* and the *Comedies of Terence.* These were chosen because they contained the words and phrases of ordinary conversation in ancient Rome. These words and expressions were copied by students in phrase books, learned by heart and were then employed as exercises in conversation. Terence was notable because of his pure Latin style and vivid portrayal of life.

The *Colloquies* imitated these ancient works by bringing into the classroom ideas which can be readily grasped by the child's mind and in dialogue form like the catechisms. The dialogue, or question and answer method, continued in textbooks the conversational method of teaching, which was practiced before printing of texts began, and had come down from Socrates. The *Colloquies* were dialogues or conversations on aspects of life familiar to children. The *Colloquies of Corderius* (Lyons, 1564) was especially popular among the Calvinists because it describes boy life in Geneva, and was the most vivid such account in the 17th century.

AMERICAN EDUCATION IN THE EARLY 18TH CENTURY

New Social Developments. At no time in the history of the western world have educational theory and practice undergone a greater alteration than in the 18th century. Many people habitually think of the

American Revolution too narrowly. They regard it as merely a political upheaval confined to the Thirteen Colonies. Many have failed to understand that what transpired on this continent was but a single episode, though highly significant, in the political transmutation which gave birth to the modern democratic state. Moreover, the political aspect was but a by-product of the deeper and more universal change in the cultural and social life and ideals of the age. In large measure, the leaders of American life and thought had come under the spell of the revolutionary philosophy of the French Enlightenment, and were no longer tolerant of the restraint imposed by British conservatism, either in government or in thought and social living.

The population of the British colonies in North America increased rapidly, and at the outbreak of the Revolution totalled about 2,500,000 people of European extraction. Cities such as Boston, New York, Philadelphia, and Charleston became important commercial centers. In the South the plantation system had greatly expanded. In New England farming, manufacturing, lumbering, fishing, and commerce flourished. Although there was much poverty, numerous financiers, merchants, and industrialists in the larger cities began to amass considerable wealth. Leadership was gradually changing from the clergymen to lawyers, business men, and planters. This shift in leadership was reflected in government, and in literature and scholarship. Scholars in increasing numbers were devoting their efforts to science, politics, and economics, and to the applications of these bodies of knowledge to commerce, agriculture, industry, and government. Abstract discussions of theological and metaphysical subtleties did not hold for the 18th century the interest that they had for the 17th.

Although the growth of population was accompanied by important effects along the Atlantic seaboard, its effect in the interior was still more significant. Hunters and trappers pushed into the back country, and were soon followed by farmers and planters. The mountains were penetrated, and settlements formed in western Pennsylvania, western Virginia, Kentucky, Tennessee, and what is now Vermont.

Pioneer life was hard, but it afforded an opportunity for the vigorous and self-reliant to make their way in the world. Leadership on the frontier depended almost solely upon the strength, hardiness, and resourcefulness of the individual. Men rose to wealth and influence, or sank to the lowest level, because of their own personal qualities; hereditary position and social connections counted for little. Unfortunately, culture and gentility were likewise too frequently unappreciated. The hard life of the frontier stripped away much that was useless and that hindered social development. It also stripped away much that is indispensable for gracious and free living. The frontiersman prized neither critical scholarship nor the fine and liberal arts, and all too frequently despised the ordinary amenities of social life. Pioneer life developed initiative, self-reliance, independence, and an intense love of freedom; hence, this back-country section played an important role in the American Revolution and in the subsequent development of American democracy.

So far as the religious complexion is concerned, a great transformation was beginning. Large numbers of Scotch Presbyterians settled in Virginia, the Carolinas, and the Middle Atlantic states. They occupied sections in which the farms were small and were not operated by slaves. Methodists and Baptists increased rapidly and minor religious groups made their homes in Georgia, the Carolinas, Maryland, Pennsylvania, and New Jersey.

Religious toleration became more common. The first half of the 18th century witnessed great spiritual awakenings. The European spirit of goodwill showed itself in missionary work, in the growth of toleration, and in the first opposition to slavery.

THE CHARITY SCHOOL MOVEMENT IN AMERICA

The Society for the Propagation of the Gospel in Foreign Parts. The S.P.G. established at the turn of the century in London by the Church of England set up many elementary schools and over 340 missions in the colonies. Work was carried on in New York from 1704 to 1782; New Jersey from 1712 to 1777; Pennsylvania from 1712 to 1778; Boston and Salem from 1707 to 1773 (three schools were in operation in Boston in 1709); and South Carolina from 1707 to 1773. Until the work of the Society in America was terminated by the Revolution, about two-thirds of its funds were expended here. Negro slaves and Indians were special objects of attention. It was a policy of the S.P.G. to admit poor children to its schools without charge, and it is estimated that from one-fourth to one-half of the pupils paid no tuition.

The work of the S.P.G. in Pennsylvania began late but is of special interest. A large number of Germans had settled in this colony and about one-third of those belonged to Quietist groups, such as the Mennonites, Moravians, and Dunkards.

The attachment of the Quietists to their native language, religion, and customs, and their antiwar sentiments made them objects of unusual concern to the political leaders. Benjamin Franklin, William Smith, first provost of the College of Philadelphia, Michael Schlatter, German clergyman of the Reformed Church, and other influential Pennsylvanians invited the S. P. G. to establish charity schools in the colony. An avowed purpose of the movement was to promote the unity of the colony by teaching the Germans the English language and encouraging them to mingle freely with their neighbors. These efforts were, however, resisted by the Quietist groups, who clung with great tenacity to their native dialect and religion. The Society did, however, succeed in establishing a system of charity schools in Pennsylvania, a system which was maintained until just before the outbreak of the Revolution. Taken all together, the Society's work represented an important movement to provide free elementary education in America. Through its efforts, the first Lutheran parish schools were established and these led, in later years, to important developments.

Benjamin Franklin (1706-1790). Author, publisher, scientist, inventor, and statesman, Benjamin Franklin was the leading figure in American educational reform before the Revolution. He led in so many new and important projects that some attention must be given to his colorful and dynamic personality. Although born in Boston, where he lived his early years, he received little formal schooling. However, by his own persistent efforts he trained himself as a writer of note, gained international recognition as a scientist, and acquired a remarkable mastery of languages. By early middle age, when he had accumulated a considerable fortune from printing, he virtually retired from private business in order to devote himself to public service. He took a leading role in the founding of the republic.

Franklin was greatly influenced by John Locke, Daniel Defoe, and by contemporary European scientists and economists. He was the moving spirit in the founding of the Junto, a society for mutual self-help; the American Philosophical Society; the Philadelphia Public Library; the Academy and College of Philadelphia, which became the University of Pennsylvania; and the Pennsylvania Hospital. He was opposed to sectarianism and also to ecclesiastical domination over public affairs.

Franklin wrote a good deal, and his views on education stress the self-reliance, public spirit, and practicality of the New England mind. As he himself was self-trained, Franklin championed self-education. He had won marked success by his industry, resourcefulness, and thrift, so he believed that studies should be pursued for their utility. This attitude was confirmed by contact with Germans in Pennsylvania who shared the realistic trend given education by Francke and other Pietists. The type of education which he advocated was, however, somewhat narrow. He proposed that the young be taught mathematics, English composition and literature, public speaking, politics, the natural sciences, morals, and religion; and he insisted especially that attention be paid to the practical applications of knowledge. He proposed that German children in Pennsylvania be taught in English, as a means of unifying the language, life, and government of the colony.

THE ACADEMY MOVEMENT IN AMERICA

A reform needed. Early in the 18th century general dissatisfaction arose with the existing colleges and the Latin grammar schools. These institutions did not meet the needs of youths preparing for careers as ships' officers, merchants, surveyors, or manufacturers. They were criticized particularly because they did not include in their courses of study the new sciences. The nonconformist academies in England had adjusted to the changes in the world of scholarship and practical affairs, offering training in keeping with the times. In the colonies a few private schools, before the middle of the century, were beginning to fit boys for business and industrial pursuits.

The Academy and College of Philadelphia. In 1749 Franklin published a pamphlet entitled *Proposals Relating to the Education of Youth in Pennsylvania,* in which he advocated establishing in Philadelphia an academy in which youths might "learn those things that are likely to be most useful and most ornamental, regard being had to the several professions for which they are intended." The institution was to include three schools: a mathematical school, an English school, and a classical school. Special attention was to be devoted to the English part of education, which Franklin thought should be the basis of the rest. The academy was opened in 1751, was chartered in 1753 and received a new charter as a college in 1755. From the beginning it was an innovation, and was notable as the first American academy—a type of institution that was to dominate American education for almost a century. Distinctive features of the institution were the attention paid to the teaching of the English language, literature, and oratory; the introduction of scientific courses; and the non-sectarian control of the institution, which has been governed from the first by a self-perpetuating board of trustees.

The academy movement. The second half of the 18th century witnessed the rapid expansion of academies in America. These institutions were destined to supplant the Latin schools as the dominant secondary schools, and to affect secondary and higher education in America in many ways. The academy provided a liberal education of a new type, and a foundation for vocations which the colonial Latin school and the college did not give. Academies were founded by wealthy philanthropists who provided for their building and support, by churches, by companies organized for the purpose, and by enterprising teachers. These institutions were for the most part governed by boards of trustees, either self-perpetuating or elected by the church or company that established them.

Among the early New England academies the most notable were the following: Dummer's, at Byfield, Massachusetts, opened in 1761; Phillips Academy, at Andover, Massachusetts, opened in 1778; and Phillips Academy, at Exeter, New Hampshire, opened five years later. After the Revolution, academies were founded in all of the states, and probably numbered more than 100 by 1800. There were separate academies for boys and for girls; but even in the 18th century some were coeducational. As pioneer institutions they sought to take care of the educational needs of the new communities.

The academies were, for the most part, quasi-public in character. Though largely supported by tuition fees, many of them received public subscriptions and sometimes state grants. For example, before 1797 seven academies in Massachusetts had received grants of land from the state government; thereupon that same year a bill was passed which provided for a grant of land to every academy meeting certain conditions. The laws of 1784 and 1787 provided for the oversight of academies by the "Board of Regents of the University of the State of New York." Until the middle of the 19th century, the academies, though charging tuition and controlled by private boards, played an important part in the education of the various states.

The academies taught Latin and Greek, as did the Latin grammar schools, but also introduced new subjects. English grammar and literature, oratory, arithmetic, algebra, geometry, trigonometry, surveying, geography, history, astronomy, "natural philosophy" (elementary physics and chemistry), and psychology, ethics, and Evidences of Christianity were studied. For girls, music, needlework, dancing, declamation, painting, and French were leading studies. Many academies organized a classical course and an English course.

The academies differed greatly in standards. Some were no better than poor grammar schools, while others prepared students for the junior year at Yale and Princeton. Students regularly proceeded from the academy to the study of law, medicine, and even of divinity. Some studied only higher arithmetic, mathematics, and surveying, with English grammar and literature and then felt that their education was completed.

The academies gained popularity because they offered courses adapted to the intellectual and practical needs of the middle class of the day, needs which the Latin schools and the colleges did not serve. Supported principally by tuition fees, they were of considerable financial benefit to the new communities in which they were located. Dependent, as they were, upon local patronage, they were necessarily responsive to the approval of the public they served.

Prior to the Civil War there were probably thousands of academies in the United States. Many early academies evolved into our most notable colleges. With the rise of the public high school after the Civil War the academy ceased to be the leading type of American school. The high school supplanted it as the "college of the people," and the academy largely passed out of existence, though a number survived as private preparatory and finishing schools, especially in the older states.

THE GROWING DEMAND FOR POPULAR EDUCATION

The aristocratic versus the democratic view. The 16th century viewed educational opportunity entirely from two standpoints: (1) cultural education for the higher classes; and (2) the elements of religion and apprenticeship training for the masses.

Religious training for the masses was demanded by Luther. He also insisted on sifting out the brighter children for classical training, which would fit them to serve the state and the social order as pastors, doctors, teachers, judges, and civil servants. Something of this same point of view was expressed by the Englishman Richard Mulcaster: [2]

---

[2] Quick, R. H., *Positions: by Richard Mulcaster,* p. 141. London: Longmans, Green and Co., 1888.

It seemeth to me verie plaine that all children be not to be sent to schoole, but only such as for naturall wittes, and sufficient maintenance, either of their naturall parentes, or civill patrones, shall be honestly and wel supported in their study, till the common weale minding to use their service, appoint their provision, not in hast for *neede,* but at leasure with *choice.*

Popular education was most advanced in the cities and towns of the Netherlands where republican government flourished.

The 17th century saw this struggle between the narrow, or aristocratic, and the broader, or democratic, views of education intensified. It was an age which took only a fitful interest in the enlightenment of the common people, and when crowned heads and their followers prided themselves on their divine right to rule and sought by every means to make their power absolute. The aristocracy had no interest in the improvement of the masses; in fact, they had no belief in the possibility of human betterment. They looked with supreme repugnance upon the republicanism of Holland and the regicide and the libertarian principles of English Puritanism.

But, nevertheless, the movements for democracy and the education of the masses increased. The same Calvinistic attitude which asserted the sovereign rights of the people demanded elementary education for the masses. In 1619, the Synod of Dort laid upon the civil authorities the duty of establishing schools where all children might learn to read. The same year, the Duchy of Weimar insisted that all children, boys and girls alike, should be compelled to attend school from the sixth to the 12th year. About this same time, Andreä, in his *Christianopolis,* described the ideal state: [3]

All the children of citizens in general, children of both sexes, are taken into training. When they have completed their sixth year, the parents give them over to the state.... As this is an institution for the public good, it is managed very agreeably as a common charge for all the citizens.

Comenius had, by all odds, the most democratic conception of education until recent times. As early as 1630, he wrote: [4]

---

[3] Held, Felix Emil, *Johann Valentin Andreä's Christianopolis,* p. 208. Urbana: University of Illinois Press, 1916.

[4] Keatinge, M. W., *The Great Didactic of John Amos Comenius,* p. 218. London: Adam and Charles Black, 1896.

> Not the children of the rich or of the powerful only, but of all alike, boys and girls, both noble and ignoble, rich and poor, in all cities and towns, villages and hamlets, should be sent to school.

This liberal attitude toward the emancipation of the masses and the education of all found little sympathy with most rulers and aristocrats. But there were special reasons why the doctrine of equality advocated by Comenius awakened no response. Comenius represented a despised sect, persecuted, powerless, and dispossessed of its homeland. The Moravian Brethren were communists and believed in Christian equality. Moreover, his contacts with the life and institutions of the Reformed Church further confirmed him in his democratic point of view. For this aspect of evangelical religion, Lutheranism generally had little more toleration than did the Catholic Church. The opposition that the aristocratic element felt toward popular education can be seen in the reply which Chancellor Oxenstierna of Sweden made to Comenius when he advocated the establishment of schools for all children.[5] "Can you stand contradiction?" he asked. Comenius replied that he desired criticism.

> The Chancellor then began to bring forward objections to the whole scheme of regenerating the world by means of Pansophia. Some of these objections were political, others rested on the Scriptural assurance that darkness rather than light was to be man's lot on earth.

Beginning of compulsory school attendance. Compulsory education came about by three steps. First was the demand of the church requiring compulsory instruction of all children in religion; second, the compulsory establishment of schools; and third, the requirement on the part of the state that children must attend school. The policy of compulsory attendance (*Schulpflichtigkeit*[6]) achieved considerable development in the latter half of the 17th century. The Calvinists of Holland took the lead in this movement. As early as 1606 The Synod of Nimeguen voluntarily requested the civil authorities to make education compulsory. The school order of Drente required attendance in 1638. A number of German principalities also adopted this policy. As already stated, the first principality to make school attendance com-

---

[5] *Ibid,* p. 50.

[6] What the Germans mean by *Schulpflichtigkeit* cannot be adequately translated by any English word. The term means literally that the children are "due at school" —that is, duty bound to be at school.

pulsory was the Duchy of Weimar in 1619. This action was influenced by the progressive attitude of the Calvinists. Duke Ernst of Gotha enacted the compulsory feature in his code of 1642. Braunschweig-Wolfenbüttel did the same in 1647. As early as 1559 the Duke of Württemberg had made attendance compulsory at the lessons in catechism, and the first compulsory law with penalty attached was passed in Württemberg in 1649. Other states to adopt this practice were as follows: Saxony, 1649; Hildesheim, 1663; Calemberg, 1681; Celle, 1689; and Prussia, 1717.[7]

Opposition to popular education. The end of the 17th century saw the democratic and aristocratic ideals in bitter conflict over education, especially among the British and French. The views of the opponents of popular education were presented by Governor William Berkeley of Virginia, Cardinal Richelieu of France, and the English philosopher John Locke.

Governor Berkeley, in answer to the question submitted by the "Lords Commissioners of Foreign Plantations" with regard to instruction in the colonies, responded in 1671 as follows: [8]

> The same course that is taken in England out of towns; every man according to his ability instructing his children.... But, I thank God, there were no free schools nor printing, and I hope we shall not have these hundred years; for learning has brought disobedience, and heresy, and sects into the world, and printing has divulged them, and libels against the best government. God keep us from both.

Cardinal Richelieu, writing in 1687, presented the French aristocratic view as follows: [9]

---

[7] Barnard, Henry, *op. cit.*, p. 519; Ziegler, T., *Geschichte der Pädagogik*, München: C. H. Beck, 1909.

[8] Henning, William Waller, *Laws and Statutes of Virginia*, Vol. 2, p. 517. Richmond, Virginia, 1819-1823.

Recent writers have sought to discredit Governor Berkeley's statement by pointing to the number of "free schools" established in Virginia. They have, however, missed the main issue. The governor had in view the free education of the common people "out of towns"—that is, in the country. In the emphatic statement of his aversion to popular enlightenment he was only expressing the attitude of aristocratic Englishmen generally. "Of 12,445 men who attached their names to deeds between 1641 and 1711 in Virginia, 5006 or 40 percent were forced to make their mark, while of 3066 women 2310 or 75 percent did the same." Bogart, Ernest L., and Kemmerer, Donald L., *Economic History of the American People*. New York: Longmans, Green and Co., 1947.

[9] Quoted by Kandel, I. L., *op. cit.*, p. 151, from Richelieu's *Testament Politique*.

> Although the knowledge of letters is eminently necessary for a country, it is certain that they need not be taught to everybody. Just as a body which had eyes on all sides would be monstrous, so the State would be if all its citizens were scholars; less obedience would be found and pride and presumption would be more common. Intercourse with humane letters would entirely banish that with commerce, would ruin agriculture, the true foster-mother of peoples, and would in a short time destroy the nursery of soldiers which rises oftener amidst rudeness and ignorance rather than in an atmosphere of polite culture; finally, it would fill France with quacks more apt to ruin private families and disturb public peace than fit to secure any advantage to the country.... If letters were profaned for all types of minds, one would see more people ready to raise doubts than to solve them, and many would be more ready to oppose truth than to defend it. It is for this reason that policy requires in a well regulated state more masters of mechanical arts than masters of liberal arts to teach letters.

The celebrated English philosopher John Locke, who helped so signally to lay the foundations for modern political democracy, was undeniably aristocratic in his educational views. In 1700 he wrote: [10] "Nobody is under an obligation to know everything. Knowledge and science in general is the business only of those who are at ease and leisure."

Forces favorable to popular education. In spite of the opposition of aristocratic powers, there awakened toward the end of the 17th century a new spirit of philanthropy, missionary zeal, and interest in the religious and educational welfare of the common people. Missionary and educational interest arose in Holland when that country became a colonial power. The Dutch companies chartered to establish colonies in Asia, South Africa, and America were required to provide for each settlement "a minister and a schoolmaster, that the services of God and zeal for religion may not grow cool and be neglected."

No force at this period was more effective in arousing interest in popular education than was Pietism in Germany. Francke's efforts bore much fruit and scattered the seeds of popular education widely. While Francke had much in common with Comenius, it must be noted that he lacked the social and scientific breadth of interest of the great Moravian. Both would educate all children. Comenius would train them together in the same schools, without distinction of class; but Francke set up special schools for the various classes of society. Comenius

---

[10] Locke, John, *Of the Conduct of the Understanding,* § 7.

would teach everyone everything; Francke taught religion to everyone, but differentiated the curriculum to train for various social strata.

The Moravian Brethren under Zinzendorf, who was influenced primarily by contact with the Pietists, became the most zealous missionaries and educators of all Protestants. In England, this new movement of Christian philanthropy expressed itself in the founding of the S.P.G. and the S.P.C.K. The fact that those two organizations were purposely international in scope is greatly significant. Many similar societies were formed in other countries. The charity school movement in England and America was due to the new awakening of Christian interest in the needs of the poor. German Pietism and the S. P. G. worked hand in hand in missionary and educational efforts in America.

The movement for popular education received its most powerful support from the evangelical elements of the Protestant Church. But it would be an error to believe that it was confined to Protestants; a similar movement was present also among the Catholics. A spirit of genuine Christian philanthropy was to be found in the work of Démia and of La Salle, who founded the order of the Brothers of the Christian Schools in France.

In all these efforts to bring the advantages of education to the common people, the dominant motive was Christian charity. The church was impelled by a sense of pity and of duty. It must, however, be recorded that the ideas of education as a right of the child, and a means of social uplift and of political preservation, had not yet dawned.

SUMMARY OF THE PERIOD

Steps of progress. In spite of serious obstacles, the 17th century made various important steps of progress in education. These may be briefly summarized in the following points:

(1) The grave weaknesses of classical Humanism became ever more apparent. Various efforts were made to revise the teaching of Latin by means of better methods of instruction, but the real enthusiasm and vital reason for Latin literature and Ciceronian eloquence had departed. The usefulness of Latin as a language was gradually confined to the learned professions. The supremacy of Latin for international exchange in diplomacy, religion, commerce, and learning had ceased.

(2) This century marked the rise of modern languages. The Spanish and Italian literatures had developed and English literature had evolved

to an extraordinary height. French literature was exhibiting promise, but German literature had not yet begun. All these languages were rapidly developing and were contesting with Latin for a place in the curricula of the schools, and for use in learned books and in university lectures. Substantial gains were made in the employment and teaching of the vernacular tongues.

(3) The most outstanding aspect of progress was the expansion of scientific knowledge. This was peculiarly true in the field of mathematics and the physical sciences; a foundation was also laid in other sciences.

(4) This period witnessed the rise of rationalism as a method of scientific thinking. At the same time empiricism received a great impetus. The adjustment of the claims of these two constituted the great problem of scientific method.

(5) The growth of the sciences and the expansion of practical knowledge led to the demand for curricular revision. The principle of utility was more and more advocated by all the educational theorists of the day. Realism was, however, important not merely as subject matter but also as a method of instruction.

(6) The early part of the century saw the writing of a number of utopias. These formed the beginnings of theories of human progress which had great significance for education.

(7) Theories of government, law, and human rights ceased to find adequate foundation in authority, and began to seek a basis in human nature. Efforts to justify monarchical government or democracy were of profound consequence.

(8) The acceptance of the principle of religious toleration in most of the countries of northern Europe gave new opportunities of development to the more progressive elements in the various religious bodies, especially to the evangelical sects. It was these people who now began to furnish education as a charity service for the poor. The most important of the new religious movements were: Pietism, in Germany; the Unitas Fratrum in Moravia; and the Puritans in England.

(9) The democratic and the aristocratic policies in education came into sharp conflict during this century. The democratic position was represented by Comenius, who urged that all children, high-born and low-, rich and poor, attend the same schools. The aristocratic tendency found its expression in the Ritter (Knightly) Academies for the aristocratic class in Germany.

(10) The education of girls received a new emphasis during the century; especially was this true in France.

(11) The training of teachers was begun. The Jesuits were the first to undertake the preparation of teachers, but the training they gave was largely confined to the curriculum and stereotyped methods. Démia and La Salle, in France, set up normal schools.[11] Francke, in Germany, gave some training to the students who were to catechize in the schools, and special instruction to those who were to teach in the Latin schools.

(12) The colonists carried to America their various educational ideals and policies. The Puritans in New England, the Dutch in New York, and the Presbyterians and Huguenots scattered in various states followed the Calvinistic ideals and practices. The English Cavaliers dominated Virginia and continued the aristocratic tradition. In the Middle Atlantic states and to some extent in the other states, Swedish, Lutheran, Mennonite, Quaker, and other colonies were established, and each had its own views and provisions for education.

---

[11] Fitzpatrick, Edward A., *La Salle, Patron of All Teachers,* Milwaukee: The Bruce Publishing Company, 1951.

Chapter 11

LOCKE AND THE PHILOSOPHY OF EMPIRICISM

INTRODUCTION. Of the leaders of thought during this era John Locke was by all odds the foremost. While no one ranks him with such exalted and constructive figures as Plato, Aristotle, or his successor, Immanuel Kant, it is far easier to underrate him than to appreciate his real worth. Coming just when he did and having fresh and sensible views on many of the deepest problems of the age, he became uniquely important. He was a pivotal figure on whose ideas the new epoch turned; for this reason, his life and contributions merit special study.

Early life and education. Locke was born in 1632 at Wrington, a small village some ten miles from Bristol, in southwestern England. His father was a capable Puritan attorney who saw to it that the boy received a good education, even in that era of political turbulence. At 14 he was enrolled in Westminster School, where Dr. Richard Busby, the notorious flogger,[1] was headmaster. Here he spent six years in the study of Latin and Greek, preparatory for college. It is supposed by some that he was among the schoolboys who viewed the execution of Charles I. This is by no means certain, but it is known that his father was a captain in the parliamentary army and that during these years of political disturbance Locke was in closest proximity to the very source of revolutionary action.

For reasons which his biographers are unable to explain, Locke did not enjoy his school life. Regardless of the cause of his unhappiness, he

---

[1] The stories of Busby are most interesting for the student of educational history. See Hazlitt, W. Carew, *Schools, School-books and Schoolmasters*, pp. 21-22. London: J. W. Jarvis and Sons, 1885.

always felt a revulsion against the common association of boys in public schools.

At the age of 20 Locke entered Christ Church College, Oxford, where a studentship provided a living. He held this appointment for over 30 years, when he was dismissed by the order of Charles II. He received the B. A. and the M. A. degrees, and for a time was a tutor in Greek, rhetoric, and ethics. He then took up medicine, a field better suited to his taste.

Locke left Oxford in 1667, and for a number of years lived as friend, confidential secretary, and physician to the Earl of Shaftesbury. This association led to his employment in various public offices. But what is more significant, he acted as tutor to the fifteen-year-old son of the Earl of Shaftesbury and later supervised the training of the grandson. These were not the only experiences Locke had with the problems of education which furnished the basis for his discussions of the subject. On account of ill health, which greatly hindered him in his work, Locke spent four years in France. Furthermore, after the fall of Shaftesbury, he felt obliged to exile himself in Holland. These periods furnished him the necessary leisure for quiet thinking and the writing of those great works which were to direct philosophy into new channels. Returning to England in the train of William of Orange, Locke was offered many flattering preferments, most of which he could not accept. He died in 1704, renowned as the deepest thinker England had produced.

Locke's writings, which cover a wide range, may be grouped under philosophy, government, education, economics, and religion. So far as government is concerned, his constitution for the Carolinas advanced views in regard to the political rights of all men, vigorously combatted the doctrine of the divine right of kings, and proclaimed the need of constitutional government. In 1690 he issued two *Treatises on Government,* which set forth his views against the doctrine of the divine right of kings, declaring: "Absolute monarchy is indeed inconsistent with civil society, and so can be no form of civil government at all." In a state of nature, he declared, all men are free, independent, and equal. He also wrote four letters on toleration, in which he urged the separation of church and state, and liberty of conscience for all who believe in God.

Locke made his most profound and revolutionizing contributions in the realm of philosophy. In 1687 he completed the *Essay Concerning Human Understanding,* on which he had been meditating many years.

This is his most enduring contribution, and its effect was incomparably great. Bourne gives the following evaluation of the essay: [2]

> The most important philosophical treatise that has been written by an Englishman—the most important because to it is more or less due the writing of nearly every other important treatise that has since appeared.

In the field of education his chief work was a series of letters published in 1693, entitled *Some Thoughts Concerning Education.* After his death a number of other writings—none of them complete—was published by friends. The most valuable of these was *Conduct of the Understanding;* usually regarded as a work in philosophy supplementary to his *Essay Concerning Human Understanding,* it is in reality, as the title implies, a treatise on the training of the rational faculty. Three less important writings on education were: *Some Thoughts Concerning Reading and Study for a Gentleman; Instructions for the Conduct of a Young Gentleman;* and a short discussion, *Of Study.* The only indication that he was aware of the general need of education for the masses is found in an essay entitled *Working Schools.*

PSYCHOLOGICAL INNOVATIONS

The origin and bounds of knowledge. The supreme barrier to the intellectual and moral progress of the day lay in the ancient myth that ideas are innate; that is to say, that they are inborn possessions of the rational faculty. This doctrine gave support to all the traditional and scholastic principles which were used as a justification for the worn-out conditions in church, state, society, and the school. It was injurious in that it discouraged every effort at the advancement of knowledge by observations and experimentation. Locke disclosed how he came to study this problem: [3]

> Five or six friends meeting at my chamber, and discoursing on a subject very remote from this, found themselves quickly at a stand, by the difficulties that rose on every side. After we had a while puzzled ourselves, without coming any nearer a resolution of those doubts which perplexed us, it came into my thoughts, that we took a wrong course; and that,

---

[2] Bourne, H. R. Fox, *The Life of John Locke,* Vol. II, p. 87. London: Henry S. King and Company, 1876.

[3] Locke, John, *Essay Concerning Human Understanding, Epistle to the Reader,* p. viii.

> before we set ourselves upon inquiries of that nature, it was necessary to examine our own abilities, and see what objects our understandings were, or were not fitted to deal with.

With this aim in view he began an inquiry into the faculties of the human mind which was to revolutionize not only philosophy but society, government, and education. In his investigation, he tells us,[4] he sought to give an

> ... account of the ways whereby our understandings come to attain those notions of things we have, and can set down any measures of the certainty of our knowledge, or the grounds of those persuasions which are to be found amongst men, so various, different, and wholly contradictory.... If by this inquiry into the nature of the understanding, I can discover the powers thereof; how far they reach, to what things they are in any degree proportionate, and where they fail us; I suppose it may be of use to prevail with the busy mind of man to be more cautious in meddling with things exceeding its comprehension; to stop when it is at the utmost extent of its tether; and to sit down in a quiet ignorance of those things, which, upon examination, are found to be beyond the reach of our capacities.

Locke could discover no innate ideas. The ideas and principles which philosophers regarded as innate are of several kinds. Some are purely abstract propositions, such as: "The whole is larger than a part"; and "It is impossible for the same thing to be and not to be at the same time." Some are religious conceptions; for example: the idea of God, which Descartes thought most fundamental of all. Others have to do with our moral nature, our sense of what is just and unjust, good and bad. Finally, there are our original mathematical axioms, which possess a self-evident certainty that transcends empirical experience. It will be perceived that, if these various ideas are all innate, then all knowledge of any importance rests upon an innate basis. Now, it was this fundamental assumption that Locke courageously, yet in scientific spirit, dared to call in question.

If these ideas are innate, they must possess certain characteristics. First of all, they must be found in the minds of infants, of idiots, and of all primitive peoples, for the very meaning of innate signifies something inherent in the soul at birth. Again, innate ideas will necessarily be found in the minds of all people everywhere, and every mind will

---

[4] *Ibid.*, Book I, Chap. 1, §§ 2 and 4.

have precisely the same idea. Thirdly, an idea that is innate will be perceived as a necessary self-evident proposition.

As a physician Locke was acquainted with infants. But he could not discover that any of them showed evidences of a precocious acquaintance with ideas supposed to be innate; in fact they did not know them until they attained the age of rationality. He studied closely the writers who had engaged in anthropological investigations. From these scholars, he concluded that not even the idea of God is to be found in the minds of all primitive peoples. He noted, furthermore, that the Greeks and the Romans did not hold the same conceptions of justice, right and wrong, and good and bad that were held in his day. Moreover, the axioms and principles of mathematics are not universally known. In fact there is not a single idea known to the human mind that can be truly said to be universal and therefore innate.

Only two sources of knowledge. Fortunately Locke did not rest content with destroying the myth of innate ideas. He assigned a different source and suggested a simpler explanation of the origin of knowledge, in place of that which he so deliberately demolished. He began by asking the following questions: [5]

> Let us then suppose the mind to be, as we say, white paper, void of all characters, without any ideas; how comes it to be furnished? Whence comes it by that vast store which the busy and boundless fancy of man has painted on it, with an almost endless variety? Whence has it all the materials of reason and knowledge? To this I answer in one word, from experience; in that all our knowledge is founded; and from that it ultimately derives itself.

Locke proceeded to point out two sources of experience: one outer; the other inner. The outer source of all man's knowledge is the five senses; the inner source is the experiences he receives from the operation of his mind in his conscious mental activities.[6]

> Our observation employed either about external sensible objects, or about the internal operations of our minds, perceived and reflected on by ourselves, is that which supplies our understandings with all the materials of thinking. These two are the fountains of knowledge, from whence all the ideas we have, or can naturally have, do spring.

The mass of sensory data which literally pours into consciousness through the eyes, the ears, and the other sense organs, acquaints the

---

[5] *Ibid.*, Book II, Chap. 1, § 2.
[6] *Ibid.*, Book II, Chap. 1, § 2.

mind with the objective world, and forms the basis of all one can know of the objects of the world.

In addition to the experiences which come from the outer world through the sense organs, there are also the experiences which the mind has of its own operations. Locke was primarily a psychologist; few men have had more profound insight into the operation of the human mind. In regard to this source of experience, he wrote: [7]

> The other fountain, from which experience furnisheth the understanding with ideas, is the perception of the operation of our own mind within us, as it is employed about the ideas it has got; which operations, when the soul comes to reflect on, and consider, do furnish the understanding with another set of ideas, which could not be had from things without; and such are, perception, thinking, doubting, believing, reasoning, knowing, willing, and all the different actings of our own minds; which we being conscious of, and observing in ourselves, do from these receive into our understandings as distinct ideas, as we do from bodies affecting our senses. . . . But as I called the other sensation, so I call this *reflection,* the ideas it affords being such only as the mind gets by reflecting on its own operations, within itself.

That there is no other source of human knowledge, Locke asserted quite positively: [8]

> These two, I say, viz., external material things, as the objects of sensation, and the operations of our own minds within, as the objects of reflection, are to me the only originals from whence all our ideas take their beginnings. . . . The understanding seems to me not to have the least glimmering of any ideas which it doth not receive from one of these two.

The *tabula rasa* theory. The mind in its original state is a sheet of "white paper, void of all characters," a *tabula rasa* or, wax tablet on which grooves are made as by a stylus. Such is the simple but graphic figure of speech which Locke employed to explain the origin of ideas. Impressions are made upon the brain through the senses, and as a result images are formed in the mind. In this process the mind is purely passive and receptive, just as a sheet of paper receives the impressions of the pen. The mind plays no active part in hearing a sound, seeing a light, or in any of the original perceptions which come to it.[9]

---

[7] *Ibid.,* Book II, Chap. I, § 4

[8] *Ibid.,* Book II, Chap. I, §§ 4 and 5.

[9] *Ibid.,* Book II, Chap. I, § 25.

> These simple ideas, when offered to the mind, the understanding can no more refuse to have, nor alter, when they are imprinted, nor blot them out, and make new ones itself, than a mirror can refuse, alter, or obliterate the images or ideas which the objects set before it do therein produce.

This passive attitude of the mind in receiving sensations is one of Locke's most dogmatic notions.

Working up the raw materials. The mind, as Locke conceived it, may be roughly likened to a mill in which rock containing various ores is treated. The mill is purely receptive in that it must have the raw materials poured into it before it can exercise its functions. By crushing the rock the different ores can be separated. So the mind, by discrimination, analysis, and association, separates and recombines the materials of sense perception into concepts, ideas, abstractions, relations, and principles. His discussion of the higher mental processes added greatly to psychological knowledge.

Implications of a denial of innate ideas. Locke's destructive attack upon the doctrine of innate ideas carried several implications of the greatest importance for philosophy and education. It is pardonable that he should not have developed these implications completely in his own thinking; that he was aware of them can scarcely be doubted. Three implications follow:

1. **Doctrine of human depravity disproved.** The traditional belief in human depravity was involved in the doctrine of innate ideas. This doctrine was held with tenacity by most educators as well as theologians, and it had a marked influence upon their educational practices. If, however, nothing exists in the mind before birth, what right is there to hold that depravity is innate in the human heart? Neither Locke nor his contemporaries had a clear conception of heredity; he declared that all children become what they are, "good or evil, useful or not, by their education." Thus his destructive criticism of innate ideas succeeded in carrying down with it the theological dogma of innate total depravity.

2. **All men are born equal.** But still another idea, world devastating in its significance, lies in Locke's innocent looking statement. If there is nothing in the soul at birth; if it is just an empty capacity into which experiences may be poured, then all individuals are exactly alike at birth; "all men are born equal." King and slave, rich and poor, the simple minded and the genius—all begin life at the same point, and

the vast differences between men are caused by their experiences and by education. Locke's empiricism placed all men on a common level.

3. **The idea of human development.** The astute observations of human development made by Comenius were evidently unknown to Locke, but without intention on his part, he provided the basis for a theory of child psychology.

The doctrine of innate ideas implies that the mind of the child possesses the same fundamental, intellectual furniture that is found in the mind of the adult. In the one, knowedge is still implicit though unrealized; in the other, it is understood. To all intents and purposes the child is a miniature adult and simply expands into adulthood. If ideas are not innate, then the child differs radically from the adult, so far as his intellectual possessions are concerned.

Locke directed attention to the character of the infant mind at birth, and traced the processes by which the child gradually builds up his knowledge and acquires the ability to think in abstract terms. He pointed out that the rational faculty is late in emerging in the life of the child. These facts tended to emphasize, as nothing had yet done, the idea of human development.

Is anything innate? Though Locke denied that knowledge is an innate possession of the human mind, he did not include in this denial all aspects of the mental life. He did not take the radical step that his followers later took, of denying the existence of the soul or mind prior to the coming of the first sensation. He not only assumed the existence of the soul or mind but that it possessed certain capacities. In his later writings he admitted the existence of all the appetites and the mental faculties, but did not enter upon a discussion of their relation to the process of sensory experience.

Springs of action and motivation. Human activity springs from inner appetites or needs, and is guided by the feelings of pain and pleasure. Inner appetites produce desires. Locke did not agree with Descartes that the mind is pure thinking substance and the body a mere machine. As to the ultimate source of activity, he wrote: [10]

> What moves the mind in every particular instance, to determine its general power of directing to this or that particular motion or rest? . . . The motive to change, is always some uneasiness: nothing setting us upon the change of state, or upon any new action, but some uneasiness.

---

[10] *Ibid.*, Book II, Chap. 21, § 29.

Locke believed the human soul is endowed with two types of propensities or desires: (1) ordinary necessities, such as thirst, hunger, heat, cold, weariness, sleep, and so on; and (2) "fantastical uneasiness," such as the "itch for honor, power, riches," "vanity of dress," emulation, "and a thousand other irregular desires." These he called "acquired habits," or "adopted desires . . . settled in us by fashion, example, and education."

Habit. *Habit,* as Locke defined it, is the power or ability of doing some one action which has been acquired by frequent repetition of the action. He laid the greatest possible stress upon this aspect of the human organism; accordingly, in his view, education may be summed up as a process of forming habits. In the building of moral character, particularly in regard to self control, habit plays the supreme role, and it is also the basis of the power of reasoning.

The faculty of reason. Locke has suffered great misunderstanding from the effort to classify his philosophy and his system of education. It may well be doubted if any thinker offers a better example of balanced common sense. His mind saw all sides of any controversy, and saved him from prejudice and narrowness of view. But, for some unaccountable reason, unless it be their inherent comprehensiveness, his writings have a strange facility for promoting enthusiastic partisanship for one-sided systems of thought. No mystic was ever more firmly convinced that man has a positive knowledge of the existence of God. Yet both atheists and theists find proofs of their conclusions in his views. Both materialists and rationalists base their ideas upon his. Similarly, varying schools of education classify him as an advocate of formal discipline and as a utilitarian.

Without any implication that he should be classified as a rationalist, it must be said that Locke did place the highest emphasis upon reason, but it was reason functioning for the sake of the moral welfare of the individual and not as an end in itself. Speaking of the pupil, Locke said: [11]

> If he shew a Forwardness to be reasoning about Things that come in his way, take care, as much as you can, that nobody check this Inclination in him, or mislead it by captious or fallacious ways of talking with him. For when all is done, this, as the highest and most important Faculty of our Minds, deserves the greatest Care and Attention in cultivating it:

---

[11] *Some Thoughts Concerning Education,* § 122.

> The right Improvement, and Exercise of our Reason being the highest Perfection that a Man can attain to in this Life.

There is nothing contradictory in Locke's view that all knowledge originates in sense perception and that reason is the highest faculty of the mind. He showed how the rational judgment combines into concepts and judgments the materials furnished by the senses. Man is both a sensory and a rational creature.

Locke's philosophy of language. From ancient times education had been predominantly, one might even say exclusively, linguistic, consisting of the acquisition of the Latin and Greek languages. But the effort to acquire these foreign tongues resulted in making education exclusively verbal and therefore memoriter. All those mental activities which are employed in the natural course of experience and the direct acquisition of knowledge found no opportunity for exercise in the school room. The inevitable result was that language was employed in a loose, indefinite, rhetorical manner, and thought was consequently crude, superficial, inexact, and frequently contradictory. To cure these defects, a philosophy of language was essential. As part of his great services in clearing away the misconceptions which hindered clearness of thought, Locke discussed the function and abuse of language.

Locke pointed out that words are arbitrarily chosen symbols. They do not possess any natural or mysterious connections with the things they signify. They do not express reality. "That which we call a rose by any other name would smell as sweet"; otherwise, it would be "rose" in every language.

He pointed out the peculiar danger to education which comes from the unusual facility with which young children learn languages. By some strange purpose of nature, young children pick up and repeat words to which they attach no mental content whatever. Later the synthesis of meaning and word may or may not be formed in their experience. In the case of abstract ideas, such as, *justice, gratitude,* the words will be learned before the ideas. But education has been greatly deceived in that it has emphasized the learning of languages, and the acquisition of words without a corresponding development of thought. This grave weakness had been pointed out by other reformers; however, until Locke's analysis of language, no one had clearly explained the difficulty. No greater blow was ever aimed at the tendency to make education predominantly linguistic. Though he had taught rhetoric at Oxford,

Locke came to hate it as much as did Plato, for he termed it "that powerful instrument of error and deceit." As for Greek, he relegated it to university study. Latin, he recommended, be made subservient to the mother tongue, and versification, composition, and Latin eloquence be entirely eliminated.

Locke had an ingrained distrust of words. He urged that thinking be done without words, in so far as possible. For words are, "in their own nature, so doubtful and obscure, their signification, for the most part, so uncertain and undetermined . . . that if in our meditations our thoughts busy themselves about words, and stick to the names of things, it is odds but they are misled or confounded." [12]

EDUCATION

Source of Locke's educational ideas. In forming his views on education, Locke was influenced largely by Montaigne, to a lesser degree by ancient writers, but most of all by the practices of English families of the higher class. It is evident that he had no acquaintance with, or it may have been sympathy for, the works of Comenius and Mulcaster, nor with those of Ascham and other Humanists. His ideas were chiefly the results of his cogitations upon his own experiences as a teacher and upon his observation of others.

Aim of education. "That most to be taken care of is the Gentleman's calling." Such, in a word, is Locke's general view of the scope of education, a training confined to the aristocratic class. He excused his narrowness by the suggestion that, if the gentry are properly trained, "they will quickly bring all the rest into order." Nevertheless, one cannot but feel that he failed to understand the deeper significance of education as an essential process of individual development and social progress. Not only that! He showed likewise no appreciation of the pleasures of knowledge as such, for he confined its advantages exclusively to the upper social classes. "Knowledge and science," he wrote, "in general, is the business only of those who are at ease and leisure." [13] Locke's statement of the aim of education was as follows: [14]

> That which every Gentleman . . . desires for his Son, besides the Estate he leaves him, is contain'd (I suppose) in these four things, *Virtue, Wisdom, Breeding,* and *Learning.*

---

[12] Locke, John, *Of Study,* § 3.
[13] Locke, John, *Conduct of the Understanding,* § 7.
[14] Locke, John, *Some Thoughts Concerning Education,* § 134.

He selected these four essentials, "virtue, wisdom, breeding, and learning," in preference to eloquence, virtue, and piety, the aim of the Humanists. Moreover, these qualities he named in order of importance. "I place *Virtue*," he declared, "as the first and most necessary of those endowments that belong to a man or a Gentleman; as absolutely requisite to make him valued and beloved by others, acceptable or tolerable to himself." *Virtue,* by which he meant good character, depends entirely upon proper religious training. It comprehends especially reverence for God, love of truth, and goodwill toward others. *Wisdom,* in Locke's thought, is prudence, sound judgment, and foresight in the affairs of life, such as managing one's estate and performing public service for the prosperity of the commonwealth. *Good breeding,* or manners, in accordance with English tradition was raised by Locke to a rank of major importance in education. It has as its inner spring proper self-regard and respect for others; its rule is: "Not to think meanly of ourselves, and not to think meanly of others." Locke placed *learning* last because, in his esteem, it was of least importance. It "must be had, but in the second place, and subservient only to greater qualities."

Though Locke minimized the importance of learning, as compared with the other objectives, he did not do so out of lack of respect for human intelligence or the rational life. Reason is man's highest faculty, but it is a faculty which functions more valuably in ethical and practical affairs than in purely speculative fields or in the amassing of knowledge. Not the scholar but the practical "gentleman whose proper calling is the service of his country" is to be the product of the education which Locke proposed. He had little respect for the scholar as such. Of him he said: "I imagine you would think him a very foolish fellow that should not value a virtuous or a wise man infinitely before a great scholar."

Private versus public education. As to the important issue, whether education is the prerogative of the church, state, community, or family, Locke preferred the family. The issue, he thought, was between the family and the public schools. He carefully weighed the advantages and disadvantages of each, and decided "the faults of a private education infinitely to be preferred" to those of the public schools. So far as a knowledge of the world is concerned, public schools are superior; but in the inculcation of morals and manners the home is more efficient and, as he declared, "Virtue is harder to be got than a knowledge of the world." Strange to say, in spite of the rigorous regimen of the so-called "public schools" of England, he objected to them because they produced a "Contagion of rudeness and vice . . . Trickery and violence," and "self conceit." He preferred the "innocence of the child by rearing him at home under the guidance of a tutor rather than the false sophistication acquired at school."

Concerning the work of the tutor, Locke wrote: [15]

> The great Work of a *Governor* is to fashion the Carriage, and form the Mind; to settle in his Pupil good Habits and the Principles of Virtue and Wisdom; to give him by little and little a View of Mankind, and work him into a Love and Imitation of what is excellent and praiseworthy; and, in the Prosecution of it, to give him Vigor, Activity, and Industry.

Physical education. In accord with his ideals of an English gentleman, Locke began with physical education. The guiding principle is a "sound mind in a sound body." Much time is to be devoted to play, especially in the open air, and to swimming. Many suggestions are given in regard to hygiene. This may have been due to his interest in medical science or to his own life-long experience in struggling with a feeble constitution. The most arresting prescription is that of the "hardening process." The naked savage inured to extremes of heat and cold, hunger and thirst, is sharply contrasted with the children of civilization weakened by too great tenderness. No covering for his head, shoes that let the water in, no gloves for his hands, clothing loose and not too warm—such is Locke's apparel for the boy. Plenty of sleep, simple diet, no medicines, and "seldom, if ever, wine or strong drink" complete the regimen of the child and insure sound health and vigor.

Education and moral discipline. English education has always exalted the disciplinary side. Locke is one of the strongest advocates of the theory that education is a moral discipline rather than a process of intellectual instruction. The truth is that Locke's chief purpose was to make gentlemen who would know how to act in conventional society.

Self-control the basis of moral integrity. The supreme secret of moral training, according to Locke, is to be found in the habit of self-control. It is the power to say "No!" to inner impulse or desire.[16]

> The great Principle and Foundation of all Virtue and Worth is plac'd in this: That a Man is able to *deny himself* his own Desires, cross his

[15] *Ibid.*, § 94.
[16] *Ibid.*, §§ 33, 45, and 52.

own Inclinations, and purely follow what Reason directs as best tho' the Appetite lean the other way....

He that has not a Mastery over his Inclinations, he that knows not how to *resist* the Importunity of *present Pleasure or Pain,* for the sake of what Reason tells him, is fit to be done, wants the true Principle of Virtue and Industry, and is in danger never to be good for any Thing. This Temper, therefore, so contrary to unguided Nature, is to be got betimes; and this Habit, as the true Foundation of future Ability and Happiness, is to be wrought into the Mind as early as may be, even from the first Dawning of Knowledge or Apprehensions in Children, and so to be confirm'd in them by all Care and Ways imaginable, by those that have the Oversight of their Education....

Motivation. In *Some Thoughts Concerning Education,* Locke set down as native propensities that originate the conduct of the child, the love of liberty, love of possession, curiosity, and desire for recreation; but the chief motivating principles are the sense of shame and the desire for honor. He considered craving for honor or social approval the most powerful agency for controlling the conduct of children and inducing them to study: [17]

Esteem and *Disgrace* are, of all others, the most powerful Incentives to the Mind, when once it is brought to relish them. If you can once get into Children a Love of Credit and an Apprehension of Shame and Disgrace, you have put into 'em the true Principle.

As to the means of developing self-mastery and the virtues, Locke does not leave his reader in doubt. He believed, on good grounds, in old-fashioned obedience, as he wrote: [18]

He that is not us'd to submit his Will to the Reason of others *when* he is *young,* will scarce hearken or submit to his own Reason when he is of an Age to make Use of it.

Usefulness determines the curriculum. Usefulness is the guiding principle in the selection of the course of study. Each study and the details of each must find their justification in the contribution they make to life. However, it is not the present life of the child, but his future life as a man that is the determining factor. Moreover, Locke did not have in view a low materialistic utility, but rather the usefulness which has significance for human conduct. the practical in its best and highest

---

[17] *Ibid.,* § 36.
[18] *Ibid.,* § 36.

sense. Religion, which is the gentleman's "calling as a man in the world," is the first and most important subject in the course of study. After religion, the conduct and interests of the gentleman will be engaged in the care of his estate, in public services to his community and country, and in the proper maintenance of his aristocratic station. He will be concerned with "moral and political knowledge; and thus the studies, which more immediately belong to his calling, are those which treat of virtues and vices, of civil society, and the arts of government; and will take in also law and history." [19]

Although Locke adopted this principle of utility, it would be hasty to conclude that the tutor will stuff the child's memory with useful knowledge. Far from it. The right attitude of the pupil toward knowledge is more important by far than possession of information. The tutor's business is not so much to teach him all that is knowable, as to develop in him a love and esteem of knowledge; and to put him in the way of knowing and improving himself when he has a mind to it.

It would seem that Locke had chiefly in view exploratory or orientation courses. An introduction is to be given into many fields. This is to be done for several reasons. First, it is intended to furnish a general acquaintance with the subjects of human knowledge, leaving detailed study of any subject to the later interest of the student. Another purpose is to avoid the narrowness and inflexibility of mind which comes when only one subject is studied. Variety makes for mental freedom and elasticity. Locke's view on this matter is highly interesting, especially since he has by some writers been considered the advocate of the doctrine of mental discipline. On this point he wrote: [20]

> The business of education, as I have already observed, is not, as I think to make them perfect in any one of the sciences, but so to open and dispose their minds, as may best make them capable of any, when they shall apply themselves to it. If men are, for a long time, accustomed only to one sort or method of thought, their minds grow stiff in it, and do not readily turn to another. It is, therefore, to give them this freedom, that I think they should be made to look into all sorts of knowledge, and exercise their understandings in so wide a variety and stock of knowledge. But I do not propose it as a variety and stock of knowledge, but a variety and freedom of thinking; as an increase of the powers and activity of the mind, not as an enlargement of its possessions.

---

[19] Locke, John, *Some Thoughts Concerning Reading and Study for a Gentleman.*
[20] Locke, John, *Conduct of the Understanding,* § 19.

Disgust with humanistic training. Locke did not hesitate to express profound disgust with the entire program of humanistic training.[21]

> When I consider, what ado is made about a little *Latin* and *Greek,* how many years are spent in it, and what a Noise and Business it makes to no Purpose, I can hardly forbear thinking that the Parents of Children still live in fear of the Schoolmaster's Rod.

With the utmost boldness he used the paring knife on the traditional curriculum. Though he had been a tutor in Greek at Oxford, he boldly proposed to do away with all study of this language, so far as general education of the young gentleman is concerned. Should he aspire to become a scholar, he could study Greek in his university course. Latin was to be retained, but its heart as a humanistic study cut out. Locke had no use for Latin eloquence or for any of those practices which fostered it, such as Latin themes, versification, declamations, and the memorizing of Ciceronian phrases. Even grammar, that age-old bugbear, is not to be spared. One thing only is to be secured, the ability to read a Latin author. Locke was quite emphatic as to the limitation of this subject. He did not want a boy to be able to speak or write Latin, but merely to have the ability to read it: [22] "You may insist on it, if it will do any good, that you have no Design to make him either a *Latin* Orator or Poet, but barely would have him understand perfectly a Latin Author." Rhetoric and logic are likewise to be cut out entirely, because they are of little advantage, for he declared: [23] "I have seldom or never observed any one to get the Skill of Reasoning well, or speaking handsomely, by studying those Rules, which pretend to teach it." Disputation, another of the medieval arts, fell under his severest censure. He objected to it for five reasons: (1) It tends to make students opinionated. (2) It develops an attitude of questioning everything just for the sake of appearing smart. (3) It develops a pride in contradicting others. (4) To overcome one's rival comes to be the chief end sought, rather than the discovery of truth. (5) It leads to captiousness and a fallacious use of words.

As already mentioned, Locke had a profound distrust of the use of words. This distrust extended likewise to the study of rhetoric.[24]

---

[21] Locke, John, *Some Thoughts Concerning Education,* § 147.
[22] *Ibid.,* § 170.
[23] *Ibid.,* § 188.
[24] Locke, John, *Essay Concerning Human Understanding,* Book III, Chap. X, § 34.

> It is evident how much men love to deceive, and be deceived, since rhetoric, that powerful instrument of error and deceit, has its established professors, is publically taught, and has always been had in great reputation; and I doubt not but it will be thought a great boldness, if not brutality, in me to have said this much against it. Eloquence, like the fair sex, has too prevailing beauties in it, to suffer itself ever to be spoken against. And it is in vain to find fault with those arts of deceiving, wherein men find pleasure to be deceived.

Study of the English language. The English language is to come into its own and to be studied daily so that the child will write and speak well. The primary reader will be Aesop's fables, especially the pictorial edition, and the Bible. French will be acquired early through the conversational method, by the employment of a governess. Latin will be learned in the same way, but after French.

Other studies. Locke recognized the value of drawing. It is especially helpful in fixing the images of objects in memory. In addition to ordinary writing, he advocated learning shorthand. Other subjects which Locke approved are geography, geometry, chronology, anatomy, and a knowledge of things. Of history he is unusually appreciative: [25] "As nothing teaches, so nothing delights more than History. . . . History is the great Mistress of Prudence and civil Knowledge, and ought to be the proper study of a Gentleman, or Man of Business in the World."

Among higher studies Locke commended especially natural philosophy, ethics, and psychology. In a rather apologetic spirit, he recommended some manual arts—especially cabinet-making, gardening, and painting as a fine art. These are to be pursued for the purpose of recreation and health, but, in addition to these values, they will be beneficial for a gentleman in directing his estate.

The education of the lower classes. In his capacity as a commissioner of the board of trade appointed by the king, Locke drew up a scheme of poor relief in which he proposed that children of the indigent be taken from their parents and kept in working schools from the time they are three until they are fourteen. After their residence in working schools, they are to be apprenticed. The advantages claimed for this scheme, according to Locke, are: (1) Mothers are set free to work. (2) Children will be better disciplined, and "from infancy inured to work." (3) The plan is economical. Children at working schools are to have

---

[25] *Some Thoughts Concerning Education,* §§ 184 and 182.

bread to eat, and in cold weather, "if it be thought needful, a little warm watergruel." They are to be taught religion and simpler handicrafts. Locke proposed a similar plan for "the children of the labouring people."

Locke's theories on education are far inferior to the best practices of the dissenting academies of his day, and likewise to the plans of Vives, Mulcaster, and Comenius. Summed up in a sentence, Locke's theory of education was characteristically British: a watered down, practical Humanism for the aristocracy, and apprenticeship training for the masses.

THE DOCTRINE OF FORMAL DISCIPLINE

Did Locke advocate the doctrine of formal mental discipline? For some years a controversy was carried on, among American historians, as to whether or not Locke upheld the doctrine of formal mental discipline. This clash of interpretation in the field of education is the more interesting in view of the disagreements which sprang up in regard to Locke's other theories. A number of contending schools of thought trace their origin to the ideas of this many-sided thinker. These divergent interpretations are the more curious when one recalls how he strove with all his might and with singular sincerity of soul to be absolutely clear and impartial and to state the truth precisely as he saw it. In view of the great importance attached to the doctrine of formal mental discipline by English and American educators, it was thought necessary to undertake a thorough analysis of Locke's position. This was done in the first edition of this work.[26]

The influence of Locke's works. The effects of Locke's ideas were profound and widespread. In philosophy, his empiricism aroused the speculative activity of David Hume and of Bishop Berkeley in England. In France it brought about the Enlightenment; and in Germany provoked the profound movement of critical philosophy of Kant. In education, his views had similar far-reaching effects upon Rousseau, Basedow, Pestalozzi, and Herbart.

---

[26] The discussion of formal mental discipline has largely ceased, and in the interest of conserving space the subject is not continued in this revision. Students who are interested can consult the first edition.

Chapter 12

THE ENLIGHTENMENT AND PHYSIOCRACY

THE French Enlightenment: revolution and progress. The drama of modern life and educational reform shifted during the 18th century to France, where the stage was set for highly spectacular as well as tragic developments. Some of the most creative movements of western civilization emerged from the seething welter of French political and social life. In certain respects, the French had been more progressive than their neighbors; in other matters, they were far less advanced.[1] It was this anomalous condition which made that land the battlefield of revolution. Here took place the climactic revolt against accepted traditions and institutions: against the prolonged domination of the ancients in literature, art, and philosophy; against the Roman Catholic Church and its formal expression of Christianity; against absolutism in government; and against highly artificial social life and impossible economic conditions and modes of education. Out of this chaos of conflicting currents there was destined to emerge a deeper knowledge of man and, in consequence thereof, a new philosophy of human life and social institutions. Only a superficial sketch can be given of the factors that produced results so momentous.

The war of the ancients and the moderns. One of the signs that a new age was about to dawn is found in the revolt against the domination of the classical literatures. In 1687, Charles Perrault (1628-1703) wrote a comparison of the ancients and the moderns, in which he asserted

[1] It will be recalled that the peoples of other countries experienced their revolutions long before; the Dutch in the 16th century, the English in the Civil War, and the Germans in the Thirty Years' War.

the superiority of the latter.[2] This was the signal for a spirited war between the two camps. Fontenelle pointed out that the unreasonable admiration of the ancients was an obstacle to progress. Literature, like art, to be creative and living, must be free to follow its own genius.

Rationalism and Empiricism. There are three sources from which man has acquired knowledge: the senses, reason, and faith. Every age and, in fact, every individual, strikes a working balance between these three, so far as light by which to live is concerned. The Middle Ages based everything on revelation; it was the era of faith and credulity. The new insight, which sharply aroused the French mind, was the integration of the rationalism of Descartes with the empiricism of John Locke. This combination, introduced into French circles by Voltaire, was more completely elaborated by a group of literary men known as the *Encyclopedists* or *Philosophes*.

The general statement of the new creed was this: [3]

> We know truth only by our reason. That reason is enlightened only by our senses. What they do not tell us we cannot know, and it is mere folly to waste time in conjecturing. Imagination and feeling are blind leaders of the blind. All men who pretend to supernatural revelation or inspiration are swindlers, and those who believe them are dupes.

Possessed by this new philosophy, the 18th century thinkers abandoned all belief in revelation and relied only on sense perception and reason. The leaders of this movement were Diderot, chief editor of the encyclopedia; Condillac; Helvetius; D'Alembert; Holbach; and La Mettrie. They were radicals who worshipped clarity, method, order, and enlightenment; and their attitude was characterized by prodigious conceit, arrogance, and intolerance.

The worship of reason. Descartes had affirmed three axioms which were universally accepted by thinking men. These were: (1) the supremacy of reason; (2) the invariability of the laws of nature; and (3) an exact method of testing or verifying truth. These ideas destroyed the throne from which tradition had tyrannized the minds of men. The

---

[2] Perrault's fame rests on another contribution, his Mother Goose stories. He was the first to put into literary form the oral traditions of Sleeping Beauty, Little Red Riding Hood, Puss-in-Boots, Cinderella, Tom Thumb, and so on. He did not create these tales; but, by publishing them, he conferred an incalculable boon upon nursery education.

[3] Lowell, Edward J., *The Eve of the French Revolution,* p. 61. Boston: Houghton Mifflin, 1892.

Encyclopedists came to have a supreme faith in the ability of human reason and understanding to discover nature's laws, to learn all truth, and, by these means, to bring in an era of human happiness. So illuminating was the effect of this rationality that Voltaire jested that reason "was born in England within this century."

The exalted achievements of human reason during the 16th and 17th centuries in mathematical and physical sciences seemed to justify the abounding confidence which philosophers now placed in her powers. The work of Copernicus, Galileo, Leibnitz, and Newton formed the most sublime victory over ignorance ever won by the human spirit. The indubitable certainty of their results stood in sharpest contrast with the uncertainty and guesswork of ethical, political, and religious thinkers. The assurance of science made an utterly different impression from that of dogmatism and obscurantism in the other fields of thought. The great scientists began to enjoy unprecedented honor. Kings and parliaments granted many of them handsome subsidies to further their researches, and ample pensions to reward them. Men began to have an exalted pride in the accomplishments of human intelligence and a vaulting ambition to extend its triumphs.

What reason had accomplished in laying bare the hidden laws of the physical universe, they believed it could accomplish equally well in other fields. An abounding confidence sprang up in the ability of man to ferret out the laws which lie at the basis of human nature. If the starry heavens so far removed from the earth can be made to yield the secret laws of their conduct, surely human reason would be equally potent in laying bare the mechanism of human nature. The central objective of the 18th century came thus to be the study of man himself. Pope celebrated this endeavor in his *Essay on Man,* in the well-known line: "The proper study of mankind is man."

Philosophers and students of government, law, society, religion, and education sought to discover a science of human nature. They believed that man was merely a product of nature, amenable to her laws and wholly explainable by reason. Hitherto man had been considered a product of two different worlds, the spiritual and the physical. Now he was found to be a product of natural forces. The new psychology explained the origin of the soul which had previously led so many philosophers astray. Furthermore, it assumed that the science of society could be deduced from a knowledge of the nature of man. Logically, it followed that, if the laws of human society were discovered, the control of society for its good would be readily attained, for the new knowledge of man could be used to mold his character and to improve his lot in life.

Empiricism and sensuality. Left to itself, the worship of reason would scarcely have brought about the convulsions of this ill-starred era. The explosive force was formed by the peculiar manner in which rationalism was blended with the doctrine of sensuousness. But a third important factor in the total situation was the fact that this new philosophic theory found a well-prepared soil in the sensuality and atheism of French life. Philosophic minds were charmed with the new doctrine that all ideas have their origin in sense impressions. They hastened to draw all the implications which flow from this conception. Condillac, Helvetius, La Mettrie, and Holbach tried to show how every human faculty develops as the result of sensation. All thought is physical, for nothing exists which is not the result of material processes. Like the animals, man, too, is a machine; his thoughts and desires are due to the impressions which things make upon his senses. Memory, imagination, and even reasoning are complex processes of perception. The brain secretes thought as the liver secretes bile. Nothing exists except what is known by the senses. No other age so blatantly denied the existence of the spiritual. It was an easy but shallow philosophy; nevertheless, it became an effective weapon to crush the life out of many of the greatest abuses that ever cursed mankind, and to bring in the new era of enlightenment.

The revolt against Christianity. No feature of the French Enlightenment aroused such passionate feeling as the vehement onslaught against a hollow and degenerate form of Christianity, which had lost touch with ethical principles, and was united with a moribund and tyrannical political order. The close alliance of church and state had produced an abundant crop of evils which only that unholy wedlock is capable of producing. The authority of the established church was guaranteed by the state. In return the church sustained the autocracy of the throne by proclaiming the divine right of kings, and granted absolution to the king and his debauched courtiers for all their crimes. Both church and state exploited the people without mercy. The moral rottenness of both can scarcely be exaggerated. Religion was an empty formalism, and the church, a mistress of all wickedness.

The leader in the attack was Voltaire, brilliant, clever, witty, vain, conceited, and sardonic, who became the undisputed literary genius of the age. He directed his sinuous intelligence and venomous wit against the Roman Catholic Church, which he invariably termed "the infamous thing." He charged that all prophets and priests are impostors and crooks and that the church is the cause of most atrocious tyranny, and of horrible human sacrifices. Voltaire did not absolutely deny the existence of God, but, like most men of his day, he took refuge in deism. He believed that, after creating the world, God withdrew and has nothing more to do in controlling its operation. Miracles, providence, and revelation, the three central tenets of Christian faith, he pronounced contrary to reason. However, he refrained from destroying religion completely, for he considered it a valuable instrument for keeping the masses under control. Thus Voltaire showed a lower ethical sensibility than the very leaders whom he so mercilessly castigated. So deep were the wounds which he inflicted upon Christianity, as he erroneously conceived it, that his memory has been the object of the most bitter execration to this day, not alone on the part of Catholics, but also of Protestants, about whose beliefs and practices he knew nothing.

The unfortunate opposition of both Catholic and Protestant official bodies to the new astronomy was highly discreditable to the cause of Christianity. It indicated a disposition to place their dogmatic assumptions above intellectual enlightenment and truth. The entire Christian system was flouted and ridiculed as a base superstition and a palpable fraud. Miracles were held to conflict with the uniformity of natural law; providence, with common sense. The Bible was considered full of errors; it could not have been an inspired work, and was thought to be wholly unworthy of confidence. The only satisfactory religion was held to be that which one derived from nature, and which is in accord with human reason.

What were the effects of these attacks upon religion and Christian faith? The Jesuits were driven out of every country in Europe but two, and finally the order as a whole was suppressed by Pope Clement XIV, in 1773. This expulsion involved the destruction of their numerous colleges, in which a large portion of the most gifted of the youth of the upper classes were being educated. Whereas many of the thinkers were favorable to deism, there was an increased trend toward out-and-out atheism. In France the leaders thought that religion should be taken out of the hands of the church entirely, and made a civic affair. Many tried to work out a purely naturalistic form of worship. Another, and perhaps the most important, result of the criticism of the church was the breaking away from empty formalism and credalism, and the return to a religion of inner light and ethical meaning.

The Enlightenment had a tremendous influence in America, where it played a part in bringing about separation of church and state. Public education was taken out of the hands of the church and became a secular and civic training. By 1790 less than 6% of the population of the United States were church members.

Conditions of social life. Everywhere in Europe standards of living were grossly unequal, and social life was shockingly corrupt. The mass of the people were in rags, and lived more like animals than human beings. For this poor and meager living they toiled to the last ounce of their strength. This was true of young children as well as those who were mature. As for the upper classes, the nobility of church and state and the *bourgeoisie,* conditions were entirely different; they lived in wanton luxury from the toil of those whom they despised.

Never had high society been more brilliant, conversation more sparkling, literature more piquant, nor science more enlightening. Manners, language, and taste were artificialized to the last degree.

Never, except in the worst days of paganism and the Renaissance, was sexual morality at a lower ebb. Fashionable women were devoid of all modesty. Ideal love and conjugal fidelity were considered *passé.* Kings maintained their mistresses openly, and with wanton extravagance. Their example was followed by the nobility of both church and state. Because the nobles had no interest in business, sports, or hunting, they occupied their time in illicit love-making. Most deplorable was the fact that nothing better was expected of them. However, their voluptuousness was refined, polished, and calculating. They adorned their vices with wit and elegance. Manners were an art, and took the place of morals. Conditions were the more unwholesome because of a cynical contempt for all virtue and idealism.

Economic conditions. Economic conditions were grim, so far as the masses were concerned, everywhere throughout Europe. Agriculture was primitive in its methods; and serfdom, actual or virtual, still obtained in most lands. In France the peasants gained a few rights, but their condition was desperate. The clergy owned one-fifth of the land; their peasants were the best treated, and their soil the best cultivated. The nobles, who owned another fifth, treated their tenants with heartless tyranny. One-third of all the lands remained idle every year. The peasants were obliged to pay extremely heavy rentals and local taxes of various kinds. Dues to the landlord, tithes to the church, taxes to local authorities and to the king amounted to four-fifths of all the produce in favorable years. Stark starvation was the peasant's lot in times of leanness. Thus he bore a staggering and inexorable burden: [4] "Starving peasants in France tried to appease their hunger with roots and herbs, and in hard times succumbed by thousands to famine." According to another historian: [5]

> Over great tracts of country the poor were reduced to living on grass and water, like the beasts of the field. When the King asked the Bishop of Chartres how his flock fared he was answered that they ate grass like sheep and starved like flies.

In the towns and in Paris the artisans fared better, because of commerce and manufacturing. Few became rich, for all forms of commercial activity were severely fettered by monopolies, imposts, duties, tariffs, and special taxes.

The political revolt. For several centuries, feudalism in France was slowly evolving into absolutism. By the beginning of the 18th century the process was complete, and the royal will was all-powerful. Every function of the government, legislative, judicial, and administrative, was under the control of the king. The claim of Louis XIV, "I am the state," was no empty boast. His court, which was the most brilliant, aggressive, and licentious in Europe, set the style for all others. Even independent spirits like Frederick the Great imitated it, and petty princes conducted their affairs according to this model. Bossuet, the most classical orator produced by Jesuit humanistic education, furnished the theory of absolutism when he asserted that monarchy under God is the most usual, the most ancient, and the most natural form of government. The king rules by divine right, and he is the embodiment of all the rights and powers of all individuals who are his subjects.

Three classes made up the nation; the king and nobility were first, the clergy and the religious orders came next, and below were the common people. The upper class consisted of approximately 150,000 people, or some 30,000 families, who enjoyed hereditary rights but were subservient to the monarch. The clergy and the religious orders accounted for

---

[4] Hayes, Carlton J. H., *A Political and Social History of Modern Europe,* Vol. I, p. 398. New York: The Macmillan Company, 1916.

[5] Higgs, Henry, *The Physiocrats,* p. 9. London: Macmillan and Company, Ltd., 1897.

some 130,000 others, who in some respects were subject to the king but in others were independent, and thus formed a state within the state. The common people amounted to about 25,000,000. Only the nobles had any share in government whatsoever. Having nothing else to do, they imitated the free living of the sovereign and his dissolute courtiers. They "devoured" the peasants "like pikes in a pond," for the peasant class was too poor, weak, and afraid to protest.

The critical revolt against autocratic power and corruption began with Montesquieu, and was advanced by Voltaire, Rousseau, and an increasing number of pamphleteers. In 1748, Montesquieu published *The Spirit of Laws,* which for the first time gave the French public an intelligent discussion of theories of government. It acquainted them with the works of Grotius, Hobbes, Pufendorf, and Locke on political organization. More particularly it drew attention to the English system of government, which was the most successful yet devised in harmonizing the power of the monarch and the freedom of the subject. This work of Montesquieu brought about an ever mounting tide of political pamphlets on every subject connected with the state.

Enlightenment the key to liberty and progress. The leaders of 18th-century thought were conscious that a profound change was taking place in the depth of the human spirit. This was a new intellectual awakening, comparable only to those momentous revolutions which history knows as the Renaissance, Scholasticism, and the Age of Pericles. The leaders bombastically called it the "Age of Reason" or "Enlightenment." They felt the thrill of emancipation from a dark and cruel past dominated by superstition, error, ignorance, and tradition. Man had been duped, misled, and oppressed because he could not think for himself. He lived a befogged existence. At last, scientific knowledge had put an end to this benighted era, and had brought Enlightenment and its twin sister Liberty. Scientific knowledge became the popular rage among the intelligentsia. It was a live topic in the fashionable salons. Ladies studied astronomy, mechanics, and anatomy. Knowledge of the operation of natural law had destroyed the mystery of the objective world, and revealed its true character to human intelligence.

The underlying current of 18th-century thought was the idea of progress through natural law. The philosophers conceived Nature as a machine governed by immutable laws. To know these laws is to be able to manipulate them for man's use. Bacon's slogan, *Knowledge is power,* had been abundantly demonstrated by science and invention. What had been done for outer nature, the philosophers felt was equally possible for human nature. Stormy as were their times, amid the storms they caught flashes which revealed a glorious new era.[6]

> It seemed as if the golden age was dawning; the human mind seemed to be awakening from the slumber of centuries to conquer the world, to unravel the mysteries of life, and to discover the secrets of the universe. Confident that only a little thought would be necessary to free the world from vice, ignorance, and superstition, thinkers now turned boldly to attack the vexing problems of religion and morality, to criticise state, society, and church, and to point the way to a new and earthly paradise. This tendency—this enthusiasm—has usually been styled "rationalism" because its champions sought to make everything *rational* or reasonable.

Descartes himself had some such dreams. The title he first proposed for his *Discourse on Method* was *The Project of a Universal Science which can elevate our Nature to its highest degree of Perfection.*[7]

The one instrument which could be trusted to lead to the perfection of human nature and happiness was, as these philosophers confidently thought, the spread of knowledge. Intellectual enlightenment, married to self-interest, was the sure instrument of human improvement. Civilization is in its infancy and not in its old age, as had been wrongly thought. Paradise is before man, and not in the past. What is the use of the achievements of science and the improvements in the arts, if man himself cannot be improved? Faith in the power of reason and knowledge to bless the lot of man was exalted into a religious fanaticism.

Attitude toward the masses. In general the upper classes despised the lower, and treated them with contempt and cruelty. The nobility looked upon the peasants as a lower order of life.

The Rationalists who, by their wits, had raised their own lot, generally came from the common ranks. Rationalism, however, is naturally cold, snobbish, and supercilious—the product of selfish, calculating egotism. The Encyclopedists generally believed the common people incapable of reason, or of enlightenment, and hence in need of control. Voltaire referred to them as *canailles* (dogs), who need a god and a king to keep them in leash. He tersely expressed his attitude in this statement: "The people will always remain stupid and barbaric; they are oxen, that need the yoke, whip and hay." He had no desire whatever to share with them

---

[6] Hayes, Carlton J. H., *op. cit.*, Vol. I, p. 418.

[7] Bury, J. B., *The Idea of Progress*, p. 67. London: Macmillan and Company, Ltd., 1921.

the benefits which arise from the advancement of knowledge and from man's power over nature. The advantages of enlightenment were for the higher classes of birth and intelligence. He always treated the people with contempt, and the Encyclopedists generally shared his attitude.

There were, however, some who took a different point of view. Furthermore, it was precisely because of this cynical heartlessness of Rationalism that Rousseau turned his back upon it and espoused the cause of Naturalism. Many of the Rationalists drew the logical conclusion of the doctrine, emphasized by Pufendorf and Locke, that all men have equality of rights. They attributed differences in individuals to social environment and training. All are equally capable of enlightenment and the development of reasoning ability. Many believed in the perfectibility of human nature. These, however, were more influenced by a belief in the potency of enlightened self-interest than in any feelings of altruism.

THE PHYSIOCRATIC MOVEMENT

Origin of movement. The philosophy of the Enlightenment failed at another point: it provided no theory of economic betterment. This need was filled by the *Physiocrats,* or *Economistes,* soon after the middle of the 18th century. The originators were François Quesnay,[8] court physician to Louis XV, and Jacques Claude de Gournay. The leading disciples and propagandists of the movement were the elder Mirabeau; Mercier de la Rivière; Turgot, the comptroller-general; and Dupont de Nemours. Dupont was the journalist of the movement who edited the works of Quesnay and managed the *Journal,* the official organ of propaganda. Americans have a special interest in him.[9]

The term *Physiocracy* literally means rule by the physical world. It has the same significance for economics that *negative education* has in the philosophy of Rousseau, and *natural law,* in the theories of the Encyclopedists. The physiocratic doctrine holds to the operation of natural law in the economic world. The importance of their work lies in the fact that the Physiocrats are the founders of economic science. Their doctrines were these:

---

[8] Quesnay's grandson came to America and undertook to establish French culture in the United States.

[9] See also page 396 of this text.

(1) Agriculture is the one and only source of wealth. It alone yields a profit. Industry and manufacturing change the form of the raw materials, but add nothing to their value. Neither does transportation of goods from one place to another.

(2) Every individual has a right to labor, and to enjoy the fruits of his labor. This is a natural right, and as such cannot be alienated or surrendered in any way whatsoever, not even by social contract. Even the state must submit to this right. Man's greatest happiness consists in the greatest possible abundance of objects suitable to his enjoyment, and in the largest freedom to profit by them.

(3) Production and exchange of goods must be absolutely free. Governmental restrictions hamper and destroy economic life. Freedom of industry and exchange of commodities are essential for maximum production and the enjoyment of goods. This doctrine, called by Gournay *laissez-faire,* has been the chief principle of economics since his day. It allows production, commerce, and trade to follow their own inherent laws without interference. Today it is called, "the free enterprise system."

(4) The sole functions of government are to protect life and property, and to administer justice. It is not within its scope to restrict or interfere with production and trade.

(5) Possession of property and security are the indispensable conditions for the full enjoyment of the products of labor. Property and security are the basis of economic liberty, and economic liberty is the basis of individual happiness.

These doctrines of the Physiocrats exercised a profound influence throughout Europe and America. These men were thoroughly upright, and were inspired by a sincere desire for the welfare of the people, especially for the material and moral elevation of the working classes. They protested the oppression of the peasants, and promoted their importance in the eyes of the rulers. They pleaded for the abolition of tolls on transportation and of restraints on agriculture and trade. They advocated the repair of roads and canals. Though they never challenged the principle of despotic government, they contended for a more intelligent and enlightened, and even benevolent absolutism. Quesnay expressed this in his advice to the Dauphin: "Do nothing, but let the laws rule."

Due to the work of the Physiocrats agriculture gained in dignity, and country life was idealized. Societies for the improvement of agriculture were formed, and it was looked upon as a means of social progress. This back-to-the-farm movement was further popularized through the works of Rousseau, Pestalozzi, and Fellenberg; by their influence specialized training for industrial and agricultural life began.

The physiocratic movement was taken up by benevolent and enlightened despots. Among these may be listed Frederick the Great, of Prussia; Maria Theresa and her son Joseph II, of Austria; Catherine the Great, of Russia; Charles III, of Spain; Gustavus III, of Sweden; and Charles Frederick, of Baden. Accepting the ideas of the Physiocrats, they relaxed the oppressive laws against the peasants, freed trade, and sought to educate the people to become productive workers and loyal subjects. In fact, in the hearts of rulers a wave of benevolence took the place once occupied by contempt and scorn for the lower classes.

These economic principles were not all sound, but they had this value: they led to more study of the subject of economic theory and laws by Adam Smith in his *Wealth of Nations,* published in 1776.

DEVELOPMENTS IN GERMANY

The Enlightenment in Germany. The Enlightenment, Physiocracy, and Naturalism, did not take the same direction in Germany that they took west of the Rhine. In Germany, these movements were confined to the ruling class; German princes and the petty nobility were completely dominated by French court life. They used the French language, bought furniture and clothes in Paris, and in every way aped French manners and ideals. The common people of Germany were wholly oblivious to all this, and plodded along like dumb cattle. They were not permitted to think of political affairs; whatever effects the new ideas were to exert came directly from those rulers who were moved by benevolent impulses to benefit their subjects. Led by Frederick the Great, the rulers saw no reason to forbid philosophical speculation, scientific research, literature, and the fine arts. In consequence of this liberty, the greatest developments of German genius are found in these fields. The *Aufklärung* forms the most brilliant era of German history in philosophy and literature.

Prussia leads in new beginnings. During the first half of the century, Germany was still a land of some 360 separate, insignificant principalities and free cities. One of the least productive and most scattered of these kingdoms, Prussia, was soon to attain political hegemony and to assume educational leadership. It did this because of the sagacity of its rulers, especially the genius of Frederick the Great.

Earlier efforts to reform the schools. Frederick came naturally by his interest in educational affairs, because of the policy of his father and grandfather. The latter, Frederick William I, had a deep attachment to Pietistic doctrines and the philanthropic reforms of Francke. He led in the establishment of some 1800 new schools in his kingdom, and even provided a small endowment for their promotion. In some instances he provided lumber for buildings, and generally took an interest in the appointment of more efficient teachers. Among his other reforms, he made education compulsory in the school law of 1717. Frederick's father took further steps to build up better schools. But all the efforts of these two did not bring satisfactory results. Lack of funds, indifference on the part of the nobility, distrust of schools by the masses because of gross ignorance, dearth of trained teachers, and political difficulties combined to destroy the fruits of their planting.

Frederick the Great (1712-1786). Frederick was a romantic and impractical youth whose genius flowered only when confronted with the responsibilities of government. He proved himself great as a general, sovereign, and practical philosopher, though he always retained a deep vein of cynicism. By his shrewd intelligence and management he extended his small and scattered domain until Prussia, in its own right, had to be rated among the first powers of Europe.

Frederick was a friend of Voltaire, and generally was very hospitable to the doctrines of the Encyclopedists and Physiocrats. He was the most brilliant of the benevolent despots, an absolutist who regarded himself as "the first servant of the state." Possessed with a discerning and independent mind, he followed the French theorists only so far as it suited his purposes. Himself a freethinker, he tolerated every form of religion, even refusing to join the general effort to suppress the Jesuit Order. He granted a large measure of freedom to the press, and permitted liberty of speech so long as it did not touch upon affairs of government. He instituted numerous reforms, but never as concessions to popular unrest. He greatly improved agriculture, and encouraged industry and other internal developments. His government was the most efficient bureaucracy in Europe. It is no wonder that education, also, made great progress under this master mind.

Efforts to reform education. Cynic though he was, Frederick believed it easier to rule an enlightened, trained, and industrious people than an ignorant and incompetent nation of serfs. With rare insight and breadth of vision, he availed himself of the expert assistance of four outstanding leaders: Hecker, the Pietist pastor and educator; Felbiger, Augustinian monk of Silesia; von Rochow, nobleman, philanthropist, and educational reformer; and von Zedlitz, efficient bureaucratic organizer, minister of justice and culture.

Hecker and the Prussian school law of 1763. As already stated, Hecker, who was trained under Francke, originated the *Realschule* and the movement for training of teachers in Germany. At Frederick's direction, he wrote the general code of regulations for rural schools, which Frederick promulgated in 1763.

This law was the first educational code for the entire Kingdom of Prussia, and forms the basis upon which later *Volksschule* legislation was built. The law touched every important subject of school organization. Compulsory attendance (*Schulpflichtigkeit*) was again decreed and more fully defined for both winter and summer. Parents and guardians were liable to a fine in case they did not send their children to school regularly. Children were due to attend school from the fifth to the thirteenth year, or until they had learned the principles of Christianity and could read and write well. They were required to pass an examination on the textbooks authorized by the church consistory. A system of child accounting was introduced. Supervision was left in the hands of the local pastors, whose duty it was to visit the schools twice every week. The church superintendents and inspectors were to visit and inspect the school once a year and to make a report on its condition. The tuition fee for the poor was to be paid by local civil or church authorities. Definite school hours were prescribed.

The real purpose of the school may be judged from the curriculum, which consisted of religion, reading, writing, spelling, and a small amount of ciphering in the upper class. The instruction in religion was laid down in some detail. It comprehended systematic instruction in catechism, Bible drill, Biblical history, Christian doctrine, and church music.

Teachers were required to obtain a license to teach, and the qualifications were raised. Good character was demanded of all teachers. From the following statement, considerable insight into the condition of the profession may be obtained: [10]

> All teachers are forbidden to keep tavern, to sell beer or wine, to engage in any other occupation by which their labor may be hindered or

[10] Barnard, Henry, *German Teachers and Educators,* p. 595. Hartford: Brown & Gross, 1878.

> the children lured by their example into habits of idleness and dissipation, such as hanging around taverns, or playing music at dinners and balls, which is prohibited under high fine and punishment.

No teacher could be employed except with the approval of the church inspector. In no other state was such a lofty standard definitely set up; but on account of too many adverse conditions it could not be attained. Frederick himself, in his later days, was obliged to compromise by placing his invalided and often ignorant soldiers in charge of the schools.

What was thus instituted in Prussia was also attempted, under the leadership of Felbiger, in the newly acquired province of Silesia. Here the population was Catholic, and certain modifications of the standards had to be made, but, in general, the school law was similar to that of Prussia. Felbiger was later employed by Maria Theresa, Empress of Austria, to put into operation similar reforms in her domain.

It is easy to overrate the importance of Frederick's interest in education, for he promised more than he actually performed. Of education for the masses of children, he stated: "In the open country it is sufficient if they learn to read and write a little; if they know too much they will go to the towns and become secretaries and such like." Moreover, he had no high regard for the value of secondary and university education. He was chiefly interested in the training school for teachers and in a military school for young nobles.

Chapter 13

ROUSSEAU: THE COPERNICUS OF MODERN CIVILIZATION

IT IS well-nigh impossible to exaggerate the influence that Rousseau has had upon the course of modern civilization. Sir Henry Maine has justly stated it: [1]

> We have never seen in our own generation—indeed the world has not seen more than once or twice in all the course of history—a literature which has exercised such prodigious influence over the minds of men, over every cast and shade of intellect, as that which emanated from Rousseau between 1749 and 1762.

His doctrines revolutionized views of government, religion, and social life; radically changed the prevailing ideas of marriage; necessitated the reconstruction of philosophy; inspired a new literary movement; and placed education on a new track.

ROUSSEAU'S LIFE AND CHARACTER

Parentage and early training. Jean Jacques Rousseau began his tragic career in Geneva in 1712, the offspring of mixed, but respectable, parentage. The father traced his ancestry to a bookseller who fled from Paris in the 16th century to escape persecution for his Protestant faith. The mother, beautiful, intelligent, and refined, belonged to an upper class Swiss family. Subjected to the rigorous regimentation which ruled the citadel of Calvinism, Rousseau was never able to attain stability either within or without. His life began with the climax of disasters, the death of his mother when he was but a week old. With an abiding sense

[1] Maine, Henry, *Ancient Law,* p. 84. New York: Henry Holt, 1885.

of grief, he long after bemoaned his loss: "I cost my mother her life, and my birth was the first of my misfortunes."

The father was a reputable watchmaker, fond of reading, but extremely eccentric and sentimental. Too poor to pay for the proper education of his son, he was likewise too busy and injudicious to train the lad himself. When Jean Jacques was six, his father taught him to read, choosing as texts some old romances which belonged to the mother. A strange sort of primer indeed! Before he was seven, the two had read aloud, in turn, "whole nights together, and could never stop until we had reached the end of a volume." These sentimental debauches over, more substantial works were avidly devoured, among them Plutarch's *Lives*, and Bossuet's *Discourses on Universal History*. In later years Rousseau drew a glowing picture of these seances: [2]

> I cannot recall to mind, without the sweetest emotions, the memory of that virtuous citizen to whom I owe my being. . . . I see the works of Tacitus, Plutarch, and Grotius, lying before him in the midst of the tools of his trade. At his side stands his dear son, receiving the tender instruction of the best of fathers.

The consequences of this overstimulation were disastrous; Jean Jacques became passionately fond of reading, but utterly incapable of acquiring the conventional habits and attitudes of normal life. According to his *Confessions*, he stole, lied, played dirty tricks, and was bright, but indolent, irritable, ill-bred, and thoroughly unprincipled.

When he was ten, his "best of fathers" ran away and Jean Jacques, together with a cousin, was sent to school for several years in the village of Bossey. This constituted the only training he was destined to receive. Here for a time he was happy, played with zest, learned to garden, and acquired that mystical love of nature which moved him frequently to tears. But even this short period of schooling ended in disappointment. He returned home with his cousin and shared lessons in drawing and coloring, and, during the time of leisure, "they made cages, flutes, kites, drums, houses, pop-guns and cross bows."

In youth, Rousseau was incapable of adjusting himself to social and vocational life. Placed in the office of the city registrar, he was quickly discharged because of incompetency. Apprenticed to an engraver, he ran away in his 16th year. The occasion was trifling; the consequences

---

[2] Rousseau, J. J., Preface to *Discourse on the Origin of Inequality.*

momentous. One Sunday evening he wandered, as he frequently did, outside the walls of the city with several companions. Returning to find the gates closed, rather than face the scolding of his master, he blithely turned his back upon home and native city to become a wanderer. If one could have looked into the heart of this careless young vagabond, he would have noted nothing which foreshadowed the future genius who was to affect the course of civilization profoundly. He was passionately fond of music, had a mystical affinity for nature, a keen sense of justice, a slight interest in handicrafts, an abnormal sex consciousness, a rather shy and diffident disposition, an unstable temperament, and an unfathomable yearning for independence.

Manhood. The next twenty years of his career have more value for the psychiatrist than for students of education. They may be passed with little detail. A priest took pity on him, tired and hungry from his wanderings, fed him, and persuaded him to accept the Catholic faith. Placed for his spiritual edification under the guidance of Madame de Warens, a charming woman, a recent convert to Catholicism, Rousseau made little progress in piety. With her assistance he put forth many efforts to find a congenial vocation. He served as a lackey, studied for the priesthood, practiced music, and became in turn a government clerk, a teacher of music, and a secretary. The reading of Locke's *Thoughts Concerning Education* led him to attempt teaching and he was employed to instruct the two sons of Monsieur de Mably, an important official of Lyons. Like all his other efforts, this, too, resulted in complete failure because of his irascible temperament. Again he returned to the hospitable roof of Madame de Warens, and in the end became her paid secretary and lover.

Two features of these years are of special significance: the experiences gathered in his wanderings, and his somewhat desultory studies. His excursions afforded a vivid insight into the revolting miseries of the French peasantry. His studies served to acquaint him with the current social and philosophical problems agitating the minds of men. Montaigne, Leibnitz, Locke, Pope, and Voltaire made the deepest impression. His range of reading included, also, scientific investigations from which he acquired some knowledge of the works of Descartes, Pascal, Kepler, and Newton. Government and education gradually came to form the central themes of his thinking. This may be traced to his study of Plato's *Republic,* which he declared "the finest work on education ever written." Among other books which had a decided influence upon him were: Montaigne's *Essays;* Pope's *Essay on Man,* and Defoe's *Robinson Crusoe.* So profoundly was he impressed with the latter that he selected it, from all the books ever written, to "constitute the whole library for the youth of Emile."

In 1741 Rousseau, in a fit of jealousy, broke with his fascinating mistress, and set out for Paris. In spite of extreme poverty, eccentricities, and awkwardness, he established cordial relations with Voltaire, Diderot, and other leaders. He thus became associated with the most brilliant literary and philosophical group in France, accepted their pessimism, and engaged in their libertarian life. By copying music, he obtained a meager livelihood. He met Thérèse Levasseur, a vulgar and very stupid servant who lived as his mistress for 23 years before a marriage was performed. Five children were born, and without delay each in turn was sent to the foundling hospital. Nor were any of them ever traced. This was one of the most unaccountable of the performances of this paradoxical genius.

The great awakening. Rousseau reached the ripe age of 37 without displaying a scintilla of intellectual superiority. Genius awakened in him with the suddenness of a bolt of lightning.

One warm evening in October 1749, Rousseau was walking leisurely along the road to Vincennes to visit Diderot, who was imprisoned in the Bastille. As he glanced through the *Mercure de France,* his attention was arrested by the offer of a prize by the scientific Academy of Dijon, for an essay on the question: "Has the progress of the Sciences and the Arts tended to the purification or the corruption of morals?" This question struck him like an electric shock, and the experience can only be described in his own terms: [3]

> The moment I read this I saw a new world, and became a new man. If ever anything was like a sudden inspiration it was the emotion within me at this reading. All at once I felt my senses dazzled by a thousand lights. Crowds of vivid ideas were suddenly presented with a force and confusion that threw me into an inexpressible bewilderment. I felt my head seized by dizziness like an intoxication. A violent palpitation oppressed me. Not being able to breathe and to walk at the same time, I dropped beneath one of the trees of the avenue, and there I passed half an

---

[3] Rousseau referred three times to this experience: Rousseau, J. J., *Confessions,* VIII; Defour, Théophile, *Correspondence générale de J. J. Rousseau,* VII, pp. 50-51. Paris: Librairie Armand Colin, 1925.

> hour in such agitation that when I arose the whole front of my coat was wet with my tears, though I was not conscious of shedding them.
>
> Oh, sir, if only I could have written even a fourth-part of what I saw and felt under that tree, with what clearness would I have set forth the contradictions of our social system: with what force would I have exposed the abuses of our institutions: with what simplicity would I have shown that man is naturally good and that it is these institutions alone which make him bad.

Rousseau wrote a scathing denunciation of civilization. The chief marvel was not that he won the prize but that the members of the Academy voted in favor of his essay; for they had in view something very different. In any case, Rousseau vaulted into fame, and felt himself seized by a holy mission for the reordering of civilization.

The next years of his life were given to writing. In response to a second prize offered by the Academy, he wrote *What is the Cause of Inequality among Men?* In 1761, he discussed marriage and family life in a romance called *The New Héloïse.* The next year, there followed the two most important works on which his claim to genius rests: *The Social Contract,* the result of many years of reflection and study of the principles of government; and the *Emile,* in which he discussed education. It has been said that Rousseau spent the last half of his life writing about the first. This is particularly true of his last work, the *Confessions,* in which he bared his soul as no other man has ever done. In spite of his great celebrity and unparalleled services to mankind, his last years were no happier than his first. He died in exile, in poverty, and in solitude, at the age of 66.

Rousseau's paradoxical nature. Of all the greatest figures of history none presents a more inexplicable puzzle. Creator of paradoxes, Rousseau's life and character were the supreme paradox. He was a creature of prodigious emotionality and uncontrollable passions. Periods of exaltation and ecstasy alternated with spells of deepest melancholy. His sentimentality reached a high degree of absurdity. He was irascible, suspicious, jealous, and quarrelsome. No friendship was lasting, for he was ever quick to pick a quarrel with the one who sought to help him. A creature of caprice, he was condemned to suffer the emotional "storm and stress" of adolescence throughout all his days.

The tendency to flashes of inspiration throws light upon the paradoxical character of his mind. Novel ideas rose to consciousness with startling suddenness and irresistible power. Here one finds an explanation of his many contradictions, his inveterate tendency to employ paradox, and his exploitation of half truths. He tried to explain his incapacity to think in wholes: [4]

> Wavering perpetually between my natural sentiments, tending to the general good of mankind, and my reason, confining everything to my own, I should have remained all my life in this continual dilemma, doing evil yet loving good, in constant contradiction with myself, had not new knowledge enlightened my heart.

Those mental traits may likewise explain his effusive repentances. In the glowing tribute to his native Geneva, he confessed he had "too late grown wise . . . vainly regretting that peaceful repose which I had forfeited in the imprudence of youth." [5] Similarly he suffered the pangs of remorse for his inhuman treatment of his own children.[6]

While writing the *Emile* the enormity of his conduct seized his conscience, as the following passage indicates: [7]

> Reader, believe me when I predict that whoever has a heart and neglects such sacred duties will long shed bitter tears over his mistake, and will never find consolation for it.

Alongside his reprobate nature existed the capacity to feel a thrill for everything that is lofty and to express these noble aspirations so appealingly that the world was inspired. If there existed no jot of information in regard to the life he lived, from his writings alone we should be constrained to judge him one of the world's noblest idealists. His firm belief in the original goodness of the human heart, his desire to preserve its innocence at all hazards, his profound sense of justice and genuine sympathy for downtrodden humanity, his interest in the preservation of virtue, his love of liberty, his passion for genuineness, all are marks of the idealist.

Rousseau's break with Rationalism was by no means a repudiation of the function of reason. He saw that the faculty of reason as the Encyclopedists conceived it was selfish, cynical, and contemptuous of the masses of humanity. "It is vain," he declared, "to attempt the establishment of virtue on the foundation of reason alone." In his philosophy

---

[4] Rousseau, J. J., *Profession of Faith of a Savoyard Vicar.*

[5] Rousseau, J. J., Preface to the *Discourse on the Origin of Inequality.*

[6] Rousseau, J. J., *Emile,* p. 16. Quotations from the *Emile,* (except Foxley's, p. 340 of this text) are from the translation by William H. Payne.

[7] Rousseau, J. J., *Confessions,* Book VII.

reason is not a primary aspect of the soul, but an acquired ability, which emerges comparatively late in human development.

ROUSSEAU'S POLITICAL AND SOCIAL THEORIES

Revolt against civilization. The actual purpose of the Academy of Dijon was to contrast the immorality of the Humanistic Renaissance with the virtues of the Scholastic era. Rousseau had no quarrel with Humanism, but seized the occasion to assert that the arts and sciences have at all times and in all lands caused the downfall of virtue. Everywhere mankind became corrupted "in proportion as the arts and sciences improved. . . . The daily ebb and flow of the tides are not more regularly influenced by the moon than the morals of a people by the progress of the arts and sciences. As their light has risen above our horizon, virtue has taken flight, and the same phenomenon has been constantly observed in all times and places." The arts and sciences make men cowardly. In proportion as they enervate the body, they decrease the vigor of mind and corrupt morals. The greatest examples of manly virtues were the Spartans, the Scythians, and the Romans. The supreme virtues are courage, temperance, simplicity, endurance, brotherhood, and justice.

Rousseau was admirably fitted to lead the revolt against the artificiality and degeneracy of civilization. A personal grievance gave him due cause to prefer an indictment against all human institutions. Consider his "terrible destitution" in all vital human relations. Neither as child or man did he enjoy the moral reinforcement that comes from a normal home life. Many offered him friendship, but his irascible disposition made it impossible to profit by their assistance. Over and over he tried to acquire the morale that comes from steady employment, but he invariably failed. He proudly acclaimed his citizenship, but was an exile most of his days. The marriage state degraded and scandalized him. A false Christianity deprived his sensitive soul of the consolations of religious fellowship. "Surely no one was ever more a solitary in the midst of society than he." Maladjusted on every side, his genius sought consolation and expression in creating pictures of a nobler civilization. "He is, so to speak, the embodied protest of thwarted individuality against a society that has failed to give manhood adequate scope." [8]

---

[8] Boyd, William, *The Educational Theory of Jean Jacques Rousseau*, p. 93. London: Longmans, Green and Co., 1911.

Man in the state of nature. By the middle of the 18th century a tremendous advance had taken place in man's understanding of his own being. There were many reasons for this. First, astronomy had destroyed the traditional conception that man is the paragon of creation. He could no longer flatter his ego by the notion that everything was made expressly for his welfare. Then, again, knowledge of the ancient Greek and Roman civilizations had shown that man could develop to an advanced point by his own natural capacities. Furthermore, close contact with the American Indians had brought new knowledge of the character of primitive races and the ideal of "the noble savage."

Out of these new conceptions emerged an interest in discriminating between what belongs to nature and what to the artificial accretions of civilization. Students of government traced its origin to a "state of nature," and to inherent "natural rights." Philosophy and theology went forth in quest of a new and better basis, and discovered it in the inner nature of man's rationality. Out of this grew likewise the concept of natural religion. With these suggestions before him, Rousseau painted his picture of the original man in the state of nature, and proceeded to show what changes and additions have been acquired by the action of civilization: [9]

> When I think of this man as he must have been when he came forth from the hands of nature, I see an animal less strong than some of the animals, less agile than others, but, taking him all in all, better organized than any of them.

As to mentality man was a creature of feeling and sensibility, and his desires "do not go beyond his physical wants." He had no relations with his fellows, spoke no language, and was devoid of all reasoning and imagination. "The only good things that he knows in the universe are his food, his mate, and his rest. The only evils he fears are pain and hunger." Like the animals he is dull and stupid, but good and happy. Rousseau agreed with Pope's description of the original state: [10]

> Pride then was not; nor arts, that pride to aid;
> Man walked with beast, joint tenant of the shade;
> The same his table, and the same his bed.

In the state of nature man lived quite unconscious of self. The sole end of his behavior was to preserve himself from pain and death, and

---

[9] Rousseau, J. J., *Discourse on the Origin of Inequality,* Part I.

[10] Pope, Alexander, *Essay on Man.*

to secure the satisfaction of his animal nature. The mainspring of his conduct Rousseau termed *self-love* (*amour-de-soi*)—that is, the instinct for self-preservation. In this animal state all individuals were free, equal, and in no wise dependent upon one another.

The state of savagery. Reason lifted man above the purely animal state. Speech, family life, and the simple arts were produced. But man was still independent; his wants were few, his strength was more than necessary, and his virtues far exceeded his vices. Thus, Rousseau imagined, the savage lived serene and happy in a condition of placid stupidity.

The evolution of society. However, man did not remain in this simple state of nature. His imagination awakened new and insatiable desires, and led him to create artificial needs. Self-assertion, self-aggrandizement, and emulation arose in the hearts of men. Primitive self-love, which was neither good nor bad, was superseded by *amour-propre,* a calculating and ambitious selfishness.

This new development was the fecund mother of all the degenerating and corrupting passions and vices of man. Social distinctions of superiority and inferiority resulted and brought in their train the horrible brood of man's inhumanities to man. In his boundless ambition, everyone sought to subordinate all others and everything to himself. Man's understanding, with the aid of a volatile imagination, expanded his desires and created new wants, limitless in extent, which he was incapable of satisfying by means of his own power and resources. Other individuals had to be used as tools in order to satisfy these wants. Individuals came to be ranked according to a social scale, and their original equality wholly disappeared.

This tendency led to the organization of social, political, and industrial life into the higher and the lower classes, and thus to slavery. Social life came to be governed by conventionality, artificiality, and snobbishness. Religion degenerated into formalism and hypocrisy. Government ended in despotism and tyranny. Prejudices and conventions pressed upon man on every side and he lost entirely the power of acting on his own initiative. "He must do as others do, and as others want him to do." Under the circumstances, independence was lost and individuality destroyed; man sank into a condition of servility to his fellows and to social institutions and customs. He discriminated himself sharply from others, and his possessions from those of others. He became acutely conscious of self, of his position in relation to others, of his power over others, and of their power over him.

Reason, the cause of man's ruin. Animals are machines run by fixed instincts which act in accord with the uniform laws of nature. Such was the conclusion of contemporary French philosophy. La Mettrie and many others accepted the logical conclusion that man, too, is just such a machine.[11] But, according to Rousseau, the animal man in his original state was no robot. He did not have a complete set of instincts capable of determining all his actions automatically. Nature acts in the animals, but man is a free agent. In this respect, man is less perfect than other creatures, but his weakness is compensated for by ability to understand and reason. In the state of nature, his understanding was the instrument of his few and simple wants.

But a tragic change took place in man's primitive condition. Out of his rudimentary intelligence, curiosity and the ability to discriminate emerged. In the beginning, one tree was as good as another, one mate as attractive, and there was no choice as to his food; for "all fed on the same food-stuffs, lived in the same way, and did exactly the same things." All men were equal.

With the new power of discrimination, choice entered and put an end to uniformity and simple equality. Preference as to his abode, mate, and food produced greater complexity of conduct. Family life evolved, language became common, and these led to the forming of human society. To these developments were then added the beginning of private property, which brought into action one of the most subtle and powerful passions of the human soul.

Man's original state of innocence and happiness was destroyed by his intelligence. Rationality was at once the cause of his moral delinquency and of all his misfortunes. It led to his first sin that drove him from his garden of happiness and placed him under a curse. The real trouble was that man substituted cleverness for virtue, and preferred self-aggrandizement to equality. In the climax of his *Discourse on Arts and Sciences,* Rousseau utters this fantastic prayer:

> Almighty God! Thou who holdest in Thy hand the minds of men, deliver us from the fatal arts and sciences of our forefathers; give us back ignorance, innocence, and poverty, which alone can make us happy and are precious in Thy sight.

---

[11] La Mettrie, J. O. de, *Man a Machine*. Translated by Gertrude Carman Bussey. Chicago: Open Court Publishing Company, 1912.

Origin of the arts and sciences. The reason the arts and sciences corrupt man lies in the fact that they are of evil origin. They arose from man's curiosity and his desire to enhance his lot.[12]

> Astronomy was born of superstition; eloquence of ambition, hatred, falsehood and flattery; geometry of avarice; physics of an idle curiosity; and even moral philosophy of human pride. Thus the arts and sciences owe their birth to our vices; we should be less doubtful of their advantages, if they sprang from our virtues.
>
> Thus it is that luxury, profligacy and slavery have been, in all ages, the scourge of the efforts of our pride to emerge from that happy state of ignorance, in which the wisdom of providence has placed us.

Institutional reforms. Rousseau declared civilization a colossal mistake, and society, the source of all evil; but, strange to say, in the end he did not demand their abolition. Though always more or less under the influence of this strange pessimism, he had hopes of realizing sweeping reforms, and of inoculating the child so that he would counteract the poison of social contacts. He pointed out the changes necessary in the state, church, marriage, family life, and school, in order to bring them back to the fundamental principles of nature.

The Social Contract opens with the paradox: "Man is born free, and everywhere he is in chains." This condition is due to an irreconcilable antagonism between the state of nature and society. In the state of nature all were free and equal, and no one exercised any control over another. To preserve this condition is the function of civil organization.[13]

> If we ask precisely wherein consists the greatest good of all, which ought to be the aim of every system of legislation, we shall find that it is summed up in two principal objects, liberty and equality.

Personal liberty belongs to man by natural right, and is forever inalienable—that is to say, it can never justly be lost, sold, or otherwise dispensed with. For this reason, when man entered into the civil state, he did so by a mutual, or social, contract. In thus forming the state, two ends were sought: first, common defense; and second, the preservation of man's original freedom. The "problem" of government is: [14]

---

[12] Rousseau, J. J., *Discourse on the Arts and Sciences,* pp. 139-140. Pages refer to EVERYMAN'S LIBRARY, volume entitled *The Social Contract and Discourses.* All references to *The Social Contract* are likewise to this edition.

[13] Rousseau, J. J., *The Social Contract,* p. 45.

[14] *Ibid.*

to find a form of association which will defend and protect with the whole common force the person and goods of every associate, and in which, each while uniting himself with all, may still obey only himself, and remain as free as before.

Rousseau conceived a society in which protection would be furnished by mass coöperation but in which there would be no limitation upon individual liberty. He had in view "the noble savage," not as the savage was in reality, but as he was romantically visualized and idealized by 18th-century writers. This figment of the imagination, "is not attached to any place, has no prescribed task, obeys no one, has no law but his own will, and is compelled to reason about every action of his life." [15]

The state exists by virtue of "the general will," which is the universal good. Laws are but an expression of this common interest and ought to be enacted only with the consent of the people. Rousseau's ideal state is small, like Sparta or Geneva. He opposed strongly the policy of representative government, for every individual must assist in making the laws. As he conceived democracy, "the people, being subjected to the laws, should be the author of them." [16] He wrote: [17]

I should have sought a country in which the right of legislation was vested in all the citizens; for who can judge better than they of the conditions under which they had best dwell together in the same society.

Representative government is wrong in principle, for "the moment a people allows itself to be represented, it is no longer free." Moreover, he added: [18] "It is doubtful whether, from the very beginning of the world, human wisdom has made ten men capable of governing their peers." These views were absolutely radical in the middle of the 18th century and they pointed a dagger at the heart of autocratic government. Rousseau was the prophet of democracy, though he was himself no true democrat.

Man in the civil state. Rousseau's views underwent a change between the time of his first essays and the writing of *The Social Contract*. He no longer idealized the primitive man but set up the civil state along democratic lines.

---

[15] Boyd, William, *op. cit.*, p. 93.

[16] Rousseau, J. J., *The Social Contract*, p. 34.

[17] Preface to the *Discourse on the Origin of Inequality*.

[18] *Discourse on Political Economy*, p. 252. EVERYMAN'S LIBRARY, *The Social Contract and Discourses*. All references are to this edition.

When the civil state emerged out of primitive barbarism, it produced many changes in the nature of man. There were some disadvantages, but these were compensated for by a preponderance of benefits. The chief cause of this evolutionary change was the rise of reason; for by virtue of this change, mankind entered into moral life.[19]

> The passage from the state of nature to the civil state produces a very remarkable change in man, by substituting in his conduct justice for instinct, and giving his actions the moral quality they previously lacked. It is only when the voice of duty takes the place of physical impulse, and law succeeds appetite, that man, who till then had regarded only himself, sees that he is obliged to act on other principles, and to consult his reason before listening to his inclinations.

One sees by this new presentation that Rousseau was now fully aware of the absurdity of his earlier principles; but his mind was never able to transcend the antagonism of nature and society. In the end he sought to do so by the theory of successive stages in the development of individual life. At one stage, the emphasis was placed upon the development of the savage and the individual; at another, upon the development of reason and duty; and at still another, upon the social man.

Religion and the church. In the *Profession of Faith of a Savoyard Vicar,* Rousseau castigated the evils of the church, and set forth a doctrine of religion based only on nature and reason. He denied miracles, revelation, dogmas, and creeds. Like his contemporaries, he was a deist, but his deism was religious and emotional. He combined a discrete agnosticism regarding the possibility of revelation with a spirit of reverence for Christianity. Religion, however, he believed to be a concern of the individual, of the heart and reason, not an institutional regimentation, or an external ritual.

Marriage and the family. These institutions also came within the scope of Rousseau's scourging. The common custom, especially in France, was that the father arranged the marriage of his children without regard for their natural feelings and sentiments. How absurd the situation frequently became we have already seen.[20] *The New Héloïse* pictures the revulsion of the heroine when about to be given in marriage:[21]

---

[19] *The Social Contract,* Book I, Chap. VIII.
[20] See page 309 of this text.
[21] Rousseau, J. J., *The New Héloïse,* Letter XXVII.

> Has my father then sold me? Yes, he has considered his daughter as mere property, and has consigned her with as little remorse as a trader would a bale of goods. He purchases his own ease and quiet at the price of all my future comfort, nay, of my life itself.

The results of this method of arranging mating were to be seen in the looseness of conjugal fidelity.[22]

> In Paris marriage is a different institution from what it is in other parts of the world: they call it a sacrament, and yet it has not half the power of a common contract. It appears to be nothing more than a private agreement between two persons to live together, to bear the same name, and acknowledge the same children. If at Paris a man should pretend to be offended with the ill conduct of his wife, he would be as generally despised, as if, in our country, he was to take no notice of her scandalous behavior.

Human nature is good. The prevailing theology held that man is totally depraved, for sin is hereditary in all parts of his nature, his emotions, will, and reason. This formed one of the central doctrines of Tertullian and of Saint Augustine and his followers; especially of John Calvin and the Port Royalists. It is of curious interest that though Rousseau was born and raised in the city of Calvinism, he never wearied of combating this pessimistic tenet. "Everything," he declared, "is good as it comes from the hands of the author of nature." Again, "Oh! let us not spoil the man of nature, and he will always be virtuous without constraint, and happy without remorse." Or, "There is not a scoundrel living whose natural propensities would not have produced great virtues if they had been better directed." Goodness is thus the original condition, evil is the acquired. If wickedness were natural, man would have to become unnatural in order to become good. The author of the laws of nature would no more create man evil than he would make the law of gravitation imperfect. The virtues, conscience, a sense of right and wrong, a sense of justice, reverence, and pity are innate in the soul. The great problem is, not to implant virtues, but to preserve the soul from the vices which society puts into it.

Origin of vices. How vice arose can now readily be seen, according to Rousseau: [23]

---

[22] *Ibid.*, Letter LXXXVI.
[23] Boyd, William, *op. cit.*, p. 315.

> Let us lay it down as an incontestable principle that the first movements of nature are always right. There is no original perversity in the human heart. There is not a single vice in it of which we cannot say how it entered and whence it came. No one ever does evil as evil!

All vices began when man entered into human relations. The original man lived an isolated existence. His needs were few and simple; and his strength and skill were ample to satisfy every need completely. Life was dull and stupid, but it was simple, happy, and unaffected.

This condition, unfortunately, underwent a radical change. A vain curiosity led man to compare himself with others, and encouraged him to conceive new wants. These desires could not be satisfied by his own unaided power and skill. Only as other individuals assisted his efforts could he secure all the desires of his heart. He became more and more dependent on others, and society thus became increasingly more complex. The original conditon of equality of men was destroyed; in its stead there arose social classes with divisions of rank and social distinctions—a few who command, and the many who obey.

Social rank produces a new and acute sense of selfhood. The individual compares himself with others, and self-love (*amour-propre*) is born. It expresses its character in self-assertion or self-aggrandizement.[24]

> But self-love (*amour-propre*) is never satisfied, and could not be, because this feeling, by preferring ourselves to others, also requires that others prefer ourselves to them—a thing which is impossible.... That which makes men essentially good is to have few needs and to compare himself but little with others.

Herein is the source of all the vices: emulation produces jealousy, pride, vanity, envy, and all other human weaknesses.

Perpetuation of evil in the individual. Thus far we have been considering the origin of evil in the race. How it is transmitted from the older to the new generation is also readily seen. The home, the school, and social environment put into the hearts of children artificial desires and ambitions that they do not have the power to satisfy. Rousseau tells how the home instils these false desires, and leads the child to domineer over others: [25]

---

[24] Rousseau, J. J., *Emile*, p. 195.
[25] *Ibid.*, pp. 14-15.

> A child cries as soon as born, and his first years are spent in tears. At one time we trot and caress him to pacify him, and at another we threaten and beat him to keep him quiet. We either do what pleases him, or we exact of him what pleases us; we either subject ourselves to his whims, or subject him to ours. There is no middle ground; he must either give orders or receive them. And so his first ideas are those of domination and servitude. Before knowing how to speak, he commands; and before knowing how to act, he obeys; and sometimes he is punished before he is able to know his faults, or rather, to commit any.

The desires and the powers of an individual ought to balance one another. If his powers are greater than his desires, he lacks a spur to self-realization; if his desires exceed his powers, a sense of frustration and unhappiness results. In the case of the young child, it is easy to implant desires out of all proportion to his power and ability to realize them.[26]

> As soon as they come to consider the people who surround them as instruments which they can employ, they make use of them to follow their inclinations, and to supplement their own feebleness. This is how they become troublesome, tyrannical, imperious, depraved, unconquerable; a progress which does not come from a natural spirit of domination, but which gives them this spirit; for it does not require a long experience to feel how agreeable it is to act through the hands of others, and to need only set the tongue a-going in order to set the universe in motion.

Again, Rousseau admonished against this danger: [27] "It is important to accustom him at an early period neither to command men, for he is not their master, nor things, for they do not hear him." Thus, it is society that early implants in the hearts of young children desires which they should not have and for the satisfaction of which they must use other persons as mere tools. It is this inculcation of the feelings of superiority and inferiority which has cursed mankind. To prevent this degenerating process in the individual is the supreme task of education.[28]

ROUSSEAU FORMULATES THE NEW EDUCATION

The new point of view. Through all centuries the theory and practice of education had been determined from the standpoint of adult interests and adult social life. No one had dreamed there could be any

---

[26] *Ibid.*, pp. 32-33.

[27] *Ibid.*, p. 30.

[28] The child is born helpless and his powers are not equal to his needs. But in providing him the help he needs, we may easily spoil him.

other point of view from which to approach the training of the young. Rousseau boldly assailed this basic assumption as not only utterly false but absolutely harmful. In place of the ideas and views of the adult, he substituted the needs and activities of the child and the natural course of development. No change could have been more revolutionary. Just as Copernicus destroyed medieval cosmology, Rousseau put an end to the traditional theological conceptions of the child, by showing that he is a creature of nature and that he acts and grows in harmony with her laws.

False assumptions of the adult point of view. The adult point of view carried numerous erroneous and misleading assumptions that were now seen to be quite absurd. Much of the treatment of children, as well as most of the methods of instruction, had to undergo radical revision.

The foremost of these misconceptions was that the child is a miniature adult, and that enlargement in size and increase in knowledge are the processes of education. As a consequence of this idea, boys and girls were treated as little men and little women. They were dressed in the absurd and injurious fashions of their parents.[29]

> The godless age of Louis XIV also inflicted upon the poor children of the higher ranks hair frizzled with powder and smeared with pomade, embroidered coats, knee-breeches, silk stockings, a sword at their sides; all of which was the severest torture for young and active children.

Little girls wore long dresses and corsets, as did the women. As people treated children's bodies, so they treated their minds. They were expected to understand the same subjects and to be interested in the same ideas as adults. They were obliged to practice the same conventionalities of polite life and, at the same time, to observe a far more rigorous standard of ethical behavior.

Departure from the adult type was regarded as an abnormality and was treated with harsh measures. Nurses sometimes bound the heads of infants to give them more shapely form. So child conduct was bound by harsh rules because it was ascribed to the innate perversity of the human heart. From all such artificiality of dress and treatment of conduct, Rousseau liberated childhood at one bold stroke.

Education had been conceived as a process by which the child must

---

[29] Barnard, Henry, *German Teachers and Educators,* pp. 479-480. Hartford: Brown & Gross, 1878.

acquire certain habits, skills, attitudes, and a body of knowledge which civilization had handed down. It was the task of the school to transfer these unchanged to each new generation. On the one hand, the stability of society depended on the success of the transfer; on the other, the success of the individual depended upon acquiring them. The fact that children are imitative, that the retentive power of memory is strongest in childhood, that they have an extraordinary ability to acquire language apart from the ideas symbolized—all these have conspired to mislead pedagogy.

It was the great service of Rousseau to demolish this false system of education. His supreme contribution to mankind lay in making the child the new center from which education must be viewed. He tells us that "we never know how to put ourselves in the place of children; we do not enter into their ideas, but we ascribe to them our own." The metamorphoses of human life—infancy, childhood, youth, and maturity—are the basis of the new pedagogy. Teaching and training consist, not in inculcating ideas, but in furnishing the child with opportunities for the functioning of those activities that are natural for each stage.

Another far-reaching assumption of the day placed the interests of society above those of the individual. "Like a saddle horse, man must be trained for man's service." The individual was sacrificed for the mass: [30]

> All our wisdom consists in servile prejudices, all our customs are but servitude, worry and constraint. Civilized man is born, lives and dies in a state of slavery. At his birth he is stitched in swaddling-clothes; at his death he is nailed in his coffin; and as long as he preserves the human form he is fettered by our institutions.

The child was trained to conform to the existing society. The ruthless crushing of individuality aroused the bitter hatred of Rousseau. The individual should never be sacrificed to the superficial whims of society.[31]

> Man is too noble a being to be obliged to serve as a mere instrument for others, and should not be employed at what he is fit for without also taking into account what is fit for him; for men are not made for their stations, but their stations for men.

The goodness and happiness of the individual are more essential than the development of his talent for social service. In setting the needs and

---

30 Rousseau, J. J., *Emile,* p. 10.
31 Boyd, William, *op. cit.,* p. 140. Quoted from *The New Héloïse,* Vol. 2.

interests of the individual above those of organized society, Rousseau reversed the universal order. In the ideal and natural society, where human nature retains its original simplicity and innocence, all individuals would be brought up together and would share the common interest.

Rousseau's new point of view began with his theory of the evolution of social organization, and was confirmed by a growing insight into the nature of children. The heart of his educational theory is the study of child nature. This he pointed out in no uncertain terms: [32]

> We do not know childhood. Acting on the false ideas we have of it, the farther we go the farther we wander from the right path. Those who are wisest are attached to what is important for men to know, without considering what children are able to apprehend. They are always looking for the man in the child, without thinking of what he was before he became a man. This is the study upon which I am most intent, to the end that, though my method may be chimerical and false, profit may always be derived from my observations. I may have a very poor conception of what ought to be done, but I think I have a correct view of the subject on which we are to operate. Begin then, by studying your pupils more thoroughly, for it is very certain that you do not know them.

Ignorant of the real feelings, thoughts, and interests of children, adults impose their own upon them. The principle of the new method is to understand what nature itself is developing in the child.[33] "You ought," he admonished parents and teachers, "to be wholly absorbed in the child —observing him, watching him without respite, and without seeming to do so, having a presentiment of his feelings in advance."

Rousseau discovers the recapitulation theory. The theory which captivated 18th century thinking was that the great epochs of the history of man must be conceived as analogous to the periods in the life of a single individual. The human race had traversed the successive stages of infancy, childhood, youth, and maturity, and was then in the period of old age.

Instead of using the epochs of individual development to throw light upon the development of the race, Rousseau turned the conception completely about and employed the evolution of the race to explain the development of the individual. In his progress from birth to maturity,

---

[32] Rousseau, J. J., Preface to *Emile.*
[33] Rousseau, J. J., *Emile,* p. 169.

the child lives over again the epochs through which the race passed in its movement to civilization. He begins as an animal; then becomes a savage, a solitaire or Robinson Crusoe; then attains rationality; and finally emerges as a social being. If we would understand childhood, we must strip off all the artificialities that man has acquired through centuries of social accretion, and look at life from the simple and direct view of the original man. What was a mere literary analogy Rousseau made the instrument of new insight into human existence. Though he was unaware of the fact, he had introduced the recapitulation theory, which was to receive increased interest and support from the Darwinian theory of biological evolution in the 19th century.

Stages of development. The recognition of stages in the development of individual life was not new. It had come down from Aristotle and had been reëmphasized by Comenius. But it was Rousseau who made it a vital principle for education, by showing its deeper significance.

According to his point of view, the various stages are sharply marked off from one another by special characteristics or functions. Rousseau was, in fact, the first to introduce the saltatory theory of development. The sudden emergence of some new function, by a leap, so to speak, was in harmony with his own temperamental experiences. The first stage, from birth to five years of age, is an animal stage. Then there emerges the dawn of self-consciousness, the earliest sense of self. "Memory diffuses the feeling of identity over all the moments of his existence. He becomes truly one." With the beginning of connected memories of self, "the life of the individual properly begins." At twelve, he suddenly becomes conscious of self in a deeper way; the rational faculty awakens, and with it the higher sentiments emerge. But the child is still an isolated being without true moral life. The next stage is reached at puberty, with the emergence of sex, which is the most important factor in the entire life history of the individual.[34]

> We have two births, so to speak—one for existing and the other for living; one for the species and the other for the sex. It is here that man really begins to live, and nothing human is foreign to him.

Sex is the key to Rousseau's whole philosophy of individual development.[35]

---

[34] *Ibid.*, pp. 192-193.
[35] Boyd, William, *op. cit.*, pp. 321-322.

The fact is that his whole account of education turns on his conception of the effects of the sex-functions on body and soul. The child, on his view, is a mere neuter, not merely in the matter of sex, but of everything truly human, and lacks passion, reason, conscience, and every other adult faculty. The real beginnings of life (and of education) await the first activities of the sex functions. When sex awakens there is an almost catastrophic irruption of the passions into the sphere of conduct, and a period of emotional stress and strain, lasting over many years, is ushered in.

With the emergence of sex the social life of the individual properly begins. Nature herself superimposes sacrifice upon individualism. The highest sentiments of the soul begin to blossom, and lead to the natural evolution of the moral life.

As the periods are sharply marked in their rise, so they are independent of each other in their development.[36]

Each age, each period of life has its proper perfection, a sort of maturity which is all its own. We have often heard mention made of a grown man; but let us now consider a grown child. This spectacle will be something newer for us, and perhaps not less agreeable.

No period should be made merely a means of getting to the next. Each is an end in itself, an independent whole, and not merely a transition to a higher period. Moreover, each stage has its own special needs and desires, and forms only the habits which are best for the perfect realization of life at that stage.[37]

The infant is an animal; treat him as an animal. The ten-year-old is a savage: expect no more from him than from a savage. Even from twelve to fifteen, be satisfied to see the boy play the game of Crusoe, since in social outlook he is still a solitary.

This being the case, Rousseau is vehemently opposed to the traditional notion which looked upon early education as a preparation for adult life.[38]

What must we think, then, of that barbarous education which sacrifices the present to an uncertain future, which loads a child with chains of every sort, and begins by making him miserable in order to prepare for him, long in advance, some pretended happiness which it is probable he

---

[36] Rousseau, J. J., *Emile,* p. 121. Cf. also pp. 46 and 122-123.
[37] Boyd, William, *op. cit.,* p. 153.
[38] Rousseau, J. J., *Emile,* pp. 44-45.

will never enjoy? Were I even to assume that education to be reasonable in its object, how could we witness, without indignation, these poor unfortunates subject to an insupportable yoke, and condemned, like galley-slaves, to never-ending toil, without any assurance that such sacrifices will ever be useful to them? The age of mirth is passed in the midst of tears, chastisements, threats, and slavery. The victim is tormented for his good.

Even in the nascent years from 12 to 15 the same principle obtains. The child is to be taught what is useful to him at the time, but not what adults imagine he will need to know when he becomes a man.[39]

> Try to teach the child what is of use to a child and you will find that it takes all his time. Why urge him to the studies of an age he may never reach, to the neglect of those studies which meet his present needs? "But," you ask, "will it not be too late to learn what he ought to know when the time comes to use it?" I cannot tell; but this I do know, it is impossible to teach it sooner, for our real teachers are experience and emotion, and man will never learn what befits a man except under its own conditions. A child should remain in complete ignorance of those ideas which are beyond his grasp. My whole book is one continued argument in support of this fundamental principle of education.

Any novice can find fault with Rousseau's theory of stages. Its value lies not in its finality, but in the fact that it laid the foundation for the genetic interpretation in such a compelling form that it must forever be considered by scientific educators.

ROUSSEAU'S EDUCATIONAL AIMS

The final end. It cannot be too strongly emphasized that Rousseau's ultimate aim is the preservation of the natural goodness and virtues of the human heart, and of society in harmony with them. In the physical world he observed order, harmony, and beauty; in the world of man, infinite conflict, ugliness, selfishness, and, as a consequence, incalculable misery. The sharpness of this contrast between the world of nature and that of man is due to the evils of society, and the kind of education given the young. The supreme end to be attained is a society in which the noble, primitive virtues—courage, endurance, temperance, equality, fraternity, simplicity, and liberty—are realized by all citizens.

---

[39] Rousseau, J. J., *Emile; or, Education,* p. 141, in EVERYMAN'S LIBRARY edition. Translated by Barbara Foxley.

Individuality the problem of education. The recognition and liberation of the individual in the modern world came slowly. The first significant expression appeared at the time of the Renaissance. It was confined to the gifted and aristocratic classes, and, even then, only the artistic and personal aspects of human life were involved. This remarkable display of individual expression in art, scholarship, and literature quickly gave place to an imitative formalism. The Protestant Reformation carried the spirit of revolt and individualistic expression over to the religious side of life.

Meantime the recognition of the individual was making rapid progress in the field of law and government. Hobbes, Grotius, Pufendorf, and Locke set forth the naturalistic basis of the personal and civil rights of the individual. But it still remained for someone to set forth the rights of individuality in the social and philosophic spheres and to correlate these with the civil and religious. Such was the profound service performed by Rousseau. By inner and outer experience he was fitted, as was no other man, to expound and defend the significance of individuality.

Rousseau was not really opposed to social life, as many believe. On the contrary, he aimed to enable the individual to enter whole-heartedly into all the basic relationships of humanity. But man was to enter a society which was adjusted to his natural virtues and capacities, and not one in which he would be but a packhorse to serve others.[40]

> There is a wide difference between natural man living in a state of nature and natural man living in a state of society. Emile is not a savage to be banished to a desert, but a savage made to live in cities.

Rousseau found it necessary to construct two systems of education for radically different social conditions. In the one case, he conceived a form of education for a state and society organized according to man's natural being. Such a state is small and compact, like Sparta and Geneva. In this state, education is a public function and extends to every child. Its purpose is to foster the natural, simple virtues, and the sense of solidarity (*esprit de corps*). Plato had this form of education in mind in his *Republic*. Rousseau sets forth this plan in his *Discourse on Political Economy*, in *The Social Contract*, and finally in *Considerations on the Government of Poland*. He declared that "education is the most

[40] Rousseau, J. J., *Emile*, p. 187.

important business of the state"; and, again, that "national education is the privilege of free men." All children, "since by the constitution of the state they are equal, . . . should be educated together and in the same way." By means of common play, songs, and patriotic training the state builds a sense of social solidarity.

The second form of education was for the existing civilization. This constituted the problem of the *Emile*. Long before he enters social life, the individuality of the child—his sense of independence, inner goodness, judgment, and resistance—must be built up to withstand the degrading influences of social life. He must live as a savage, in order that he may keep unscathed the primitive virtues which distinguish man's estate.

Rousseau had in view the education of the upper classes. The lower classes, he stated, do not need an education. The circumstances of life produce in them the sense of equality, simplicity, spontaneity, and all the other virtues of which they stand in need. But it is the children of the rich and high-born, who are brought up in luxury and artificiality, who stand most in need of natural education. Here is seen the influence of Plato, Montaigne, and Locke on the mind of Rousseau.

General versus specialized education. Hitherto, education had aimed to produce the gentleman-scholar to serve the church and state. This involved the specialization of the powers of the individual and his subjection to others. Rousseau saw in this a direct threat against the fundamental integrity of man. In making a citizen or a laborer, education made him less a man. It was a choice between the natural individual and the distortion of his original nature. In all this opposition to the aims of education of the past, Rousseau was pleading for a generous, liberal cultivation of the native endowments of the child. He is to be developed as a whole, before the cramping molds of specialization have an opportunity to distort his being.[41]

> In the natural order of things, all men being equal, their common vocation is manhood, and whoever is well-trained for that cannot fulfill badly any vocation connected with it. Whether my pupil be destined for the army, the church, or the bar, concerns me but little. Regardless of the vocation of his parents, nature summons him to the duties of human life. To live is the trade I wish to teach him. On leaving my hands, he will not, I grant, be a magistrate, a soldier, or a priest. First of all he will be a man.

[41] *Ibid.*, p. 8.

Education is to fit man for a changing fortune and a changing environment. The child is not to be trained for a definite vocation or a definite social position. The variation of individuals in wealth and station makes such training for a single position extremely hazardous. Rousseau drew attention to the fact that society itself is always changing and that man is not a creature fixed and unalterable, because human nature is still in process of development.[42]

> Considering the mutability of human affairs, and the restless, revolutionary spirit of this century, which overthrows the whole existing order of things once in each generation, can we conceive a more senseless method than that of educating a child as though he were never to leave his chamber, and were always to be surrounded by his attendants?

As we do not know what society or the future environment will be, nor yet what the fate of the individual will be, we cannot intelligently educate for the future. It follows from this reasoning that the child is to be educated, not for some "uncertain future," but only to act in the present. No one rejected so utterly and boldly the appeal to the child's future good. Rousseau's reason is that the child is wholly incapable of visualizing such future good. Moreover, in being trained to use his powers in the changing conditions of life, he is best prepared to meet any situation when it shall arise.

The educational institution. What institution shall train the child? Is education a public or a family function? Rousseau felt no sense of contradiction in advocating each, according to the needs involved. There is a form of public education that is good for the attainment of the end he held in view, and there is a form distinctly bad. There is one form of family training that is bad, and another that is good. The system of public instruction in the colleges of his day Rousseau dismissed with the curt and stinging comment that it is a "ridiculous establishment." In the *Discourse on Political Economy,* he wrote of public education as follows:[43]

> Public education, therefore, under regulations prescribed by the government and under magistrates established by the Sovereign, is one of the fundamental rules of popular or legitimate government.
>
> I know of but three peoples which once practiced public education, the Cretans, the Lacedemonians, and the ancient Persians; among all

[42] *Ibid.,* p. 9.

[43] Rousseau, J. J., *Discourse on Political Economy,* pp. 268-270.

these it was attended with the greatest success, and indeed it did wonders among the two last.

Some years after the publication of the *Emile,* he was given the opportunity to plan a system of education for Poland. The system he formulated was national in scope, and aimed to mold every child according to a national stamp, by means of play and the emotions which result from communal activities. The important thing is to get them accustomed from an early age to discipline, to equality and fraternity, to living "under the eyes of their fellow citizens and seeking public approbation." In the section on "Education," Rousseau wrote: [44]

> National education is the privilege of free men.... At twenty years of age, a Pole ought to be a Pole and nothing but a Pole. When he is learning to read, I want him to read about his own country. At ten, he should be acquainted with all its provinces, highways, and towns. At fifteen, he should know all its history; at sixteen, all its laws. There should not have been a fine action or an illustrious man in all Poland, whose fame does not fill heart and memory so that he can give instant account of them....

It does not appear that Rousseau was aware how sharply this program contradicted his views as presented in the *Emile.* As a matter of fact, he would not have admitted any contradiction. Both systems were designed to preserve those fundamental virtues which constituted the supreme end of life and the chief good of the state.

Family education. In the *Emile,* the father and mother are declared the natural teachers. Speaking of Emile, Rousseau said: [45]

> He will be better educated by a judicious though ignorant father than by the most skillful teacher in the world; for zeal will much better supply the place of talent than talent, the place of zeal.

In lauding the virtues of domestic education, Rousseau had in view the home of Calvinistic Geneva.[46] Writing of this he declared: [47]

> It is there the children ought to be educated, the girls by the mother, the boys by the father. This is exactly the education suited for us, midway between the public education of the Greek republics and the domestic

---

[44] Boyd, William, *The Minor Educational Writings of Jean Jacques Rousseau,* pp. 141-146. London: Blackie & Son, Ltd., 1910.

[45] Rousseau, J. J., *Emile,* p. 15.

[46] Eby, Frederick, *Early Protestant Educators,* pp. 250-252. New York: McGraw-Hill, 1931.

[47] Boyd, William, *The Educational Theory of Rousseau,* pp. 25-26.

education of monarchies in which all the people have to remain in isolation with nothing in common save obedience.

The conflict between state and home education can be readily explained. They are cooperating factors in a small state, and through both the common life, habits, and sentiments are communicated to the young. Both unite in developing equality, fraternity, simplicity, liberty, and all the other virtues.

The *Emile* and isolation. The problem which Rousseau discussed in the *Emile* is quite different from that which he had in view in his other writings. It is not the problem of training all children, rich and poor, high-born and low, for a common lot. It is not the communication of the habits, customs, ideals, and sentiments of national life. It is not a preparation for citizenship in a small commonwealth where all are already on a level. Emile is a scion of wealth and aristrocracy and is not intended for any other fortune. The education he is to receive is not needed by the children of the poor. He is to be educated as a savage to enter society as it is and not as it ought to be. The chief purpose is to inoculate him so that he can successfully resist all the evils which he must inevitably encounter in adult life. To this end he must be trained for independence of judgment and of will power. In this situation individuality is more necessary than sharing the communal sentiments. Emile is an orphan, isolated from family relationships and from other children. He is to live in the country where life is simplest, and social relations are reduced to the lowest degree. The tutor is his only companion.

One can now see the full significance of Rousseau's conception. Emile represents, at once, the species in its evolution and the individual in his need of freedom in passing through the earlier stages of development. The hypothesis of the *Emile* is that the boy stands on the moral and intellectual plane of the primitive man. He is not as yet fully moral or rational. He must be left free to follow his own bent and to develop according to nature. He should be dependent on things only, and not rendered artificial or precocious by premature training and instruction. His education, like that of the savage, depends upon his physical environment and inner nature, and not upon social conditions.

EDUCATION AND THE PERIODS OF DEVELOPMENT

The education of children is determined by the various periods of development. Each stage has its own dominant faculty, which emerges and becomes the mainspring in organizing life. The principles to be followed in one period do not hold for another, for the task is to foster the budding activities and interests of the child's nature—not to give him the conventional habits and ideas of society.

(1) INFANT EDUCATION

The method of nature in training infants. Education begins at birth or before; and the first period of five years is concerned primarily with the growth of the body, motor activities, sense perception, and feeling. The method of nature must be followed in everything. With impassionate pleading, Rousseau recalled mothers to their natural duties, and even made it fashionable to breast feed their offspring.

The individuality of each child must be respected. It is wrong to model different minds after one common pattern. Our concern should not be to alter the natural disposition of the mind, but to prevent degeneration. The doctrine of individual differences is fundamental to Rousseau. He wrote: [48]

> One nature needs wings, another shackles: one has to be flattered, another to be intimidated. One man is made to carry human knowledge to the farthest point; another may find the ability to read a dangerous power.

Rousseau condemned the prevailing style of dressing infants in swaddling clothes, which hindered the free movement of body and limbs. On the one hand, he liberated helpless babies from the bondage of dress; on the other hand, he accepted the hardening process for the body. Even in infancy, the meeting of hardships is nature's method: [49]

> Observe Nature and follow the route which she traces for you. She is ever exciting children to activity; she hardens the constitution by trials of every sort; she teaches at an early hour what suffering and pain are. . . . Harden their bodies to the changes of seasons, climates, and elements, as well as to hunger, thirst, and fatigue.

---

[48] *Ibid.*, p. 254.
[49] Rousseau, J. J., *Emile*, p. 13.

For "the weaker the body, the more it commands; the stronger it is, the better it obeys."

Nothing must be done for the child that he can do for himself. Such is the one principle which should guide in the treatment of infancy. Life is a struggle for existence; this is the most fundamental biologic law—a law to which the child must learn to conform. Skill in walking, in talking, and in self-help is to be developed in direct relation to his needs, and with as little assistance as possible. Rousseau frowned upon medicine, and considered hygiene less a science than a virtue or habit of right living.

Moral and social life are absolutely foreign to the infant mind. But, for this very reason, "the most dangerous period in human life is the interval between birth and the age of twelve. It is the time when errors and vices germinate." All vices are implanted by unwise coddling or pampering of infants. By permitting them to domineer, one germinates in their little hearts the spirit of caprice and an insatiable appetite for self-aggrandizement.

Nature of the educational process at this stage. Just what sort of process is education? We are not left in doubt as to Rousseau's views. The truth, as he saw it, is that education does not arise from without; it springs from within. "It is the internal development of our faculties and organs" that constitutes the true "education of nature." The first education is the free and unhampered expression of the natural activities of the child in relation to the physical environment. The important thing is that the infant be allowed to obey the inner impulse to action and that he experience directly the results of his behavior.

(2) EDUCATION FROM FIVE TO TWELVE

Current methods of teaching and learning. Rousseau was a severe critic of the methods then in fashion in the schools. For most children, childhood was a sorrowful period, for instruction was heartlessly severe. Grammar was beaten into the memory. Teachers had not as yet imagined that children could find any pleasure in learning, or that they should have eyes for anything but reading, writing, and memorizing. The only form of learning that teachers knew was learning by rote. Rousseau saw in this a fearful error; for the child, as he believed, has no real memory, and purely verbal lessons mean nothing to him.

The ruling philosophy of education of that day was that of formal discipline. This was very clearly stated by one of Rousseau's contemporary critics: [50]

> Education is the same thing for man and for beast. It can be reduced to two principles, to learn to put up with injustice, to learn to endure *ennui*. What does one do when one breaks in a horse? Left to himself, the horse ambles, trots, gallops, walks, but he does it when he wishes, as he pleases. We teach him to move thus or thus, contrary to his own desires, against his own instinct—there is the injustice: we make him keep on at it for a couple of hours—there is the *ennui*. It is just the same thing when we make a child learn Latin or Greek or French. The intrinsic utility of it is not the main point. The aim is that he should habituate himself to obey another person's will: that he should be beaten by a creature born his equal. When he has learned all that, he can stand on his own feet, he can go into society.... All pleasant methods of teaching children necessary knowledge are false and ridiculous. It is not a question of learning geography or geometry: it is a question of learning to work, of learning the weariness of concentrating one's attention on the matter in hand.... Develop these ideas and then you will have a book the precise opposite of the *Emile* and worth very much more.

Rousseau saw in such a method only a means of enslaving mankind. This was the education which depended on books and upon the authority of others, and against all of these Rousseau revolted with all the vehemence of his being.

Rousseau's opposition to books. Of his bitter aversion to books Rousseau expressed himself vigorously: [51]

> I hate books; they merely teach us to talk of what we do not know. ... There exists one which, to my way of thinking, furnishes the happiest treatise on natural education. This book shall be the first which my Emile will read; for a long time it will of itself constitute his whole library.... What, then, is this wonderful book? Is it Aristotle? Is it Pliny? No; it is *Robinson Crusoe.*

This distrust of books is not confined to any one stage of child life. The book comes between the child and things. Moreover, the knowledge that the child learns from books takes the place of the exercise and formation of his own judgment. *Robinson Crusoe* alone is valued because it pictures the natural unfolding of the child's life at this stage of boyhood.

---

[50] Abbé Galiani, letter to Madame d'Epinay. Quoted by Boyd, William, *The Educational Theory of Jean Jacques Rousseau,* p. 306.

[51] Rousseau, J. J., *Emile,* pp. 161-163.

Negative education. "Do nothing and allow nothing to be done." "Take the very reverse of the current practice, and you will almost always do right," [52] is the new method proposed by Rousseau for education at this stage. It is not that Emile is to learn nothing; the prohibition is directed only against the traditional procedure.[53]

> The first education, then, ought to be purely negative. It consists not at all in teaching virtue or truth, but in shielding the heart from vice, and the mind from error. If you could do nothing and allow nothing to be done; if you could bring your pupil sound and robust to the age of twelve years without his being able to distinguish his right hand from his left, from your very first lessons the eyes of his understanding would be open to reason.

"Negative education," which Rousseau called this method was adopted for several reasons. First, it followed logically from the principle that human nature is good and that it unfolds by virtue of inner compulsion. Any interference with this natural unfolding would be corrupting. In truth the evils of man are directly due to the bad education which he has received. Accordingly he demanded: "Prevent anything from being done." Above all, he was incensed at the bad methods of motivation and discipline employed. He disapproved sharply of rebukes, corrections, threats, and punishments. Even stronger was his anger at the rewards, promises, and prizes that were dangled before the eyes of children to induce them to do or to learn something that was foreign to their active interests. Similarly, the use of rivalry Rousseau regarded as the basis for all that social system which formed mankind into competing groups or classes, and filled the human heart with jealousy, suspicion, and illwill.

Nor did he accept Locke's counsel to reason with children. Before the age of 12 the child cannot reason, and he has no moral sentiments; consequently all appeal to judgment and moral incentives are premature and wrong. Experience alone will form his course of study. He learns what he likes, when he likes, and how he likes. He is not even conscious that he is learning, for he is absorbed only in his activities. He must be doing something, and, as he acts, he learns.

Naturalism is not soft pedagogy. One is liable to conclude that, in adopting a system of doing nothing and allowing nothing to be done,

---

[52] *Ibid.*, p. 60.
[53] *Ibid.*, pp. 57 and 59.

Rousseau became the advocate of a soft and easy-going pedagogy. Some of his statements would seem to favor this interpretation. Emile is not subjected to any regimen whatever, and no commands are given him. He follows his own inclinations and learns only by experience. However, Rousseau had in view something quite different from the ordinary conception of the easy-going life. He aimed to avoid not only a *laissez-faire* policy on the one hand, but also that of the martinet on the other. He relieved his fictitious pupil of the harsh yoke of the conventional system of education, but in its place he put the severe yoke of getting food, clothing and shelter.

Criticisms of the elementary curriculum. Rousseau was not eager to have Emile, before 12, learn anything of a conventional character, not even reading. He did, however, expect a live boy to pick up reading incidentally. He opposed fairy tales and fancy for the pre-school age, because they were not real; and he objected to fables for the age of boyhood. Aesop's fables, chosen particularly for their moral value, had for many centuries formed the first reading text. But it was precisely because of their supposed moral significance that Rousseau cast them aside. The boy is not a moral being as yet, and, in any case, the fables are misleading.

Moreover, the reaction against the extreme application to ancient languages reached its climax in Rousseau. He did not believe a boy could learn more than one language, and that must be his mother tongue.

History is another study to which objection was raised for this stage, and on several grounds. Children do not have true memory; they are, therefore, unable to form correct ideas of human conduct or to judge historic situations. Furthermore, history is confined too much to wars, kings, dates, and political facts of secondary importance; it does not treat of the significant events of real human value. Again, history deals with society, and the child is incapable of understanding social phenomena. History must, therefore, be excluded from this stage of development. Geography, also, is too advanced for children.

Thus Rousseau rules out not only the older subjects which had formed the curriculum for centuries but also the new materials of the realistic era. In no respect did Rousseau violate universal tradition so much as in the rejection of religious instruction. The child is not to hear of God until he attains the age of reason. This idea had farcircling consequences on education.

Practical activities form the curriculum. The activities which spring naturally from the needs of life form the curriculum at each stage. The needs of boyhood are simple, having to do merely with the preservation of existence. First come play and sports, which improve the body, bringing health, growth, and strength. Then, too, the child engages in securing a livelihood.[56] "Agriculture is the first employment of man; it is the most honorable, the most useful, and consequently the most noble that he can practice." The child learns how to handle the spade and the hoe, the lathe, hammer, plane, and file—in fact, the tools of all the trades. These activities lead him to measure, count, weigh, and compare the objects with which he deals. He judges distances, learns to observe accurately and to draw the things he observes. Speech, singing, arithmetic, and geometry, are learned not as formal schoolroom subjects but as activities that are related to life situations.

Before 12, the child cannot reason. His needs are simple and few, and easily satisfied. His power to secure satisfaction is not yet commensurate with even these simple needs, and accordingly a feeling of weakness and dependence is experienced. He is still a pre-social, premoral stage of being, and is capable only of responding to things and to necessity. The general policy for his education is: [57]

> Exercise his body, his organs, his senses, and his powers, but keep his soul lying fallow as long as you possibly can. Be on your guard against all feelings which precede the judgment that can estimate their value!

As yet he does not know the will of another, and should not be subjected to either commands or punishments. His activities are caused by necessity, and he can have no real sense of responsibility or of duty.

Objective of boyhood education. Rousseau's ideal for Emile at the close of boyhood is this: [58]

> His form, his bearing, and his countenance bespeak self-assurance and contentment. A glow of health is on his face. In his prompt but sure movements you may see the vivacity of his age, the firmness of independence, and the experience coming from his multiplied activities. His manner is open and free, but neither insolent nor vain. His face, which has not been glued down to books, does not rest on his stomach, and there is no need of telling him to hold up his head.

---

[56] Rousseau, J. J., *Emile,* p. 178.
[57] *Ibid.,* p. 60.
[58] *Ibid.,* pp. 123-124.

(3) THE AGE OF REASON

Emergence of reason. When he broke with the leaders of the Enlightenment, on account of their exaggerated emphasis on reason, Rousseau reacted to an extreme positon and denied the value of the rational nature. Later he saw his error and assigned to reason a genuine, though subordinate, function. As he conceived it, reason does not arise from sensation, as the materialists held; nor is it an original and innate principle, as the rationalists believed. It is a natural faculty that had its origin in the emotional life.

The period from 12 to 15 Rousseau called the "Age of Reason," for the emergence of the rational judgment is its signal characteristic.

Self-preservation is the fundamental urge of life, the spontaneous expression of inner, biological animality. Our first impulses are naturally self-ward, and all our behavior is for individual well-being. Sensory experiences do not form the origin of the mental life, as Locke and others thought. It is not what comes from without, but what issues from within that produces human behavior and determines the course of development.

The rise of self-consciousness is a fact of deeper significance than the mere increase of sensory experiences. It is a higher principle of life, one which imparts unity and continuity to all the varied movements and experiences of the mind. It marks the departure from the stage of mere animal feeling to the higher sentiments and faculties of the soul. From these sentiments arises man's higher life, for they form the motives of all adult activities. Rousseau's psychological views were formed as a direct protest against both the current materialism and rationalism.[59]

---

[59] Rousseau told the Pastor de Montmolin that one of his objects in projecting the *Emile* was to "raise himself clearly against the infernal book, *De l'Esprit,* which according to the detestable principle of its author pretends that feeling and judging are the same thing, which evidently amounts to establishing materialism." Rousseau wrote concerning this work published by Helvetius in 1758: "At the first appearance of the work *De l'Esprit,* I resolved to attack the principles I found dangerous. I executed the enterprise. When I learned that the author was persecuted, immediately I threw my leaves into the fire. . . . When all was quieted, I had the occasion of expressing my sentiments on the same subject in other writings (*Emile* and *La Nouvelle Héloïse*) but I have expressed it without mentioning the name of the author of the book." Here unquestionably is one of the real secrets of Rousseau's writings. Quoted by Grossman, M., *The Philosophy of Helvetius,* pp. 152-153. New York: Teachers College, Columbia University, 1926.

What causes the emergence of the rational judgment at this particular stage? The explanation that Rousseau offered is one of the deeper theories which he evolved. The inner life of the child is conditioned by the relation which his needs bear to the strength that he can exert for the satisfaction of those needs. In infancy, his needs are simple and few, and his strength is feeble.[60] "At the age of twelve or thirteen the strength of the child is developed much more rapidly than his needs."

Owing to this pre-pubertal increment in muscular power, the youth is much stronger than is necessary to satisfy his needs, which have as yet remained few and simple, providing his nature has not been corrupted by a precocious imagination.[61] "He whose strength exceeds his desires has some power to spare; he is certainly a very strong being." It is this preponderance of strength beyond the satisfaction of his needs, that causes reason to emerge.

Relation of intelligence to activity. Our needs or desires are the original cause of our activities; in turn, our activities produce intelligence, in order to guide and govern our strength and passions, for "reason is the check to strength."[62]

> In proportion as a sensitive being becomes active, he acquires a discernment proportional to his powers; and it is only with the power which is in excess of what is needed for self-conservation that there comes to be developed in him the speculative faculty suited for employing that excess of power for other uses. If, then, you would cultivate the intelligence of your pupil, cultivate the power which it is to govern.... Let him be a man in vigor, and soon he will be such by force of reason.

Reason, an accessory faculty. Inasmuch as intelligence evolved in relation to activities, it is necessary that these be developed to a high degree before reason appears. "Childhood is the sleep of reason." Furthermore, Rousseau declared: "Of all the faculties of man, reason is that which is developed with the most difficulty and the latest."[63] Only when the child reaches the age of 12 does reason begin to stir, and the time for its uninterrupted development is exceedingly brief. When the strength of youth is augmented out of proportion to his needs, reason awakens in order to furnish guidance, for this is the function of the rational life.

---

[60] Rousseau, J. J., *Emile,* p. 133.
[61] *Ibid.*, p. 131.
[62] *Ibid.*, p. 84. We now know that Rousseau was in error in regard to the increase of strength prior to puberty; and also that puberty comes earlier than he thought
[63] *Ibid.*, p. 52.

Education during the age of reason. Reason then is not some divine entity, but only an accessory faculty. This is the age when real education by human agency begins. Up to this time, the unfolding of the child has been determined by natural laws; and with the action of these laws the educator must never interfere. However, the new stage, "is the period of labor, of instruction, and of study."

Teachers have made numerous mistakes because they have not understood the nature of reason and the time when it arises. (1) The first blunder was the attempt to educate the child through reason. Even Locke advised this. But this practice places the cart before the horse: "It is to begin at the end, and to confound the instrument with the work." All effort to reason with children before reason emerges is not only foolish but injurious.[64]

> The common error of parents, . . . is to suppose their children capable of reasoning as soon as they are born, and to talk to them as if they were grown persons. Reason is the instrument they use, whereas every other means ought first to be used in order to form their reason; for it is certain, that of all the knowledge which men acquire, or are capable of acquiring, the art of reasoning is the last and most difficult to learn.

The design of nature is obviously to strengthen the body before the mind. When allowed to awaken at its proper time, reason projects the future of the child.[65]

> What, then, shall our pupil do with that surplus of faculties and powers which he has on hand at present, but which he will stand in need of at a subsequent period of life? . . . He will project into the future, so to speak, that which is superfluous for the time being. The robust child will make provision for the feeble man.

(2) A second blunder has been to substitute authority for the child's own mental efforts.[66]

> If you ever substitute in his mind authority for reason, he will no longer reason; he will be but the sport of others' opinions. . . .
>
> Compelled to learn for himself, he uses his own reason and not that of others; for in order to grant nothing to opinion, you must grant nothing to authority. . . . He has a mind that is universal, not through its knowledge, but through its facility of acquiring it; a mind that is open, intelligent, ready for everything.

---

[64] Rousseau, *The New Héloïse,* Letter CXXXIX.
[65] Rousseau, J. J., *Emile,* p. 133.
[66] *Ibid.,* pp. 137 and 188-189.

(3) The greatest mistake of traditional pedagogy consisted in attributing to reason a power of control which it does not possess. This was the error of the rationalists. As reason appears later than the passions, and as it emerges out of them, it is subordinate to them. It is not the reliable guide for conduct. Rousseau startled philosophy by declaring that "the divine voice of man's heart and his inner conscience alone are the infallible guides and capable of bringing him happiness."

Imagination. Of all the faculties which emerge at this stage, Rousseau had a positive aversion for the imagination. He never thought of imagination as producing anything that is good. It creates unnecessary and artificial needs which spring from social rivalry. It inflames the passions and is, therefore, the one faculty that is responsible for the vices and evils of social and moral life.

Curiosity and utility as motivations. As the feeling of need causes the activity of the body, so curiosity causes the activity of the mind. It is the motivating power for intellectual life. The child is curious, because every object or situation has significance for his struggle for life and well-being. As curiosity is caused by desire for well-being, it relates only to that which will be of real service to the child. Utility is, therefore, the one and only principle that determines the curriculum at this stage.

All the artificial means that teachers employ to induce children to work, such as the sense of honor, pride, rivalry, or the approval of elders, are useless and injurious. The true motive for learning is the desire to know or the usefulness and service of knowledge. Rousseau agreed with Bacon and Locke in exalting utility as the best motivation.

Rousseau's hatred of rivalry. Rivalry, or emulation, had always been one of the chief motivations in the schools. Rousseau regarded it as the arch evil of social life and utterly prohibited its employment.[67]

> Let there never be comparisons with other children; as soon as he begins to reason let him have no rivals, no competitors, even in running. I would a hundred times rather he would not learn what he can learn only through jealousy and through vanity.

There can be no doubt that it was this severe onslaught of Rousseau which discredited the use of emulation in modern pedagogy.

The curriculum. For intellectual instruction no definite course of study is projected! The most accurate delineation is to be found in

[67] *Ibid.*, p. 161.

Robinson Crusoe. By force of circumstances Crusoe must utilize his intelligence in order to live. He is not interested in human relationships, for he has none. The phenomena of nature absorb his thought, but only those that make a genuine contribution to his self-preservation receive attention. Geography and astronomy are the first subjects of interest, these to be learned directly from nature. Then follow the various phenomena of physical science. These in turn lead to agriculture and to the manual arts and crafts. But when Emile has a good acquaintance with these, he is to be trained more expertly in cabinet-making. Such is the curriculum from 12 to 15.

It will be seen that Emile has acquired only physical knowledge. He does not know even the term *history,* nor what ethics and metaphysics mean. He learns the essential relations of man to things, but nothing of human relationships. The central concern of Rousseau was threefold: (1) to implant a taste for knowledge, that is to say an abiding curiosity. "My purpose," he asserted,[68] "is not at all to give him knowledge, but to teach him how to acquire it when necessary, to make him estimate it exactly for what it is worth, and to make him love truth above everything else." (2) To think clearly. Reflecting Descartes' principle of clearness, he wrote,[69] "The spirit of my system is never to allow anything to enter his mind save ideas which are accurate and clear." (3) To furnish the right method.[70] "It is not proposed to teach him the sciences but to give him a taste for them, and methods for learning them, when this taste shall be better developed. Without doubt this is the fundamental principle of all good education."

The method of training. One must turn to Rousseau's method in order to appreciate how fully he anticipated the pragmatic philosophy of purposeful learning: [71] "Without doubt we derive much clearer and much more accurate notions of things which we learn for ourselves than of those which we gain from the instruction of others."

The great principle of Rousseau's method was that nothing should be learned on the authority of others.[72] "Subject in everything to an authority that is always teaching, your pupil does nothing except at the word of command. . . . To what purpose do you desire to have him think if

[68] *Ibid.*, p. 189.
[69] *Ibid.*, p. 143.
[70] *Ibid.*, p. 144.
[71] *Ibid.*, p. 157.
[72] *Ibid.*, pp. 84-85

you do all his thinking for him?" This principle of independent research was probably the result of Montaigne's influence. For the same reason the use of books was discouraged.[73] "Let there be no book but the world. . . . The child who reads does not think—he merely reads; he is not receiving instruction, but is learning words."

Central principle of method. Rousseau placed Emile in situations that obliged him to depend upon his own strength, to get his own bread, to think his own thoughts, to reach his own conclusions, in fact, to use his own brains and never to depend on the opinions of others. Like Crusoe he must depend on his own powers and intelligence.

To the objection that such a method would be too burdensome and require too great a length of time, Rousseau responded as follows: [74]

> You fear lest I weigh down his mind under this mass of knowledge. The very contrary is true: I teach him much more to ignore these things than to know them. I show him the route to learning, easy, in truth, but long, boundless, and slow to traverse.
>
> Compelled to learn for himself, he uses his own reason and not that of others; for in order to grant nothing to opinion, you must grant nothing to authority.

Substitution of symbol for object condemned. Rousseau's second principle is equally positive: Everything must be learned by direct observation of concrete things.[75] "Why not begin by showing him the object itself, so that he may know, at least, what you are talking about!"

Rousseau could not too vigorously condemn the ancient practice of substituting the word, or some other symbol, for the object. Of this he said: [76] "Never substitute the sign for the thing itself save when it is impossible to show the thing; for the sign absorbs the attention of the child and makes him forget the thing represented." And again: [77] "Things! Things! I shall never repeat often enough that we give too much power to words. With our babbling education we make nothing but babblers."

Pupil must invent apparatus. Another principle which Rousseau repeatedly insisted upon is that the pupil should make all of his own apparatus. After observing geographic facts, he is to make charts, maps,

---

[73] *Ibid.*, p. 137.
[74] *Ibid.*, pp. 188-189.
[75] *Ibid.*, p. 137.
[76] *Ibid.*, p. 141.
[77] *Ibid.*, p. 157.

and globes. Similarly, the microscope and telescope are to be "invented" by the pupil.[78] Again,[79] in another connection he wrote,

> I wish we might make all our own apparatus; and I would not begin by making the instrument before the experiment; but, after having caught a glimpse of the experiment, as by hazard, I would invent, little by little, the instrument which is to verify it.

Picture of ideal youth. Rousseau pictures the ideal boy at the end of this stage of life as industrious, temperate, patient, firm, and full of courage and endurance.[80]

> [He] has every virtue which is related to himself. In order to have the social virtues also, all he lacks is to know the relations which exact them. . . . He has no faults, and no vices. He has a sound body, agile limbs, a just unprejudiced mind, and a heart that is free and without passion.

(4) EDUCATION FROM FIFTEEN TO TWENTY

Puberty. The most crucial event in the entire life-history of the human being is the emergence of sex.[81] "We are born twice, once for existing and again for living; once for the species and again for sex." This marks the birth of the soul. Hitherto, life has been an animal existence; now, human sentiments emerge.

The social period. The genetic principle is the most constructive doctrine that Rousseau gave to the world. His plan of isolation, his insistence upon individuality, and his naturalism are after all only relative, and preparatory for something more important. His real goal was idealistic, the development of the highest virtues, such as sympathy, generosity, friendship, equality, gratitude, and universal justice. But these are the products of human relations and are capable of development only in the adolescent heart.

Limitations of the child mind. The mind of the child is limited to a low level of experience. He knows things but does not understand their relation to one another or to man. He does not yet fully know himself, and, in consequence, he cannot judge others. He is, accordingly, incapable of social and religious experience; and, therefore, cannot appre-

---

[78] *Ibid.*, p. 188.
[79] *Ibid.*, p. 151.
[80] *Ibid.*, pp. 190-191.
[81] *Ibid.*, p. 192.

ciate and comprehend the meaning of life. The world of the spirit, morality, art, and philosophy is as yet sealed to him. Nevertheless, these are the interests that raise mankind above the level of the savage. Up to the age of 15 Emile knows nothing of history, morals, or society; he can generalize but little and can comprehend but few abstractions.

The crucial development. All the highest experiences and sentiments arise as the result of the emergence of the sex life.[82] "As soon as man has need of a companion, he is no longer an isolated being, his heart is no longer alone. All his relations with his species, and all the affections of his soul are born with her." The sex life arouses many other sentiments which are secondary to it. Among those are the appreciation of beauty and the sublime, the perception of human relations, the sense of moral and social life, and the religious emotions.

Social and moral life. Having, through his own unfolding feelings, become conscious of his dependence, Emile is now obliged to begin a study of his own nature and of his relations to others.[83] "The study proper for man is that of his relations. . . . When he begins to feel his moral nature, he ought to study himself through his relations with men, and this is the occupation of his entire life beginning at the point we have now reached."

Discussing education during the period of adolescence, Rousseau wrote, "It is at this age that the skillful teacher begins his real function as an observer and philosopher who knows the art of exploring the heart while attempting to mould it."[84] First of all is the need of warding off evil passions:[85]

> My Emile having thus far regarded only himself, the first look which he throws upon his fellows leads him to compare himself with them, and the first feeling which the comparison excites within him is to desire the first place. This is the point at which the love of self changes into self-love, and where begin to arise all the passions which depend upon it. But in order to decide whether those of his passions which shall dominate in his character shall be humane and beneficent, or cruel and malevolent, whether they shall be passions of benevolence and commiseration, or of envy and covetousness, it is necessary to know to what place he will aspire among men.

---

[82] *Ibid.*, p. 196.
[83] *Ibid.*, pp. 195-196.
[84] *Ibid.*, p. 205.
[85] *Ibid.*, pp. 210-211.

Second, Rousseau would now arouse the higher emotions such as friendship, sympathy, gratitude, love, justice, goodness, and philanthropy. These emotions are to be awakened by the study of the mental, social, and moral nature of man. These subjects are not only to be studied indirectly through books, but to be experienced in life. Rousseau remains true to naturalism, even in the unfolding of the highest activities. Everything must come from the genetic unfolding of the inner feelings, for all is subjective. The true work of education is the inner emergence, growth, exercise, and integration of the feelings, sentiments, and passions. It is not so much outer discovery, or observation of reality, as the evolution of inner feelings which invests outer phenomena with meaning, use, and value.[86]

> The living spectacle of Nature is in the heart of man; and to see it, it must be felt. . . . How will the song of birds cause him a rapturous emotion, if the accents of love and pleasure are still unknown to him? . . . How will he be affected by the beautiful spectacle of Nature, if he does not know the hand that has taken care to adorn it?

The awakening of inner feelings must precede the attributing of these feelings to outer causes. The inner integration of feeling, thought, and will must take place before the intuition that the world without is likewise a unity. The youth must "rise from the study of Nature to the search for its Author." With this inner development and integration, the world of spirit, morality, duty, art, religion, and philosophy dawns. It is this inner unfolding and enrichment of experience which have raised civilization above the level of the savage.

The curriculum. The curriculum of this period will include knowledge of human nature and of the social order, which today one would classify as psychology, sociology, and ethics. Rousseau did not have in mind primarily the study of these subjects in books; but in concrete life situations, the warm experiences of the actual relations of living men. History in the form of biography and what we now know as social history, he would admit. Of literature Rousseau would favor the ancients, though a glance is given at the moderns as well. For moral training of young men he prescribed fables. Religion, also, is to play a role; but it is to be the natural religion of the human heart and not the dogmas and creeds of the church.

---

[86] *Ibid.*, p. 139.

The education of girls. The education of the boy begins with radical naturalism and individualism, but ends by evolving a romantic idealist. The education of the girl remains hopelessly traditional. Rousseau justified himself by rather commonplace arguments.[87]

> The whole education of women ought to be relative to men. To please them, to be useful to them, to make themselves loved and honored by them, to educate them when young, to care for them when grown, to counsel them, to console them, to make life agreeable and sweet to them —these are the duties of women at all times, and what should be taught them from their infancy.

This strange denial of independent personality to women can only be explained on the ground that Rousseau had no contact with women of character and his conception of human personality was not broad enough to include the female virtues. He thus concludes with an anticlimax.

CONCLUSION

Education a series of antinomies. In reaching a final judgment of the philosophy of Rousseau, it is necessary to understand that he found in human nature, in society, and consequently in education conflicting principles and tendencies. That he endeavored to transcend these conflicts and reach some higher level of reconciliation gives one a deeper respect for his genius.

First of all, he found in the depth of his own nature a conflict of the real and the ideal which reminds one strongly of the similar struggle of St. Paul.[88]

> On contemplating the nature of man it seemed to me that I could discern two distinct principles, one of which raises him to the study of eternal truths, to the love of justice and of moral beauty, to the regions of the intellectual world on which the wise man delights to meditate, while the other thrusts him back on his own pettiness, subjects him to the dominion of the senses and to the passions which serve them, and by means of them frustrates all that the sentiment of the first principle inspires in him. I wish and yet I do not wish. . . . I feel myself at once a slave and a free man. I see the good and love it; and yet I do evil. I am active when I listen to reason, passive when my passions lead me astray; and my worst torment when I succumb is to feel that it was in my power to resist.

---

[87] *Ibid.*, p. 263.

[88] Rousseau, J. J., *Profession of Faith of a Savoyard Vicar.*

A similar conflict is found between human nature and society. This struggle appears between the general education for manhood and the making of a citizen.[89] "Compelled to oppose nature or our social institutions, we must choose between making a man and a citizen, for we cannot make both at once."

Again, general education and vocational training are antagonistic. Rousseau pleaded the cause of general culture in preference to vocational training.

Among the numerous other conflicts which he sought to resolve are: the freedom of nature and the conventionality of society, the original spontaneity of the child and the system of formal discipline, naturalism and idealism, the sense of freedom and that of duty or obedience, the natural goodness of the human heart and social depravity, the psychology of memory and that of reason, the power of imagination, or fancy, and the sense of reality, sensibility and reason, and male and female. Rousseau struggled to find some means of reconciling these various antinomies in human nature. He attempted to reconcile them by assigning them to the successive stages of development. He was far from successful; but, as a matter of fact, neither has any other educator been entirely successful in harmonizing these conflicting principles.

---

[89] Rousseau, J. J., *Emile*, p. 5.

Chapter 14

TRANSITION FROM CHURCH TO STATE CONTROL OF EDUCATION

CHIEF causes of the transition. The latter decades of the 18th century saw astonishing change in the attitude of many rulers towards the rights of the people, and of states toward education. These changes were due to several causes, the chief of which were (1) the growth of philanthropic sentiment; (2) the doctrines of the Physiocrats; (3) the deepening sense of the rights of individuals and the significance of personality; and (4) the study of the origin and the nature of civil government.

The New Humanitarianism. The most signal fact in the situation of the western world at the close of the 18th century was the spontaneous concern for the moral and religious improvement of the destitute classes. This interest in the welfare of the masses, and particularly of young children, was not so much a religious affair as it was in the previous century. At that time, Father Démia and La Salle and the Brothers of the Common Schools had represented the Catholic Christian spirit in assisting the young. Among the Lutherans it was the Pietistic movement with Francke as leader, and in the Anglican Church the S. P. G. and the S. P. C. K., which established charity schools in England and America. But none of these movements, admirable though they were, received general support and met the deplorable needs of the time. It was from another quarter that a larger movement was to spring, namely, belief in the dignity of human personality and its improvement through enlightened intelligence.

Benevolent despotism and education. The new attitude toward man issued in two forms of government: benevolent despotism, east of the Rhine; and democracy, in France, England, and America. The benevolent despots were chiefly influenced by the principles of the Physiocrats; the republicans followed British and French political thinkers. Many of these thinkers were under the delusion that legislation has unlimited power to mold the individual and to control society by means of education. The general plan of the universe, as they conceived it, provided natural laws for the government of all things, including man and society. Newton had discovered the universal law governing the physical world; there must be similar laws regulating the moral and social order. All the ills of mankind could be speedily cured by the discovery of these fundamental laws, and by their use in controlling and educating the race. Accordingly, the art of government was to be founded upon an exact science, and all the affairs of men were to be brought into perfect order and efficiency. Who, then, was to place these laws in operation?

The Encyclopedists and the Physiocrats looked to intelligent and benevolent rulers. They were the natural social engineers of all human affairs. "It is an obligation laid upon sovereigns," announced Dupont de Nemours, "to promulgate by positive ordinances the natural and essential laws of the social order." Kings existed for the welfare of their people, not the people for the benefit of the kings.

The *Philosophes* and *Economistes* had no confidence in representative parliaments elected to make laws. Such a democratic process was too slow, laborious, and subject to political uncertainty. It was, in fact, an absurdity. An enlightened despot could issue a few rationally devised laws which would speedily bring order into social and economic life. But, despite their distrust of democracy, its principles triumphed in France and America.

The nationalization of education, however, took place under both the republican and the bureaucratic forms of government. Under the one, education was promoted in order to procure obedient, contented subjects and efficient producers; under the other, to train citizens who possess the intelligence to perpetuate free government for their own good.

The rights and new significance of the individual. The emancipation of the individual from ecclesiasticism, philosophic dogmatism, and economic and political thraldom had reached its climax soon after the middle of the 18th century. The doctrines of equality and of inalienable natural rights had operated as a subtle leaven throughout the middle and upper classes of western Europe and America. The passionate demand of Rousseau for the emancipation of the individual from social bondage resounded everywhere. It was amplified in power by the speculative philosophy of the profound German philosopher Immanuel Kant, whose ethical principles required that an individual must never be used as a mere instrument for another's profit, for each man is an end in himself in the kingdom of social ends.

Shift from church to state control. The period from the Reformation onward showed a marked interest in the philosophy of government. So long as the influence of the Renaissance remained uppermost, attention was centered upon Plato's *Republic,* Aristotle's *Politics,* and the democracy of Greece and Rome. As for the church, it clung tenaciously to the Old Testament doctrine that kings are divinely chosen and authorized to rule.

These philosophies of government were challenged and the people of England and France were bold enough to show their defiance of ancient tradition by beheading two despotic kings. The writings of Grotius, Milton, Pufendorf, Locke, Montesquieu, and Rousseau on civil liberty and democracy were read with avidity by ever widening circles of people. The inevitable result was that they turned from the theocratic theory to a naturalistic theory of its origin and powers, and the control of church authorities over civil governments declined to its lowest level. The transition to public control of education came more slowly and was not uniformly attained. Although there were many who saw in state control of education the promise of a new world order, others, like Kant and Schiller, opposed this method of solving the problem.

THE NATIONALIZATION MOVEMENT IN FRANCE

Plans for national education in France. From the middle of the 16th century to the middle of the 18th century, education in France was conducted almost entirely by the Jesuits and several other religious orders which they largely dominated. An educational revolution then took place, and in 1763 the numerous Jesuit colleges were summarily suppressed, thus leaving the French people quite destitute of schools. Immediately, La Chalotais, Diderot, Mirabeau, Talleyrand, Condorcet, and others began to present plans for a complete system of national schools to replace the teaching orders. Numerous as were these plans down to the end of the century, they all followed the same type of organization, which required the centralization of all culture under public control.[1]

French ideas of educational organization. The ideas of French writers and political reformers on the organization of education during the latter half of the 18th century may be summed up in the following points:

(1) Education must be taken out of the hands of the church and be wholly controlled by the state. All French savants agreed that lay instructors must be substituted for the religious teachers and orders. La Chalotais, the French statesman, in his *Essai* in 1763, threw down the challenge to the church in striking terms: [2]

> I claim the right to demand for the Nation an education that will depend upon the State alone; because it belongs essentially to it, because every nation has an inalienable and imprescriptible right to instruct its members, and finally because the children of the State should be educated by members of the State.

(2) Education must be universal. The writers of the period were in favor of public enlightenment. But the extent of free schooling brought forth a variety of opinions. La Chalotais feared too much education for the common people. His plan was quite reactionary: [3]

> The welfare of society requires that the education of the common people should not go beyond its occupations. Any man who looks beyond his trade will never work at it with courage and patience. It is hardly

---

[1] WORKS ON FRENCH EDUCATION

Date	*Author*	*Title*
1757	Helvetius	*On the Soul (De l'Esprit)*
1762	Rousseau	*Emile*
		The Social Contract (Contrat Social)
1763	La Chalotais	*Essay on National Education*
1768	Rolland	*Plan of Education (Plan d'éducation)*
		Report on Education to Parliament
1772	Helvetius	*Treatise on Man (De l'Homme)*
1775	Turgot	*Memoirs (Mémoires)*
1776	Diderot	*Plan of a University for the Russian Government*
		Provision on Education
1792	Condorcet	*Report on the General Organization of Public Instruction Presented to the National Assembly*

[2] La Fontainerie, F. de, *French Liberalism and Education in the Eighteenth Century,* p. 53. New York: McGraw-Hill Book Company, Inc., 1932.

[3] *Ibid.,* p. 60.

necessary that any of the common people should know how to read and write except those who earn their own living by these arts, or whom these arts help to earn their living.

Roland, in his report to Parliament, recommended: [4]

> Education cannot be too widely diffused, to the end that there may be no class of citizens who may not be brought to participate in its benefits. It is expedient that each citizen receive the education which is adapted to his needs.

Diderot and Condorcet also favored universal instruction.

Opinion was at variance as to how far education should extend in the life of the child. Most writers desired only primary education to be universal and free. They did not expect many children, especially girls, to go beyond that stage.

(3) The objectives of education were radically revised in accord with the new philosophy; civic virtues took the place of the religious and humanistic. The chief objectives were enlightenment, the development of a national spirit, fraternity, the ability to guard one's own rights and to serve the state in civil offices.

(4) Secularization of instruction must take the place of religious indoctrination. Of this, Compayré remarks: [5]

> As a matter of fact, the whole pedagogy of the eighteenth century is dominated by the idea of the necessary secularization of instruction. Thorough-going Gallicans like La Chalotais or Rolland, dauntless free-thinkers like Diderot or Helvetius, all believe and assert that public instruction is a civil affair. . . . All wish to substitute lay teachers for religious teachers, and to open civil schools upon the ruins of monastic schools.

(5) Five grades of instruction were recognized: (*a*) the primary school; (*b*) the secondary school, corresponding to the intermediate grades; (*c*) institutes or colleges for higher general instruction, corresponding to our modern high schools and colleges; (*d*) professional schools for law, medicine, theology, and other learned professions; and (*e*) the National Society of Sciences and Arts.

(6) The general opinion held that instruction should be free, even

---

[4] Roland's *Report on Education*. Quoted by Compayré, G., *History of Pedagogy*, p. 356. Boston: Heath, 1885.

[5] Compayré, G., *op. cit.*, pp. 344-345.

for adult and professional training. Diderot and Condorcet demanded that tuition "be absolutely free" throughout. Talleyrand would make primary instruction free; others would place the limit of free instruction at a higher level. Where there was not free instruction for all, children of marked ability were to be given scholarships.

(7) Talleyrand and Mirabeau did not favor compulsory education, but Diderot would make attendance obligatory.

The later educators were more practical minded. In order to make France republican and to overcome the indifference of the ignorant masses, they believed instruction should be "imperative and forced." Lepelletier, at the close of the century, represented this view: not only would he make education compulsory but complete equality must be sought: [6]

> Let us ordain that all children, girls as well as boys, girls from five to eleven, and boys from five to twelve, shall be educated in common, at the expense of the State, and shall receive, for six or seven years, the same education.... In our system the entire being of the child belongs to us; the material never leaves the mould.... Whatever is to compose the Republic ought to be cast in the Republican mould.

Like Plato, Lepelletier would rear all children in state barracks. All education is to be free; and all pupils to have precisely the same studies and regimentation, in order to acquire *esprit de corps*.

(8) A number of other features were demanded by some of the reformers: freedom of teaching, uniformity of instruction for all classes, adult education, and scholarships for poor but brilliant students. The dearth of textbooks was frequently mentioned. The revision of the curriculum received marked attention. The emphasis came to be placed upon the natural sciences, history, and geography, but the central feature of the course of study was generally government and the duties of the citizens.

Popular demands for a national system. The demands for a national system of education became insistent by the time of the Revolution. The recommendations for reform voiced in the *cahiers* sent up from the people in 1789 included the following resolutions: [7]

---

[6] *Ibid.*, p. 398.

[7] Gréard, O., *Education et Instruction Secondaire,* Vol. II, p. 41, note. Paris: Librairie Hachette et Cie., 1889.

Instruction should be organized to suit the present. Instead of allowing the youth to exhaust himself in the arid study of a dead language, he will be taught morals, *belles-lettres,* the languages, sciences, history, the law of nations and the law of nature. [*The People,* Bordeaux.]

There should be taught the exact sciences, physics, chemistry, natural history, history, geography, fine arts, living languages, by giving to these studies the time which is devoted to the almost useless work of logic. [*The People,* Vouvant.]

These resolutions concerned only secondary training. The demand for primary instruction for all was more widely urged. The Constitution of the Republic, in 1791, has this provsion for national education: [8] "There shall be created and organized a system of public instruction, common to all citizens, and gratuitous with respect to those branches of instruction which are indispensable to all men."

REFORM MOVEMENTS IN ENGLAND

Great Britain in transition. Throughout the 18th and well into the 19th century, England was in a period of transition—not the catastrophic type that revolutionized France, but the slow evolution of conflicting forces in constant interaction. These changes were social, political, religious, industrial, and philosophical. The development of education attendant upon this complex background was entirely in accord with the English way of life.

Social changes. Internally, Britain was stabilized; English, Scotch, Welsh, and Irish; and Anglicans, Calvinists, Catholics, and Dissenters had reached a working accord that permitted great expansion along all lines. The population rapidly increased: in England from 5 million in 1700 to 9 million in 1800. In Scotland and Ireland the increase was not quite as great. These increases took place despite large emigration to the colonies, and the losses from wars.

Wealth mounted for the upper class, but so also did poverty for the masses generally; for economic feudalism still continued by which those who have, receive more, and those who have little lose that which they had.

British character has always been a most unusual combination of antithetical qualities. Politically they moved steadfastly toward com-

---

[8] Compayré, *op. cit.,* p. 372.

plete democracy; socially and economically they remained divided into widely separate classes. An hereditary aristocracy at the top, a substantial middle class of some independence at the center, and a growing mass of "those of the inferior sort" at the bottom, were all ruled by a profound devotion to form, prestige, and snobbery. While politically democratic, they were economically individualistic and socially worshipers of aristocracy. It was this social ideal that constituted their unity and strength.

Political evolution of Britain. The resort to violent political measures recessed in England with the execution of Charles I, in 1649. The Revolution of 1688 determined that Britain should be Protestant, that the sovereign should reign but not rule, and that the absolute, arbitrary power of the sovereign would no longer be tolerated. Henceforth, the power of government was lodged in Parliament; the throne was only a symbol of the unity of empire and of devotion to an aristocratic ideal.

At this time the Parliament represented only the upper classes who owned property and adhered to the established church. The House of Commons was not yet accountable to its constituents. It voted in secret and the votes of members were readily purchased, so that government was easily controlled by the upper class. Complete democratization of the Parliament was on the way, but it took a century before universal suffrage was granted and two centuries before the power of the House of Lords was curbed. Of this evolution of government in Britain the American Revolution was a part and exercised far-reaching influence.

Henceforth, in Great Britain political democracy and a medieval social system, religious liberty and an established church, economic individualism and surviving feudalism, lay down in peace to work for the realization of the empire. In his home, his conscience, and in the directing of his energies every Englishman was master of his destiny. But the rules of social behavior were as rigid as the laws of the Medes and Persians; he was judged by his speech, his dress, his manners, and the way he played the game, whether he was bred a gentleman or a menial. England was a unique achievement in human engineering.

The Industrial Revolution. The economic is not the central force in history but it certainly is a potent one. Changes of greatest consequence were afoot in "Merry Old England," more particularly in the last half of the momentous 18th century. Methods of farming and stock raising were improved, but this led to enclosures of property and the consolidation of holdings. Tenants and owners lost their land and gravitated to the cities to swell the laboring class in the slums.

This was the most active period in the amazing expansion of the empire; the few million people of these little islands carved out the greatest empire in history. India fell to Britain in 1757 and Canada in 1759, placing most of North America in her hands. Her navy sailed all seas unchallenged, and her possibilities for trade and exploitation were limitless.

Toward the end of the century a series of inventions began to industrialize England and revolutionize western civilization. In 1765 Watt invented the steam engine as a driving power. Within two decades this resuscitated the coal industry of Cornwall, and later changed transportation on land and sea. In 1733 John Kay invented the mechanical shuttle which made mechanical weaving possible. Arkwright took out a patent on a spinning machine and the first spininng mill was set up in 1768. Finally, Whitney invented the cotton gin in 1794. Equipped with coal and the steam engine, England became the ship-building and textile center of the world.

These various social conditions and inventions brought on what is called the "Industrial Revolution." At the middle of the century the production of goods in England was still largely manual and confined to the cottages. A large number of independent artisans and proprietors were engaged in manufacture on a small scale. Many of these owned their homes in the country, where they got the raw materials from the farmers, wove it into cloth and sold the goods to the consumer. Soon, however, production was performed by machines and centered in large mills, shops, and factories; and the small independent operators without capital were forced into the laboring class. A middle class of entrepreneurs shared the profits with the executives and capitalists.

Progress in literature and philosophy. The last half of the 18th century was marked by great activity along literary lines. It produced a resplendent array of authors who gave England the most superior literature in the modern world. Novelists, poets, historians, and essayists built the largest reading public. The first newspaper appeared late in the 17th century, and in the 18th a deluge of pamphlets, tracts, and popular books followed, discussing especially public issues of the greatest consequence.

English philosophic thought made commendable progress. Among the most noted thinkers were Hume in critical philosophy, Blackstone in law, Adam Smith in economics, and Bentham in moral and political science. British philosophy was predominantly individualistic and utilitarian, despite the humanitarian movements in religion and education, and the strong underlying *esprit de corps* which welded the varied citizens into national unity.

Utilitarianism was indigenous to British culture. It was advocated by Bacon, fully endorsed by Locke, and accepted universally by the British public. At the time when German thinking produced the idealism of Kant, Fichte, and Hegel, British thought evolved the individualism and utilitarianism of Bentham, Hamilton, and James and Stuart Mill. Utilitarianism is based upon a hedonism which holds that the good is at once pleasurable and useful. Priestly gave it an educational turn as the aim of education: "The chief and proper object of education is not to form a shining and popular character, but a useful one, useful according to the sphere in which a person lives." Jeremy Bentham developed the principle of utility into a system of utilitarian ethics which was everywhere accepted by liberals in the British world.

In the field of education Priestly's *Essay on a Course of Liberal Education for Civil and Active Life* (1765) was in line with the policy of the dissenting academies and had great influence in England and America. None of the leading thinkers such as Blackstone and Adam Smith gave unqualified support to the policy of state education. They were all too thoroughly individualistic and utilitarian to advocate state ownership of children like the Frenchman, Lepelletier, or compulsory state schools and attendance like the Dutch and Germans; or even the parish system of Scotland. The religious leaders of all bodies were unalterably fixed on two propositions: first, education is inseparable from religious instruction and must not under any circumstances be secularized. Second, the teaching of religion cannot be entrusted to the state. The result was inevitable, for no efficient state system of education was possible as long as the church was in control.

Religious conditions during the 18th century. Religious life in Britain and America was about as chaotic as it could possibly become. Christianity lost its appeal for intelligent and progressive minds. The main reasons for this were: First, both Catholic and Protestant theologians stubbornly opposed the Copernican astronomy. They could not accept the idea that the world moves, much less that it moves around the sun, and that it is not the center of the universe. These ideas contradicted the Scriptures, which they held to be inerrant.

Again, the Newtonian celestial system disclosed that the physical universe is entirely mechanical. No energy is ever destroyed, and no new energy is ever created. This material order is under the absolute rule of cause and effect. There is, therefore, no possibility of miracles, and whoever teaches otherwise dupes the people. Intelligent minds cannot accept the notion of a deity interfering with the mechanism of nature.

Third, both Catholics and Protestants had clung with utmost tenacity to the doctrine of the divine right of kings to rule and the divine duty of subjects to obey. Thoughtful men could no longer accept these principles as the basis of social order. They revolted not only against the established order itself but likewise against Christianity for fostering these falsehoods.

The entire system of Christian truth was therefore brought into disrepute with the consequent rise of Deism, Unitarianism, and atheism. To be sure, the masses were not much disturbed by these academic questions; they did have spiritual instincts calling for satisfaction and religious emotions to express, but the formalism of church services and the dreary sermons on morality did not arouse any spiritual fervor. Religious emotions, like all others, seek expression in action, and the formal, conventional, theoretical discourses and services of worship gave little opportunity for response. Methodism in England and the wildest revivalism in the colonies, the rapid growth of Sunday schools, and the planting of Christian missions in foreign lands represented the popular expression of religion.

In connection with the onslaught upon religion a book was written which was followed by momentous consequences. Joseph Butler, Bishop of the Church of England, challenged the rationalistic criticism which threatened to destroy all confidence in Christianity. He did so with a calm and logical trenchancy superior to their own. His chief work, *The Analogy of Religion, Natural and Revealed, to the Course and Constitution of Nature* (1736) does not figure sensationally in the history of philosophic thought; but let there be no mistake, its role in British and American education marks it among the most resultful publications ever to come from the press. The study of Christian Evidences which it initiated saved Christianity in England and America. *The Analogy* became the one text most used in the colleges, academies and even in many high schools. The course in "Evidences of Christianity" was required for graduation in practically every college and academy.

Widespread pauperism. The last half of the 18th century brought increased pauperism all over Europe, but especially in England, France, and Switzerland. Not only the Industrial Revolution, but the multiplication of population, drunkenness, debauchery, ineptitude, and, above all, ignorance caused the worsening of social conditions.

It was a common practice in the congested centers and in the mining districts of England to employ large numbers of children as young as five and six years to work all day in the mines, mills, and shops. They had no opportunity to attend school. These shocking conditions were counteracted to some extent by a corresponding upsurge of benevolence; and a variety of educational means were evolved to relieve the situation.

Charitable education characteristically English. English reformers were incapable of conceiving education as other than a charity. The result was that throughout the 18th century all movements for the improvement of schools had to come from the efforts of benevolent individuals or societies. Four of these, the charity school, the Sunday school, infant schools, and the socialistic movement were due to the new spirit of benevolence; a fifth, the monitorial system, did not root directly from charity but arose because a cheap means to supply instruction was necessary. The charity school movement in England reached its climax during the 18th century.

Sunday schools. Robert Raikes, publisher in Gloucester, conceived the novel idea that instruction might be given laboring children without loss of wages by using the only holiday they had in the week, Sunday. In 1780 he opened the first such school by employing a paid instructor. It was a regular charity school in which the secular studies, reading, writing, numeration, and spelling were taught together with the usual religious instruction, singing of hymns, the catechism, and the Scriptures. The movement spread rapidly over the land and in 1785, the *Society for the Establishment and Support of Sunday Schools throughout the Kingdom,* including in its members people of all denominations, was organized.

Others quickly followed Raikes' example, but they depended upon volunteer instruction. The most enthusiastic instigators of Sunday schools were the Methodists and Baptists. For them this new plan was not a charity in which the well-to-do expressed their pity by patronizing paupers and permanently giving the children an inferiority complex, but a means of building their self-respect. Trevelyan writes of these dissenting congregations: [9]

> Many of the more self-respecting of the new proletariat found in the Baptist or Wesleyan chapel the opportunity for the development of talents and the gratification of instincts that were denied expression elsewhere. The close and enthusiastic study of the Bible educated the imagination.... And in the chapel life working men first learnt to speak and to organize, to persuade and to trust their fellows. Much effort that soon afterwards went into political, trade union and co-operative activities, was then devoted to the chapel community. It was in Little Bethel that many of the working-class leaders were trained. In a world made almost intolerable by avarice and oppression, here was a refuge where men and things were taken up aloft and judged by spiritual and moral standards that forbade either rage or despair.

The monitorial systems. The Society for Promoting Christian Knowledge and many other organizations collected large sums for the education of children. But, despite the various efforts to establish Charity Schools, there were in England large numbers of children who had no opportunity to get an elementary education. Two outstanding difficulties stood in the way: the expense of teaching all the children was too great; and even had there been funds, there were too few teachers available. Finally a plan of organizing instruction was hit upon which gave promise of meeting the situation. This was the system of monitorial instruction. This method of solving the education of the masses of children was conceived first by the Rev. Andrew Bell and later, independently, by Joseph Lancaster. The plan was for the headmaster to teach the lesson to a group of the more mature and intelligent boys. Then the entire body of pupils was divided into small groups and these were taught the lesson by those whom the master had taught. One head teacher could in this way instruct many hundreds of children.

The system quickly attained great popularity in England. Lancaster in later years went to South America, to Mexico, and later to New York City and Philadelphia, where he had some success.

Mutual instruction solved the problem of expense, for it was cheap. It demonstrated that large numbers of children could be handled in the same school building, which was an important contribution to pedagogical wisdom. As to the main point, the utilization of one boy, however

---

[9] Trevelyan, G. M., *British History in the Nineteenth Century* (1782-1901), p. 160. London: Longmans, Green and Company, 1922.

intelligent, to teach what he has just learned to a group of fellow pupils, did not prove very successful. The question of the contribution which one pupil can make in inducing his fellows to learn is a matter of great moment for pedagogical theory, but it still remains unresolved in practice. The method of Bell and Lancaster did not succeed in producing a substitute for trained teachers.

Socialistic efforts. Robert Owen (1771-1858) was one of the most colorful, romantic, and dashing figures in the history of education. Sent to school at a very early age, at seven he assisted his teacher, and from ten supported himself; he was a self-made man. Before 30 he became head of a cotton manufacturing plant where he showed outstanding executive ability. Owen manifested a profound interest in the welfare of ignorant laborers and the underprivileged children of the parish. He organized the community at New Lanark near Glasgow for the improvement of living conditions by a socialistic program which enforced cleanliness, temperance, and religious toleration; and he added a school to provide free instruction for all children from five to ten. He was especially able to sympathize with the boys and girls who were placed in the mills and factories at the age of five and six and deprived of instruction.

Owen's school at New Lanark, called *The New Institution* and conducted on Lancasterian principles, attracted wide attention; similar schools were set up elsewhere. James Buchanan, who taught in *The New Institution,* was called by a group of benevolent men to open an infant school in London. Inspired by Buchanan, Samuel Wilderspin developed new methods of instruction and popularized infant schools in the city. Later, Wilderspin achieved such a reputation that in 1824 he was chosen agent of the newly founded *Infant School Society* which established infant schools in great numbers throughout England. *The British and Foreign School Society, the National Society,* and *the Irish Commissioners* promoted schools at this level both at home and abroad. The *Glasgow Infant School Society* was founded in 1826 and under its auspices David Stow began his celebrated work of teacher-training.

About this time Owen got a fuller vision of the reconstruction of human society by means of the right kind of education; he thereupon renounced Christianity and started English socialism. He published his chief book, *A New View of Society;* or *Essays on the Formation of Human Character,* to popularize this new point of view. Like the enthusiasts of all eras he was absolutely confident that human society could be regenerated by means of education. "All poverty and crime," he asserted, "are the effect of error in the various systems of training and government." Despairing of success in the Old World he promoted an experiment in coöperative socialism at New Harmony, Indiana. where he expended some $200,000 before the project failed.[10]

The first English compulsory education law. The first approach made by England toward compulsory education was the law passed by the Parliament in 1802, entitled "An act for the Preservation of the Health and Morals of Apprentices and others employed in Cotton and other Mills, and Cotton and other Factories." In section 6 it was stipulated that every apprentice must be instructed for a part of each working day "for the first four years at least of his or her apprenticeship . . . in the usual hours of work in reading, writing, and arithmetic, or either of them." Employers had to pay the teachers, who in turn provided rooms in which instruction was given. Children were to attend divine worship at least once each week. Binding out children less than nine years of age was prohibited, as was night work. The number of hours children could labor in a day was limited to twelve. This act asserted for the first time the right of the state to protect children and provide for their welfare. It was, however, evidently lacking in adequate power of enforcement. This method of providing education for the mass of children was a miserable makeshift at best, and an evidence of the lack of genuine insight into modern educational standards of instruction and organization. Childhood cannot be exploited while receiving an education.

PROGRESS OF GERMAN NATIONALIZATION

New German leaders and trends. In the background of the Germanic nature reposed a pietistic spirit, a profound sense of subservience to the authorities and the state, and an inveterate tendency toward idealism combined with a certain practical interest in realism. It was these qualities which saved the Germans from the superficial materialism which dominated the volatile temperament of the French and led to bloody revolution. The Naturalism and Romanticism of the French were not without influence but these turned in the direction of neo-Humanism.

Interest in education, long dear to the hearts of the political leaders

---

[10] Owen then approached the government of Mexico with the request that he be granted the state of Texas, where he might regenerate humanity by the organization of a new social order and the proper education of children. Mexico declined his petition.

of Germany, now became all-powerful. The Pietistic-realistic movement had been carried forward by Johann Julius Hecker; the influence of the Enlightenment was represented by Frederick the Great; Johann Bernhard Basedow attempted to put into practice the principles of Rousseau; and Friedrich Eberhard von Rochow and Johann Ignaz von Felbiger applied the benevolent reforms of the Physiocrats. When these various French influences had spent their force the profounder insights of the Germans captured modern philosophic and educational thought. German thought had received a decided rationalistic trend from the philosophy of Leibnitz and Wolff, and was readily transformed into ethical idealism by Kant, Schiller, and Fichte. The work of several of these leaders needs to be studied further in order to secure a satisfactory view of educational progress in Germany.

BASEDOW AND THE PHILANTHROPISTS

Basedow's career. Johann Bernhard Basedow (1724-1790) was by far the most notable of the German school reformers of the 18th century. He was born in Hamburg where his father was a wigmaker in poor financial circumstances. Basedow's early education was deficient, for the harshness of his father finally caused the boy to run away from home. A philanthropic individual discovered that, in spite of glaring faults, he had remarkable intelligence. Persuaded to return home, he attended the gymnasium, and in due time entered the University of Leipzig. He did not apply himself to his studies consistently but gave attention to education and later became a private tutor in the family of Herr von Quaalen, of Holstein. His pupil was a boy of seven, whom he taught informally, lessons being given as they walked, rode, or played. Tutor and pupil learned to speak Latin together in daily conversation about commonplace objects; but, as might be suspected, it was not very good Latin. This experience as a tutor turned his attention quite definitely in the direction of the reform of educational methods. So deep was his interest that he wrote his master's thesis in this field at the small University of Kiel. Appointed professor of ethics and *belles lettres* at the knightly academy at Soroe, in Denmark, he was soon transferred to the gymnasium at Altona. Here his heterodoxy gave offense and he was removed from office.

The reading of Rousseau's *Emile,* in 1762, and of La Chalotais' *Essay on National Education* the next year turned his attention once again to the reform of education. These two books profoundly influenced him. He was familiar to a certain extent with the pedagogy of Comenius, but he knew far better the ideas of Locke and Francke. The truth is that Basedow became an eclectic who pieced together with remarkable skill a pedagogical creed which attracted great attention.

Pedagogical writings. Basedow was a voluminous writer, but only a few of his works were of abiding importance, especially in education. In 1768 he issued a ringing message entitled: *Appeal to the Friends of Mankind and to Men of Power Concerning Schools and Studies and their Influence on Public Welfare.* This work outlined his views of reform in educational organization, curriculum, and methods. It was an appeal to benevolent men to furnish the funds that would enable him to write a textbook for the guidance of parents. His appeal met with tremendous response. Kings, princes, literary men, and statesmen became subscribers not only in Germany but elsewhere. Among others who took part were the Swiss notables, Iselin and Lavater; and the Austrians, Abbot Felbiger and Moses Mendelssohn. His proposal brought a favorable response from Catholics, Jews, and Protestants, as well as from the Masonic and other fraternal orders; a considerable sum was quickly provided.

The result of his labors was entitled *Book of Methods for Fathers and Mothers of Families and for Nations* (1770). *The Elementary Book* followed half a year later. In 1774, the two works were combined and published in four volumes with one hundred engravings. This was the greatest textbook since the time of Comenius. The entire work was designed to cover the education of children up to 18 years of age; its purposes were as follows: [11]

1. Elementary instruction in the knowledge of words and things.
2. An incomparable method, founded upon experience, of teaching children to read without weariness or loss of time.
3. Natural knowledge.
4. Knowledge of morals, the mind, and reasoning.
5. A method, thorough and impressive upon the heart, of instructing in natural religion.
6. A knowledge of social duties, of commerce, etc.

The *Elementarwerk* aroused tremendous enthusiasm, and Basedow was hailed by many as "the greatest benefactor of mankind."

---

[11] Barnard, Henry, *op. cit.*, p. 458.

The *Philanthropinum*. Basedow now urged that a school be set up to demonstrate his principles. Struck by this suggestion, Prince Leopold of Anhalt-Dessau invited him to organize an institution in his capital city, Dessau; and he provided buildings, salaries, and other facilities for the project. Accordingly, in 1774, Basedow set up a small school for boys of the upper class of society, and christened it with the pretentious but significant name *Philanthropinum*. By this term he sought to express the idea that the institution was the child of philanthropy, the love of men for mankind and for the training of the young to humanitarian ends. The school for a short time became celebrated but it always had within it the seeds of dissolution.

Basedow's educational aim. The aim of his school was simple and yet comprehensive: to prepare boys of the upper class for useful and happy living. He proposed to produce citizens of Europe with the cosmopolitan outlook which characterized idealistic Germany at the close of the 18th century.

State education completely independent of the church. When Basedow read the work by La Chalotais he became an ardent advocate of state education. The schools, he was convinced, must be opened to children of all religious views: Jews, Catholics, Protestants, and even those of no religious convictions, and he believed the state alone can successfully operate such schools. He declared: [12]

> In a country containing different religious bodies, where public schools are supported at the general expense to which each inhabitant contributes, fairness requires that the benefit of these schools should be shared in common, and that no children should be excluded from them on account of religion or sect.

Basedow urged that a "State Superior Council for the Supervision of Public Instruction" be established. This suggestion doubtless had weight in the establishment of the *Oberschul-Collegium* in 1787, when the control of Prussian schools finally passed to the state.

Basedow's methods. As to principles of method, Basedow chose with deep insight the best that had been suggested by other writers, and he skillfully put them together. The chief points which he emphasized may be summarized as follows:

(1) Everything should be taught by means of objects, pictures, and

---

[12] Adamson, J. E., *Short History of Education,* pp. 217-218. Cambridge: Cambridge University Press, 1919.

models. In line with this, his book on elementary methods contained one hundred copper engravings, which formed the basis of instruction. In his master's thesis he wrote the following statement, which goes to the heart of the principle of sense experience or visual instruction:

> All our knowledge comes from the senses, and experience of things is our teacher. Many things in all studies remain obscure to children for this reason alone: that they have neither been seen nor heard.

That words must be taught together with things or pictures of things was the central feature of his practical method.

(2) Basedow was not a linguistic scholar. He really had little interest in Latin, and less in Greek. However, on account of the popular demand for Latin, he taught this language, as well as French and German. All languages were taught by the direct or conversational method and by means of games. In 1776, to demonstrate the success of his methods, he held a public examination to which he invited men of the greatest celebrity. The detailed account of this occasion is intensely interesting.

(3) Education is more important than instruction. This signifies that mere learning is not the most significant attainment, but that the child is more to be trained by means of discipline and good environment. The truth is that Basedow did not have a high regard for learning as such.

(4) Another principle which he took from Realism was that all learning must be useful. Education must prepare for life, but not necessarily should it anticipate life.

(5) Following the theorists of several centuries, Basedow insisted that discipline must not be harsh. He did use some punishments and also rewards, and he advocated making the punishment fit the delinquency. But he believed in making training so pleasant that there would be little need of harshness. The other schools of the day were universally noted for their cruelty.[13]

The curriculum. The curriculum, which was encyclopedic, included Latin, French, and German; though, as already indicated, Basedow's aim was not humanistic in the classical sense. Other common subjects, which he included, were arithmetic, geography, geometry, and history. The realistic studies received the greatest attention. Included in these were natural history, anatomy, physics, carpentering, and *Turnen*. The

---

[13] The greatest illustration of the inhuman schoolmaster, we are informed, was the Swabian Häuberle. See Barnard, Henry, *German Teachers and Educators*, p. 479.

pupils went on excursions to studios, farms, mines, and military camps. They visited the shops of artisans to observe the work of the various industries, and the markets to learn of commerce and exchange.

Social relations were likewise observed in the concrete. The boys regularly attended the court of the prince to learn manners. In fact, manners and morals formed the most important part of training. Like Rousseau, Basedow revolted against the use of fables for the teaching of morals.

The teaching of religion was undenominational, and laid the chief emphasis upon morals. It may be regarded as a transitional step to the secularized instruction of today. Basedow went so far as to suggest teaching the religion of the most numerous body of the people. But he would exempt from attendance upon such instruction, children whose parents objected to this form of religion. Moreover, he insisted that occasion should not be taken to advance the truth or falsity of any religious view.

Textbooks. Basedow emphasized the need of textbooks and of literature at the level of the child's comprehension. As there were no trained teachers, he felt that textbooks should be so ample in materials and so clear in method that the parent, though unskilled in teaching, would not err in instructing children. La Chalotais before him, in his *Essai,* had gone so far as to assert that suitable texts might help mankind to dispense with teachers entirely. In writing his textbooks, Basedow tried to include all the knowledge necessary for elementary instruction.

A new literature for children. One of the finest contributions made by the Philanthropinists was the creation of children's literature in German. This was largely due to the extravagant praise which Rousseau had heaped upon *Robinson Crusoe.* J. H. Campe, one of Basedow's chief fellow-workers, wrote *Robinson the Younger.* Later, Wyss produced *Swiss Family Robinson.*[14]

> Basedow's *Elementarwerk* was the basic cause of an entirely new type of pedagogical literature; children's books for instruction and entertainment. The literary market was flooded with an enormous mass of storybooks, and magazines, picture books and instructive books for youth in several-volume sets, romances, dramas, histories, geographies and physics books for children and for use in the schools, an industry which in the course of time reached gigantic proportions.

---

[14] Heman, F., *Geschichte der neueren Pädagogik,* p. 229. Osterwieck: A. W. Zickfeldt, 1913.

Physical education. Physical exercise received more attention than it had ever received in the schools since the days of ancient Greece. Basedow thought that most of the training to be offered in the people's schools should be physical. Free play in the open air, foot races, wrestling, swimming, riding, hunting, and even fishing formed part of the ordinary activities of the school.

Basedow, like Rousseau, emancipated child life in the upper classes from the bondage of conventionality and artificiality. Ordinarily, pupils wore a simple uniform which in no wise restricted freedom of movement. Following Locke and Rousseau in making garments more comfortable, he also accepted the hardening process. His pupils were obliged to fast one day each month, to live in cold rooms, to be out in storms, and to sleep at times on the ground.

This interest in physical education was fully developed by Salzmann, Basedow's associate, in his work *Gymnastics for Youth,* which was popular in Germany and was translated and widely used in England. In his school at Schnepfenthal, Salzmann trained Gutsmuths, who became the creator of the *Turnen* system of physical training, which has been followed ever since in Germany.

Chief contributions of Basedow's system. The work of Basedow began a new epoch in German education. The following results sum up its chief contributions:

(1) It mobilized and concentrated the scattered interest in educational reform. At this time a wave of philanthropy reached its climax. Many men and women of the upper classes were eager to help the lower, and they saw in education the most promising means to this end.

(2) Basedow set forth a definite system of reform and worked out his principles in a concrete program. Imitators of the system sprang up everywhere, and many similar institutions were established in Germany and contiguous countries. Campe established a school near Hamburg. Salzmann, Basedow's closest associate, set up a school at Schnepfenthal. He emphasized gardening, agriculture, animal culture, geography, nature study, and gymnastics. Two of Germany's greatest educators came out of this school: Ritter, the geographer; and Gutsmuths, the father of the German system of gymnastics. Pestalozzi, also, was definitely influenced by Basedow's efforts and writings.

(3) The *Philanthropinum* assisted greatly in making the transition, from a poor system of schools under the dual management of church and state, to the full control of the state. Basedow strongly favored this

great change. His recommendation of a supreme school council influenced the policies of von Zedlitz, the Prussian minister who brought about the law which gave the state full control of the schools. He was enthusiastic over the principles and practices of the Philanthropinists.

(4) The most important contributions were those of realistic studies and physical education. Realism was given a position of genuine significance. Basedow corrected the error of Hecker and, for trade training, substituted the higher realistic culture. The *Real*-school was transformed into a modern school and placed in competition with the humanistic *Gymnasium*.

Reasons for the decline of the system. (1) The *Philanthropinum* held on fitfully for some years. Basedow was too erratic, temperamental, and quarrelsome to get along with anyone who had the capacity to run it successfully, and his forced withdrawal ended its usefulness. With the passing of this experimental school, the enthusiasm for the system declined.

(2) Again, one may well surmise, the vulgarity, amounting to obscenity, of some of his object lessons may have alienated many people of refined taste.

(3) The looseness of the system favored the growth of charlatanism in many institutions which pretended to copy his methods. His soft pedagogy alienated men of exact and laborious ideals of scholarship. The idea of play education did not suit the German spirit.

(4) The leaders of the new Humanism sharply opposed the *Philanthropinum* because of utilitarianism and neglect of Greek. Moreover, Basedow's lack of serious attention to Latin and his poor scholarship in this language offended many.

BARON VON ROCHOW

Von Rochow and rural education. What Basedow did for the reform of education for the upper classes and the people of the towns, von Rochow attempted for the peasant class. He was a country squire with a large estate, a man of generous and compassionate heart. From personal experience he knew the stupidity, superstition, stubbornness, and suspicious nature of the peasants. They were afraid even of the most benevolent efforts to assist them in their misery, poverty, and disease. Von Rochow decided that the trouble was due, not to a lack of intelligence, but to the fact that they had not received any education.

Confident that the peasants could be elevated to a higher condition of life, he threw himself with enthusiasm into the improvement of schools. In 1772 he published a work entitled *School Book for Children of Country People and for the Use of Village Schools.* Its object was to elevate the intelligence of teachers and to give them practical skill. This work became popular, and made a profound impression on Baron von Zedlitz, the Prussian minister of state and the most outstanding official in the Prussian bureaucracy. Thereafter von Zedlitz undertook no reform of the Prussian schools without first consulting von Rochow.

Von Rochow began to improve the schools on his estate. Filled with missionary zeal he established a teachers' seminary, and required that the teachers should share the same spirit. His second publication was a reader which bore the name *Children's Friend.* Von Rochow shared many of the principles of Basedow. He believed especially in state education, of which he said: [15]

> My principle is: children belong to the State,—the State must provide for their education, and that they learn reading, writing, ciphering, and how to think correctly. The proper school period can not be replaced in after life.

He translated, into German, Mirabeau's *Discourse on National Education.* Among his other writings were: *Schools for the Poor; Abolition of Public Beggary;* and *Formation of National Character by Popular Schools.* Through these works and his schools, von Rochow exerted a greater influence than did any other man of his time on the education of the peasantry of Germany.

THE NEW HUMANISM AND NATIONALIZATION

A new Humanism arises in Germany. The most consequential results for the progress of education came from the new-born interest of the Germans in classical art, literature, and philosophy. The traditional Humanism had simmered down to the study of Latin grammar and Ciceronian phraseology, in the vain expectation of inspiring a new outburst of classical eloquence. So far as the study of Greek was concerned, early Humanism was content with the Greek New Testament and the usual works of Aristotle. The beauty and meaning of classical antiquity

---

[15] Barnard, Henry, *op. cit.*, p. 502.

had not been appreciated. This condition was now to undergo a profound change.

First, Johann Winckelmann (1717-1768) traveled in Italy and wrote a work on Greek sculpture, drawing attention to its wonderful beauty. This aroused the interest of Lessing (1729-1781) and inspired his *Laocoön*. These works awakened German students to a new world, the world of esthetic value. Soon, the interest was broadened to the intensive study of Greek literature in all its forms—poetry, drama, eloquence, history, and philosophy. Men like Gesner, Ernesti, Herder, and many others studied Hellenic antiquity with a zest unknown since the Italian Renaissance. Fortunately they did not try to rival the ancients in the ancient tongues, but were content to yield to their inspiration. These men felt within them that same creative urge which was the inner cause of the artistic expression of the Greeks. From this enthusiasm and admiration for classical art sprang several important movements.

Creation of German literature. German literature as such did not exist before the second half of the 18th century. The higher schools of Germany had devoted attention to the formalism of Latin, but had utterly failed to arouse a creative literary and scientific spirit. The consequence was that the German language still remained a poor instrument of literary expression. Even Frederick the Great wrote only in French, and regarded German as a rude and uncouth tongue. Leibnitz, also, enthusiastic as he was for the vernacular, published his chief works in French. The conception that literature is something more than sterile imitation of Latin authors began with the introduction of the German students to Shakespeare, Milton, Addison, and Pope. Just then they came into contact with the classical Greek world. Out of this contact sprang the greatest era of German literature, including the works of Lessing, Herder, Goethe, Schiller, and Humboldt.

The new ideal of manhood. Former ideals of manhood now ceased to charm the upper middle class which was rising in the Fatherland. The "other-worldliness" of the Pietists was incompatible with the scientific spirit and the awakening creative and esthetic urge. At the same time the cynical sycophants of French society were repulsive to the younger, more serious Germans. The individualism of the natural man, conjured up by Rousseau, was boorish and lacking in grace and humanity; but his doctrine of freedom from the tyranny of conventionality, his defense of sentiment, and his love of nature and trust in its unfolding process, won heartiest approval. Rationalism, which considered everything from the standpoint of utility and judgment to come, now seemed harsh and mechanical. It had banished play, poetry, sentiment, and joy as a waste of time. Even the Englishman Locke had no place for poetry and music. But Rousseau, whose writings touched off a deeper response in Germany than in France, astonished the Germans by his assertion that reason is no reliable guide for man's conduct, and cannot take the place of "the divine voice of his heart." A new ideal of cultured manhood was desired to fill the yearnings of young Germans, instinct with fresh but unexpressed life and genius.

Forming or culture. *Bildung,* forming or culture, was the new word which, at the close of the 18th century was on every tongue to designate the ideal that dominated education in Germany. It superseded the ideals of former epochs. Winckelmann had glorified "the noble simplicity and calm greatness" of Greek manhood. "Beautiful manhood" (*schöne Menschheit*) was the spontaneous product of the natural harmony of the Greek spirit. It was the rhythmic beauty that springs naturally and spontaneously from a happy constitution. The new ideal of the German literary class was not a mere imitation of the Greek; but, emulating the Greek spirit, it was the free and natural expression of that which is most ideal in human nature. All-sided, harmonious, spontaneous self-activity, self-discovery, and expression are the characteristics of this new ideal. It aimed at the true, the beautiful and the good in humanity. Everything man undertakes must have its source in the union of all his powers; everything isolated is ugly. To live one's life as an organic, rhythmic whole is the highest end. The forming of a complete personality, adjusted to all sides of human life by the harmonious development of all the powers of the individual, is the ideal. This new cultural objective was most adequately described by Herder in his *Philosophy of the History of Human Culture* (*Philosophie der Geschichte zur Bildung der Menschheit*). This ideal of life was best expressed by the term "culture for humanness" (*Bildung für Humanität*), or "pure manliness" (*reine Menschlichkeit*).

The new ideal had a transforming influence upon German schools, especially upon secondary and higher education. Since their establishment in the 16th century, the Latin schools had failed to receive any new impetus. Their work had long been a deadening drudgery. Admission to the universities was by special examination. The arts or philosophic faculties in the universities were on a low level, largely performing the work which should have been done by the Latin schools. The teachers of the Latin schools were usually young men who were poorly trained and who expected to take up the pastoral office after serving their apprenticeship in teaching. They were not definitely interested in the education of youth. All these conditions were changed by the new spirit of scholarship and literary productivity.

The new Humanism was introduced into the University of Göttingen by Johann Mathias Gesner and Christian Gottlob Heyne. Johann August Ernesti promoted it in Leipzig, and Friedrich August Wolf in Halle. These men gave thoroughgoing courses in the Greek and Latin languages and literatures. Along with this intensive instruction, they provided some training in the art of teaching. The young men who pursued the new training no longer had the pastorate in view, but expected to spend their lives teaching in the gymnasiums. The study of philology and literature was pursued for its own sake, independent of theology. The teaching office became better paid; the tenure, life-long; and the post of *Oberlehrer,* as the teacher was called, took its place among the learned professions. The office was raised in respectability, and, as a servant of the state, the *Oberlehrer* ranked with the higher public officials.

The tendency to separate the Latin school from the church had consequences of the greatest moment. It meant that there had arisen a new class of people who were not primarily devoted to the church. Baron von Zedlitz, the great educational leader of the Prussian bureaucracy, introduced the new Humanism into Prussia in 1771. This ascendancy of the state over the church came to a head in the famous school law of 1787. This law, placing the schools of Prussia under the supreme school board (*Oberschulkollegium*), marked the beginning of a new organization of education in Germany.

Three types of schools were recognized: the first were in the villages and country places; the second, in the towns; and the third, in the larger cities. The last were high-grade classical secondary schools. The rural schools were of elementary grade and were modeled after the type conducted by von Rochow on his private estates; the second, after the model of Francke's town school.

The next big step in the standardizing process was the introduction of the school "leaving-examination" (*Abiturientenprüfung*) for students who completed the classical gymnasium course. All students who passed this stiff test were admitted without further qualification to the universities. As a result of this the universities dropped all entrance examinations. Those Latin schools that were sufficiently strong to train their students for the "leaving-examination" became classical gymnasiums; those that could not do so remained in a lower rank.

The effects of all these developments upon the universities must not be overlooked. The new training of philologists raised the standard of work in the gymnasiums, and relieved the universities of all secondary school work. They were then in a position to devote their strength to the highest level of scholarship, the search for new knowledge. This gave the arts and science faculties a status equal to the professional faculties of law, medicine, and theology.

State regulation and centralization of all schools was definitely reaffirmed in the general state law (*Allgemeine Landrecht*) of 1794. It stated that: [16]

> Schools and universities are state institutions.... Such institutions may be established only with the knowledge and approval of the State. All... are under the supervision of the State and are at all times subject to its examination and inspection.

By these laws, Prussia effected the transition from the church-state school of the Reformation period to the public school of the 19th century. Teachers became state servants; and civil authorities replaced consistories, church superintendents, and pastors as supervisors for the schools.

NATIONALIZATION IN OTHER COUNTRIES

Benevolent despots. Similar efforts to establish national systems of education in other countries were made by various benevolent despots. While they extended state initiative and control generally in Europe, they did not add any reform of great significance.

Maria Theresa and school reform in Austria. The Empress Maria Theresa imitated in Austria the educational reforms of her great rival, Frederick of Prussia. She attempted to introduce more centralization of government. This, however, could not be carried out fully because of the differences in language, customs, and political condition of the peoples of her heterogeneous domains. But she cautiously introduced some reforms in agriculture, education, religion, and finance. The Jesuits

---

[16] Kandel, I. L., *History of Secondary Education,* p. 239. Boston: Houghton Mifflin, 1930.

were expelled; persecution was restrained; and Felbiger undertook the reform of schools, as he had done for Frederick in Catholic Silesia.

Joseph, the son of Maria Theresa, educated in government by Karl Anton Martini (a disciple of the rationalism of Wolf and a leader of the Enlightenment in Austria), carried on the work begun by his mother. He accepted the doctrines of the Physiocrats, but found difficulty in introducing their policies. He favored toleration in religious affairs, liberated the serfs, and put through other measures of reform. He likewise held enlightened views on educational reform. The curriculum was revised, and the teachers became civil servants. The system was strongly paternalistic. The press was censored, and foreign periodicals were excluded.

Denmark. As early as 1721, a decree of Frederick IV reformed education in his Kingdom. Among other progressive measures adopted was that of compulsory attendance. Children between five and eight years were required to attend school daily for five or six hours; after eight they had to attend half of each school day. Religion and reading were required, writing and arithmetic were optional.

Reform in Sweden and Baden. Gustavus III of Sweden, a friend of Mirabeau, put into operation a number of principles of the Physiocrats. It was at his request that Mercier de la Rivière, one of the leading Physiocrats, published his work *De l'Instruction Publique* (1775).

Charles Frederick of Baden (1748-1816) was in regular communication with Mirabeau and Dupont de Nemours. He was the best example of a despot who put into operation the tenets of the Physiocrats. He believed that poor peasants make a poor kingdom, for serfdom is not only unjust but economically unsound and harmful. Under his application of economic principles, Baden became one of the most prosperous and enlightened states.

Educational reform in Spain and America. Charles III of Spain (1759-1788) received his early training under the influence of the French *Philosophes* and *Economistes*. He belonged to the new type of enlightened monarchs, and was noted for honesty, conscientiousness, and deep interest in his responsibilities. He expelled the Jesuits, curbed the power of the church and Inquisition, redressed political grievances, and gave encouragement to science and literature, as well as trade and industry.

In education he initiated three efforts: (1) an experiment in a physiocratic utopia in Spain; (2) the general reform of education; and (3) the establishment of education throughout the Spanish possessions in the New World.

Following the doctrines of the Physiocrats, he promoted an experiment in agricultural colonies in Spain. These were planned to be communities in which priests and monks would be excluded, and simple and industrious farmers would till the soil and live happily together under a constitution based entirely upon the laws of nature. The experiment, however, did not meet with success, and was finally abandoned.

Under the control of the Roman Church, instruction in Spain had long been sadly neglected. Charles planned to take education entirely out of the hands of the clergy and to make it a function of the civil government. He effected marked reforms in university education, professional training, and in the establishment of schools. He required examinations of all candidates who wished appointments as teachers in the state-supported schools.

In his efforts to promote education in America, he stimulated Spanish colonization by offering royal subvention to settlers. In 1771, he undertook to establish a school in Louisiana, which at the time was a part of his domain in the New World. He sent a "director" and three teachers, under contract, to New Orleans to conduct a school. The French inhabitants did not relish these Spanish instructors; yet the school remained in existence for some time. It is held that this "director" was the earliest example of the city superintendent in an American school system.[17]

Charles also planted education in other parts of America. He attempted colonization in California, in accordance with physiocratic ideas. In these colonies he promoted schools; owing to special conditions, the educational activities were carried on by the Franciscan Fathers. In 1784, Father Lazuen introduced schools wherein religion, reading, writing, and Spanish were taught. Every boy was taught some trade and girls also received instruction. By royal order, schools were a regular feature of every California mission. In 1785, the Franciscans opened a school at St. Augustine, in Florida, and Charles supplied the necessary funds. A similar effort was made in Texas.

Thus, Charles' educational interest had a special significance for our

[17] Noble, Stuart, "Early School Superintendents in New Orleans," in *Journal of Educational Research,* November 1931, pp. 274-279. Public School Publishing Company, Bloomington, Ill. This view overlooks the work of Michael Schlatter as "superintendent" of charity schools in Pennsylvania some years earlier.

country. Moreover, even before these last developments, he had issued a royal order looking to the establishment and maintenance of schools everywhere in Spanish America at public expense. It is true that little was accomplished, but this was due to unfavorable conditions and not to lack of interest on the part of Charles.

National life and education in Switzerland. About the middle of the 18th century J. J. Bodmer and J. J. Breitinger, of the College of Zurich, became interested in English literature and led the way to a higher order of literary production in the German tongue. Zurich became the center of a new life which regenerated the whole Swiss people. In 1758, Franz Urs Balthasar, of Lucerne, published *The Patriotic Dreams of a Confederate of a way to rejuvenate the old Confederation,* recommending the creation of a national institute of education. Inspired by his work, a group of zealous patriots formed the *Helvetic Society,* in 1762. Among the members were Bodmer, the literary leader; Gessner, the Swiss poet; and Iselin, a nobleman-philanthropist. Among the younger set were Lavater, a poet, and the youth Pestalozzi. These men opposed the tyranny of the oligarchical party in the various cantons, and labored for liberty, fraternity and justice. The society represented, moreover, a growing desire for a central government. But foremost among the activities of the group were its efforts on behalf of the improvement of schools.

The French Revolution struck a responsive chord in the hearts of many Swiss of all levels, even of the patrician class. The French craftily fanned the flames of revolt among the discontented. At this time Switzerland was a loose confederation of eighteen small sovereign and twenty-seven semi-independent states. In 1798, the Helvetic Constitution was adopted, and a unified government called the *Swiss Directorate,* like that of France, was established.

Internal progress, especially in education, immediately claimed the attention of the new central government.[18] Albrecht Stapfer, who was made minister of arts and sciences, set himself with untiring endeavor to improve the educational system. He began by requiring all the cantons to send in reports of the condition of their public schools, and also suggestions for improvement. A system of federal regulations was drawn up, uniting all scientific and cultural institutions into a single organization. Local councils and inspectors were authorized, and in every canton

---

[18] Dändliker, Karl, *A Short History of Switzerland,* p. 225. New York: The Macmillan Company, 1899.

a seminary was to be established for the training of teachers. At the request of Stapfer, Pestalozzi began to publish a paper on educational reform. Such was the national framework in which the simple-hearted Pestalozzi was to become the most renowned world educational figure.

SPREAD OF EDUCATION

Europe and South America. The spread of modern educational activities activities and organizations during the 19th century is one of the outstanding phenomena of history. All civilized lands have found it necessary to revise their educational programs. In addition to the countries already mentioned, other countries in northwestern Europe early established state systems. In Holland, Norway, Sweden, and Finland, illiteracy has long been a thing of the past. Southern Europe has also undergone a great revival, as have likewise eastern European countries. Similarly, in South America, all the republics have established systems of schools. During the past few years Mexico has worked out a most successful state system.

British dominions. Throughout British Dominions, modern education has been everywhere established. The large immigration from Scotland and Ireland, as well as from England, has resulted in educational activity of a high order. The various dominions have not been hampered by the encrusted traditions of centuries as is old England, and their systems consequently are more progressive.

The Dominion of Canada offers one of the finest examples of educational progress. The national constitution provides that education shall be the concern primarily of each province; while the various school systems are not all on the same level of efficiency, they are highly developed. In general they have succeeded in combining much of the best of the education of Scotland, England, and the United States.

Chapter 15

THE TRANSITION MOVEMENT IN AMERICA

CONSTITUENT FACTORS IN THE EDUCATIONAL REVOLUTION

LEADERS of thought. Independent thinking on educational matters—history knows of no absolute innovations—did not appear in America until after the Revolution. The most aggressive agitator prior to this time was Franklin, and despite his independence in other lines, in education he obviously derived his ideas from English and German sources. Five factors must be recognized in regard to proposals for education in the young republic: (1) The American Philosophic Society; (2) individual writers on education; (3) Americans who contacted the new educational ideas in France and introduced them in their several states; (4) the direct participation of French teachers and thinkers in the United States; and (5) Thomas Jefferson.

1. The Philosophical Society. In 1727 the industrious Franklin formed a *Junto,* a debating club, and in 1743, *The Philosophical Society.* In 1769 the two were merged into the *American Philosophical Society for Promoting Useful Knowledge.* The purposes of the organization were to promote scientific knowledge and political discussion on the broadest scope by mobilizing the interest of the leading men of America and Europe. By the end of the century over 650 of the greatest leaders had been elected members. Among the Europeans were Buffon, Condorcet, Lavoisier, Lafayette, and Dupont de Nemours. The organization was instrumental in acquainting the members with the most advanced discoveries and events in Europe; and, still more important, in creating a sort of national consciousness in American Society.

The deepening interest in the subject of the relation of popular government to education led the society to offer a prize for "the best system of liberal Education and literary instruction adapted to the genius of the Government of the United States." The prize was divided between two essays: Samuel Knox's *An Essay on Education* (1787) and Samuel H. Smith's *Remarks on Education; Illustrating the Close Connection Between Virtue and Wisdom; to which is annexed a system of liberal education.*

2. *Other important writers.* Even before the *Philosophical Society* brought out these two essays, other men began to discuss the need for educational institutions. Benjamin Rush, a man of excellent education and a leader in the Revolution, published *Thoughts upon the Mode of Education Proper in a Republic* (1786). Another author of note was Noah Webster, famous for his speller and dictionary. The Blueback Speller, it is estimated, sold 25 million copies. His *Essays* (1790) discussed education. Following in the same vein, Robert Corams wrote *Political inquiries; to which is added a plan for the general establishment of schools in the United States* (1791). Joseph Priestley, the scientist-educator, published *The Proper object of education in the present state of the World* (1791). William Godwin wrote *The Enquirer, Reflections on Education, Manners and Literature* (1797).

3. *Americans visit France.* The new theory of government which captured the American mind came directly from English writers who championed the rights of the individual. But the new American theory of education had its origin in France. Strangely, English thinkers and writers were slower in grasping the vital connection that links the exercise of suffrage in a democracy to an enlightened populace. French educational ideas spread in several ways, but more by personal contact than by literature. Prominent Americans sojourning in France during the era of its educational revival caught its enthusiasm and broadcast the new ideas at home. Among these were Benjamin Franklin, John Adams, Thomas Jefferson, John Jay, and Ezra L'Hommedieu.

Adams spread French conceptions in New England, where, after his return from France, he formed the *American Academy of Arts and Sciences* (1780). Moreover, this same year, he led in the rechartering of Harvard to make it a university. John Jay and Ezra L'Hommedieu originated the University of the State of New York. Thomas Jefferson attempted to establish a complete system of public schools in Virginia, and became the father of the University of Virginia, which was strongly influenced by French ideas of organization.

4. Frenchmen come to the United States. Again, French teachers and educators came to this country and attempted to do for culture what Lafayette had done for political life. In 1780, Simon Paulin was appointed to teach French at Harvard; two years later, he was superseded by Albert Gallatin, who became celebrated in American statecraft. Columbia University established a chair of French in 1779; William and Mary, in 1793; and Union College, in 1806.

Among the Frenchmen who attempted to organize education in the new Republic two were outstanding. One, Chevalier Quesnay de Beaurepaire (grandson of Quesnay, founder of the Physiocratic movement), came to America with Lafayette and fought in the Revolution. Remaining in America, he conceived the idea of linking the United States with French culture. To this end he established the *Academy of Sciences and Fine Arts of the United States of America,* with headquarters at Richmond, Virginia. It was an institution at once national and international, being affiliated with the Royal Societies of London, Paris, and Brussels; but it was, unfortunately, of short duration. The other figure was Dupont de Nemours, also a Physiocrat, who, in, 1800, at the suggestion of Thomas Jefferson, published a work, *National Education in the United States* (*Sur l'Education Nationale dans les Etas-Unis*), which had considerable influence upon American students of education.

5. Thomas Jefferson. More than any other one person, Thomas Jefferson (1743-1826) determined the democratic character of our American way of life. Born near Charlottesville, Virginia, when it was a border settlement, Jefferson was more influenced by the frontier and the backwoods than other leaders of the Revolution. He received a good education in the College of William and Mary and studied law in the office of George Wythe. His scholarship was so efficient that he could use with facility Latin, Greek, and several modern languages. His views were influenced chiefly by British constitutional law, the philosophic works of Locke and Shaftesbury, natural science, and the educational ideas of the French. He was stoutly attached to the economic principles of the Physiocrats. "I have sworn," he declared, "upon the altar of God, eternal hostility against every form of tyranny over the mind of man."

Jefferson had a powerful influence on the development of public education in the United States. He founded the University of Virginia, and worked for the establishment of a system of schools supported and controlled by the state and local governments. The great motives which dominated his life were: faith in the ability and goodness of the common man; belief in the possibility of improvement in human life by reform in law, government, and education; and an intense zeal for the cause of human freedom.

Jefferson spent his life in public service. As a member of a committee to revise the laws of Virginia, Jefferson wrote measures which greatly promoted education. He was particularly proud of the establishment of religious liberty by the separation of church and state. He drew up three bills for the establishment of a state system of public schools. The system was to include elementary schools in every locality, secondary schools in every section, and a state university. The elementary schools were to be locally controlled and supported, and were to be open without tuition to all white children. The secondary schools and the university were to be built with state funds, but supported chiefly by tuition fees. The education of poor boys of intelligence was to be made possible by a system of state scholarships. One of these bills for the establishment of elementary schools, was passed in 1796-1797, but the time for the opening of the schools was left to the discretion of the county courts. No county set up schools under the law.

Jefferson always contended that popular education is the business of the state, and vital to its welfare. As early as 1786, he wrote to Washington: [1] "It is an axiom in my mind that our liberties can never be safe but in the hands of the people themselves, and that, too, of the people with a certain degree of instruction." He worked assiduously for a number of years to establish the University of Virginia, in which all useful sciences were to be taught on the highest levels. No other American at that day or since felt so profoundly the necessity of academic freedom, as well as the significance of high standards of scholarship, for national and human welfare.

Principles of the Revolution. The chief leaders of the American Revolution formed a new and definite philosophy of government. It was to the best interest of civilization for America, they asserted, to separate from the Old World, and to establish a government and way of life ordered on wholly new principles. These principles were that human life is capable of the greatest improvement; that governments exist to effect this end, by respecting the natural rights of man and by limiting the

---

[1] Randolph, T. J. (Editor), *Memoirs, Correspondence, and Miscellanies from the Papers of Thomas Jefferson.* Charlottesville: F. Carr and Co., 1829.

practices of government; and that life, liberty, and the pursuit of happiness are inalienable rights inherent in the nature of human personality.

All leaders were agreed that education was the indispensable means to procure the common weal. But they held very diverse views respecting the fundamental principles of educational organization and practice. One group following the French idea believed that government and education should be highly centralized, and that children should be prepared for citizenship by being carefully indoctrinated in democratic principles. Another group held that localities should manage their own schools as far as possible; and that the central government, instead of teaching a system of ideas, should cultivate the minds of the young and encourage them to think for themselves on public affairs.

THE FEDERAL GOVERNMENT AND EDUCATION

The Federal Constitution and education. The Constitution of the United States contains no direct reference to schools. This is surprising in view of the influence of French educational ideas. President Washington favored a national university, in which students from all parts could come in contact with one another so as to unify the country. He left it an endowment. But Jefferson and the great body of people feared the domination of a central government, and desired local control of lower schools, and separate church and state colleges and universities. As a consequence decentralization and local autonomy prevailed in American education.

Two amendments to the Constitution, the First and the Tenth, are of greatest significance for education. The First Amendment declares: "Congress shall make no law respecting an establishment of religion, or prohibiting the free exercise thereof; or abridging the freedom of speech or of the press." This fundamental principle of the separation of church and state was intended to free America from the religious bitterness that fragmented and weakened the Old World. The unforeseen result of this amendment was the complete secularization of public education.

The Tenth Amendment declared: "the powers not delegated to the United States by the Constitution, or prohibited by it to the States, are reserved to the States respectively, or to the people." The opponents of a powerful central government conducted in the interests of a privileged class voted this amendment in order to safeguard local autonomy and individual liberty. As a consequence American education was left to the prerogative of the states, and supported and controlled by state and local governments and private agencies.

The Federal land grant policy. From ancient times it had been the practice to donate lands for the establishment of schools and colleges. The Spanish sovereigns early adopted this policy in their government of the New World. The Puritans did the same in New England. Individuals early laid plans to use the income from the sale of the vast lands of the West not only for the support of state and local governments, but for schools and internal improvements as well.

As early as 1783 a plan for the utilization of the lands was proposed in Congress with the provision that a portion of the revenues from their sale be used to establish schools. Two years later, Congress passed an ordinance making possible the sale of land in the Northwest Territory. This law provided for dividing the lands into townships, six miles square; and the townships into lots, each a mile square.

In 1787 an immense area was sold to a land company, and an ordinance adopted for the government of the region declared: "Religion, morality, and knowledge being necessary to good government and the happiness of mankind, schools and the means of education shall forever be encouraged." Later the same year, the *Northwest Ordinance* regulating the utilization of land was adopted. Lot 16 in each township was given for the school of the township; and two entire townships were set apart for the endowment of a universtiy. This established the precedent of the Federal Government of granting lands for encouragement of schools and colleges.

STATES LAY THE FOUNDATIONS OF SCHOOL SYSTEMS

Educational provisions in state constitutions. By 1800 eight of the 16 states had adopted constitutional provisions for education. The constitution of Pennsylvania, adopted in 1776, directed the legislature to "establish a school or schools . . . in each county of the state." It further directed: "All useful learning shall be duly encouraged and promoted in one or more universities." In 1790 a new constitution directed the legislature to provide for the free education of the poor, and to see that "all the arts and sciences [were] promoted in one or more seminaries of learning."

Articles on education are especially liberal in the state constitutions of North Carolina (1776), Georgia (1777 and 1798), Massachusetts (1780), New Hampshire (1784), and Vermont (1793). Interest in founding systems of public schools was by no means confined to those states with constitutions referring to the subject. The constitutions of New York and Connecticut, until well into the 19th century, were silent on the subject of schools; but these were among the earliest and most enterprising states in pioneering for education.

Public education in Massachusetts. The state constitution of Massachusetts, adopted in 1780, confirmed Harvard College in its ancient powers, rights, and privileges; and designated the governor, lieutenant-governor, council, and senate of the state, with six ministers of the Congregational Church, as overseers of the college. Furthermore, it charged the legislature to "cherish the interests of literature and the sciences, . . . especially in the University of Cambridge, public schools, and grammar schools in the towns."

In 1789, the legislature of Massachusetts legalized the *district* system, which had gradually developed from the town system of colonial days. The law required an elementary school in towns of 50 or more families, and grammar schools in towns having 150 or more families. Teachers were to be college graduates or, if not graduates, they were to be certificated by ministers of the Congregational Church. Only citizens of the United States were allowed to teach in town schools. Fines were imposed on towns failing to provide schools.

In 1797, the legislature enacted a law which gave to academies a recognized place in the public school system. All academies meeting certain standards stipulated in the law were to receive from the state an endowment of half a township of land. To receive this grant, an academy was required to have a permanent endowment of at least $3,000.

New York lays the foundation of a state system. No mention of education was made in the constitution of New York down to 1894. From the Revolution the state has, nevertheless, pursued a liberal policy in promoting private educational agencies and in the support and control of public schools.

Governor George Clinton initiated the educational program in 1784. The legislature ordered that unappropriated lands in the state be surveyed, and 690 acres in each township be reserved for the support of schools. At the same time an act was passed establishing the *Board of Regents of the University of the State of New York,* whose duty it was to promote and supervise secondary and higher education. After three years this feature was changed and the University was established with oversight of "all the colleges, academies, and schools." This organization has had a continuous existence to the present time and is the oldest in the country. The Regents chartered a number of academies before the close of the century. In 1790, the Regents were authorized to expend for schools funds received from the sale of certain state lands. This marks the beginning of the state fund for education in New York.

The act creating the Board of Regents gave it power over secondary and higher education only, but the board early urged the importance of establishing a system of common schools. In 1795, the legislature appropriated £20,000 a year, for five years, to be distributed to common schools in the state. A school was to be established in each district. The English language and grammar, arithmetic, and "such other branches of knowledge as are most useful and necessary to a complete education," were to be taught. Funds were to be distributed to the counties, and then by the counties to the towns. Within the towns, funds were distributed to districts on the basis of the number of days in each year that a school was maintained. Two school commissioners and district trustees selected and approved teachers, and exercised supervision of the schools. By 1800 there were in New York 1,350 public schools. The purpose for which the 1795 act had been passed, the general diffusion of the elements of an education, was rapidly being attained. The act met, however, strong opposition, and when it expired, in 1800, it was not renewed.

THE UNIVERSITY MOVEMENT IN THE UNITED STATES

The multiplication of colleges. The early part of the 18th century experienced a widespread religious revival known as the "Great Awakening." Various Protestant denominations increased in membership and began to organize for more aggressive action, by making provision for training ministers. As an outcome of this development, a number of new colleges sprang into existence. Among these were The College of New Jersey (later Princeton), established in New Jersey by the Presbyterians in 1746; King's College (now Columbia University), in New York City, founded by the Episcopalians in 1754; Brown, by the Baptists in Rhode Island in 1764; Rutgers in New Jersey, by the Dutch Reformed Church in 1766; and Dartmouth, in New Hampshire, by the Congregationalists in 1769, in order to missionize the Indians.

Every one of these institutions owed its existence to Christian ministers, just as did the three original colleges. Moreover, each had as its chief function, to train young men for the pulpit. In other respects, too, they followed the ideals and practices of their predecessors. They were obliged to seek their charters from English officials who were already waxing suspicious of deviations from established customs.

The one institution of this period that did not directly stem from religious influences was the Academy and Charity School founded by Franklin in 1751. Four years later its scope was broadened and the new charter invested the Trustees with authority to confer degrees under the name "The College, Academy and Charitable School of Philadelphia."

Character of the pre-Revolution colleges. Colonial colleges followed the English model in practically all particulars down to the Revolution. Every student was required to live in the dormitory under the master's charge. Daily religious observances, obedience to a long series of rules, and a common mode of life and discipline were required. Down to 1767, each tutor carried a group through the college course, teaching them in all subjects. Only at that late date were tutors appointed for each individual class. Yale, in 1767, and Harvard, in 1773, abandoned the listing of students in the catalog according to the rank and social standing of their parents—another custom brought over from English university life.

The pronounced English character of our first colleges has been purposely dwelt upon because it fixed the type that all higher education was to follow on this continent. Variations crept in as the decades passed, but this basic conception prevailed everywhere down to the middle of the 19th century. It was college education, implying regulation of conduct rather than professional instruction: residence under restrictions; daily religious exercises; a common dining hall; the forming of a special type of character; a liberal education of limited scope; and formal discipline for the mind as well as morals. Such were the objectives of the traditional American college, which everywhere was the instrument for higher culture.

Something of the character of these early colleges can be guessed from the youthful age of the students. The average age of graduates in the class of 1681 at Harvard was about 19½ years. In 1753, 29 students entered Harvard, and the average age was 15 years and five months. One of these was 12½, eight were 14 to 15 years, and 12 were 15 to 16 years. It was not uncommon for students to graduate at 15 years of age. All these institutions were teaching what we now regard as the secondary school age. Their enrollments were small, and most students were preparing for the ministry.

Summary of colonial colleges: 1636-1776. Before the American Revolution, nine colleges had been founded in the colonies. Most of these received public subsidies, and each (save one) was closely associated with a particular Protestant church. Some of these institutions have changed their names, and some have changed their locations, but every one is still in existence, and all are rendering distinguished service.

COLONIAL COLLEGES, 1636-1776

Institution	*State*	*Religious Alignment*	*Date*
Harvard University	Massachusetts	Congregational	1636
College of William and Mary	Virginia	Anglican	1693
Yale University	Connecticut	Congregational	1701
Princeton University	New Jersey	Presbyterian	1746
University of Pennsylvania	Pennsylvania	Non-sectarian	1749
Columbia University	New York	Anglican	1754
Brown University	Rhode Island	Baptist	1764
Rutgers University	New Jersey	Dutch Reformed	1766
Dartmouth College	New Hampshire	Congregational	1769

As to the spirit of these institutions, two most significant changes had occurred. First, they had begun to be far more democratic than formerly. Harvard and Yale gave up the policy of listing their students according to the social status of the father. Sectarian requirements were gradually abolished. King's College (later Columbia), from its establishment in 1754, was liberally disposed; Brown University, founded in 1764 by Baptists, had the following in its charter: "Into this Liberal and Catholic Institution shall never be admitted any Religious Tests but on the contrary all the Members hereof shall forever enjoy full free Absolute and uninterrupted Liberty of Conscience," and "that the Sectarian differences of opinions shall not make any Part of the Public and Classical Instruction."

Second, the curricula of the newer institutions became much broader than in the older institutions. The French language was added. In addition to the ancient languages and the philosophic branches, psychology, logic, ethics, and metaphysics were offered. More attention was devoted to the mathematical branches, algebra, geometry, and trigonometry. History was a new interest, and also the sciences, especially geography and astronomy. Several institutions added, also, such practical lines as surveying, navigation, husbandry, commerce, and government.

Beginning of the university ideal. Concurrent with the Revolution there appeared a quickening of academic interest; in rapid order the existing colleges attempted to transform themselves, while at the same time many new ones were planned on the university model. British authorities had repeatedly refused to grant the people of North Carolina a chartered college. This caused bitter feeling among them. Grasping the very first chance in 1776 they placed in the constitution of the state a provision for "one or more universities." It was chartered in 1789 and began teaching six years later, and is the oldest State University. The first constitution of Vermont (1777) likewise provided for the creation of a state university.

In 1779, the College, Academy and Charitable School of Philadelphia was, by act of legislation, converted into "The University of the State of Pennsylvania." This action is notable as it was the first specific legislation establishing a state university. In 1791, the institution adopted as its permanent name, The University of Pennsylvania, but it was returned by the legislature to private management. In 1780, Harvard was rechartered and designated a university, although it did not for many years use this title, an action not without significance. In 1784, New York passed an act establishing the University of the State of New York. Georgia did the same the following year. In 1790, a "National University" was proposed, to be created and supported by the Federal Government. President Washington urged its establishment and left $25,000 in stocks for its endowment. By an act of the General Assembly of Kentucky, 1798, Transylvania University was established, which in 1845 was consolidated with the University of Kentucky. In 1802, the legislature of the Northwest Territory chartered the American Western University. Brown University took its present title in 1804. Louisiana established the University of New Orleans as a state institution in 1805; Michigan was founded in 1817; and Virginia, in 1819. Thus, after the Revolution, the university ideal as opposed to the traditional church college took strong hold upon the minds of American leaders. These universities represented a wholly new order of affairs in higher education, and had little in common with the narrow religious college of former days. The curricula were to be as broad as the new purposes which inspired them; modern languages and the physical as well as the social sciences were to be emphasized as central features.

Totalitarianism. The most extraordinary proposal at this period has yet to be mentioned. This was the plan of combining all educational institutions, together with the other agencies of culture into one grand organization, to be designated the *University* of the state.

The president of Dartmouth College proposed (1777) that this college should become a state university,[2] "And that there be two or three Charity Schools or Academies in connection with this university." An effort was later made to do privately what was here proposed to be done publicly: this led to one of the most historic decisions of the U. S. Supreme Court.

As early as 1785 the charter of the University of Georgia empowered the *Senatus Academicus* to establish, control, and supervise all the public schools to be supported by the state. It was to select all the teachers, prescribe the branches to be taught, and, finally, to examine the results.[3]

The University of the State of New York. In 1784 the New York Legislature passed an act entitled "An Act for establishing a university within this state." Far-reaching authority was granted the Regents, for they were "empowered to found schools and colleges in any part of this State" and to endow them, "every such school or college being at all times to be deemed a part of the University and, as such subject to the control and direction of the said Regents."[4] It was the hope of many powerful friends that King's College, discontinued at the time of the Revolution, would become the apex of the system. As it turned out, the central institution alone is missing; otherwise, the system, as it was constituted, accomplished the plan of unification of all educational agencies into what is known as the *University of the State of New York*.

The University of New Orleans. In 1805, the legislative council of Louisiana took action establishing the University of New Orleans. The

---

[2] Chase, Frederick, *A History of Dartmouth College and the Town of Hanover*, p. 473. Cambridge (Mass.): J. W. Wilson and Son, 1891-1913.

[3] Hull, A. L., *A Historical Sketch of the University of Georgia*, p. 8. Atlanta: Foote and Davies Company, 1894.

[4] Sherwood, Sidney, *History of Higher Education in New York*, p. 53. Washington: United States Bureau of Education, 1900.

Regents were instructed to establish in each county one or more academies for boys, and others for girls; also, a public library for each county was planned. The expense was to be cared for by two lotteries, which were then the popular method of financing public instruction. The college was put into operation, but the entire scheme was abandoned in 1826.

The University of Michigan. Nowhere did this movement for a centralized system find fuller expression than in the case of Michigan. The governor and judges who constituted the first legislature passed an act, in 1817, creating the University of Michigan.[5] Power was granted the president and professors "to establish colleges, academies, schools, libraries, museums, atheneums, botanical gardens, laboratories, and other useful literary and scientific institutions consonant to the laws of the United States of America, and of Michigan, and to provide for and appoint directors, visitors, curators, librarians, instructors, and instructrixes in, among, and throughout the various counties, cities, towns, townships, or other geographical divisions of Michigan." All these subordinate teachers and officers were to be paid from the university treasury. Under its bizarre charter, the university established a number of primary schools and a college in Detroit, which was called the first college of Michigan; no less than ten branches or preparatory schools were opened by the Regents. As in Louisiana, this educational scheme was to be supported by lotteries.

French educational plans. What explanation can be offered for these peculiar developments? Why did Americans turn suddenly from the traditional church college to the secular state university—from the local and individual institutions to the centralized organization embracing all elementary schools, academies, libraries, museums, and lyceums throughout the entire state? What changed their idea as to the aims of education and broadened the curricula of the schools? There is but one explanation: the influence of French educational plans. Little importance has been attached to this development. Everyone knows how French philosophy and political ideas dominated the 18th century on both shores of the Atlantic, but few understand the spread of French

---

[5] This scheme, the most quixotic and grandiose in American educational history, may be found in full in Hinsdale, Burke A., "Notes on the History of Foreign Influence upon Education in the United States," in *Report of the United States Bureau of Education* (1897-1898), Vol. I, pp. 591-629.

educational theories and plans of school organization on this side of the water.[6]

In his *History of the University of Michigan,* Dr. B. A. Hinsdale explained its quixotic charter: [7]

> Students of educational history know very well where to find the original of the Catholepistemiad of Michigan. That original is the Imperial University that the First Napoleon gave to France in 1806—which was not, in fact, a university at all, but rather a highly centralized organization of state instruction, having its center in Paris.

French contributions to American education may be summarized as follows: (1) The term *university* came into general usage for designating institutions of higher learning. (2) The idea of state support and state control of education was accepted as a logical necessity of republican government. (3) Higher education took as it new aim the training of lawyers, judges, legislators, and civil servants for the state, rather than ministers for the church. (4) The view that secular education should replace religious training under the control of the church was adopted. (5) Instruction was everywhere to be gratuitous. (6) All the agencies necessary for the diffusion of knowledge—schools, academies, libraries, and other institutions—were to be organized into an articulate system. (7) The curriculum was more broadly conceived, taking in modern languages, and the natural and the social sciences; professional training in law, medicine, and engineering was also to become a part of university training. (8) A complete system of schools required three levels: elementary, secondary, and higher.

The importance of the final deposit from the French educational interest is difficult to estimate. Due to this influence, a number of states took the first step toward establishing universities under public control and with purely secular aims in view. These institutions, however, remained rather feeble for many decades and did not exert a very wide influence; in fact, most of them reverted eventually to the traditional college type.

---

[6] Consult Herbert B. Adams in *Thomas Jefferson and the University of Virginia;* Sidney Sherwood in *History of Higher Education in New York;* B. A. Hinsdale in "Notes on the History of Foreign Influences upon Education in the United States"; and Charles F. Thwing in *A History of Higher Education in America.* The French plan is discussed fully in the next chapter of this text.

[7] Hinsdale, Burke A., *History of the University of Michigan,* p. 10. Ann Arbor: University of Michigan Press, 1906.

A
In Adam's Fall,
We sinned all.

B
Thy life to mend,
This Book attend.

C
The Cat doth play,
And after slay.

D
A Dog will bite,
A thief at night.

E
An Eagle's flight
Is out of sight.

F
The idle Fool,
Is whipped at school.

An Alphabet of Lessons for Youth.

A WISE son maketh a glad father, but a foolish son is the grief of his mother.

BETTER is a little, with the fear of the Lord, than great treasure, and trouble therewith.

COME unto Christ, all ye who labour and are heavy laden, and he will give rest to your souls.

DO not the abominable thing which I hate, saith the Lord.

NEW ENGLAND PRIMER, PAGE 13.

COLLEGES ESTABLISHED AFTER THE REVOLUTION, TO 1799

Date	Name	State	Auspices
1782	Washington College	Maryland	Non-sectarian
1783	Dickinson College	Pennsylvania	Non-sectarian
	Hampden-Sidney College	Virginia	Presbyterian
1784	St. John's College	Maryland	Episcopal
	Cokesbury College	Maryland	Methodist
1785	College of Charleston	South Carolina	Non-sectarian
	University of Georgia	Georgia	State
1787	Franklin College (1835, Franklin and Marshall)	Pennsylvania	Non-sectarian
1789	Georgetown University	Dist. of Columbia	Jesuit
	University of North Carolina	North Carolina	State
1791	University of Vermont	Vermont	State
1793	Williams College	Massachusetts	Congregational
1794	Greeneville and Tusculum College	Tennessee	Presbyterian
	Blount College (1807, University of Tennessee)	Tennessee	State
	Bowdoin College	Maine	Non-sectarian
1795	Union College	New York	Non-sectarian
	Washington College	Tennessee	Presbyterian
1799	Transylvania University	Kentucky	Presbyterian

TEXTBOOKS

The most interesting textbook ever printed in America was the *New England Primer*, which was preceded by the English Calvinistic primer, *The Protestant Tutor. The New England Primer* was first printed between 1685 and 1690 and quickly won great popularity. It is a small book of 88 pages, 3½″ x 5″ in size. It contains the letters in Roman and italic types and in script; a number of illustrations, each of which is accompanied by a rhymed couplet; and verses taken from the Bible, each of which begins with a successive letter of the alphabet. Obviously it was an adaptation of the *Orbus Pictus* of Comenius. Included in the *Primer* is *The Westminster Shorter Catechism,* the most widely used of all epitomes of Calvinistic doctrine; and John Cotton's *Spiritual Milk for American Babes.* "Easy Syllables for Children," a list of words to be spelled; and verses, poems, and selections from the Scriptures complete the text.

Two texts in arithmetic were in early use, one by Cocker and the other by Hodder. In 1792 Isaac Greenwood, Hollis professor of mathematics at Harvard, brought out his *Arithmetic,* the first book on the subject to be written by an American. Grammars written by English authors were used. Franklin speaks of Greenwood's and Brightland's books on the subject. *Lily's Latin Grammar* was popular until the close of the 18th century; and in New England, Cheever's *Accidence* was commonly used. Cicero's *Orations* were read in schools more than any other selections from Latin literature, although Horace, Caesar, and Livy were also widely read. In the Greek, Xenophon and Homer were read, but the most popular Greek text was the New Testament.

The most famous of all 18th century American texts was Webster's *Speller* (1783), which formed the first part of his *Grammatical Institute of the English Language.* The second part was a grammar, and the third a reader. By far the most widely used grammar was that of Lindley Murray, published first in 1795. It was reprinted many times. Caleb Bingham's *Young Ladies' Accidence* (1785) was another popular grammar. The most popular American arithmetic was that of Nicholas Pike. It contained also a short introduction to trigonometry and surveying. Dilworth's *Schoolmaster's Assistant* was greatly used. Caleb Bingham published *The American Preceptor and Columbian Orator,* widely used as a reader.

Conclusion. The period of the Revolution was marked by great enthusiasm for the diffusion of knowledge.

The period witnessed significant educational achievements. Church and state were separated. The academy and the state university were established as parts of the American educational system. A real effort was made to throw off outworn practices in schools and colleges, and to make these institutions more effective agencies for promoting human welfare. Administrative machinery was transformed; schools were made responsive to the will and needs of the people; and the system of support and control of education that has since been developed in this country had its beginning. Connecticut and New York and the Federal Government laid plans for promoting schools from revenues derived from the sale of public land. Everywhere was an atmosphere of faith in republican government, and in education as one of its most effective agencies. Plans took shape slowly, and their realization required even more time; but the American people had established the foundation of a school system of a new type.

Chapter 16

THE REBIRTH AND REINSTATEMENT OF IDEALISM

KANT, THE FORE-RUNNER OF THE NEW PHILOSOPHIC IDEALISM

THE new idealism. Descartes had contended that all knowledge is innate, and Locke that no knowledge is innate but everything that any man can know comes from experience, especially sensory experiences. This flat contradiction necessitated a thorough-going restudy of the origin of knowledge, or how the mind comes to know. French thinkers were content with a superficial, materialistic rationalism hastily deduced from empiricism. The celebrated German philosopher, Immanuel Kant (1724-1804), penetrated deeper into the problem. The result of his cogitations were presented to the world in three treatises: *The Critique of Pure Reason* (1781), *The Critique of Practical Reason* (1788), and *The Critique of the Judgment* (1790). It is doubtful whether any other writings in all the history of human thinking have been so provocative and arresting as these. They called for a revolution in our conception of mind as transforming as the conception of the physical universe by Copernicus.

It is obviously impossible in a few pages to acquaint anyone with even a glimmering of the profound conclusions reached by this new sage in the far-off, insignificant University of Königsburg. He denied the Platonic-Cartesian theory that all knowledge is innate; but he did reach the conclusion that something of the greatest significance is innate. He contended that knowledge of the outer world comes only from our senses, that is, by experience of things. But he just as firmly asserted that mathematical conceptions and our sense of duty and of beauty are not the result of the functioning of our senses. All such ideas or forms of knowledge belong to the nature of the mind itself; they are *a priori*, that is, prior to sense experience.

Sensory knowledge is of phenomena. Probably Kant's most devastating conclusion was the undreamed of idea that space and time do not exist as realities outside the mind, but only as forms in which the mind thinks the things presented by the senses. Moreover, all our judgments about things and their relations to one another are made because of categories inherent in the structure of the mind. For example, we do not perceive one object causing a change in another object; all we can see is that one change follows another. The mind itself supplies the idea of causal relation. Though Kant did not deny that the senses supply the crude materials of knowledge, he did assert that the mind itself completed the process by adding factors that do not come from without. The mind is unable to know the ultimate nature of things, but only their outer appearance and how they act.

Kant held with the materialists that there is an outer physical universe which is wholly mechanistic in character. Man's body is a part of such a universe. But what the real nature of the physical universe may be we cannot know. The mind receives something through the senses but proceeds to add from its own inner constitution so much that the resultant thought of the object can have no similarity to the outer object. For illustration, objects do not have color. It is our way of sensing them that adds the color. That is to say, man's intellectual comprehension does not give him knowledge of what things are in themselves, but only how they appear to him. The mind is not able to know metaphysical realities but is limited to appearance. In experiencing an object the mind supplies so much and the senses so little that knowledge is more a product of inner than of outer causation.

The practical is reason in the moral sphere. The original purpose which Kant had in view when he began was to prove the reality of God, immortality, and freedom, which the materialists denied. But he concluded that so far as knowledge of the outer world goes, it cannot be proved that God created it, nor that man has a soul, and inasmuch as the outer world is a closed mechanism, there can be no such thing as freedom in nature.

But there is more to man than the capacity to think and reason about things. He is a creature of action and his reason makes judgments on what is good and bad, that is to say, decisions as to what should or should not be done. Reason then functions in the realm of morals; it sets up ideal values and demands that the will seek to realize these values. In other terms, it tells man what duty, or the "categorical imperative," is. Man is free in that he has choice to obey or disobey what conscience commands.

But the fact of supreme import is that man finds in his nature a perfect norm or ideal to which his acts should conform. It is part of his rational structure and not the result of experience. He is no more left to pure chance experiences to tell him what is good and what is bad than he is left to judge what a perfect circle is from the imperfect circles which his eyes have seen. Mathematical science derives from the reason and not from the senses. Similarly, duty is the ideal of conduct implanted in man's rational being and not the result of contingent or accidental experiences of the pleasant or profitable.

Man has a moral feeling that he ought to obey duty regardless of whether it is pleasant or unpleasant. His sensations and interests have nothing to do with the issue. These high conceptions of religious and moral values came to Kant as a consequence of the influence of Pietism His desire to find the truth about God, freedom, and duty, which the philosophers of the Enlightenment had denied, led him to assign a certain limitation to the speculative capacity of the mind. The intellect functioning in the realm of empirical knowledge has to do only with an outer world of changing phenomena; it cannot prove that God caused the world or that it was created in time; it does not know that man is free or that good and evil exist. So far as man's reason goes, it upholds the conclusions of the freethinker and the agnostic.

In his *Critique of the Practical Reason* Kant discloses the basis for moral and religious life. God and duty exist in man's rational nature as perfect forms, presuppositions or ideals which are implanted in his nature to guide his conduct. He is not forced to obey them; but, if he does not, he suffers consequences which make him aware that he has done something wrong. In basing the moral and religious life upon action or will, Kant assigned to will a metaphysical competency that gives it priority over the intellect. In the field of phenomena, or nature, we act on knowledge. But moral values have to do with an entirely different realm. Here action is not by intelligence but by faith. Kant humbled reason, but exalted will and personality. Faith, not sensory experience, is the true source of mental and moral illumination. We do not know God as an object of sensory experience, but if we act as if He exists, the reality of His being will become evident. Such is Kant's conclusion.

Kant accepted the existence of two entirely separate world orders, the physical and the ethical. Man exists in both. In the one mechanism rules and there is no freedom or intelligence. In the other the ethical universe, freedom and intelligence are found and these are essential for moral life.

In the moral universe or kingdom, every individual is an end in himself and never a means for another's ends. Every man is an ethical, independent personality in whom the moral struggle of the universe is fought. Kant insisted upon the maxim: "Be a person and respect all others as persons." He exalted the individual and humanity and not the state or society. Moreover, he declared that "the only good thing in the world is a good will." In taking this position he made moral responsibility depend upon the motivation of the agent more than upon the results of the deed itself.

From another angle it should be pointed out that Kant was in harmony with the contemporary movement of altruism, which swept the world during this era. This was the basis for charity education, the establishment of orphanages, Christian missions, religious toleration, the abolition of slavery, and the beginning of socialistic schemes. Kant's views exercised a profound effect upon education as well as philosophy.

SCHILLER THE FORE-RUNNER OF THE NEW EDUCATIONAL IDEALISM

Introduction. Heretofore Friedrich Schiller has never received more than passing mention in the history of education. To pick him out now for special notice requires justification, and adequate explanation for the neglect of his contributions by historians. That he exercised the decisive impact at a most crucial moment in the development of modern educational theory can be clearly shown.

Sketch of Schiller's career (1759-1805). Schiller was born of humble stock. His father wanted him to become a physician, and for a time he did study medicine, but his real interest was in literature, in which he early showed marked talent, and quickly became the best loved poet of the German people. In 1789 he accepted the professorship of history at the small University of Jena and established his home a few miles away at Weimar, the center of the most brilliant literary coterie in the world. In addition to Schiller, who was poet, historian, and philosopher; there were Goethe (one of the ten men of greatest genius of all times); Herder; Wieland; Schelling; Fichte; Hegel; Humboldt; and the Schlegel brothers.

Schiller was a devoted admirer of Shakespeare, and was well acquainted with English literature and philosophy. As a historian and dramatist, he was alert to the momentous events of that tempestuous age which saw the American Revolution and the French Enlightenment, followed by the bloody Reign of Terror. On the quieter front of literature his interest was profoundly stirred by the *Aufklärung* and, especially, the three epochal treatises of Kant.

Obviously civilization was at the crossroads with no certainty as to what should guide the future course. Some men wanted the old religion, some a new one, and the vast majority wanted none at all. Some wanted a republic based upon liberty, equality, and fraternity, some wanted absolute monarchy, while others desired the unabridged liberty of the savage. Some wanted totalitarian, practical education controlled by the state, some a religious training by the church, and the majority of the people were indifferent to all efforts to educate the young. Schiller shared Kant's profound confidence in the power of education to rescue all humanity and produce a nobler people.

In 1793 Schiller discussed the beautiful and the sublime and two years later he published *Letters on the Aesthetic Education of Man*. This was an epochal deliverance which had much to do with launching education upon the new direction taken by Pestalozzi, Herbart, Froebel, and the German humanists. The five outstanding educational problems of the day Schiller defined as follows: (1) Shall education be nationalistic and practical, controlled by the interest of the state, or shall it be private and interested in perfecting an ideal humanity? (2) Shall it be passive and receptive making human beings docile puppets, or shall it render them active and creative agents? (3) Recognizing the antithesis between sensory experience and abstract thinking, what method of instruction will bring about the transition from the one to the other? (4) How can man be raised from the level of sensory appetites to action on moral principles and sublime motives? (5) As a part of the physical universe, man's behavior is mechanically determined. How then can he be educated for freedom?

Schiller's views were the result of profound reflection called forth by the grim social, political, and economic conditions of the day. It is rare indeed that a situation so complex has been integrated so completely by any thinker. The politico-moral crisis was naturally uppermost in the mind of this historical dramatist, as he witnessed the "Age of Reason" reach its apogee in the horrors of the "Reign of Terror."

Political reconstruction and stability rest on moral character. Schiller definitely apprehended the magnitude of the revolution that was taking place in the relation of the individual to the state. "Man," he declared, "has awakened from his long lethargy and self-deception, and with impressive unanimity demands that his imperishable rights be restored to him." The state must cease suppressing individuality, for the individual has become sovereign, and in consequence the actual man must be ennobled to become the ideal man.

All improvement in the political sphere must proceed from the moral improvement of the individual; this was Schiller's basic conviction. Instead of the state being able to make a more perfect humanity, it must be based upon it. How can character be improved under the influence of a barbarous form of government which destroys the unity of manhood and prevents the full development of human personality?

As Schiller viewed the situation, contemporary society had "dissolved into its elements" and two types of manhood had emerged. One was the crude man of brute force, who gave rein to his sadistic impulses in acts of blind rage and savage vengeance. Angered by years of grinding tyranny he undertook to seize a liberty which he could not wisely employ. The other type was the sensual man who was too besotted with debauchery to care what became of himself and the world. Schiller's sympathies were wholeheartedly with downtrodden humanity, and he passionately believed in political freedom, but the state was giving its subjects only a one-sided training in order to exploit their productive capacities. Schiller felt that true liberty can rest only on the all-sided development of the individual. Here, unquestionably, is the origin of the doctrine of the harmonious development of all the powers.

The position of philosophy and religion. While human society was thus passing through one of its periods of utter despair and blind groping for light, neither philosophy nor religion had any sure guidance to offer. Dogmatic theologisms, both Protestant and Catholic, had unwisely chosen to defend both the Ptolemaic astronomy against the precision of Copernican demonstration, and the divine right of kings to exploit their subjects, and were ingloriously repudiated by men of intelligence. On the philosophical side the doctrine of innate knowledge was shattered by the empiricism of John Locke. Then came Kant with his critical examination of the competency of the human mind and his proof that God cannot be known by the intellect but is only an intuitive assumption of the ethical will. His doctrine of morality as a transcendental command that comes from the rational nature and has no relation to our ordinary life split man into two irreconcilable and unrelated levels. On the one hand is the lower, animal, or sensuous nature, which is intrigued only by things and the satisfactions they bring. On the other hand there is the rational-moral nature which commands man to do right because it is right, and not because it brings either pleasures or profit. It was the moral law, or categorical imperative, with all its sublime dignity and cold rigor against weak, pleasure-seeking human nature; it was external authority against sensuous inclination.

The supreme problem and Schiller's remedy. The supreme problem to which Schiller addressed his thinking was how to implement the rational-moral capacity and relate it to the sensuous side of human nature. Kant's philosophy had sharpened the dichotomy of the physico-sensuous versus the rational-moral to the point where all interrelation seemed impossible. Man was viewed as a creature compounded of two natures and existing in two sharply separated worlds, the material world on the one hand and the ethical-rational on the other. His body, his senses, and appetites belong to the physical world; his rationality and moral being are of the ethical world. Men generally live on the low level of the physical, which is moved mechanically by instincts. How can they be made to live on the level of spiritual freedom?

"Shall philosophy withdraw, dejected and hopeless, from this field, while brute force dominates in every direction? Must the most important of all goods be abandoned to sheer accident? Shall the conflict of blind forces continue forever in the political world and shall social law never triumph over malevolent selfishness?" Schiller asks these arresting questions, and then proceeds to state that reason cannot oppose these physical powers directly, but must find some other power to oppose them. According to his view the two levels can be reconciled only by a third that partakes of the nature of both, namely, the esthetic or the sense of beauty. He stated it this way: "If truth would wrest the victory in the strife with force, she must first become a force herself and appoint an instinct as her champion in the realm of phenomena, for instincts are the only active forces in the sensuous world." [1] Schiller proposed to use man's esthetic interest to implement his moral and spiritual capacities.

The origin of self-activity. What is the source and nature of human activity? This constitutes the central question of education and also of all social progress. The nature of activity, whether it be physical force or mental process, spontaneous emotionality or spiritual self-activity, depends upon its origin. Kant's division of the universe into the physical and the ethical-rational did not shed light on the problem. His doctrine of will did, however, bring its importance into full view and it is at this point that Schiller made his most significant contribution.

Like everyone at that time, Schiller accepted the empiricism of Locke, who asserted that the mind in sensation is purely passive and receptive, for, as a part of the physical universe, it is subject to the law of cause and effect. Man's physical movements are, therefore, the result of outer forces and are all determined. In sensation the soul is wholly receptive; something is done to and through the individual rather than by him. Moreover, sensibility causes sensuous appetites (Stofftreibe), that is to say, nature necessitates the somatic activities, but these are merely outer nature acting in and through us as a part of the physical forces of the universe. Our desires, emotions, and passions are the result of animal instincts and are mechanical and determined. Sensibility, then, offers no explanation of the origin of higher mental and moral processes, especially those resulting from ideal motives.

The basic problem is this: If the mind is passive and mechanical in sensory experience, how can it become active in art, moral conduct, and rational thinking? Reason in itself consists of empty forms which are without power to bring about action. They are like the polar star and the compass: they tell the mariner which way to go, but they have no power to make him go. Ideas, images, and principles are powerless in and of themselves. How then does man become active? How can he will to change things?

It was here that Schiller turned philosophy and education in a new direction by pointing out that the real source of activity in man is an original tendency to impose his mental forms upon matter. This emotive force Schiller called the "form drive" (Formtrieb). It is none other than a spontaneous impulsion or instinct to impose inner images upon outer

---

[1] *Schiller's Complete Works, Vol. II, Eighth Letter, On the Aesthetic Education of Man.* Tr. by Chas. J. Hempel, Philadelphia: I. Kohler, 1861.

matter, that is, "to make the inner outer." This instinct to form shows itself in two ways, in imagination and in artistic creation. Consider some illustrations. One looks at the clouds, which are in themselves quite shapeless. But the "formative impulse" of the mind imposes its own imaginary patterns upon them. Those clouds are a herd of buffalo stampeding before the driving storm. Those stars are the "Great Bear"; to some one else they are "the Dipper." That man with the princely bearing "is the angel of the Lord." That quite ordinary girl is, to the lover, the most glamorous paragon of creation, the object of ecstatic devotion. Thus our emotional states impose their imagery upon outer matter and impart to it deepened significance.

The creative imagination. Singularly gifted with creative imagination, Schiller was able to understand the psychology of this volatile function. He had a distinct advantage in the fact that he could look introspectively on his own constructive imagination at work creating projects of great dramatic interest. How marvelous it would have been if Shakespeare had possessed a power of introspection commensurate with his genius. He might have revealed how his mind worked in producing Hamlet, Lady Macbeth, and Romeo and Juliet.

In regard to the order and connections of its imagery the imagination, according to Schiller, obeys no law, but is entirely free:

> It is the interest of the creative imagination to change its objects spontaneously; the interest of the understanding is to unite its objects with strict logical necessity.... Imagination passes unfettered and without rule from one conception to another conception and seeks not to be bound by any other connection than that of time.[2]

Everyone knows how utterly bizarre is the order of his own imagery. Memory follows one pattern of association, purposive thinking follows another, and logical thinking still another. No one can assign any reason for the order of mental imagery.

Transition from the passivity of the sensibility to activity. It is the function of art through the stimulating power of beauty that causes the soul to act. Believing, as Schiller did, that the mind is passive in sense perception, and that will or creative activity is the chief function of the soul he was obliged to accept the idea that self-activity could originate only in a process that partakes of both the sensory and the rational. The inner eye of the soul sees a figure of beauty in the block

---

[2] Schiller, *"On the Necessary Limitations in the Use of Beauty of Form."*

of marble; the architect envisions a cottage nestling in the clump of trees on the hill. Or it may be that it is the idea of a bridge, or a mental image of a vase to be made or a tragedy to be written. Art changes matter to a form that it would not assume without the interposition of man's imagination and will. Thus the artistic impulse or will to form is the factor that unites inert ideals or concepts with the crude data of sensory experience.

Art, like science, is independent of momentary impulse or caprice, for it acts on principles that are fixed and eternal. The supreme function of art is to free men from thralldom to nature. "So long as man is merely percipient, he is a slave to nature; as soon as he thinks her, he becomes her law giver. So far and so long as he imposes form upon matter, he vindicates his own freedom by shaping the formless, by transforming it into an object of his own choosing." The reality of things is inherent in themselves, but the appearance of things is man's affair, and the state of mind that is nourished by appearance takes more pleasure in its own activity than in anything that it receives. The creative mind has passed from the pleasure of the senses and of possession to the much greater enjoyment that arises from creative action. To create is far more delightful to the artist than to possess.

What Schiller is telling us is that the movement of art by which inner form is voluntarily imposed upon outer matter is an instinct or inner impulsion that has its primary origin in will, that is, the mind seeking and willing order, relation, and ideals. As long as the mind is content merely to imagine such forms it remains quiescent. But to be true to itself, mind must find expression in the voluntary activities which change matter so as to make it conform to the patterns conceived by the creative imagination. According to Schiller the function of play consists of playing with beauty, that is, of artistic creation.

Theory of play. It will be hard to find a theory that has been so misinterpreted as Schiller's theory of play. That it is based upon the surplusage of energy is true, as Herbert Spencer stated, but that is the barest fringe of it. Moreover, one must not confine his idea to the play or make-believe of young children. It includes that, of course, but is far richer as a concept. By the same token, it must not be confined within the narrow range of adult recreational activities. Schiller was trying to account for the forces that have made man human and he assigns the first place to the play spirit in the creation of beauty.

> No one will ever err if he seek the ideal of beauty on the same road on which he satisfies the play impulse. . . . Reason tells us that man shall *play* only with beauty, and he *shall only play* with beauty. For to speak out once for all, man only plays when in the full meaning of the word he is a man, and he is only completely a man when he plays.[3]

By play, Schiller obviously meant the creative faculty. Manhood is fully integrated and harmonized when he expresses his inner ideals of beauty and morality in outer forms. Upon this proposition Schiller constructed his entire theory of art and education.

> Reason makes the following demand: there shall be interaction between the impulse-to-form and the material impulse—that is, there shall be a play instinct—because it is only by the unity of reality with form, of the accidental with the necessary, of the passive state with freedom, that human nature is completed.[4]

Man realizes his complete self only when he creates. In place of being overwhelmed by the welter of sensory experiences of things, he takes his experiences of things up into himself and changes them according to patterns in harmony with his rational nature. Thus by creation, beauty knits together thought and feeling in the unity of matter and spirit.

The esthetic reconciles the sensuous and the rational. Accepting the view that man is a dualistic creature, Schiller contended that it is necessary to unite the sensory and the rational by some intermediary function that partakes of the essential nature of both. He assigned this task to the esthetic impulse. He declared that:

> Man cannot pass directly from perception to thought. . . . The transition from the passive state of sense perception to activity of thought and will can take place only through an intermediate state of aesthetic liberty. In one word, there is no other way to make sensuous man rational except by first making him aesthetic. . . . Through the aesthetic frame of mind the self-activity of reason is already disclosed in the sphere of sensuousness.

Thus it is the function of esthetic activity or the creation of the beautiful that harmonizes or coördinates the lower order of sensibility with the higher, or rational, order.

Perception of form. In his pursuit of medical science Schiller must have devoted some time to the study of biology, and he came to attribute to the eye and ear a major role in the evolution of man. These distance

---

[3] *Op. cit., Fifteenth Letter, On the Aesthetic Education of Man.*
[4] *Op. cit., Fifteenth Letter.*

receptors remove the subject from immediate contact with objects: they do not give an experience of the reality of things, but only of their form or appearance. Consequently mere form and color make a much deeper impression on man's mind, and give an opportunity for greater esthetic appreciation and expression.

The effects of beauty and play with beauty. Beauty operates directly on man's emotions and through them it is enabled to affect character and personality. Reason and moral principles, that is to say, ideals, cannot directly participate in this process of organizing the personality, but must function through the emotions. Schiller recognizes that beauty arouses emotional activity, but it acts also to restrain the more violent emotions or passions. By controlling instincts it has lifted man from the coarseness and passion of savagery. Taste demands moderation, grace, and dignity; it requires good breeding. This tempering action of good taste was the basic principle of Greek culture, which Schiller passionately admired.

Schiller attributes the fact that beauty operates both to excite and relax the soul to the existence of two kinds of beauty. There is, he claimed, "an energetic beauty" (*energische Schönheit*) and also a "relaxing" or "softening beauty" (*schmelzende Schönheit*). These operate upon the sensuous and the rational nature to bring about different results. The tempering action is directed to keep the sensuous and the formal impulsions within proper limits; the *exciting*, to maintain both of them in their full force.

Beauty sublimates passion. According to Schiller man's esthetic susceptibility explains the evolution of the spirit of romance. Reverence for beauty has evolved the tender passion as well as awakened feelings of affection. The effects of the esthetic sense in refining the sex instinct Schiller described as follows:

> Delivered from the heavy fetters of passion, the eye, with calmer vision attends to the form, the soul peers into the soul, and out of a selfish exchange of pleasure comes a magnanimous interchange of affection. Passion broadens and sublimates to love, in proportion as it sees humanity dawn in its object.... The beautiful reconciles the external contrast of the two sexes in the whole complex framework of society.[5]

Feeling of the sublime. Concerned, as he primarily was, with the ordering of the emotions, Schiller regarded the sublime as the highest

---

[5] *Op. cit., Twenty-seventh Letter.*

and most spiritual of all experiences. Appreciation of beauty is partly a sensuous and partly a mental process, but the response to the sublime is the highest act of man, for it transcends the sensuous and is an act of pure spirituality.

Schiller ascribed great power to beauty, but a still more exalted power to the sublime. Both, as he pointed out, affect emotions and lead to the implementation of the higher life.

> There are two genii which nature has given us as companions throughout this life. The one, lovable and gracious, shortens the tiresome journey by his cheerful play, renders the chains of necessity light for us, and leads with joy and good humor to the most dangerous places, where we must act as pure spirits, and must lay aside all that is physical, even to the apprehension of truth and the performance of duty. Here he leaves us, for the sensory world alone is his field of action, beyond this his earthly wings cannot carry him. But at this point the other enters, grave and silent, and with strong arm bears us over the giddy deep.
>
> In the first of these genii we recognize the feeling of the beautiful, in the second the feeling of the sublime. . . . In the presence of beauty we feel free, because the sensory impulse is in harmony with the law of reason. In the presence of the sublime we feel free because sensory impulses have no influence on the jurisdiction of reason, because spirit alone is active here as though it operates under no other laws but its own. . . . Nature has herself actually used a sensuous means to teach us that we are more than sensory.[6]

The use of the sublime in education. When Schiller advocated beauty and the sublime as educational instruments, he not only went beyond most modern educational theories, but he obviously gave education a new interpretation, for he viewed it as a process of emotional development. In this he allied himself with the Athenians, who considered the Graces and Muses as the real educators of men.

Schiller urged emphatically the use of the sublime in elevating man's nature from savagery to moral liberty.

> The sublime opens to us a road to overstep the limits of the world of sense, in which the feeling of the beautiful would forever imprison us. It is not little by little, it is suddenly and by a shock that the sublime wrenches our spiritual and independent nature away from the net which feeling has spun round us. . . . One single sublime experience often suffices to break all this tissue of imposture, and at one blow gives freedom to the fettered elasticity of spiritual nature, to reveal its true destination,

[6] *Op. cit., On the Sublime.*

and to oblige it to conceive, for one instant at least the feeling of its liberty.[7]

In order to clarify Schiller's meaning one must understand something of what is meant by the sublime. This feeling comes over most people as they view for the first time some grand spectacle of nature, such as the Grand Canyon of the Colorado, Niagara Falls, a beautiful sunset, or the Northern Lights. In history it is found in contemplating the death of Socrates, the crucifixion of Jesus, and other great dramatic events. It may be said that the birth of Christianity was a series of sublime experiences. Schiller probably had in mind the celebrated statement of Kant that two things always aroused in him the feeling of the sublime, the ordered stars above and the moral law within.

The sublime finds its greatest example in the intuition of the infinite or universal. When this conception bursts upon the consciousness of the individual it stirs the most profound emotions known to man. It may come as the thought of infinite time, infinite space, or a being of infinite power. It is at once terrifying, humbling, and attracting. The individual becomes the subject of conflicting emotions; on the one hand he feels a sense of his own utter insignificance and impotency; on the other he is inspired by a sense of dignity and a desire to express his exalted vision.

Schiller's application of esthetics to personality. Schiller's theory of esthetic education was equally applicable to mankind as a whole, or to any one people or to an individual. Progress must necessarily be from the lower level of animality to the sense of personality as outer appearance and from this to the inner moral-rational. The Graces precede the Muses; or, in other terms, improvement of outer form must precede the inner organization of personality. Schiller contended that there is no other way to make a sensuous man rational or moral than by first making him esthetic. What he meant is that before becoming rational the mind must pass into a stage in which the imagination becomes active in creating new images not furnished by the senses. In other words the mind must become spontaneously creative by the exercise of the imagination. The development from the lower level of the sensuous to that of the esthetic must come first and is more difficult than the later transition from the esthetic to the rational-moral.

In art man gives form to nature and by doing so he transcends the

---

[7] *Ibid.*

laws of nature. The point of greatest moment, however, is that man learns to apply art to his own personality; he undertakes to make himself over after a pattern pictured in his imagination.

> Man is a person, therefore, a being which is the cause of himself, and indeed the absolutely final cause of his conditions; a being which can change himself according to grounds that he draws from his own being. The type of his appearance is dependent upon the type of his perceptions and volitions, therefore upon conditions which he himself determines freely.[8]

By education man determines his own destiny. Moreover, he does his utmost to make his children after a more beautiful pattern; he brings them up to act and express themselves according to forms of grace, dignity, and truth.

The way esthetics affects the moral nature. It is well again to recall that the great motive that inspired Schiller's expedition into education was to find a new basis for the political life of man; and that he believed that the very possibility of popular government rests upon the moral nature of personality. If then the rational-moral factor in man is dependent upon the esthetic, the question arises as to how the esthetic life contributes to the awakening and development of the moral nature. This Schiller believed, is accomplished by the inculcation of moral ideals or forms of beauty into the mind and heart.

In ancient Greece the poets were the early educators, and through poetry they transmitted the ideals of manhood and womanhood. An ideal is a mental picture, image, or form of personality that society selects for the individual to follow and achieve in life. It is a product of the creative imagination in harmony with esthetic sensibility. Rhythm, dancing, poetry, music, drama, and art are all involved in its production, especially in the early stages of life. It was to this original humanism of the Greeks that Schiller turned for his educational program. Poetry is the chief means for inculcating ideals, and the poet knows better than anyone how effectively his art can exercise this power.

> Poetry acts on the whole of human nature, and it is only by its general influence on the character of a man that it can influence particular acts. Poetry can be for man what love is for the hero. It can . . . form a hero in him, call him to great deeds, and arm him with a strength to be all that he ought to be. Thus the degree of aesthetic energy with which

---

[8] *Op. cit., On Grace and Dignity.*

sublime feelings and sublime acts take possession of our souls, does not rest at all on the interest of reason. But it rests on the interests of the imagination.[9]

Stages of development. Schiller indicates that there are three stages of development which the individual as well as the whole species must of necessity traverse "if they are to fulfill the circle of their destiny." These are the physical, the esthetic, and the moral. The first two can be shortened, but neither can be omitted or their order changed. By means of the esthetic experience man freed himself from the rule of nature, and imposed his forms or patterns upon the external matter. In the moral state he acquires controls of his sensuous life and imposes an ideal form upon his entire nature.

In his sketch *"Out of the History of the Individual,"* Schiller terms the three periods, the Child, the Boy, and Youth and Man.

The child is still an animal. "He is altogether passive"; his thinking is wholly on the sensory level, and he is motivated only by pleasure and pain.

> We may, then, repeat: Man needed to be an animal before he knew that he was a spirit; he needed to crawl in the dust before he ventured in a Newtonian flight through the Universe. The body, therefore, is the first spur to action; sense the first step on the ladder to perfection.[10]

In boyhood reflection begins, but only in so far as it relates to the satisfaction of animal impulses. His conduct is motivated by the amount and degree of pleasure derived from his activities, and the good things of the spirit are valued only because they are the means to a sensuous end. During childhood the individual is in harmony with himself and with nature; for nature acts in and through him. "All his being acts together as a simple unity on the sensuous level, and is a harmonious whole. The senses and reason, the receptive faculty and the spontaneous active faculty, have not as yet come into contradiction with each other." As soon as he begins to prefer form to substance and consciously foregoes reality for appearance the barriers of animal life fall, and he finds himself on a path that has no end. The exact period when the esthetic instinct or the artistic interest develops, depends entirely on the attraction that mere appearance has for the boy.

In youth and young manhood, Schiller believes, the individual loses

---

[9] Schiller, *op. cit.*
[10] Schiller, *op. cit.*, p. 423.

his unity and becomes acutely conscious of the beauty of the perfect, and, as a consequence, the conflict of his inner self with the ideal begins. There is now revealed to him "the whole worth of spiritual pleasures." For the first time he becomes aware of moral beauty and it arouses him to great activity. The desire for perfection now comes to its height. He must henceforth be a moral unity and aspire to harmony with the ideal. "At first he loved his fellows because he believed they could be of use to him; he loves them now far more—because he looks upon good will as the condition of the perfect mind." In all of his conceptions of development Schiller expressed the idea that the child recapitulates the cultural history of the species. This formed the culture epoch theory, which was widely accepted at that time as the basis of neo-Humanism.

Stripped of elaboration two sharply antagonistic systems of education bid for favor on the fundamental level. The first is the pragmatic, or practical. It is based upon the needs of the organism for food, shelter, and clothing, and, despite the denial of its advocates, it is utilitarian and industrial. It is in reality the traditional apprenticeship system streamlined and brought up to date.

The other system is historical Humanism. Its greatest expressions were the age of Pericles in Greece and the Italian Renaissance. No one in modern times has so fully caught its real spirit as Friedrich Schiller, and through him it revitalized education in the works of Pestalozzi, Herbart, and Froebel. The transition of the ideas of Pestalozzi from the practicality of Rousseau to his search for "the harmonious development of all the powers" can best be explained by studying Schiller's conceptions. As for Herbart, his ideas of "the aesthetic revelation of the world," the theory of education of taste, the culture epoch theory, and the development of sympathy were all derived from Schiller. Froebel's principles of play, creative activity, self-realization, and socialization evidently came from the same source.

SUBJECTIVE AND ABSOLUTE IDEALISM

Materialism. Heretofore thinkers had accepted the existence of a material world and a spiritual world without much reflection upon the dichotomy. But the human mind does not readily rest content with such a dualistic universe, especially as the two are obviously related in many ways. One group of thinkers assumed that everything is material and attempted to explain mind, thought, feeling, and will as the result of physical processes. They achieved an undivided world by doing violence to man's mental and spiritual nature. In fact they denied the existence of anything supernatural.

Subjective idealism. Kant's astute suggestion that in perception the object itself makes a contribution, but that the mind from its own capability makes a still more significant contribution, was a profound observation. Space, time, causation and other relations, he asserted, are not outer realities but only forms in which we experience and think things. This conception threw a new light upon a very dark problem. Fichte boldly took a further step; he denied that the object is outside the mind at all; that is to say, the mind creates the object without assistance from outside. Experience then is wholly due to the mind and not to an outer world. This is the exact opposite of the materialistic philosophy and at a stroke it wipes out the external physical universe altogether and leaves only mind, thought, or ideas. This philosophy is termed subjective idealism.

Hegel's absolute process. Behind the course of human events the moving forces are invariably ideas; men live by them, are governed by them, and strive to realize them. They are the hidden factors which make history. The most effective thinker whose ideas shaped events during the last century was a man who has been scarcely mentioned in the history of education, George William Frederick Hegel (1770-1831). He taught most of his life as a private tutor, a rector of a gymnasium, and a professor of philosophy, and was successful in all his efforts. His ideas on education were expressed in his works on philosophy and in his addresses to students and, as rector, to the public. But it was not his educational views that have given him an exalted position in education; it was rather his general philosophy.

To present a satisfactory account of Hegel's theory of the universe in a history of philosophy is difficult enough; but in a history of education, it is impossible. His system is the ultimate abstraction. His conceptions, especially along the line of law and government, were accepted as the official philosophy of Prussian bureaucracy, and finally produced modern German totalitarianism and the dialectical materialism of Karl Marx. In America his philosophy exerted a profound influence upon a few New England thinkers such as Emerson, and on education through William T. Harris. Later it helped to form the basis for the pragmatic or instrumental views of John Dewey. In view of such an array of consequences to keep silence about Hegel's philosophy is inexcusable; but to give it any fully satisfactory presentation is impossible.

Absolute idealism. After Fichte had demolished the idea of a world external to the mind it remained for Hegel to perfect the structure of a cosmic totalitarianism. He viewed the universe as one vast system of processes or ideas in eternal change, a night in which all individual objects lose their identity, an ocean in which the drops of water that compose it are ideas standing in logical relation to one another. This was an ultimate synthesis of things and ideas, God and nature, the real and the ideal, the material and the spiritual. This conception of the unity of all things in an eternal process of evolution dominated philosophic thinking during the 19th century. This is the basis for the doctrine of change or process without ultimate end that has been popularized by 20th century pragmatism. This blind, cosmic evolutionism preceded by some years Darwin's doctrine of biological evolution.

This welter of change is, however, not lawless, a chaos of unrelated ideas, for a dialectic law governs the forward movement. The steps are always from a thesis or affirmation to an antithesis, and the resultant conflict generates a movement to unite the two in a new and higher synthesis. This is primarily a psychological and logical process, but Hegel extended it to explain all processes in the universe, physical, chemical, biological, mental, and spiritual.

Things, Hegel concluded, are ideas which have not as yet become conscious of themselves. Nature is not an absolutely different kind of being from mind or idea, but is only the form ideas take before they appear in the conscious mind; that is to say, nature is mind, intelligence, mental process that is unconscious. The processes of physics and chemistry obey the same logical law of thesis, antithesis, and synthesis that is found in the movement of ideas because they, also, are mental.

Hegel was profoundly interested in law and government and this was the aspect of his philosophy which has had the most momentous consequences in the world today. In early years he became disgusted with the stupid bureaucracy of the petty German states and desired to see government established upon an orderly, rational basis. He expressed this conception in two works: *The Philosophy of Right* and *The Philosophy of History.* In these treatises he showed how the evolutionary process of the world-spirit has evolved upward through a number of stages. Its final product has been the totalitarian state which is the personification of rational order. The state embodies the overall spirit or ideal of manhood which is shared by all individuals. The sovereign with his advisors or council represents intelligence which makes laws, and the people represent the body which obeys. All work together as a totality for the good of the entire organism. Here is the dynamic ideal which constituted the formative principle of Prussia and the German Empire in their reach for world hegemony during the past century.

In its highest form the "world-spirit" shows itself in art, science, and philosophy. In these processes the universal is sought and realized. Hegel constructed an educational theory in harmony with his absolute idealism. The momentous consequences of Hegel's philosophy did not, however, result from his educational views but from his conception of the process of cosmic evolution. He explained the universe as a process of universal change according to the dialectic of thesis, antithesis, and synthesis. This conception was early adopted by Karl Marx as the course to be followed for socio-political progress by means of conflict (antithesis to existing conditions) and revolution, or the principle of dialectic materialism. It found final expression in Russian Communism.

In America where socio-political conditions were less inflamed, John Dewey interpreted the process in a less militant fashion. His theory of mind and "how we think" is based upon action, conflict, crisis, and hypothesis. It was nonetheless economic and utilitarian, for Dewey had, also, socio-political progress in view. To bring about change in an orderly way, he used the schools, where children were taught to produce and meet problems in accordance with the dialectic of utilitarian pragmatism

Chapter 17

PESTALOZZI AND THE COMMON SCHOOL MOVEMENT

FOREWORD. Those interested in debating will find a subject of unusual possibilities in the question whether Rousseau, the vagabond genius of Geneva, or Pestalozzi, the philanthropic educator of Zurich, has exerted the greater influence upon modern society. Both were dreamers moved by a deep sympathy for downtrodden men. The one influenced education profoundly through his books, but failed as a teacher; the other exerted little power through his writings, but won the world for universal public education. However, had there been no Rousseau, we probably would never have heard of Pestalozzi. The former was a model of what a teacher ought not to be; the life and character of the other form the most inspiring biography that can be studied by anyone interested in education.

No other great historical character can be said to have succeeded so remarkably and failed so miserably. Selfish impulses were seemingly left out of his nature; his altruism was unbounded. He was "All for others, nothing for himself." Such was the final eulogy of his grateful countrymen. But out of his failures, he succeeded in awakening the world, as no other was able to do, to a faith in the school as the supreme instrument for saving man from misery and prostration.

PESTALOZZI'S LIFE AND WORK

Early life and training. Johann Heinrich Pestalozzi was born in Zurich, Switzerland, in 1746, the son of a physician. His father died when Heinrich was only five, leaving the devoted mother with a slender fortune and three children, a girl and two boys. Pestalozzi wrote thus of his home training: [1]

> My mother devoted herself to the education of her three children with the most complete abnegation, foregoing everything that could have given her pleasure. In this noble sacrifice she was supported by a poor young servant whom I can never forget. On his deathbed, agonized at the thought of what the consequences of his death might be for his family that he was leaving almost penniless, he sent for her, and said: "Babeli, for the love of God and all His mercies, do not forsake my wife! Her noble, simple heart was touched, and her soul accepted the sacrifice. "If you die," she said, "I will not forsake your wife, but I will remain with her, if needs be, till death."

The rigorous economy of the home and the dominating influence of mother and nurse gave his character the peculiar bent which it retained through life. Affectionate, emotional, sensitive, and generous by nature, feminine characteristics were far stronger than the masculine in Pestalozzi's personality. Unfortunately, his mother and nurse increased these natural inclinations of the boy. They appealed to his sentiments and devotion rather than to his reason and manliness. "See," Babeli would say, "how your mother goes without everything for your sakes, and how she never leaves the house for months together, how she is saving every farthing for your education?" This appeal to his feelings and the constant examples of self-sacrifice of the mother and of Babeli left the most ineffaceable impressions upon young Heinrich's memory. Without the influence of a masculine character to counterbalance, he grew up an impractical, emotional dreamer. Yet it was the influence of his home life that gave his nature the altruistic bent which was the source of all his strivings, failures, sorrows, and equally of his imperishable success. As Niederer, his friend and helper, said: "In Pestalozzi there was as much of the woman as of the man." Puny from birth and from always living indoors, deprived of a father's influence and of contact with boys of his own age, and all outdoor games and interests, Pestalozzi remained small and weak, shy and awkward, impressionable and quixotic.

School life. The school failed to correct the one-sided influence of the home; unfortunately, it further accentuated the character he had been forming. In his relations with other pupils he developed no power of self-assertion, no discernment of character, nor the ability to under-

[1] DeGuimps, Roger, *Pestalozzi: His Life and Work,* pp. 2-3. Translated by J. Russell. New York: Appleton, 1895.

stand the actual conditions of life and to distinguish his own impracticable notions from the world of stern reality. He described how he was always the sport of his fellows: [2]

> From my childhood I have been everybody's plaything.... The day of the earthquake at Zurich [Dec. 19, 1755], when masters and boys rushed pell-mell downstairs, and nobody would venture back into the class-room, it was I who went to fetch the caps and books. But, in spite of all this there was no intimacy between my companions and myself.... And so I could not take it amiss that they dubbed me Harry Oddity of Foolborough.

Pestalozzi attended the ordinary elementary school, and later the Latin school. But he did not learn much at these institutions, and they made little impression upon him. A more powerful influence came from his experience with his grandfather, Andrew Pestalozzi, who was the pastor at Hoengg, a small village three miles from Zurich. From the time that Pestalozzi was nine years of age, he spent a portion of his summer vacations there. This gave him close contact with nature and a satisfaction which he could obtain nowhere else. More important were the impressions left on his youthful mind when he accompanied his grandfather on his daily visits to the schools and to the sick and poor of the parish. Hermann Krüsi, Jr., son of Pestalozzi's first associate at Burgdorf, says of these experiences: [3]

> In this village, where many mills were in active operation, he first witnessed the contrast between extreme wealth and abject poverty. He saw the children of the village playing before the school-house, with eyes sparkling with pleasure and innocence, contented and happy even in their rags; but when he compared them with those of more mature age, the victims of overwork and manifold vices, with hollow cheeks and sunken eyes, and with the appearance of constant misery upon their faces, his young soul was incensed against the selfishness of wealth built upon such ruins of health and happiness.

Brought thus early into contact with the suffering and degradation of the people, he experienced such deep pity for their lot that he was never to forget it.

College experiences. The higher school at Zurich consisted of two parts: the *Collegium Humanitatis,* which gave a two-year course in the

---

[2] *Ibid.,* p. 6.

[3] Krüsi, Hermann Jr., *Pestalozzi; His Life, Work and Influence,* p. 16. New York: American Book Company, 1875.

arts; and the *Collegium Carolinum,* which gave professional courses with the emphasis upon theology. Pestalozzi attended both institutions and came into contact with the many political and social currents of his time. Two members of the small faculty exerted profound influence upon the students: J. J. Breitinger, professor of Greek and Hebrew; and J. J. Bodmer, professor of history and politics. The latter made Zurich the greatest resort of literary personalities in the German world.[4] His teaching was concerned with the heroic history of Switzerland and inspired the students with a passionate love of justice and liberty. Roger DeGuimps furnishes a vivid picture of the influence of these professors: [5]

> So great was the influence of these professors on their pupils, that the latter came to despise wealth, luxury and material comfort, and cared for nothing but the pleasures of the mind and soul, and the unceasing pursuit of justice and truth. For a long time Pestalozzi and his friends slept on the bare ground, with no other covering than their clothes, and ate nothing but bread and vegetables.

J. A. Green relates that young Pestalozzi "whipped himself till he bled that he might be able to bear the pain for any punishment his ardour might bring upon him." [6]

Pestalozzi had entered upon higher instruction with but superficial preparation. There has always been a question as to his scholarship, largely attributable to his frequent references to his own defective knowledge. At the college, it would seem, he made a little progress and attained mastery of several lines of thought. On one occasion, one of his professors, who had a good knowledge of Greek but poor command of the vernacular, published a translation of some of the orations of Demosthenes. Pestalozzi himself had the boldness to translate one of these orations and to hand it in as an examination exercise. DeGuimps is the authority for the statement that this translation was deemed so excellent that the college published it. That Pestalozzi attained some degree of scholarship can be judged from his writings at this time. As a matter of fact, he never mastered orthography and grammar.

---

[4] Bodmer was one of the first to introduce German scholars to the creative spirit of English literature and thus to lay the basis for the new Humanism. In 1732 he translated Milton's *Paradise Lost.*

[5] DeGuimps, Roger, *op. cit.,* p. 10.

[6] Green, J. A., *Life and Work of Pestalozzi,* p. 22. London: University Tutorial Press, Ltd., 1913.

Pastor, lawyer, and agriculturist. Stirred in early childhood by the inexpressible misery and ineptitude of the people, Pestalozzi looked at first to the pastoral office as the vocation that offered most opportunities for ameliorating poverty and suffering. After he broke down in his trial sermon, he shifted his interest to the study of law and politics. He imagined that, by becoming a statesman, he could direct legislation and bring about a better social and political world. But here again he was quickly disillusioned. His activity as a student marked him as a dangerous radical, who could not hope to have the support of the very people he desired to help.

Several movements after the middle of the 18th century focused the interest of people generally upon agriculture. First, there was a reaction, among many of the more thoughtful, against the artificialities and evils of society. Rousseau advocated a return to the simple life of the peasant, and held up agriculture as not only the original but the noblest and happiest of all the arts. Prior to this widespread reaction, the French Physiocrats spread their theory that farming was the only industry which produces a real profit. In addition, several other ideas were at work. The growth of population and the depletion of the soil made the food supply a serious problem. However, the science of chemistry offered promise of improved crops. From all these ideas, there spread over Europe, especially in university circles, a deep interest in agriculture, and many students responded to this new enthusiasm.

Pestalozzi spent a year with a practical agriculturist, Tschiffeli, to equip himself as a farmer. With glowing hopes, he borrowed money and purchased 100 acres near the village of Birr, in Aargau. Here he constructed a comfortable home and settled down to raise madder and vegetables to sell in the city of Zurich. He christened the place Neuhof, and here, for thirty years, he took part in a slow-moving drama which caused him to drink to the very dregs the cup of bitter frustration. He consoled himself with the thought that he had to live like a beggar that he might learn how to make beggars live like men. It may be added that he was not alone in his destitution, for when he settled in Neuhof, he married a woman of much ability and a little fortune. In 1770, his first and only child was born. This event recalled him to his early dreams of doing something for the assistance of the poor.

By 1775, the experiment at Neuhof had miserably failed, and Pestalozzi lost everything except the house. Captivated by a new enthusiasm, he now turned his home into an orphanage, and this ideal, above all else, became the life-long idol of his heart. "It has been said," remarks his biographer DeGuimps, "that had this not been an act of such monstrous folly, it would have been an instance of the most sublime self-sacrifice." After several hectic years this dream faded, and Pestalozzi was again completely down and out.

Development of his educational ideas. Interest in education as the supreme means for the uplift of mankind unfolded slowly in his thinking. The first contact with this idea came in his student days when he read Rousseau's *Emile,* shortly after its publication. The birth of his son strongly revived this interest, and he decided to rear the boy according to the principles of Rousseau. In his experiment in the orphanage he had tried to unite training in gardening, farming, cotton spinning, and housework, with instruction in reading and writing. The failure of the orphanage did not weaken his confidence in the plan, and as all other hopes of realizing the noble dream seemed lost, Pestalozzi decided to give his ideas to the world in written form.

In 1782 he published *Leonard and Gertrude,* his first important book. This is a vivid portrayal of a Swiss village of the day with its drunkenness, poverty, hunger, misery, loutishness, meanness, and autocracy. In striking contrast to this dark scene is the sweetness, order, and efficiency of Gertrude, the wife of the village drunkard. In her home she trains in various domestic and industrial arts not only her own but also her neighbor's children. Moreover, she unites with these handicrafts reading, writing, arithmetic, and other studies. This simple book aroused the greatest enthusiasm as a descriptive novel. Kings and potentates read it; queens shed tears over it; and literary men hailed the new author. To Pestalozzi's utter chagrin and disappointment, no one saw it as a treatise on education. He tried to remedy the error on the part of the reading public by publishing several sequels which explained his ideas on education more definitely. But the more earnestly he made the attempt, the more dismally he failed, for readers were not interested in the reform of education.

The next years were spent in desperate poverty. About 1792 he came into contact with the youthful German philosopher, Fichte, who was destined to become the brilliant Idealist and reformer of Germany. The two men became devoted friends, with consequences of greatest importance. At his suggestion, Pestalozzi wrote his most scholarly book, *My Investigations into the Course of Nature in the Development of the*

Human Race. He always regarded this as his most important work, but the scholars of the world, and even his ardent admirers treated it with indifference. Yet, it was those three years of intensive thinking which issued in his celebrated declaration: "I want to be a schoolmaster." Under this impulse he took charge of the orphanage at Stanz, which in the few brief months of its existence became "the cradle of the modern elementary school."

What was this remarkable new insight which produced such a profound revolution in Pestalozzi's thought and drove him, when already well beyond fifty years of age, into the primary classroom? It was the conviction that the regeneration of society can be accomplished only by the slow process of raising each individual to a higher level of self-respect and sense of power. In his early plans for education Pestalozzi had placed his confidence in the learning of a trade or handicraft, and the ability to read and write. Many had staked their faith upon the diffusion of knowledge, but did not show how this was to function in the lower class of people. From all other plans of reform, Pestalozzi turned coldly away; he now pinned his faith to the possibility of improving even the lowest rank of human society by the psychological development of the capabilities of each individual. He aimed to produce in each child a deep sense of personality and dignity by making him aware of his own inherent powers.

Personality of the man. Pestalozzi was far from attractive. In physique he was small, and his countenance was ugly. His health was never good. Added to this was an absolute indifference to dress and appearance. He wore knee breeches, and his stockings were frequently down and his shoes unbuckled. His eyes were wild and roving; his manner was nervous and, in conversation, excitable. He was utterly informal and approachable, equally ready to explain his principles to a king or a peasant. Yet, with it all, there was such a spirit of goodwill and devotion to his purpose that instinctively everyone loved and trusted him.

Pestalozzi's schools. It would be a mistake to conclude that Pestalozzi had in view, when he began to teach, a complete system of new educational principles. Far from it! He knew his main purpose; and in the orphanage at Stanz and later in his schools, he gradually felt his way to a sound pedagogical practice. Out of his experiences he formed certain fundamental principles; but, in truth, he was always an experimentalist. The two chief institutions which established his fame were the institute at Burgdorf, from 1800 to 1804, and a similar one at Yverdun, from 1805 to 1825.

Yverdun, like Burgdorf, was a boarding school for boys. At its best, it enrolled from 150 to 200 pupils, ranging from 6 or 7 to 18 years of age. The majority were Swiss, but many nationalities were represented—French, German, Italian, Polish, English, and others. The prevailing languages were French and German.

Pestalozzi, his wife, and the unmarried teachers lived in the institution, and conducted it as a well-ordered family. The long rooms located in the upper story of the old chateau provided dormitories for the boys.

Pestalozzi never wavered in the conviction that the home is the ideal educational institution, the most effective medium for social experience; the foundation of all moral, political, and religious life. "Our educational machinery," he declared, "has only a value in so far as it approaches the character of a well-ordered house in all its details." A peasant who came to Pestalozzi's institution to visit his son, out of surprise exclaimed: "Why, this is not a school but a family!" Filled with delight, Pestalozzi replied: [7] "That is the greatest praise you can give me. I have succeeded, thank God, in showing the world that there must be no gulf between the home and the school."

The daily program shows how completely the life of the boys was directed. The masters slept in the same rooms with them. Half an hour was allowed for dressing. From 6 to 7 morning prayers and the first lessons took place. Then followed washing and breakfast. From 8 to 10 the lessons continued, one hour being devoted to a period. A sandwich was eaten in the five- to seven-minute interval between the class periods. From 10 to 12 o'clock further lessons followed. From 12 to 1:30 the pupils had dinner and recreation; then classes were resumed until 4:30 or 5. A short period of recreation was again given, and lessons followed until 8. From 8 to 9 o'clock evening prayers were held, and then the boys went to bed. It will be seen that the day was fully occupied. A much longer period of time was devoted to class work than is usual in schools today, between nine and ten hours daily being spent in classroom exercises.

Care was taken to avoid overworking the children. The more difficult subjects, such as arithmetic, came in the morning when the mind was

---

[7] DeGuimps, Roger, *op. cit.*, p. 210.

freshest, and the lighter—music, drawing, fencing, and manual training—in the afternoon. Special private lessons in languages and other subjects also had to come at this time. Recreation played a large part in the school life. Wednesday and Saturday afternoons were free, and quite frequently were employed in a picnic trip to some place of interest in the valley. Rigid adherence to the daily schedule was not followed. The life of the place was quite informal, simple, and variable. At times, Pestalozzi became so interested in the after-breakfast plays that he allowed them to continue until 10 o'clock. Swimming in the river which ran by the chateau was a common practice in the summertime.

The organization of the school was quite simple. Boys under eight years of age were combined in a primary class. Above this was the school proper, consisting of two groups: the lower class of boys, from 8 to 11 years of age; and the upper class, from 11 to 18.

The course of study and the time allotted to each subject weekly were as follows:

Lower Class		Upper Class	
Subject	*Hours*	*Subject*	*Hours*
Nature Study	2	Natural History	2
Description of Products of Art	2	Technology	2
Geography	2	Arithmetic	6
Knowledge of Country (walk)	2	Geometry and Drawing	4
Arithmetic (mental)	6	Language	4
Drawing	4	Singing	3
Reading and Language	6	Religion	9
Singing	3		
Religion	6		

Discipline and worship. The discipline of the school was paternal. Believing that learning must be wholly natural, Pestalozzi was opposed to coercion. In general there were neither punishments nor rewards. Rivalry and fear were not used as incentives. The masters were forbidden to punish any boy, and corporal punishment was resorted to by "Father Pestalozzi" only in extreme cases. The evening assembly hour, usually led by Pestalozzi himself, was employed in giving the boys moral and religious instruction. Questions of discipline were discussed in the assembly.

Last years. The Burgdorf institute came to an end because the old castle was needed by the town authorities for other purposes. But its end did not come any too soon, for its vital power had already declined.

Pestalozzi's new effort, at Yverdun, had its period of greatest prosperity from 1805 to 1810, when the institution attained a celebrity unparalleled in the history of education. From this time until it was finally closed in 1825, there was an increasing struggle against the forces which were tearing at its heart. The last years were full of bitterness and sorrow. It is deeply pathetic to read of Pestalozzi's final efforts to save the institution, and of attempts to begin a new institution when this had collapsed. Exhausted by an effort to answer his critics, he came to his death in 1827 at the age of 81.

PRINCIPLES OF EDUCATION

School conditions. Pestalozzi's educational reforms can best be appreciated in contrast with the existing school conditions, which for the education of the common people were incredibly bad. The church was still largely in control of the schools everywhere and exhibited no real concern for improvement. Instruction consisted of little beyond the catechism. Memorization was the only method, and teachers possessed no fitness for their task. The privileged classes looked upon the common people as cattle, and, in view of the horrors of the French Revolution, they feared to enlighten them. Moreover, it is a mistake to assume that the people, on their part, were eager for knowledge. Steeped in ignorance and superstition, they had profound suspicion and distrust of all the philanthropic efforts to ameliorate their lot. More than one noble effort at their education was thwarted by lethargy or sullen opposition.

School buildings for the lower classes were generally lacking. In the canton of Zurich some 350 schools were in existence; but less than 100 had buildings of their own, and these were unfit for their purpose. Most of the schools were conducted in private houses, an example of which is given by Morf: [8]

> As I opened the door, an oppressive feeling of dampness struck me. Packed in a dark corner our country's greatest treasure—its youth—were sitting, compelled to breathe the hot air, reeking with foul mist. The windows are never cleaned, the room is never aired. The children are so closely heaped together that it is impossible to get out without climbing over the seats and tables.

---

[8] Morf, H., *Zur Biographie Pestalozzi's*. Vol. 1, p. 18. Quoted by Green, J. A., *op. cit.*, p. 16.

The schoolroom was frequently also the family living room, where domestic duties were carried on during school hours. Similar conditions were found in most European countries.

Teachers were usually selected for reasons other than ability to instruct. No special fitness was required. Disabled soldiers were appointed by Frederick the Great. Tailors, tavern keepers, bricklayers, and other artisans were often employed. Sometimes the choice was determined by the possession of a room where the children might assemble.

The following gives a picture of conditions when Pastor Stouber visited the school.[9]

> ...He was taken to a miserable cottage where a number of children were crowded together without any occupation, and in so wild and noisy a state that he could with difficulty get a reply to his inquiries for the master. "There he is," said one of them, pointing to a withered old man who lay on a bed in one corner of the room. "Are you the schoolmaster, my good friend?" inquired Stouber. "Yes, sir." "And what do you teach the children?" "Nothing, sir." "Why, then, were you made schoolmaster?" "Why, sir, I had been taking care of the pigs for the countryside for many years, and when I got too old and feeble for that, they sent me here to take care of the children."

Aim of education. Pestalozzi's theory and practice came from his desire to change the horrible condition of the common people. They lived in indescribable degradation, more like animals than men. This was due to the feudalistic social and political situation which still survived in Switzerland. In the canton of Zurich, 5,000 citizens lorded it over 140,000 peasants who were little better than serfs. Political office, industry, production, and trade were monopolies of the few. When the revolution in Switzerland abolished these privileges and emancipated the people, agriculture and industry began to develop. But poverty, squalor, misery due to ignorance and incapacity continued. It was Pestalozzi's purpose to raise the people from this degradation to the level of humanity. It was not their poverty which hurt him; it was rather the degraded lives they led. Their shiftlessness, their feeling of frustration and hopelessness, their want of purpose, and their utter lack of human dignity stirred his soul to its depths. This deplorable situation, he firmly believed, could be cured by properly devised measures. "Ah!" he said,[10] "ever since my

[9] Green, J. A., *op. cit.*, pp. 16-17.

[10] Pestalozzi, J. H., *How Gertrude Teaches Her Children*, p. 9. All quotations from *How Gertrude Teaches Her Children* are from the translation by L. E. Holland and F. C. Turner. Syracuse: C. W. Bardeen, 1894.

youth, has my heart moved on like a mighty stream, alone and lonely, towards my one sole end—to stop the sources of the misery in which I saw the people around me sunk!" And again [11] "Long years I lived surrounded by more than fifty beggar children. In poverty I shared my bread with them. I lived like a beggar in order to learn how to make beggars live like men."

After the Swiss revolution (1799), which liberated the downtrodden class, Pestalozzi came to feel more deeply than ever that a better education for every individual was the only means of conserving the advantages gained by the political change. The winning of political, social, and economic rights meant little unless accompanied by the development of their capacities to profit by and utilize their liberties. The right to individual development must be prior to any other right whatsoever. Without the development of a child's capacities, all other rights are useless and a mockery.

There were abundant plans for ameliorating the desperate plight of humanity in those hectic days. Some advocated a new religion; some, old religions; and some, no religion at all. Some advocated new forms of government; others a new social order and new economic conditions. In the snarled web of conflicting ideologies, Pestalozzi seized upon several fundamental principles, on which his reforms were based:

(1) First, all genuine reform must begin with the individual and not with society. On this point he said: [12]

> Those who wish to make the community virtuous and strong, before virtue and strength are developed in the individual, may frequently lead the State into wrong action, because they try to fix the external forms of virtue and strength upon men without making sure that the essence of the thing is theirs.

The elevation of every individual is the only certain means of elevating the whole. The reform of social organizations, governments, economic conditions, and the church is futile unless the individual is developed so that he can use these institutions to advantage. This principle was the ripened fruitage of the movement which had been in progress since the Reformation—the growing sense of the dignity and importance of the ethical worth of every man.

(2) Second, the individual can be elevated only by putting into his

[11] *Ibid.*, p. 213.
[12] Green, J. A., *op. cit.*, pp. 141-142.

grasp the power of helping himself. Philanthropy renders him dependent and weak, and robs him of self-respect, which is the dearest possession of human life. The greatest service that society can render to an individual is to teach him, first, to respect himself, and second, to help himself.

(3) Third, the only means of attaining the end desired is through the process of development. The seeds of independent action latent in every child are merely awaiting an opportunity to grow. Education must furnish the opportunity for this growth.

The ultimate aim of education, Pestalozzi believed, was to insure a happier and more virtuous life for every individual. The process by which he hoped to bring about this desired end is the harmonious development of all the powers of the individual. Education is the only effective philanthropy, the first of all the human rights. For this reason, Pestalozzi chose education as the means for social reform.

Organic development. If one seeks the inner secret of Pestalozzi's general theory of education, he will come closest to it in the idea of organic development. The child is an organism that unfolds according to definite, orderly laws. This conception was inherent in the idea of man as a human plant, popularized by La Mettrie and others. But Pestalozzi gave the idea a new and fuller significance. He never wearied of using this interesting analogy: [13]

> In his speeches, in his explanations of his views, and especially in his fables, he is constantly comparing the education of man, even from the intellectual and moral point of view, to the development and growth of a plant. It is evident that in his eyes the analogy is complete. He even states it once in these words: "Man, formed from the dust of the earth, grows and ripens like a plant rooted in the soil."

It was Pestalozzi's main purpose to discover the laws according to which the child develops. These laws, he believed, are as definite as the laws of the physical world.

Pestalozzi held that the organism has three basic aspects. First, there is the intellectual side, which results from man's relation to his surroundings, for the environment determines "the kind of sense impressions" he experiences. Second, there is the physical side, especially that aspect of it which expresses itself in motor activities. These activities, as Pestalozzi viewed them, arise from within and are the result of man's

[13] DeGuimps, Roger, *op. cit.*, p. 123.

inner wants. Third, there is the moral-religious side, which may best be termed the ethical. This aspect has its basis in the relations with other human beings and with God. These three aspects are popularly named "the head," "the hand," and "the heart." Each develops in its own characteristic way and according to ascertainable laws. To find these laws and to utilize them in the training and instruction of the child are the tasks of education.

From this conception of organic development, Pestalozzi deduces certain general principles of method that are to be observed in the processes of training and instruction.

(1) **Development must be harmonious.** The three aspects—intellectual, ethical, and executive or constructive—normally function together, and must be developed in unison. "Only that is truly and naturally educative which appeals to the whole of our being, heart, head, and hand together." Human nature is a unity, and each capacity is an essential part of the unity. Pestalozzi insisted emphatically on this point of view.[14] "To consider any one capacity exclusively [head or heart or hand] is to undermine and destroy man's native equilibrium."

Whenever any one of the three elements of human nature does not receive proper emphasis, the unity of the organism is disrupted and the individual is unable to live a completely normal life, and to adjust himself to civilization. Pestalozzi was keenly alive to this danger, and blamed it for the supreme weaknesses of the age.[15]

> I cannot leave these gaps untouched. Perhaps the most fearful gift that a fiendish spirit has made to this age is *knowledge without power of doing and insight without that power of execution or of overcoming* that makes it possible and easy for our life to be in harmony with our inmost nature. Man! needing much and desiring all, thou must to satisfy thy wants and wishes, *know* and *think,* but for this thou must also (and can) *do*. Knowing and doing are so closely connected that if one cease the other ceases with it.

Head, heart, and hand are different organs; yet they must function in harmony. In his early writings and practice, Pestalozzi emphasized the executive side. After more reflection, he came to see that mere train-

---

[14] Pestalozzi, J. H., *The Swan Song*. Edited by J. A. Green, in *Pestalozzi's Educational Writings,* pp. 268-269. London: Edward Arnold, 1916. All *Swan Song* quotations used in this chapter are from this edition.

[15] Pestalozzi, J. H., *How Gertrude Teaches Her Children,* p. 173.

ing in "doing" will be ineffective unless the other sides of life are also developed. An individual trained only to produce, no matter how expertly, will become a mere mechanical creature.

The three constituents of human nature do not stand on exactly the same level of importance. They are all essential, but one must have priority. In this, Pestalozzi agreed with the views of Immanuel Kant and Friedrich Schiller. In accordance with Kant's doctrines Pestalozzi held that the ethical life of man must have primacy, and the physico-motor and the intellectual are subordinate. The human being must develop to the fullest extent his intellectual capabilities; but this is not an end in itself. Similarly, man must acquire skill in applying knowledge; he must engage in constructive activities; he must learn to produce. But this also is not an end in itself. The supreme end is the realization of a complete personality that lives in harmonious relations with other personalities and with the Supreme Being. It is the business of the moral and religious life to correlate and unify the other powers of the organism with itself.

(2) General education must precede the vocational. In his earlier views, Pestalozzi sought the beginning of education in the utilitarian activities which center in the home, in agriculture, and in industry. Later, he receded from this position and concluded that education of a general character must precede the acquiring of specific skill. Human nature needs to be uplifted and ennobled by the development of its fundamental capacities for thought and moral behavior, before the individual is trained for a specific vocation.[16] "The development of mind and heart precedes any particular branch of industry; that is to say, we need first of all a general education of head, heart, and hand." That general education must precede the vocational was one of the chief principles of Rousseau; not until Pestalozzi became acquainted with the ethical conception of Kant and the new Humanism of Schiller did this idea fully dawn upon him.

In his institutions Pestalozzi endeavored to work out a system of general intellectual instruction, while his earlier emphasis upon industrial and domestic activities no longer received attention. It is obvious, however, that he was never entirely satisfied with his results; he was always conscious that constructive activity was not receiving the attention it

---

[16] Green, J. A., *op. cit.*, pp. 352-353. Whether Pestalozzi learned of Schiller's views of aesthetic education directly, or indirectly through Fichte we do not know. Nevertheless, there are so many points of similarity that the presumption is that he was influenced in his thinking by the German poet.

deserved. As a consequence he kept looking for an opportunity to promote the constructive aspect of child nature.

(3) **The increase of power is most essential.** Education by organic development placed the emphasis upon the growth of power rather than on the acquisition of knowledge. Pestalozzi was in full agreement with this view. It was not so much that he minimized the value of knowledge, but rather he saw that to force knowledge upon the mind is unnatural and injurious. He fought with all his might against the old education, which furnished the child with the finished judgments of others' thinking. He explained: [17]

> It is a principle of ours that the teacher should aim rather at increasing the powers of his pupil than at increasing his knowledge.... Even to know what is right and what is best, unless it is combined with the will and capacity to act accordingly, can be only a source of weakness; it is in fact rather a hindrance than a help. Learning in youth should always be a spontaneous process, a result of free activity, a living and original product.

The traditional process of teaching had a detrimental effect upon the child. It gave the appearance of culture and knowledge without the reality. But far more injurious even than this false and egotistic sophistication was the fact that the real powers of the child were left undeveloped because they had never been called into function. How can he acquire the ability to form sound judgments when he has never been made to judge for himself? Pestalozzi said: [18]

> I was wholly against making the judgment of children upon any subject, *apparently ripe before the time,* but rather would hold it back as long as possible, until they had really seen with their own eyes, the object on which they should express themselves.

(4) **The child's powers burgeon from within.** The powers of the child burgeon spontaneously from within, because of the awakening of innate impulses; they are not the product of outer environment, as the materialists would have us believe. Once awakened the innate powers strive to unfold to maturity, as naturally as the acorn grows into an oak.

By laying bare to inspection the fundamental course of unfolding in each aspect of child nature, the educator secures a blue print to guide him in his methods. Development must be spontaneous and free, and "all

---

[17] *Ibid.,* pp. 348-349.

[18] Pestalozzi, J. H., *How Gertrude Teaches Her Children,* p. 48.

educative instruction must be drawn out of the children themselves, and be born within them."[19] All efforts to force the child, before his own powers are ready to develop are injurious. In his practice Pestalozzi did not rely upon punishment, rewards, fear, or rivalry. All these are external incentives.

(5) **Grading an essential principle.** Grading has its basis in the manner in which all development takes place. Nature makes no sudden leaps; she slowly unfolds, by scarcely perceptible additions, whatever is to be produced. The significance of this for education was strongly emphasized by Pestalozzi in several points of view. Instruction must be graded, "according to the degree of the growing power of the child," so as to fit his needs.[20]

> In all matters of instruction, it is necessary to determine, with the greatest accuracy, which of those constituents is fit for each age of the child, in order, on the one hand, not to hold him back if he is ready, and on the other, not to load him and confuse him with anything for which he is not quite ready.

Gradation involves arranging the subject matter in a series of transitional steps from the easiest to the most difficult; that is to say, the demands on the child shall be commensurate with his ability to achieve.[21]

> Try to make in every act, graduated steps of knowledge, in which each new idea is only a small, scarcely perceptible addition to that which is already known. . . . Everything which the child has to learn must be proportioned to his strength, getting more complicated and difficult in the same degree as his powers of attention, of judgment and thought increase.

Gradation involves mastery. As each step depends on the one that preceded it, each step must be well mastered before the next is taken. This procedure insures accuracy and thoroughness. In accordance with this demand, repetition and drill played a large rôle in Pestalozzi's practice. He endeavored to treat each subject in orderly sequence so that the child would readily master each step and thus acquire real power. The grading of the school followed as a consequence of the grading of subject matter. Although grading had been worked out in the secondary schools, it had been wholly neglected in the common school.

---

[19] *Ibid.*, p. 17.
[20] *Ibid.*, p. 26.
[21] Green, J. A., *op. cit.*, pp. 174-175.

(6) In method, follow the order of nature. The method of all education may be summed up in one simple rule: Follow nature. The teacher is a gardener who provides the conditions necessary for the growing plant. Reflecting upon the question: "What is the true type of education?" he answered: [22]

> It is like the art of the gardener under whose care a thousand trees blossom and grow. He contributes nothing to their actual growth; the principle of growth lies in the trees themselves. He plants and waters, but God gives the increase.... So with the educator: he imparts no single power to men. He only watches lest any external force should injure or disturb. He takes care that development runs its course in accordance with its own law.

Pestalozzi believed that nature has provided birds and animals with an instinct for the training of their young. Just as birds teach their young to fly and sing so nature prompts parents to act in certain ways for the education of their offspring. Pestalozzi would have parents become conscious of these natural promptings by taking them out of the hands of blind nature, and would see to it that the acts to which they lead are consciously and purposely performed. All instruction is, then, only the scientific art of helping nature to unfold in its own way.

Pestalozzi was confident he had discovered the right principles and method of elementary intellectual instruction. Deeper than most of his other cravings was his desire to put into the hands of illiterate mothers a method for developing their infants' powers of sense perception, constructive activities and social and moral life. The *Book for Mothers,* which he hastily endorsed, did not satisfy him. A mechanically perfect and simple method was left for others to attempt, but it always remained one of Pestalozzi's fondest dreams.

INTELLECTUAL DEVELOPMENT AND INSTRUCTION

By the irony of Pestalozzi's fate, he accomplished most in the field of intellectual education, although he was more profoundly concerned about the practical and moral. He labored to discover the roots in all these fields; yet, it was the emphasis upon sense perception which created most stir in the world. Of this he wrote: [23] "Sense impression of Nature

---

[22] Green, J. A., *Pestalozzi's Educational Writings,* p. 195. London: Edward Arnold, 1912.

[23] Pestalozzi, J. H., *How Gertrude Teaches Her Children,* p. 200.

is the only foundation of human instruction, because it is the only true foundation of human knowledge." Summarizing his achievements, he declared: [24]

> When I now look back and ask myself: What have I specially done for the very being of education? I find I have fixed the highest, supreme principle of instruction in the recognition of *sense-impression as the absolute foundation of all knowledge.*

The scholarly world agreed with this appraisal of his contributions so far as the principles of method were concerned. It has also recognized that this was no new doctrine. Quite the contrary! What, then, was the reason that such special credit should be given to Pestalozzi for introducing this principle?

The reason lies partly in the new insight with which he invested the idea, and partly in the practical method he employed. Comenius and Basedow relied to a large extent upon pictures of objects. Pestalozzi saw that, for the beginnings of experience, objects are indispensable and must precede pictures. The picture comes later, and performs the function of assisting the child in making the transition to drawing, writing, and reading. But if the first experiences are to be adequate, the senses must come into contact with the objects themselves.

A more important reason lies in Pestalozzi's insight that sense experience is an active process. The mind is not passive or merely receptive, as Locke declared. The whole mind is implicated in sense experience. The fact that every object which is perceived is at once placed in an ordered world of space and time indicates that perception is a mental process. Moreover, when the child begins to discriminate, analyze, and abstract the qualities of objects, the mind is especially active. By this new interpretation, Pestalozzi showed that inner, active forces are related to the functioning of the sense organs. The child does not wait passively for the objects of nature to impress him; on the contrary, his inner being pushes out to greet, conquer, use, and put into order the world of sensory experiences.

Again, the relation of perception to conception had to be made clear before the function of sense perception in education could be made definite and practical. The penetrating insight of Immanuel Kant was necessary before the relation of perception to conception was fully under-

---

[24] *Ibid.*, p. 139.

stood. His analysis of the intellectual faculty showed that "percepts without concepts are blind, and concepts without percepts are empty." It was this insight which led Pestalozzi to discover the chief weaknesses of modern education. The traditional method of teaching and learning had taught children words, on the assumption that they were acquiring concepts or ideas. But lacking the necessary sensory experiences, children attached no precise meanings to the words. Pestalozzi knew that only by beginning with objects could the child build up clear concepts. Hence, he concluded that the art of early instruction lies in the selection of the right objects for the active observation and analysis of the mind of the child. To accomplish this, Pestalozzi developed his system of object lessons.

Beginnings of the curriculum. Pestalozzi attached the greatest importance to right beginnings. For this reason he sought most diligently the starting points of all instruction and these he found in the perception of objects by the senses. Clear perception and discrimination of objects through touch and vision lead the mind naturally to the sense of number. Again, from the form of objects, the mind learns measurement; and from measuring, it develops drawing and geometry. Moreover, drawing is the natural antecedent to writing. Through the sense of hearing, the child recognizes sound, from which music and language are derived. The linking up of language with objects, that is to say, the integration of visual perception with the word or name, has a profound effect for awakening the intellectual life. The beginnings of all instruction are found in form, number, and words. Of this, Pestalozzi wrote: [25]

> *Number, form,* and *language* are, together, the elementary means of instruction, because the whole sum of the external properties of any object is comprised in its outline and its number, and is brought home to my consciousness through language.

Accordingly, Pestalozzi spent much time in training children to observe, analyze, count, and name objects.

From the three starting points just mentioned, Pestalozzi derived his curriculum for intellectual development. It included object lessons, which were always accompanied with training in language; for perception and word form an integrated whole. Arithmetic, both written and mental, was of the highest importance, for this study insures clear and accurate

---

[25] *Ibid.*, p. 87.

thinking. Object lessons led to the study of nature generally, and included in this was geography. In another direction, sense observation led to the study of the products of man's own making, to objects of manufacture and art. The study of form brought about drawing, interest in color, modeling, and geometry. Vocalization is the origin of language; and this must always be connected with sense observation and intellectual activity. Music, especially singing, was considered a form of language.

It will be noted that Pestalozzi emphasized the mathematical and realistic aspects of the curriculum. Language was stressed as a means of communication and of thought, but not as a fine art. The objects of nature and science were uppermost in his evaluation. Religion, morals, manual production, plays, and gymnastics received attention, but they were not considered forms of intellectual development.

In disregarding Mother Goose, fairy tale, story, history, and literature, Pestalozzi exposed two grave weaknesses in his efforts to construct a system of education. First, he had evidently not observed the intensity of the children's interest in these forms of activity. Surely he did not appreciate that the mind of the child stands as much in need of mental play as his body does of physical play. Again, dominated by his principle of direct sense impressions, he failed to understand the function of imagination in developing conceptual thinking.

Pestalozzi agreed with Rousseau in the outright rejection of history, though not for the same reason. He contended that the facts of history are too remote from living experience.[26]

> It is utter nonsense that men who have no living acquaintance with the world as it stands before their eyes, should wish to be made acquainted with the spirit of a by-gone world, removed from the world of today by hundreds and even thousands of years.

Obviously Pestalozzi did not fully appreciate that man is essentially an historical and social creature. It has not been outer nature alone that has made him human, but also the millenniums of social intercourse, and the interaction of human beings throughout a million years.

Principles of intellectual instruction. Several principles of special application to mental development were recognized. The first of these is that one must proceed from the known to the unknown. When once

---

[26] Quoted by Green, J. A., *op. cit.*, p. 182.

stated, this idea appears so self-evident that it seems incredible that anyone should ever have pursued the opposite course. And yet, absurd as it certainly was, much of the instruction of children before this time attempted, as someone has remarked, "to teach the unknown by means of the incomprehensible." A most flagrant example of this was the practice of teaching children to recite Latin or the catechism before giving them the meaning of the words. Against all such instruction Pestalozzi vehemently protested.

Another principle which Pestalozzi recognized is that instruction must proceed from the concrete to the abstract, or from the particular to the general. This principle formed the central theme of all his ideas on intellectual culture. The practice of teaching words before the child has a direct experience of the things they designate, he looked upon as a terrible mistake—a mistake which was to blame for most of the evils of the time. Clearly, however, as he recognized this principle, he did not show how the process should be carried to its completion. His absorption in the art of sense impression kept him from explaining how the mind develops the power of abstract thinking.

Logical and psychological order of subject matter. In the attempt to follow out these principles in actual instruction, Pestalozzi encountered a subtle difficulty which never ceased to baffle his thought. The lack of psychological knowledge, together with his inability to express his ideas clearly, greatly misled him. He never perceived the distinction between the logical and the psychological order of subject matter. It was largely this failure to discriminate between these two methods of approach which made him constantly declare that "the art of instruction" depends "on the existence of physico-mechanical laws." It was this confusion, which made him say that he would "mechanize instruction." His methods never got away from this grievous error.

It is recognized today that instruction may adopt and follow out one of two divergent lines of procedure. These have been called the *psychological* and the *logical* order of subject matter. They may be readily illustrated by language and drawing.

Yielding to his passion to search for the beginnings of every subject, Pestalozzi recognized vowel sounds as the simplest elements of language. By sounding vowels and consonants together syllables are formed, and words constituted. In consequence he had the children repeat meaningless syllables interminably. He was not aware that the psychological origin of language was the complete word or expression, which has meaning attached to it. The development of language results, not from the practice of nonsense syllables, but from the use of words which express ideas.[27]

Drawing furnishes another example. Pestalozzi traced all form to its component elements, which are points, lines, angles, and curves. He required his pupils to practice the drawing of lines and angles in a systematic, but tiresome, way until they could draw them perfectly. They were then gradually led along until they could construct highly complex and intricate figures. However, the truth of the matter is that the psychologically simple for the child is never a straight line, which, in fact, he is incapable of drawing. The first drawing is always a formless scribbling, which is more an emotional expression than an idea or object.

Methods in the common school branches. Much of Pestalozzi's great influence was due to the changes he introduced in the common school branches. Especially in arithmetic, drawing, geography, singing, and language did he arouse intense interest by the application of his principles.

Reform in teaching arithmetic. The teaching of arithmetic had not been readjusted after the adoption of the Arabic notation. Numeration was rendered more difficult, though the understanding of arithmetical processes was greatly facilitated. The chief difficulty arose in teaching the new symbols to young children. The Roman notation was closer to the primitive practice of counting the fingers on one's hand, or the counters of the abacus, and was accordingly easier for the child to grasp. The Arabic symbolism was somewhat strange and, being farther removed from concrete experience, was less directly suggestive of its significance. As a result, the understanding of simple numbers by the young was poorer in the 18th century than in the 14th. As Dr. David Eugene Smith explains: [28]

> The effect on the teaching of arithmetic was not fortunate in one respect, since the giving up of the counters led from the concrete, visual, palpable arithmetic to the abstract arithmetic of figures. Counting and reckoning came to be more matters of words and abstract rules than before, and arithmetic was probably more poorly taught than it was under the abacus system.

---

[27] The infant's play in making sounds when he is just learning to talk is quite a different matter.

[28] Smith, David Eugene, "Arithmetic," in Monroe, Paul, *Cyclopedia of Education,* Vol. I, p. 205. New York: Macmillan, 1913.

The real trouble lay in the practice of ignorant teachers who presented the meaningless symbols to young children and blandly assumed that their pupils understood their significance. It was this stupid practice which excited the bitter protest of Pestalozzi, and led him to bridge the gap from concrete object to numeration. When once the child has clearly grasped the significance of the symbol, he can readily make progress in the fundamental operations. Pestalozzi elaborated his method of teaching arithmetic by graded steps of progress that accorded naturally with his principles of instruction. He began with the concrete, insisted upon clear insight into every step, and fixed each step indelibly in memory by repetition and drill. Prior to Pestalozzi's reform, arithmetic was not taught to children before they were ten years old. His method enabled him to teach it successfully in the first grade, where it has been taught ever since.

Arithmetic was given the position of preëminence in his curriculum because Pestalozzi believed it the most effective means for the development of accurate thinking. Modern education followed him in this practice and viewpoint. In order to insure proper understanding at every step, Pestalozzi required all operations to be done mentally. This practice led to a new emphasis upon mental arithmetic.

Geography. This is another subject in which Pestalozzi introduced innovations, which were widely accepted. He boldly dispensed with the aid of charts, maps, and textbooks, and began with nature itself. One of his pupils has given a graphic account of his method: [29]

> For the first elements of geography we were taken into the open air. They began by turning our steps to an out-of-the-way valley near Yverdun, through which the Bûron flows. This valley we had to look at as a whole and in its different parts, until we had a correct and complete impression of it. Then we were told, each one, to dig out a certain quantity of clay, which was embedded in layers on one side of the valley, and with this we filled large sheets of paper, brought with us for the purpose.
>
> When we got to school, we were placed at large tables which were divided up, and each child had to build with the clay, on the spot assigned to him, a model of the valley where we had just made our observations. ... Then, and then only, did we turn to the map, which we had only now gained the power of correctly interpreting.

By insisting on this concrete approach, Pestalozzi made geography an arresting subject of elementary education. It may be stated that the

---

[29] Quotation from Vulliemin; in Green, J. A., *op. cit.*, p. 367.

celebrated geographer Karl Ritter held Pestalozzi in the greatest veneration.

Drawing. Pestalozzi's interest in drawing grew out of his doctrine of sense impression as the foundation of all instruction. He was the first in modern times to accord this subject a regular place among the skills which form the elementary curriculum. As he viewed it, drawing is connected with the perception of form and, therefore, trains the child in accuracy of observation. It thus lays the foundation for clearness and precision of thought. In the experience of the child, making pictures or outlines of objects is the first attempt at linear symbolization. Hence, drawing is the natural approach to writing.

So far as method of teaching drawing is concerned, Pestalozzi did not contribute much of permanent value. The fact is that he could not draw. As a consequence, he was obliged to rely on his assistants to carry out his instructions, which were not always successful. For drawing, he attempted to form "an alphabet" by copying lines, angles, and curves. These the children were required to practice, with interminable repetition, until they had acquired thoroughgoing skill. Then, in accordance with his principle of "unbroken continuity and scarcely perceptible advance," they gradually drew more complex figures. The free drawing of objects was rigidly excluded. That Pestalozzi should have sanctioned such a stupid, unnatural, and deadening procedure is strange; yet it appeared to harmonize with his principles, and with his desire to "mechanize instruction."

Language. It was logical for Pestalozzi to prefer modern languages to the ancient, because the ideas expressed are nearer to the experiences of the child. His own institutions, by necessity, had to be bilingual, using both French and German.

Many before him had pointed out the danger of teaching the child words dissociated from content. This has been the most grievous error of the traditional schools, and it was roundly condemned by Pestalozzi as follows: [30]

> Whenever we put empty words into a child's mind, and impress them upon his memory, as if they were real knowledge, or genuine means of acquiring it, even when neither his feelings nor his experience of things are in a position to furnish clues to their meaning, we are obviously deviating from the principle, "Life Teaches." We are sowing the seeds

[30] Pestalozzi, J. H., *The Swan Song,* p. 293.

> of an artificial use of the Divine gift of speech. We are sowing the seeds of callous insincerity and shallowness to which is due so much of the blundering arrogance which is characteristic of our time.

Symbols must not precede the objects they signify, nor must words precede things. Similarly, memorizing definitions without the mental activities which formulate the definitions is not only meaningless, but positively harmful. Mere book knowledge is an actual hindrance to the development of the mind.

All this had become clearer after Locke explained the relations of ideas and words. Pestalozzi, however, was the first to recognize the real function of language in the development of the mind by associating the sense image with the name of the object. This practice, of integration of language with perceptive processes, at once fixes and clarifies ideas. Pestalozzi boasted that his method made "greater use of language as a means of raising the child from vague sense-impression to clear ideas" than had ever been attempted before. He trained elementary teachers and pupils to talk in familiar terms about objects in the school, the home, and nature. These informal discussions were designed to give children positive skill in the expression of ideas.

In correlating language with perception of objects, Pestalozzi made a basic advance, but he erred in that he considered this the only way in which the child could learn the use of language. He said: [31] "The natural progress in learning his mother tongue, and the educational advantages thereof, are limited by his sensory acquaintance with the things about him." Pestalozzi became so deeply absorbed in the beginnings of education, and consequently so restricted in his vision, that he could not see how advanced instruction might proceed with little or no direct contact with things. He considered knowledge of nature the center of the course of studies for intellectual growth. He did not understand that social life played a larger role than did external nature in man's evolution upward from the primitive level. It was this lack of insight that caused him to undervalue play, fairy tales, story, history, and literature as means for the cultivation of language.

Music. Like language, music springs from the perception of sound. Pestalozzi did not himself work out the method of singing, but permitted others to do so in accordance with his principles. The lessons began with

---

[31] *Ibid.*, p. 293.

the observation of tone, and proceeded to the relation of time and melody. Notation followed. In his institutions he made much of music and wished to see it developed by gradual steps from "the nursery lullabies to a series of national songs, that should rise in the cottages of the people, from the gentle cradle song to the sublime hymn of praise." [32] His followers who worked out the system had remarkable success, and the Pestalozzian method became popular in both Europe and America.

DEVELOPMENT OF PRACTICAL POWER

Productive efficiency. Pestalozzi believed the causes of the misery of the people lay in their lack of competence to do things. This incapacity was due to the impractical training that they received in home and school. His "pet scheme," he said, was "that of a school for poor boys" which would train them in various industries. To the end of his days his mind always reverted to this central dream. The riper insight of middle life and his own practical experience brought him to see that mere trade training of itself would not be sufficient to lift up shiftless humanity. The real disease of human incapacity was too deeply seated to be eradicated by giving men a certain degree of technical skill. A deeper need must first be met. The individual must become a self-respecting, intelligent, social unit. He must possess a conscious sense of morale arising from efficient participation in communal life. Pestalozzi saw what later educational experience has confirmed, that the development of the lower classes can be brought about only when they have opportunity to speak the language and to know the thoughts of cultured life. Such training is even more essential than industrial efficiency. For this reason Pestalozzi turned his attention to general education of the masses.

Strange to say, no English term has been found which expresses what Pestalozzi meant by *Fertigkeit.* "Motor activity," "practical power," "productivity," "industrial training," "creative activity," and other words have been used, but none of these has found general acceptance. *Fertigkeit* means skill, readiness, or capacity for production. What Pestalozzi had in view was that knowledge is developed in and by means of the common activities of life. "One learns to do and know by doing." This insight came to him in his experience at Stanz: [33]

---

[32] Pestalozzi, J. H., *How Gertrude Teaches Her Children,* p. 204.

[33] DeGuimps, Roger, *op. cit.,* p. 151. See quotation on page 444.

I knew how useful the common needs of life are in teaching man the relations of things, in bringing out their natural intelligence, in forming their judgment, and in arousing faculties which, buried, as it were, beneath the coarser elements of their nature, cannot become active and useful till they are set free. It was my object then to arouse these faculties, and bring them to bear on the pure and simple circumstances of domestic life, for I was convinced that in this way I should be able to form the hearts and minds of children almost as I wished.

Pestalozzi desired to work out a system of lessons for the development of practical power in the child. He would begin with the earliest movements of arms and hands, and gradually advance to constructive activities. The mind and the bodily activities would be associated with felt needs. The opportunity never came to construct such a system. However, his disciples, Fellenberg and Froebel, evolved this aspect of his pedagogy.

THEORY OF MORAL AND RELIGIOUS DEVELOPMENT

The social. The third constituent of the organism recognized by Pestalozzi is the moral-religious. The development of this important side, he explained, is "the Keystone of my whole system." This aspect he called "the heart," by which he meant especially those emotions which have to do with the will and the social life, in other words, the relations of the individual to other persons. In spite of the peculiarity of his ideas and the fervent language in which they are expressed, Pestalozzi has given the world a plausible view of the origin of these most significant human capacities. Unfortunately for education, the development of ethical life from the standpoint of personal relationships did not receive the attention it deserves.

In formulating his view of the process of moral-religious education, Pestalozzi proceeded just as in the case of the intellectual and practical powers: he sought the beginnings in experience. These elements are the instinctive feelings which arise in the infant because of his relation to his mother. At birth the human is the most helpless of all creatures. This helplessness and its prolongation over many years create the qualities which are distinctively human. From his close relation to the mother, the infant derives a sense of dependence; and out of this, in response to her care, emerges a feeling of love for the mother. Her protection in time of danger produces a feeling of "trust" and "gratitude." The firmness of the mother in her ministrations stimulates an attitude of "patience" and "obedience." Such is the genesis of the emotions, which make the child human and personal. From these original virtues, love, trust, gratitude, patience, and obedience, develop the higher aspects of the moral, social, and religious life.

As the activities of the child increase with his growing powers, his dependence upon the mother decreases, and finally vanishes. The expansion of his activities brings with it many new and higher needs, which can be satisfied only by dependence upon other people and upon the goodness of the Creator. It is the supreme art of pedagogy to transfer the original emotions, which have grown out of dependence upon the mother, to mankind first and then to God Himself. In this way, love, trust, gratitude, and obedience become the basis of social life and institutions, and the motivation for all conduct and learning. Sympathy and altruism are the higher, sublimated developments. From these arise man's sense of the ideal and his conscience.

In basing religion on these emotions, Pestalozzi agreed with Schleiermacher, the celebrated German theologian, who defined religion as a feeling of dependence upon God. This point of view opposed the dogmatism of the traditional theology and the deism of the Enlightenment. Belief in God is not the result of reasoning processes, nor an intuition. It is the product of a will that finds itself impelled to seek perfection and is dependent upon the Infinite for the satisfaction of its strivings. Faith, not reason, is the faculty by which man apprehends his Maker.

If religion is an emotion, it cannot be taught. Such was the startling conclusion drawn by Pestalozzi. This placed him in opposition to the most cherished views of the theologians. During all the centuries the church had taught religion by catechism, sermons, Psalms, and the Scriptures, by attendance at church services, and the partaking of sacraments. Morals, too, had been inculcated by instruction. There was great dudgeon when Pestalozzi abandoned the Heidelberg catechism. True to his theories, he asserted, "I taught neither morality nor religion." He believed that emotions must be aroused by personal situations, and must be experienced before they can become the subject of intelligent discussion with young children.[34] "I strove to awaken the feelings of each virtue before talking about it, for I thought it unwise to talk to children on subjects which would compel them to speak without thoroughly understanding what they were saying."

---

[34] *Ibid.*, p. 159.

Furthermore, it is important to understand that the development of these fundamental emotions comes, in point of time before intellectual growth.[35] "The first instruction of the child should never be the business of the *head* or of the *reason;* it should always be the business of the senses, of the *heart,* of the *mother.*" The priority of the development of the emotions is likewise required by the controlling position they occupy in the functioning of the organism as a whole.

Moral virtues rank first. The three aspects of human nature—intellect, practical power, and the moral-religious nature—are not of equal rank in the organism. All are essential to man's well-being, but the emotional life is primary. It furnishes the power and motive for the activity of the intellect and practical life. Only when these two function in subordination to the first, does man have the harmonious development which brings inner peace and happiness.

Home life the center of education. The only place where the human being can unfold his powers in a perfectly natural way is the home. The love of the mother evokes the emotions of the child, and develops them in their proper relation. The activities that center in the home furnish opportunities for awakening the senses and for the exercise of judgment and knowledge. They are also the best means for training practical power.

It is well to bear in mind that Pestalozzi had in view the home as it existed before the Industrial Revolution. At that time it was the place of varied industries, which have since been transferred to specialized factories. To give mothers a method of education so simple and definite that every one could develop her own child "in the sanctuary of the home" was the sublime ambition of Pestalozzi's heart.

SUMMARY OF PESTALOZZI'S PHILOSOPHY

Education's most successful failure. Pestalozzi must be awarded the prize as the champion of successful failures. Every enterprise he undertook came to grief. Yet he was honored by kings, governments, and savants, and his system of instruction was put into operation in many lands. Moreover, no one had more to do with the spread of the common school system. Surely here is a paradox which requires explanation.

---

[35] Pestalozzi, J. H., *How Gertrude Teaches Her Children,* p. 189.

Causes of failure. There are numerous reasons to account for Pestalozzi's failures. His bizarre personality and idiosyncrasies caused many to ridicule him. His loquacity, emotionality, and slovenliness turned others against him. An inability to express himself clearly, and, back of this, a certain confusion in his ideas produced misunderstanding and lack of confidence. Only those who looked deeper were captivated by the nobility of his purposes, and saw in his principles the only dependable means for human progress.

The Yverdun institute was his greatest and most enduring achievement. Yet, it was not in operation very long before signs of weakness appeared; it lasted only 20 years. Many weaknesses contributed to its failure. (1) First, the duality of language caused difficulties. Both French and German were commonly used in the institution. (2) Second, the universal interest of the public in the institution, and the exalted approval of royal personages, celebrities, and governments—shown by their visits and by sending students to the school—turned the heads of Pestalozzi and his associates. So numerous were the visitors who came to see the new methods that the regularity of instruction suffered. The school became a showplace. (3) Third, bad as were these conditions, even more serious causes of discord were present. As the school grew in size and complexity, Pestalozzi was unable to retain the simple home spirit. Pupils came from many lands; hence it was difficult to unify the spirit of the group. The home atmosphere on which he counted so heavily was forgotten. As early as 1808, when standing beside an open coffin, as though he expected to die immediately, Pestalozzi moaned: "This work was founded by love, but love has disappeared from our midst." [36]

So long as the institute remained small and simple, Pestalozzi was able by force of his amiable personality to quash every incipient discord. But when the school entered into an experiment in institutional self-government as a constitutional state, the atmosphere of home life ceased. Discussing the decline of the home spirit, Ramsauer, a student and teacher, wrote: [37]

> This ceased when the family life was transformed in the institution into a constitutional state existence.... Egotism made its appearance every day in more pointed forms. Envy and jealousy rankled in the breasts of many.

---

[36] DeGuimps, Roger, *op. cit.*, p. 277.

[37] Holman, H., *Pestalozzi; An Account of His Life and Work,* p. 108. London: Longmans, Green and Co., 1908.

(4) Fourth, with the passing of the personal control exercised by Pestalozzi, there arose between two of the staff bitter dissension as to which one better represented Pestalozzi's ideas. It was these quarrels of his chief assistants and their friends that paralyzed the work for many years and finally destroyed this celebrated experimental school.

Results and criticism. When one undertakes to set down in concise form the central contributions of Pestalozzi, he is apt to do what others have done—take refuge in the excuse that, after all, the distinctive feature was the life and not the doctrine of the man. Holman has emphasized the tentative nature of his principles: "It is not too much to say that Pestalozzi began everything, though he finished nothing."[38] Pestalozzi himself was not unaware of the unsatisfactory statement of his principles: "To my grave," he acknowledged, "I shall remain in a kind of fog about most of my views."

Summary of his principles:

(1) Pestalozzi had an indomitable and infectious faith in education as the supreme means for individual and social betterment. Von Raumer has stated the point as follows:[39]

> He compelled the scholastic world to revise the whole of their task, to reflect on the nature and destiny of man, as also on the proper way of leading him from his youth towards his destiny.

His enthusiasm made kings and rulers take an interest in the education of children in hovels. He democratized education by proclaiming that it is the absolute right of every child to have his God-given powers fully developed.

(2) He psychologized education. When there was no psychological science worthy of the name, and although he had but the vaguest notions of the nature of the human mind himself, Pestalozzi saw clearly that a correct theory and practice of education must be based upon such a science.

(3) He was the first to try to base education on organic development rather than upon the transmission of ideas.

(4) He sought the fundamental laws of development.

(5) Education begins with the perception of concrete objects, the

---

[38] *Ibid.*, p. 312.
[39] *Ibid.*, p. 307.

performing of concrete acts, and the experiencing of actual emotional responses. Pestalozzi regarded this idea as his greatest contribution.

(6) Development is a gradual building up of power. Every form of instruction must proceed in a slow, gradual course, concurrent with the unfolding powers of the child.

(7) Religion is deeper than dogmas or creeds, or the memorizing of the catechism or the Scriptures. Pestalozzi demanded that religious feelings be awakened before words or symbols are brought to the child.

(8) Several new devices of method were originated by Pestalozzi. He employed the letters of the alphabet fastened on cards, and introduced slates and pencils. The most important innovation was that of simultaneous, or class, instruction. This was not new, but it had not been generally practiced.

(9) Pestalozzi revolutionized discipline, basing it upon the mutual goodwill and cooperation of pupil and teacher.

(10) Pestalozzi gave a new impetus to the training of teachers and the study of education as a science.

PESTALOZZI'S INFLUENCE

Respect paid to Pestalozzi. He was the recipient of many honors. As early as 1792, he was made a "Citizen of the French Republic" along with Kosciusko, the Polish patriot; Schiller, the German poet; Wilberforce, the philanthropist; and George Washington. In 1814 he was knighted by Alexander, Tsar of Russia, who sent him an autographed letter. Nothing, however, so signalized the exalted position he held as the reverence and respect paid to him by many of the greatest minds of the times. Among those who knew him best and revered him most were Fichte and Herbart, both celebrated philosophers; Nicolovius and Süvern, high officials of the Prussian Government; Friedrich Froebel, the educator; and Karl Ritter, the celebrated geographer. Ritter wrote of his indebtedness: [40]

> I have seen more than the paradise of Switzerland, for I have seen Pestalozzi, and recognized how great his heart is, and how great his genius; never have I been so filled with a sense of the sacredness of my vocation, and the dignity of human nature, as in the days that I spent with this noble man.

---

[40] DeGuimps, Roger, *op. cit.*, pp. 263-264.

Speaking, forty years later, of his own work, Ritter said:

> Pestalozzi knew less geography than a child in one of our primary schools; yet it was from him that I gained my chief knowledge of this science, for it was in listening to him that I first conceived the idea of the natural method. It was he who opened the way to me, and I take pleasure in attributing whatever value my work may possess entirely to him.

Nothing shows better the great admiration in which Pestalozzi was held than the inscription on his tomb: [41]

Here Rests
HENRY PESTALOZZI

Born at Zurich, the 12th of January, 1746
Died at Brugg, the 17th of February, 1827

Saviour of the poor at Neuhof, at Stanz the father
of orphans, at Burgdorf and Munchenbuchsee
founder of the popular school, at Yverdun
the educator of humanity; man,
Christian, and citizen. All for
others, nothing for himself.
Peace to his ashes.

TO OUR FATHER PESTALOZZI

Grateful Aargau

The spread of the method in Europe. The influence of Pestalozzi's reforms upon education was far reaching. Deputations were sent from many lands to examine and report upon his methods. In 1807-1808, when Prussia was crushed under the heel of Napoleon and while French soldiers paraded *Unter den Linden,* Fichte boldly addressed the German people and urged them to adopt his system. In 1808, the Prussian Government, under the authorization of the king, sent carefully selected young men to Yverdun to be trained by the master himself. Pestalozzi's old friends, Nicolovius and Süvern, were in charge of this movement to secure trained teachers. No less than 17 young men were sent to Yverdun, and all of them spent three years there at the expense of the government. The schools of Prussia were reorganized, Pestalozzian methods were adopted, and normal schools were established to train new

---

[41] *Ibid.,* p. 367.

teachers. So great was the influence of Pestalozzi in reshaping Prussian education that Diesterweg was constrained to call it the "Prussian-Pestalozzian school system." And he has stated: "Whatever of excellence or eminence they have, they really owe to no one but to him." [42] Scores of other young Germans found their way to Pestalozzi, and later became the leading teachers in Germany.

The cantons of Switzerland accepted Pestalozzi's methods for public instruction, and established normal schools to train teachers. Economic and social conditions were transformed, and the Swiss people became a living testimony to the success of the ideas of their indomitable compatriot.

The influence of Pestalozzi was increased in Switzerland by the success of the institutions of Baron von Fellenberg, who conducted an agricultural and industrial institute at Hofwyl, after the plans set forth in *Leonard and Gertrude*. He had in view especially practical training and vocational preparation for all grades of society. In addition to farming, there were established printing, tailoring, shoemaking, and other lines of work. With this practical training went instruction in common school branches. Fellenberg's school exercised an importance next to that of Pestalozzi, not only in Europe but in America as well. Its influence in popularizing manual labor and agricultural education in America was very great.

France and England were less affected by Pestalozzi. The various efforts to interest Napoleon utterly failed; he was too busy with his own affairs to care for Pestalozzi's childish *ABC*'s. But a few more discerning Frenchmen introduced the new system to the French people. M. A. Jullien, a knight of the Legion of Honor and a man of wealth and influence, took 24 students to Yverdun for an entire year.

So far as England was concerned, about the same interest was manifested as in France. But the movement in England was of greater moment for American education, since it became one of the connecting links for the entrance of Pestalozzianism into our country. J. P. Greaves, an Englishman, spent some years at Yverdun, and later carried the new principles back to his native land. At his request Pestalozzi wrote *Letters on the Early Education of the Child,* which is one of the best statements of his views on infant education. It was, however, Dr. Charles Mayo

---

[42] Diesterweg, A., "Pestalozzi and the Schools of Germany," in Barnard, Henry, *American Journal of Education* (1857), Vol. 4, pp. 343-358.

and his sister, Elizabeth Mayo, who had most to do with the planting of the system in England. Dr. Mayo long conducted a school for boys and was active in the establishment of the Home and Colonial Training College for training teachers in the Pestalozzian method. He lectured and also published texts and other books. There are two special reasons for directing attention to this activity of the Mayos. First, they formalized and mechanized all genuine life out of the Pestalozzian method; secondly, through their work the system finally made its chief impact upon American education.

THE LITTLE GRAMMARIAN, ILLUSTRATING AN ABSURD USE OF THE SENSE-PERCEPTION PRINCIPLE.

Other countries affected by the new method were Russia, Poland, Spain, and Italy. Compayré, who has written most appreciatively of the work of Pestalozzi, states: "There is scarcely a district of Europe, in the North as well as in the South, which has remained foreign to the movement." [43]

Pestalozzianism in the United States. A knowledge of Pestalozzi's principles and practices came to the attention of American educators in disconnected ways. The various efforts to introduce the new ideas may

---

[43] Compayré, G., *Pestalozzi and Elementary Education,* p. 105. Translated by R. P. Jago. New York: Crowell, 1907.

best be divided into four phases: (1) The work of Maclure and Neef; (2) Educational literature on Pestalozzi; (3) The teaching of special subjects; and (4) The Oswego movement.

The work of Maclure and Neef. The first attempt to introduce the Pestalozzian system into America was made by William Maclure, who came to Philadelphia as a youth to engage in business. He accumulated a large fortune before he was 40, and spent the remainder of his life in the pursuit of two dominant interests, the reform of education and the study of the geology of North America. He made the first geological surveys on this continent. While engaged in 1804 in a diplomatic mission to France, his attention was called to Pestalozzi's method of instruction. He visited Pestalozzi at Yverdun and Fellenberg at Hofwyl a number of times, and invited Pestalozzi to come to Philadelphia to establish a school. Pestalozzi declined, on account of age and other difficulties, but recommended Joseph Neef, who at the time was conducting an orphanage on Pestalozzian principles in Paris.[44] He had been a soldier under Napoleon, and later had taught music, gymnastics, and French at the Burgdorf institute under Pestalozzi. Neef accepted the invitation and came to Philadelphia in 1806. It may be added that Maclure published during that same year, in the *National Intelligencer,* the first account of Pestalozzi to appear in America. Two years later, and as a forecast of the opening of the school, Neef published a *Sketch of a Plan and Method of Education.*

The school was opened in a suburb of Philadelphia in 1809, and proved an entire success. Unfortunately, due to his desire to have his pupils in the country, Neef removed the institution to Village Green near Chester, Pennsylvania. In the new setting it rapidly declined in patronage. Neef was induced to make a fresh start in Louisville, Kentucky, a struggling frontier town. This effort was likewise a failure, and for a time Neef engaged in farming.

---

[44] The story told by P. Pompee, in his *Etudes sur la Vie et les Travaux de J. H. Pestalozzi,* is substantially as follows: Having expressed to the American ambassador a great desire to see Napoleon, Maclure was invited to accompany him on the occasion when he knew the emperor and Talleyrand had arranged to visit the Pestalozzian orphanage conducted by Joseph Neef. During the occasion Maclure was so absorbed in watching Napoleon that he failed utterly to observe the school work. When the party was leaving, he heard Talleyrand remark to the Emperor, "It is too much for us." Struck by this statement, Maclure returned to study the method of the school and became deeply interested. The story is probably true, but it has lacked final confirmation. See Monroe, Will S., *History of the Pestalozzian Movement in the United States,* pp. 66-68. Syracuse: C. W. Bardeen, 1907.

In the meanwhile the restless Maclure visited New Lanark, Scotland, and made the acquaintance of Robert Owen and his experiment in industrialism and education. These two philanthropists found they had much in common. Maclure renewed his visits to Fellenberg's institute at Hofwyl, and became more and more deeply interested in plans for industrial and agricultural education. He and Owen, who, by the way, had his two sons educated in the Hofwyl school, now embarked upon the most fantastic educational experiment ever undertaken in this country. This has already been explained in connection with the Charity School movement. Neef was called to conduct the work of education in the socialistic experiment at New Harmony which afforded an excellent opportunity to demonstrate Pestalozzi's principles and methods.

Educational literature on Pestalozzi. Another means for the spread of Pestalozzi's views in America was through educational literature, especially magazine articles and reports. In 1813, Neef published *Method of Instructing Children Rationally in the Arts of Reading and Writing.* In 1819 a number of articles, written by an anonymous author, appeared in a magazine called *The Academician.* This writer had never visited Pestalozzi, but he was quite familiar with the literature available. In 1818 and 1819 John Griscom visited Europe, and four years later published the result of his observations in two volumes entitled *A Year in Europe.* He gave an elaborate account of the schools of both Pestalozzi and Fellenberg. These volumes made a deep impression. Another educator who visited Pestalozzi and spread his doctrines was William C. Woodbridge, who for many years edited the *American Annals of Education.* However, the principles of Pestalozzi were chiefly spread, so far as literature went, indirectly through the writings of Americans who studied the effects of his methods on the schools of Europe. The reports of Victor Cousin, Calvin E. Stowe, A. D. Bache, Henry Barnard, and Horace Mann gave the widest currency to the new system, even though they did not treat directly of Pestalozzi's principles.

The Manual Labor movement already referred to in connection with Fellenberg will be discussed in connection with the growth of American colleges.

The teaching of special subjects. The Pestalozzian geography and music were the first to be introduced into America. The credit for this work belongs to William C. Woodbridge (1794-1845), a graduate of Yale. He visited Pestalozzi in 1820, and on several other occasions between 1825 and 1827. Woodbridge's enthusiasm centered in geography and music. As a result, he published, in 1822, the *Rudiments of Geography,* and, two years later, the *Universal Geography.*

Geography had not been a regular subject of the American school curriculum, and Woodbridge produced a revolution in the teaching of the subject. About the middle of the century a further development took place due to the work of Arnold Henry Guyot (1807-1884), a Swiss professor of geography trained by Karl Ritter. He was employed by the Massachusetts State Board of Education to lecture on geography in the state normal schools. He helped to spread among a large group of teachers Pestalozzi's method in this subject, and his texts were the first works in the common school to treat geography as a science.

Woodbridge was likewise interested in music. At the first meeting of the American Institute of Instruction, in Boston in 1830, he gave a lengthy address on the Pestalozzian method of teaching this subject. Woodbridge did not develop this work himself but he succeeded in arousing the interest of Lowell Mason (1792-1872), who had been teaching vocal and instrumental music in Boston. The new method "changed his whole manner of teaching, as well as his theory of the educational value of music." Woodbridge placed at his command the books and directions which he received from the associates of Pestalozzi who had worked out the method in detail. Music, long neglected in Puritan education, soon reached a high point of development under Mason's influence; in fact, he became America's foremost pioneer in the field of public school music.

William Russell and Hermann Krüsi, Jr., did much to spread Pestalozzian methods in this country. Russell established the *American Journal of Education,* which was the first educational publication to attain success. It featured a number of articles on Pestalozzi and also his *Letters* to Greaves, which was the first of his own writings to be published in America. For many years Russell conducted a private normal school at Lancaster, Massachusetts, in which he used the Pestalozzian system. His greatest contribution in this direction was in bringing Hermann Krüsi, Jr., son of Pestalozzi's assistant, to teach in his school. Krüsi was also employed to lecture in the state normal schools of Massachusetts on Pestalozzian drawing and arithmetic. He engaged in this work for about ten years before going to the normal school at Oswego, New York.

The Oswego movement. Up to 1860 Pestalozzi's system had not been prominently introduced into American education. The closer acquaintance with the central features of his philosophy and practices came in a round-about manner. For years Edward A. Sheldon (1823-1897) had been superintendent of the public schools of Oswego, New York. Dissatisfied with the methods in vogue and casting about for something better, he chanced to visit the provincial normal school in Toronto. Here he found a display of materials for object lessons such as was employed by the Home and Colonial Training College in London. He learned of the work of the Mayos in England and of the Pestalozzian methods in the college. He procured their publications and appliances, and put the new method into practice in the training of his teachers. He induced the school board to employ Miss M. E. M. Jones of the Home and Colonial Training College to come to Oswego and train teachers in the methods of Pestalozzi, especially the method of object-lesson teaching. She remained only a year, but was followed by Hermann Krüsi, Jr., who continued the work for twenty-five years. With this new and vital idea, Oswego became the hot-bed of educational progress. The enthusiasm of its students was boundless, and the new method was carried by them to all parts of the country.

Chapter 18

HERBART AND THE SCIENCE OF EDUCATION

HERBART'S LIFE, WORK, AND WRITINGS

SIGNIFICANCE of his biography. The life story of a great educator may be of interest either for inspiration or for information—to increase enthusiasm for the teacher's task or to explain the genesis of a particular theory. Pestalozzi and Froebel are examples of the first; Herbart, of the second. The first tasted the bitterness of innumerable failures and frustrations, and suffered like the heroes of faith. Herbart lived a placid existence of easy success and great honor. Only those facts necessary to explain his system of education and philosophy will, therefore, be presented here.

Early life and education. Johann Friedrich Herbart was born in Oldenburg, in northwestern Germany, in the year 1776. His mother was beautiful and had superior intelligence and literary ability; his father, a lawyer, rose to the rank of privy councilor. When about five years of age, little Johann fell into a tub of boiling water; he had, in consequence, a delicate constitution all the rest of his days. The mother devoted herself unreservedly to his care and training, even to the supervision of his studies. She was present at every lesson, and studied Greek in order to accompany him in his work.

Elementary instruction was given young Herbart by Pastor Ulzen, who had a short but effective educational philosophy: "The aim of all instruction is to cultivate clearness, definiteness, and continuity of thought." One may well believe that Pastor Ulzen had a strong influence in shaping Herbart's own theory of instruction.

From 12 to 18 years of age, Herbart attended the Oldenburg gymnasium, where he was graduated with the following official report:

"Distinguished among his school-fellows for order, good conduct, and increasing industry in developing and improving his excellent natural abilities." In addition to marked ability in mathematics, languages, and philosophy, he was a gifted musician and possessed rare literary taste. His mentality ripened verly early: at 11, he studied logic; at 12 metaphysics; and at 14, he wrote an essay on the *Freedom of the Will*. As a mere youth of 19, he dared to measure his philosophical acumen against the most exalted figures of contemporary thought, Schelling and Fichte. It may readily be concluded that a mind so penetrating would be deeply conscious of the psychological processes of its own development, the basis of his discerning pedagogical insight.

His father sent him to Jena to prepare for the practice of law. Herbart certainly had a mind sufficiently judicial, but he possessed no taste for law. From 1794 to 1797 he attended the university, with his mother as his companion. Here lived the most brilliant and creative minds in the literary and philosophical history of Germany. Among this group were Herder, Wieland, Goethe, Schiller, Schelling, and Fichte, to mention only the leaders. Most consequential, Madame Herbart cultivated a special friendship between her son and Schiller, who at this time was writing his *Letters on the Aesthetic Education of Man*. Under the influence of this idea, young Herbart reached his decision to devote his life to the study of education and philosophy.

Private tutor. At the suggestion of his mother, he left Jena early in 1797 to become private tutor to the three sons of the governor of Interlaken, Switzerland. This was one of the most decisive steps of his life. It had two highly important results: first, he gained the experience in teaching which was to determine his pedagogical theory; and second, his educational interest had a decisive influence upon his philosophy, especially upon his psychological and ethical theories. The three boys were eight, ten, and fourteen years of age. His teaching was, therefore, concerned with early adolescence. From his experience as an instructor he came to believe that the period of greatest susceptibility to instruction extends from the age of ten to seventeen, the period in which general education is completed.

Herbart and Pestalozzi. Herbart is usually represented as a disciple of Pestalozzi. It is true that he held the quixotic sage in high esteem, but it is easy to overstress the actual influence of Pestalozzi on Herbart. The truth of the matter is that several years before he came into contact with Pestalozzi, he had formulated his educational views. At the time when Herbart met Pestalozzi, the latter was still teaching in an elementary school belonging to the municipality; nor had he formulated his principles or written his chief educational works.

Herbart had all the resources of a subtle dialectician and introspective powers of the highest order. He is called the "father of modern psychology," and also the "father of the modern science of education." How greatly he is respected may be learned from the notable French educator, Compayré: [1]

> It is a hundred years since Herbart published his treatise on *General Pedagogy;* it dates from 1806. And yet, this book, now old, answers perhaps better to the needs and aspirations of the hour than any other. At this time, in fact, when democratic peoples are seeking more and more to base their morality on science, it is surely worth while to listen to the voice of a philosopher who believed and tried to demonstrate that all education depends alone on instruction, and that ideas and knowledge are the source of good feeling and virtue.

Herbart an educational philosopher. Herbart was both a skilled teacher and a profound philosopher. Like Plato, he was an educator before he became a philosopher, and it was the problems of education that led to the construction of his speculative theories. Furthermore, it may be said that he is the only educator in modern times on an equality with the greatest thinkers in the realm of philosophy.

Herbart's life fell into three periods of university work and scholarly productivity. From 1802 to 1809, he taught at Göttingen and wrote his chief works on education. In 1809, he was called to the University of Königsberg, in East Prussia, to occupy the world's most distinguished chair of philosophy; distinguished because it had been occupied by Immanuel Kant. Of this signal honor Herbart wrote: "How happy I was to receive the offer of this, the most renowned chair of philosophy, the place which, when a boy, I longed for in reverential dreams, as I studied the works of the sage of Königsberg." Here, in connection with the lectures on education, he conducted a pedagogical seminar, in which students learned to apply the principles which they discussed in the classroom. During this era his chief publications were along psychological lines. In 1833, Herbart returned to the University of Göttingen, where

---

[1] Compayré, G., *Herbart and Education by Instruction,* Preface, p. ix. New York: Crowell, 1907.

he died in 1841. His literary productions during this period were few and relatively unimportant.

HERBART'S SCIENCE OF EDUCATION

Approach. Herbart's approach to the study of the science of education was direct. While tutoring his three pupils, he faced the practical situations of instruction; and, because he was required every month to furnish his employer a written report of his methods and results, he thought through his work with clarity and system. The consequence was that his entire thinking was dominated by the search for a satisfactory theory as well as effective practice.

Recognizing that education is an art, the first task of educational science is to discover its ultimate end or objective. Having set up a clear view of the aim to be attained, Herbart proceeded to discover the proper means for its realization. It was this practical investigation that revealed to him the principles of psychology, ethics, and metaphysics that were to guide him in his undertaking. He was well aware that any philosophy that hopes to throw light upon the deeper problems of life and the world must likewise be adequate to solve the problems of education.

Aim of education. *"The one and the whole work of education may be summed up in the concept—Morality."* Such was the emphatic statement of the aim of education as Herbart viewed it when he wrote the *Aesthetic Revelation of the World the Supreme Business of Education.* "Morality" meant for Herbart five basic ideas: freedom, perfection, good will, right, and retribution. It did not mean mere amiability or an unintelligent compliance with conventional manners, but positive personality that clearly perceives the ideal and follows it from choice. Goodness of will must be constant and unwavering. To express fully this idea of steadiness, he employed the peculiar term "memory of the will."

Herbart was strongly under the influence of Schiller's conception of esthetic manhood. By beginning instruction with Homer's Odyssey in Greek rather than with Latin grammar, he proved to his utmost satisfaction that Schiller's view of cultural recapitulation was correct. Furthermore, he had accepted Schiller's theory that esthetic taste, not Kant's categorical imperative, opposes the lower appetites and gives the individual moral control over himself.

For Herbart, the end of education and instruction is the production of the man of culture, who is persistently constrained by a sense of taste to strive to attain the highest ethical ideals. It is not that the uneducated man cannot be good; he may be mechanically good, or good under certain situations; that is to say, he may be good by habit or by imitation; but he cannot be so intelligently, freely, and constantly good, nor good in so many minute ways, as the educated man.

Having fixed upon character as the aim of education, Herbart endeavored to discover, by the deductive method, how to realize it. The will is the seat of character and the kind of decisions the will makes determines the kind of character. "A good man commands himself." His nature contains two factors, a commanding self and an obeying self. To educate the youth to will the good, freely and constantly, until it has become his very nature to do so; such is the fundamental endeavor of education.

Many-sidedness of interest. At a later period Herbart expanded his view of the aim. He came to see that it was necessary to explain more clearly the relation of the ideal to vocational and other activities of mature life. The teacher cannot foresee what choices the future man will make, in what activities he will engage, or what vocation he will follow. Yet, by virtue of his deeper knowledge of life, the teacher can foresee what principles should guide the future interests of the normal man. For this reason the teacher must present to the boy the character of man. Consequently the teacher, who naturally sees farther and deeper than the pupil, will take care that the future aims which the boy will later place before himself are fully anticipated. He must prepare the boy not only to desire those aims, but to have the ability to attain them. For these reasons it is essential to give the boy the broadest possible training. This is termed by Herbart "many-sidedness of interest." Only that individual who has the broadest range of experiences and interests, who has studied life at the greatest number of points, can make with confidence the choices which are best.

Good character and many-sidedness of interest form the complete objectives of education. They are not in conflict, but, as Herbart thought of them, they form a unity, for many-sidedness of interest is a guarantee not only of sound choices in all the varied moral situations of life, but of wise choice of vocation as well.

Interest. In many ways the most significant and permanent of Herbart's contributions to pedagogical theory is his doctrine of interest. Others before him had noticed a mental set or readiness which may now be identified as interest, but no one had explained its true character. For

Herbart, interest became the basic principle upon which depended all his other principles.

Interest is an inner tendency making for the retention of an object of thought in consciousness, or for its return to consciousness. This force resides in the idea. It is the nature of ideas which have once been in consciousness to strive to return. This tendency is increased by two laws of the mind: the law of frequency, and the law of association. The more frequently a concept or idea has been brought into consciousness, the easier becomes its return, and the greater is its power over the mind. This is due to the law of habit. Again, where a number of ideas are associated, the combined power of the mass determines what ideas shall enter consciousness. Interest is, therefore, the active power, residing in the content of the mind, that determines what ideas and experiences shall receive attention.

The supreme art of the educator is, therefore, to bring constantly to attention those ideas that he wishes to dominate the life of his pupil. By thus controlling the child's experience, the instructor builds up masses of ideas which, in turn, develop by the assimilation of new materials. The interests of a physician are in medicine and surgery; of a banker, in money; of a theologian, in religion. The difference of mental content is due to the fact that through the years each has been building a different mass of ideas.

Having definitely set up these ultimate ends, Herbart moved forward with clear vision toward their realization. Morality and interest have to do with objects to be desired, choices to be made, acts to be performed, and ends to be realized. It is, accordingly, the business of education to instil the proper interests and desires, in order to build inner control, to give the child insight into life in all its phases, and to mature his judgments. This complex task can be performed only by what Herbart designated as "educative instruction."

Educative instruction. The profound effects of education upon human life and happiness demand that this art be based upon a positive, scientific procedure. Herbart felt that it would be unfortunate indeed if the prolonged toil of the educator could be overturned by some sudden caprice within the child or some seductive force from without. Education must be based upon an unshakeable foundation, and must give confidence that, the inner soul-life of the child having once been stabilized by means of instruction, the results of education will endure.

The greatest of modern educational reformers, Rabelais, Montaigne, Locke, and Rousseau, had been guilty of disparaging the importance of instruction. First, they insisted that all learning should be made not only pleasant but easy. It must involve no hardship, no effort. All learning must be play. In a word, they advocated what at the present time is called "soft pedagogy." They exalted discipline and training above instruction, and belittled the value of learning. The Germans came to employ two words to differentiate these two conceptions: *Erziehung* and *Unterricht,* education and instruction.

Herbart was positively opposed to any such distinction. In his view, whatever imparts clear and true ideas will inevitably issue in good conduct. Right thinking will produce right action. Therefore, he contended, there is no real discipline without the knowledge and insight which come from instruction. Insisting absolutely upon the unity of the soul, Herbart could not logically admit two different processes of education; the one, for discipline and moral training through the will; the other, for intellectual enlightenment through ideas and learning.

The denial of faculties and the assertion of the unity of the soul emphasize the fact that in the educative process all mental functions coöperate in a common task. That is to say, the intelligence is not educated at one time by one process, and the will, at another time by an entirely different process. As a matter of fact, will and intellect develop synchronously and by the self-same process of educative instruction. Herbart did not believe that knowledge is an end in itself and that it stands apart from will. The true end that the educator sets before himself is the producing in the child of a steady will, or purposefulness. Knowledge or ideas are the necessary means to this end of an enlightened will. Therefore, in making goodwill the aim of education, Herbart did not place the end outside of the process, but rather within it. Discipline is not a matter of some occasional and extraneous checking of misconduct, but the continuous persistent cultivation of right ideas and acts.

By implanting interests and desires in the soul by means of instruction, the educator furnishes the power of inner self-control. The real work of instruction is, therefore, the imparting, not merely of knowledge, but of inner discipline by means of insight.

The clearest statement of educative instruction is in the explanation of Compayré, who described it in this manner: [2]

---

[2] Compayré, G., *op. cit.,* pp. 46-47.

> The governing idea of Herbart's pedagogy . . . is that the only foundation of the whole of education, is instruction. There exist, then, no longer two distinct educations, an intellectual and a moral education. . . . To instruct the mind is, he considers, to construct it. It is no longer a question, as under the old hypothesis of faculties bestowed by nature, of overloading a more or less trustworthy memory, of causing literary or scientific knowledge to enter an understanding more or less open. Knowledge is no longer a mental ornament, it is a mental element. Knowledge builds and produces mind. . . . It is a consequence of this theory that instruction assumes a profound and delicate meaning, and that quite new duties are imposed on teaching; its office is no longer confined to developing the intellect, since it must create it, and since by the association of memories by regular "series" of ideas, those mental forces are aroused whence spring not only strength of intellect but strength of will.

Herbart, therefore, recognized no other method of educating than by causing the growth of ideas in the mind of the child. This must be brought about in conformity with psychological laws. Education as a science and an art depends on a clear-cut psychology.

HERBART'S PSYCHOLOGY AN EDUCATIONAL PSYCHOLOGY

Herbart was the first to formulate a science of education based directly on ethics and psychology. From ethics he derived the end of instruction; from psychology, its method. His greatest contributions in this field may be summarized as follows:

(1) He turned psychology from the speculative or philosophic method to the empirical examination of mental processes. (2) He was, also, the first thinker to abandon the idea of separate faculties, and to insist upon the unity of the mind in all its operations. (3) He attempted to apply mathematics to psychology, though not with marked success. Nevertheless, his work along this line led to the development of experimental psychology. (4) Another field which owes its origin to this great mind is that of physiological psychology.

Herbart's psychology developed out of his experiences as a teacher, and shows at every turn his pedagogical interest. It is a psychology, not merely of mental, but chiefly of educational processes. It shows, not so much how the mind works when free to follow its own unrestrained course of thinking, as the process which must be utilized in reaching a goal, beyond the experience of the present—a new and better life.

The origin of knowledge. In the conflict of rationalism and empiricism Herbart chose a middle position. He agreed with the rationalists that the soul is an entity (*Real*); but he refused to accept their doctrine that knowledge is innate. He agreed with the empiricists that knowledge arises from experience, but he turned against the sensationalism of Locke and the materialism of the French philosophers.

The soul is endowed with a special capacity to react to things (*Realen*), and by this process "presentations" are experienced. Presentations result from a threatened collision of things with the soul, bringing about an inner reaction or creative process of recognition. Presentations are objects of thought which have been "presented," that is, brought into consciousness. The "apple" is presented when one has the sensations of sight, touch, taste, and so on, which make up the experience "apple." Without such presentation through the sense organs, the mind can never experience a living thought of "apple." Herbart insisted, along with all the modern sense-realists, on the indispensable need of sense perception for clarity of thought. But, as we shall see below, he showed that sensory experience is only the first step in the process of knowing.

To grasp this conception of presentations is the first requirement for an understanding of Herbart's psychology and his theory of education. All mental life originates with presentations. In thinking of "presentations," however, Herbart meant not so much the mental states themselves, as the significance, the meaning, or the content of the experience. In other words all percepts, concepts, ideas, or meanings come within the definition of presentation. The soul finds its highest existence in concepts. The development of the mind comes with the elaboration of percepts into concepts, for life functions in and through concepts or ideas.

But Herbart did not hold that experience is the only source of knowledge; he was too much of an educator for that conclusion. Once the primary elements are experienced, further knowledge is acquired by "intercourse" with others. Most of the ideas that constitute knowledge come from this source, and especially from teachers in the work of instruction. The first objective of the teacher is to control the presentations that are brought to the mind of the educatee and to make them as clear and impressive as possible.

Three fundamental mental functions. Herbart recognized the three basic functions of the mental life: knowing, feeling, and willing. So far as it represents or conceives, the soul is called mind; this is the function of knowing. So far as it feels and desires, it is called the heart, or disposition; these are the functions of feeling and willing.

Herbart's psychological standpoint. Two contradictory views have been held by philosophers as to the relation of these three fundamental processes.

On the one hand, there are those psychologists who look upon the soul as originally empty and devoid of all content. According to these thinkers, until the first sensation or perception arises, there is nothing whatever present in the soul or the mind; it is really born when the first sensation is experienced. By the addition of one sensation to another, all the varied mental processes emerge; perception, imagination, conception, judgment, and reasoning are but the results of experienced sensations, and are due to association or other processes. Moreover, feeling and willing arise from the relations that sensations or perceptions bear to one another.

The other point of view looks upon the soul as constituted by various capacities, functions, or activities. These are the most original competencies of soul life. From the activities of the organism arise sensations, perceptions, and all the other processes of intellect. Many modern psychologists belong to this group. Of the educators, Rousseau, Pestalozzi, and Froebel based their theories upon this voluntaristic view. Their theories of education assume that feeling, impulse, and instinct are the innate elements of mental life.

In this controversy Herbart occupied a middle position. The active aspect and presentational or objective aspect are never separate, but part of the same state of mind. Feeling, thinking, and action are never divorced.

The stream of consciousness. There is this peculiarity of all objects presented to attention: they do not remain long in consciousness. No experience is more indisputable than that the objects occupying consciousness are constantly changing. What was thought of a moment ago has now faded, and a new idea claims the attention. Observing how objects of thought come into the attention, Herbart introduced into psychology the idea of the "limen," or threshold, of consciousness. At any moment four or five objects or ideas can be in consciousness. Some will be sinking below the threshold, one will be in the focus of attention and others will be emerging into consciousness seeking to become dominant. Thus the mental life is made up of a sequence of presentations, which ever rise into consciousness and are, then, again superseded by other ideas.

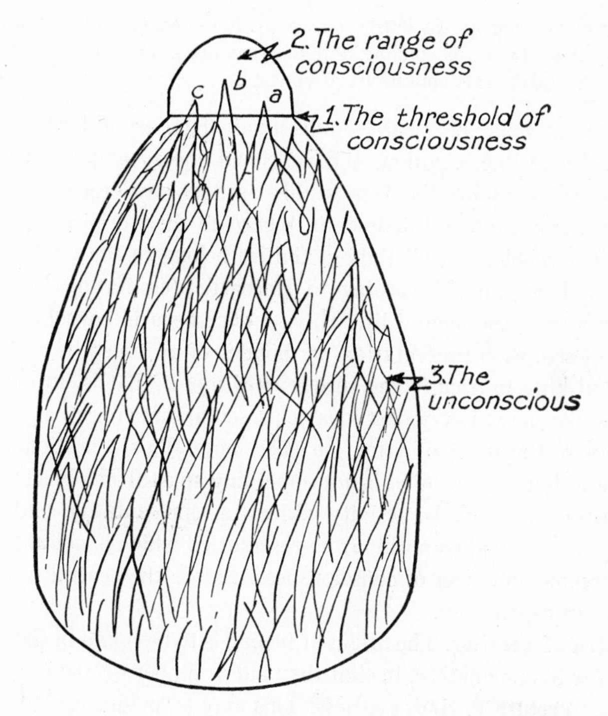

HERBART'S SCHEME OF PSYCHOLOGY.

Realm of unconscious mentality. No object once presented to consciousness is ever forgotten. All presentations fall back into the unconscious vault of the mind. This realm contains that immense store of perceptions, images, and ideas which embraces all our past experiences. They are not dead, or inactive, but dynamic entities, ever ready to spring back into consciousness when a propitious opportunity is presented.

Nature of mental activity. We come now to the most characteristic of Herbart's psychological conceptions. According to his point of view, feeling and willing accompany presentations and ideas, but are not their source or cause. They are derived, and not original states. They are, therefore, not coördinate in origin with knowledge, but originate from the relation which presentations or concepts bear to one another; that is to say, they spring from objects of thought. Herbart stated it in these terms: [3]

> *The disposition of the heart* [*Gemüth*], *however, has its source in the mind*—in other words, feeling and desiring are conditions, and for the most part changeable conditions of concepts.

This point must be clearly understood: Herbart did not deny the existence of feeling, emotion, and volitional energy which are found in experience. He admits them as readily as does any other psychologist. But there is a notable difference in regard to their origin. For the one group of psychologists, all these activities belong to the original nature of the soul or mind. According to Herbart, presentations furnish the only activity of the mental life. Having once been in consciousness and been deposed, each presentation or thought of an object is as active as an ousted king to occupy the throne once more; that is, to come back into consciousness. Every past idea or presentation is pushing, or striving to return to the focus of attention once more. This condition indicates that the activity of the mind is not something apart from objects or ideas, but inherent in them. An activity without a representative content, that is, a meaning, would be nothing; a presentation which is not active could never become an object of consciousness. This is the central principle of Herbartian psychology.

Origin of feeling. The origin of feeling is to be found in the relations ideas bear to one another, in that they aid or hinder one another in their struggle to return to consciousness. This may be made clear by an illustration. A person goes to the city to perform five errands. Four of them are accomplished when he suddenly recalls an imperative engagement. This thought rushes into consciousness, takes full possession of attention, and thrusts aside the fifth errand, which is either forgotten for the moment or causes only an inner uneasiness to arise. The person may have been so anxious to perform the promised task that a conflict of the two ideas produces a strong feeling of dissatisfaction. But, suppose he then recalls that the pressing engagement was postponed. This new idea then combines with the idea of the errand to bring the latter into full consciousness. The result is a feeling of pleasure or satisfaction. In case the engagement hinders the performance of the errand, a feeling of pain results.

---

[3] Herbart, J. F., *A Text-Book in Psychology*, p. 26. Translated by Margaret K. Smith. New York: Appleton, 1891.

Feeling, therefore, arises from a furthering, or arresting, of an idea which seeks to get control of consciousness. When one idea tends to further another in its struggle upward, a feeling of pleasure results; when it hinders, a feeling of pain. Feeling may then be defined as the consciousness of the rising or the sinking, the furthering or the hindering, of the life interests of the soul. Feeling, therefore, is a secondary or derived phenomenon, and has its source in ideas.

Desire and will. These active functions of the mind are related to feeling, and, like feeling, they have their origin in the activities of ideas, in what Herbart called the "circle of thought." He described it in this way: [4]

> The circle of thought contains the store of that which by degrees can mount by the steps of interest to desire, and then by means of action to volition.

Herbart did not believe in a special faculty of will. It was his opposition to this doctrine that drove it finally from modern psychology. Nevertheless, he does recognize will as the highest and most important function.[5]

> Man's worth does not lie in his knowing, but in his willing. But there is no such thing as an independent faculty of will. Volition has its roots in thought; not, indeed, in the details one knows, but certainly in the combinations and total effect of the acquired ideas.

The will of the individual is the self, the totality of ideas which constitute experience and express themselves in action.

In general, desire is a state of mind which seeks to bring about some other state of mind. Desire is always directed toward some particular object, which it strives to bring into consciousness in such a concrete and substantial way that it will completely satisfy the craving. An illustration will make this clear. A person suffering from fever desires a dish of ice cream. The desire is not satisfied with the mere idea, or image of the cream. It can only be completely satisfied when the patient sees, handles, and tastes the cooling object. If he is convinced that it is impossible to secure the object, the desire remains but a wish. If there is a confidence that it can be realized, the desire may become a volition.

---

[4] Herbart, J. F., *The Science of Education*, p. 213. Translated by Henry M. and Emmie Felkin. Boston: D. C. Heath, 1902. This translation is used for all *Science of Education* references.

[5] Herbart, J. F., *Outline of Educational Doctrine*, pp. 40-41. Translated by Alexis F. Lange. New York: The Macmillan Company, 1901.

When some other idea comes in to interfere with the realization, the desire is arrested or hindered, and a feeling of pain or frustration results.

When a desire is accompanied by the belief that the object can be realized, and there is no hindering presentation, it passes directly over into volition. Any idea, therefore, that fills consciousness to the exclusion of all other ideas will result in immediate action. In the case of the mental experience which is termed "deliberation," two opposing claimants for action compete for attention at the same time, and thus hinder each other. First, the one is uppermost and the results of its action are projected by the imagination; then, the other has its innings. After this process of appraising the value of each is completed, the mind chooses one of the two concepts and excludes the other completely from consciousness. To allow the one idea or concept to fill the consciousness, to the exclusion of the second, constitutes an act of choice, which immediately results in a volitional act.

Herbart's theory that feeling and willing are the outcome of presentations or ideas gives instruction a significance which it cannot have under any other system. He stated it as follows: [6] "How this circle of thought is being formed is everything to the teacher, for out of thoughts come feelings, and from them principles and modes of action." It is a fact that there is no way in which the educator can impart feelings or volitions directly to the child. He can control the environment to a certain extent, and thus secure a certain reaction from the child. But according to the Herbartian theory, the educator has almost complete mastery. The pupil feels and wills in accordance with his dominant thoughts or presentations; and it is precisely these thoughts or ideas of the child with which the teacher deals. By manipulating ideas he constructs the child's circle of thought. By thus controlling what the child thinks, the teacher determines what he feels and wills. Only on the basis of such a pedagogy, in which he can be certain of the results, can the educator have full confidence in his art.

Analysis, comparison, and generalization. Presentations do not remain separate and distinct, as they originally came into experience. Two changes affect them: (1) They are analyzed into constituent parts; and (2) these parts are regrouped, or synthesized, into masses of similar ideas or meanings. These two mental processes, which are known as "analysis" and "apperception," are of the greatest moment to the teacher,

---

[6] Herbart, J. F., *The Science of Education,* p. 84.

for upon their employment hangs the entire art of instruction. It is necessary, therefore, to look at these processes in some detail.

The process of analysis may be briefly sketched by the first experience of an orange. When one sees a certain shade of yellow, feels a moist softness, and has a taste of orange flavor, the various impressions unite to form a single presentation or object of thought. By some peculiar gift of the mind, although these various impressions come from separate sense organs and nerves, they are, nevertheless, thought together as one single object. Experience always begins with such wholes. Later these wholes are analyzed into their constituent elements, and each quality is thought of separately. This analytic process is facilitated by means of the comparison of different kinds of oranges with that which has already been experienced. In this manner the mind acquires the notion of particular qualities or abstract ideas. All experiences are subjected to this process and their various elements abstracted or isolated.

Although Herbart recognized fully the importance of analysis, he placed greater emphasis upon the process of synthesis or integration, for he felt that the teacher's art depended upon it to a higher degree. By synthesis Herbart meant that mental activity which "thinks things together." When the same quality is found in various objects—for example, the yellow of an orange, a flower, and a bird—the quality is analyzed and separated from the objects, and is then conceived as a single idea or an abstraction. Similarly, when various objects of the same kind are associated in the mind, they form a generalization or a concept.

EDUCATIONAL PRINCIPLES AND METHODS

"The circle of thought." Education as a science finds its governing principles in ethics and psychology. The former points out the goal; the latter makes clear the way. For Herbart, education is not a process of guiding or developing the activities of the child, as other theorists hold. The teacher works directly with objects, ideas, concepts, judgments—in a word, with "presentations." He cannot influence feelings or volitions directly; for these, according to Herbart, can be aroused only through the ideas and judgments to which attention is directed. Psychology reveals how the teacher may skillfully manipulate the ideas which are to be brought to attention, and how he may weave the new ideas into the texture of the mind. In this way, "the circle of thought" is built up.

For Herbart, there is a profound difference between the mind of the educated and that of the uneducated man. The untrained mind, however rich and varied its experiences may be, is invariably atrophied on a lower level of mentality. He visualized three levels in the systematic development of the mind: first, the stage of sensations and perceptions; second, the level of imagination and memory; and third, the highest level, which has to do with conceptual thinking and judgment. It is the function of instruction to elevate the mind from the first to the highest stage. Concerning this Herbart wrote: [7]

> Uncultured men, to say nothing of savages, have hardly any other faculty of understanding than that of their passions. But among educated men there are other concept masses elaborated to the stage of thought called "understanding."

Not only does the work of instruction bring new ideas, but its chief task is to bring about a closely knit, highly systematized circle of thought. It does this by the process of apperception.

Apperception and apperceptive masses. How the factors of thought are associated, whether loosely or closely, depends entirely on how knowledge is acquired. The experience of the uncultivated man is loosely integrated; the knowledge of the well-educated is so presented that its parts are logically related to one another.[8]

> Those only wield the full power of education, who know how to cultivate in the youthful soul a large circle of thought closely connected in all its parts.

If new presentations are systematically brought before the attention and linked to previously experienced presentations, the new presentation may be expected to unite closely with similar ideas already experienced.

This principle of apperception is one of Herbart's prize contributions to modern pedagogy. The idea that he had in view is so valuable to instruction that it should be understood by every teacher.

What Pestalozzi meant by going "from the known to the unknown," and what other psychologists mean by "assimilation," Herbart expressed by the term "apperception." Two factors enter into the process: first, the datum, idea, or object new to experience; and second, the mass of organized experience that has already been in consciousness and has been relegated to the realm of the unconscious. The body of past experiences,

---

[7] Herbart, J. F., *A Text-Book in Psychology*, p. 185.
[8] Herbart, J. F., *The Science of Education*, pp. 92-93.

which is most closely related, takes up the new datum and assimilates, or relates, it with itself. The story is told of a child who saw for the first time a pot of ferns; he called it a "pot of green feathers." He did not know ferns, but he had had some experience of feathers. This former experience of feathers came into attention to interpret the new object. Another illustration may be given: The savage looks at an eclipse of the sun, and feels that the forces of darkness and evil are conquering the force of light, goodness, and life. The scientist looks at the same eclipse, and is delighted with the harmony of "celestial mechanics." Both have had the same visual image. It is the background of experience which causes the difference in interpretation. The ideas already in the memory, which come forward to assimilate the new presentation, are termed the "apperceptive mass." The process of assimilation of new ideas by apperceptive masses is the learning process and has been likened by Dr. Paul Monroe to the process of the digestion of food.

> The apperception of Herbart is like the assimilation of food by the body. As new material is assimilated, it becomes part of the living tissue, by contact with which new food can be made to live.[9]

Present-day educational psychologists no longer recognize a special mental function called "apperception," and the term is rarely used in works on psychology. In place of "apperceptive mass," the terms "mental set" and "pattern" are found. The Herbartian idea of apperception was so dominated by his belief in the primary character of presentations or concepts that it does not accord readily with a psychology which places less emphasis upon the ideational side and more upon the motor and volitional aspects of mental phenomena.

The significance of apperception for instruction will be most readily appreciated by teachers in the fields of secondary and higher education. Herbart was not directly interested in primary instruction, but rather in the training of the age at which the rational life emerges and actively constructs a general body of knowledge. The connecting of new ideas with former experiences and knowledge was for him the supreme art. By the welding of the new to the old, the "circle of thought" is closely organized and expanded into a compact, logically related body of dynamic knowledge. Thus there is formed the mental background from which right interests and desires will arise, and bad ones will be excluded.

---

[9] Monroe, Paul, *Cyclopedia of Education*, Vol. I. Article: "Apperception." New York: The Macmillan Company, 1913.

Culture-epoch theory. The theory that the race has passed through certain stages which are repeated in the unfolding development of each individual appealed to the literary and philosophic world of the 18th and early 19th centuries. Loosely formulated by Rousseau, it was more definitely urged by Schiller as the fundamental principle of culture. It was at the basis of the new Humanism, which led to the reorganization of the German gymnasium. Herbart and his followers not only accepted the theory as a psychological guide for understanding the nature of child life, but based their curricula and methods upon it. For them, the cultural products of the race furnish the best materials for the development of ethical ideals and the emerging personality.

Herbart recognized three stages in the development of character. The first stage is that of sensation and perception, when emotionality is strong and the impulsiveness and caprice of the child must be curbed; the intermediate stage, of memory and imagination, when the child responds to systematic training; last the stage of judgment and universal concepts, when the will has been formed by instruction. In order to understand Herbart's culture-epoch theory, it is necessary to see its application in the forming of social relations and moral ideas in relation to these three stages.

One must never lose sight of the fact that Herbart was formulating a social and ethical pedagogy. He believed that the social and ethical relations, the moral purposes and judgments, of adults are altogether too remote and too complex to become the natural desires and interests of youth. They must have something far simpler; that is to say, they must have life situations which are easy to grasp.

The simple ideas which are most suitable for children are expressed in the literature produced by early peoples. Herbart, and more especially his disciples Ziller and Rein, believed that, as the past was simpler than the present, it must, therefore, be closer to the child's experience and appeal more directly to his interest. The culture of each epoch in human history is based upon that of the former epoch. In the portrayal of the lives of the heroes of each epoch of history, one finds the increasing complexity of human life and relations. The lives of great heroes are presented to the child that he may perceive, understand, and form judgments of life in situations increasing in complexity. It is, accordingly, not in the study of nature or of science that the education of the young finds it chief materials. It is rather in literature and history. If education is to reach its end, which is the cultivation of character, it is necessary that the moral world should be revealed to the child. This revelation can be made only as the child comes to know the lives, conduct, and ideals of men of former ages. The decisions they made, their ideals of life, and their moral conduct furnish the concrete situations for the evolution of the moral nature of the child. By these means the pupil acquires the capacity to understand and to judge what is right and good in conduct. By viewing in imagination the good and the bad, his insight is clarified, his moral taste is refined, and he forms right ideals. Thus, the natural history of the moral life of the race furnishes the chart for the growth of the moral life of the individual.

For his task of tutoring adolescent boys, Herbart selected Homer's *Odyssey* as the text. There he found, in the heroic characters of primitive Greece, the simplicity of life and the primitive moral situations which fitted the ethical level of his pupils. Later Herbart's followers worked out this culture-epoch theory for younger children. They proceeded from fairy tales, Mother Goose stories, and the Old Testament, to the epic literature of the Greeks and the New Testament, and finally to modern literature.

The curriculum. If soul-life is comprised primarily of the ideas which form the circle of thought, then the curriculum of studies becomes all-important. There are, in general, only two kinds of presentations: (1) those that arise from experiences of things, and (2) those that come from social intercourse or personal relations. These two comprehend the totality of all that the human mind can know. From the first is derived all knowledge of the objects, the forces, and the laws of nature; from the second is learned the nature of man, his personal relations, morality, and religion. The first is "empirical knowledge"; the other, Herbart calls "sympathy."

Experience begins with sense perception of objects. In this view Herbart was wholly in accord with Locke and Pestalozzi. The child gathers much of his sensory experience before the period of formal education begins. But the knowledge that he brings to school is faulty in several ways. It is inaccurate; it is partial or narrow in range; and it is wholly lacking in system. The task of instruction must be to fill in the weak places by bringing the pupil into direct contact with a wider range of objects, which will round out his information.

Furthermore, the child's mind must be lifted from the sensory level of the concrete to the higher level of scientific knowledge, from sensation and perception to concept, judgment, and thought. He must ascend from the particular to the universal. This step, which Pestalozzi failed to provide for in his pedagogy, becomes central in Herbart. In forming his more complete science of education Herbart adopted Schiller's conception of the esthetic. He gave the development of "taste" a position right alongside of empirical experiences. He failed, however, to appreciate the creative aspect of art.

The second kind of knowledge, coming from social intercourse, is the more important because it is the basis of all the higher intellectual and moral development. It ascends from sympathy with individuals and judgments concerning individuals to the broader sympathy with society in general, and lastly has to do with the relation of both the individual and society to God. This kind of knowledge and the development of the moral judgment are found in history, literature, languages, religion, and art. History and literature furnish the opportunities for exercising ethical insight and judgment; for the one presents the characters and conduct of men, and the other pictures in imagination the ethical situations and conflicts which occur in human life. Both history and literature describe concrete, personal situations which call into action the moral judgment of approval and disapproval. Languages, religion, and art likewise reveal the inner nature of man, and promote the moral life.

The followers of Herbart worked out the secondary curriculum, in infinite detail. The subjects they included were: geography, religion, natural sciences, history, German, Latin, French, and Greek. Among the natural sciences they included: geology, botany, physics, chemistry, and mathematics. The historical interest formed, however, the backbone of the whole body of knowledge. The culture-epoch principle was followed in large measure, and all subjects were correlated into a systematic body of knowledge. For the elementary field, the following statement of principles governed their choice of materials: [10]

> 1. By following the order of the national culture, and presenting it in the light of ethical judgment, we shall call forth permanent interest in the developing child; hence, *chronological progress from older and simpler, to newer and more complicated stages and conditions.*
>
> 2. As a basis for this material we must use child-like classical, religious, literary, and historical matter (Folk Stories and *Robinson Crusoe* in the first two grades). "Periods which no master has described, whose spirit no poet has breathed, are of small value for education."

---

[10] DeGarmo, Charles, *Herbart and the Herbartians,* pp. 142-143. New York Scribner's Sons, 1912.

3. Only large, connected unities of subject-matter are able to arouse and keep alive the deep sympathy of the youthful mind, thereby contributing to the development of character. "Great moral energy is the effect of entire scenes and unbroken thought masses."

Doctrines of concentration and correlation. We are indebted to Herbart for two pedagogical doctrines which have played a conspicuous role in educational science, the principles of concentration and correlation. Herbart did not state either of these principles in precisely the way in which they have been formulated and applied by his followers. By "concentration" he meant the complete absorption of the attention in single acts of thought; it is that mental experience by which the mind is wholly immersed in a single idea to the exclusion of every other interest. It is the focusing of one's whole consciousness upon a single object of thought.

The disciples of Herbart have given a broader application to the term. They regard "concentration" as the grouping of all studies in the curriculum around one common central study. Such a central subject might be evolution, around which biology, physics, geology and other sciences would be correlated. For elementary education, history, geography, literature, or manual activities have been used by different theorists as centers. Herbart himself looked upon the ethical enlightenment of the youth as the central process of education. History and literature are the dominant means, while nature study and mathematics are subordinate.

Such a central core is necessary for several reasons. First, the number of studies that press for a place in the curriculum is too large to treat each of them with equal fullness. Second, the unity of the mental life requires that there be a unity in the knowledge of the individual. Third, as has been stated above, the ethical life is the unifying principle of the soul.

"Correlation" is the process which accompanies concentration. It is this process that makes one subject central, but sees to it that each topic studied receives full support from all other objects. For example, in connection with the discovery of America, history and geography may well be assisted by drawings and maps and by facts taken from nature, literature, and even arithmetic. These two doctrines, concentration and correlation, have played a large part in forming our conception of the scientific educational method of instruction.

Method of instruction. Herbart's method of instruction is thoroughly unique; for his fundamental philosophy, psychology, and ethics and principles of education form a closely-knit system which finds practical application in organizing the mind and character.

Like all the reformers, Herbart had been struck by the obvious uselessness of much that was taught. Most knowledge learned in the schools was merely retained in the memory and had no significance for life, in other words, no significance for action. Herbart held that the acquisition of such knowledge is due to a wrong method of teaching, and is harmful to the mind. Such knowledge has not been properly assimilated because it was not related to the experience of the individual; it has not been apperceived. All knowledge which is rightly assimilated will be learned with genuine interest and pass over into appropriate application. Mere information contains no guarantee that it will affect the will of the individual and find its way into function. It is stored in the memory as so much waste material. To be made serviceable for action, it must be integrated with the other ideas so as to form masses of thought and interest. The method of instruction which Herbart set forth was designed to build a living mind in strict accordance with the fundamental laws of human thinking.

The Herbartians recognize five steps which are indispensable in every process of instruction. Usually termed the "five formal steps of the recitation," these are: preparation, presentation, association, generalization, and application.[11]

The five formal steps are the result of the application of the principles of Herbart's psychology and ethics to the process of instruction. The pupil's experience, at the beginning of education, is haphazard, unsystematic, and faulty in emphasis. Things and events crowd into the mind in masses, and the result is a chaotic conglomeration of ideas. In order that experience may be systematized so that all of its resources will be usable, instruction must perform its function. It must fill in with further concrete experience wherever information is lacking. It must analyze the old experience, and recombine and systematize its materials into concepts. Only by such processes can knowledge become the ready instrument of the mind.

Preparation. This process requires that past ideas, or memories, related to the particular topic which is to be treated in the lesson be recalled to attention. In order that proper assimilation may be assured,

[11] Herbart united the first two steps into what he termed "clearness." The last, which is now termed "application," he named "method."

the apperceptive masses which are necessary for assimilation must be brought into consciousness. Only in this way can a vital interest in the new material be aroused, and the pupil be prepared to give full attention to the new lesson material.

Presentation. The second step in the psychological ordering of the lesson materials is that of presentation. This process involves the presenting of new material so that the pupil clearly and fully apprehends it. It requires that the concrete object or experience should always be used unless there is already ample sensory data. Herbart called these first two steps "clearness," because he insisted upon the presentation of the idea in concrete form. In the approach to every new subject, the concrete must always be provided. But not only in the field of sensory objects does experience begin with the concrete; Herbart insisted that in the field of sympathy or human relationships, that is, in the moral sphere, experience must begin with the simplest and most understandable situations.

Association. This process involves the thorough assimilation of the new idea, and this takes place by the apperceiving of the new by the old ideas. Points of likeness with former ideas are brought forward, differences are pointed out, and the new idea takes its place in the structure of the mind. This involves comparison, which is the logic of induction.

Generalization. Herbart improved upon Pestalozzi, who dealt only with concrete and individual objects of experience. Herbart was well aware that real thinking can take place only as sensory experiences are analyzed, abstract characteristics are sifted out, and general conceptions are formed. Generalization is a necessary step in the development of the mind to its highest capacity; otherwise, it will remain always on the low level of perception and the concrete. This process is especially necessary for instruction on the adolescent level.

Application. The final step in the acquisition of knowledge in accordance with psychological processes is exercise in using the knowledge that has been acquired. This term does not stress use in a purely utilitarian sense; rather it means that every idea which is learned shall form a part of the functional mind, and that it shall aid in the interpretation of life in a clear and vital way. It can do this only if the child learns immediately to apply the new idea and to make it his own. The proper assimilation of knowledge and its use in apperceiving still further knowledge is the only assurance that dead information will not accumulate to burden the mind.

THE RESULTS OF HERBARTIAN PEDAGOGY

Herbartian principles and methods had an incalculable effect on education. Although delayed for some time in their influence even in Germany, they finally were almost universally adopted. A vast literature, much of it controversial in character, has been produced in the elaboration of the system. Next to Germany, the system had its most extensive reception in America. Like a tidal wave, interest in this elaborate methodology swept over American teachers and students of education during the last decade of the 19th century. Four American teachers, dissatisfied with the superficial pedagogy of the time, sought deeper insight from the universities of Germany. These were Charles DeGarmo, C. C. Van Liew, Charles McMurry, and his brother, Frank McMurry. Returning to America, all these men occupied important positions in some of the foremost universities and teachers' colleges of this country. They introduced American teachers to the principles of Herbartian pedagogy, and began a remarkable and voluminous outpouring of literature on the subject, which came from the press between 1889 and 1901.

Not only were the works of Herbart and his disciples translated from the German; there were, likewise, numerous other books, pamphlets, and articles published explaining or applying the Herbartian principles. Furthermore, the *National Herbartian Society* was organized in 1892, in imitation of a similar organization in Germany. It enrolled many of the leading educators of this country and published a year-book.

Dr. Charles McMurry published *General Method* in 1892, and with his brother published *The Method of the Recitation* in 1897. A large number of other works followed. The wave of enthusiasm for Herbartian pedagogy assisted, in large measure, in stimulating independent study of the science of education by American students. Rather suddenly, however, the works of William T. Harris, United States Commissioner of Education; of G. Stanley Hall; and of John Dewey put an end to the spread of the system. In 1902 the *National Herbartian Society* changed its name to the *National Society for the Scientific Study of Education*—a change which may well symbolize the coming of age of American educational science.

Evaluation. The psychological and pedagogical theories of Herbart have been discredited and superseded for various reasons. His psychology was formed before the time of Darwin's biological evolution. No one today would accept his fundamental thesis that feeling and willing are secondary functions derived from ideation. Feeling and action are unquestionably older and deeper than knowledge. But it must be acknowledged that Herbart did away with the faculty psychology, introduced the scientific and mathematical method of approach to education, promoted the training of teachers, and gave the methodology of secondary education a new meaning.

Herbart had in view the education of the youth in his adolescent years, when his mind and character are reaching maturity. At this period the intellectual life is undergoing its most rapid growth. While there is a vast amount of emotionalism, there can be no question that, for the higher moral life as well as for the intellectual, emphasis must be placed upon grafting onto his nature as many interests as possible. Ideation, or thought, and will cannot be separated. The higher will is an informed will. Impulse and desire, however, do not spring from ideas, as Herbart imagined, but they cannot become will, in any high sense, without the assistance of ideas. Herbart was right when he endeavored to form the circle of thought as the surest means of forming character. Ethical personality is, after all, not the product of biological, but of social evolution. It has not come from the struggle with nature, but has been wrought in the crucible of interaction with other humans. The processes of idealization and of self-consciousness have assisted in developing insight and moral ideals. Viewed from this angle, no theory of pedagogy has yet risen to compete with that of Herbart on the secondary and higher levels.

The Herbartian terms which were on every teacher's lips at the beginning of this century, "interest," "apperception," "circle of thought," "concentration," "correlation," "culture epoch," and "formal steps of instruction," have gone the way of all fetishes. New terms and ideas have now taken their places. Nevertheless, these principles of Herbart have not been entirely abandoned. Transmuted into new forms of thought and into statements of greater scientific accuracy, they can still be detected in most textbooks on methods and curriculum.

Chapter 19

FROEBEL AND EDUCATION BY ORGANISMIC EVOLUTION

A UNIQUE educator. Of all the first-rank educational reformers of modern times, or of any time, for that matter, Froebel has been most exalted by the few and least understood by the many. His followers revered him as the most perfect man who ever lived, and looked upon his writings as inspired. Others condemned him as a pantheist, a mystic, a symbolist, and an eccentric old fool who spent his time playing with small children. The Prussian Government viewed him as a dangerous revolutionist, and prohibited his educational practices.

Today the most common misconceptions in regard to Froebel are that his principles have to do only with infant education; that he is merely the founder of the kindergarten, nothing more important. Another widespread error is that, because he was a symbolist, his ideas are doctrinaire and valueless. Despite all the misrepresentation and misunderstanding, Froebel's principles are more widely received and his methods more fully incorporated into western educational practices today than ever. Herbert Quick candidly acknowledged that he "very imperfectly" understood Froebel, but at the same time he added significantly: [1] "All the best tendencies of modern thought on education seem to me to culminate in what was said and done by Friedrich Froebel." Froebel stands today as the most comprehensive and vitalizing educational reformer of the 19th century. Students who become dizzy at the thought of mysticism are warned to avoid him, but the one who makes the effort to pierce beneath a somewhat forbidding exterior will find an insight that illumines the entire field of education.

[1] Quick, R. H., *Essays on Educational Reformers,* p. 384. New York: Appleton, 1891.

FROEBEL'S LIFE AND EDUCATION

Childhood and youth. Froebel's childhood was extremely unhappy. But it was probably this circumstance which aroused his genius. The result of his unhappiness was twofold: he formed a deep and abiding attachment to nature, and at a very premature age he became acutely conscious of his own inner life. These two experiences, the unfolding panorama of outer nature, and the awakening of his inner impulses and feelings account for the two sides of his philosophic and educational theory.

Friedrich Froebel was born April 21, 1782, in the village of Oberweisbach, in the mountains of Thuringia, in southern Germany. His father, pastor of an extensive parish, was too busy and lacking in paternal instincts to enter into the life of this son. When Froebel was nine months of age, his mother died. "This loss," he wrote long afterwards, "a hard blow to me, influenced the whole environment and development of my being; I consider that my mother's death decided more or less the external circumstances of my whole life." It was not so much the loss of his mother which adversely affected him, but the attitude of his stepmother, who treated him with undisguised hostility. Persuaded that young Friedrich was stupid, the parents let him grow up without the usual attention to education. Deprived of parental affection and playmates, the boy soon became moody and subjective. Thrown thus upon his own resources, the lad's sensitive heart turned to the hills, flowers, trees, and clouds for companionship.

Moreover, an overwhelming tendency to introspection as a young child prepared him to observe and interpret the experiences of child nature, and gave him a sympathy for children which people generally do not feel. He was not permitted to attend the regular school for boys, but was placed in the school for older girls, which was under the charge of his father.

From 10 to 14 Froebel spent the only happy years of his childhood in the home of his maternal uncle, Pastor Hoffman, of Stadt-Ilm. Here he lived the normal life of a boy and attended the parish school, where he received the only systematic instruction of his whole career. Of greater moment, however, was the benign religious instruction given him by his uncle; this awakened within him spiritual aspirations of the most profound character. At 15 he was apprenticed to an expert forester, who failed to train him as he contracted.

Young manhood. In the spring of 1799, Froebel was sent on a mission to his brother, who was studying at the University of Jena. He decided to remain there for some months and gave himself over to hard study, though it was chiefly along elementary lines. At the time Jena, as has been pointed out, boasted the most remarkable group of celebrities ever to be found at a modern German university.[2] It is impossible to estimate with any degree of precision just how deeply may have entered into Froebel's experience the rich and varied intellectual and literary activity that centered about the little university. His lack of systematic preparation prevented him from appreciating very fully the more profound currents of intellectual activity that swirled about him. The great similarity of his ideas and those of Schiller poses a most intricate problem.

Leaving the university, Froebel made various attempts to find a vocation that would be permanently agreeable. But he always felt a deep dissatisfaction with everything until by a happy accident he was invited by Herr Grüner, of Frankfort, to teach drawing in his normal school. Froebel immediately recognized that educational work was the only activity that answered his longings and was in harmony with his aptitudes.

The most significant stages of progress in the ripening of his educational genius appeared gradually. From 1807 to 1810 he undertook the training of three young boys. Most of this time he spent with his charges at the school of Pestalozzi at Yverdun. Together with his pupils, Froebel attended classes and thus had the opportunity to learn in detail the methods and principles of the celebrated "father of modern education." By 1810 he had reached the conclusion that, while Pestalozzi had made a remarkable advance beyond his predecessors, yet his ideas were far from forming a perfected science of education. Of this experience Froebel declared: [3]

> I soon saw much that was imperfect.... The powerful, indefinable, stirring, and uplifting effect produced by Pestalozzi set one's soul on fire for a higher, nobler life, although he had not made clear or sure the exact way towards it, nor indicated the means whereby to attain it.

---

[2] See page 472 of this text.

[3] Froebel, F., *Autobiography,* p. 79. Translated by E. Michaelis and H. K. Moore. Syracuse: C. W. Bardeen, 1889.

There can be no doubt that this contact with Pestalozzi furnished the preparation for Froebel's own educational reforms.

Scientific investigations. Dissatisfied with Pestalozzi's principles and practices, Froebel decided upon a new and radical step. His mind was many-sided, introspective, observant, and critical. Above everything else was an insatiable craving for principles that would explain fully the underlying laws of all phenomena. His great contemporaries in the field of philosophy, Fichte, Schelling, and especially Hegel, endeavored to reach a knowledge of the universe by means of philosophical speculation alone. Froebel, on the contrary, began to form his philosophy by a study of the empirical sciences.

The last decades of the 18th and the first of the 19th century witnessed a remarkable forward movement in the various realms of human knowledge. The study of philology by F. A. Wolf, Boeckh, and Schlegel had revealed the original unity and the subsequent development of all languages. Chemistry had divorced itself from its primitive theories, and Black and Priestley had set it on its triumphant path toward positive science. Physics and geology had made astonishing progress.

Froebel plunged with burning zeal into the study of all these fields, as well as mathematics, in which he was already fairly proficient. Especially, however, did he devote himself to the study of mineralogy, which more than anything else satisfied his deeper intellectual cravings. For a time he studied at the University of Göttingen, but later went to Berlin to work under Professor Christian S. Weiss, celebrated for research in mineralogy and natural history. Froebel also heard lectures by Fichte, the most renowned philosopher of the time. The fact that Froebel rose to be assistant curator of the mineralogical museum at Berlin under Weiss, and the further fact that he was offered a professorship in mineralogy are evidence of his attainments as a student of science.

Froebel's work at Berlin was interrupted by the renewal of the Napoleonic wars (1814). He volunteered for service, to save the fatherland. He did not see any actual fighting, but this experience brought him several friends who were to be his life-long associates in his educational enterprises.

Educational institutions. After a preliminary experiment, Froebel opened a school for boys at Keilhau (1817), in Thuringia, similar to Pestalozzi's famous institution at Yverdun. In this venture he incorporated his principles of elementary education. The school, however, was not a great success. In 1831, Froebel left Keilhau to his assistants and went to Switzerland, where he conducted several institutions. In 1836, partly because of the ill health of his wife, but more because he had reached a decision to devote his life to the reform of pre-school training, he returned to Germany.

The following year, in an old mill in the mountain village of Blankenburg, he opened the first kindergarten. From this time until his death, he devoted his efforts to founding kindergartens, the training of kindergartners, the elaboration of his methods, and the creation of apparatus for these institutions. His views were enthusiastically received by a few people, but were not widely adopted in Germany because they were not understood and because they were considered to be politically radical. The kindergarten was banned from Prussia for some years.

FROEBEL'S EVOLUTIONISTIC PHILOSOPHY

Sources of Froebel's ideas. The originality of Froebel's ideas was discounted from the start. German authorities dismissed his pedagogy with the curt remark that he had nothing which was not in Pestalozzi. That he was an independent thinker with creative ability can no longer be doubted. That his thought was influenced by contemporaries, he was frank to avow. One may recognize four sources from which he drew: (1) the general movement of post-Kantian philosophy; (2) the developments of science; (3) the writings of the great educators; and (4) his own keen scientific observation of human development.

Froebel was exposed at Jena and later at Berlin, to the most dynamic movement in the history of modern philosophic thought. Among others he studied especially the systems of Bruno, Fichte, Schelling, and Schiller. While these systems harmonized in general with the trend of his experience, they did not completely satisfy him. It was rather the philosophy of K. C. F. Krause which furnished him a world orientation (*Weltanschauung*). He had always been deeply introspective and a keen observer of human nature. At the same time he was profoundly interested in all the phenomena of the external world, and the unification of the subjective and objective. Froebel believed that Krause harmonized more successfully than others the different methods and the various fields of knowledge. Most important of all, he utilized his knowledge more satisfactorily in an explanation of human evolution.

In Krause's comprehensive system Froebel found his own views of life quite fully expressed in philosophic form. Krause was not what philosophers call an Idealist, like Fichte and Hegel. He may be more accurately termed a spiritualistic Realist. His system is not materialistic nor naturalistic, and it skillfully avoids pantheism. It has been most aptly termed *Panentheism,* that is, everything is in God, and is an expression of His creative will. It is noteworthy that Krause's philosophy was treated by the Germans with the same cold indifference as Froebel's educational theories, and for the same reasons. Both of these thinkers were sympathetic with democracy and, accordingly, in direct opposition to the totalitarian movement. Froebel's life-long striving for all-sided unity found most satisfying expression in Krause's spiritualistic system.

The second source of Froebel's general philosophy was scientific knowledge. He studied languages to discover the genetic development of human experience; mathematics for the light it sheds on the laws of astronomy, physics, and mineralogy; botany for the evolution of plant life; the child in order to learn the course of human development.

The third source of Froebel's views was the literature of education. That he read Rousseau seems clear, though there is no direct statement to that effect. The likeness of their principles and methods warrants the conclusion that Froebel was a Teutonic Jean Jacques. His direct contact with Pestalozzi's ideas and practices naturally colored his whole thinking, but to class Pestalozzi with Froebel is to confound the blossom with the ripened fruit. There was also a little known author who contributed much to Froebel's philosophy, Johann H. G. Heusinger, who in 1797 published an educational work entitled *On the Utilization of the Powerful Impulse in Children to Activity* (*Über der Benutzung des bei Kindern so thätigen Triebes, beschäftigt zu sein*). Heusinger followed out in practice the ideas of Rousseau and Basedow. Froebel's copy of this work was much used, and the margins were filled with comments. It is probable that he knew Heusinger as an instructor of mathematics at the University of Jena.

Critical comparison of the ideas of Froebel and Schiller shows many similarities that cannot be purely coincidental, but so far no one has studied the influence of Schiller upon Froebel's views.

Froebel's mind was too independent, too original, to accept with docile spirit the views of others. In combining ideas from these various sources, he was unquestionably constructive; and in working out the implications of his fundamental conceptions in educational principles and apparatus, he showed marked creative ability. The chief educational principles of

Froebel are to a large extent assignable to his direct observation of the activities of children. Especially in his maturer years was Froebel strongly intent upon the observation of children's activities, and the interpretation of these in a genetic theory. Especially did he seek to know what things children produce, and how they act when left to their own spontaneous devices. He aimed to base his methods and his kindergarten apparatus upon such objective scientific knowledge.

Froebel was the chief modern thinker to view education as an element in the process of cosmic evolution. For him, education is not the passing on of the funded experience from one generation to the next, nor the development of certain capacities or powers, nor the adjustment of the individual to his environment. It is, rather, a process which includes all these and goes far beyond them. In his first important book, *The Education of Man* (1826), Froebel indicates that education is the process by which the individual develops self-conscious manhood, with all his powers fully and harmoniously functioning in relation to nature and society. Furthermore, it was the same process by which mankind as a whole originally rose above the animal level, and has continued to develop to his present condition. It comprehends both individual and universal evolution.

Froebel's philosophy begins with what the philosophers term the Absolute and the theologians call God. He conceived this original being as an active, energizing, creating, intelligent, and self-conscious agent. Creation is not an act performed once for all; it is rather a continuous process of productive activity. Fichte derived nature from mind, and Schelling derived mind from nature. Krause and Froebel, on the contrary, derived both nature and mind from an original unity, from self-active, spontaneous spirit. In the physical universe, this creative urge is experienced and known as force; in man, it rises to the highest level as spirit and thought, and becomes conscious of its own nature and ends.

In their essence, physical force and thought are both the activity of God. Divine energy unfolds into the manifoldness of nature and into the complexity of man. Seeing that it is God's nature to express itself in creative activities, it is necessary for Him to individualize His being. So it is imperative for God to express Himself by creating a world of particular objects and beings.

The doctrine of unity or "part-whole." The consummate doctrine of Froebel's philosophy is the conception of unity. It had its roots in his innermost experiences but found its best exposition by Krause, who universalized the idea of organismic unity and development. This conception was so novel that Krause was obliged to invent the term "part-whole" (*Gliedganzes*) to express it.[4] One may illustrate its meaning in this way: The finger is a unity when considered by itself, but a part of the hand. The hand is a unity in and of itself, but it is part of the arm. Thus, every object in the universe has this twofold aspect. The entire universe is a living organism, the unity of which is God. He has unfolded into the manifold universe without losing His unity, just as the life energy of a single cell unfolds into the complex organism without losing its functional integrity.

Krause and Froebel agreed in extending the principle of organic evolution to the mind and its relation to the physical order. They maintained that man is a unity and not a duality. The functioning of man's diverse organs and mental capacities springs from the unity of the organism. An example of functional unity may be seen in any productive activity, in which physical movements and mental processes function together. For illustration, in the making of any product, the memory, imagination, perception, reasoning, will, and feeling coöperate with the nerves, muscles, and sense organs. Owing to this functional integration, Froebel considered productive activity the most efficient means of education. Traditional methods of instruction which called into action separate faculties were destructive of unity and, consequently, injurious.

This doctrine of unity may also be seen in the objects that man produces. Each product is a unity by virtue of the distinctive purpose or function that it performs. The chair, the hoe, or the bridge—each is a unity in itself because the mind of man has ordered the materials for the attainment of a certain end. The automobile, composed of a multitude of parts or of mechanisms within mechanisms, has many unities within the one comprehensive whole, which is a means of transportation. By virtue of its function the automobile is one, and not many.

The idea of unity rises to highest significance in the case of human relations. It is the explanation of all social, institutional, and religious life. The individual is a unity or whole when considered by himself. When he acts in relation to others and participates in the general life he maintains his unity but is also a part of the larger whole. The hand is a unity when it performs its functions in relation to the organism. Severed from the body, it loses its identity and becomes just decaying

[4] *Glied* is the German for "part" or "member," and *Ganzes* is "whole."

flesh and bone. So it is with human beings. Individuals enter into relations one with another, and form organizations for the realization of certain purposes. Such organizations are functional unities in so far as they realize their ends. God is the original organism, the primordial unity from which the entire universe has evolved by virtue of His creative self-expression.

General theory of development. In trying to grasp what appears to be so mysterious in Froebel's philosophy, it is well to keep in mind that all his thinking was surcharged with the conception of organic evolution. He looked upon man as the "human plant." He shared this conception with Pestalozzi and others before him, but he extended it to a wider range than did any of them. To understand his view, picture a seed planted in the warm earth in springtime; observe the living green shoot which comes out of the seed, the division of this shoot into several branches, and the burgeoning of buds or leaves on these branches.

In considering this unfolding of the seed into the plant, it is important to look deeper than the outer appearance. In the seed and plant there are at work certain unseen forces which are building the structure of the plant out of the particles of matter that are taken in by the roots. These creative forces are directed and governed in their action by an inner law. Such is the background idea.

Now, let this picture of the natural, gradual unfolding of the plant organism be generalized; apply it to everything in the entire universe. Because of his detailed study of the formation of crystals, Froebel was led to extend the principle of development downward through the entire inorganic creation. Whether it be the forming of a crystal, a rock, or a planet, all are evolved in precisely the same way, and because of one and the same unfolding force. Froebel believed that this same principle or law is operative in the realm of life, animal as well as vegetable.

But Froebel was not content to apply this idea of development to the inorganic and the biological realms. He took a further momentous step. He declared that the same law of development reigned in the spiritual realm, in will and mind. He looked upon the activity of man's mental nature as caused by the same force that forms the crystal or the living organism. Moreover all human activities and behavior are subject to the process of unfolding from simple, primitive conditions to the most complex. This conclusion means that productive activity and human behavior in the race and in the individual have followed a course of orderly evolution. Productive skill and ethical conduct are subject to the universal law

of growth. This conception is one of the most significant in tł
of modern education. Its implications are manifold.

The same law of unfolding that governs in the biological and ina-
mate world is, therefore, found in our voluntary acts and in all our processes of thought. Back of all these processes, the force that forms the crystal, the animal body, the act of will, the thought in the mind, is one and the same force; it is the energy of the Creator spontaneously pushing outward and upward.

Child development is not an unimportant phase of life, a mere transition which unfortunately intervenes between birth and maturity; it is in line with the very nature of the universe itself, the method of creation.

The law of development. The great quest of philosophy at the beginning of the 19th century was to discover some unitary law or principle that would explain the organization of the entire universe. Schiller held that the sensuous and the rational-ethical are harmonized by the creative power of beauty. Fichte and Hegel thought they found an integrative drive in the dialectic process of thesis, antithesis, and synthesis. They contended that the physical and mental worlds are both a process of thought. Having reduced everything to thought, it was easy to conclude that the dialectic process could be invoked to explain the evolution of everything in the universe.

Froebel also searched for a single principle that would explain the process of the creative activity of the universe. As he conceived it, the principle, according to which spiritual energy evolves, is the "law of opposites" or "the law of contraries." It is similar to the law of thesis, antithesis, and synthesis, except that this is a process of logical ideas or meanings. Froebel's law is a dynamic principle; the law of action, reaction, and equilibrium. It is, therefore, broader in application than the ideational process of thesis, antithesis, and synthesis, which is applicable only to ideas. Froebel's law is universal in its scope. It explains the creation of all things in the physical and the spiritual worlds. Its greatest value, however, is in explaining the course of development of human conduct. According to Froebel, the universe is not pure thought or idea, as Hegel taught; nor physical force, as the materialists believed. It is a spiritual organism that shows itself alike in the force of the physical world and in the will and thought of the mental world.

Human development. In the unfolding of the cosmos, man is "the last and most perfect product of evolution." In him the body "appears in highest equilibrium and symmetry." As the original source of all creative energy is spiritual, man combines the mental, or psychological, with the physical. In him "the primordial force is fully spiritualized." It has come to consciousness of itself. By this self-consciousness "man feels, understands, and knows his own powers." Self-consciousness is the greatest step of progress in the cosmic process; for, by virtue thereof, man knows his own experiences, chooses his own ends, attains freedom, and has become capable of seeking perfection.

The attainment of self-consciousness and freedom carries two resulting implications of the highest consequence. By a knowledge of his own nature and of the laws of his development, man can understand the right system of education by which to rear children. He is no longer blindly following instinct, but can act in a scientific or rational way in training the young.

The second implication is that the species is still evolving to a higher order of being. As the botanist, by the selection of seed, can vary his plant production, so man, knowing the law of cosmic evolution, can develop the human race to a nobler state. Belief in unlimited progress for man was one of Froebel's most cherished convictions.[5]

> Man, humanity in man, as an external manifestation, should, therefore, be looked upon not as perfectly developed, not as fixed and stationary, but as steadily and progressively growing, in a state of ever-living development, ever ascending from one stage of culture to another toward its aim, which partakes of the infinite and eternal. It is unspeakably pernicious to look upon the development of humanity as stationary and completed.

Again, he declared: [6] "We are ignorant of the nature of Humanity which lives only in its continuous development and cultivation."

Mental and spiritual development. As has been stated, the same law of organic development which operates in the unfolding of the physical world operates in the same manner in the inner life of man. In his experiences man comes to know this cosmic law or process in the most intimate way. His activities grow or unfold in precisely the same way as does the plant, from the simple unity to finer and finer discriminations in action. This may be illustrated by the example of the child's reaction to people. At first, he reacts to all in the same way. Then, he begins to discriminate, and his responses grow more varied

---

[5] Froebel, Friedrich, *The Education of Man*, p. 17. Translated by W. N. Hailman, New York: Appleton, 1892.

[6] *Ibid.*, p. 146.

and complex as he notes differences in people. The same is true of his purposes. To begin with, he has only a vague general attitude toward life. Gradually his purposes evolve, and become more and more differentiated.

The process of evolution is primarily one by which activity becomes differentiated, and increasingly better able to express life. The law of development is the law of the evolution of creative activity. It holds primarily for will, conduct, purpose, and, consequently, for thought as accessory to these processes.

Evil due to faulty education. Contending that the child is inherently good, that the essence of his being is divine energizing, Froebel was obliged either to deny entirely the existence of evil in man, or to account for its origin. If he could not successfully account for it, his system was open to an accusation which was frequently made against it; if he were a pantheist, his strong insistence that the goal of educational process is freedom would be rankly inconsistent. Before considering his view of the cause of depravity it is advisable to understand his conception of virtues and vices.

The virtues which Froebel extolled are of different ranks of importance. Those of the lower order are courage, perseverance, resolution, prudence, and industry. These are related closely to the physical life. The next group are the virtues of the heart, mind, and will: simplicity, gentleness, friendliness, justice, moderation, self-control, truthfulness, loyalty, brotherly love, and impartiality. These are social virtues and are developed chiefly by the games of childhood. Of a still higher order are forbearance, consideration, compassion, and the encouragement of the weak, which are due to the feeling of common sympathy.

The chief evils are willfulness, deceit, falsehood, defiance, obstinacy, stubbornness, mental and physical indolence, sensuality, vanity and self-conceit, dogmatism and despotism, an unbrotherly and unfilial spirit, superficiality, aversion to work and even to play, disobedience, ungodliness, carelessness, frivolity, and egotism. These are not due to any principle of original depravity as the theologians taught. Froebel believed that each vice is a virtue which has been perverted in its unfolding.[7]

> A suppressed or perverted good quality—a good tendency, only repressed, misunderstood, or misguided—lies originally at the bottom of every shortcoming in man. Hence the only and infallible remedy for counteracting any shortcoming and even wickedness is to find the orig-

[7] *Ibid.*, pp. 121-122.

> inally good source, the originally good side of the human being that has been repressed, disturbed, or misled into the shortcoming, and then to foster, build up, and properly guide this good side.

All evils, therefore, are caused either by (1) the complete neglect of the development of certain aspects of human life; or (2) "the distortion of originally good human powers and tendencies by arbitrary and willful interference with the original orderly and logical course of human development." [8]

The germ of wickedness comes from the sense of neglect by the mother or nurse. Out of this feeling springs "willfulness, the first and most hideous of all faults . . . a fault that soon becomes the mother of deceit, falsehood, defiance, obstinacy, and a host of subsequent sad and hideous faults." [9]

Neglecting to develop any power destroys the fundamental harmony of the child's being, and causes a divergence of his real self from his ideal self—that is to say, what he has actually become is not consistent with what his essential nature requires him to be. All the evils of the human heart are due to faulty development, and the lack of development must be charged to a wrong method of education.

The individual repeats the racial development. In his unfolding life, on all sides, the individual repeats the stages of development the race has passed through. This theory—known in the Herbartian philosophy of education as the *culture-epoch theory,* and in biology as the *recapitulation theory*—follows logically from Froebel's view of cosmic evolution. The rhythmic beginnings of language, the animistic attitude toward nature, superstition and other early religious experiences, the late emergence of reason, the awakening of the moral sense, in fact, all the epochal developments of the race, are definitely repeated in the unfolding life of the individual. Froebel explained the theory in this way: [10]

> Thus, in the mind of man, in the history of his mental development, in the growth of his consciousness, in the experience of every child from the time of his appearance on earth to the time when he consciously beholds himself in the Garden of Eden, in beautiful nature spread out before him, there is repeated the history of the creation and development of all things. Similarly, in each child there is repeated at a later

[8] *Ibid.,* p. 119.
[9] *Ibid.,* p. 22.
[10] *Ibid.,* pp. 40-41.

period the deed which marks the beginning of moral and human emancipation of the dawn of reason—essentially the same deed that marked, and inasmuch as the race was destined for freedom, must mark, the moral and human emancipation, the dawn of reason in the race as a whole. Every human being who is attentive to his own development may thus recognize and study in himself the history of the development of the race to the point it may have reached.

But while each individual must pass through all the preceding phases of human development, Froebel warned that "this should not be done in a way of dead imitation or mere copying, but in the way of living spontaneous activity." Thus the boy loves to play at cave life, not as imitating someone, but because such play expresses the inner craving of his nature. Moreover, the discovery that the individual travels the same highway of experience as the race leads to several valuable conclusions. First, one is enabled to see mankind as a whole; that is, to feel the unity of all humanity. Again, one is enabled to understand more sympathetically the unfolding life of his own children.

Human development by stages. Like other advocates of genetic development, Froebel held that human growth takes place by stages. He was, however, strongly averse to Rousseau's belief in the sudden emergence of new features. This so-called *saltatory theory* did not meet with his approval. Catastrophic changes and emotional storms were not characteristic of his experience. Moreover, such sudden changes would contradict his idea of a uniform law governing all unfolding. Froebel was impressed, rather, with the gradualness and continuity of development, and the unity which embrace all stages of growth.

The particular stages which he accepted are: infancy, childhood, boyhood, youth, and maturity. He declined to assign definite age limits, for the stages are marked by certain central tendencies rather than by years. The central tendency or nascent feature of each stage controls all the other developments, and defines the educational aim for the particular stage. The completion of each stage is essential to the proper development of the next. It cannot be claimed that any one stage is more important than any other. Each stage must be what that stage calls for, and should not be regarded merely as a preparation for the next. Each stage depends on the one preceding it, and consequently "in its place and time each stage is equally important." Froebel further expressed the idea in this way: [11]

---

[11] *Ibid.*, pp. 28-29.

> The vigorous and complete development and cultivation of each successive stage depends on the vigorous, complete and characteristic development of each and all preceding stages of life. . . . The boy has not become a boy, nor has the youth become a youth, by reaching a certain age, but only by having lived through childhood, and further on, through boyhood, true to the requirements of his mind, his feelings, and his body.

Man's creative nature. The most enlightening idea that Froebel has contributed to modern pedagogy is that the human being is essentially dynamic or productive, and not merely receptive. Man is a self-generating force and not a sponge which sops up knowledge from without. The core of his being partakes of the creative, spiritual energizing of the Absolute. He is an organism of spontaneous activities and must of necessity express his nature, not in capricious or arbitrary ways, but in accord with the fixed law of development. As a creature of nature, his activities are, first of all, unconscious and instinctive, and guided by the purposefulness of nature. As man emerges from nature, he becomes more and more fully aware of its ends, and accepts these ends for his conscious striving. He thus combines the unconscious and spontaneous with clear, conscious purposefulness. Man's genius and life work are realized by expressing all the inherited promptings of his divine essence. By means of this self-expression he grows in self-realization.[12] Froebel's classic statement of this principle is as follows: [13]

> *God creates and works productively in uninterrupted continuity.* Each thought of God is a work, a deed, a product, and each thought of God continues to work with creative power in endless productive activity to all eternity. . . . The Spirit of God hovered over Chaos, and moved it; and stones and plants, beasts and man took form and separate being and life. *God created man in his own image; therefore, man should create and bring forth like God.* His Spirit, the spirit of man, should hover over the shapeless, and move it that it may take shape and form, a distinct being and life of its own. This is the high meaning, the deep significance, and great purpose of work and industry, of productive and creative activity. We become truly godlike in diligence and industry, in working and doing, which are accompanied by the clear perception or even by the vaguest feeling that thereby we represent the inner in the outer; that we give body to spirit, and form to thought; that we render visible the invisible; that we impart an outward, finite, transient being to life in the spirit.

---

[12] *Ibid.*, p. 2.
[13] *Ibid.*, pp. 30-31.

Man acts in order to express his inner emotions. The very essence of his nature is spiritual energy, which is clearly seen in all purely human activities. Activity realizes inner purposes in terms of outer form and structure. Moreover, the results of such activity enrich man's knowledge in a normal, functional manner and lead to self-consciousness.

It is highly noteworthy that Froebel did not derive the urge to activity solely from physical need, as so many thinkers do. His theory of evolution is spiritual and not mechanistic; it is esthetic and not utilitarian. In this respect his whole philosophy is a direct challenge to pragmatic and naturalistic schools of thought. He gives no comfort to the economic interpretation of history. Froebel was emphatic in disavowing the principle of utility as the mainspring of human conduct: [14]

> The debasing illusion that man works, produces, creates in order to preserve his body, in order to secure food, clothing, shelter, may have to be endured, but should not be diffused and propagated. Primarily and in truth man works only that his spiritual, divine essence may assume outward form, and that thus he may be enabled to recognize his own spiritual divine nature and the innermost being of God. Whatever food, clothing, and shelter he obtains thereby comes to him as an insignificant surplus.

Thus, for Froebel, it is not the natural appetites which furnish the drive for action and consequently the basis of education. There is a transcendental urge, an imperative which is superior to physical appetites; this driving force is spiritual being, unity with God. Froebel accepted the principle of Jesus, "Seek ye first the Kingdom of God and His righteousness, and all these things shall be added unto you."

Is man's development predetermined? Froebel's theory of development by inner unfolding might readily be construed as a doctrine of strict determinism, especially in view of his constant insistence that man's development is analogous to that of lower organisms. No one, however, would more vehemently repudiate this interpretation than Froebel himself. Nothing was farther from his belief. To him, indeed, freedom is the breath of man's life. He is not a machine determined, from within, by inner law, nor yet from without, by physical forces. Man has attained consciousness of his own inner being. He knows and evaluates ends, purposes, and results; he chooses the ultimate type of selfhood which he would express and realize. He is self-determined be-

[14] *Ibid.*, p. 32.

cause he can choose his final goal and, in a large measure, create the environment necessary for its attainment. The one thing which differentiates man from the lower orders of being and which makes him free is self-consciousness. This is the fulcrum by which man is raised to the higher level of existence. To make the child conscious of himself is, therefore, one of the prime objectives of education.

FROEBEL'S THEORY OF EDUCATION

Educational objectives. The objectives which Froebel set for education are in harmony with his fundamental principle of self-realization through self-activity. Perfect living and culture, all-sidedness, and harmony within and in all life's relations are to be sought; likewise, a knowledge of self, of nature, of God, and of the inner law which relates them all is essential. These objectives are set forth in his own peculiar language. Several passages may be quoted: [15] "Education should lead and guide man to clearness concerning himself and in himself, to peace with nature, and to unity with God." From this it can be seen why Froebel insisted upon knowledge of oneself, of nature, and of the law of organic development. The child must utilize this law to achieve harmony within himself and with nature, and the incorporation of the general in the particular. Froebel summed it up in these terms: [16]

> The representation of the infinite in the finite, of the eternal in the temporal, of the celestial in the terrestrial, of the divine in and through man, in the life of man by the *nursing* of his originally divine nature, confronts us unmistakably on every side as the only object, the only aim of all education, in all instruction and training.

Another aspect of Froebel's objective remains to be discussed: the development of will, which forms the most essential function of the school.[17]

> To give firmness to the will, to quicken it, and to make it pure, strong, and enduring, in a life of pure humanity is the chief concern, the main object in the guidance of the boy, in instruction and the school.

In insisting that the effects of education upon the will are more important than the effects upon the intellect, Froebel was in accord with the trend of modern philosophy and pedagogy since Kant.

---

[15] *Ibid.*, pp. 4-5.
[16] *Ibid.*, p. 16.
[17] *Ibid.*, p. 96.

Philosophy of the curriculum. The basis of the curriculum is found in the unfolding activities of child nature. These activities are the necessary expressions of his normal life as a biopsychic organism. The child learns by doing and through doing. Learning is the result of his active life. For Rousseau, the importance of an object rests in its usefulness; for Pestalozzi, in its value in training the sense organs; for Herbart, in its contribution to knowledge. But for Froebel, an object is important for what the child can make from it through self-expression. The real purpose of instruction is not to acquire knowledge, but, by means of activities, to build up habits, skills, and power of will and character. Learning which does not come as a result of constructive or productive activity violates the unity of the organism, and remains as a dead experience. Activities which are truly educative spring from the effort to realize some purpose or ideal. That purpose may not be necessarily clear to the consciousness of the child, but it is nevertheless the propulsive power which causes him to act.

The unfolding of activities. The activities in which the normal child engages are not caused by outer stimulation or because of an imitative instinct. Froebel had a strong aversion to externalism in every form. Moreover, the various activities are not independent of each other; they form a unity and unfold, from the child's basic nature, in the same manner in which the leaves and branches of a tree unfold from the earliest shoot. Activities follow a genetic order of developing, and bear a functional relationship to the inner life of the child. They spring from the original unity of the infant organism; and diversify into a variety of activities which, in turn, integrate into a higher and more significant unity. Wholly new functions do, however, emerge, and bring about radical transformations in the unfolding life.

Faithful to this organic view, Froebel believed that every new interest buds from some activity already functioning. In a very true sense the child must be looked upon as an organism or body of activities. The burgeoning of any new activity or interest is of the greatest moment, for it signifies the beginning of a new subject. In other words, one subject or interest leads by a natural emergence to another. For this reason it is absolutely essential that the educator know at what time in the pupil's experience the new should spring forth from the old. Froebel explained his conception in this manner: [18]

---

[18] *Ibid.*, p. 255.

> For the purpose of a living, life-giving, and life-stirring instruction, it is most important to note the moment, the proper place, for the introduction of a new branch of instruction. The distinctive character of a natural and rational... system of instruction lies in the finding and fixing of this point.... Therefore, the whole attention of the teacher must be directed to these budding-points of new branches of instruction.

What Locke meant by times of special "readiness" when the mind is "in tune", what Herbart meant by "preparation", Froebel meant by "budding-points" of new interests. For Locke and Herbart, it was a new mental interest; for Froebel, it was the emerging of a new activity.

Furthermore, it would be a grave misinterpretation to think of the child at any stage as an individual struggling alone to survive and develop. For Froebel, all the activities of the child, even the most common physical ones, are directly related to the social life which surrounds him. As he is an organism in and of himself, so also he is a part of larger organisms, the family, and humanity as a whole. From the beginning of life, he acts in a social medium and all his conduct has immediate relation to others. In consequence, the development of his social feelings go hand in hand with the development of his productive power. The expression of inner aims and needs must always be integrated with social unity and communal purpose.

The educational process: the directing of self-activity. All genuine development comes from inner spontaneous activity. Froebel's whole educational system was a protest against the idea that learning or culture can be imposed from without. He declared that all those figures of speech which regard education as coming from the outside misrepresent the process.[19] "God neither ingrafts nor inoculates. He develops in accordance with eternal self-grounded and self-developing laws."

Froebel thus completely reversed the traditional idea of the educational process. He endeavored to draw out of the child, by means of self-prompted activity, every potentiality. On this point he was very positive: [20] "The purpose of teaching and instruction is to bring ever more *out* of man rather than to put more and more *into* man." The child is replete with potentialities: [21] "All he is ever to be and become,

---

[19] Hughes, James L., *Froebel's Educational Laws for All Teachers,* p. 13. New York: Appleton, 1898.

[20] Froebel, F., *The Education of Man,* p. 279.

[21] *Ibid.,* p. 68.

lies in the child, and can be attained only through development from within outward."

Froebel was strongly insistent that the child shall not be introduced to any new subject until he is ripe for it. He is ripe only when he desires to act in relation to particular situations. He should not learn to draw or read or write except from a spontaneous urge for the activity. Whatever is learned as a result of a need for action, or through action, has a genuine significance for life. But what is learned from someone else is of little value. On this point Froebel declared: [22]

> Experience and history, too, teach that men truly and effectively promote human welfare much more by what they put forth from themselves than by what they may have acquired. . . . To learn a thing in life and through doing is much more developing, cultivating, and strengthening, than to learn it merely through the verbal communication of ideas.

The perfect life "would have each human being develop from within, self-active and free, in accordance with the eternal law." [23] Human nature in the child is inherently wholesome and good; it can be trusted to unfold rightly, for it is the divine nature expressing itself in free self-activity and self-determination: [24] In harmony with this principle, Froebel stated his theory of method: [25]

> Therefore, education in instruction and training, originally and in its first principles, should necessarily be *passive, following* (only guarding and protecting), *not prescriptive, categorical, interfering.*

This principle of non-interference, or of "negative education," as Rousseau termed it, is characteristic of that group of thinkers who view education as a process of unfolding the inner powers of the organism. This point of view is more pertinent to infancy and early childhood than to youth.

Later stages. In the later stages of development the unfolding is no longer organic and simple, but depends upon prescription, self-conscious choice, and ideal purpose. Froebel recognized this fact when he declared that "all prescription should be adapted to the pupil's nature and needs, and secure his coöperation." In the later stages of development, as well as in the earlier, there must be harmony between

---

[22] *Ibid.*, pp. 278-279.
[23] *Ibid.*, p. 13.
[24] *Ibid.*, p. 8.
[25] *Ibid.*, p. 7.

the inner and outer factors. This harmony is brought about by the interaction of teacher and pupil within the sphere of the ideal and in obedience to its commands.[26]

> All true education in training and instruction should, therefore, at every moment, in every demand and regulation, be simultaneously double-sided—giving and taking, uniting and dividing, prescribing and following; . . . between educator and pupil, between request and obedience, there should invisibly rule a third something, to which educator and pupil are equally subject. This third something is the *right*, the *best*.

Froebel was not interested in transmitting knowledge that has no direct meaning for life. But by developing his activities when young, the youth is prepared to gather knowledge more readily when he is older; and in this preparation the teacher plays a vital role.

Religion. The most fundamental striving of any organism is to preserve its own integrity, that is, its inner unity and life. Inasmuch as the child must develop in harmony with his environment, it follows that he must act in obedience with God and nature: "The new-born infant is asleep in God," and in perfect unison with Him. The child's first and deepest interest must be the preservation of this unity; for "religion is a living in the soul that finds and feels the One in All." This interest, which is religion, forms the first subject at every level of education.[27]

> Religious instruction quickens, confirms, explains the feeling that man's own spiritual self, his soul, his mind and spirit, have their being and origin in God and proceed from God; it shows that the qualities and the nature of the soul, of the mind and spirit, have their being in and through God; it gives an insight into the relation of God to man, as it is clearly manifested in the mind and life of every one, in life as such, and particularly in the life and development of mankind, as they are preserved and revealed in the sacred books.

Religion, for Froebel, is a vital personal relationship. The relation of the obedient child to his father is the best preparation for understanding his relation of sonship to the divine Father. For Froebel, therefore, normal home life is the best means for the development of the religious nature. It may well be doubted whether any other educator has been so profoundly religious and uncompromisingly Christian.

Period of infancy. Infancy is the period of dependence and of the "fostering care" of the parents. Spiritually and emotionally the child

---

[26] *Ibid.*, p. 14.
[27] *Ibid.*, p. 140.

is still one with his parents, just as the living shoot, emerging from the branch, is in unity with the branch. The growth of the infant recapitulates more definitely than later stages the history of the race. The earlier developments are those of the senses and of motor activities, which unfold in organic relation to each other. The senses of hearing and vision have most to do with the development of knowledge and the higher spiritual nature. For a time hearing must have the precedence because of its connection with language; for without language there can be no development of the spiritual nature.

Period of childhood. In general this period begins at three years of age and ends at about six or seven. Up to this stage the activities of the organism are still an undifferentiated unity. The onset of childhood is marked by a change in the character of the child's activities.[28]

> As soon as the activity of the senses, of the body and the limbs is developed to such a degree that the child begins self-actively to represent the internal outwardly, the stage of infancy in human development ceases and the stage of *childhood* begins.

Froebel designated this period as the time when real education begins, and he elaborated it to the fullest extent in his kindergarten training. The idea of a method which could be put into the hands of mothers had been an interest close to the heart of Pestalozzi. That Froebel got it from him is unquestionable. But it did not capture his full interest until some years after his association with the sage of Yverdun. Then he gradually came to feel that the most glaring weakness of all education lay in the wrong foundation which is laid in childhood. For this reason, in 1836, he turned away from the training of teachers in which he was engaged, to establish a new institution, which he named *Kindergarten.* The name is characteristic of Froebel's view of children as young plants raised in a garden under the cultivation of the teacher. The idea is expressive of the doctrine of organic education which Froebel shared with Pestalozzi, but of which he was himself the greatest exponent. The most fundamental instincts of the child's nature awaken during this period and must be unfolded according to definite principles and in a definite order. The most important forms of expression in this stage of development are sense perception, language, and play.

Language the earliest form of expression. Language is the earliest means which the human being uses to express his inner feelings

---

[28] *Ibid.,* p. 49.

and images. The naming of objects accompanies his growing contact with nature, and all his relations with others. Childhood "is preëminently the period of development of the faculty of speech." Language causes that awakening of the mind which lifts man above the animal world. Language and nature study are to be tied together by the memorizing of short poetical representations of nature and life. These consist of short poems about objects and the incidents of home life.

Play as self-expression. Froebel was the first educator to discern the true function of play in child development. His point of view is almost exactly that of Friedrich Schiller. Here is his statement: [29]

> Play is the highest phase of child development—of human development at this period; for *it is self-active representation of the inner—representation of the inner from inner necessity and impulse.* Play is the purest, most spiritual activity of man at this stage.... It gives joy, freedom, contentment, inner and outer rest, peace with the world. A child that plays thoroughly, with self-active determination, persevering until physical fatigue forbids, will surely be a thorough, determined man, capable of self-sacrifice for the promotion of the welfare of himself and others.... The spontaneous play of the child discloses the future inner life of the man. The plays of childhood are the germinal leaves of all later life.

Froebel's preëminence in regard to play rests not only on the recognition of its theoretical value, but on its practical applications. He elaborated many types of play and showed how they were to be used in preschool education.

Drawing. Another deeply significant activity of this stage is drawing. In truth, Froebel believed it is as essential to child life as language. Of this he said: [30] "The faculty of drawing is, therefore, as much innate in the child, in man, as is the faculty of speech, and demands its development and cultivation as imperatively as the latter." Drawing is, in fact, a language or form of expression which stands between the perception of the thing and written symbols. "What man tries to represent or do he begins to understand." Drawing is a means of increasing knowledge and of exercising judgment and reflection. In one direction it is an important step in the growth of the ability to think abstractly; and in another it leads to the study of colors and painting.

---

[29] *Ibid.*, pp. 54-55.
[30] *Ibid.*, p. 79.

Rhythm. Movement is the source of the sense of rhythm. No educator has imputed higher cultural value to rhythm than did Froebel. As Miss Susan Blow expressed it: "The infant, a rhythmic soul in a rhythmic body, is born in a rhythmic universe." Rhythm is the basis of language and music. But, as Froebel clearly saw, the most important moral qualities, such as firmness, moderation, and self-control, are likewise based upon it. Rhythm is essential to all appreciation of art. The ripening activities of the child lead over naturally from rhythmic movement to song.

Ripening activities. The first effort of the mother in obedience to her own instinctive prompting is to direct the child's attention to the members of his own body; arm, hand, finger, tongue, and so on. This is the earliest step in the process of learning about himself on the way to self-consciousness. From the members of his body she will lead him to understand the movements of the various parts of the body. Then awakens an interest in the objects about him and how they act.

According to Froebel each new activity grows out of some earlier activity. For illustration, drawing sharpens and makes more discriminating the child's power to perceive objects. In its turn, clear perception of objects leads over to the knowledge of number. The number sense is the beginning of mathematics, on which Froebel placed great emphasis. Thus all activities and capabilities unfold from one another by a genetic process.

Kindergarten apparatus. In his later years Froebel worked out the series of building blocks and other apparatus for the use of kindergarten children in their creative activities. These were carefully graded so as to form an ascending series from the simple to the most complex. In addition to building blocks, he used paper, cardboard, sand, clay, sawdust, and other materials for making objects of interest. The use of these materials in productive activity followed his fundamental law, according to which all evolution takes place. Froebel's real purpose was to find a series of constructions that would parallel the unfolding of the child's creative impulses and would harmonize the logical and psychological order of development. Such constructive activities form the most perfect means for the development of the inner capacities. They call into function all the physical, mental, social, and spiritual aspects of the child's being.

Froebel recognized as important the "collecting instinct" and also the "instinct of research" found in the tendency of children to take apart everything on which they can lay their hands.

In all his activities at this stage the child has no ulterior motive. He plays spontaneously for the sake of the activity itself, and not for any result which may come to him. His activity is, therefore, not consciously purposeful, and he is wholly oblivious of the end which nature has in prompting his activities.

Gifts and occupations. Froebel was the first educator to invent systematic apparatus for the expression of the child's activities. The first series he called "gifts," because, as he suggested, they were divinely given to fill the needs of the young at this stage.

The first gift is the ball, "the most universal plaything of children." It is first, because it is the symbol of the unity of the universe, the representative of all things. The second gift consists of the ball, the cube, and the cylinder, which symbolize the dialectic process: thesis, antithesis, and synthesis. The third, as well as all succeeding gifts, is formed by dividing the cube in various ways. These divisions form blocks for the child's building activities.

Children were not permitted to use these blocks as they pleased. The constructive activities of the kindergarten were so meticulously formulated that they were robbed of spontaneity. The occupations were by no means so formalized. Among them were clay modeling, paper cutting, coloring of pictures, sand-pile play, drawing of life forms, cardboard work, sewing, weaving, and many other forms of simple hand work.

Period of boyhood. This is the period from six or seven to nine or ten years of age, and Froebel designated it the "period of learning," in which "instruction predominates." This is the time when the fundamental human emotions and interests should be developed as a preparation for the development of what Froebel termed "firmness of will," but what is now meant by "steadiness of character." The training received in the preschool period is marked by spontaneous development from within. To this end, the unfolding activities of child nature need freedom of expression. But in this new period the outer environment plays a larger role. Self-expression now, more than ever, takes the form of constructive or productive activities which are purposeful.[31]

> What formerly the child did only *for the sake of the activity*, the boy now does *for the sake of the result* or product of his activity; the child's instinct of activity has in the boy become a *formative instinct*.

[31] *Ibid.*, p. 99.

Constructive activities. The constructive activities in which the child is now to engage are of many varieties. The sharing of the work of the home has the greatest value in producing physical vigor, developing purposefulness, and promoting a sense of communal unity. The boy should engage in constructive work for an hour or two daily. Building with blocks, sand, sawdust, and materials of all sorts is also to engage his attention. Each boy is to cultivate a garden of his own. The projects in which the individual engages will soon branch out into more pretentious undertakings, in which two or more boys will coöperate. In such activities Froebel saw the ripening of the sense of community purpose, which is of the highest importance for social life.

Plays. The games of boyhood have a richer significance than those of the period of childhood. They show more purpose and indicate, consequently, more intelligence. However, the most valuable results of games at this period are the moral qualities which they foster.[32]

> Justice, moderation, self-control, truthfulness, loyalty, brotherly love, and again, strict impartiality—who, when he approaches a group of boys engaged in such games, could fail to catch the fragrance of these delicious blossomings of the heart and mind, and of a firm will; not to mention the beautiful, though perhaps less fragrant, blossoms of courage, perseverance, resolution, prudence, together with the severe elimination of indolent indulgence?

Froebel's enthusiasm for play made him the prophet of our own day. Only in recent years have cities and towns begun to measure up to his ideals of the organization of play.[33]

> Every town should have its own common playground for the boys. Glorious results would come from this for the entire community. For at this period games are common, and thus develop the feeling and desire for community, and the laws and requirements of community.

The story interest. Stories, myths, legends, fairy tales, and fables receive a higher educational rating in the Froebelian pedagogy than they do in any other system. He recognized the significance in the heart of the boy of "the desire and craving for tales, for legends, and for all kinds of stories. This craving especially in its first appearance is very intense." The meaning of the desire for stories is far reaching and complex. It is an awakening of the individual's interest in the past, the

---

[32] *Ibid.*, p. 113.
[33] *Ibid.*, p. 114.

beginning of a sense of time, and of history. But of still greater value are its effects upon the mind, the imagination, and the growing consciousness of self. Stories are the play of the mind; they develop the powers of mind, as physical play gives strength and power to the body. Froebel described the effects of stories on the growing personality as follows: [34]

> Mind breathes mind; power feels power and absorbs it, as it were. The telling of stories refreshes the mind as a bath refreshes the body; it gives exercise to the intellect and its powers; it tests the judgment and the feelings.

Study of nature. According to Froebel, the study of nature forms one of the deepest of boyhood interests. He was himself as passionately fond of nature as was Rousseau, but more intelligently so. The normal boy spends most of his time in contact with the outer world and finds an increasing interest in its varied phenomena. Excursions into the mountains and valleys are exhilarating to his spirit as well as to his body; hence these formed a regular feature of the weekly program of Froebel's school at Keilhau.

Froebel believed that an intuition tells the boy, even at an early age, that the objects of nature have a hidden meaning. This feeling of the inner significance and unity in all things produces a natural longing to understand the secrets of the objective world. "Nature is the work of God," and "a revelation of God." It represents His spirit and purpose, and acts according to the law of His unfolding will. The boy should come to understand that "all the objects of nature are organically united members of one great living organism." Of even greater importance is the fact that man himself is a product of nature, and that the law of the evolution of nature is also the law of the unfolding of man in his physical, mental, and spiritual being.

The study of nature is valuable, first of all, for the light it sheds on man; in this way it assists the growing boy to understand himself and other human beings. Thus a knowledge of nature leads to self-consciousness. The observation of nature divides into the study of natural history, physics, and chemistry. But among all the sciences, the chief means to reveal the inner law of nature is the science of mathematics. "The mind and mathematics are as inseparable as the soul and religion." Froebel's view fully agrees that "God is a mathematician." Arithmetic

---

[34] *Ibid.*, p. 307.

and geometry are not abstractions remote from real experience, for mathematics "is the expression of life as such." Froebel was deeply impressed by the correspondence of the mathematical construction of the universe with the mathematical insight of the human mind. He regarded this parallelism as an evidence that man and nature are both the result of the same law of evolution.

The memorizing of poetic descriptions of nature leads over, on the one hand, to song and, on the other, to language proficiency. Thus there is omitted from the curriculum of the boy nothing that might have some meaning for his active nature. He studies each subject because his nature demands it, and not because his teachers are interested in it. He sings, not to become a musician; paints, not to become an artist; makes a garden, not to become a horticulturalist, but because his active spirit is exploring the possibilities of human experience.

The family. Pestalozzi looked upon the family as the most ideal educational institution, and he endeavored to have the school conform in spirit and organization to its life. Froebel derived much of his enthusiasm for family life from Pestalozzi; however, he went far beyond the latter's idea on the functions of the family. For him, "the family is the center of all human endeavor." Biologically, industrially, religiously, educationally, as well as socially, it is the chief human institution. This esteem for the family is interesting in view of Froebel's unhappy experiences in childhood.

In order to grasp his exalted estimate of the far-reaching significance of the family, it is well to recall that Froebel spent most of his life in the small communities of the mountain regions of Thuringia. There, life retained its medieval simplicity and integrity, and the family was still the center of industrial and social activity. Most articles that were used were made by the members of the family, for Froebel lived before the dawn of the Industrial Revolution. The complete separation of industrial production from the family was still unknown. Yet, while much of Froebel's view of the activities of the family would need some modification to fit present conditions, his fundamental conceptions of the biological and social functions of the family need not be altered.

The family is a living organism in which father, mother, and child "constitute a complete, unbroken unity." All the activities of life grow out of the needs of the family, and return again to center in it. Like the biological process by which the tree produces the seed which, in turn, produces another tree, and so on indefinitely, so the circle of family life insures the continuous progress of humankind.[35]

> Only the quiet, secluded sanctuary of the family can give back to us the welfare of mankind. . . . With the foundation of every new family there is issued to mankind and to each individual human being the call to represent humanity in pure development, to represent man in his ideal purity.

Because the family is the focus of all human activity and the source of the humanizing process, the cultivation of childhood is man's supreme task. Devotion to the task of human cultivation brings to man the most lasting and deepest satisfaction.

Nature has ordered that the mother shall be the chief educator of the young child. The instincts which nature provided to guide her efforts in developing the infant must now be lifted into the light and become a rational method of procedure. The father is the educator in the period of boyhood when the child enters into the stage of constructive activities. In the school the master directs instruction, but the school does not supplant the home. At best, it merely supplements the work of the home, which always remains the central institution for human cultivation.

Family life furnishes a favorable medium in which the activities of the child begin to germinate and unfold. These activities are not mere imitative reactions, copied mechanically from others; they are acts of self-expression and spring spontaneously from the inner nature of the child. Gradually he becomes aware of the yearnings and desires which prompt his actions; as a result, he chooses the purposes upon which he wishes to act, and thus develops a firm will. In this process the child becomes more fully conscious of his own inner life and experiences, and more aware of the ideal perfection to which he must aspire.

The family is well fitted to meet the need of personal relationship. It "alone secures the development and cultivation of a good heart and of a thoughtful, gentle disposition in their full intensity and vigor." Goodwill leads the child to view everything in terms of family life and to refer everything to the family circle. It is this unity with the family which gives the child his earliest sense of communal feeling and com-

---

[35] *Ibid.*, p. 232.

munal purpose. These sentiments and attitudes are basic for all later social living.[36]

> The aim and object of the parental care of the child, in the domestic and family circle, then, is to awaken and develop, to quicken all the powers and natural gifts of the child, to enable all the members and organs of man to fulfill the requirements of the child's powers and gifts.

The common activities of the home coördinate with the unfolding interests of child nature and arouse the all-sided activities of life. Nothing is done there as a deadening exercise, or without genuine significance or purpose. Moreover, every one of the activities essential for the conduct of complete life is present in the home. The child, having learned to participate in the purposes of the home, is fitted to engage in the communal purposes of all other institutions, school, church, state, industry, and society.

The home has special significance for the cultivation of religious life. Pestalozzi traced the germination of religious feeling to the sense of dependence which the infant feels toward his mother. Froebel believed that religion begins in the sense of relation of father and son. Religion is the craving for unity, for harmony of purpose, and this spirit is awakened first of all in the home environment. Out of this conception of child culture as the supreme biological and humanizing activity of man, Froebel gave expression to his admonition: "*Come let us live with our children.*"

Social education. Froebel was the first educator to perceive the deeper significance of education in human relations. The growth of individualism, which began in the Renaissance and the Reformation, reached its climax during the revolutionary period of the 18th century. The note of educational isolation sounded by Rousseau had captured educational theory, but its one-sidedness was soon apparent. Froebel lifted the problem of the individual and society out of any contemporary setting, and treated it in a purely philosophic way. To him, the individual and society are not at all absolute contraries; in the interest of life they must be harmonized in a rightly educated personality.

Froebel's conception of social education was a corollary of his central doctrine of "part-whole" (*Gliedganzes*). Man is an individual in so far as he is a self-conscious being with his own feelings, thoughts, and

---

[36] *Ibid.*, p. 64.

volitions. But he enters into living relations with other people in all he does and thinks. Such relations with others impart genuine significance to his existence. The child can emerge from the animal state and grow into a human being only as he enters into human relations and acquires ability to coöperate in communal purposes.

Froebel had a large circle painted on the floor of the kindergarten room to unify the group. The first exercise of the day required the teachers and all the children to toe this circle and to engage in song, prayer, and play together. In this way unity of feeling and of purpose were infused into the group and dominated the activities of every individual. Social education was no mere theoretical idea; it trained the child to engage with others in group activity for common ends. Froebel was not the first to organize the school as a little "republic" or "state," but he did appreciate more deeply than others what the purposes of group organization ought to be.

Not only in the school do social relations develop the child. Froebel believed that all human activity and thought are the direct result of human relations. A child raised apart from contact with others cannot possibly become human. The relations to the mother and father cause the germination, in the infant, of the sense of dependence, of language, of affection and other social values. At the later stages the child shares the various activities of the home, the church, the playground, and develops, to a still higher degree, community of purpose, religious spirit, and industrial and civic efficiency.

Symbolism. From his childhood Froebel showed a tendency toward symbolism, and this increased markedly in the latter part of his career. Words, flowers, casual events, everything, in fact, was looked upon as possessing an inner significance. He chose plays and games, and invented kindergarten apparatus to symbolize some law, relation or object. No other educator has attributed so significant a role to symbols.

He devised his gifts in order to convey to the mind of the child the idea of the law of development. The ball is the first and universal plaything, because it symbolizes God, the unity of all things or any one thing. It is "b-ALL." The circle, painted on the floor of the kindergarten, represented the inner unity of the group. Any three similar objects of slightly different sizes might be used to symbolize the family relationships, father, mother, and child. Likewise, by means of symbolic representation, the church, industry, the state, and other institutions were brought vividly to the child's consciousness.

Froebel believed that child nature has a peculiar affinity for symbolic representation. He had repeatedly observed that young children in their plays always use one object to represent another. A stick must do service for a horse; a few blocks, for a train of cars.

Because of this emphasis upon symbolism, the most severe criticism has been directed against his ideas and practices. Just why critics should summarily dismiss such symbolic representation is difficult to understand. There can be no question whatever that Froebel correctly observed in the spontaneous activities of children a natural penchant for symbols. For this reason he considered symbolism a necessary function of the growing understanding, and felt that it betokens an active and creative mind. It is essential, not only for the activities of young children, but also for the subsequent ripening of their ideas.

Froebel believed that symbolization is a form of language. As the child has a natural affinity for words, which are auditory and written symbols, so he has a spontaneous urge to create other symbols.

Furthermore, it must be pointed out that, as a matter of fact, man has become what he is mainly through the use of symbols. Without them no progress above the brute would have been possible. The flag, the cross, the uniform, the wedding ring, and spoken words, are all merely symbols. Mathematical science is pure symbolism. No one objects to their use. There can be no doubt, however, that sometimes Froebel overemphasized the use of symbolism and, in some respects, pushed it to the point of absurdity.

Other criticism of Froebel's theory and practice. Froebelianism, in both theory and practice, has been the object of violent criticism. Even in his own day, it was scorned by the great majority of educational leaders. Prussian authorities objected to the socialistic and liberalizing tendencies of Froebelian training. Before his death Prussia placed a ban upon the establishment of kindergartens.

Among the chief criticisms raised are the following:

(1) Froebel's emphasis upon play as a regular part of school work has not been favored by many educators. The statement has commonly been made that it results in detracting from serious learning.

(2) Froebel's principles underrate the importance of true knowledge. His insistence upon constructive work and his frequent denunciation of useless knowledge have led to a disrespect for learning as such.

(3) He has usually been discredited as a mystic and pantheist. He forcefully defended his position as neither pantheistic nor mystical,

but the lack of a clear-cut statement has left his critics more or less victorious.

(4) His devotion to drawing and cubic building blocks has caused some to object to his kindergarten methods as overemphasizing form and mathematical knowledge.

(5) Freobel's law of evolution imparts little illumination regarding the unfolding of nature or life, but is largely a useless formula. It does not tell definitely how to proceed in the development of child life.

It is not necessary to evaluate any of these criticisms. Each has, in a greater or lesser degree, discredited and weakened the influence of his system. Even the kindergarten principles and practices which formed the most systematic application of his philosophy have undergone radical changes. But while all this is true, no educational theory has been more followed in actual practice than that of Froebel. His principles have been accepted as basic for all education, from infant training through the graduate school. Stripped of its eccentricities, Froebelianism fits remarkably well into modern genetic psychology, sociology, industrial evolution, and democracy. Among its permanent contributions are the following doctrines:

(1) Education must be based upon the natural evolution of the child's activities.

(2) All real development stems from inner self-activity.

(3) Play is an essential process of early education.

(4) Constructive activity is the chief means for integrating the growth of all the powers, physical, mental, and moral.

(5) It alone can harmonize spontaneity and social control.

(6) The curricula of the schools must be based on the activities and interests which are nascent at each stage of child life.

(7) Mankind is still in the process of development, and education is the essential means for future evolution.

(8) The further development of the race depends essentially upon the education of women.

(9) Knowledge is not an end in itself but functions in relation to the activities of the organism.

HISTORY OF THE KINDERGARTEN MOVEMENT

Founding of the kindergarten. This was Froebel's most important single contribution to education; his theory, practices, methods, and apparatus outstripped in popular favor all rivals in the field of infant education. He seriously turned his attention to this work in 1828, according to a letter to his co-worker Barop: [37] "For a long time my thoughts have been occupied with the right education and treatment of little children between three and seven years of age."

It was not, however, until 1837 that he established, at Blankenburg, his first institution of this kind. This effort failed, but a permanent establishment was effected in 1840. It bore the symbolic name *Kindergarten.* From this time until his death in 1852, Froebel was able to establish a few other kindergartens and also a training school. Much of his interest was directed to the education of women, on the theory that the improvement of mankind depended upon mothers who can intelligently train their children.

In spite of every effort, very few institutions of the kind were organized in Germany. It is to other lands and peoples that one must look for the fuller reception of Froebelian pedagogy. There were not wanting, however, some most enthusiastic German adherents, among them the great educator, Diesterweg, who favored the novel system. A number of young women who received the training carried the new system into other lands. The Baroness Bertha von Marenholz-Buelow, a woman of marked ability, came into contact with Froebel in 1849, and was at once captivated by his ideas. Visiting many of the countries of Europe, where she established kindergartens and associations, she gave international scope to the movement.

The kindergarten movement in America. Froebel prophesied that only in America would his ideas find fullest acceptance. This forecast was correct. The kindergarten was introduced into the United States by Germans who came to this country after the Prussian revolution in 1848. Among these was the wife of the noted German-American statesman, Carl Schurz. As a young woman, Mrs. Schurz, together with her sister, who introduced the kindergarten into England, had been pupils in Froebel's training school. Mrs. Schurz opened the first American kindergarten in her home at Watertown, Wisconsin, in 1855. Three years later Caroline Frankenburg, also a student under Froebel, opened the second institution at Columbus, Ohio. Later, a number of "German-English" schools conducted in thickly populated German settlements

---

[37] Hanschmann, A. B., *Friedrich Fröbel; Die Entwicklung seiner Erziehungsidee in seinem Leben,* pp. 161-162. Dresden: Bleyl & Kaemmerer, 1900.

added the new institution. Through his writings on Froebel, Dr. William N. Hailman, in charge of the "German-English" school at Louisville, Kentucky, did most to acquaint Americans with the new doctrine. On the suggestion of Henry Barnard, who had his initial contact with the kindergarten in England, Miss Elizabeth Palmer Peabody started the first English-speaking kindergarten in Boston in 1860.

The movement in the United States has followed three steps of progress. The introduction of the kindergarten into new communities has usually been accomplished by individual teachers or mothers who have had contact elsewhere with the new principles and practices. The second step has been the formation of an association, which had in view a free kindergarten for under-privileged children. The last stage has been the incorporation of the kindergarten with the public free school system. The first school system to take this final step was that of St. Louis, Missouri, in 1873. The leader in this important action was Dr. William T. Harris who was the superintendent.

The period of private enterprise in the establishing of kindergartens lasted from about 1855 to 1880. The period of philanthropic interest, under the associations and churches, had its largest development from 1880 to 1900. In all, over 400 associations were formed. During this era several hundred city school systems adopted the kindergarten as an integral part of public education.

Modification of theory and practice. Down to the beginning of the present century the kindergarten strictly maintained the integrity of its doctrines and practices. The struggle for its introduction naturally caused it to remain aloof from other schools. Its leaders fostered the system as an esoteric cult, and practiced the methods which they had learned in a ritualistic, formal manner. Primary school teachers, on the other hand, did not understand the new system, and were naturally critical of its results and hostile to its methods. They found it difficult to teach children who had kindergarten training with those who did not.

About the beginning of the century, through the efforts of G. Stanley Hall, the vast accumulation of new knowledge from genetic psychology, biology, sociology, neurology, and hygiene was brought to bear upon the kindergarten. From that time the aloofness of kindergartens gradually decreased, and during several decades there was a rapid fusion of kindergarten and primary work.

What is most significant in this readjustment is the fact that the principles of Froebel have in large measure dominated primary work.

Among the chief contributions of the Froebelian philosophy have been the full adoption of the principles of self-expression, play, physical culture, creative production, dramatization, drawing, and social education.

The influence of Froebel's views has extended far beyond primary school education. The Sunday school, missionary methods, methods of Americanization, manual training, and many other cultural movements have been deeply affected. The makers of toys, games, textbooks, play apparatus for children, and even the sections of the newspapers for children, have been greatly influenced by his ideas. Moreover, much of the educational thinking of such leaders as G. Stanley Hall and John Dewey has been the outgrowth of Froebel's philosophy.

Chapter 20

GREAT NATIONAL SCHOOL SYSTEMS

INTRODUCTION. During the past 150 years the type of education developed by the peoples of western Europe has spread to all civilized lands. It became increasingly nationalistic and everywhere tended to separate from ecclesiastical control. The countries that led in the progress of education were Germany, Great Britain, France, and the United States.

FORMATION OF THE GERMAN SCHOOL SYSTEM

Prussian hegemony. The outstanding fact of European political history during the 19th century was the rise of the German Empire and its emergence as a world power. This achievement was due chiefly to the development of Prussian hegemony among German states. It has been generally recognized that the rise of Prussia was due primarily to the efficiency of its school system, which became the model for all states. Its influence extended far beyond the confines of the Fatherland. The Government of France commissioned Victor Cousin to make a study of the system. His report had powerful effects not only in France but in America as well.

German *Volksschulen.* A transforming impetus was given to elementary education in Germany at the beginning of the 19th century. When, in 1806, Prussia lay bleeding from the defeat by Napoleon, the philosopher Fichte, within sound of the French sentries on *Unter den Linden,* delivered his stirring addresses to the German nation. He declared that the only hope of salvation for his stricken people lay in the adoption of the Pestalozzian system of education. As a result Prussia became a nation of schoolmasters and pupils. Within three decades

Prussian schools became the models for the world. All elementary education became public and free. Illiteracy disappeared. School attendance was required of all children from six to 14 years of age. The teachers, who were almost all men, were selected and trained with great care. Methods were humane and adapted to the cultivation of practical intelligence. The system was directed especially to the instilling of national ideals.

Enrichment of the elementary curriculum. Down to the time of Pestalozzi, elementary education was lacking in content. It consisted only of the four *R*'s—religion, reading, writing, and arithmetic. It was Pestalozzi's great service to bring enrichment to the curriculum by adding content and activity studies. The German elementary schools offered a broad and informing culture as well as the tool subjects.

In the later decades of the century this system of popular elementary instruction was followed by special continuation and trade schools that furnished vocational training in the various arts and trades.

An aristocratic system. All German children did not attend the same elementary schools until after World War I and the establishment of the republic. The *Volksschulen* were designed only for the common people. The upper classes, who were to be trained for commerce, higher technical positions, state offices, and the professions, were educated under a different system. To all intents and purposes the system was designed to continue the aristocratic order. But it is easy to misjudge the German practice so far as educational opportunity was concerned. Children of superior intelligence have always been selected from the *Volksschulen* to receive higher instruction in order to advance to a station commensurate with their abilities.

Secondary school system. The efficiency of the secondary school system is one of the best means of measuring any system of education, for it is usually the last level to be highly organized. The German states have been noted for the efficiency of their high schools. During the early part of the 19th century, secondary instruction was confined chiefly to the gymnasiums, which were classical in type. Under the impetus of the neo-humanistic revival they had been brought to a high standard of efficiency. The realistic schools, on the other hand, were of little significance during this time.

By the middle of the century three important influences appeared to challenge the monopoly of the classical gymnasium. (1) The first of these was the vast increase in scientific knowledge and the application

BERLIN ELEMENTARY SCHOOL PROGRAM [1]

	Lower			Middle		Higher		
	VIII	*VII*	*VI*	*V*	*IV*	*III*	*II*	*I*
1. Religion	3	3	3	4	4	4	4	4
2. German	8	7	7	6	6	6	6	6
3. Object-Lessons	2	2	2	—	—	—	—	—
4. History	—	—	—	2	2	2	2	3(*2*)
5. Arithmetic	4	4	4	4	4	4	4(*2*)	4(*2*)
6. Elementary Geometry	—	—	—	—	—	3	3(*2*)	3(*2*)
7. Natural Science	—	—	—	2	2	4	4(*3*)	3
8. Geography	—	—	—	2	2	2	2	2
9. Drawing	—	1	2(*1*)	2	2	2	2	2
10. Writing	—	2	2	2	2	1	1	1
11. Singing	1	1	2	2	2	2	2	2
12. Gymnastics	2	2	2(*1*)	2	2	2	2	2
13. Needlework	—	—	—(*2*)	—(*2*)	—(*2*)	—(*3*)	—(*4*)	—(*4*)
Total	20	22	24(*24*)	28(*30*)	28(*30*)	32(*35*)	32(*32*)	32(*32*)

[1] This course is typical, though there were variations from state to state. In the table, the classes are indicated in ascending order. The number of hours devoted to each subject of instruction is given for each week. Boys and girls attended separate schools. The italic numbers in parentheses in the table indicate the variation in amount of time required of the girls in the particular subject.

of science to industrial production. A similar attitude of superiority on the part of the Classicists and opposition to the sciences and the modern languages that arose in England and the United States also arose in Germany; yet an increasing demand likewise appeared for the incorporation of these modern studies in the higher schools.

(2) The second movement was the Industrial Revolution. Up to the middle of the century, Germany remained predominantly an agricultural country. But the population became congested and was obliged to seek an outlet either through emigration or in some different form of society. Large numbers began to leave the Fatherland, and the princes sought to establish colonies in various portions of the earth. The Industrial Revolution offered a better means of caring for the increasing numbers. The vision of a grand industrial empire reacted directly on the school setup.

(3) The third development was an awakening of the democratic spirit, which culminated in the revolution (1848) in Prussia. The revolutionary movement was quickly crushed, but the absolutism of the monarchy was changed in favor of a constitutional government. Among other objectives, the revolutionists expressed a demand for the reform of the classical gymnasium.

This demand for the reform of secondary instruction increased in volume as Germany became an industrial and exporting nation. A prolonged struggle ensued between those who felt that the perpetuity of German culture and the stability of the institutions depended upon the discipline and ideals realized by the gymnasial course and those who sensed the need of modern culture to meet the problems of the growing empire. Grudgingly the conservative element agreed to the study of some modern foreign language and of the sciences. But this slight adjustment was far from sufficient.

It was under these conditions that efforts were put forth to reconstruct the old but feeble realistic schools which followed the type founded by Hecker. In 1870, following the establishing of the empire, the *Realgymnasien* were given enlarged privileges in preparing students to enter the universities. Gradually, further recognition was accorded them. But the dominating attitude of the Classicists was not overcome until the celebrated Conference on education in 1890.

The stage was set by the reactionary element to restrict again the hard-won privileges of the modernistic group. Then, a new and powerful factor entered. The young emperor, William II, unexpectedly threw the weight of government to the side of the progressives. He appeared in person at the assembly of educators and, on the basis of personal experience, took the gymnasiums to task in a memorable address. Above all else he stressed the national character of education. Among other points was this decisive statement: [2]

> Whoever has attended the gymnasium and has looked behind the scene, knows wherein it has failed. Above all a national character is lacking. We must make German the foundation; we should bring up young Germans and not young Greeks and Romans. We must get away from the basis that has existed for centuries, the monastic education of the Middle Ages, where Latin and a little Greek formed the standard. The German exercise must be the center around which everything revolves.

After this the *Realgymnasium* and the *Realschule* enjoyed greater prestige and witnessed rapid growth.

Secondary school organization. The arrangements for secondary education in Germany have always been very elaborate and detailed. The pupils who were to take up higher studies spent the beginning years from six to nine years of age, in a special primary school. Then they had the choice of entering one of three different types of school. First, there was the *Gymnasium,* which remained the strictly classical institution, with Latin, Greek, and mathematics as the backbone of the course of study. Students who attended this school could enter the university and prepare themselves for one of the learned professions. The second institution open for their choice was the *Realgymnasium.* This was a compromise institution, with a high-class modern scientific course. The third opportunity was the *Oberrealschule,* which offered a curriculum entirely of modern languages and scientific studies. It was this school which was designed to train for the higher technical and commercial vocations.

Curriculum. The accompanying tables present the full courses of study in these institutions, and the hours per week given to each. Inasmuch as the student practically determined his vocation with his choice of school, there was no election of studies within the particular institution. The fact that these schools have been noted for their thoroughness and for the continuity of their studies in the secondary field has added to their importance in the estimate of many American educators.

Influence on America. The educational system of Germany was of special significance in the evolution of schools in America during the

---

[2] Paulsen, F., *Geschichte des gelehrten Unterrichts,* Vol. II, p. 597. Leipzig: Veit and Company, 1896.

19th century. No other system had such profound influence. Over 10,000 Americans studied in German universities and returned as enthusiastic advocates of German educational organizations and methods. These

GYMNASIUM

	VI[a]	*V*	*IV*	Lower *III*	Upper *III*	Lower *II*	Upper *II*	Lower *I*	Upper *I*	Total
Religion	3	2	2	2	2	2	2	2	2	19
German	4	3	3	2	2	3	3	3	3	26
Latin	8	8	7	7	7	7	6	6	6	62
Greek	—	—	—	6	6	6	6	6	6	36
French	—	—	4	3	3	3	2	2	2	19
History and Geography	2	2	2;2	2;1	2;1	2;1	3	3	3	26
Arithmetic and Mathematics	4	4	4	3	3	4	4	4	4	34
Description of Nature	2	2	2	—	—	—	—	—	—	6
Physics, Chemistry, and Mineralogy	—	—	—	2	2	2	2	2	2	12
Writing	2	2	—	—	—	—	—	—	—	4
Drawing	—	2	2	2	2	—	—	—	—	8
Total	25	25	28	30	30	30	28	28	28	252

[a] These Roman numerals represent the classes, nine in all. The lowest is the sixth. The three higher classes are divided into lower and upper divisions, with a year's work in each.

REALGYMNASIUM

	VI	*V*	*IV*	Lower *III*	Upper *III*	Lower *II*	Upper *II*	Lower *I*	Upper *I*	Total
Religion	3	2	2	2	2	2	2	2	2	19
German	4	3	3	3	3	3	3	3	3	28
Latin	8	8	7	4	4	3	3	3	3	43
French	—	—	5	5	5	4	4	4	4	31
English	—	—	—	3	3	3	3	3	3	18
History and Knowledge of Earth	2	2	2;2	2;2	2;2	2;1	3	3	3	28
Arithmetic and Mathematics	4	4	4	5	5	5	5	5	5	42
Description of Nature	2	2	2	2	2	2	—	—	—	12
Physics	—	—	—	—	—	3	3	3	3	12
Chemistry and Mineralogy	—	—	—	—	—	—	2	2	2	6
Writing	2	2	—	—	—	—	—	—	—	4
Drawing	—	2	2	2	2	2	2	2	2	16
Total	25	25	29	30	30	30	30	30	30	259

OBERREALSCHULE

	VI	*V*	*IV*	Lower *III*	Upper *III*	Lower *II*	Upper *II*	Lower *I*	Upper *I*	Total
Religion	3	2	2	2	2	2	2	2	2	19
German	5	4	4	3	3	3	4	4	4	34
French	6	6	6	6	6	5	4	4	4	47
English	—	—	—	5	4	4	4	4	4	25
History and Knowledge of Earth	2	2	2;2	2;2	2;2	1;2	3	3	3	28
Arithmetic and Mathematics	5	5	6	6	5	5	5	5	5	47
Description of Nature	2	2	2	2	2	2	—	—	—	12
Physics	—	—	—	—	2	2	3	3	3	13
Chemistry and Mineralogy	—	—	—	—	—	2	3	3	3	11
Writing	2	2	2	—	—	—	—	—	—	6
Freehand Drawing	—	2	2	2	2	2	2	2	2	16
Total	25	25	28	30	30	30	30	30	30	258

institutions were unequalled for the study of philosophy, psychology, the classic languages, education, theology, law, medicine, and the sciences. Their degrees were the highest in standard. Germany was likewise the music school of the world. All levels of our school system, from the kindergarten through to the graduate school of the university, were profoundly affected by their policies and practices. There was still another way in which German culture and education directly affected the development of our institutions. During the century over six million German immigrants settled in the United States. Their descendants formed a significant portion of our total population.

The Germans were not rapidly assimilated into the American culture. It was their habit to continue their cultural life by establishing their own distinctive institutions. Nevertheless, they have been loyal Americans in spite of their devotion to their inherited cultural life. Among the institutions which they set up were their parochial and German-American schools. Many progressive German educators were instrumental in introducing our people to the principles and practices of Pestalozzi and Froebel.[3]

[3] Consult Schuricht, Hermann, *Geschichte der deutschen Schulbestrebungen in Amerika*. Leipzig: F. Fleischer, 1884.

FRENCH EDUCATION IN THE 19TH CENTURY

The results of the Revolution. The radical plans for educational reconstruction so triumphantly announced during the days of political and social upheaval did not soon become a reality. France was forthwith projected into the swirling tide of Napoleonic wars which did not furnish the mood for an educational program that required order, tranquility, national unity, steady growth, and above all, money for buildings and teachers' salaries. The immediate results of the Revolution on educational plans were primarily negative in that it permanently swept away the colleges and schools of the Catholic orders. Several ineffective efforts were made to fill the vacancy. The law of 1795 founded secondary schools after a fashion, and a subsequent enactment in 1802 made provision for state secondary schools known as lycées, and for municipal and private colleges of secondary school level. Primary education was left to the *Communes* without direction.

The Napoleonic system of education. In 1808, Napoleon launched the first national system of education in France, the most unique and totalitarian organization called the "Imperial University." The law stated: [4]

> There shall be constituted a body charged exclusively with instruction and public education throughout the whole extent of the Empire.... No one can open a school or teach publicly, without being a member of the Imperial University and without having been graduated from one of its Faculties.... No school can be established outside of the University, and without the authorization of its head.

This grandiose scheme combined in one colossal machine all the means of secondary and higher instruction, academies, lycées, and colleges throughout the Empire. At its head was a *Grand Master* who was responsible only to the Emperor. He was assisted by a chancellor or secretary, a treasurer, and a University Council of 30 members. Together they had absolute control of the system. A large staff of inspectors kept the Grand Master and Council informed about the conduct of the schools. France was divided into districts known as "academies," each under the control of a rector and council of inspectors. A higher normal

---

[4] Compayré, G., *op. cit.*, pp. 510-511.

school was established to train teachers for the system. Technical science was recognized on an equal plane with the scholarly arts.

The purpose of this great administrative machine was not enlightenment or knowledge for its cultural value but the control of the minds of men. "My aim in establishing a teaching body," declared Napoleon, "is to have a means of directing political and moral opinions."

The writers on education of the Revolution were intent upon primary instruction universally applied. Not so Napoleon! When Pestalozzi made an effort to interest him in primary instruction he treated the matter with contemptuous indifference. Primary education was omitted from his university system for some years.

This imperious scheme formed the basis of the educational system of France, which was not fully realized for more than half a century. Strangely enough, the plan was carried to the United States and had a widespread influence in the organization of a number of state school systems.

The Restoration Monarchy (1815-1830). The fall of Napoleon saw the restoration of the Bourbons to the throne under a constitutional monarchy, and the reinstatement of the church with its traditional privileges, particularly education. Primary education was granted 50,000 francs for its encouragement. But as this was divided among 37,000 communes, each got only the equivalent of about 30 cents. During this period the Grand Master of the Imperial University was designated *Minister of Education.*

During this transition the Bell-Lancaster method of mutual instruction became very popular in France. Two reasons added greatly to its acceptance; it was cheap, and trained teachers were not available. The mutual system assisted the people in getting some instruction for their children.

The July Monarchy (1830-1848). At this time Guizot was made Minister of Education and began the reform of the school system. The first notable action was to commission Victor Cousin, a distinguished professor at the Sorbonne and member of the State Council of Public Instruction, to visit Prussia and report on its system of schools. His report (1832) was the most consequential educational document of the time. As the survey of elementary education revealed that no system existed, the Parliament, in 1833, for the first time took steps to organize elementary schools. A primary school was made imperative in every commune and was to be inspected by the state. Religion was to be taught in accordance with the wishes of the majority of the parents of the commune, but children were not required to attend. The church returned as a factor in education. Normals for the training of teachers were set up. But, despite these measures, the schools were not free.

Education in the Third Republic (1870-to date). France owes her system of schools to the Third Republic, and it was Prussia and the United States which influenced the final establishment. All fees for the lower public schools were now abolished, and primary instruction was free for all children. The 1882 law required school attendance of all children from six to 13 with the condition that children over 11 could be excused by showing their competency by passing an examination. This was one of the most formidable steps for the French to take; but it was too long delayed, and in the end it was a final compromise between the forces which sought a unified and progressive republic and the conservative forces of reaction. The course of study was greatly enriched, and gradually, by a series of laws extending over some years, the schools were secularized.

THE EVOLUTION OF PUBLIC EDUCATION IN ENGLAND

The development of the Empire. The 19th century witnessed the organization of the most extensive empire ever known under one sovereign rule. It embraced approximately one-fourth of the surface of the earth with large portions of every continent except Europe. This dominion was made possible because of the British genius for conquest and colonization. At the beginning of the 19th century England and Wales had a population of around 14 million; at its close, of 30 million. Peace prevailed for the great portion of the century, and because of British competence in production, exchange of goods, and the organization of government, England became the greatest industrial nation on earth. Wealth increased phenomenally, but it was chiefly in the hands of the aristocracy and the barons of industry.

Essential factors in the evolution of education. English education has always been based upon the integration of two factors, Humanism and utilitarianism, or form and practicality. It has been a strict system of apprenticeship so far as the method of transmission is concerned. The higher and ruling classes educated their sons in the great public schools and in the colleges of Oxford and Cambridge. Here they acquired the ideals and manner of life of the gentleman, together with a certain amount of classical knowledge. This apprenticeship of life fitted them to act their part in the strict social life of their class and to serve in the offices of the church and state, the army, navy, and government, both at home and abroad.

The common people were likewise apprenticed in their particular forms of service of army, navy, and industry.

Another characteristic of the English way of life is their devotion to religion as an absolutely essential aspect of education. Time and again the problem of secular state education has come up but there has never been any serious deviation from sectarian control of schools. The voluntary principle and vested interests invariably prevailed against a system of public support and control.

The Great Reform Act. After prolonged political agitation, the Reform Act was passed in 1832, which set England on the road to genuine political democracy. It abolished the "rotten boroughs" system by which the Tory party made an utter farce of the elective system; put an end to secret voting in Parliament; made members of Parliament responsible to their constituents; and extended the suffrage to nonproperty owners. This was the first of a succession of measures which gradually made England a truly representative democracy. It was a triumph of the middle class, and for the first time it gave a direction to reform that was ultimately to make manhood suffrage a reality.

The first step toward state elementary schools. The Great Reform Act was followed the next year by the beginning of state participation in, rather than mere control of, education. Englishmen of all groups had always instinctively opposed state participation in elementary education, relegating it to the church and home on a purely voluntary basis. A system of state elementary schools was roundly condemned by the most radical thinkers such as Thomas Paine, Priestley, and Goodwin who feared the employment of such instruction for the suppression of freedom of thinking. The Tories, who saw no need for the enlightenment of the poor, were just as violently opposed to its establishment. But the extension of suffrage to lower class citizens contained a menacing threat, namely the enfranchisement of the unenlightened masses. The education of the children of the poor was therefore a political necessity.

Investigation showed that England was far behind other peoples in provision for popular schools. Of 12,000 parishes in England and Wales, 3,500 had no schools, 3,000 had endowed schools of different grades, and 5,500 had unendowed schools. Three-fifths of the children of the poor were without schools of any sort. The duration of schooling for those who did attend was only two to three years.

Confronted with these grave conditions in 1833, Parliament voted a small fund to be used to encourage the building of schoolhouses. This provision was insignificant, but it broke the stubborn resistance against state subvention of schools for the poor and created a precedent that grew from year to year until it ultimately brought full state support and control.

Social schizophrenia. It is a strange circumstance that at the very time when England was moved by a philanthropic impulse to abolish slavery in her Empire she allowed the rapacity of her economic barons to impose a fate worse than slavery upon her helpless infants. The Factory Act of 1833 forbade the employment of children under nine in mills and factories. Children under 13 could not work longer than 8 hours daily; from 13 to 18 the limit was 69 hours a week. To insure their education the factory must instruct these children two hours daily. Despite these measures, which applied only to mills and factories, the parliamentary inquiry of Lord Ashley in 1840-1842 later exposed unbelievable conditions: [5]

> "Little children," we are informed, "spent twelve and thirteen hours daily in the dark, opening and shutting doors in the mines; boys and girls on hands and knees dragged trolleys of coal along the ways, children of six and seven carried coal in sacks." Children were apprenticed from the age of four to seven, and they received only food and clothing but no wages.

Even when Parliament took action on this horrible and stupid cruelty only half measures were adopted.

Later progress. In 1868 the franchise was again extended among the common people, and was followed by a new measure of popular education in 1870. The same step was taken in 1885 with an education bill some years later. It can be said that through the 19th century the extension of suffrage to the lower class of people was invariably followed by the extension of state education.

---

[5] Adamson, John William, *English Education,* 1789-1902, pp. 132-133, Cambridge: Cambridge University Press, 1930.

SOME OTHER COUNTRIES

Scandinavian countries. This block of northwest Europe includes Sweden, Norway, Finland, and Denmark. These peoples followed Lutheran doctrines and the plans and policies of education evolved in Germany. Finland's greatest leader was Uno Cygnaeus (1810-1888) who received inspiration from the ideas of Pestalozzi and Froebel. He gave Finland one of the best systems of elementary education in Europe. He was especially interested in the Swedish system of manual training (sloyd), which was borrowed by Russia and later introduced into the United States from there. The Danish Folk High School System has become notable for carrying education of workers beyond the general school levels.

Canada. As it did in the United States, education in Canada became the function of the individual provinces. Ontario, which is the leading province, organized a superior system of schools compounded of features from English and American ideas and practices; the other provinces followed.

Japan. Of all modern peoples, the Japanese stand first in the rapidity of their transition from a backward feudalistic organization to the forefront of scientific knowledge and technology. This tremendous leap took place in less than two generations, an unbelievably sudden transition. Feudalism was abolished in 1871, and a new social order came into existence. Contrary to its former practice of extreme isolationism, the Japanese government now sent a commission to the chief nations of Europe and America to study their forms of government, industries, and education. The first educational code (1872) establishing equality of all classes followed the next year. The preamble to the code contains this astonishing statement of educational policy:

> It is intended that henceforth universally without any distinction of class or sex, in a village there shall be no house without learning (education), and in a house no individual without learning. . . . As for higher learning, that depends upon the capacity of individuals, but it shall be regarded as a neglect of duty on the part of fathers or elder brothers, should they fail to send young children to primary schools without distinction of sex.

The overall organization of schools they borrowed from France, but certain features of American and more especially of German education were incorporated. The people of Japan responded to these efforts to bring them up to the highest level of scientific instruction with astonishing interest and energy. They not only learned to imitate western civilization, but showed a high degree of intellectual creativity.

The compulsory attendance law required children to be at school from six to 14 years of age. Its enforcement was so rigorous that the enrollment about 1911 and 1912 was 98 per cent of all children of school age, and the average attendance was 92.6 per cent. In fifty years the illiteracy rate had fallen from a high level to 0.09 per cent, which placed them among the most literate people in the world.

Public education becomes worldwide. By the end of the 19th century, some form of public education had been organized in practically every independent country in the civilized world. Commerce, invention, government, and international relations had made it necessary that the people be educated. Christian missionary efforts played an increasing role in promoting the interest in literacy among the backward peoples of the world, but never reached more than a small fraction of the population. The emigration of many millions of people from Germany, Britain, France, Italy and other European countries to other lands had an important effect in the transmission of culture. The English language largely replaced French as the international tongue, but it was the German system of education which was most often copied.

ILLITERACY IN VARIOUS COUNTRIES

Country	*Date*	*Percentage of Illiteracy*
German Empire	1905	0.03
Denmark	1921	0.1
Finland	1921	0.1
Sweden	1921	0.2
Switzerland	1905	0.5
France	1904	3.5
Great Britain	1907	13.52
Italy	1905	30.6
Russia	1894	61.7

The basis of these statistics in every case was the literacy of the army recruits. Other bases used at the time were the signing of the marriage certificate and the ability to read at some particular age. In several cases the literacy of the people generally was higher than that of the recruits and in some cases it was lower.

Chapter 21

BUILDING THE AMERICAN SCHOOL SYSTEM

AMERICAN educational outlook. Pioneers have the opportunity to be transformers; most American colonists came to this country because they harbored ideas of religion and political order that were considered subversive and intolerable at home. Out of the welter of ecclesiastical, social, and racial differences, they formed a new ideal of human relations. By the end of the 18th century they had ample opportunity to reflect upon European conditions and the new liberal principles set forth by Milton, Locke, Montesquieu, and other reformers. They felt the necessity of establishing human society on an entirely different basis. For a while many American leaders were swept off their feet by the brilliancy of French conceptions of society, economics, religion, government, and education; and the fortune of the New World swayed in the balance.

The decline of the French influence. The passion for the new French culture declined as suddenly as it had arisen. After all it had little kinship with the sober genius of the new Americanism. The causes of its failure were many. The bloody Revolution together with the Napoleonic wars and the collapse of his imperialistic ambitions turned Americans against French ideas generally. The effort of the French to spread atheistic propaganda was offensive to the religious people in America, who, despite their enfeebled condition, remained the only power which could build the nation on a solid democratic basis. Unlike France, where centralization in Paris was inevitable, the United States had half a dozen cities surrounded by expansive territory, each of them competing for national leadership. The number of Americans who came into contact with French ideas of education was after all quite limited and the language difficulty acted as a formidable barrier. Finally, Jefferson threw the force of his prestige staunchly against totalitarian control and in favor of democratic local government. What could primitive pioneering America have in common with France with its luxury-loving aristocracy, its mercurial intelligentsia, and its plodding peasantry?

Distinctives of American ideals. The chief distinctives of New World thinking were as follows:

1. All men are created free and equal; therefore, all distinctions of class and race are contrary to the laws of nature and of God. The tyranny and snobbishness of aristocracy must be abolished, for men must be subject only to laws which they have themselves established and which are the same for everyone. The European system of different schools to perpetuate class distinctions of high-born and commoners must not be given public approval in America, but educational opportunity must be equal for all children at public expense.

2. The true basis for a commonwealth is enlightened intelligence. "Cultivated mind," as Mirabeau B. Lamar eloquently phrased it, "is the guardian genius of Democracy and while guided and controlled by virtue, is the noblest attribute of man. It is the only dictator that freemen acknowledge and the only security that free men desire." Americans pinned their faith to the intellectual enlightenment of all citizens.

3. Not only had European education been class education, but for the masses it had always been vocational. The American policy was to provide the masses with a general development of all capacities rather than trade or vocational training.

4. European nations always kept the control of education in the hands of the ecclesiastical hierarchy or of the national government; and for that reason it was generally centralized. Americans reversed this practice and placed the schools, so far as possible, under local and popular control. The danger of totalitarian control arose early in the Calvinistic policy, and again in a more formidable way in the French national program. Both these temptations were resisted. Thomas Jefferson strongly opposed centralization in government and education; he believed local government was the best guarantee of freedom. No federal control and a minimum of state control has been the American school policy.

5. The American people were convinced that education was so indispensable for the success of democracy that they determined the schools should be free to every child. Furthermore, the opportunity of secondary and higher instruction was insisted upon for all who desired it. No people

in the history of man have had such a large proportion of their youth receiving higher instruction.

6. The most radical departure of all was the separation of church and state, with the consequent secularization of the public schools.

7. The programs of public schools were arranged to give ample time for religious instruction in the home and church. Moreover, church bodies that desire to do so are at liberty to establish schools of all grades and levels in order to give their children and youth whatever religious training they desire.

This pattern of education was not entirely clear at first, and only gradually have the main features been achieved. A knowledge of the condition of education at the beginning of the 19th century and of the factors in the social, economic, and religious life is essential for understanding the school system as it developed by the end of the 19th century.

Changing social conditions. So far as social and economic conditions were concerned the changes were many and profound. Not only did the population grow by leaps and bounds, but its character changed radically. In 1793 it was 3,819,846; in 1815, 6,800,000; and in 1860, 31,443,321. Most of the increase came by immigration from England; Scotland; Germany; Scandinavia; and, particularly, from Ireland, where famine prevailed for a time. Most of these peoples settled in the industrial centers of the Northeast, though large numbers settled in the middle-northern states. Meanwhile, the area of the country was greatly expanded by the addition of the Northwest Territory, the Louisiana Purchase, Florida, New Mexico, Arizona, California, and the Republic of Texas.

The industrial revolution in England was followed later by a similar but slower movement in the United States. The enormous territory open to settlement long made this country predominantly an agricultural civilization, dependent to a large extent upon goods manufactured in Great Britain and elsewhere. Slowly at first, and by leaps and bounds after the Civil War, the transition took place which was to make this the greatest industrial civilization of all times. This tremendous change or revolution took the industries out of the homes and transferred them to specialized shops and plants; it shifted most of the population from the open country, the villages, and the small towns to the cities. This transformation decreased the economic importance of the home, but increased that of the community. All these changes exerted profound influence upon the school and heightened the need for educational readjustment.

The extent to which science and inventions have altered the conditions of life is too well known to need discussion. The transformation is still proceeding and no man has the prophetic vision to tell how far it will go. It promises to deliver man from abject drudgery and afford all the leisure necessary for genteel if not also creative living.

Changed civic conditions. In the political area equally great changes were taking place. The logical consequences of the doctrine that all men are born free and equal were that no man is wise enough to rule over or make laws for another man and that suffrage must, therefore, become universal. At the time of the Revolution suffrage was limited to property owners. Vermont, at the adoption of her first constitution, became the first state to accept full manhood suffrage. New York and Virginia remained strongholds of conservatism, but popular pressure led to the reform of the constitution of the former in 1821 and of the latter in 1829. The sweeping victory of Andrew Jackson (1828) signified the acceptance of the democratic principle everywhere.

The religious situation. The religious life of America was likewise in a process of transformation. The traditional bodies had been conservative, formal, and ritualistic. To keep firm hold upon the people, they placed reliance upon their status as established churches. Both in England and America the 18th century witnessed the collapse of religious interest generally. Antitrinitarianism and agnosticism became general within the upper class, and atheism or indifference among the people generally. The church fell to an all time low so far as membership was concerned; the first U. S. census taken in 1790 showed only 6 per cent of the population were church members. The proportion was even less in the colleges, which were hotbeds of free thought. And, it will be recalled, these very colleges were the only source for the supply of pastors for the churches of the formalistic bodies.

Not only was it a time of transition when the power heretofore exercised by the church was being taken over by the state, but it was a transition of leadership from the more conservative and formal religious bodies to the new and nonritualistic types. The New England Church divided sharply into the Unitarian and Congregational bodies. The Methodists represented the enthusiastic position and were growing with great rapidity among the common people. The same can be said of the Baptists. Meanwhile, large numbers of Presbyterians emigrated from

Scotland, Lutherans from Germany and Scandinavia, and Catholics from Ireland and Germany. These forces of Christianity now swung into action to build a new social order with free churches in a secular state.

In contrast with the colleges, academies, and high schools, which required the study of Christian Evidences, it is a curious circumstance that the elementary schools became more and more thoroughly secularized. The elementary texts, which in the 18th century were almost completely religious in content, switched first to materials that emphasized morality, and then, as time went on, to an emphasis on the things of nature and the civic virtues.

Education at the beginning of the century. At the close of the 18th century the schools and colleges of the land were thrown into great confusion by the political, social, and philosophic revolutions of the times. Some 28 or 30 colleges were in existence, three-fourths of them established by religious bodies to train ministers. But religion had reached its lowest level in history, and the percentage of college students who professed to be Christians was at its lowest; from these were to come the ministers of the orthodox churches. Bewildered by the confusion, the colleges could do little more than mark time until their objectives became clarified. From 1800 to 1829, 48 new colleges were established, distributed as follows: nonsectarian, ten; state, nine; Presbyterian, nine; Baptist, seven; Methodist, six; Catholic, four; and Episcopal, three. This shows quite clearly the swing away from the traditional religious bodies and from sectarian control. Although the ministry remained the chief objective sought, teaching was the aim of an increasing number of students.

The Latin grammar schools were in a declining state. They did not change their function, which was to train students for college; but in this task they had more and more to compete with the rising academies and also with learned ministers who tutored young men for college entrance examinations.

The academies were exceedingly aggressive up to the time of the Civil War. They proved to be far more adaptable than either the Latin grammar schools or the colleges to existing conditions in the older settlements and likewise on the frontier. Many of the states subsidized academies that were under private management. In addition to general education at all levels, they offered something of vocational training, preparation for college, religious education, and the training of teachers for elementary schools.

Morse, in his *Geography*, 1798 edition, furnished some interesting facts about the schools of Boston, which at that date had a population of 18,000. He wrote,

> In Boston there are seven public schools supported wholly at the expense of the town, and in which the children of *every* class of citizens freely associate. In the Latin grammar school, the rudiments of the Latin and Greek languages are taught, and boys are qualified for the universities; into this school none are admitted till ten years of age, having been previously well instructed in English grammar. In the three English grammar schools, the children of *both* sexes, from 7 to 14 years of age are instructed in spelling, accenting and reading the English language, both prose and verse, with propriety, also in English grammar and composition, together with the rudiments of geography; in the other three the same children are taught writing and arithmetic. The schools are attended alternately, and each of them is furnished with an Usher or Assistant. The masters of these schools have each a salary of 666 2/3 dollars per annum, payable quarterly.

Elementary schools were not held in high esteem, for the plans of the reformers of the Revolution had not yet materialized. New England had evolved the district organization by dividing the towns. As a consequence, the number of school districts was multiplied to an absurd extent and brought about the "moving school," which divided the time of the teacher into a few months, or even weeks, at each school. Most schools had only a few pupils, poor buildings and equipment, and little money to pay the teachers. However, when schools were properly spaced, the district system became the soundest method of organization, and was ultimately adopted in every state. The teachers at this time received no professional training.

THE COMMON SCHOOL MOVEMENT

Beginnings and men. The new movement for universal public education began in the state of New York, under the leadership of DeWitt Clinton. It then spread to Massachusetts, where Horace Mann gave it the widest popularity, and to Connecticut and Rhode Island, where it was promoted by Henry Barnard.

The fresh start in New York. The evolution of education in New York State was affected by the necessity of reconciling the strong Dutch tradition of elementary instruction; the English interest in private and church initiative in education; and the French plan of university organization, which aimed to unify all cultural activities. The result was something of a compromise, a dualistic system; on the one hand a strong interest in state encouragement of common schools for all children; on the other an interest in private academies and colleges for more advanced instruction which were placed under the control of "the Regents of the University of the State of New York." The compromise signified that the people had outgrown the English policy of class education and declined to accept the French innovation of complete centralization.

The provisions of the common school law (1795) lapsed in 1800 and the state was left without any arrangement for public schools. This left the way open for private interests to promote schools as best they could. Friends of education became active in establishing academies. By 1805 some 25 academies were incorporated under the Regents of the University. In 1828 the number increased to 44, and in 1839 to 106. The rapid increase in this type of school was due to the Literary Fund set up in 1813, the income of which was used for their assistance.

Elementary education was promoted by the establishment of the "Common School Fund" by the legislature in 1805. This fund was recruited from many sources such as the sale of school lands, lotteries, income from bank stock, federal funds, and other sources.

In 1805 DeWitt Clinton, then Mayor of New York City, organized the New York Free School Society to promote free schools in the city for the poor children who were not given instruction by the churches. The organization was interdenominational but under Protestant auspices, and Clinton was its president for 21 years. Twice he served as governor of the state, 1817-1822 and 1824-1828. During his administration, state funds for schools were greatly increased and many improvements made, and, most important of all, popular interest in education was intensified. This policy of free education for all children, though not immediately adopted in New York, was in line with the aspirations of the people.

In 1811 the legislature instructed Governor Tompkins to appoint a commission to report on a plan for the establishment of "common schools." The law of 1812 followed and formed the elementary school system of the state. All towns (in the New England sense) were to be divided into school districts which should elect three district trustees to look after the school. The interest on the school fund was to be apportioned to the counties and to the cities on the basis of population. The system of schools was placed under a State Superintendent of Common

Schools to be selected by the Council of Appointments. The Superintendency was unfortunately abolished in 1821.

In 1832 New York City took over the schools of the Free School Society and made all schools free. That event marked the birth of a new era in the struggle for common schools. From that time onward the other cities of the state followed suit, and the movement triumphed.

The common school revival in New England. In placing New York ahead of Massachusetts in the establishment of the common school an explanation is needed to forestall objections. As has already been noted the latter had early taken steps to make provision for education, in accordance with the high ideals of Calvinism, ideals all too high for struggling pioneers in a wilderness. But these early provisions were tied up with a most zealous religious spirit, and during the 18th century their religion underwent a serious recession and the interest in education greatly declined.

Originally the New England town (township) was a large area with the population huddled together somewhere in the center for protection and for religious and communal life. As time advanced and the need for protection lessened, when crude roads were formed and homes were established over the territory, it was no longer feasible for the town school to function as originally designed. Moreover, many new towns with scattered populations were formed in the western portion of the state. In these it became the practice to divide the territory into smaller and smaller districts, which still belonged to the town. The situation was carried to absurdity. Each district set up a school; so that some schools were only half a mile apart, and at times had only one pupil. The buildings were usually miserable and teachers were scarce, poorly paid, and without training. But poor as he was, the teacher of the town had to move from district to district "squadroning out the school," giving several months to one and then to another school, according to the proportion of his salary paid by the various school districts. In one case a school had the services of the teacher only a month and a half every three years. Every taxpayer wanted to get his money's worth of instruction for his children even if it were only six weeks every three years.

Originally, the General Assembly had control of all education, but after statehood, control passed more and more into the hands of the local districts. In 1789 the General Assembly enacted a law permitting districts to set up school committees to supervise the schools. But the most disintegrating enactment was the law of 1801 which granted the district control over taxation for the school. Such local control invariably caused the schools to decline. By 1827 the movement for democratization reached its highest point, but the schools were at their lowest level. The school law of 1827 marked the turning point. Support of schools by taxation was made compulsory, all rates were abolished and the schools made entirely free for all children. This action by the legislature was the first step in the "Common School Revival" in New England. But no substantial progress could be effected until the state took bold action and provided expert leadership.

Horace Mann (1796-1859). The most epochal event in the development of 19th century American education was the appointment of Horace Mann to direct the public schools of Massachusetts in 1837. Never did client have a more eloquent, sacrificial, and comprehending pleader; never did pleader feel he had a cause more appealing, consequential, and complex. *"The Common School is the Greatest Discovery Made by Man"* was the thesis which he elaborated at great length and by every medium of expression.

Mann was a product of the Massachusetts schools and graduate of Brown University, where he got his only teaching experience for a period of two years. He was president of the state Senate when the State School Board was established in 1837. He had chosen law for his career, but was unexpectedly elected to the secretaryship of this Board and for twelve years gave himself exhaustively to the prosecution of the office. Each year he published a report discussing the needs of the school system and its improvement. At home and abroad these reports were avidly read, for they marked a new epoch in educational literature. In 1843 Mann spent five busy months in assiduous study of the schools of the various countries of Europe. His observations and conclusions were given in the 7th annual report which has become an educational classic.

The innovations and reforms which he advocated are voluminous and only the barest summary can be attempted here. He urged the following:

1. Improvement in physical equipment: better buildings; sanitary conditions in heating, lighting, ventilation, and toilets; hygienic seats and desks; teaching aids, such as blackboards, maps, charts, and so forth; and more spacious grounds for play.

2. Higher standards for training of teachers; normal schools, institutes, and teachers' associations.

3. Greater care in the examination and selection of teachers.

4. The employment of more women teachers, on the ground that they

are by nature more sympathetic and better adapted to deal with elementary pupils.

5. More intelligent supervision of instruction and discipline.

6. The placing of a library in every school and community; more books written expressly for children, and more dealing with history, science, and the mechanical arts; and the cultivation of the reading taste of children.

7. Improved methods of instruction in all fields; reading to begin with the word method rather than the alphabet; spelling of words in common use and not technical terms; and concrete methods of teaching arithmetic, grammar, composition, and other subjects difficult for beginners.

8. The consolidation of small districts into larger units for economy and better supervision. "No substantial progress," he asserted, "could be made so long as the district system existed."

9. The introduction into the curriculum of vocal music, history, geography, physiology and hygiene, and moral instruction. The reading of the Bible without comment was also recommended.

10. Insistence upon punctuality and regularity in attendance; the resort to compulsory attendance.

11. Higher compensation for teachers.

12. Uniform textbooks.

13. The enactment of stringent laws against child labor.

14. A longer school year, ten months being necessary for the best results.

15. More secondary schools with more state aid.

16. The abandonment of corporal punishment.

17. Provision for the education of defective and dependent children.

In addition to his twelve reports Mann established (1838) the *Common School Journal,* ten volumes of which were issued during his term as secretary. He was a most eloquent speaker and delivered many notable addresses on education. Due most largely to Mann's influence, three normal schools for the training of teachers were established; two in 1839 and one a year later.

An effort so intensive as that of Mann for the alteration of traditions could not proceed far without arousing furious opposition. His report on European education provoked a bitter controversy with some of the schoolmasters of Boston. Even more prolonged and acrimonious was the conflict over the teaching of religion in the public schools. History has fully vindicated his position in both cases.

America's first great educational scholar aids movement. Second in rank in the promotion of the common school movement was Henry Barnard (1811-1900), who did for Connecticut and Rhode Island what Mann did in Massachusetts. At the age of 19 he graduated from Yale; after studying law for some time and teaching in an academy for a year, he went to Europe where he visited Fellenburg at Hofwyl. Returning he became Secretary of the Connecticut State School Board, and later held the same position in Rhode Island. He established the *Connecticut Common School Journal* and, in Rhode Island, the *Institute of Instruction,* which was the first teachers' institute.

Barnard was a greater scholar than Mann and his works are the most comprehensive treasury on education. In 1855 he began the *American Journal of Education* which contains 32 volumes on the history and theory of education. No other man has equalled him in volume of publication. He was appointed the first United States Commissioner of Education in 1867 and served for three years.

Other important factors advancing common schools. Sentiment in favor of the common school was incited by an ever increasing tide of pamphlets, newspaper articles, reports, and books, which kept the attention of the public upon this subject. As early as 1819 John Griscom published *Year in Europe* in which he described European education. Henry Barnard said, "No one volume in the first half of the 19th century had so wide an influence on our educational measures directly and indirectly as this." But it was rivaled by Victor Cousin's Report on the *State of Public Education in Prussia,* made for the French government (1831), published in 1832, and translated into English in 1834. Other important reports and discussions came from Wm. C. Woodbridge, Calvin G. Stowe, Horace Mann, and Henry Barnard.

Of educational journals there were a goodly number, beginning with *Academician* in 1818, *The American Journal of Education* by William Russell from 1826 to 1831, and its successor, the *American Annals of Education,* edited by Woodbridge until 1839.

Educational associations. It will be recalled that there had been organized, in the period of early nationalism, various societies for the promotion of education. From 1825 onward, friends of education organized a large number of associations which had for their objects the mutual improvement of their members and the promotion of the cause of popular education. The most important were the Western Academic Institute and the Board of Education, established at Cincinnati in 1829; and the American Institute of Instruction, founded at Boston a year later. These societies, by their publications, conventions, and resolutions addressed to the public and to office holders, developed a solidarity of sentiment for public schools, and contributed to the popularity of the movement. These societies were forerunners of the National Education Association.

The educational problem and the choice of solutions. After the Revolution and the War of 1812 various solutions of the educational needs of the young republic were offered:

1. The states could go on as they had been doing with wholly inadequate systems of schools. However, this could not satisfy the demands for knowledge in a growing civilization.

2. The French totalitarian system had obtained a foothold in many states, most notably in New York and Michigan. It was rejected on the national level but not on the state level.

3. The Lancasterian system of mutual instruction made a bold bid for acceptance and was given a trial in several of our American cities and in Mexico, but while it solved the problem of economy, it was not efficient and, consequently, was everywhere discarded.

4. The method of collaboration with the religious bodies by dividing out funds to churches on the basis of the number of pupils was tried in New York City and in other places, but it encountered religious prejudices and sharp rivalry and had to be abandoned.

5. The "pauper school system" was the most formidable aspirant for adoption. By this plan the state provided the tuition of children of paupers, while all others were required to pay the rates. This plan was tried in New Jersey, Pennsylvania, Georgia, Texas, and other states, but it encountered numerous difficulties. The method of deciding who were paupers was a major problem; most objectionable was the stigma branding children, which was wholly un-American.

With none of these plans could the American people be content; they therefore turned to the common school system as the only plan which satisfied all conditions. It involved "taxing all the wealth for the education of all the children." It made the schools free for all children regardless of their circumstances. It favored convenient school districts that made schools accessible to all. It harmonized the interests of the state as the centralizing overall agency with local and family responsibility and interests; and it prepared the way for the adoption of compulsory attendance.

The spread of the common school system. The action of Massachusetts' law in abolishing rates and declaring all schools free in 1827 set the pattern for the other states of the Union. New York City followed in 1832, New York State in 1867. The Pennsylvania law of 1834 permitted the establishment of free schools in districts which were willing to support them. Rhode Island followed in 1848; Vermont in 1864; Connecticut in 1868; and New Jersey in 1871.

State after state secularized its schools; many, if they had not entered the Union with such provisions in their constitutions, adopted amendments which forbade sectarian instruction in public schools. By the time of the Civil War, free common schools of a secular character had become the fixed policy of the country.

The special circumstance that forwarded the public school system throughout the Middle West and the Far West was the Federal Ordinances (1785 and 1787) granting lands for new states from the Northwest Territory.

Ohio was the first state admitted to the Union from the old Northwest Territory after the ordinances were drawn. When, in 1802, Ohio adopted its constitution, Congress gave to each township, for the support of schools, one square mile of land out of the 36 square miles in the township. Special acts were passed creating the University of Ohio, at Athens (1803), Miami University (1809), and various school societies. In 1825, the foundation of the Ohio school system was definitely laid in a law which required the formation of school districts, provided a county tax, and required that teachers be certificated for each county by county examiners. In 1827, Congress passed a law which provided for the sale of Ohio school lands, the proceeds from which were to be placed in the state treasury to the account of the respective townships; the state was to pay interest to each township on the sum deposited to its credit. Schools were made free in 1853.

The constitution of Indiana (1851) directed the legislature "to provide by law for a general and uniform system of schools, wherein tuition shall be without charge and equally open to all." The next year the law made schools free. The same took place in Illinois in 1855, and in other western states as they entered the Union.

The development of common schools in the South was retarded by social and economic conditions. North Carolina, which may be taken as an example of Southern practices generally, established its permanent school fund in 1825, and its system of elementary schools in 1839. Many of the southern states did not accept the common school policy until after the Civil War.

Compulsory attendance. The idea of compulsory attendance was obnoxious to the English. Luther advocated it in a limited way. Calvin insisted upon compulsory instruction by the pastors, parents, and the state, and the implied attendance of children upon such instruction. But the acceptance of this imposition had been lost when the people of New England lost their fervor for Calvinistic theocracy.

Horace Mann discovered the practice of compulsory attendance in Germany and urged it upon Massachusetts. He argued that it is absurd for the state to go so far as to establish, support, and conduct schools and then permit parents to keep their children away to grow up in ignorance.

Compulsory attendance was adopted first by Massachusetts in 1852. In the next half century it was legally accepted by 34 Northern states; and between 1905 and 1918 it was belatedly adopted by all the states in the South that had not already acted.

Although many of the Southern states did not respond to the common school movement until after the Civil War, it is an error to think that education was totally neglected or that opportunity was absent in that part of the country. It was, however, less available for all classes of society than in other portions of the country.

A new philosophy of government involved. The policy of supporting common schools by direct taxation upon all property for the education of all the children of the community involved the acceptance of a revolutionary philosophy of government.

Establishment of schools under the direction and control of the church-state was accepted by the colonists of New England and New Amsterdam as a religious principle. The Massachusetts law of 1647 not only required towns to establish schools but likewise the levying of a tax for their support. So long as schools were endowed privately by individuals or by large legacies, or by government grants of lands, or by the right to tax some commercial monopoly, the people generally favored their establishment. Under such circumstances a free school for the children of the community was wholly acceptable. But the school was free only by virtue of charity. Rates were abolished in town schools in Massachusetts during the first half of the 18th century and later in Connecticut and New Hampshire.

Subsequent changes altered the educational situation radically. First, a great slump in spiritual and educational interest took place which caused the people to lose confidence in their traditional religious principles. Moreover, between 1700 and 1770 some 168 new towns were formed in Massachusetts, nearly all in the western portion. The people in these new settlements were not familiar with the Calvinistic philosophy of the church-state relation, and they did not establish schools in compliance with the 1647 law. Furthermore, the people in the 18th century were generally animated by a new sense of individual freedom, and claimed the right to make the laws under which they were to live.

The right to control taxation now became the sorest point in government. The policy of taxing the property of all the people to provide free schooling for all the children involved an organismic theory of the state that was not unfamiliar to those with a Calvinistic background but conflicted sharply with the theory of the parental right to determine the child's education.

When the state law (1801) of Massachusetts empowered the local districts to levy a tax for school purposes, it enabled individuals to determine what the rate of taxation for the free school should be. It thereupon became necessary to convince the voters of the necessity of free public education. The transition from the church-state concept of education was not difficult in New England where the Calvinistic organismic tradition had prevailed from its beginning as a colony. But it was hardest to bring about in Rhode Island, Pennsylvania, and the Southern states, where a different philosophy of government and of individual independence was most deeply entrenched. Combined with these prejudices was the snobbish idea, inherited from England, that public education is a charity.

Under these circumstances the most frequent argument for the acceptance of the common school policy was the claim that education would eliminate delinquency and crime. Horace Mann used this point most effectively to bring about the improvement of schools. He held the belief that the greatness of the common school lay in its power to prevent children from becoming criminals, which was far better than trying to reform them after they had fallen. This argument was used in all the states.

THE AMERICAN HIGH SCHOOL

Origin of the secondary school. As a broad generalization it may be stated that secondary education usually arose in connection with higher education. Historically it furnished a preparation for advanced knowledge; never was it merely an extension of elementary training. The American high school had quite a different origin; it was instituted directly as the answer to the demand for vocational preparation. It had a singleness of purpose all its own, namely, to fit boys to become more efficient in business and industry. The Latin grammar school prepared for college; the college prepared for the ministry and for other professions in a general way; the academies were general utility institutions functioning in pioneering society and paralleling the Latin grammar schools and the colleges. Most frequently an elementary school was attached to the academy. The writing schools evolved into the English grammar school, which, when a primary school was attached, finally produced our grade school.

Founding of the Boston High School. By 1820 some people of Boston became convinced that the training given in the writing schools was not at all adequate for the boys who were going into "mercantile or mechanical" pursuits. Nor did the 26 academies incorporated before 1821 (114 before 1840) suit their purpose because, as the committee charged to study the problem stated, "Children are separated from their parents . . . to acquire that instruction which cannot be obtained at the public seminaries." A new institution was thereupon recommended and opened in May 1821. To be admitted, boys had to be at least 12 years old, which was the age at which the colleges admitted many of them. The Latin grammar school admitted boys at seven before 1825, at nine afterward, with the course shortened to five years. The general pattern of the Latin grammar schools in New England was entrance at nine and a three year course of study.

The age of admission to the first high schools varied. Some of them imitated the Latin grammar schools and made nine years of age the lower limit. Others made 12 the age of admission; among the latter were: Boston, in 1821; Salem, in 1827, and Providence (recommended plan), in 1837. The Hartford and New Haven high schools placed the age at 13. A boy had to be 12 to enter the English department of Phillips Exeter Academy. In setting age limits these institutions had no thought of the elementary school as preparatory to the high school.

So far as the student's knowledge was concerned he had to "be well acquainted with reading, writing, English grammar in all its branches, and arithmetic as far as simple proportions." After three years, English

The First High School in the United States, Established in Boston, 1821.

literature and geography were added to the requirements. In the course of study English was the only language; other subjects were declamation, science, mathematics and its applications, history, and logic. To insure a high quality of work it was required that the teachers be educated at some university.

Naming of Boston High School. For three years this new educational venture was known as "The English Classical School" which distinguished it from the Latin School and Harvard College. In 1824 it was designated "The English High School." The term "high" was for a long time commonly applied to certain schools in Europe, but John Griscom, in an article in the *North American Review,* gave an account of the "High School" of Edinburgh, and this evidently furnished once and for all the name for this new American free public institution.

It is a singular glimpse behind the façade of educational organization which reveals that in 1826 Boston opened a high school for girls, but found it so popular that after two years it was abandoned because of the expense. The elementary school course was then revised to take care of the needs of girls. Nevertheless, the public high school eventually proved to be the most popular form of training for young women in America; in recent years a larger proportion of girls than of boys has graduated.

By 1826 Massachusetts was so convinced of the value of the high school that a law required every town of 500 households to employ a master to teach U. S. history, bookkeeping, geometry, surveying, and algebra. Towns of 4,000 inhabitants were required to employ a master to teach Greek and Latin, history, rhetoric, and logic. The purpose was to increase the opportunity for high school education. Similar steps were taken in other states some decades later.

The high school becomes popular. That the High School was the answer to the American demand for full public education on the adolescent level was quickly demonstrated by their rapid spread over the whole country. There was much experimentation with age of entrance, length of course, course of study, and specific aims and purposes. Exact statistics of the early growth of high schools are impossible to secure. A rapid increase began after 1850 when many private academies were replaced by public high schools. After the Civil War the increase was accelerated, and in the last decade of the century it became phenomenal.

Legality of free high school tested. Opposition to taxation for the public high school was met in a number of states. In 1872 suit was brought at Kalamazoo, Michigan, to test the constitutionality of a tax levied by the school board for the support of the public high school. In a decision handed down by the State Supreme Court, Chief Justice Cooley upheld the authority of the board and the right of the people of the school district to follow their judgment in the maintenance of a high school. This decision established the American policy that secondary and higher education are constituent parts of a state's free school system.

THE INTEGRATION AND CORRELATION OF SCHOOLS

The educational pyramid. At the close of the 19th century public education in the United States consisted of a series of institutions superimposed one above the other, all graded and articulated. These were: the kindergarten, the primary school, the grammar grades, the four-year high school, the standard four-year college, and the professional schools. This educational pyramid, so simply and prettily arranged, was not constructed at once. Far from it. Not one of these institutions was originally planned to articulate with another. Each arose as a separate and independent unit, and only after lengthy processes of adjustment were they welded into what appeared as an integrated system. It is essential to see how this coördination was accomplished and diverse objectives fused into a general concept of education.

Schools instituted for specific purposes. The schools of the past were mainly established to effect specific purposes and not as instruments of general education. Needs for special skills arose at different times and under varied social conditions; and institutions were established to train the young along each particular line. During the later Middle Ages commerce, business, and industry advanced in a big way. Out of the need for exchanging information, defining contracts, and keeping accounts arose the demand for schools to teach writing and arithmetic. As late as 1682 several writing schools were established by the Boston authorities and they continued well into the 19th century.

At the time of the Reformation Protestants were especially interested in teaching the masses of people to read the Scriptures for themselves. This emphasis upon reading led to the creation of the reading schools of the Lutherans, Calvinists, and other groups. The French Enlightenment imparted new zeal to the spread of literacy as an instrument for the liberation of men politically and socially. The emancipation from ignorance, superstitution, and political tyranny became the objective of the state, which has everywhere superseded the church in the control of men. Since that day the ability to read has been the common measure by which the advancement of all people is judged.

Grading of schools. At the beginning of the 19th century there existed a variety of schools to teach different things. The vast majority of these were one-teacher schools to teach reading and religion. In cities like Boston there were in addition more advanced schools of three kinds: (1) Latin grammar schools, (2) English grammar schools, and (3) writing schools in which expert penmanship and arithmetic were taught. Until well into the century these schools were ungraded and the curricula limited. Individual instruction was the rule everywhere, and dependence on the textbook was universal. In the Latin schools pupils were classified by their stage of advancement in reading Latin classics and in grammar, but in the English grammar schools and the writing schools grading had not yet been introduced.

Five movements tended to consolidate the elementary schools into unity and to bring about graded instruction: (1) the change from individual to simultaneous or class instruction, (2) the grading of subject matter by the writing of better textbooks, (3) the monitorial system, which showed how large numbers of children could be taught in the same building, (4) the expansion of the course of study, and (5) the employment of better trained teachers. Pestalozzi had insisted upon class instruction and grading, and the system had been accepted everywhere in Europe and brought to a high point of perfection in Germany. Moreover, David Stow advocated a separate teacher for each grade, and organized on this basis the schools connected with his Glasgow Training School for teachers.

Horace Mann, Henry Barnard, Calvin Stowe, and a host of others who had become impressed with the German schools kept insisting upon the advantages of classifying pupils and of a closer organization of instruction. Grading was successfully introduced into American schools between 1820 and 1850.

The coordination of the reading school with the writing school. The forming of the elementary graded school began in Boston (1789), with the reading schools and writing schools occupying the same building. Each school pursued its own program of work but taught the same pupils. The writing master taught downstairs while the reading master taught upstairs, or vice versa. In this "double-headed" system the pupils attended both departments alternately, half a day for each.

Girls were allowed to attend these reading and writing schools from April 20th to October 20th. In some other places the girls were taught upstairs and the boys downstairs in the same building. The welding of these various factors into our present unified elementary school took several decades.

Primary instruction. The teaching of young children to read and write was everywhere despised as a trivial task and was for a long time relegated to the home and to private teachers. From this came the common practice of mothers teaching children to read before sending them to school. Mulcaster, Brinsley, Comenius, and Hoole in the 17th century were the first to dignify primary education.

The law of Massachusetts provided that "no youth shall be sent to the Grammar Schools, unless they shall have learned . . . to read the English language, by spelling the same." This same requirement was made for the writing school and the Latin grammar school. For this reason city school authorities considered primary instruction outside their responsibility.

School authorities in Boston felt no official interest in teaching young children to read and write. This was left to the parents and women who taught the dame and infant schools. In 1817 Boston had 4,132 pupils in 162 private schools of primary grade, i.e., in infant and dame schools. More disconcerting was the fact that 529 children between four and 14 years of age were not in any school. The next year the city appropriated $5,000 for primary schools, and a special Primary School Committee was assigned the task of providing schools of this rank. These schools were to be taught throughout the year by women. Children were admitted as early as four years of age, and they were prepared for admission to the grammar and writing schools at seven. In 1819 the new primary schools were opened, entirely separate from the older schools and managed by their own Board until 1855, when they were consolidated with the grammar schools to form the eight-grade elementary school. Similar consolidations took place in other places and set the complete pattern.

The coordination of the primary with the grammar and writing schools. Animated by a progressive spirit, the Boston School Board led the way in the unification of the grammar school, the writing school, and the primary school. In 1848 it organized the "Quincy School" on an entirely new plan and built a four story structure of 12 rooms to house the primary school and the reading and writing schools. John D. Philbrick, a most progressive administrator, was placed in charge of the experiment. The new building provided a separate room for each of the 12 teachers (four for the primary grades, and four for each of the other schools). The final step was the fusing of the reading and writing departments into the same grades in the grammar school. By this process the standard eight-grade school finally emerged. Boston adopted this new

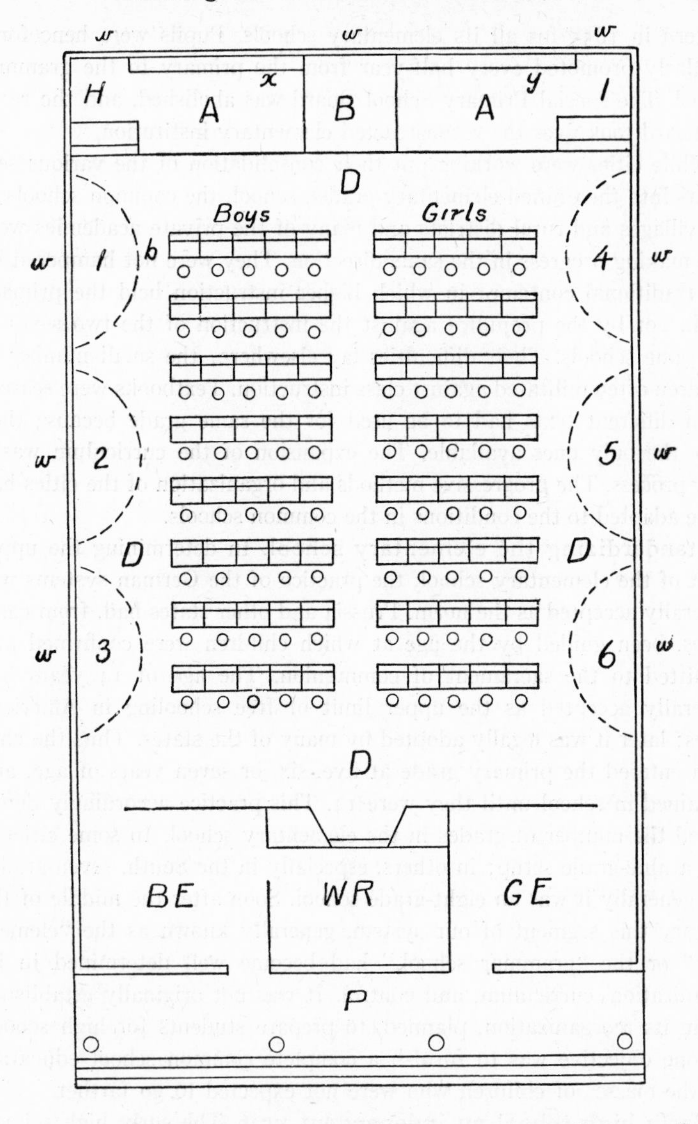

PLAN OF A SCHOOLROOM SUBMITTED, IN 1831, TO THE AMERICAN INSTITUTE OF INSTRUCTION. *Key: P,* portico; *D,* doors; *BE* and *GE,* entrances for boys and for girls; *H,* master's desk; *I,* assistant's, or monitor's desk; *1, 2, 3, 4, 5, 6,* stations, marked on the floor, to be used by classes when reciting to monitors.

pattern in 1855 for all its elementary schools. Pupils were henceforth regularly promoted every half-year from the primary to the grammar school. The special Primary School Board was abolished, and the regular board took over the reconstructed elementary institution.

While cities were working out their consolidation of the various segments into the unified elementary graded school, the common schools in the villages and rural districts and many of the private academies were also making progress in the same direction. They were not hampered by the traditional contempt in which higher instruction held the primary work, nor by the prejudice against the instruction of the two sexes in the same schools. Their difficulties lay elsewhere, the small number of children often militated against class instruction. Textbooks were scarce; often different texts had to be used for the same grade because they were the only ones available. The expansion of the curriculum was a slow process. The progressive methods and organization of the cities had to be adapted to the conditions in the common schools.

Standardizing the elementary school. In determining the upper limit of the elementary school, the practice of the German systems was generally accepted as the norm. Prussia and other states had, from early times, been guided by the age at which children were confirmed and admitted to the sacrament of communion. The age of 14 years was generally accepted as the upper limit of free schooling in American cities; later it was legally adopted by many of the states. Thus the children entered the primary grade at five, six, or seven years of age, and remained in school until they were 14. This practice accordingly determined the number of grades in the elementary school. In some cities it was a nine-grade setup; in others, especially in the South, seven-grade; but generally it was an eight-grade school. Soon after the middle of the century this segment of our system, generally known as the "elementary" or the "grammar school," had become well determined in its organization, curriculum, and control. It was not originally established or, in its reorganization, planned, to prepare students for high school. Its one objective was to furnish a complete common school education for the masses of children who were not expected to go farther.

Early high school an independent unit. The early high schools were entirely unrelated to the grammar grades on the one hand, or to the college on the other. They even taught pupils of the same ages as those in the upper elementary grades. Their original purpose was to furnish a more advanced form of training for those boys who were to enter commercial pursuits. Later, imitating the academies which they replaced, they aimed at a broad training for life and vocations and at furnishing a new terminal education for the majority of children.

EVOLUTION OF HIGHER EDUCATION

Growth of colleges and universities. Throughout the 18th century the higher institutions of America were still small, simple colleges, whose objective was to discipline the youth and to offer a literary training for students who desired to become ministers, lawyers, doctors, teachers, and leaders of public affairs. Despite the powerful impact of French free thinking, the ideals and traditions of the church colleges quickly reasserted themselves and returned them to conservative paths.

Several significant movements occurred during the first third of the 19th century, when conditions were plastic and American civilization was searching for its own path of development. Several great religious awakenings aroused the people in all parts of the country, and began to check the spread of irreligious thinking that accompanied the French Enlightenment. The separation of church and state and the adoption of complete religious liberty were among the most transforming changes which took place. The colleges that had formerly imposed religious tests now opened their doors to all male students, without respect to their religious beliefs. It was not that they were less religious; they merely discarded formalism in exchange for a more genuine piety. This was distinguished as a period of far-reaching revivalism; but probably the most consequential religious events were connected with the rise of the foreign mission movement in the colleges. Not only did young men become interested in carrying their religion "to the heathens," but many colleges were started with the purpose of training them for the task.

During the early decades of the new century the religious bodies were the chief promoters of higher institutions; the states of the Middle West came next with their universities. By 1830 some 48 new colleges and universities thus came into being. In the North Harvard, Yale, and Princeton were generally the models. Through their graduates these became prolific mothers of new colleges. In the South also numerous institutions opened their doors to eager students. The model here was the University of Virginia (1825), brain-child of Thomas Jefferson. Another influence that affected many of the new colleges was the agricultural movement. The Physiocratic theory and the example of Pestalozzi and

Fellenberg induced American educators to connect farms with the colleges, and students earned their keep by laboring in the fields.

The period from 1830 to the end of the century was one of great expansion of American colleges. Progress was inspired by a brand new conception which came from an unexpected quarter.

Influence of German universities. During the 19th century, higher education in the United States was profoundly affected by the scholarly universities of Germany, which aroused an entirely fresh spirit and an exalted enthusiasm, destined to transform the traditional college. The readiest way to understand this new inspiration will naturally be to study the character of the German university system, to note particularly how it differs from the English organization in aims and method, and finally to study the ways in which this new and powerful influence laid hold upon the backward institutions of this country.

Character of German universities. "The education of the German Universities," says a French writer, "begins where that of most nations in Europe ends." How did it happen that the higher institutions of Germany were so far in advance of others at the beginning of the 19th century? German scholars proudly ascribe this superiority to two conditions: freedom of investigation (*Lernfreiheit*), and freedom of teaching (*Lehrfreiheit*). Curious as it may seem, the German universities were scholarly republics within autocratic kingdoms. German professors were accorded opportunity for free and unbiased research; they were less enslaved by dogmatism and traditionalism, and were granted a breadth of liberty in teaching that was unknown in other lands. Not only were they free to search for truth and to impart it without let or hindrance, but they evolved a form of university organization which necessitated scholarly industry and progressive thinking on the part of all members of the faculty. How these fortunate conditions were brought about has already been indicated, in part, in the study of educational reforms in the German university system.

In two important respects, the German universities had come to differ from the higher institutions of Europe and America: (1) German universities did not exist to furnish general education. That was supplied by the gymnasium, or secondary school. (2) They did not furnish technical or practical training. They aimed to produce theologians rather than pastors; jurists rather than lawyers; medical scientists rather than mere practitioners; investigators, scholars, and thinkers rather than technical experts and schoolmasters.

The German university professor was not a tutor in the English sense, or a teacher in the American sense of the term. He was a specialist in his field—chosen not because of his ability to impart knowledge, but because of his ability to organize and increase knowedge. No man could become a professor in a German university without having given evidence that he had mastered a certain subject of study and produced valuable new results as an investigator.

Periods in the development of university ideals. The effects produced by German influences on American institutions divided into two more or less distinct periods. The first began in the early part of the century and lasted until about 1875.[1] The second period began about 1875, when the situation of higher education became somewhat clearer.

The influence of American students who had received their higher training in Germany is well stated by Dr. Charles F. Thwing, in his *History of Higher Education in America.*[2]

> The men, therefore, who went from American colleges to German universities in the threescore years and ten from 1815 to 1885, returning to their native land, profoundly influenced American education. They brought back with them a spirit of freedom in learning and of freedom in teaching, together with a keen and large appreciation of scholarship. The university inspired each of these men to engage in independent research and thought; it quickened the instinct of creation; it aroused a sense of scholarship; it gave an appreciation of the value of scholastic tools, such as libraries and laboratories.
>
> *Wissenschaft, Lernfreiheit,* and *Lehrfreiheit* were the rallying cry which inspired American students trained in Germany for doing their great work as teachers and as leaders in their native country.

The beginning of the crisis. The controversy over the organization of higher education, which had been raging more or less vigorously for a generation, flamed to its climax at the time of the inauguration of Charles W. Eliot as president of Harvard in 1869. Several years of

---

[1] The first edition of this work went to some length to show the upward development of the standard American four-year arts college in its effort to become a university, the subsequent establishment of graduate instruction, and the forming of the junior college. This evolution formed the most consequential movement in higher education in the 19th century. In order to conserve space and because the junior college is now accepted, much of the discussion is deleted from this revised edition.

[2] Thwing, Charles F., *A History of Higher Education in America,* pp. 321-322. New York: Appleton, 1906.

European study, much of it in Germany, had broadened and clarified his vision. In a ringing proclamation his inaugural address definitely set forth the university ideal.

If any date indicates the final dominance of German ideals and the consequent beginnings of the modern period, it was that of Eliot's inauguration. Immediately, Dr. Noah Porter, soon to become president of Yale, leaped into the arena in defense of the venerated ideals of the traditional college. In his book *The American College and the American Public,* he attacked every important innovation that had been adopted during the preceding half-century. He pointed to the failure of the Amherst College plans for reform and to the reaction which had followed the adoption of the elective system at Harvard and Brown. He warmly espoused the fixed curriculum rather than the policy of free electives; the study of Latin, Greek, and mathematics rather than modern languages, English, natural sciences, and social studies; the textbook and the textbook method of instruction rather than the university lecture and laboratory practice; the inflexible, lock-step, four-year class system rather than the course system; the common dormitory and strict surveillance rather than ordinary life in unsupervised lodging houses; institutional religion rather than individual piety; preparatory work in academies or under private tutors rather than in affiliated public high schools; college tutors rather than university professors; and separate education of boys and girls, rather than coeducation. Verily he was the apostle of things as they were. With the zeal of a religious fanatic, he declared: [3]

> The writer holds that it is vitally important to the culture of this country, he would almost say to the existence of this country as a country, that the American college, with its class system, its fixed curriculum, its generous and earnest common life, and its enforced discipline, should be retained and re-enforced.

Following President Porter, Dr. Andrew Ten Brook, for some years a member of the Michigan faculty, took up the cudgel from the standpoint of the state university. His *History of the American State Universities* marked a new era in the evolution of public education at the university level.

It must not be assumed that the right was wholly on either side of

[3] Porter, Noah, *The American College and the American Public,* p. 325. New Haven: Chatfield & Co., 1870.

the great collegiate controversy. The leaders of the university party looked upon American colleges as little better than high-grade secondary schools. They saw in the scholarly activity of the German universities the ideal of higher learning, and they expected to infuse this new spirit into the old college. They believed that a complete change of aims and methods, as well as the raising of standards of work, was imperative. The monotonous learning of prescribed lessons must give way to the enthusiastic pursuit of knowledge determined by the student's interest and resolution. The formal drill system must be replaced by scholarly training. The university leaders were determined to bring about these changes by a thoroughgoing transformation of the college.

The college party, on the other hand, looked upon these innovations as a ruthless and radical departure from the methods of training which the light of experience had shown to be best. A thoroughgoing preliminary training, such as the American college offered, was deemed absolutely essential before students could profit by the freedom and specialization of the German university system. The college leaders were not opposed to the university type of work, but they held that it was not for America, since our students were not prepared for such training and since they needed the strict regime of traditional college instruction.

Chief innovations. The two most significant innovations that marked the change from the traditional college to the university were the elective principle and coeducation. It is necessary to trace, in a general way, the development of each.

The elective principle. The elective system was the cause of most heated and prolonged controversy in academic circles. As a matter of fact, free election was the established principle at the University of Virginia from its opening in 1825. Its fundamental policies and standards were far in advance of any other American institution. But, owing to circumstances, Virginia did not play a leading part in the evolution of university organization. There were sporadic attempts, in several other institutions, to introduce the modern languages and the sciences as electives, but these were incidental events; the leaders in the adoption of the elective principle were Harvard and Michigan.

At Harvard, up to 1825, the course of study had remained the same for all students. Latin, Greek, and mathematics formed the major portion of the curriculum. Beginning with the academic year of 1825-26, some elective studies were introduced, and the principle was then gradually extended for some years. From one-half to three-fourths of the work of the upper years was made elective.

Under the presidency of Edward Everett, a reaction began, and by 1849-50, "the ancient order of things had been so far restored that with the exception of one elective of three hours in the junior and senior years, all the studies were required." Finally, in 1856, the single elective in the junior and senior years was abolished, and Harvard was again on a fixed curriculum for all four years.

In 1867, the elective principle was again introduced, and it was forcefully advocated by President Eliot at his inaugural address in these terms: [4]

> It were a bitter mockery to suggest that any subject whatever should be taught less than it now is in American colleges. The only conceivable aim of a college government in our day is to broaden, deepen, and invigorate American teaching in all branches of learning. It will be generations before the best American institutions of education will get growth enough to bear pruning.

By 1886, the only requirement in the arts course was that of English composition in the freshman year. Later this free system was again modified by the adoption of the group system.

The elective principle was first introduced at Michigan in 1855 and 1856, but it was limited to the senior year. Later it was extended to the junior year also, and opportunity for specialization in a few branches was allowed. By the eighties, the upper years had been made elective and the fixed curriculum abandoned.

The education of women. Traditionally girls were not given the same education as boys. All of them were trained in the home for home management; for personal adornment, including dancing and music; and for religious and moral behavior. It was generally believed that woman, being weaker physically, was therefore mentally inferior to man, and not capable of understanding higher learning. For a long time the practice was to establish separate institutes, seminaries, or "finishing schools" for girls of the higher economic brackets. Wesleyan Female College, Macon, Georgia, "the oldest chartered college for women in the world" opened in 1837. Mary Lyon established Mount Holyoke Seminary in South Hadley, Massachusetts, the same year. Later Vassar

[4] Eliot, Charles W., Inaugural Address (1869).

(1861), Smith (1871), Wellesley (1875), and Bryn Mawr (1880) were founded for the education of women in higher scholarship similar to that of the colleges for men.

The first trend was to establish separate schools for girls; then came the tendency, following the example of the University of Alabama (1820), for universities to have two departments under one management and to build the two of them a short distance apart. This became the practice in several states, and also at Radcliffe (1884) and Barnard (1889). The early course of study was quite different and led to different degrees. Maid of Arts, Maid of Philosophy, Mistress of Arts, and Mistress of Humanistic Literature degrees were commonly conferred in the colleges for women. In one instance the Mistress of Piano degree was conferred.

Oberlin College (1833) at Oberlin, Ohio, was the first college to admit young women on the same basis as men and to confer on them the same degrees. It was, therefore, in the Middle West that coeducation began. It was quickly demonstrated that girls are as capable mentally as boys. The fact that in this country women soon came to outnumber men in the teaching profession made coeducation the rule rather than the exception. Another factor was that of expense; separate institutions for the sexes with equal equipment for both were found economically impossible.

Coeducation. Nothing—not even the passing of the dormitory or the introduction of the elective system—heralded so conclusively the new order of collegiate life as did the adoption of coeducation. This practice had been common in some of the academies and in most of the early high schools. The general policy in the East and the South, where college education for women began, was to establish separate institutions. Oberlin College was the first institution calling itself a college to enroll women on an equal basis with men; this was in 1837. Not until 1867 did the University of Indiana begin to admit women, and it was the first state higher institution to take this step. The University of Michigan reluctantly followed three years later. Other western universities, both state and private, generally organized on the coeducation plan. It is now agreed that coeducation is the American way. Even though segregation had some advantages, it had to be abandoned, in the interest of higher values; especially was this the case in public institutions. Today universities universally admit women to graduate instruction.

Results of the university movement. The main facts in regard to the effort to make the colleges into universities after the German pattern have been presented. The leaders did not succeed in the effort. There was a deplorable tendency to add the higher instruction rather than to improve the quality of the work the colleges were doing. Concerning this tendency, Dr. Tappan complained: [5]

> We feel the want of universities; hence, we are continually struggling to give our colleges as much of a university character as possible....
>
> Our Colleges grasp at a University amplitude of studies, at University capacities and functions, and take the name of Universities, and yet Universities they cannot be within the prescribed limits, with the general paucity of learned material and appliances, and while offering themselves as institutions for students in the elementary course. They were elementary schools of a higher grade in their inception, such they have ever continued to be, as such their existence will ever be demanded, and as such they require to be perfected. By retaining their original designation, while endeavoring to graft upon them what belongs properly to a University, we have only embarrassed them in their proper and possible functions, given them an equivocal character, and lessened their usefulness.

However laudable may have been the ambition of the colleges to become universities, one must note in this tendency the pregnant source of future problems. In taking on university functions and methods before it was able to do so efficiently, the college laid itself open to the charge that it had become a hybrid institution—part college and part a weak imitation of a university. This step precipitated a new problem by the end of the century.

A humorous incident related by James Bryce, the famous English author, in *The American Commonwealth,* illustrates this passion for university reputation: [6]

> I remember to have met in the far west a college president who gave me a long account of his young university, established by public authority, and receiving some small grant from the legislature. He was an active, sanguine man, and in dilating on his plans frequently referred to "the faculty" as doing this or contemplating that. At last I asked of how many professors the faculty at present consisted. "Well," he answered, "just at present the Faculty is below full strength; but it will soon be more numerous." "And at present?" I enquired. "At present it consists of Mrs. Johnson and myself."

---

[5] Tappan, Henry P., *University Education,* p. 78. New York: Putnam, 1851.

[6] Bryce, James, *The American Commonwealth,* Vol. II, pp. 671-672. New York: The Macmillan Company, 1897.

The university versus the college ideal. During the period between 1825 and 1875, a heated struggle raged in regard to the ideal for higher education in this country. A number of causes were slowly transforming the character and purposes of the colleges. Among the chief of these were: (1) the increased number of students preparing for secular vocations; (2) the demand for instruction in modern languages, natural and applied sciences, and social studies; (3) the development of professional training; and (4), above all, the coming of the German ideals of productive scholarship or research.

The summary issue of the struggle was whether the university ideal or the ideal of the traditional college should dominate. The actual conflict, however, was waged over a number of specific points:

UNIVERSITY IDEAL		TRADITIONAL COLLEGE IDEAL
1. Free elective principle	*versus*	Fixed curriculum, uniform for all students
2. Modern languages and sciences	*versus*	Classical languages and mathematics
3. Course system with individual progress	*versus*	Lock-step class system
4. Specialization and professional training	*versus*	General culture
5. Lecture and laboratory method	*versus*	Textbook and recitation
6. Instruction by professors	*versus*	Instruction by tutors
7. Voluntary lodging in boarding houses	*versus*	College dormitory life
8. Individual responsibility for conduct, including class attendance	*versus*	Surveillance by college authorities
9. Voluntary religious observance	*versus*	Institutional religion
10. Preparatory work, broader and more advanced in scope	*versus*	Fixed and narrow prescriptions
11. Coeducation	*versus*	Segregation of sexes

Graduate instruction in America. The first provision for graduate instruction in this country came from the generosity of Bishop Berkeley, the celebrated English philosopher, in a gift to Yale college. As early as

1814, Yale separated her few graduate students from the others. In 1861, she conferred the first doctorate of philosophy degree. The University of Michigan, rather prematurely, one must imagine, in the fifties announced a "University Course," in which no less than twenty subjects were offered. From 1856-1857 onward, a small number of students returned for advanced work, which required an A.B. or a B.S. degree for admission. At Harvard, also, an early beginning was made, but the chief development came after Eliot assumed the presidential office in 1869.

The real credit for launching work of the highest level of scholarship must go to Johns Hopkins University, which was opened, under the guidance of President Daniel Coit Gilman, in Baltimore in 1876. Here, the German ideal of research and creative learning began, for the first time, in this country. In both Harvard and Yale, the graduate schools were closely related to powerful undergraduate colleges with their settled traditions. These graduate schools were necessarily small, and their significance was disparaged; their very existence was parasitic, in that they were dependent upon the undergraduate college. Not only were they subordinated to the college, but they imitated the methods and ideals of the college. Johns Hopkins, on the other hand, was an institution of a higher order, with no college to overshadow it.

Other institutions soon followed. Clark University, under the inspiration of President G. Stanley Hall, copied the German ideal, and for many years existed as the freest American center for research along a few lines. The success of graduate work at the University of Chicago, which was opened in 1892, was a powerful factor in the growth of genuine university instruction.

UNIVERSITIES AND COLLEGES ESTABLISHED TO 1900 [7]

Period	*Number*	*Period*	*Number*
Before 1780	9	1840-1849	42
1780-1789	10	1850-1859	92
1790-1799	8	1860-1869	73
1800-1809	11	1870-1879	61
1810-1819	11	1880-1889	74
1820-1829	25	1890-1899	54
1830-1839	38	Total	508

[7] The number of colleges established was actually much larger. The history of many of the efforts to establish colleges has never been, and probably never can be, written, for many of the institutions have long since become defunct.

NEW FEDERAL INTEREST IN EDUCATION

Union sentiment and education. It has been pointed out that in the early years of the Republic many leaders desired the establishment of a general system of education under the control of the Federal Government. Efforts were made from time to time to endow state colleges by the sale of Federal lands, but such efforts were uniformly defeated. The opposition to this policy came from private institutions which feared that public colleges would destroy their institutions; and from the belief that education was properly a function of the states, not of the Federal Government.

The Morrill Act. In 1862 Congress passed the Morrill Act which provided for a grant to each state of 30,000 acres of land for each Congressional seat of that state. The proceeds were to be used to establish a college in which agriculture, mechanical arts, and military science and tactics were to be taught, or to add departments for these subjects at existing institutions. Eighteen states used the grants to develop departments at their state universites; four supported work in engineering and agriculture in private institutions; and the remaining states established separate "land-grant colleges." In 1890 Congress passed an act providing annual grants from the Federal treasury for the support of these colleges.

The United States Commissioner of Education. In 1867 Congress created a national department of education with a United States Commissioner of Education. The next year it was made a Bureau of the Department of the Interior, and Henry Barnard was appointed the first commissioner. Under President Hoover, the Bureau became the United States Office of Education. Despite numerous restrictions this Federal agency has rendered most efficient service.

PROFESSIONAL AND VOCATIONAL TRAINING

Professional education. Great strides were taken in establishing schools of law, medicine, theology, music, and technology. Sometimes these institutions were attached to universites, but frequently they were independent foundations; sometimes they began with substantial endowments, but often they were promoted by the energy and insight of individuals.

At the inauguration of President Eliot, James Bryce is said to have told him that Harvard was "no real university, but only a struggling college, with uncertain relations to learning and research, loosely tied to a congeries of professional schools." The original simple college, founded by the Puritans to train preachers, had by this time evolved into a multiplicity of cultural and professional institutions, more or less loosely related, but under the management of the corporation of Harvard University. Practically all our larger American universities have developed this same character, though the number of professional schools varies greatly in the different institutions. Around the college of arts and sciences have usually been grouped between 15 and 25 professional schools. Many new degrees have been set up to satisfy the demand for recognition of distinctive curricula. Some of these adjunctive schools admit students from the high schools; some require one year of college work; some, two years; some, three years; and a few now require a complete college course for entrance.

The American university. The resultant institution, the outgrowth of these innovations, exhibits a quixotic patchwork representing mainly the compromises of divergent interests. It accommodates all levels from the freshmen and sophomores, who make up the greater body of students, to those who pursue the highest graduate and professional work. The college of arts and sciences remains as the standard institution and it clings to the traditions of general culture; but its methods, curriculum, and spirit are controlled by the interests of the professional schools about it and the graduate school above it.

Teacher training in America. The training of teachers grew into prominence in the 19th century. Some experimental efforts were made to use private academies for this purpose, but did not prove successful. The normal school was an importation from France. The first to be established were at Lexington (1839), Barre and Bridgewater (1840), all of them in Massachusetts. So far, teacher training had in view only preparation for the elementary schools and the instruction was not of college grade.[8]

The first College teacher training course, "Didactic," was offered by President Francis Wayland at Brown University (1851), but it was not

---

[8] In 1839 Andrew J. Yates, a professor of government, set forth a plan recommending that no one be allowed to teach who did not graduate from an academy in which he was taught pedagogy, and no one be allowed to teach in an academy without graduation from a university. In the university, along with other graduate departments, would be one on "public instruction" leading to the M.A. degree.

continued. When President (1852) of Antioch College, Ohio, Horace Mann offered an elective course to sophomores on "Didactics or Theory and Art of Teaching." He used Potter and Emerson's *School and Schoolmaster* and Page's *Theory and Practice of Teaching* as texts. The University of Iowa conducted a Normal Department from 1856 to 1873. Illinois Normal University was established in 1857.

The first university chair of education in the English-speaking world was established in the University of Michigan (1879). Graduate instruction was offered by G. Stanley Hall as an elective in Johns Hopkins (1881). New York University began graduate instruction in 1888. The same year Dr. Nicholas Murray Butler opened New York College of Teachers (later Teachers' College, Columbia University). The University of Chicago made pedagogy a part of the Department of Philosophy under John Dewey in 1895. His famous elementary school was opened in 1896.

Thus by the end of the 19th century the normal school was everywhere accepted as the training school for elementary teachers. Moreover, education had attained a foothold in the college curriculum, and in the graduate schools of a number of first class universities.

Chapter 22

EDUCATIONAL THEORY AND PROBLEMS AT THE END OF THE 19th CENTURY

THE end of the humanistic era. Toward the end of the century dissatisfaction with current systems of education arose both in Europe and America. This had many causes, among them the enormous expansion of knowledge, the intensification of nationalism, the conflict between various philosophies of education, and the impact of the theory of biological evolution.

In 1891 young Kaiser Wilhelm, himself the product of the classical *Gymnasium,* attacked the system at the December Conference of the teachers. "Above all," he declared in Latin, "the national basis is lacking. We must educate young Germans and not young Greeks and Romans." In consequence the emphasis was henceforth shifted to the *Realgymnasium* and the other schools which prepared German youth for industry, commerce, and world conquest.

In England the existing institutions remained largely unmoved by the change of events, but a new order of schools and universities arose to take care of modern progress. Moreover, the bastions of Humanism and Idealism were vigorously attacked by the champions of scientific evolutionalism.

REALISM WINS BATTLE AGAINST HUMANISM AND IDEALISM

The sciences move into the spotlight. After the middle of the 19th century the biological and physical sciences moved into the spotlight, taking precedence over humanistic culture. Three immortal names are linked with this new era which has had its culmination in our own day: Charles Darwin, Herbert Spencer, and Thomas Henry Huxley, all of them Englishmen. Each made a contribution to the new scientific point of view that radically affected the basic conception of education.

Biological evolution. Theories of evolution had been under discussion for many years. The boldest and most comprehensive of these was the effort of Hegel to explain the world, man, and God, as a process of cosmic evolution. The universe, he believed, is the unfolding of mind on an absolute scale. At first this mind took the form of blind, unconscious force which evolved the infinite forms and processes of nature; then, it became conscious of itself in man, the individual, then in society in general, and finally in the organic life of the state.

This comprehensive synthesis or cosmic process captured the philosophic minds of the early 19th century. It guided the course of German imperialism, and used the school as a tool of national policy.

Hegel's hasty absolutism was altogether too speculative and lacking in objective confirmation to satisfy the insatiable but critical curiosity of the scientific mind. Lyell, English geologist, had a much clearer approach in his explanation of the changes of the earth's surface. This theory had tremendous advantage because it showed the process of evolution of the earth's surface in phenomena that were already familiar or readily observable, but the key to naturalistic evolution of life was missing.

The extending of the evolution theory to all forms of life was hindered by the lack of insight into the origins of different species. This crucial link was supplied by Darwin's principle of "natural selection" in his momentous work, *The Origin of Species*, published in 1859. Alfred R. Wallace, who had reached the same conclusion, termed it "the struggle for existence," and Herbert Spencer, "the survival of the fittest."

One thing is certain: no scientific theory other than that of Copernicus ever brought such immediate, catastrophic, and universal disturbance to the entire range of human thinking. Biological investigation henceforth took first place in human interest for two generations. Revision of ideas was required in every field of study, and new theories of psychology and of education on a naturalistic basis were an outcome of the changed conception of the nature of mind and its place in the universe. An explanation of the place of childhood in the general scheme of things was now possible.

Herbert Spencer (1820-1903). Younger than Darwin by a few years, Spencer independently worked out a theory of evolution on a philosophic basis. He wrote voluminously but his general ideas did not make the tremendous sensation that Darwin's did. His treatment of psychology and sociology were eventful but not epochal. His work *Education* was a best seller in its field for half a century. It was used in normal schools, teachers' institutes, and universities as a text in the training of teachers in Britain, the United States, and elsewhere. No other work in this field had such universal popularity.

Spencer's educational views. This work consists of four essays: *What Knowledge is of Most Worth, Intellectual Education, Moral Education,* and *Physical Education.* Written in a vigorous and authoritative style, the conclusions of the author are devastating because of their originality and pragmatic approach. Only the first essay need be considered here.

Spencer's primary thesis is that knowledge must be valued on the basis of what it contributes to life. "How to live?—that is the essential question for us. . . . To prepare us for complete living is the function which education has to discharge." An analysis of the activities which constitute "complete living" yields five classes: "1. Those activities which directly minister to self-preservation; 2. Those activities which by securing the necessaries of life, indirectly minister to self-preservation; 3. Those activities which have for their end the rearing and discipline of offspring; 4. Those activities which are involved in the maintenance of proper social and political relations; 5. Those miscellaneous activities which make up the leisure part of life, devoted to the gratification of the tastes and feelings." The order of these activities is the order of their descending importance from the most to the least.

Spencer proceeded to inquire what knowledge will be of greatest value for each of these activities, and in every case the answer was, unquivocally, "science." The value of scientific knowledge was contrasted with the information which was given to young men in the traditional schools, confined largely to Latin, Greek, and mathematics.

For direct self-preservation a knowledge of things and all that pertains to health is essential; for indirect preservation, which involves getting a living, all the sciences which deal with the production of food and other commodities are of special value. In particular, physics, chemistry, and biology are of most assistance; but the mathematical sciences are necessary for building and other constructive activities.

For the proper rearing of a family Spencer was profoundly concerned, and he urgently advised that preparation be made in advance by training all young people to be intelligent parents. This calls for a lengthy program of studies such as physiology, anatomy, psychology, and methods of intellectual and moral culture. For citizenship quite a different series of studies must be utilized. History, he warned, should not consist of kings, warriors, their battles, and other such "squabbles for power," but rather of the "science of society," "facts which help us to understand how a nation has grown and organized itself." "The only history that is of practical value is what may be called Descriptive Sociology."

For the leisure part of life which has to do with play, with following a hobby, and the enjoyment of art and literature, the best preparation again is science. Even though the appreciation of the fine arts, beauty and literature, foreign languages and cultivation of taste demand attention to something other than science, it must be noted that these leisure activities must be subordinated to the activities which are most essential to happiness. "Accomplishments, the fine arts, *belles-lettres,* and all those things which, as we say, constitute the efflorescence of civilization, should be wholly subordinate to that knowledge and discipline on which civilization rests. *As they occupy the leisure part of life, so should they occupy the leisure part of education.*"

Recognizing the subordination of the esthetic or ornamental aspects of living, Spencer yet contended "that the highest art of every kind is based upon science, for without science there can be neither perfect production nor full appreciation."

Effects of Spencer's views. The unparalleled popularity of Spencer's essays, especially of his effort to compare the values of different kinds of knowledge, is evidence that he had sounded a note welcome to many minds. His was not by any means the first appeal to the English world in favor of the instrumentalist or utilitarian philosophy of education; but it was the beginning of the movement that led to the downfall of the traditional humanistic monopoly of secondary and higher education. In an age of implicit faith in formal discipline, Spencer contrasted the mental power gained by learning science with that acquired from learning Latin and Greek languages and literature.

Thomas Henry Huxley (1825-1895). Next to Darwin as a pure scientist, Huxley occupies the chief honor for placing science in the school program. He began as a physician and surgeon, then accepted a position to teach geology, and later taught comparative anatomy, in which he rose to eminence as a scientist. Huxley was the first authority who embraced a knowledge of contemporary scientific thought in Britain, France, and Germany; and still more significantly, he was the earliest champion of Darwin's theory in England.

Huxley's outstanding service to education was the popularizing of scientific knowledge. His post as Dean of the Royal College of Science in London provided the opportunity to spread the idea of science most widely. He lectured to working men, gave scientific addresses, delivered popular lay sermons, published textbooks and outlined programs of study for schools. His election to membership and chairman of the first London School Board put him in a position to formulate a new curriculum for all the city schools. He championed infant schools, elementary schools, continuation and technical schools, that is to say "an education ladder from the gutter to the university." Huxley wrote much on education; his most important book is *Science and Education.*

Results of the scientific drive. The results of the drive to give science a more prominent role in education were highly successful. By the end of the 19th century Latin and Greek no longer enjoyed the exclusive position they had held since the Renaissance, not even in England. Greek was already being abandoned in the American high school curriculum and Latin was becoming elective; both were to be subordinated to science and other subjects.

The traditional Arts course in the American college underwent profound alteration. The physical and biological sciences which began to be admitted into the curricula around the middle of the 19th century, but were not credited toward the Bachelor of Arts degree, were given full equality by the end of the century. Laboratories were set up, and scientific experiment and observation were considered the only method of reaching truth.

THE PREDOMINANCE OF EUROPEAN EDUCATION ENDS

European philosophies pass. During the latter part of the 19th century the chief American schoolmen, Francis W. Parker, Edward A. Sheldon, and William T. Harris, were under the spell of European educational philosophies and methods. Parker was a pedagogical evangelist of marked power who followed out in practice the principles of Pestalozzi, with which he became acquainted as a student of education in Germany. He revolutionized methods of instruction in the schools of Quincy, Massachusetts, and made them the most progressive and liberal in the country. For many years Parker served as head of the Cook County Normal School in Chicago, which enabled him to missionize on a broad field. Meanwhile, Sheldon introduced Pestalozzian methods into the normal school at Oswego, New York, and popularized the new method of instruction by training teachers. Important as were the contributions of Pestalozzianism, in theory and practice, they were thoroughly absorbed and transcended before the end of the century.

As superintendent of schools in St. Louis and later United States Commissioner of Education, Harris wielded an unparalleled influence for many years. He was the chief advocate of the Hegelian philosophy in America and endeavored to rationalize school organization and the curriculum in accordance with its principles. But his efforts had little consequence; and the real power of Hegelianism later emerged from a different quarter.

Parker and Harris helped to make the kindergarten a constituent part of education and promoted manual constructive work. Superintendent J. L. Hughes of Toronto, in his work, *Froebel's Educational Laws for All Teachers* attempted to extend this system to all levels. How far Froebel's principle of creative activity has influenced 20th century education is impossible to determine.

As we have already seen, the most systematic educational theory at the time was that of the German philosopher, J. F. Herbart. Because of its scientific psychology it furnished the paramount method of instruction for the German schools. During the 1880's, four young Americans found their way to the little University of Jena to study Herbartian pedagogy under its chief exponent, Wilhelm Rein. These men, Charles C. Van Liew, Charles De Garmo, Frank McMurry, and his brother Charles A. McMurry, spread over the United States a knowledge of Herbart's philosophy and education with religious fervor. They also established the *National Herbart Society*. Under incisive criticism, the movement soon wilted, and in 1902 the organization was changed to the National Society for the Scientific Study of Education.

From these examples it was evident that American educators were becoming independent of European domination.

THE ARTICULATION OF AMERICAN SCHOOLS

Articulation of elementary school and high school. From 1840 to 1850, some of the high schools of Massachusetts began the practice of basing their entrance examinations upon the grammar school subjects —a policy which had not been thought necessary at first. In some cases the requirements specifically stated that the subjects for the admission examinations were the grammar school studies. This was true of the following high schools: Worcester, 1844; Nantucket, 1848; Quincy, 1853; Westfield, 1854-1855; Taunton, 1855-1856; and South Danvers and Plymouth, 1857. It was not until some years after the Civil War that the admission examination was generally abandoned, and that children were allowed to enter the high schools by virtue of having completed elementary school.

Results of the correlation. The unified city school system was formed by superimposing the high school directly upon the graded school. No effort was made to articulate the curricula of the two institutions; the unification was, therefore, largely superficial and mechanical.

One of the chief results of the correlation of these two schools was the delay in entering upon the high school course. Instead of entering at from nine to 12 years of age, the pupils generally did not enter until they had completed the eight grammar grades, usually at 14 or 15. The average age of admission to the Lowell High School in 1846 was 13 years 11 months. This high school had been articulated with the grades. In 1860, the average age of entrance to the Danvers High School was 14 years 8 months; in 1861, the average age at South Danvers was 14 years 11 months, and at Worcester, the first-year high school students averaged 15 years 7 months. In 1858, the school system of Cambridge, Massachusetts, was planned to carry the child through the grade school by fourteen and one-half years of age.

High schools became preparatory schools. The originators of the first high schools had no intention of preparing students for college; that was the function of the Latin grammar schools. It had also been a secondary function of the academies; much college preparatory work was also done by private instruction. The Boston High School did not offer instruction in Latin and Greek, and consequently was not designed for preparing students for college. The high schools, in New England especially, took their aims and curricula chiefly from the academies. However, they soon came to be influenced by the objectives and curriculum of the Latin grammar school as well. This was particularly true in those places that had never established Latin grammar schools.

The first suggestion that the high school serve as a college preparatory school was made in Plymouth, Massachusetts, in 1826; it was proposed to change the Latin grammar school into a high school for the purposes of a good, practical, English education as well as for the study of Greek and Latin. It is uncertain whether this proposal was put into operation. At any rate, Lowell, Massachusetts, in 1831 established a high school "designed both to perfect the English Education . . . and also to fit young men for college." Portland, Maine, followed about the same time; and Providence, Rhode Island, in 1838.

> It is evident that by 1840 with a few exceptions such as Boston and Salem (until 1855) the high school had assumed the dual role of a college preparatory school and a training for practical life activities.[1]

In the Middle West, the high schools performed both functions from the time they were established; in the South, private academies controlled education. The two functions were carried out by offering two distinct courses of study: the *English course* and the *classical course.*

College entrance requirements. Meanwhile the colleges continued in complete isolation and independence; admission by examination was the practice everywhere. Even in Michigan, where the university supported a number of branch preparatory schools, students were required to pass the admission examination. But a change took place in the character of the examination. Formerly it had been oral; it now became a written test. Formerly it was confined to a knowledge of Latin, Greek, and some arithmetic, but by the end of the Civil War it was based upon so many subjects that a good high school course was practically essential to pass it.

Correlation of college and high school. The final correlation of high school and college began at Michigan in 1870. President Frieze advocated giving admission certificates to the best high school students. The faculty thereupon adopted a plan of accepting students from certain high schools that had been inspected by a faculty committee. Thus it came about that most colleges required only graduation from high school with a certain number of hours.

---

[1] Grizzell, E. D., *Origin and Development of the High School in New England before 1865,* p. 279. Philadelphia: University of Pennsylvania Press, 1923.

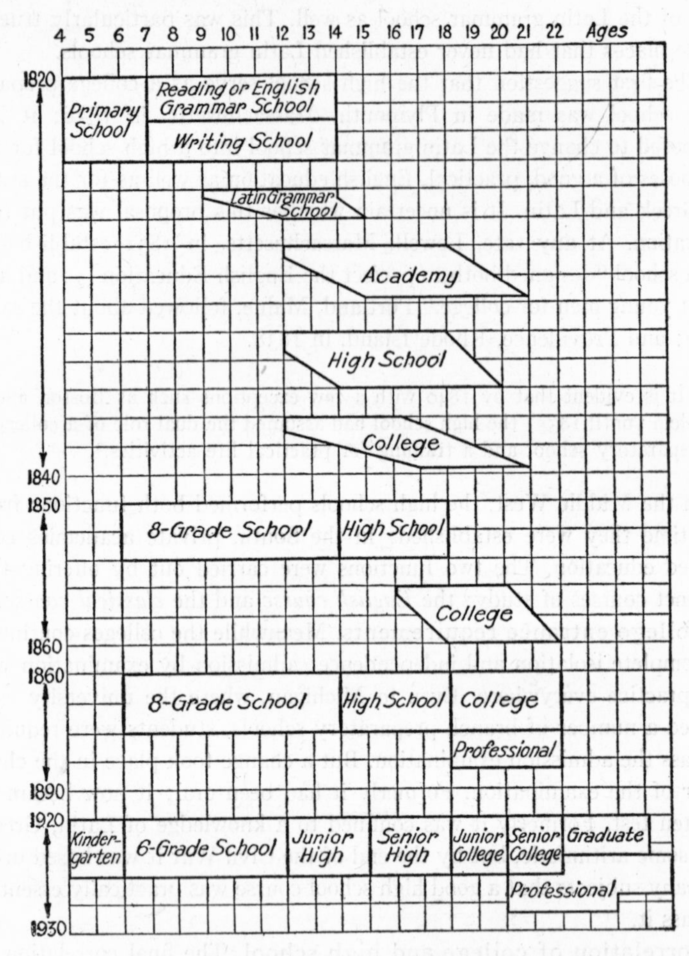

Development of the American School System.

The demand for reorganization. About 1880 the American school system, after half a century of effort, formed a pyramid of articulated institutions, kindergartens, elementary schools, high schools; and college, graduate, and professional instruction. Leading educators now began to look at it in a critical way, and did not find it satisfactory. Two weaknesses were apparent. One had to do with the curriculum, the other with organization. The first was due to the overemphasis of the traditional humanistic basis of education, and the consequent lack of attention to English and modern languages and the sciences; the other came from a comparison of the scholarship and age of the graduates of the secondary schools with European graduates of the *Gymnasium.* These defects precipitated a crisis and began consequences of the greatest magnitude.

The new crisis. In 1888 Charles W. Eliot, President of Harvard University, brought the weaknesses of the system to public attention in an epochal address at the Washington meeting of the Department of Superintendence. His subject was: "Can School Programmes be Shortened and Enriched?" He opened his address with the following challenging statement: [2]

> In the process of improving the secondary schools, colleges, and professional schools of the United States,—a process which has been carried on with remarkable energy since the Civil War—certain difficulties have been created for the higher education in general, and particularly for colleges. These difficulties have to do with the age at which young men can get prepared for college, and therefore with the ages at which boys pass the successive stages of their earlier education. The average age of admission to Harvard College has been rising for sixty years past, and has now reached the extravagant limit of eighteen years and ten months. The average college graduate is undoubtedly nearly twenty-three years old at graduation; and when he has obtained his A.B. he must nowadays allow at least three years for his professional education.

Dr. Eliot pointed out that the highly organized school systems of Europe graduated their students from three to five years earlier than the American. In his report as president of Harvard for 1888-1889, he stated: "Wherever the fault and whatever the remedy it is clear that the degree of Bachelor of Arts is taken in the United States later than in any other country in which the degree is used, and too late for the best interests of the individuals who aspire to it, and of the institutions which confer it."

In an incisive address before the annual session of the N.E.A. (1890), entitled "The Gap between the Elementary Schools and the Colleges," President Eliot placed the blame for the prolongation of education and its inefficiency upon the public elementary and high school. In consequence of these criticisms, the Association (1892) appointed a committee of ten noted educators, with President Eliot as chairman, to make a study of the situation and recommend changes.

[2] Eliot, Charles W., *Educational Reform,* p. 151. New York: Century, 1898.

The committee selected the nine fields of study usually taught in the high schools of the United States, and then induced ten experts in each field to hold a series of conferences and draw up their conclusions as to where, how long, and by what methods each of these nine fields should be taught. "The Committee of Ten" then undertook to correlate these recommendations into a program of reform. This was the first time in American education a group of 100 educators had undertaken to formulate a unified system of instruction for children and youth from six to 18 years of age. The report was one of the most important educational documents ever issued in the United States.

The unanimity of these 100 is truly astonishing as was the moderation of their claims and their cautious conservatism. But this report dynamited the log-jam and in the prolonged discussion which followed all the schools were subject to examination, criticism and reconstruction.

THE RECONSTRUCTION OF THE HIGH SCHOOL

Report of the Committee of Ten. The Report was full of interesting suggestions and recommendations, many of them reactionary, and all based upon the theory of formal mental discipline. The primary objective was to secure uniformity in curricula for admission to college, and to shorten the period of preparation. It was unanimously agreed that "many secondary studies should be begun earlier." This was the germ which some years later was to bring about the formation of the junior high school. The teaching of science and, especially, English and history was favored. The report urged laboratory work for all sciences. A more immediate effect was that it led colleges to adopt the "unit system" for entrance requirements. Industrial and commercial subjects were unfortunately omitted. The report also urged that good training in English be required for all pupils entering college, and that English should be given as much time in the high school as Latin.

The conferees were almost entirely college professors, and as such were subject-matter specialists. They viewed the problem from the standpoint of when the various subjects should be introduced into the experience of the child and not from the standpoint of existing institutional organization. The line separating the elementary and the high school was no longer considered sacrosanct. But the entire proceeding was weakened because they viewed the problem from the standpoint of preparation for college and not from that of the needs of children and youth.

Some of their principles look quite absurd today. The Committee "unanimously declared that every subject which is taught at all in a secondary school should be taught in the same way and to the same extent to every pupil so long as he pursues it no matter when education is to cease." Again, "All subjects are of equal educational value if taught equally well." Obviously the members of the famous ten believed that subjects are of value more because of the process of learning than because of the information.

In order to shorten the time of college preparation, the traditional lock-step, four-year, fixed-course curriculum was abandoned and the hour credit system adopted. Some subjects were required, beyond which the additional units could be chosen more or less freely. Bright students could accumulate the necessary credits at a more rapid rate than others; and summer school work likewise gave opportunity for rapid advancement.

The report and the consequent reform of the high schools resulted in a long conflict over the control of the curriculum of the high school for college preparation and for other objectives.

THE ELEMENTARY SCHOOL

Committee of Fifteen. Elementary education was also affected by Dr. Eliot's reports. In 1893 the National Education Association appointed the Committee of Fifteen to study the organization of the elementary system, the coordination of studies, and the training of teachers. The results of the report of this committee were not so far reaching as those of the committee on secondary education, but they brought about, nevertheless, a study of various means to break up the lock-step system and to facilitate the progress of more gifted pupils. From the two studies eventually arose the junior high school movement.

THE JUNIOR COLLEGE

Origin of the junior college. All in all, the junior college movement is the most significant event that has taken place in higher education since the establishment of Johns Hopkins University, in 1876, as a graduate university. The original gestures for such a movement were made by Dr. Henry P. Tappan, president of the University of Michigan, and by Col. W. W. Folwell, president of the University of Minnesota. But these gestures were quite premature. The necessary conditions for the realization of such ideals of secondary and higher education did not appear until the end of the century, when the articulated high school and the graduate university had developed. The junior college was fundamentally due to the realization, on the part of American educators, that the first two years of the standard four-year college belong to the secondary field. In the effort which was made between 1825 and 1875 to raise the old-fashioned college to the level of the European university, the standard of scholarship had advanced two years above what it had been. When the graduate school appeared, however, it was clear that the colleges had not been wise in aspiring to university rank. In curriculum, methods, and age of students, the first two years of the standard college remained on the secondary level. The situation became acute during the last decade of the 19th century, and demanded reorganization to meet the new complexity in student needs and encyclopedia scholarship.

The chief leaders in the movement to establish junior colleges were Dr. William Rainey Harper, first president of the University of Chicago, and Dean Alexis F. Lange, of the University of California. There was no collaboration; yet, although they worked independently, they had the same objective in view. At the time of the organization of the University of Chicago, Dr. Harper gave the work of the first two years of the College of Arts and Sciences a separate status, with the title "Academic College." Students who passed the courses of these years were given the recognition of "Associate in Arts."

Dr. Harper also undertook a movement to affiliate a large number of small colleges with the University of Chicago, by accepting their work through the sophomore year. In response to his efforts, Lewis Institute was opened in Chicago in 1896, as such an affiliated junior college. The next year, Bradley Polytechnic Institute, of Peoria, Illinois, was established on the same basis. Dr. Harper was a member of the boards of these institutions. Through the American Baptist Education Society, whose policies he dominated, he influenced the establishment of the first denominational junior colleges in Texas and other states. Another aspect of his plan was to induce public high schools to add two years of college work to their curricular offerings. Some half-dozen high schools took this step, but the only one that continued was the township high school at Joliet, Illinois. In 1902 this became the first public junior college. From these beginnings the junior college movement later spread throughout the Middle West and the South.

THE ARTS COLLEGE

The reorganization. In the field of higher education reorganization of the standard four-year college came under warm discussion. The rapid growth of graduate instruction and of the professional schools gave an added incentive to the movement to shorten the time for general education, without, however, making it less effective. Some college presidents favored shortening the college course to three years, and some, even to two years. In the end it was decided not to shorten the time but to change the form of organization of the college course. The "lock-step" class system together with the fixed curricula, was abandoned, and in its place the course or hour credit system was adopted. This change furnished a much needed elasticity; it permitted the brilliant student to shorten, by more intensive work, the time necessary for securing a degree. The most far-reaching result of the discussion was, however, as we have just seen, the emergence of the junior college.

EARLY ADULT EDUCATION MOVEMENTS

Adult cultural needs. Throughout the 19th century various movements arose to supply a growing demand for cultural opportunity for adults who had not been so fortunate as to enjoy a full course of training. This was true especially of women but many men were also interested.

Women's societies and clubs. Women began to form organizations as early as the 1830's. First came the missionary and philanthropic associations, later the educational, and after the Civil War the women's clubs and societies for the cultivation of talents and social welfare. The first of these clubs for self-improvement was the Sorosis Club formed in New York City in 1868. The number of societies and clubs is now legion and their purposes embrace all the interests of womanhood. This movement may be said to have culminated in the forming of the Woman's Christian Temperance Union (1874), the Federation of Women's Clubs (1893), and the granting of suffrage to all women on an equal basis with men (1920).

The Chautauqua movement. This movement had its inception in an effort to help Sunday School teachers become more efficient. A two weeks session of lectures and study courses was held at Chautauqua Lake in southern New York state under the leadership of Lewis Miller, a wealthy manufacturer, and Bishop John H. Vincent of the Methodist Church. The first meeting was in August 1874 and over 1000 people attended.

The movement met with instant and enthusiastic approval and expanded along a number of lines. The combination of popular lectures, short study courses, recreation, and enthusiastic religious services appealed to many people. Soon Correspondence Courses and Home-Reading Circles were formed for those who could not attend the sessions at headquarters and to care for the year-round interest. The success of the Chautauqua Assembly led to the setting up of similar groups in many places to promote courses of lectures by popular teachers and speakers.

William Rainey Harper of Yale University became the organizing genius of the parent Chautauqua, and when he formed the University of Chicago (1891-92), he introduced the Summer Session, the Correspondence School and the Extension Department all of which had been tried out at the parent Chautauqua Assembly.

Chapter 23

G. STANLEY HALL AND GENETIC PHILOSOPHY

HALL'S importance for psychology and education. Was he a "playboy of scholarship," a sophistic "Hippias Pedagogicus," or "the prophet of a new era"? Such varied judgments were passed upon him while he was still alive. Did he give a permanent redirection to education, or were his ideas fruitless? His name has received scant attention in works on the history of education. Outside of his immediate disciples, few have even remotely sensed what Dr. Hall was attempting to do. His scholarship was at once so comprehensive and idiosyncratic that he baffled people of conventional habits of thought. The truth is, he was a psychological and pedagogical Columbus who undertook to explore the paleontology of the soul, but most psychologists have not been convinced that the world he undertook to explore was more than a mirage.

Life, work, and writings. Granville Stanley Hall was born of Mayflower stock at Ashfield, Massachusetts, in 1844 or 1846. Though his father was a man of intelligence, he had no particular desire to have Stanley go to college. Nevertheless, for poor farming people, the family was one of unusual culture. Despite his father's lack of interest, Stanley went to Williams College, where he graduated in the class of 1867. Setting out to enter the ministry, he enrolled in Union Theological Seminary, New York City. Through the good office of Henry Ward Beecher, a wealthy friend made it possible for young Hall to go to Germany for graduate study. First at Bonn, and later at Berlin, he studied philosophy and theology. Returning to America in 1871, he accepted a position as a private tutor, and from 1872 to 1876 he was a professor in Antioch College, Ohio, where he taught English literature and psychology.

Becoming deeply interested in psychology, Hall resigned at Antioch and spent two years at Harvard University studying under William James. He received the Ph.D. degree in 1878. He then proceeded once more to Berlin, where at first he specialized in physiology. The second year he went to Leipzig to study psychology, under Wilhelm Wundt; theology, under Dorner; and philosophy, under Trendelenburg.

During his many years at Harvard and at German universities, Hall received a training unequalled in its comprehensiveness. It included theology, philosophy, anthropology, biology, physiology, anatomy, psychology, and neurology, under the most noted experts of Germany and America. No other man of his time could feel at home in so many diverse and yet related fields of science.

Returning to Boston in 1880, he wrote his first notable study, *Contents of Children's Minds on Entering School*. From 1882 to 1888, he taught psychology and education in Johns Hopkins University. Elected president of Clark University in 1888, he revisited Europe for nine months to study the organization of higher education in various countries. For the next 30 years he was the center of the most unique institution of higher education in the world, a select group of students who possessed the pioneering type of mind. Stimulated by his indefatigable spirit and creative genius, they explored the regions of genetic psychology and education. Dr. Hall himself published some 14 volumes and over 350 articles touching a wide range of subjects. He died in 1924.

Genetic psychology. When Darwin published his celebrated work, *The Origin of Species*, a new epoch began in human thinking. It is impossible for anyone today to understand how revolutionizing was the theory of biological evolution. Every subject of human interest came in for reorganization in the light of this new point of view. One of the most difficult problems that faced the theory was to account for the human mind and soul. It was this challenge of reconciling man's mental life with the evolutionary hypothesis that motivated all of Dr. Hall's thinking. He described the experience as follows: [1]

> As soon as I first heard it in my youth I think I must have been hypnotized by the word "evolution"; which was music to my ear and seemed to fit my mouth better than any other.

---

[1] Pruette, Lorine, *G. Stanley Hall; A Biography of a Mind*, p. 208. New York: Appleton, 1926.

Nothing quite so fully expressed his ambition as to become "The Darwin of the Mind." What Darwin and his followers did to piece together the evidences for the evolution of biological life from single cellular forms to the complex human body, Hall endeavored to do for the mind. He was a scientific pioneer in the world of psychic phenomena, who undertook to explore the uncharted areas of mind in the animal and human world. In this adventure he possessed all the dash, the courage, and the expectancy of a discoverer of new continents. He made mistakes that shocked petty and conventional souls and brought ridicule upon him. For the technicalities of systematic scholarship he cared little. His was the romance of primal discovery, an aerial survey from a high altitude; others were to follow with their yardsticks and cartography.

Fundamental theory. Dr. Hall's fundamental theory was that mental and physical life are always parallel; in technical language, there is no psychosis without neurosis. Mind and body have evolved together through millions of years on the earth. Physical life began in a single unicellular creature, and mind began with the same creature. Through infinite changes the body has evolved to what it is today; and at every step mental life accompanied the physical. To chart the nascent developments of psychic life through all the past, and to assist in the future growth of the soul formed for Dr. Hall a colossal task to which he dedicated his life with religious fervor.

In the first living cell resided all the potentialities which, through millenniums, have evolved into the complexity of life in the world today. Hunger was the most original and inherent cause of activity. The quest for food was the origin of mentality, because it caused action.[2]

> Every thought and feeling has as its *motif* the feeding of the hunger of some group of cells. . . . The *amoeba has a soul or else man has none.* We must be vitalists or mechanists all the way along the series; we cannot shift our point of view when we come to man.

After the one-celled animals came the many-celled. Along the shore lines of the world there appeared highly complicated organisms of myriads of cells. Life was moving up the scale. Locomotion made them more efficient for seeking food and escaping enemies. Subsequently, a nervous system developed in the worm, and mental life began a new epoch. Finally, the vertebrate forms appeared with the greatest complexity of

[2] *Ibid.*, pp. 210-211.

the nervous system. "At some stage of the great drama, cold-blooded, scaly reptiles were transformed into warm-blooded mammals," and in due time man was evolved. As the hand was used, the brain began to develop, "for the mind of man is handmade." Then, language and primitive arts sprang up. Such, in a sketchy outline, was the gradual evolution of life and activity; in and through the entire process the mental life was evolving step by step along with the body and its activities. First, there unfolded the great basic instincts: food-getting, reproduction, and avoiding enemies. Correlated with these was the evolution of the senses. Then followed the growth of the intermediate mental organs and the basic emotions. Finally, with the development of tribal society, man's higher soul life was realized.

Child study and the recapitulation process. The evolution of mind and activity in the race is of the greatest value as a scientific theory explaining the origin of man. But it has also a more practical application. The child-study movement and adolescent psychology are areas of the immense field of genetic psychology; Dr. Hall was spurred on in his investigation of mental evolution by a profound interest in education.[3] "He strove to understand the history of mind that he might understand the possibilities of a single child."

Genetic life and psychology had a deep significance for Dr. Hall because he believed that all the evidence showed unmistakably that the child repeats the evolution of the race. This theory, as already indicated, was not new at all. It began with Rousseau in a general way; for Schiller and Herbart, it took the form of the culture-epoch theory; for Froebel, it was the law of recapitulation of spiritual development. Dr. Hall now viewed it in the clearer light of biological evolution, and added thereto the idea of the recapitulation of the instincts and mental processes of past ages. The individual inherits the stored-up results of all the experiences of the past. More particularly, the practical activities, ritualistic performances, and those actions which, because of repetition, tended to become habitual were stored up and handed down to the new-born through heredity. The human embryo passes through stages similar to those through which the race passed in its earliest history. The infant repeats the life period of the primitive social group. The child passes through a hunting period, a cave period, a building period, and so on.

[3] *Ibid.*, p. 221.

Such is the origin of man's instinctive responses and impulses. Many of them are retained in the soul as vestigial organs are in the body.

Dr. Hall must be credited with the parable of the tadpole's tail. Frogs do not have tails, but tadpoles do have tails. If the tail of a tadpole is cut off, the back legs of the frog will not grow, because the nutriment for their development comes from the tail. It is absorbed and gradually disappears; but it has been essential for the later development. So it is in human growth generally. Many activities and organs of childhood must disappear or undergo great modification in order to insure the full development of the body.

An analogy of this biological fact may be found in the mental life. There flash across the consciousness or in dreams strange ideas, emotions, or images that come from ancestral experiences and are, so to speak, the fossilized mental remains of the far-away past. Many of the experiences and impulses of children are remnants of psychic habits long since forgotten. Our fleeting fancies often afford glimpses of the ancestral life. These have been retained in man's unfolding heredity, just as he retains some particular facial feature, bodily characteristic, or mannerism from his ancestors.[4]

> The evidence for the truth of such a conception of the mind and body of man is now so great, and so corroborative one part to another, that it is hardly possible to doubt it. Both mind and body are full of observable traces of their ancient origin.... The evidence that the mind as well as the body retains vestiges of the past is now beyond dispute.... Rudimentary psychoses are as evident as rudimentary organs.
>
> Human courtship, care of the young, crime, fears, subconscious habits, demand for their explanation an evolutionary theory. Many actions of the infant can be explained in no other way.... We must see that mind and body alike are teeming with the traces of ancient life, both human and prehuman, knowledge of which is of the greatest importance for a comprehension of the most common facts of daily life; and for education.

Such is a brief summary of the theory of psychic evolution, or genetic psychology, which Dr. Hall elaborated.

Study of child nature. Before Dr. Hall's studies little systematic investigation of child nature had been done. The most important studies made were in the field of infant development. Darwin had written *A Biographical Sketch of an Infant* (1877). The German psychologist

---

[4] Partridge, George E., *Genetic Philosophy of Education,* pp. 25-27. New York: Sturgis and Walton Company, p. 191.

Preyer had published *The Mind of the Child* (1880), a work of systematic observation. The same year Hall made his study on the *Contents of Children's Minds on Entering School.* After assuming the presidency of Clark University, Dr. Hall began the publication of *The Pedagogical Seminary,* largely devoted to articles on child study and on education from this new standpoint. Later, one of his students at Clark, Dr. Frederick Tracy, published *The Psychology of Childhood.* From this time the movement ripened with rapidity and with mounting interest. Many child-study societies were formed all over the country. Similar movements took form in European lands. Dr. Hall was the acknowledged leader of the movement for the scientific study of child nature and development. Not only did he publish numerous articles, but through his students a great number of investigations were made.

Adolescence. Dr. Hall's two-volume study, *Adolescence; Its Psychology and Its Relations to Physiology, Anthropology, Sociology, Sex, Crime, Religion and Education,* must be considered the most comprehensive treatment of this subject ever made. While Dr. Hall must share with others the honor of initiating the study of child nature, he was the real creator of the science of adolescence. The few scattered studies of special topics made before Hall's day were largely inconsequential and gave no indication of the great significance of the subject as a whole. Hall's study will long remain an imperishable monument to his deep sympathy and profound insight. Only a man with his intimate knowledge of all aspects of the human organism was capable of launching such a new science or combination of sciences.

The study of the phenomena of adolescence has had marked effect upon secondary education in our country. It aided greatly in bringing about the organization of the junior high school and the junior college, altered fundamentally the secondary curricula, and in many ways affected methods of instruction and discipline. The popularizing of knowledge of adolescent life has profoundly changed the attitude of parents, teachers, and religious workers in regard to the treatment of youth.

New theory of play. Hall took his stand with the great educational reformers who favored play. Next to thirst, hunger, sex, laughter, and crying, play must be regarded as the most general of all activities. In play the child repeats the central activities of the race. Play is an expression of the past habits of the race that have been stored up in the nervous system and handed on by heredity. It is the inner force which makes for the expression of all early movements and activities, and for the acquisition of control and skill. Play is purely instinctive; it has no conscious ends in view. Education must utilize the play motive, for it is the most natural force in the development of child life. Early education must be chiefly play, and throughout life, play is the necessary restorative of human energies. Of the educational value of play, Dr. Hall wrote: [5]

> Play is the best kind of education, because it practices powers of mind and body which, in our highly specialized civilization, would never otherwise have a chance to develop. To understand the play instinct we must know something of the past life of the race.

Again, in explanation of play as recapitulation, he says: [6]

> In children, especially, most of their lives consist in rehearsing the rude history of their race. The most persistent plays and games are not, as Groos says, practicing for future occupations, but are nothing but repetitions in abridged and sportive form of the serious occupations of their ancient forebears. The best definition we have of child-life is that it is early human occupations epitomized: for the child relives the history of the race in his acts, just as the scores of rudimentary organs in his body tell the story of its evolution from the lower forms of animal life from which he has inherited his every organ and tissue. Let us, then, grasp the vast and significant fact that wherever we find any interest, instinct, or impulse to act that is strong and spontaneous, it is always an expression of the momentum of the past. The all-dominant, but of course mainly unconscious, will of the child is to relive this past, as if his early ancestors were struggling in his soul and body to make their influences felt and their voices heard.

The reason play is so pleasurable to both young and old is because it is instinctive. The more activities are the expression of the oldest and most deep-seated instincts, the more pleasurable they are.

Fancy, the play of the soul. Educational theorists have been sharply divided upon the question of the use of fancy and fairy tales. Factualists, like the Puritans, Rousseau, and John Dewey, oppose the use of fairy tales and literature of fancy. They regard all make-believe, not only as false, but even as injurious to the mind. Others like Plato,

[5] Hall, G. Stanley, "Play and Dancing for Adolescents," in *The Independent*, Vol. 62, pp. 355-356.

[6] Hall, G. Stanley, "The Natural Activities of Children as Determining the Industries in Early Education," in *Proceedings of the National Education Association* (1904), p. 444.

Froebel, Andersen, and Hall, look upon myths, fairy tales, and Mother Goose as the play of the mind. They are as essential for the wholesome development of the mind as physical play is for the growth and the coordination of muscles and nerves which leads to motor control.

Feeling and emotion affect the intellect most directly through the imagination. They express themselves in faith and belief, which represent the life of the race. These are more powerful by far than the experiences of the individual, and become the deciding factor in all important life situations. The inherited background is the drive behind all the activities of imagination, dreams, and spontaneous interests. It guides the attention in all its flittings, and governs the apperceptive processes.

Imagination is of two kinds, the reproductive and the creative. In the one case, it merely reproduces images of objects experienced by the senses; in the other, it creates forms such as we know in myth, fairy tale, and Santa Claus legends. The mind of the child is highly animistic. This is the factor which reads into things the feelings, the sense of self, and power of which the child is becoming conscious. This mental play of the child has a vital relation to his later interpretation of life in terms of religion and morals. The imagination is most creative in the realm of the ideal.[7]

> The intellectual life is a growth, a series of stages in which there is always a partial adaptation to the practical needs of the individual, while all the time there is progress, by an apparently circuitous route, toward a permanent adjustment, in adult life, to the demands of the environment. Thought at each stage is in excess of the needs of that stage; but from the excess of thought and fancy the practical intellect is shaped by the needs of life; and the mind, which is inclined by nature to roam everywhere, to be free and to follow the instincts and racial feelings, is finally domesticated and harnessed to definite tasks.

Myth. The best example of the dominance of the intellect by the background psychic life, the unconscious will, is the myth. Myths have grown out of the feelings of the race, and have created a world of unreality. The growing mind of the child recapitulates the myth-making instinct of the race. The child lives in two worlds at the same time: the world of sense or things, and the world of fancy; the world of hard reality, and the world of ancestral experiences that well up within him. Truth, for the child, is only in part a matter of sense experience. He is

---

[7] Partridge, George E., *op. cit.*, p. 63.

constantly at work creating, out of his own instincts, a body of truth; he does this in ways but little controlled by his environment.

Stages in child life and education. Along with Rousseau and Froebel, Hall recognized that individual human development proceeds in distinct stages which represent the great eras in history. Furthermore, Hall believed in special developments, when particular organs or functions suddenly burgeon and bring about new activities and experiences. He divided child life into four general stages—infancy, childhood, youth, and adolescence.

Infancy is the period from birth to about four years of age. It is the time of most rapid physical growth and of the acquisition of such fundamental activities as walking, talking, and the movements necessary for self-preservation. The senses are most active in this period.

The stage of childhood extends normally from about four to eight. The sensory life is now no longer dominant, but gives place to the activity of the imagination. The education most suitable to this period, as recommended by Dr. Hall, is as follows: [8]

> Now for five years or more the chief educational need of the child is that his mind be provided with rich cultural material stimulating to the imagination, and that he should be left free to work this out and express it in free play. The child must now live through the stage of myth-making and poetic fancy of the savage; the receptive faculties must be steeped in nature lore, story, and those inventions of natural religion which the race has now outgrown, but which are suited to the child's needs. It is only in such a way that the mind, acted upon by the environment, adds a stratum above the merely sensory plane, and begins to work in a larger field, both in time and space, than the senses can grasp. It is all-essential now that the child's world be made rich and full; and consequently it must be crude, unfinished, disjointed, and illogical. Fancy must roam free, thought must grapple with all the problems of the practical and ideal worlds, but there must be no forcing, nor strain after precise knowledge.

This statement indicates that Dr. Hall fully appreciated the role which fancy and imagination play in the evolution of mind.

Youth is the period from eight to 12 or 13, the pre-pubertal age. In this stage the child is recapitulating the humdrum life of savagery, which endured several hundred thousand years. Physical growth slows, and his intellectual powers become less active. Life now demands that the fundamental habits of society and the rudiments of learning be acquired. Drill,

---

[8] *Ibid.*, pp. 206-207.

repetition, ritual, and regimentation are necessary for the stabilization of character. Moreover, such routine is actually pleasurable. Partridge sums up Hall's view of this period and its training as follows: [9]

> The method of teaching should now be mechanical, repetitive, dogmatic, and authoritative. The powers of retention are at their greatest height, and they have greater capacity, by far, than we yet employ. We have much to learn in this particular from the schoolmasters of the past. The greatest possible stress, short periods, few hours, incessant insistence, incitement, little reliance upon interest, reason, or work done without the presence of the teacher—these are the correct methods in imparting the essentially formal elements of knowledge.

Thus, according to Hall, the education of youth is quite the opposite of that of children, and also of that of adolescents.

Adolescence begins with puberty and extends to full physical maturity, at from 22 to 25. This corresponds in race history to the period of modern civilization; its education must follow quite a different philosophy from that followed in the earlier stages.[10]

> At adolescence the aspect of all education must radically change. Once more the need is for free play of interests, developing from within. Now ... feeding the mind must take the first place, and all drill and discipline must be subordinated. Appeal must be made to enthusiasm and inspiration. The powers of appreciation and intuitive understanding must be depended upon, and too much must not be asked from the child in return. Examinations have but little place. The method of teaching must be to present large conceptions, rather than details. The world must be taught as a whole, rather than in its minute parts. Quantity and enrichment are more to be desired than accuracy. The purpose must be to bring out the child's own interests and enthusiasms, and so to nourish and lead them as to raise them to the highest possible level. Culture must be all-sided and at every point the emotional life and the intellectual life must be kept in close contact with one another.

Range and detail of Hall's studies. Dr. Hall was not content to elaborate a general theory of genetic psychology. He strove to explore the entire range of child nature and activities, and, as far as possible, to study certain aspects in detail.

Among the emotional expressions and other activities of children that he traced were fear, anger, pity, curiosity, interest, collecting, cave-build-

---

[9] *Ibid.*, pp. 209-210.
[10] *Ibid.*, pp. 211-212.

ing, doll play, sand pile, and other forms of play. Physical growth, moral and religious developments, growth of the will, social nature, rhythm, and feelings were discussed. Other subjects that he treated were the early sense of self, showing off, bashfulness, love of nature, speech development, early memories, children's lying, and imagination and fancy.

Hall was convinced that every advance in modern education was directly caused by a more definite knowledge of children, and a deeper sympathy for their needs. His books and articles, almost 400 in number, present an amazing array of topics. He discussed the regimen of the nursery, the reconstruction of the kindergarten, the vitalization of primary and elementary education, the reform of the high school, the reformation of the Sunday school, the reorganization of the normal schools for the training of teachers, and many phases of college and university education.

His interest in everything pertaining to health and physical development marked him as one of the pioneers in physical and mental hygiene. He discussed overpressure in schools; the heating, lighting, and ventilation of school buildings; dancing and other forms of recreation; sex information, abnormalities of mind, social hygiene, morale, and eugenics.

Hall's discussions of adolescent life and training were especially voluminous; all aspects of development were included. He wrote numerous articles on the education of adolescents at the level both of the secondary school and of the college. No other writer in modern times has been intimately conversant with the varied phenomena of human development at so many points. His many-sided specialization gave him comprehension and insight that were unparalleled.

In the field of teaching, Hall discussed methods of teaching history, religion, morals, reading, rhetoric, literature, and other subjects. Methods, he claimed, must be adapted to the subject and also to the dominant psychology of the particular period; the instruction of the adolescent must be quite different from that of the pre-adolescent child.

Fundamental principles. (1) The continuance of the race is supremely important; the individual is incidental. Education must recognize this fact and direct its course in accordance with this principle. Sex life, reproduction, and the rearing of children are the supreme functions of life, and must occupy a central position in education.

(2) The emotional life is far more fundamental than the intellectual. Intelligence is a comparatively late development, while emotion is as

ancient as life itself. Emotion furnishes the motivation for the development of the intellect. Consciousness and thought owe their origin to the emotions. The emergence of intelligence and its subsequent development have grown out of the activities of man in securing food, avoiding enemies, seeking shelter, and exercising imagination. It transcends the mere needs of the organism and builds a structure of higher thought.

(3) Human development is a process of recapitulating the racial developments. It proceeds from the fundamental to the accessory. The child in his progress upward shows first the simpler, more ancient forms of activity, and then gradually develops the more accessory functions. The movements of trunk and shoulder develop earliest; later, the finer movements of wrist, hand, and finger. Similarly, in the development of the mind, the more general and simpler things come first; later, the more detailed and specific. This order must govern the procedures of education.

(4) Education must be based upon the development of the child's own activities, capabilities, and interests. It should be all-sided and lead to a well-balanced, normal personality.

(5) All the sciences which throw light on human nature form the basis of a science of education.

Hall's influence. No American scholar has so frequently been called a genius as Dr. Hall. Certainly he was our most daring and most comprehensive thinker in philosophy, psychology, and education. His knowledge of many sciences gave him the power of integrating ideas from many fields of science that are not usually correlated. His ideas have entered vitally into the thinking of present-day educators, and have vastly modified our educational procedures. It may never be possible for historians to evaluate definitely his influence on education, because of the vast complexity and diversity of present-day educational ideas.

Criticisms of his theories. Among the criticisms which have, at least, temporarily, dimmed his fame and decreased his influence are these: (1) The questionnaire method which he used extensively in securing data on child life is not sufficiently accurate for scientific purposes. (2) The recapitulation theory, on which he based his views, has not been found true except in a very general way, and many of the developments supposed to be recapitulations are more easily explained in other ways. Few of the educational historians and philosophers of the past half-century are aware of the explorations of G. Stanley Hall and the references to his views have been derogatory and often quite false.

He is charged with being a Herbartian, while in fact nothing could be farther from the truth. His method was called unscientific, despite the fact that he introduced Wundtian experimental psychology into this country; and despite his monumental volumes on adolescence, the credit for introducing this science has strangely been attributed to another. A conspiracy of silence and disparagement has kept the past generation from knowing the significance of this colossal figure.

Chapter 24

JOHN DEWEY'S INSTRUMENTALISM

AMERICA'S philosopher. For fifty years Dr. John Dewey was the foremost educational thinker of America. He is regarded by many the greatest philosophic thinker the New World has produced. No other philosopher has devoted so much attention to the discussion of educational questions, nor has any other exercised so profound an influence on the schools not only of America but of other lands as well.

Life and work. John Dewey was born at Burlington, Vermont, in 1859. He received his early training in the public schools of the town, and his college education at the University of Vermont. He graduated in 1879, but after teaching a country school for a brief interval, returned to the university for another year to continue the study of philosophy. He then entered Johns Hopkins University, where, at the conclusion of two years, he received the Ph.D. degree. Dewey specialized in political and institutional history under Herbert B. Adams; in philosophy, under George S. Morris and Charles S. Pierce.

For some years Dr. Dewey taught in the University of Michigan; in 1894, he was called to be head of the department of philosophy at the University of Chicago, where he remained for 10 years. From 1904 until he was made emeritus, Dr. Dewey was professor of philosophy in Columbia University.

His fame as a philosophic thinker and educational reformer spread to foreign countries. In 1919, he was invited to lecture on philosophy and education at the Imperial University of Tokyo, Japan. He lectured for two years at the University of Peking, China. The Turkish Government requested him to reorganize its school system, and similar recognition came from Russia, Mexico, and Turkey. No modern educational thinker since Pestalozzi has been so universally renowned at home and abroad. He died June 1, 1952 at the age of 92.

The University Elementary School. In January 1896 Dr. Dewey opened the University Elementary School as an experimental laboratory. The purpose was to found a school where "theories and ideas might be demonstrated, tested, criticized, enforced and the evolution of new truths" discovered.

The children in this school varied in age from four to 14, and were divided into small groups, of eight or ten to the group. No rigid scheme of grading was adopted. Several instructors who had had kindergarten and primary experience conducted the work under Dewey's direction. A "Plan of Organization" was formulated "to define the general spirit in which the work is undertaken," but "not to give a rigid scheme." In accordance with the object of the school, every effort was made to discover new and more natural methods. As Dewey stated: [1]

> The teachers started with question marks, rather than with fixed rules. ...We started upon the whole with four such questions, or problems:
>
> (1) What can be done, and how can it be done, to bring the school into closer relation with the home and neighborhood life—instead of having the school a place where the child comes solely to learn certain lessons? What can be done to break down the barriers which have unfortunately come to separate the school life from the rest of the everyday life of the child?...
>
> (2) What can be done in the way of introducing subject-matter in history and science and art, that shall have a positive value and real significance in the child's own life?... Some statistics have been collected showing that 75 to 80 per cent of the first three years of a child in school are spent upon form—not the substance—of learning, the mastering of the symbols of reading, writing and arithmetic. There is not much positive nutriment in this....
>
> (3) How can instruction in these formal, symbolic branches—the mastering of the ability to read, write and use figures intelligently—be carried on with everyday experience and occupation as their background and in definite relation to other studies of more inherent content, and be carried on in such a way that the child shall feel their necessity through their connection with subjects which appeal to him on their own account?
>
> (4) Individual attention. This is secured by small groupings—eight or ten in a class.

---

[1] Dewey, John, *The School and Society* (Third Edition), pp. 116-119. Chicago: University of Chicago Press, 1900.

From the beginning, this experiment produced phenomenal effects. First, it helped to clarify Dr. Dewey's principles as to the underlying processes of education. Then again, it attracted extraordinary attention from educational leaders, and became the stimulus for similar experimentation in a number of places. The results of the investigation were published in a small book, *The School and Society,* which ran through numerous editions. No other educational work of recent date has been so widely read.

Dewey's writings. Dr. Dewey was a prolific writer. A large number of volumes and hundreds of articles came from his pen during sixty years. Many of his publications had to do with pure philosophy, and are of interest to students who wish to acquire a more accurate knowledge of his fundamental theories.

FUNDAMENTAL PHILOSOPHICAL PRINCIPLES

Nature of mind and knowledge. Like other speculative thinkers, Dewey had a general system of philosophy in which he explained the nature of the mind and of knowledge. Although it is abstruse, one must understand this basic view to appreciate his principles of education.

(1) *Instrumental character of the mind.* Dewey based his educational principles and practices upon the pragmatic theory of the evolution of the mind and knowledge. In harmony with the hypothesis of biological evolution, he held that mind and intelligence have evolved in a purely natural way. They have evolved because of the activities of human organisms in meeting the varied practical and social situations of life. Men soon found that perceiving objects, remembering them, and reasoning about them greatly increased the power of controlling objects and situations. The employment of mental powers in connection with the ordinary activities of daily existence brought results which otherwise could not have been enjoyed. Mind is, so to speak, a most effective tool or instrument; by its use man raised himself above all other creatures.

But when one says that mind or intelligence is a tool, it is understood that the term includes all aspects of the mind—thinking, feeling, and willing. Knowledge is not something apart from the mind; ideas are modes or activities of the mind. They are developed and retained by the individual to assist him in controlling the objects of the environment, and to avoid pain or to secure satisfaction. Such, in brief, is the instrumental theory of intelligence which Dewey and his followers elaborated.

(2) *Relation of knowledge and action.* From what has just been stated, it is clear that, in the course of human development, knowledge did not precede action, as is generally believed. Just the reverse is true: action always preceded experience which is the source of knowledge. A simple illustration will make this principle clear. The child thrusts his hand too close to the fire, and is burned. He thus learns that the movement of his hand under this circumstance brings a painful experience. So it is with all learning. The individual acts upon the impulses and instincts that he, along with others, has inherited, and in each case a definite experience results. In precisely the same manner, all the way back through the biological scale, action was spontaneous and primordial, and, as a consequence, experience, knowledge, or learning arose. In a sense, therefore, knowledge is incidental to action; it is a by-product of action.

The ordinary conception has always been that knowledge arises apart from action, that it has an independent existence. For example, consider the well-known fact "Washington is the Capital of the United States." This is a single, definite piece of knowledge. It is distinguishable from every other fact, and apparently it exists apart from any action of the reader. But, as Dr. Dewey viewed it, this fact exists only as related to the reader's action and the actions of other people. Among its many implications are these: If one acts in a particular manner he will come to experience visual and tactile contacts with the city of Washington, and will know it as the Capital of the United States. In truth, it does not exist at all apart from his action; any significance or meaning that it possesses has reference only to what he does or wishes to do.

If knowledge is thus derived from action and as a by-product of action, it should not be dissociated from the activity that produced it. In fact, it has no real and continued existence or significance when thus dissociated. This idea has some profound educational inferences that will be brought out later. But it is necessary, at the moment, to look still further into the relation of an idea to the activity which produced it. As experience or knowledge grows from action, in turn it is fused with the activity itself in order to redirect, modify, or nullify the repetition of the act. This is the innermost secret of the learning process. The original activity undergoes a change because of the results which follow it. In the simple illustration already suggested, the child thrusts his hand close to the flame. A dire result follows, a sharp pain. Any tendency to repeat this action is naturally inhibited; the child has learned one of the salutary lessons of life. A creature of much lower intelligence that cannot resist the fascination of the flame, will repeat the experience, to its own destruction. Thus, it has been concluded: first, that action is primordial, and that experience follows action; also, that experience modifies action, either by inhibiting it entirely, or by redirecting or repeating it.

(3) *Knowledge developed from the central activities of the race.* All knowledge has been the result of activities of individuals in their struggle for existence. The dominant activities thus engaged in because of man's felt needs were directed toward securing food, shelter, and clothing. These activities exerted by our ancestors all the way back have resulted in forming powerful tendencies that are inherited by the offspring today as instincts, impulses, and interests. These inherited tendencies are not definite, fixed, instinctive activities in man, as they are in the animals; they are urges that can be modified in adjusting to the environment. Furthermore, as already noted, it was through the expression of these activities that human intelligence was brought into function, and was developed. According to Dewey's view, it follows, therefore, that the basic activities of the home and social life constitute for the child the starting point of the education process.

(4) *Social relations of knowledge.* Another fundamental principle, and in many respects Dewey's chief contribution, is that knowledge is always a social instrument. This will be discussed at length later. In the meantime it is necessary to consider further the processes of securing knowledge, especially in its higher aspect as the result of thinking.

HOW WE THINK

In his book, *How We Think,* Dr. Dewey analyzed the conditions under which the mind does its thinking. He takes issue with the vague notions of the past that thinking is a process which takes place apart from the ordinary affairs of life. Thinking does not just happen; it does not take place in a vacuum; especially, it does not result from pure contemplation as Plato and the idealists believed. Nor yet does it come from just amassing sensations and assorting them into classes. There must be something to cause thinking—that is, to oblige the human organism to think. So long as the activity flows along smoothly in an easy course, there is nothing to cause the individual to think. But when some change in his conditions takes place, when his action no longer fits the circumstances or is entirely blocked, or when he is uncertain what course to pursue, he is compelled to think. The following are illustrations: the window sash will not close; the automobile will not start; the stomach will not digest its food; the monetary system no longer performs its accustomed function. Each of these changed situations is a challenge to thought, a demand that the individual bestir himself and discover what new kind of action is necessary to restore the satisfaction formerly enjoyed.

Thinking, therefore, takes place only when a problem comes up. Problems are the necessary conditions for aggressive mental activity. Dewey explains, in the following passage, how a problem causes thinking: [2]

> A question to be answered, an ambiguity to be resolved, sets up an end and holds the current of ideas to a definite channel. Every suggested conclusion is tested by its reference to this regulating end, by its pertinence to the problem in hand.

When a problem is presented, one begins to analyze the situation and to discover what readjustments must be made, or what hypothesis will explain the situation, and what remedy must be applied. Thereupon the individual frames a conclusion and tries it out. If it works, well and good; experience has been enriched, and activity has been readjusted and moves forward again serenely, until some new difficulty arises. Thinking is, accordingly, a result of activity; it is a continuous process of experimentation and of readjustment of experience.

Thinking and inductive reasoning. In analyzing the processes of thinking, in the higher aspects of the term, Dewey recognized "five logically distinct steps."

(1) First there occurs the consciousness of a difficulty, or a problem, or a felt need.

(2) Next comes the brooding of the mind over the situation until, by an analysis of its various elements, the mind locates the heart of the difficulty and defines the factor of greatest significance.

(3) Then follow suggestions as to possible solutions.

(4) The bearings of each suggested solution are developed, and the most probable solution is submitted to action, that is, to experimentation.

(5) Further observation and experimentation lead to the acceptance or rejection of the solution.

---

[2] Dewey, John, *How We Think,* pp. 11-12. Boston: D. C. Heath, 1910.

Such is the course that all normal minds pursue in the practical affairs as well as in the theoretical problems of life.

Some have suggested a similarity between these steps and the five formal steps of the Herbartian methodology. Such a view is, however, far-fetched. There is in Dewey's analysis nothing more than the well-known method of reasoning according to inductive logic: it involves recognizing a problem, analyzing its elements, framing an hypothesis, testing out the hypothesis by the amassing of more facts, and the continuation of the process until a solution is found. In other words, this is the method of experimentalism.

The application of this principle is quite old and comes from the doctrine of the useful, as advocated by Bacon, Locke, Rousseau, and others. But Dewey deserves credit for making educators more fully aware of the significance of the process in the development of the mind. This principle has formed the basis for his insistence upon methods of instruction that are in accord with the normal course of mental activity. From this analysis of how the mind works there have come into recent methodology the so-called *functional method, project method, problem method,* and the activity program.

DEWEY'S PHILOSOPHY OF EDUCATION

Education a process not a product. A system of philosophy is of little value, nor is it worthy of credence, however logical it may appear, until it has been tested in the field of education. If a theory does not hold true in its doctrine of man, its explanation of human development, and in its views of moral and social progress, it is worthless. Dewey belongs with those thinkers whose general philosophy and philosophy of education aspire to form a consistent whole.

Education is not in any way a trivial affair that can be relegated to old women and nursemaids. It is an indispensable social process, a means for the orderly ongoing and progress of human society. All education must proceed by the participation of the individual in the activities and purposes of society. It is a process by which civilization is preserved and carried forward in its attempts to complete itself. Education is, therefore, the most consequential of all the activities of society.

Dr. Dewey defined *education* as "the process of the reconstruction or reconstitution of experience, giving it a more socialized value through the medium of increased individual efficiency." He has repeated this definition consistently throughout his works. Because it is a rather abstract statement and different from the traditional definitions based upon the etymology of the word *educatio,* an explanation of its meaning may be necessary.

Everyone knows that his own experience is changing from moment to moment, and from day to day. New situations are always confronting one; and with each change in conditions or in environment, his activities must change to fit the new situation. New problems demand solution, choices must be made, and readjustments attempted. These changes in activities bring about an increasing diversification and enrichment of experience; in other words, experience is revised, reorganized, and reconstructed. This growing, changing, or revising of experience is what Dr. Dewey understood by education.

Dr. Dewey believed that this conception of education as a process has several important advantages over the idea of a product to be sought. First of all, it "puts the meaning of education within the process." Again, it does away with the old-fashioned, formal notion that education begins when the child enters school and stops when he withdraws. According to the new view, education begins as soon as the child is born, and proceeds throughout life. Furthermore, this view of education corrects the erroneous idea that "education is a preparation for life." It insists that education is life.

Educational end or aim. It has been customary for educational philosophers to set up some ultimate aim and often also to define intermediate aims for each particular stage of development. One is surprised to learn that Dewey did not countenance any such aims. As he himself stated in writing of education.[3]

> It has all the time an immediate end, and so far as activity is educative, it reaches that end—the direct transformation of the quality of experience. Infancy, youth, adult life,—all stand on the same educative level in the sense that what is really *learned* at any and every stage of experience constitutes the value of that experience; and in the sense that it is the chief business of life at every point to make living thus contribute to an enrichment of its own perceptible meaning.

From this point of view, the aim of education is found within the process itself, and not as an ulterior goal to be reached; or rather one may say

---

[3] Dewey, John, *Democracy and Education,* p. 89. New York: The Macmillan Company, 1916.

that the aim is always the particular goal or end that is immediately before the attention and that elicits thought and activity. Education proceeds by constantly remaking experience, and it is this reconstruction which constitutes its value and accomplishes its aim.

As a process of continued revision or reorganization of experience, education is always moving forward to further activity and revision. As Dr. Dewey explained: [4]

> Since life means growth, a living creature lives as truly and positively at one stage as at another, with the same intrinsic fulness and the same absolute claims. Hence education means the enterprise of supplying the conditions which insure growth, or adequacy of life, irrespective of age. The process of education is a continuous process of adjustment, having as its aim at every stage an added capacity of growth.

There never comes a time when new experiences fail to take place, when learning absolutely ceases. So long as the individual is readjusting himself to the changes in the environment, just so long he is learning and education is going forward. There is, therefore, no final end or goal when education is completed. Furthermore, the aims set up by the teacher or education are not the aims which the child chooses for himself. They are foreign to his nature, and consequently cannot be the aims of his education. Educational aims can be determined only by the child's own being, and are always approximate, never ultimate.

Education a process of living. This conception of the continuous reconstruction of experience emphasizes the principle that education is not a preparation for life at some future time; rather, it is the process of actual living, here and now. The idea of educating for the future always presented a challenge to Dewey, and provoked a combat which he never wearied fighting.

Another reason why one must not set up a final goal for education is: such a remote aim cannot be made a functional purpose for the child himself. On this point, Dewey emphatically declared: [5]

> It is nonsense to talk about the aim of education—or any other undertaking—where conditions do not permit of foresight of results, and do not stimulate a person to look ahead to see what the outcome of a given activity is to be.

---

[4] *Ibid.*, p. 61.
[5] *Ibid.*, p. 119.

The child lives in the present, and cares nothing for the future; in fact, he is wholly incapable of imagining the remote time "when he will be a man." It is absurd, therefore, to require him to do things today for the sake of what he will be years from now. The adult is forever trying to make the child act upon ends which only the adult can foresee, but of which the child knows nothing.

As the child acts only in the living present, setting up approximate aims and readjusting his experiences as he goes along, the process of education is identical with the process of living. The continuous enrichment of experience by readjusting to the complexities of the environment constitutes, therefore, the heart of education.

Two essential factors of the educational process. Dewey recognized two fundamental factors in the educational process; one is the psychological, and the other, the social factor. There is, on the one hand, the individual child with all his native powers, capacities, and instincts; on the other, there is the social world with all its ongoing activities, institutions, customs, and attitudes.

(1) *The individual factor.* Education begins with the activity of the child. If he is incapable of normal activity, he is incapable of education. Dewey explained: [6]

> Education must begin with a psychological insight into the child's capacities, interests, and habits. These powers, interests, and habits must be continually interpreted—we must know what they mean. They must be translated into terms of their social equivalents—into terms of what they are capable of in the way of social service. . . .
>
> The child has his own instincts and tendencies, but we do not know what these mean until we can translate them into their social equivalents. We must be able to carry them back into a social past and see them as the inheritance of previous race activities. We must also be able to project them into the future to see what their outcome and end will be.

From this and similar statements, one might have expected Dewey to give a full account of the rise and development of the instinctive activities of children. But this he never did, except in a very general way. The fact is, these instincts do not exist in the child as mechanical forces that unfold in a predetermined way. They are mere tendencies to activity, and develop a real character only as they are brought into

---

[6] Dewey, John, *My Pedagogical Creed,* Article I. Reprint, The Progressive Education Association, Washington, D. C.

exercise in social situations. Their nature is constituted in and by social activity. Dr. Dewey mentioned four such instincts, or fundamental interests, as the basis of education. These are: "the interest in conversation, or communication; in inquiry, or finding out things; in making things, or construction; and in artistic expression." [7]

Concerning the language interest, he noted that it "is the simplest form of the social expression of the child, hence it is a great, perhaps the greatest of all educational resources." But all these interests are brought into function in pursuing the great social activities, getting food, shelter, and clothing. These are the activities which have brought about the evolution of the human organism and of society, and which must form the curricula of the schools. The following passage fully illustrates this: [8]

> The primary root of all educative activity is in the instinctive, impulsive attitudes and activities of the child, and not in the presentation and application of external material.
>
> That these individual tendencies and activities are organized and directed through the use made of them in keeping up the coöperative living already spoken of, taking advantage of them to reproduce on the child's plane the typical doings and occupations of the larger, maturer society, into which he is finally to go forth; and that it is through production and creative use that valuable knowledge is secured and clinched.

(2) *The social factor.* The nature of society and its relations to individuals are usually conceived in a wrong way. Individuals are thought of as separate entities or units; society is thought of as composed of so many separate individuals who come together to form an organization. They are like separate bricks in a wall. An individual cannot be regarded, according to Dewey, as a being apart from society. A brick might exist even if there were never a wall in the world, but a human individual could not exist if there were no society. The human being is an organism whose capacities for acting have been developed or brought into functional activity in relation to his fellows. It is the acquisition of the characteristic social activities, responses, and modes of conduct that make the child human, and at the same time make him individual.

On the other hand, society is not just individuals huddled together in an organization. In Dewey's theory, "society is an organic union of

---

[7] Dewey, John, *The School and Society* (Revised Edition), p. 45. Chicago: University of Chicago Press, 1916.

[8] *Elementary School Record,* p. 142. Chicago: University of Chicago Press, 1900.

individuals." The organic life, activities, and purposes of society reproduce themselves in individuals. This reproduction takes place as the child comes to understand, appreciate, and appropriate, as his own, the purposes, ideas, and attitudes of the society about him.[9]

> *Mind* as a concrete thing is precisely the power to understand things in terms of the use made of them; a socialized mind is the power to understand them in terms of the use to which they are turned in joint or shared situations. *And mind in this sense is the method of social control.*

Social intercourse, relations, and interactions are the central factors in the evolution of the activities of the individual. The character of man's mind and all his knowledge has been the result of social living. Without such relations none of his powers would ever have developed. Knowledge, as such, has importance only because of its social significance. Language is the indispensable means of social intercourse; for this reason it plays a significant part in education.

Social living and the child's powers. It is peculiarly the social situations of the family that first awaken into activity the powers of the child. Of this, Dewey said: "True education comes through the stimulation of the child's powers by the demands of the social situations in which he finds himself." The child engages in the home activities because he discovers they have a social meaning or satisfaction for himself and others.

At the beginning of his life, the capabilities of the child are as yet undeveloped. They are expressed and developed only as the child enters into relations with other people. It is, accordingly, through entering into social relations in the home that the individual's powers are first developed.

However, there remains another danger of misinterpreting this relation of the individual and society. In acquiring the social activities, the child utilizes them only for his own security and pleasure. He is self-centered, selfish. But the continuance of society, the general good, the common weal demand that individuals shall consider the good of the whole. Individuals must be so developed that they will attempt to realize the ends and purposes of society. To accomplish this end, Dewey sought to organize the school for cooperative action.

Dewey's conception of the importance of social life was probably the result of three influences. First, he was originally an adherent of the

---

[9] Dewey, John, *Democracy and Education,* pp. 39-40.

Hegelian philosophy, which looks upon society as an organism. Secondly, his graduate study at Johns Hopkins University brought him into contact with institutional history and the social evolution of man. Thirdly, his study of the Industrial Revolution and his contact with the rampant individualism of American life made him see that the greatest need of mankind at the present age is a new type of cooperative living.

The school as a social instrument. The ordinary conception of the school vizualizes it as a place where children go to learn certain skills and acquire information for their individual needs. Dewey considered the school an institution essential to society. It is not a mere temporary device but an absolute necessity for socializing individuals.[10]

> The school is primarily a social institution. Education being a social process, the school is simply that form of community life in which all those agencies are concentrated that will be most effective in bringing the child to share in the inherited resources of the race, and to use his own powers for social ends.

Dewey pointed out that the Industrial Revolution took the various industries away from the home, thereby robbing it of one of its chief functions. Industries had a direct social and educational significance, in that they stimulated the activities of the child. By contact with these activities, his intelligence was awakened; and through participation, social purposefulness was exercised.

The office of the school is to furnish a social environment in which the real, vital, meaningful activities of the race are "simplified," "purified," and "balanced," so as to appeal to the interest of the child. "The primary business of the school is to train children in cooperative and mutually helpful living." It reduces society "to an embryonic form." Existing life is too complex for the child to grasp and enter into. As a "simplified social life, the school life should grow gradually out of the home life." It should "take up and continue the activities with which the child is already familiar in the home."[11]

Direct experience the basis of all method. None of the modern educators, except Rousseau, have been more insistent than Dewey upon direct experience. However, it is not so much the objects that he valued as it is the concrete and meaningful situations. Inasmuch as learning

---

[10] Dewey, John, *My Pedagogical Creed,* Article II.
[11] *Ibid.,* Article II.

comes indirectly in response to action, the situations which arouse activities furnish the natural condition for the growth of knowledge. Dewey emphasized this point of view:[12]

> The first approach to any subject in school, if thought is to be aroused and not words acquired, should be as unscholastic as possible. To realize what an experience or empirical situation means, we have to call to mind the sort of situation that presents itself outside the school; the sort of occupations that interest and engage activity in ordinary life. And careful inspection of methods which are permanently successful in formal education, whether in arithmetic or learning to read, or studying geography, or learning physics or a foreign language, will reveal that they depend for their efficiency upon the fact that they go back to the type of situation which causes reflection out of school in ordinary life. They give the pupil something to do, not something to learn; and the doing is of such a nature as to demand thinking, or the intentional noting of connections; learning naturally results.

Not only did he demand that concrete situations be furnished the child in order to call forth his activity, but he insisted that all learning come to him as a by-product of his actions, and never as something to be learned directly for its own sake. The Egyptians had to reset the boundaries of their farms after the annual innundation of the Nile. From this practical situation they learned to measure and to count. Similarly, the Phoenicians, in making records of their commercial accounts, had to operate rapidly and accurately, and thus originated the cursive script. The separation of fiber from the bolls of cotton was a most laborious process, and made the price of cotton goods excessive. This practical situation challenged Eli Whitney, and the result was the cotton gin. Need, or necessity, is the mother of all invention, and of all knowledge or new experience.

Interest, effort, and motivation. In the last decade of the 19th century, American education was introduced to the Herbartian doctrine of interest. Combined with the Froebelian doctrine of self-activity, as practiced in the kindergarten, and the new emphasis upon child development, the doctrine of interest everywhere challenged the traditional pedagogy. The traditionalists believed in formal discipline. They held that the new doctrine was a "soft pedagogy," and would not prepare children to face the difficulties and hardships of actual life. Moreover,

---

[12] Dewey, John, *Democracy and Education,* p. 181.

allowing the child to learn only what was pleasant to him would break down the high standards of scholarship and open the schools, especially the secondary and higher schools, to effortless work. This conflict challenged the philosophic insight of Dewey. He undertook to clarify the problem by showing that all true effort springs from a deep, native interest in the task. He asserted that, where such genuine interest is absent, it is necessary to arouse it; for to depend on artificial stimulation is functionally bad. Moreover, he declared that all learning which results from such artificial motivation is morally wrong.

In order to be sound and moral all learning must arise from the normal experience of the child. Only those objects and ideas should solicit attention which are of genuine interest in the organism and necessary for its life. Concentration of attention and effort of will can be put forth only for that which is of genuine value. In this way, Dr. Dewey explained the weakness of the position which holds that, because a thing is distasteful and uninteresting, it is therefore by some magic pedagogically strengthening. From Dewey's doctrine of interest came a new doctrine of motivation by "felt need."

The curriculum. One may readily guess that Dewey had little sympathy with the traditional curriculum, or any course of studies that divides knowledge into particular branches. There is nothing in the outer world corresponding to the departmentalization of subject matter. It is only the logical interest of the adult that has divided the world into abstract compartments of knowledge. According to Dewey, the mind of the young child does not make divisions of its fund of experiences into various subjects.[13] "We violate the child's nature and render difficult the best ethical results by introducing the child too abruptly to a number of special studies, of reading, writing, geography, etc." The child is not interested in the logical ordering of subject matter. The correlating center is his own living interest, the problem confronting him, his felt need.[14] "The true center of correlation of the school subjects is not science, nor literature, nor history, nor geography, but the child's own activities." The underlying element that unifies life and activities must, therefore, be found in the child's active life and not in logical formulations.

The school should not begin with the three *R*'s, but with the activities

---

[13] Dewey, John, *My Pedagogical Creed,* Article III

[14] *Ibid.,* Article III.

that the child has seen in the home, the activities that constitute the great racial functions.[15]

> The beginning is made with the child's expressive activities in dealing with the fundamental social materials—housing (carpentry); clothing (sewing); food (cooking). These *direct* modes of expression, at once require the derived modes of expression, which bring out more distinctly the factors of social communication—speech, writing, reading, drawing, molding, modeling, etc.

In his primary school, Dewey began with the activities with which the child is familiar in home life; getting food, shelter, and clothing. These activities make the most natural appeals to his interest. They arouse the constructive instinct, and bring not only nerve and muscular coordinations but all aspects of mentality into functional action. In the first six grades Dewey emphasized numbers, music, art, woodwork, cooking, sewing, science, geography, reading, writing, history, and gardening. It must be understood, however, that all of these were learned in connection with the situations and problems that arose in connection with the production of food, shelter, and clothing.

Among the things constructed in connection with woodwork were: sandpaper blocks, boxes for pencils, boxes for matches, plant trellises, paper cutters, bookstands, and similar articles. The food interest led to cooking, baking, studying sources of food materials, and so on. The clothing interest furnished opportunities not only for hand work but also for study of the origin of fabrics and their manufacture.

By these constructive activities the attention of the child was directed to the actual world, where he learned from observation agriculture, transportation, industrial activities, and the problems of distribution, the buying and selling of commodities. He was led back into history to find the origin of all these activities in primitive life. In his constructive activity the child acquires the facts of arithmetic, geography, history, botany, chemistry, the use of language, and other formal subjects.

The school itself demanded cooperative action in constructing things that the children needed—such as equipment for the laboratories, bicycle stands, apparatus for physical exercises, bird houses, gins for cotton, Indian tents, racks, and so on. All these activities and many others brought each child into active relation with his fellow workers and

---

[15] Dewey, John, *Plan of Organization of the University Primary School.* Privately printed.

furnished opportunity for cooperative effort. In fact, the entire management and work of the school were designed to make the child conscious of community purposefulness, and to train him in cooperative action.

Conclusion. It is impossible as yet to estimate the historic significance of Dewey's innovations and ideas. There have been attributed to him many ideas and practices which actually are due to other reformers. Moreover, it is too early to foresee just how much of his special point of view will endure the test of reflection. The functional theory, doctrine of interest, and the project and problem methods are important contributions, but they are not particularly original. How far each should be utilized is still a matter of dispute. The movement for constructive activity had its origin in Froebel, but was confined to the kindergarten. It would seem that Dewey's emphasis on socialization has come nearer to an enduring contribution. But this also was not new, for it was found in different forms in all the great reformers. Moreover, it caused the most determined effort ever made to place public education under strict control of reactionary forces. Dewey, however, clarified the relation of all knowledge and productive activity to social living.

Dewey claimed that his theory of pragmatism or instrumentalism was a Copernican revolution in educational theory. The analogy was not, however, a happy one. The acceptance of the doctrine of heliocentricity was followed by an era of unanimity, peace, and unparalleled progress in astronomy. Just the opposite is true in education; confusion, dissatisfaction, and downright distrust have been the chief characteristics of American education for half a century. Opposition to many of Dewey's fundamental principles has mounted to a feverish condition. In later years he modified many of his early conceptions in view of criticism.

Chapter 25

EDUCATIONAL PROGRESS IN THE 20th CENTURY

GENERAL social and intellectual conditions. The 20th century ushered in the greatest revolutionary transformation since the fall of the Roman Empire in the 5th century of our era. It has included the termination of European domination over civilization and the assumption of leadership by American democracy. European philosophies of education, Hegelianism, Pestalozzianism, Herbartianism, Froebelianism, and the superiority of Germanic schools passed just before the beginning of the century. Scientific realism deposed the belated Humanism of the schools and colleges, and seized the direction of human affairs. Christianity, yielding to its inherent tendency to formalism and institutionalism, tied its fortune to the existing social, political, and economic conditions, and to a traditional biology; and, though it maintained a show of official respectability by becoming the tool of imperialistic exploitation, it declined in genuine power and service to mankind. Its inability to discern its unique function in an evolving world and to transmit its spiritual values was apparent, and as a consequence secularism gained the upper hand.

The most vigorous intellectual activity manifested itself in the pursuit of the sciences. Biology occupied the spotlight and dominated psychology, sociology, and political science. The biological principles of the struggle for existence and the survival of the fittest led to the belief that might makes right. This gave justification to an intensified nationalism.

Monarchy and imperialism were uppermost but felt the challenge of growing socialism. In order to keep the masses in subjection, Germany sought world domination, and in the attempt plunged humanity into two devastating wars.

Wealth, leisure, standard of living. When a thoroughgoing inquiry has been made, and all pertinent facts are garnered, the most basic and significant fact in regard to 20th century life is that its greater per capita wealth has provided America a higher living standard and more leisure for all its people than any other in all history. It has more mechanical horsepower per capita to do the drudgery and perform the work than any people with many slaves to every household. It has better school buildings, more and better equipment, and ampler opportunity to produce superior culture so far as such physical instruments can aid in advancing culture. More children have been enabled to continue their education through adolescent years than ever before in history. It has been an age of power and leisure beyond the reach of utopian imagination.

CONTEMPORARY PHILOSOPHIES OF EDUCATION

Reaction against all philosophy. The 19th century brought an end to the construction of comprehensive systems of philosophy founded upon metaphysics. The conception has generally prevailed that ultimate reality is unknowable, and the human mind must content itself with a knowledge of the contingent, temporal, changeable, and relative—in a word, with the phenomenal. The fact is, the mind of man is limited in its capability and it is not only impossible to transcend experience but unprofitable to attempt to do so. The effort to deduce knowledge from general principles results only in stark failure. While a few thinkers continued to thrash over the old straw, the most constructive minds threw themselves into the detailed pursuit of the natural sciences with an avidity never approached. Those who continued to feel the need of philosophy concluded that man is predominantly a creature of action and that reflection, though valuable in a way, should not become morbid in pursuit of ultimate reality. Philosophy, it has been generally accepted, is the study of the methods of learning from experience.

So far as the study of education was concerned the leaders generally adopted the scientific methodology and the philosophy and history of education were subordinated to psychology, administration, curriculum, and methods. Experimentalism was the guiding philosophy, so far as there was any. However, as the years advanced, protests against this program of naturalism have become increasingly powerful. The progress in educational philosophy will now be sketched.

Pragmatism. The pragmatic philosophy of John Dewey, known also as instrumentalism and experimentalism, has prevailed to an extraordinary extent not only in America but elsewhere as well. It is essentially the New England descendant of the realism of Bacon combined with the utilitarianism of Bentham and Mill. Among the innumerable disciples of Dewey who have carried on his views, the most influential have been Boyd H. Bode, Ohio State University; William H. Kilpatrick, John L. Childs, Harold Rugg, and George S. Counts, all of Teachers College, Columbia University. These men have promoted the pragmatic philosophy in somewhat different ways and have been highly successful in clarifying its principles and making it practical in the program of the schools. Their writings, which are numerous, have adhered to the Dewey tradition. They have influenced to a marked degree the curriculum and method of instruction and the social aspects of education; its metaphysical and epistemological implications they have not advanced. The study of how minds work in learning and cooperation in bringing about social reform are their chief contributions.

In many ways instrumentalism has identified itself with the Progressive Education movement; and it has relation also to Realism and to one aspect of neo-Humanism.

During the past few years an increasing tide of criticism has arisen against pragmatic education from philosophic thinkers, religious leaders, practical educators, and even parents. Several national organizations have taken up the cudgels against this system, especially in its social and moral application.[1]

The Progressive Education movement. Three factors caused this movement: (1) the spirit of radicalism and reform begun by Francis Parker in Quincy, Massachusetts, and let loose more completely by Dewey's school at the University of Chicago; (2) the new Froebelianism, which emphasized self-realization through self-activity, and, probably, the sudden exploitation of the Montessori method, which for

---

[1] Hulburd, David, *This Happened in Pasadena.* New York: The Macmillan Company, 1951.

Nock, Albert Jay, *The Theory of Education in the United States.* Chicago: Henry Regnery Company, 1931.

Smith, Mortimer, *And Madly Teach.* Chicago: Henry Regnery Company, 1949.

Lundberg, George A., *Can Science Save Us?* New York: Longmans, Green and Company, 1947.

Breed, Frederick S., *Education and the New Realism.* New York: The Macmillan Company, 1939.

a brief time aroused still further confidence in the *laissez faire* theory and practice; and (3) the widespread study of child nature strengthened the view that the innate interest and activities of the child, unhindered by external compulsion or authority, are to be trusted implicitly. With such conceptions in mind, Stanwood Cobb and a number of parents and teachers at a meeting in Washington, D.C., organized the "Progressive Education Association" in 1919.

Through some misunderstanding early in its history the new movement became identified in the popular mind wtih the pragmatic philosophy as expounded by Dewey and his followers. It is true the term "progressive education" had been used by Dewey in *Democracy and Education,* and it was generally assumed that the new movement represented his philosophy. Superficially the two movements appeared identical—each of them was a sharp break with traditionalism, formalism, and imposition. But a close study reveals they were based upon entirely different conceptions.

The Progressive Education movement actually sprang from the spiritualistic and creative principles of Froebel and of Montessori, together with the new science of child development. It insisted that the spontaneity of the preschool child and child-centeredness be extended upward through the grades. Its fundamental drive was humanistic and not utilitarian; and although it was activistic, it was the play spirit and not industrial production that was sought. It was, moreover, dominantly individualistic. In 1928 Dewey [2] definitely repudiated the movement.

His objections to Progressive Education were: first, that it overemphasized the education of the individual, a view which was reiterated by Drs. Bode and Counts; second, that the Progressive classroom situation is "artificial" and not, as it should be, "a substitute for the life outside of the school;" third, that the Progressive method depends upon "immediate and spontaneous interest," which is a misinterpretation of the nature of interest; fourth, the pupils plan everything themselves and they are not held responsible for the performance of their tasks; they should not be permitted to reduce the teacher's function to continuous improvisation. The jumping from one interest to another violates, Dewey pointed out, the principles of mental growth which demand continuity of effort; fifth, he insisted that the school exists to

---

[2] Dewey, John, "Progressive Education and the Science of Education," *Progressive Education,* 1928, Vol. V, pp. 197-204.

build a better social order through constructive activities, but Progressive Education had no such purpose in view.

Four years later George S. Counts challenged the Association policy by his radical and provocative addresses, *Dare the School Build a New Social Order?* Dr. Boyd H. Bode followed some six years later with a similar criticism.[3]

In consequence of the attacks by the instrumentalists and others, the Progressive Education Association changed its name to the *American Education Fellowship,* and with the new name its objective underwent a profound alteration. It now undertook as its chief purpose the building of a new social order.[4] In 1933 the Association launched one of the most far reaching movements, known as the "Eight Year Study." The Fellowship continues to publish as its organ the magazine *Progressive Education.*

Realism. Among the educational thinkers of the 16th century Renaissance were a number of outstanding men who repudiated Scholasticism, but turned avidly to the ancients to satisfy their craving for knowledge. They were not interested in Humanism for esthetic, moral, or religious reasons but for the scientific knowledge, the intellectual content of the classical writers. Similarly during the past half-century a number of writers have favored freedom of thought and opposed traditionalism, but their deeper interest is the advancement of science. They believe in knowledge for its own sake regardless of where the chips may fall. Among these are Bertrand Russell and Alfred North Whitehead, both Englishmen who came to the United States because the freedom of life and thought here was more favorable to their ideas. As professor of philosophy for many years at Harvard University Whitehead elaborated a system of thought that cannot be adequately

---

[3] Bode, Boyd H., *Progressive Education at the Crossroads.* New York: Newsom and Company, 1938.

[4] *Progressive Education:* A quarterly, Review of the Newer Tendencies in Education, Vol. 1, 1924, to Vol. 16, 1939.

Burr, Samuel E., *An Introduction to Progressive Education.* Cincinnati: Gregory Co., 1933.

Cobb, Stanwood, *The New Leaven: Progressive Education and Its Effect Upon the Child and Society.* New York: John Day Co., 1928.

Progressive Education Association, *Creative Expression; the Development of Children in Art, Music, Literature and Dramatics.* Gerland Hartman and Ann Shumaker, Editors, Milwaukee: E. M. Hale and Company, 1939.

——— Commission on Relation of School and College, 5 vols.

——— *Adventure in American Education.* New York: Harper Brothers, 1942-1943.

represented by the term Realism. Its organismic character marks it as a new trend in scientific and philosophical construction. It is, however, so abstruse that few can understand it. Despite its high value for education its influence is limited. Here belongs also Robert Millikan, the physicist, who took a profound interest in education and religion.

These thinkers saw the escape from a low, immoral, and humdrum existence in zeal for scientific knowledge. They had confidence that this pursuit was the road to the "good life." They were not averse to the application of knowledge, but they did not cultivate it for the sake of the loaves and fishes, but for the pure joy of intellectual conquest and more especially for understanding the universe in which we live.

Essentialism. The trend toward pragmatism and progressivism was vigorously opposed by William C. Bagley, of Teachers College who took a conservative point of view. Primarily a student of teaching, he emphasized method, content, and management rather than creative thinking. While his position was more in harmony with common sense, it lacked a basic philosophy, and as a consequence was unable to effect a strong reaction to progressive trends.[5]

Efforts to resuscitate Humanism. Various attempts have been made to revive humanistic education or to salvage some of its values from the flood of changes in aims and curricular offerings. These have come chiefly on the college level but the implications of the theory reach to lower education as well. But in the various efforts the original idea has been distorted and little of the true Humanism remains.[6]

The chief originator of the new humanistic movement was Irving Babbitt, Professor of French at Harvard. He bewailed the decline of classical Humanism, advocated the cessation of the conflict between ancient and modern languages, and desired to restore the conception of the well-balanced scholar. Another undying humanist is Alexander Meikeljohn, sometime President of Amherst College, who directed a strange experiment at the University of Wisconsin (1926-38) in an effort to revive a knowledge of Greek language, literature, and life.

A still later experiment has been carried on at St. John's College,

---

[5] Bagley's chief works were: *Education and Emergent Man.* New York: Thomas Nelson and Sons, 1934; *The Educative Process.* New York: The Macmillan Company, 1926.

[6] F. C. S. Schiller, philosopher at Oxford espoused the pragmatic philosophy of William James, but termed it Humanism. See *Humanism, Philosophic Essays.* London: Macmillan and Company, Ltd., 1903.

Annapolis, Maryland, by President Stringfellow Barr, whose curriculum consists of 100 books which are chosen because they are the most important from the standpoint of an all-around acquaintance with liberal culture.

The Humanism of the 1920's was a strong protest against the exaggerated emphasis upon science. Its advocates were under the influence of English conceptions of education which were introduced after World War I.

Another aspect of Humanism has been advocated by a number of writers who believe the improvement of society lies in the use of science in inventing instruments which will do away with drudgery and make the lot of man more pleasant. They especially decry the idea that the otherworldliness of Christianity can bring man a happier life. They scorn the supernatural as the source of a better existence.[7]

Roman Catholic philosophy of education. Secular education in France and the United States, and the naturalistic systems of pragmatism and the new Humanism were alike objectionable to Catholic traditions because they denied the supernatural. The conviction that to it alone were committed the oracles of divine truth and the authority to teach have necessitated that the Church establish its own system of elementary, secondary, and higher schools so that all subversive influences might be rigidly withheld from Catholic children.

Roman Catholic scholars have been unusually active during the past quarter-century in redefining the position of the Church in all matters of education. Naturally the most authoritative statement on the subject was the papal encyclical *On the Christian Education of Youth* issued by Pius XI in 1929.[8] In addition to this a large and scholarly literature has been published by American Catholic writers.

---

[7] Babbitt, Irving, *Humanism*. Providence, R. I.: Brown University Press, 1926.
Flexner, Abraham, *The Burden of Humanism*. Oxford: The Clarendon Press, 1928.
Potter, C. F., *Humanism, A New Religion*. New York: Simon and Schuster, 1930.

[8] A translation will be found in *Current History Magazine*, 1930; it was also published by the American Press, 1936.

Marique, P. J., *The Philosophy of Christian Education*. New York: Prentice-Hall, Inc., 1939.

Fitzpatrick, Edward A., *Readings in the Philosophy of Education*. New York: D. Appleton-Century Company, 1936.

Guthrie, Hunter, and Walsh, G. G., *A Philosophical Symposium on American Catholic Education*. New York: The Fordham University Press, 1941.

Redden, John D., and Ryan, Francis A., A *Catholic Philosophy of Education*. Milwaukee: Bruce, 1932.

On the practical side, Catholic schools have likewise made great advancement during the past half century. The right to operate Christian schools was sustained by the U. S. Supreme Court decision in the Oregon case. In 1922 the legislature of that state enacted a law requiring every child from 8 to 16 years of age to attend the state public schools. This measure was appealed to the Federal Supreme Court by several of the Orders of Sisters, and the ruling handed down nullified the law. The decision permitted parents to meet the state compulsory attendance law by sending their children to parochial schools, provided such schools meet the scholastic standard set up by the state for the education of children.

Since the Oregon decision Catholic teachers in increasing numbers have qualified for teachers' certificates by pursuing professional courses in education, and they have frequented gatherings of teachers and collaborated with voluntary standardizing agencies.

Of 2,468,390 children enrolled in non-public schools during 1947 and 1948 approximately 93 per cent were Catholics. Some 476,425 Roman Catholic youth were enrolled in 2,185 Church secondary schools this same year. The proportion of Catholic children attending Church elementary and secondary schools has continued to increase annually; this is particularly noteworthy in the separate high schools for boys and girls.

SOME CHANGES IN EUROPEAN EDUCATION

1. European school systems have become more exclusively nationalistic and propagandistic as imperialistic ambitions ripened. This was true to a degree in England and France, but especially in Germany, Russia, and Italy. Japan followed this trend in the Far East.

2. The religious problem has given considerable difficulty in England, France, Germany, and Russia, and continues to be unsettled everywhere.

3. The curriculum was changed from the traditional humanistic program to the more realistic, practical, and technical.

4. The importance of directing youth was increasingly felt. The Hitler youth movement was a notable example.

5. As technology advanced children and youth were less needed in the ranks of labor; and more advanced training was necessary to equip them to enter industry. The consequence was that the period of compulsory school attendance was lengthened in many countries and con-

School Year
13 12 11 10 9 8 7 6 5 4 3 2 1

Universities and professional colleges of university rank (including schools of commerce)

Various types of vocational and continuation schools (including commercial schools)

Various types of Mittelschule

Volksschule

Aufbauschule, type of Deutsche Oberschule

Aufbauschule, type of Oberrealschule

Deutsche Oberschule

Oberrealschule
Realschule

Realgymnasium
Realprogymnasium

Gymnasium
Progymnasium

Grundschule

School Year
13 12 11 10 9 8 7 6 5 4 3 2 1

PRESENT GERMAN SCHOOL SYSTEM.

tinuation schools were set up. The Education Act of 1944 in England extended the age of compulsory attendance from 14 to 15, and in time to 16 years; and, for one day a week, to 18 years. France copied American education after World War II, and the compulsory attendance limit was upped from 13 to 15; part time attendance was required to 18 for those who had employment. Primary education in Germany was increased one year, and graduation from Gymnasia put at 19 years. Junior colleges have been established in large numbers in England, Japan, and the Philippines.

6. The trend everywhere has been socialistic. The intellectual enlightenment which motivated popular education from the time of Rousseau and Pestalozzi was at its heart a principle of social fermentation and emancipation. The autocratic states promoted education to produce skilled workmen and subservient subjects. But the rulers generally were well aware that education was a dangerous instrument, which was likely to lead to a socialistic state. To perpetuate control of the masses the leaders of Germany promoted imperialism in the hope that prosperity would keep the people subservient.

The common school is the seed plot of democratic government. France became socialistic, England elected a labor government, and socialism gained markedly in other countries. In Germany the nazi government (1933) took control of the schools away from the cities and federal states and effected a totalitarian regime. The state governments and the church were both forced to retire from participation in education. The elementary school was seized upon as the organ of political partisanship and propaganda, and secondary and higher education received a setback. Nazi Germany, Fascist Italy, and Communist Russia rivalled one another in using education for political ends.

7. In England (1944) the National Board of Education was transformed into a Ministry of Education with centralized powers, control, and direction over the local councils. French education had always been over-centralized, and it was now proposed to bring in more flexibility by recognizing some local initiative.

8. Nursery schools became a necessity as more mothers were engaged in industry. England (1944) provided nursery classes for children from ages two to five. In setting up its first real system of schools, Russia established nurseries (often in factories) for children under three, and all-day kindergartens for children from three to eight. In 1948 and 1949 Poland had 5,960 kindergartens, with 270,000 children between four and seven years enrolled. In 1951 they were open nine hours a day instead of five to accommodate working mothers, and for 11 months of the year.

9. The English 1944 law virtually placed all schools under public control and made them free. France began to eliminate tuition fees from the lycée (1933). Schools in Russia have been nationalized and secularized. In 1929 the enrollment was 15,000,000; in 1936, 35,000,000; and 1939, 47,000,000. In Poland the number of schools and universities has greatly increased and the enrollments multiplied.

THE SCIENTIFIC EDUCATIONAL REVOLUTION

The educational situation. No age can equal the past half-century in the expansion and diversification of the education of children and adults. Tradition, the *status quo,* and past policy, have been chiefly useful as points of departure, the fixed locus by which we assure our vision that change, which has been identified with progress, has taken place. Experimentation, reconstruction, criticism, controversy, and confusion of ideas have prevailed; but out of it all more deep study, discussion, profound and varied thinking, and a veritable deluge of literature have come. A survey such as this cannot give a satisfactory account of even the main events in a drama so extensive and volatile.

The causes of the advance of the science of education. Examination of the phenomenal advancement of education as a science during the past half-century leads to two explanations: for the first time men of creative capacity commensurate with those in the other great fields of knowledge were appointed to the graduate faculties of the leading universities to investigate and teach education. Outstanding examples in addition to G. Stanley Hall, Nicholas Murray Butler and John Dewey were William H. Burnham in Mental Hygiene at Clark University; Edward L. Thorndike in Educational Psychology and George D. Strayer in Administration at Teachers College, Columbia University; Charles H. Judd at the University of Chicago; and Arnold Gesell, director of the Yale Clinic of Child Development.

The second factor was that for the first time the rigorous methodology of science was applied to the theories and problems of education. During the last half of the 19th century German psychologists had employed the most meticulous technique of laboratory investigation and mathematical measurement to physiological psychology. Fechner, Wundt, and Helmholtz gave the study of the mental life a wholly new status by separating psychology from philosophy and making it an independent science.

A number of Wundt's students introduced his methods to American universities. G. Stanley Hall established the first American laboratory for the study of psychology at Johns Hopkins, and later made Clark University the center for the study of human development. James McKeen Cattell, who was Wundt's assistant at Leipzig, became professor of psychology at Columbia. E. B. Titchner, who united a background of English culture with training under Wundt, was located at Cornell; and Charles H. Judd was for many years at the University of Chicago.

Meanwhile William James, from an early specialization in physiology adapted the scientific approach to psychology at Harvard and trained a host of teachers for American colleges and universities. Among these was Edward L. Thorndike, who as professor of educational psychology at Teachers College, Columbia, gave the subject a wide development as an independent science.

PSYCHOLOGY AND EDUCATIONAL PSYCHOLOGY

Changing psychological views. No science has equalled psychology in the radical changes through which it has passed during the last hundred years. Long termed "Mental Philosophy" by the English and American world, it shed its connection with philosophy and, borrowing the term "psychology" from German usage, it became a natural and experimental science under Wundt, Fechner, and Helmholtz. Meanwhile, in America, under the impact of biological evolution, William James of Harvard gave the subject a decidedly physiological turn, and G. Stanley Hall placed the emphasis on the genetic point of view. Throughout the early decades of the 20th century these various approaches were vigorously pursued by the disciples of Wundt, James, and Hall. Each in his own way made an effort to show that mind is a natural phenomenon which has evolved in harmony with the laws of nature. Obviously it was necessary to include the mental processes of the lower levels of life, and animal mentality from the amoeba to the great apes was investigated with painstaking precision in scientific laboratories.

Mechanistic psychology. Many new psychologists viewed mind as a phenomenon of nature in the Newtonian sense, that is to say, as the result of pure mechanism. But since some of the foremost physicists more recently have come to doubt the mechanical view of the world and adopted a more creative explanation, psychologists have revised their positions. Not only was the physical analogy pulled from under their feet, but an even more disconcerting thing happened: the investigations of the neurological laboratories failed to substantiate their claims.

Educational psychologists took a lively interest in the learning process; this led to the study of animal learning. John B. Watson, following the Russian, Pavlov, and the pragmatic view of mind, elaborated the "Behavioristic Theory"; and Edward L. Thorndike developed the "Stimulus-Response (S-R) Bond Theory." Both of these theories were later abandoned, and educational psychology has turned to other explanations.

Structural and functional views have been widely held, and in recent years the Gestalt theory has attained popularity. During the past several decades social processes, creative thinking, integration, and the study of personality have crept into works on psychology. The tremendous demand for knowledge of the mental life in connection with education has far outrun the purely scientific interest.

Psychoanalysis and psychotherapy. Contemporarily with the physiological, experimental, genetic, pragmatic, and Gestalt psychological movements, there sprang up still another of momentous value, the analytic. Its origin was different, however, for it originated in the realm of pathology. Some European physicians, confronted with cases of hysteria, sought to trace its histology in order to find its therapy. Sigmund Freud, an Austrian physician, found the approach by analyzing the childhood experiences of his patients. Many of his ideas were fantastic, but he hit upon the simple fact that somewhere in the history of the patient something had gone wrong with neuropsychic developments. To probe as deeply as possible into the past, he believed, might furnish the clue to the beginning of the trouble. Psychopathology, psychoanalysis, psychotherapy, and psychiatry sprang from this basic source. For the educator two valuable contributions resulted. First, psychoanalysis was a form of archeology, an excavation of the lower strata of the mind, the digging into the past for facts by which to explain behavior. Second, it confirmed the conclusion of the geneticists that the psychic nature is basically emotional. It was in the natural order of events that G. Stanley Hall should introduce Freud and his doctrine to American scholars.

As to the place of sex in the unfolding life of the human organism, Freud's view was an exaggeration, or better, an overemphasis upon the minor aspect of this central function. The pragmatic philosophy on its side made a similar blunder when it underestimated the importance of sex and made food, shelter, and clothing the only basic motivations.

Genetic psychology. G. Stanley Hall left no succcessor to carry on his research into the development of child nature in a comprehensive way. His fundamental theory of recapitulation was discredited, his method of using questionnaires was condemned as unscientific, and his general conclusions as to educational reform neglected. Educational theory and practice, it must be acknowledged, has been dominated by the pragmatic-instrumentalist philosophy. However, interest in the study of children has not been entirely neglected and in these later years it has shown a new vigor, and has become more scentific in method.

The general tendency has been to cultivate small areas more intensively. Dr. H. H. Goddard, who studied under Hall, became the first leader in clinical and abnormal psychology by his research work at the Training School for Feeble-Minded Children at Vineland, N. J. He was one of the first in America to use the Binet-Simon scale and greatly advanced the science of intelligence testing. Dr. Arnold Gesell, another of Hall's protégés, specialized in the physical and mental growth of infants and is the world's outstanding authority in the field.

The elementary school age has not been studied so intensively by American scholars. But in Europe Piaget, Director of the Rousseau Institute at Geneva, has given the world the most remarkable insight into the development of the pre-pubertal stage. Among his books are *The Child's Conception of Physical Causality, The Child's Conception of the World, Judgment and Reasoning in the Child, The Language and Thought of the Child* and *The Moral Judgment of the Child.*

No field of genetic research has attracted more attention than that of adolescence. But no one has attempted to equal the two large volumes in which Hall summed up all aspects of the subject at the time (1904). Innumerable texts on the subject have been published, and in recent years several new investigations have been made.

The deepening conviction that in the final analysis all education must base its procedures not so much on experience in general but upon the ripening factors of the personality has caused educators to seek more definite knowledge of genetic processes. In the field of adolescence this has stimulated a number of investigations. From 1934 to 1939 the Progressive Education Association authorized a Study of Adolescence by the Commission on Secondary School Curriculum. The findings of the Commission, which are numerous, have been made available.[9] These investigations are based upon case studies. A few years later The National Society for the Study of Education devoted its 43rd Yearbook (Part I) to Adolescence.[10]

Still later a group of professors at the University of Chicago, representing biology, physiology, nutrition, pediatrics, psychiatry, anthropology, sociology, education, and psychology, formed The Committee on Human Development, which is exploring a number of different phases of child and adolescent development. The projects of the Committee are

---

[9] The most important of these are as follows:

Thayer, V. T., *et al., Reorganizing Secondary Education.* New York: D. Appleton-Century Company, 1939.

Zachry, Caroline B., *Emotion and Conduct in Adolescence.* New York: D. Appleton-Century Company, 1940.

Blos, Peter, *The Adolescent Personality; A Study of Individual Behavior.* New York: D. Appleton-Century Company, 1941.

[10] Chicago: The University of Chicago Press, 1944.

supported by the Lilly Endowment.[11] The first work to appear is a study of sixteen-year-old youth in a small city not far from Chicago. Many methods were used to secure data.

Educational psychology. It has always been assumed that educational psychology is merely the application of scientific psychology to classroom and pedagogical situations. It is now beginning to appear that educational psychology is perhaps an entirely different and independent field of science. It has for its purpose the art of departing from what would naturally happen in order to produce an artificial product. Scientific psychology is analytic and explanatory; educational psychology is the science of the integration of the organism to produce a harmonious personality. The science of the natural operation of the mind is one thing, but the task of education is not to follow nature in its simple operations, but to build up higher functions which do not come of their own accord.

Educational science has carved out its own field, and is not only experimental but to an increasing degree genetic. The greatest advance has been made in the effort to bring more of precision and accuracy into our knowledge of the mental processes and how they can be controlled.

THE DEVELOPMENT OF TESTS AND MEASUREMENTS

The historical background of the movement. This highly consequential movement had its roots in various settings, in all of which, however, there was a sorely felt need for more accurate knowledge of mental processes. The unfruitful effort of Herbart to apply strict mathematical calculation to the recall of ideas led after many years to the extreme toil of Wundt, Ebbinghaus, Fechner, and Helmholtz in measuring sensory discriminations, memory, time reactions, and other psychological phenomena. In England the same desire for definite and objective knowledge induced Sir Francis Galton to originate the idea of using the mathematical technique in measuring human traits in his works, *Heredity Genius* (1869), and *Natural Inheritance* (1889). The advances of Galton were followed by the work of Karl Pearson. These two movements, the German and the English, were instrumental in producing

[11] Havighurst, Robert J., *et al.*, *Adolescent Character and Personality.* New York: John Wiley and Sons, Inc., 1949.

the first article published in this new field in America by James McKeen Cattell, entitled "Mental Tests and Measurements" (1890).[12]

Another beginning of a different sort was made in America by J. M. Rice, editor of *The Forum.* Interested in promoting efficiency in school teaching, he investigated for some years the spelling achievements of 33,000 pupils, and published several articles in 1897. He proved that children who were taught 15 minutes a day by a rational technique could spell as well as those who were taught 40 minutes by the drill method. This astonishing fact, objectively demonstrated by technical investigation, aroused heated discussion and objection. It initiated the scientific movement of testing by accurate measurements the results of teaching the various subjects in the curriculum, and it led to the forming of various measurements of achievements.

A substantial advance was made by the publication in 1904 of *The Theory of Mental and Social Measurements* by Edward L. Thorndike. This was the first general work to set forth the statistical approach in the study of problems of anthropology, vital statistics, economics, sociology, biology, and education. This treatise made clear to new students what is meant by average, median, mode, scale of measurement, probable error, standard deviation, and coefficient of correlation. This work added greatly to the clear understanding of the data which now flowed in ever increasing volume from precise laboratory experimentation and statistical method.

Thorndike promoted the measurement of the ability of school children and established scales for spelling, handwriting, arithmetic, and other subjects. S. A. Courtis, Leonard P. Ayers, and others produced many subject-matter measuring scales. This movement did not, however, continue to exert great influence, for at the time a profound change of attitude toward all subject-matter in the curriculum came along. Moreover, interest in measurement suddenly took a different direction.

The measuring of intelligence. The French psychologist, Alfred Binet, for some years had explored various aspects of the psychophysical organism. In 1904 the Minister of Public Instruction for France appointed him to a committee to find a scientific method for discovering the subnormal children in order to separate them from others in the schools. With the assistance of Theodore Simon he tested children in the Paris schools, and in 1905 published *A Method of Measuring the*

[12] *Mind XV,* pp. 373-380.

Intelligence of Young Children. Binet was able with a high degree of accuracy to discriminate the idiot, the imbecile, and the moron, and to establish what is called "mental age." The tests were revised in 1908 and 1911 to apply to the higher levels of intelligence. Before his death, Binet forecast the course that mental tests should take.

The work of Binet in testing intelligence was promoted in the United States by H. H. Goddard and Lewis Terman. In 1916 Terman published the Stanford Revision of the Binet-Simon tests. The idea of "Intelligence Quotient" (I.Q.), which is the child's "mental age" divided by his chronological age was the suggestion of William Stern. The use of the Army Alpha and Beta group intelligence scales in World War I had a profound effect in demonstrating the value of the measurement movement. From 1910 to 1930 the number of different tests formulated to test achievement, memory, factual knowledge, skills, interests, attitudes, and aptitudes reached phenomenal proportions. Since then the effort has been directed more to the evaluation of the higher mental processes, interests, and general personality traits.

Today measurement has been expanded to the utmost and is used in connection with choice of studies, college entrance, vocational placements, discovering aptitudes, and in all educational activities. All aspects of the personality are now being subjected to measurement.[13]

GUIDANCE, COUNSELING AND PERSONNEL WORK

Relation of guidance and instruction historically. The function of the guide is to conduct the novice to the object of his search so as to save time and effort in useless experimentation. The Athenian Greeks separated the function of guidance (pedagogy = child guidance) from

---

[13] Terman, Lewis M., *The Measurement of Intelligence.* Boston: Houghton Mifflin, 1916.

Varon, Edith J., "The Development of Alfred Binet's Psychology," *Psychological Monographs,* Vol. 46, No. 3, 1935.

Binet, Alfred, and Simon, Th., *A Method of Measuring the Development of the Intelligence of Young Children,* translated by Clara Harrison Town. Lincoln, Ill.: The Courier Company, 1913.

Freeman, Frank N., *Mental Tests; Their History, Principles and Applications.* Boston: Houghton Mifflin Company, 1939.

Lindquist, E. F., (Editor) *Educational Measurement.* Washington: American Council on Education, 1951.

Committee on Measurement and Guidance, *New Directions for Measurement and Guidance.* Washington: American Council on Educational Studies, 1944.

instruction. Such a division did not, however, become universal, probably because it is felt that guidance is inherent in the process of education. The need of guidance in the choice of school and of studies has been frequently pointed out by reformers. Nevertheless the present movement for guidance and counseling did not spring directly from school situations but from the changing conditions of industrial-professional life.

Changes in vocations and vocational training. Modern civilization has produced profound changes in the number and nature of vocations and in the preparation needed to fit youth for their life-work. The few and simple pursuits of the past have been complicated and evolved by science and technology:

1. Few children today are brought up in conditions where they can observe and participate in any of the industrial and other pursuits that sustain society.

2. Most of the professions and vocations have become highly specialized and are now divided into a number of technical specialties. The total number of vocations runs into many thousands.

3. The assembly line of the superindustrial plant has many tasks absurdly simple, repetitious, and correspondingly fatiguing. They require practically no mental activity. Others require a high degree of technical knowledge and skill.

4. Both general education and technical training are more and more needed to equip young people for their vocational careers.

5. Under these conditions choice of vocation, preparation, and the acquisition of skill require guidance which teachers and school officers ordinarily cannot give. Vocational guidance belongs to specialists.

6. The selection of employees for large industrial, mercantile, and other establishments can be performed efficiently only by officials who know the requirements, and can judge the abilities and competency of individuals.

Educational and personal guidance. In 1882 President Daniel Coit Gilman of Johns Hopkins University appointed a board of advisers, consisting of one professor from every undergraduate department, so that every student "may have a friend to consult in the perplexities which arise." Later this officer was called dean. His function was to maintain the close personal touch with students; this was no longer feasible for the president because of his mounting administrative duties. President W. R. Harper of Chicago advanced the work of deans along the line of guidance. The complicating of college life and the expansion of the curriculum to thousands of courses required that students be given help in the selection of courses best suited to their needs.

But Harper, who had a deep intuition of the relation of the student's intellectual capacity to his personal attitudes, interests, and traits, went further and advocated basing the curriculum upon the development of the adolescent life.

The beginning of the guidance movement. In 1908 Dr. Frank Parsons, under the beneficence of Mrs. Quincy A. Shaw, daughter of Agassiz, began "The Vocation Bureau" in the Civic Service House, Boston, Massachusetts. For several years, it may be added, he had been interested in securing jobs for young immigrants. In stating the aims of the Bureau, Parsons used the term "vocational guidance" which quickly became popular usage. The next year the Boston School Committee requested the Bureau to outline a program of vocational guidance for the Public Schools of the city. The program was forthwith initiated and has been in operation ever since.

The vocational guidance movement was backed by Harvard University, especially by President Charles W. Eliot and Paul Hanus, Professor of Education, and courses were introduced into the summer session. Under such favorable auspices the movement gathered speedy momentum, and a national conference was held in Boston in 1910. Three years later The National Vocational Guidance Association was organized, and its official organ, *The Vocational Guidance Magazine,* began publication.

The integration of the test-measurement movement with the guidance movement. These two movements did not reach their crescendo until they were united in the 1930's. Binet early foresaw that the diagnosis of the interests and intellectual aptitudes of youth led naturally to discernment of vocational competence and placement. In 1910 he wrote:

> I hope in 1912 to be able to publish a study already begun a long time ago on the different aptitudes of children; it will be the logical complement of the measurement of intelligence. I think the knowledge of aptitudes is the finest problem of pedagogy. It has as yet been treated nowhere... and at the moment we possess no sure procedure for investigating the aptitudes of any subject, child or adult.... There would be immense profit in knowing the worth of each one and the vocation for which his nature destined him; methods and tests which would throw light on vocations, aptitudes, and also inaptitudes, would render immeasurable service to all. As soon as the theoretical part of the problem was

solved, practical applications would not delay, and a whole intelligent organization of placement would be made.[14]

Few students of education, fewer still of the laymen have any comprehension of the vast development of these movements. But despite their significance, it must be remembered that the human personality has not yet been completely dissected and charted.[15]

THE ADVANCEMENT OF SCHOOL ADMINISTRATION

Beginning and expansion. The conducting of schools has expanded into a business of gigantic proportions and of intricate performances requiring over a thousand separate functions and activities. From the simple art of managing a small school it has grown into the most elaborate technique of administering huge systems of schools in cities and states. Concurrent with the increase in complexity has been the growth of accurate knowledge of management. This colossal expansion took place in the first quarter of the century and was facilitated by the employment of professors who specialized in educational administration in the leading universities. Teachers College, Columbia University, was foremost in recognizing the necessity of amassing precise information by careful investigation in this area. The early authorities in the subject were Samuel T. Dutton, David Snedden, George A. Strayer, and N. L. Englehardt.

The fields of administration. Gradually the various areas of organization, administration, supervision, statistics, financing, building, staff-

---

[14] Varon, Edith J., "The Development of Alfred Binet's Psychology," *Psychological Monographs,* Vol. 46, No. 3, p. 91, 1935.

[15] Bloomfield, Meyer, *Readings in Vocational Guidance.* Boston: Ginn and Company, 1915.

Brayfield, A. H., *Readings in Modern Methods of Counseling.* New York: D. Appleton-Century Company, 1950.

Brewer, John M., *History of Vocational Guidance.* New York: Harper & Brothers, 1942.

Froelich, Clifford P., *Guidance Services in Smaller Schools.* New York: McGraw Hill Book Company, Inc., 1950.

Vocational Guidance Magazine, Vol. I, 1922 sq.

Warters, Jane, *High School Personnel Work Today.* New York: McGraw-Hill Book Company, Inc., 1946.

Williamson, E. G., *et al., Trends in Student Personnel Work.* Minneapolis: The University of Minnesota Press, 1949.

Wrenn, C. Gilbert, *Student Personnel Work in College.* New York: Ronald Press, 1951.

ing, public relations, and child accounting were investigated and the thousand different detailed functions differentiated.

The American Association of School Administrators, an affiliate of the N.E.A., at its annual sessions presented the most vital problems as they arose in importance and instituted intensive study of each. This has added greatly to the progress of the science and art of education. The Federal Office of Education, begun in 1867, has done invaluable service by compiling statistics and publishing reports and monographs on a wide variety of topics.

Surveys. The surveying of schools has been taking place for a long time. Today surveys are made of the details of state school systems, county schools, city systems, colleges, and universities. Probably the first was made during the Lutheran Reformation to determine the condition of the Latin Schools and universities, which declined because of the violence of religious and vocational changes. It was quite simple but brought out the facts.

The first in our country to be made as a means of evaluating the efficiency of a school system was that of the schools of Boise, Idaho, by Calvin N. Kendall, Superintendent of the schools of Indianapolis, in 1910. This was a short and simple evaluation of school practices.

In 1911 and 1912 the schools of New York City were surveyed under the direction of Dr. Paul H. Hanus, Professor of Education of Harvard University. Since that time innumerable surveys have been made. Today they are carried out by a group of specialists armed with statistics, graphs, and technical information on all aspects of the schools: score cards to measure adequacy of buildings, playgrounds, equipment and so on; achievement tests to measure the efficiency of instruction; and all the other aspects of schoolwork. The results are not always beneficial, for authorities do not always follow through with reform measures. But without such investigations and recommendations little progress would take place.

New study of school administration. In 1950 the W. K. Kellogg Foundation (see p. 652) set out to improve the administration of public education on a nationwide scale. The project is called The Co-operative Program in Educational Administration (the C.P.E.A.).

This investigation was the result of three years of discussion by the American Association of School Administrators. It will extend over five years and its significance may be guessed by the fact that a grant of more than $3,000,000 has been allocated for it. The objective of the project is to learn as much as possible about the administering of schools so that it may be made more efficient. Some six or more universities have divided the country into regions and have organized groups of institutions, each of which is pursuing some one aspect of the total project.[16]

AGENCIES PROMOTING EDUCATIONAL PROGRESS

Participation of Federal Government in education. At the beginning the originators of the Federal Government did not regard education as one of its direct concerns and consequently did not mention it in the Constitution. This policy accorded fully with English philosophy and tradition which held public education to be strictly a domestic, local, and charitable interest. In any event it was highly unlikely that any federal system of education could have been formed that would have won the approval of the diverse groups which formed the Republic. Benevolent neutrality was the wisest policy, although the early provision of land given each new state under the laws of 1785 and 1787 for the promotion of schools was a salutary gesture and in harmony with English precedent.

The Morrill Act of 1862, endowing agricultural and mechanical education in each state, was another act in pursuance of the original policy of the Federal Government. Numerous private colleges, copying the plan that Fellenberg had established, adopted the manual-labor-agricultural feature but they failed to follow through with this aspect of training. It became apparent that neither the states nor private interests were willing to promote vocational education. It was, accordingly, encumbent upon the Federal authority to take the initiative, if anything was to be accomplished. The establishment and continued support of the land-grant colleges proved to be the most far-reaching educational measure ever taken by the Federal Government; for the first time it gave public higher education prestige and thus greatly encouraged the progress of state universities.

During the past half-century the Federal Government has extended

---

[16] Brubacher, J. S., *Modern Philosophies of Education.* New York: McGraw-Hill Book Company, Inc., 1939.

Monroe, Walter S., Editor, *Encyclopaedia of Educational Research,* Revised Edition. New York: The Macmillan Company, 1950.

National Society for the Study of Education, *Philosophies of Education.* Bloomington, Ill.: Public School Publishing Company, 1942.

its promotion of education and child welfare in various ways. In 1912 it established the Children's Bureau of Education to look after the welfare of children generally. Vocational training and agricultural education, however, continued to be the major concern of Congress in the field of education. In 1914 the Smith-Lever Act initiated extension work in home economics and agriculture. In 1917 Congress established the Federal Board of Vocational Education to bring about vocational training in all the states; and it passed the famous Smith-Hughes Act to forward vocational training in schools below the college level. The Smith-Hughes Act marked a new era in the Federal promotion of education: aid was given to states on the basis of a contract; education was promoted below the college level; the standards, methods, and policies were formulated on which public aid would be granted; and, finally, approval of the work was kept in the hands of Federal agents. Many new enactments have extended this type of work so that vocational training is now on a satisfactory basis throughout the states.

The Great Depression compelled the Federal Government to take extensive action to help young men support themselves, and at the same time to advance their vocational knowledge and skill. The first of these agencies to be organized (1933) was the Civilian Conservation Corps (CCC). The other agency was The National Youth Administration (1935) which assisted unemployed young men and women to earn money while they pursued their education. Both these agencies were terminated during World War II.

In 1944 Congress, with the desire of assisting men who had been in the armed forces, passed the Servicemen's Readjustment Act, generally called "the GI Bill of Rights." It granted up to $500 a year to ex-service men and women to pay the tuition and supplies for study in school or college. A subsistence fund was also provided.

Repeated efforts to speed up the educational progress over the nation have caused many people to desire more centralization of power. It is much easier to have a law passed by Congress favoring reform measures than it is to persuade 48 state legislatures to do it. Others are fearful of the pressure of Congress and the encroachment of Federal control in education. In 1929 the Bureau of Education became the Office of Education.

At the beginning of the century, it was discovered that the various state school systems varied greatly in efficiency. The Southern states generally were deplorably low in their standards. The ability of many of these states to finance their schools so as to make them more efficient was far below the average for the nation. The reason for this lies in the fact that the amount of taxable wealth behind each child shows very great inequality. In order to equalize educational opportunity great pressure has been brought upon Congress to provide funds for the states whose per capita contribution to their schools is below the average of the nation as a whole. Many measures have been introduced into Congress but no action has yet been taken.

Presidential participation in educational affairs. Educational centralizers have for many years endeavored to enlist the tremendous power of the President of the United States to promote the reforms these people desire. Pressure from such sources has increased greatly during the past quarter-century because of the depression and war. President Hoover instituted in 1931 a special committee to study social trends. It made an elaborate report and recommended the establishment of a "Department of Education with a Secretary of Education" with cabinet rank at its head. In 1938 President Roosevelt set up an "Advisory Committee" to study the school situation. According to Adolph E. Meyer, "This was by far the most comprehensive analysis of educational conditions ever undertaken by any nation." Following this report in 1940, President Roosevelt called The Conference on Children in a Democracy. In 1947 President Truman authorized the "Commission on Higher Education for American Democracy," and in 1951 the White House Conference on Education.[17]

EDUCATIONAL FOUNDATIONS, ASSOCIATIONS AND OTHER AGENCIES

Early funds set the policy. When George Peabody (1867) set up the Fund named after himself, he not only perpetuated his name and set

[17] *President's Research Committee on Recent Social Trends in the United States* New York: McGraw-Hill Book Company, Inc., 1933.

White House Conference on Child Health and Protection (called by President Hoover). New York: The Century Company, 1931.

White House Conference on Child Health and Protection, Section III, (1) *Education and Training Committee on Special Classes,* 1931; *Committee on the Family and Parental Education,* 1932; *Committee on the School Child,* Washington, 1932.

White House Conference on Children in a Democracy (called by President Roosevelt). Washington, 1940.

White House Conference on Rural Education (called by President Roosevelt). Washington, 1944.

a noble example of philanthropy, but he laid down a liberal policy and method of management which has guided later foundations. Between 900 and 1,000 educational funds, foundations, and agencies have been established, many of them with local application and with various objectives in view. Their combined assets are around $2 billion. Only a few can be touched upon here.

1. **The General Education Board.** Organized in 1902 and incorporated by Act of Congress, this body set as its objective "the promotion of education within the United States of America without distinction of race, sex, or creed" and "in general to do and perform all things necessary or convenient for the promotion of the object of the incorporation." The design of John D. Rockefeller, founder of the Standard Oil Company, was to establish an agency to distribute part of his immense wealth and also the funds of others entrusted to it. Mr. Rockefeller started the fund with $32 million. The Board has promoted projects at home and abroad. Agriculture, high schools, colleges, universities, medical education, Negro education, and research in many fields have been assisted. It has published a number of important books dealing with educational problems. It also assisted in establishing the Lincoln School of Teachers College, Columbia University.

2. **Carnegie Foundation for the Advancement of Teaching.** This was originated by the great steel industrialist and philanthropist, Andrew Carnegie (1905), to provide retiring allowances for college and university professors in the United States and Canada. The total gift amounted to $15 million. This Foundation greatly affected all the institutions of learning, but especially aided the progress of higher education.

No sooner did the trustees of the Foundation begin to study the distribution of the annual income than they found themselves confronted by the necessity of deciding what is a college. They did not desire to assume the responsibility of standardizing institutions, but in the end they gave a great impetus to this task. The rules they adopted to guide them had great weight in promoting private college retirement systems and also state retirement systems for public school teachers.

3. **Russell Sage Foundation (1907).** The income from $15 million is used "to promote the improvement of social and living conditions in the United States." Research on adverse social conditions and publication of information on social welfare are among its chief operations.

4. **Carnegie Corporation of New York (1911).** $125 million was originally set apart; now the assets are over $170 million. The pur-

poses include the advancement of knowledge and understanding among Canada, the British Commonwealths, and the United States. It aids technical schools, higher institutions, libraries, scientific research, publication of books, and so forth.

5. **The Rockefeller Foundation (1913).** This was one of the largest endowments and its objective was one of the broadest, namely the welfare of mankind throughout the world. Public health, medical and natural science, fellowships and scholarships, and health education are its main pursuits.

6. **Commonwealth Fund (1918).** $10 million, given by Mrs. Stephen V. Harkness and Edward S. Harkness, formed the basis of this important agency. A variety of activities "for the welfare of mankind" have engaged this organization through the years: medical education, the California curricular study by W. C. Bagley (1925), the teacher-training study by W. W. Charters, nursing education, criminality and delinquency, child guidance, mental illness, school surveys, and, more recently, European fellowships and publication of educational works. Its present assets are over $50 million.

7. **The W. K. Kellogg Foundation.** This was established (1930) "for the promotion of the health, education, and the welfare of mankind, but principally of children and youth . . . without regard to sex, race, creed or nationality." The fund is around $48 million, and some $30 million from the income has already been expended. The Foundation has three chief interests: 1. "The development of health education in the public schools"; 2. "The general improvement of rural schools"; 3. "School camping as a function of public education." In 1950 the Foundation began a five-year study of school administration (see p. 647).

8. **Ford Foundation (1936).** $232 million in assets in 1949. Its purpose is scientific, educational, and charitable by means of studies, research, and other activities which meet human social need.

Over 120 foundations grant fellowships or scholarships to promote the education of capable students. Among the chief of these are The American Association of University Women, The Guggenheim Foundation, Institute of International Education, and the National Research Council.

Management of Foundations. In an age when the forces of education and social innovation and radicalism and those of conservatism and reaction are engaged in deadly struggle, it is remarkable that these powerful foundations, backed by hundreds of millions of dollars, have not been made the subject of any charge of partisanship or defalcation in their beneficent task of human betterment.[18]

Adjunctive agencies. From the beginning of the century, education in its innumerable aspects has been the passionate hobby of more groups of people than ever before. The list of organizations which seek to promote the education of children will fill a volume. Only a few of the front leaders can receive mention. The National Education Association (N.E.A.), founded in 1857, enrolls today about three-fourths of the one million teachers of the country. With its numerous affiliated groups it is the most powerful professional organization. For some years the most active organ of the N.E.A. has been the Education Policies Commission which has published a number of studies.

Among those that are national in scope are the National Congress of Parents and Teachers (begun as the National Congress of Mothers in 1894). With branches in all states and a membership close to 3,000,000 it has been, through the years, one of the most effective organizations in the United States for the improvement of schools. Similar organizations have been formed in many foreign countries. The Child Study Association of America with its many branches has been of service in spreading knowledge of and sympathy for child life. Among the chief agencies for research are The National Society for the Scientific Study of Education, The American Association of School Administrators, a department of the N.E.A., The National Association of Directors of Educational Research now known as The Educational Research Association, The Progressive Education Association, and The Association for Childhood Education. A number of agencies concern themselves with interracial, interreligious, and international relations.

CHIEF DEVELOPMENTS WITHIN THE SCHOOLS

The fortunes of the kindergarten. In July of 1892, a small body of women animated by the principles and practices of Froebel came

[18] For list of foundations, etc., see *World Almanac.*

American Foundations for Social Welfare. New York: Russell Sage Foundation, 1946.

"*Foundations and Charitable Trusts,*" Social Work Year Book, 1949.

Monroe, W. S., *Encylopaedia of Educational Research.* New York: The Macmillan Company, 1941.

Rich, Wilmer Shields, and Neva R. Deardorff, *American Foundations and Their Fields.* New York: Raymond Rich Associates, 1948.

together in Saratoga Springs, N.Y., to form *The International Kindergartners Union.* It was a deeply solemn occasion, for an intuition of destiny pervaded all hearts. No groups of religious devotees ever consorted with more sublime faith in their cause. Three years later 35 leading Kindergartners met in Chicago in a session to hear President G. Stanley Hall discuss child education from the standpoint of the new genetic psychology. At the conclusion of his address all but two of the 35 withdrew from the meeting. Hall profoundly admired Froebel's ideas, but he was critical of his symbolism and sought to give kindergartners a more objective and scientific point of view, and to bring kindergarten technique into articulation with child nurture generally. But the fanatical reverence of the kindergartners at that time for the formal practices and mystical symbolism of Froebel's philosophy was so overwhelming that they were in no mood to listen to the calm voice of science. From that day onward a rift in the ranks of the adherents of Froebelianism never healed until the devotees of the system lost their assurance.

Setback for the kindergarten. World War I dampened the ardor for the kindergarten system and for all things Germanic. Synchronous with that depressing event came the arresting technique of Dr. Maria Montessori. Froebelianism might readily have withstood all these onslaughts, but it could not survive the acid logic of the educational philosophy of John Dewey. Froebel staked the validity of his system of training on the assumption that the age from three or four to six or seven forms a unique stage in the life history of the child. It has, he insisted, a psychology of its own in which the inner experiences laid up during the years of infancy break forth into expression in outer forms, that is to say, in play activities. It was not the genetic philosophy of Hall, nor those other disturbances that brought confusion into the camp of Froebel worshipers; it was rather the opposition of the educational theory and practice of Dewey. He replaced the panentheistic dialectic of Froebel—the law of opposites—with the Hegelian dialectic or the law of process, the rise of concrete problems and the consequent reconstruction of experience. In his school at the University of Chicago (1896-1903) he brought together children from four to fourteen years, and ignored the idea of any distinct mental differences or stages of development. He contended that the same process of thinking holds for the infant, the preschool child and the adult. The notion that the child from three to six or seven is motivated to action and thinking in a way other than that which motivates experience at all levels he considered absurd.

Meanwhile, in 1916, the National Council of Primary Education was formed, and the view grew that a common interest obtained between workers in the nursery, the kindergarten, and the primary school. This bond finally brought together these various organizations to form the Association of Childhood Education (1931).

Preschool education. Great progress has taken place in the spread of preschool education, but despite these advances there was never again that fervent sense of mission which possessed the women who knew Froebel themselves or knew those whom he inspired. It possesses no philosophy of its own, no magic technique which distinguishes it from education in the other stages. But it must be recorded that the enthusiasm of earlier days led to the enactment of laws in all except a few states providing for this level of education.

Increase in kindergarten enrollment. Enrollment in public kindergartens decreased slightly during the depression years of the 1930's, but increased slowly during World War II and reached an all-time high of 988,680 by 1947 and 1948. The popularity of the kindergarten as an instrument of public education varies extremely. In 1947 and 1948 Michigan had more children enrolled in public kindergartens than in the first grade and Maine had almost as many. West Virginia, North Carolina, South Carolina, Tennessee, Alabama, Mississippi, Arkansas, and Idaho reported no enrollment. New York had 183,987 in the first grade and 135,571 in the kindergarten; Texas, on the other hand, had 195,420 in the first grade and only 6,261 in kindergarten.[19] Some states made considerable advance before the depression in the establishment of public kindergartens, but these were abandoned, and those that operate today are largely in private hands.

PROGRESS IN ELEMENTARY EDUCATION

Conditions at end of the century. Elementary education had attained a high degree of efficiency under the traditional philosophy as the century drew to its close. The Committee of Fifteen (1893) directed by the National Educational Association to propose reform measures in organization and curriculum brought in an inconsequential report.

The main objective of the school at this time was the acquisition of subject matter. Stress was laid on acquiring skill in the fundamental

---

[19] Statistics of State School Systems, 1947-48, p. 50. Washington: Federal Security Agency, 1950.

operations; in reading it was effective oral presentation; in writing it was a fine Spencerian hand; in spelling it was accuracy in spelling tricky words, many of which the child did not use; in arithmetic it was the mastery of the tables, measures, and processes, some of which were no longer in common use, and in rapidity of addition and subtraction; in history and geography it was learning the disconnected facts of American geography and the wars of English and United States history; and in literature it was memorizing poetry and reading excerpts from noted authors.

Learning was memorization, and rigorous regimentation marked the conduct of the school. The textbook was followed slavishly. These practices were based on the slogan "Knowledge is power," and on the theory of formal mental discipline.

This technique was challenged for a time by the Herbartian methodology, which held that the main purpose of instruction was to help the child to rise from the concrete objects of experience to abstract concepts by means of expert instruction. The Herbartian cult was, however, soon abandoned.

Progress in organization. Substantial advancement has been made in the universal acceptance of the regular features of the state school system. Compulsory attendance laws were enacted in all remaining states, especially in the South, which had lagged behind. By 1918 all states required attendance. The eight-grade elementary school became the standard, but not until the 1930's did the seven-grade setup disappear. Great interest was manifested in rural education; and consolidation of school districts proceeded to a large extent in the South and West. The kindergarten was incorporated into the grade school in many states and cities as an integral factor. The junior high school began to take the seventh and eighth grades from the elementary school.

The most important innovation in organization was that at Gary, Indiana. Superintendent William Wirt induced the Board to organize on a new plan, which has been known as "the platoon school" or "the work-study-play" movement.[20] The Gary System evolved from Wirt's conviction that education embraces all aspects of child nature. He felt that it is incumbent upon the school to provide for the exercise of all the capacities of the children, all the way from the nursery through

---

[20] Spain, C. L., *The Platoon School.* New York: The Macmillan Company, 1923; Bourne, Randolph S., *The Gary Schools.* Boston: Houghton Mifflin Company, 1916.

the junior college. The school plant contained playgrounds, gardens, swimming pools, drawing and music studios, science laboratories, carpenter and machine shops, library, and auditorium.

The classes alternated between the various activities, all of which were considered to have the same educational value. By this alternation for work, study, and play, the usage of the school building was increased about 40 per cent. Furthermore the school was in session 20 per cent longer daily in order to keep children occupied and keep them away from the detrimental influences of the town. Moreover it ran on Satday and throughout the entire year.

Outside agencies that provided educational activities were used as integral parts of the program. Children could go home for special lessons in art or music, to the scouts, or to institutions or industrial or commercial plants of interest. Those whose parents approved went to the churches or the YWCA for religious instruction.

The Gary system was the sensation in the American educational world after the demise of the "Dewey School" at the University of Chicago. Over 120 schools, several of them in New York City, adopted this form of organization. Large as was the interest it aroused and salutary, withal, it has not been able to revolutionize the schools of the nation.

Emphasis upon the individual. The intensified study of child nature and intelligence tests and measurements led to exalted emphasis upon individual differences. The old system of grades assumed that all pupils should progress at the same rate; this came to be known as a lock-step system. Those who did not pass at the end of the year were required to take the grade over. The lock-step system received sharp criticism, because it kept bright and precocious children in grades with mediocre and dull children and made dull children repeat the early grades, in some cases several times, or until they dropped out of school.

Various plans were explored to amend these evils. The two most prominent plans staged to fit the school to the capacity of individual children were the Winnetka Plan and the Dalton Laboratory Plan. The lock-step system was abandoned. Individuals were promoted on the approval of the principals; sometimes the intellectually superior and the slow were placed in different classes. This was classification by ability.

The Dalton Laboratory Plan. Early in the century Helen Parkhurst became interested in the revolution in methods of instruction then stirring in the world. Her desire was "to equalize the pupil's individual difficulties and to provide the same opportunity for advancement to the slow as to the bright child." Individual learning was the common characteristic between the Montessori system which she studied, the scientific laboratory, and the eager pursuit of a project which a child sets up for himself. Miss Parkhurst conceived the idea (1911-1920) of applying the laboratory technique, by which the experimenter learns at his own rate and by direct experience, to all subjects of the curriculum. Each subject was divided into projects and each pupil entered into a contract to learn these stints as rapidly as he could do so.

This was known as the "Dalton Laboratory Plan" because of its introduction into the high school of Dalton, Mass., in 1920. It attained some popularity in America for a time but was criticized as being too individualistic and was in time given up in Dalton. It attained, however, greater influence in England and France.

The glaring weakness of the lock-step graded school system came to a head during the first two decades of this century. In 1919 the schools of the town of Winnetka, Illinois (about 10,000 population), determined to do something about the matter. They installed a fairly elaborate plan. The curriculum was set up in two parts: "the common essentials," and "the group and creative activities." In the first the work of each grade was divided into a series of specific tasks to be performed or learned by each pupil. This work was wholly on an individual basis. The pupil progressed through the grades as rapidly as he learned the assignments. The other field included the appreciation of literature, music, art, playground activities, assemblies, handwork projects, and dramatization. In these the pupils got as much as they could, but no standards of achievements were set up. Under this plan a pupil might be doing work in several grades.

This school system was carefully surveyed (1923-24) to discover the results of the plan.[21]

---

[21] Washburne, Carleton, "The Winnetka System," in *Progressive Education*, Vol. I, No. 1, p. 5.

Washburne, Carleton, Vogel, Mabel, and Gray, William S., *A Survey of the Winnetka Public Schools*. Bloomington, Ill.: Public School Publishing Company, 1926.

Parkhurst, Helen, "The Dalton Laboratory Plan." London: Dalton Association, 1926.

Parkhurst, *Education on the Dalton Plan*. New York: E. P. Dutton & Company, Parkhurst, *Exploring the Child's World*. New York: Appleton-Century-Crofts Co., 1951.

The great transition in method. The most momentous transition in education has been from acquiring information by means of instruction and skill by means of drill to the development of power to act and think by meeting situations and doing things. It has been from repeating or imitating the past to learning to adjust to the living present. The main problem is the relation of stored-up knowledge to the exercise and functioning of intelligence. The pragmatic philosophy makes action, adjustment to environment, or problem-solving primary, and getting knowledge incidental. The acquisition of past knowledge becomes subsidiary or even unimportant. This change severed the individual from the great task and legacy of group ideals from which the motivation of the individual must arise.

From a fixed curriculum of orderly subject matter, class work has been changed to seeking ends to be realized, situations to be met, and problems to be solved. The stable curriculum has been changed to living situations, felt-needs, and interest in direct thought. Only knowledge that functions is treasured and only for the time being.

Shift of emphasis of subject matter to functionalism. Oral reading was given up, and silent reading to gather information substituted. The child used many readers in place of one. Formal grammar was abandoned and emphasis upon correct writing and speech habits favored. Fine handwriting was no longer insisted on. Spelling was learned as a functional subject, and only words used by the children were learned. Arithmetic was confined to practical operations.

The curriculum has been enlarged to include history, geography, literature, social studies, physical training, drawing, shopwork, art, music, sciences, physical and health-education, and cooperative activities. In recent decades the emphasis has been upon acquiring social and democratic attitudes.

EVOLUTION OF SECONDARY EDUCATION

High schools broaden their functions. At the beginning of the century about 75 per cent of the high school graduates prepared to enter college. Today only about 25 per cent have college in view. It is clear that the high school is no longer chiefly a college preparatory school. On the other hand the high school is holding its students better and is today the recognized completion point for general education. One's social and vocational competency is now largely rated by graduation from high school; but its most important function is to prepare for vocational training by laying a broad but fitting foundation.

Increase in high school attendance. The increase in the number of pupils in high schools has been one of the great social phenomena of education history.

INCREASE IN SECONDARY SCHOOL ATTENDANCE
(CONTINENTAL UNITED STATES)

Schools	*1890*	*1900*	*1910*	*1920*	*1930*[a]	*1945-46*
			Number of Schools			
Public	2,526	6,005	10,203	14,326	23,930	24,314
Private	1,632	1,978	1,781	2,093	2,760	3,053
Total	4,158	7,983	11,984	16,419	26,690	27,367
			Number of Pupils			
Public	202,963	519,251	915,061	2,199,389	4,399,422	7,140,164
Private	94,931	110,797	117,400	184,153	341,158	594,236[b]
Total	297,894	630,048	1,032,461	2,383,542	4,740,580	7,734,400
			Pupils per 1,000 of Population			
Public	3.2	6.8	10.0	17.6	35.8	
Private	1.5	1.5	1.3	5.7	2.7	
Total	4.7	8.3	11.3	23.3	38.5	
			Number of Graduates			
Public	21,882	61,737	111,363	230,902	591,719	
Private	8,070	12,216	14,409	24,166	51,447	
Total	29,952	73,953	125,772	255,068	643,166	

[a] "Biennial Survey of Education, 1928-1930," in U. S. Office of Education Bulletin (1932), No. 20.

[b] U. S. Office of Education, Report for 1947-48.

At the beginning of the century only around 10 per cent of the youth were enrolled in high schools; today about 75 per cent are in attendance. This enormous increase in the attendance upon high school, while a most gratifying sign of the prosperity and high civilization of the American people, has several other significant angles. It means that an age of mechanical power and industry can spare its youth from the ranks of labor, that is to say, industry no longer needs our young people. This has come about because of the increase of production through the use of machines.

Another meaningful fact is that a larger proportion of the young people now attending the high schools are from the lower intellectual and economic bracket. This influx has created new problems, especially along curricular and social lines. New methods have become necessary to interest the lower intellectual types and vocational education has had to be introduced on a broadened scale.

The rapid growth of the high school during the early years of the century led to the setting up of the Commission on Reorganization of Secondary Education (1918) to bring about a more rational form of training. It was essential to transform it from a school predominantly preparatory to an institution educational in its own right. The most celebrated feature of the report was the formulation of the *Seven Cardinal Principles of Secondary Education.* These famed objectives turned out to be a poor revision of Aristotle's conditions of happiness.

Still another momentous effort to render high schools more effective was the cooperative program by the Commission on the Relation of School and College (1930-1938), and that of the Commission on Secondary School Curriculum, both promoted by the Progressive Education Association. Generally entitled the "Eight Year Study," the first was an experiment carried on in 30 high schools located in different parts of the country. These schools conducted their work on "progressive education plans" and their graduates were admitted without further requirements by 200 colleges.

Originally American high schools had no commerce whatsoever with the colleges; but by some quirk of fate by the beginning of our century they had become chiefly institutions to prepare students for college. This objective was clear-cut; and the schools were annually examined by the accrediting agencies to keep up their efficiency. Accrediting set an objective standard and brought prestige and recognition, and made college entrance requirements more important than all other functions of secondary education. This system of exploitation enabled the colleges to stultify and domineer over high schools and confine them to a narrow groove. A widespread revolt arose against this hide-bound method and subject matter of instruction, which was first challenged by the "Eight Year Study." This was the most extensive effort to compare the results of a more liberal and progressive form of training with those of the older system. The investigation was made as scientific, objective, and free from criticism as possible.

The conclusion reached by the "Eight Year Study" was that the college entrance requirements, which were the result of grinding toil by college professors and secondary school executives for 40 years, did not prepare students as well qualified for college as those produced by the new method and curricular electives of Progressive Education. Although there has been no wild rush to alter college entrance requirements, nevertheless the punctilious adherence to traditional requirements has been abridged and students who show intellectual superiority are now admitted even if they have not absorbed all the minutiae of knowledge demanded by the standardizing agency.[22]

The junior high school movement. Out of the general fermentation which began with President Eliot's onslaught upon the American system of schools of the last century came a disposition to experiment with new patterns of organization. President W. R. Harper opened the University of Chicago (1892) with the freshman and sophomore years as the "Academic College," and he urged that this junior unit be united with the regular four-year high school. John Dewey fused the kindergarten with the primary school and grammar grades. The Committee of Ten (1893) urged that a number of high school studies be offered earlier in the curriculum. The Committee of Fifteen studied the revision of the elementary school (1895), and was followed in this four years later by the Committee on College Entrance Requirements. The reports of these committees and innumerable other conferences added fuel to a strong desire for innovation in the organization of American education.

Charges continued that the schools were wasting the precious time of the young; that they did not keep the pupils profitably employed; that the youth were dropping out of school too early; that bright children were retarded by association with the average and dull in the same classes; and that languages, mathematics, and the sciences should be taught lower in the grades so as to prepare earlier for college.

Alert superintendents sought to reorganize the elementary and high school. Richmond, Indiana, reorganized on a 6-2-4 grade basis in 1896; Chicago experimented with special high schools to prepare for college; some cities tried a 6-6 form of reorganization; finally Berkeley, California, adopted a 6-3-3 plan, which came to be preferred. The reason for

---

[22] Aiken, W. M., *The Story of the Eight-year Study*. New York: Harper & Brothers, 1942.

Diederich, Paul B., "The Eight-year Study: More Comments," *Progressive Education,* Vol. 28, No. 5, March 1951.

Redefer, Frederick L., "The Eight Year Study After Eight Years," *Progressive Education,* Vol. 27, No. 2, November 1950.

Thayer, V. T., Zachry, C. B., and Kotinsky, R., *Reorganizing Secondary Education*. New York: Appleton-Century-Crofts, Inc., 1930.

this was that a functional basis for the new unit was grounded in the development of the child. The junior high school found its real basis as a transitional school which takes the child just before the pubertal upheaval and carries him over the emotional period of early adolescence. The publication of the voluminous study, *Adolescence,* by G. Stanley Hall (1904) furnished a basic functional philosophy for the junior high school.

In the reconstruction, four types of secondary organization came to be accepted: junior high schools, junior-senior high schools, senior high schools, and the traditional four-year type. The separate junior high school form of organization increased from 387 in 1922 to 1,842 in 1930 and 2,647 in 1946. It was a boon for states with many small towns or consolidated school districts which did not have enough children for a regular high school. The junior-senior schools are organized on the basis of two divisions in the same institution.[23]

NUMBER OF THE VARIOUS TYPES OF PUBLIC HIGH SCHOOLS, 1922-46 [24]

Type	*1922*		*1930*		*1938*		*1946*	
	Number	*Percent of Total*	*Number*	*Percent of Total*	*Number*	*Percent of Total*	*Number*	*Percent of Total*
1	2	3	4	5	6	7	8	9
Junior high school	387	2.8	1,842	8.3	2,372	9.6	2,647	11.1
Junior-senior high schools	1,088	7.7	3,287	14.8	6,203	25.2	6,358	26.5
Senior high schools	91	.6	648	2.9	950	3.9	1,317	5.5
Regular high schools	12,490	88.9	16,460	74.0	15,056	61.3	13,625	56.9
Total	14,056	100.0	22,237	100.0	24,590	100.0	23,947	100.0

[23] Bunker, Frank Forest, *The Junior High School Movement—Its Beginnings.* Washington: W. F. Roberts, 1935.
Bunker, *The Functional Reorganization of the American Public School System.* Washington: Government Printing Office, 1916.
Smith, William A., *The Junior High School.* New York: The Macmillan Company, 1932.
[24] Office of Education, *Statistics of Public High Schools 1945-46.* Washington: Federal Security Agency, 1949.

HIGHER GENERAL EDUCATION

The junior college from infancy to maturity. From its birth in 1892 to 1910 the junior college remained an anemic infant dependent upon its mother, the University of Chicago. It did not gather momentum until it took new root in California under the leadership of Dean Alexis F. Lange.

The California movement. Dean Alexis F. Lange came in contact with the idea of the junior college during his student days at the University of Michigan, where it had been suggested by Dr. Tappan. Through his efforts, originally, the California Legislature enacted the first junior college law in 1907. Under this law the establishment of public junior colleges began in 1910. Soon the number of junior colleges in California increased with startling rapidity, and the movement spread to a number of other states. The work of the American Association of Junior Colleges has had a marked effect in the rapid growth of the movement since World War I. The following table is approximately correct; though it takes into account only the colleges established since 1900 and still existing. A considerable number of the early ones have ceased to exist, and some have become senior colleges. The latter have not so far been tabulated. There are in existence today in the continental United States, according to the latest statistics, 621 junior colleges with an enrollment of 558,162 students. This movement has shown a tendency to spread to our insular possessions and also to several foreign lands.

GROWTH OF THE JUNIOR COLLEGE[25]

Year	*Number of Colleges*	*Enrollment*	*Percentage Increase in Enrollment over Previous Year*
1900	8	100	
1915	74	2,363	
1922	207	16,031	
1930	429	67,627	24.2
1935	521	107,807	4.1
1940	575	196,710	26.4
1950	648	465,815	—6.9
1951	634	562,786	17.2

[25] *Junior College Directory, 1951,* American Association of Junior Colleges. These figures include 13 colleges with 4,624 students outside the United States.

Causes of the junior college movement. The underlying cause of the movement was the realization that the first two years of college work belong to general education and are secondary in character. But the rapid and extensive establishment of junior colleges during and after World War I has been due to a number of contributory causes. Among these the following have been the most potent:

(1) The movement for standardizing higher institutions of learning brought about by the Carnegie Foundation was directly responsible for changing the status of many private institutions struggling to be standard colleges. Numerous private colleges found they could not maintain the standards adopted by degree-granting institutions. The small institutions did not have funds adequate for efficient instruction in the upper years; and when they did offer such work, it was not accredited by the higher institutions.

(2) Many professional schools required just two years of college training prerequisite to entrance. This practice stimulated some colleges to restrict the level of their offerings to these two years.

(3) The early age at which many youths graduated from high school by taking summer courses led many people to favor local junior colleges in order to keep their children at home until they were more mature.

(4) The long distance to the universities in many western states favored the growth of local institutions of junior rank.

(5) The increase in post-graduate work in the high schools favored the development of this new institution.

(6) The popular demand for a higher completion point than the high schools was supplied by the junior college.

(7) The increased expense of university attendance, especially after World War I, caused many students to go to the junior colleges.

(8) The increase in freshmen and sophomore enrollment induced a number of large western universities to favor the establishment of junior colleges as feeders.

(9) The desire to keep wealth at home induced the leaders of the local community to establish local colleges.

(10) The failure of the universities to adjust their methods and discipline to the needs of freshmen necessitated a new institution with different objectives.

(11) The desire for more personal attention to the needs of the individual student, the overcrowding of the university classes, and the lack of university dormitories have had far-reaching influence.

(12) The demand for vocational preparation for many minor professions and for hundreds of technical vocations above the high school level has greatly stimulated junior college development.

Recent trends in junior colleges. The most recent trend in this field is the establishment of the four-year junior college. This plan of organization unites the last two years of the standard high school with the first two years of the college, and thus forms a new unit. The new plan has been effected most widely in the Middle West and in California. The University of Chicago some years ago separated the junior division from the senior years of its college of arts and sciences, and organized a four-year junior college. This reorganization was begun in 1928 and completed in 1931.

The establishment of the four-year college unit in connection with public schools has brought about a regrouping of the grades in a number of instances. Many public school systems have reorganized on a "6-4-4" plan, which calls for a six-year elementary school, a four-year intermediate school, and a four-year college. This development is still in the experimental stage. The chief obstacle to the adoption of such a plan is that the junior college has not determined its function in relation to the totality of the educational process; it is not yet grounded in a general philosophy of education.[26]

UNIVERSITY EDUCATION AND PROFESSIONAL TRAINING

Higher education. Turmoil has characterized higher education in the United States for a long time, but at no period has it been so continuous as in the first half of the present century. At the same time, nowhere in the world has the growth of colleges, universities, and technical schools been so tremendous. The term "higher education" loosely includes junior colleges, standard senior (four-year) colleges, normal schools, universities, theological schools, and research and technical institutes.

---

[26] Bogue, Jesse P., *American Junior Colleges,* Second Edition. Washington: American Council on Education, 1948.

Boucher, Chauncey Samuel, *The Chicago College Plan* (Revised and enlarged by A. J. Brumbaugh). Chicago: The University of Chicago Press, 1940.

Sexson, John A., and Harbeson, John W., *The New American College, The Four-Year Junior College, Grades 11 to 14 Inclusive, Organized and Administered as a Single Institution.* New York: Harper & Brothers, 1946.

Increase in institutions and enrollment. The increase in higher institutions and in the number of students enrolled has been persistent and virtually uninterrupted for the past 60 years. In 1900 some 977 institutions were listed; the figures for 1947 and 1948 show a total of 1788 of which 472 were junior colleges. Moreover, junior college publications show several hundred more not counted in the Biennial Survey of higher institutions by the Federal Office of Education.

It is, however, the student enrollment that is most phenomenal. In 1900 the number of students was 237,502; in 1947 and 1948 it was 2,378,670, a gain of 1,001 per cent. More than one million of these were veterans whose education was subsidized by the Federal Government. But even after subtracting this group, the number of enrollees increased with every decade and was vastly more in proportion than in any other country in the world. In 1900 the percentage of the population in higher institutions was 0.31 percent, in 1948 it was 1.79 per cent, although the population had doubled meanwhile.

The colleges and universities became secularized. Most of these institutions now shunted religion into the background.

Among the far-reaching results of the Carnegie Foundation (1905) was the weakening of church control of higher education. This great benevolence had in view the pensioning of college professors at the age of retirement at 65 years. Soon after it began to organize for action it discovered that it could not provide for the large number of institutions which applied to be beneficiaries of its funds. Under its terms no church-related college could participate in its retirement benefits. This caused a number of institutions to relinquish their denominational ties and to declare themselves nonsectarian. Such action was not at all contrary to the spirit of the times, since higher education for some decades had been gradually abandoning its religious objectives and adopting a purely naturalistic view of life. The course of study abandoned the teaching of Christian Evidences, made ethics an elective, gave up the chapel service and otherwise relinquished moral control.

Experiments in curriculum. The number of major experiments in collegiate instruction have been many, and over 100 less pretentious efforts have been tried out. From the time of the adoption of the principle of broad electives and the credit-hour system the feeling has persisted that college education has lacked integration. The University of Wisconsin carried on for some twelve years an "Experimental College" under the direction of Dr. Alexander Meikeljohn, whose underlying motive was to furnish students a unitary, integrated course of study during the freshman and sophomore years. The basis of the curriculum was literary and classical. An attempt with somewhat similar purpose was made in the University of Minnesota "General College." This was a special curriculum pursued by a group of students during the first two years of college and had in view a better distribution of subject matter. St. Johns College, Annapolis, Md., has established its curriculum on the "100 best books" from ancient times to the present. Harvard and Yale Universities have restudied their college curricula and effected changes in the first two years to secure a better "general education."

Hundreds of less ambitious investigations and experiments have been made during the past decades. All pale into insignificance, however, before the radical reorganization which was made by the University of Chicago. Following out the plans of William Rainey Harper at the founding of the institution, the freshman and sophomore years have been completely separated from the upper years. A new four-year college has been formed combining the two upper years of the high school with the freshman and sophomore years of college work. The course of study has been unified. The credit system has been discarded and attendance upon classes is not required. The class system is not followed and students can complete their course as rapidly as they pass a series of comprehensive examinations. The most devastating radical step is the granting of the traditional bachelor's degree (B.A.) at what amounts to the end of the sophomore year. This consequential step may in time lead to the complete abandonment of the traditional standard college. Somewhat liberal plans for the pursuit of undergraduate work have just been announced at Johns Hopkins University.

EXTENSION, CORRESPONDENCE WORK, AND NIGHT SCHOOLS

Extension of school work. No more marked change has occurred in the schools than the expansion of the functions, services, organization, and curricula. The traditional institution as it evolved during the 19th century was simple and sequestered in its operation. The University of Chicago, when it opened in 1892, introduced four changes which have become well-nigh universal in the United States and Canada. These are the year-round functioning of the university (by adding the summer session), the night school, the extension work, and correspondence instruction.

Confined at first to the university level, summer session work has become almost universal in the colleges, the high schools, and, to a certain extent, in the elementary schools. The night school has greatly expanded the opportunity for education among the employed. Many junior colleges in getting started operated as night schools. Correspondence courses and extension work are not confined to the college and university level. These services not only have enabled multitudes to continue their education while making a living, but have enabled students to take their academic work at a pace to suit their circumstances and abilities.

Research. The most distinguishing quality of the American universities during the past half-century, other than athletics, has been the passion for research. Our age takes nothing as fixed, settled, unchangeable; every situation and every idea is only a starting point. Innumerable individuals are feverishly busy inventing new gadgets, devices, and conceptions. Medicine, dentistry, psychology, science, and technology are fields of continuous observation and experimentation. Universities have demanded evidence of research and production for degrees and for the appointment and promotion of faculty members. Commercial establishments employ staffs of investigators to bring out new products to sell the public. The Federal Government has promoted research by huge subventions. Billions of dollars are going into investigations of all sorts. It has furthermore been proposed that an international organization be founded to pursue research on a world-wide scale.[27]

Libraries and new usages. Horace Mann made eloquent pleas for libraries and for teaching children to love to read. As a consequence, a number of states enacted laws encouraging the establishing of school libraries. The change in college methods of teaching, particularly the new emphasis upon research, gave a powerful impetus to the use of reference reading and as a result the higher institutions took greater interest

[27] Report of the Harvard Committee, *General Education in a Free Society.* Cambridge: Harvard University Press, 1945.

Meikeljohn, Alexander, *Education Between Two Worlds.* New York: Harper & Brothers, 1942.

Report of President Truman's Commission on Higher Education, *Higher Education for American Democracy,* Vol. I, pp. 514-515. Washington: Government Printing Office, 1947.

in enlarging their library facilities. The adoption of a standard number of books in the library and an annual increment in order to receive accreditation of their work brought speedy results in high schools and colleges.

The forming of the American Library Association (1876) was followed by better techniques in the conduct of libraries and the professional training of librarians. Women's organizations because of their literary proclivities began promoting public libraries. But the most substantial and vital stimulus came from the gifts of Andrew Carnegie for the construction of libraries. The Carnegie Corporation donated over $43,665,000 for this purpose.

THE REVOLUTION IN CURRICULA AND METHODS

Curricular changes. The traditional curriculum had been constructed over a period of many years, and was the result of many different influences. Each subject had been evolved on the basis of its own materials and by specialists interested in full analysis. The result was an aggregation of studies: reading, writing, spelling, grammar, arithmetic, literature, geography, history, drawing, physiology, and natural science. The high school had two main courses of study: the commercial, which prepared for practical life; and the humanistic, which prepared for college. The college had two curricula: the traditional humanistic, which led to the B.A. degree; and the scientific, which led to the B.S. degree.

The end of the century witnessed a tremendous expansion of knowledge along every line, and, as a consequence, a number of problems came to the front. The plethora of materials led to the question of the relative values of the various kinds of knowledge. William T. Harris, in accordance with the idealistic philosophy, sought to find a logical basis for the selection of the curricula in the nature of knowledge. G. Stanley Hall advocated the genetic principle with a course of study to fit the needs of the growth of the child. Herbert Spencer argued that the natural sciences were by all counts of most worth. Dewey based the curriculum on the utilitarian needs of the individual and society.

The first half of our century has been a period of heart-searching emotions in regard to the curricula of the schools at all levels. The pragmatic principle and the doctrine of self-activity introduced profound changes. Manual constructive work, play, creative activity, practical subjects, and other lines were tried out. The expansion of the sciences called for survey courses. The middle decades saw a new emphasis on the fine arts: drawing, art, music and, later still, on drama. The world condition has brought into the spotlight the civic and other social aspects of education.

The present trend of thought is to emphasize the democratic principle, and also to employ a curriculum fitted to the needs of the emotional nature of the growing child.

Dewey deplored the separation of subjects from one another into compartments as unnatural and unpsychological. The introduction of the pragmatic principle of proximate goals of action and thought introduced the teleological form of integration in which means and end take precedence over the logical categories. As a consequence the psychological order of subject matter, that is to say, the order of felt-need, experience, and problem solving become paramount. This dispenses with the conception of a fixed body of knowledge to be acquired by the educatee. He acquires knowledge as a byproduct of action, not as a changeless body of truth. Information is secured by gathering and interpreting data, laboratory work, and group discussion. Formal lessons, lectures, and bookishness are no longer considered valuable.

Still another development, far-reaching in its use, came about in the wake of the invention of apparatus for visual and audio-visual instruction. What the telescope and the microscope did three centuries ago, these inventions and television are doing on a broader scale today. The possibilities, dangers, and limitations of this new aid to direct experience can not as yet be estimated.

PHYSICAL AND HEALTH EDUCATION

The new status. During the past fifty years educators have become much more acutely conscious of the need of physical education, partly because of the intensified interest in biology, and partly because the wars have shown the physical deficiencies of our young men and the need of better health. As a consequence physical and health education have been advanced as never before, and along with these has grown a practical interest in public recreation and outdoor education or camping. To these fields of physical education, health, public recreation, and camping, some institutions have linked safety education. So far no name has been found to bind these five different interests.

Physical education. Three systems of physical cultivation have flourished in our modern world: the English system of athletics and sports, which has come down from the Renaissance; the German *Turnen,* promoted by the followers of Basedow; and the Swedish system of calisthenics. All of these were introduced into various American schools and colleges during the latter half of the last century.

The two World Wars have given occasion to appraise more accurately the physical condition of our people and as a consequence greater emphasis has been placed upon systematic physical training in schools and colleges, and the entire subject has been investigated and given a higher evaluation. The training of teachers to direct the games, play, and physical activities at all levels of school life has been greatly advanced by the universities. Interscholastic Leagues in various states have been formed for the promotion of athletic contests between high schools. Intercollegiate athletics has also been organized on a universal scale. The entire system, however, has become professionalized and commercialized and, to some extent, corrupt as did the Greek system of Gymnastics. This trend to train winners of contests and the neglect of direct physical training for every growing child and youth have reached a climax.

Health education. Interest in hygiene goes back about a century in American education to Horace Mann; but it received its greatest impetus with the establishing (1885) of what is now The American Association for Health, Physical Education and Recreation.

Medical inspection in public schools. Medical inspection of school children began in Europe during the last half of the 19th century. By 1899 the large cities of Germany employed school physicians. Inspection began in the United States in the closing decade of the century. For some years attention was centered upon the control of infectious diseases, and vaccination was optional with local authorities; but later it became a universal requirement.

Progress in this century. The first two decades produced an increasing interest in hygiene. A tremendous advance was made in public health, immunology, nutrition, nursing, and in teaching health education. During the past quarter-century more interest has centered in public health. The most extensive survey of health ever made in this country was conducted by the Works Progress Administration under President Franklin Roosevelt in 1935-36. The National Health Conference followed at Washington, D.C., in 1938.

Every state in our country now has laws pertaining to child health.

Some require health examinations of pupils and of teachers. Usually the administration of the health program is lodged with the superintendent. In some cases the program is state financed. Dental examinations are sometimes included. The training of special teachers of health is included in the physical education program. Repeated efforts have been made to induce Congress to vote funds for the expansion of this type of work but so far it has not responded.

Public recreation. Large cities have long had parks in which people cooped up in tenement houses and apartments could find a breathing place. In late years, especially because of interest of civic clubs, playgrounds, swimming pools or beaches, and apparatus have been added to furnish children and youth the opportunity to exercise. But these facilities were quite useless without someone to put on a program to direct these sports. The expense of these workers has usually devolved upon the city governments.

Safety education. The grim fact that more children die by fires, drowning, and automobile accidents than by disease has aroused public attention within the past few years. To meet this situation schools have added courses in safety education so as to train children to avoid accidents.

Outdoor education. For many years summer camping has flourished on a private basis for children of the wealthier class. Scouts and Campfire clubs also have camping opportunities, but poor children do not. The cooping up of children in cities during the hot summer vacation presents a difficult problem to large cities. Recently some city schools have begun to take an interest in the situation and a movement has arisen to provide opportunity for more children to have camping experience.

Training of directors. The training of athletic and physical education directors for the schools and for these newer services has devolved upon the universities. Schools of education and teachers' colleges have added departments of physical and health education and have integrated training along these lines with their courses in professional education.[22]

---

[28] Fitzgerald, G. B., *Community Organization for Recreation.* New York: A. S Barnes and Company, 1948.

Leonard, Fred Eugene, and Affleck, George B., *A Guide to the History of Physical Education.* Philadelphia: Lea and Febiger, 1947.

Meyer, Harold D., and Brightbill, Charles K., *Community Recreation.* Boston D. C. Heath and Company, 1948.

VOCATIONAL AND PROFESSIONAL EDUCATION

Vocational training. This term is usually employed to designate any training whose purpose is to equip individuals to support themselves and contribute to the welfare of society by specific occupations. It stands against general education, which has the development of the individual in all his human functions in view; and against technical and professional education, which require a much higher and broader preparation and a prolonged period of scientific and technical study. Historically, all forms of education followed the apprenticeship method and little general education was offered. Only in the modern age, and particularly in the United States, has general education been paramount and provided free for all children through the high school.

During the 19th century technical and vocational training reached a high state in Germany, and many different schools were functioning. Toward the end of the century some manual training schools and a few trade schools were established in some of the cities of the United States.

In 1906 Massachusetts authorized a Commission on Industrial and Technical Education, and began to promote vocational training in that state. Generally, the American states were slow in taking action. New hope arose when the N.E.A. (1908) formed The National Society for Promotion of Industrial Education, with the object of seeking action by the Federal Government.

The advance of vocational training along all lines was chiefly the result of the participation of the Federal Government through its distribution of funds which are matched by the states. The Smith-Hughes Act (1917) began the new era by furnishing financial support for teaching agriculture, mechanical arts, and home economics below the college level. Its distinctive impetus came from the fact that the Federal Government entered into definite contract with each state; and it set up

---

Neumeyer, Martin H., *Leisure and Recreation*. New York: A. S. Barnes and Company, 1949.

Oberteuffer, Delbert, *School Health Education*. New York: Harper & Brothers, 1949.

Paterson, Robert G., *Foundation of Community Health Education*. New York: McGraw-Hill Book Company, Inc., 1950.

Williams, Jesse F., and Abernathy, Ruth, *Health Education in Schools*. New York: The Ronald Press Company, 1949.

Williams, Jesse F., and Brownell, Clifford, *The Administration of Health and Physical Education*. Philadelphia: W. S. Saunders Company, 1945.

standards for achievement and specified the right to share in the supervision of the work. The World Wars and the Great Depression of the 1930's greatly increased interest in all forms of vocational education. The George Deen Act (1936) expanded Federal aid.

Meanwhile, this country has changed from an economy chiefly agricultural to a land combining agriculture and industry as does no other country except Germany. The application of science to industry has transformed the entire economy. Industrial chemistry, physics, biological research, and the other sciences have transformed our lives beyond the capacity of the individual mind to comprehend. The professions have split into many fields of specialization, and many technical vocations now are adjunctive to professions. The varied lines of vocational practice are numbered by the thousands.

The advancement of the teaching profession. In the general upswing of interest in education and the expansion of knowledge in all its fields, the advancement of the training of teachers has participated. At the end of the century the kindergartners were the best equipped for their task in both theory and technique. Next came elementary school teachers who had attended good normal schools. High school teachers who were college graduates knew more of subject matter but had little or no professional training. The training of administrators was just beginning.

Gradually, after 1900, the requirements for teachers' certificates were increased and standardized. Graduation from a normal or some college credit was generally required. More and more professional knowledge as well as other learning was demanded by state certificating bodies.

Between 1910 and 1930 many normal schools increased their standards and became regular arts colleges with departments of education, and offered first the bachelor's, and later the master's degree. In addition practically every liberal arts college and university added professional courses in education for prospective teachers. The coordination of the liberal arts courses and professional education courses was gradually worked out.

At the beginning of the century, teacher training was chiefly historical and theoretical. Soon, however, schools added courses in methods and curriculum and, most significantly of all, "practice teaching." Today the training in methods and practice and in administration, measurements, and other practical lines has outrun the study of theory and subject matter.

Gradually kindergarten and elementary teaching came to be monopolized by women, with men only in administrative positions. In recent decades the percentage of men in the profession has wavered between 10 per cent and 18 per cent, with the great majority of them in supervisory positions and in the high schools. Now that women and men are paid the same salaries for the same work and women fill many administrative positions, the proportion of men is still further decreased.

Great efforts have been made by state legislatures, departments of public instruction, and various national organizations to improve the quality of teaching. Over 20 such organizations exist, and a number of organizations have been set up, specifically to inquire into the training of teachers. Probably the most important of these has been The Commission on Teacher Education, appointed by The American Council on Education, and financed by the General Education Board.

Teachers institutes. Much professional uplift came from the teachers institutes, which were initiated by Henry Barnard in Hartford, Connecticut, in 1839, and by Jacob S. Denman in Ithaca, N. Y., in 1845. These annual meetings, usually lasting about a week, obtained great popularity and accomplished much, but as teachers became better equipped the institute was eliminated during the early part of this century. Of greatest benefit to the profession has been the summer session, the work-shop and in-service training.

SEX EDUCATION AND BIRTH CONTROL

New topics for the curriculum. On the list of most crucial problems confronting present-day society these stand high. Neither has yet received the sympathetic and impartial consideration it must get in the schools for the welfare of the individual and humanity.

The study of sex from a scientific standpoint is itself relatively new. Havelock Ellis in England and Sigmund Freud in Austria led in bringing it to attention. Due to the work of these and other brave adventurers, the appreciation of the centrality of sex in individual and social existence has increased greatly during the present century. The iron curtain of reserve behind which it has always moved and the delicacy of feeling against revealing the facts of life to young children have prevented proper instruction. Now, however, the imperative need to combat perversion, hysteria, prostitution, rape, illegitimacy, and disease has made knowledge of sex essential for every adult. To the greatest extent, the happiness and welfare of every individual is wrapped up in his or her sex life.

How, where and by whom "the facts of life" are to be communicated to the young are crucial problems. The consensus of progressive thinkers agrees that knowledge of sex must be imparted to children but the details of the program are not agreed upon, and some bodies of the Christian Church are vehemently opposed to such instruction. A dispassionate disclosure of the physical facts of fertilization, such as the scientists and physician know them to be in vegetable and animal life, does not make a great impact upon the mind of the adolescent. The story of the bees and birds is one thing, the violence of animal passion is quite another. So far no consensus has been reached; and while discussion and experimentation in instruction goes on among the educators, the overstimulation of sex consciousness among children has been anything but wholesome.

How widely sex instruction may now be in vogue in the schools is not known, for no statistics as to its inclusion are available. This may be due in part to the fact that the subject is approached in a number of ways and integrated with various other fields of interest. Among these are physical education, health and hygiene, biology, pets and animal husbandry, manners and morals, ethics and religion, sociology, family life, and special moving picture demonstrations. The intense opposition of some branches of the Christian Church to the teaching of this subject may be an even stronger reason for the neglect to gather information.

The question of birth control has likewise met with powerful resistance by conservative church bodies. Two points need to be presented: First, among the cultivated peoples of Europe and America the higher intellectual and moral classes of society are not reproducing themselves; on the other hand, the lowest economic and intellectual class, the class most given to criminality and delinquency, is greatly overproducing. This ominous fact presents gravest dangers for mankind. It is increasingly imperative that the species aim more at quality and less at mere quantity, at the wholesome and not the psychotic.

Second, birth control has become an alarming problem. Many countries, such as Puerto Rico, China, India, Indonesia, Japan, and many European peoples are increasing their populations at a rate far beyond the possibilities of food supply. The future prospect can be only black and horrible tragedy: large numbers of people living their entire lives in hunger. Scientists and responsible statesmen are increasing their warnings, as every year the population of these lands jumps by millions. Statistics predicting future populations by 1970 and 2000 are frightening in their implications. The results to civilization, it is conjectured, may be devastating. India, where the population per square mile is abnormally high and increasing by millions yearly, is the first nation in its five-year plan of improvement to adopt a program of birth control.

CHANGES IN MORALS AND IN CHARACTER CULTIVATION

The decline of western moral life. The history of 20th century morals presents a theme of greatest perplexity. Whether only moral standards have slipped or whether the ethical fiber of the people has deteriorated: these are questions too vital and immense to be handled in a few paragraphs. A battery of scientific investigations would be needed to deal adequately with the inquiry and the very yardsticks for accurate measurements are not available. Even if these were at hand, statistics of earlier days are not available for comparison. That momentous changes have occurred, which imply decline, is beyond question.

The revolt against the past. The first half of the 20th century will go down in history as the age of revolt against the past. The spirit of the age concentrated attention upon the present, on the theory that life is adaptation to changing situations. Biologically, to live is to adjust to the contemporary environment. The bridges with the past were cut, trails obliterated, ties ripped asunder; and forms of good taste and guidance were thrown into the garbage with the tinsel and flowers of last night's party. Piety, which is respect for the virtues of the fathers, became regarded as sheer hypocrisy, or as a naïve and docile subserviency. The past has been preparatory to the present and for that very reason it is inferior and outmoded; it was simple and can, therefore, furnish no sure guidance in a more involved present.

Revolt against external authority. The profoundest shift in feeling has been the violent reaction against all forms of external authority. It resembles the tempestuous, irrational rage of the three-year-old or of the first-stage adolescent against the parent who blocks his capricious acts. Moreover, this revolt has shown itself in family life, classes of society, government, religion, and the backward peoples of the earth.

This great shift has taken place in one generation. Rome fell slowly through several centuries, but modern imperialism and monarchy crashed in less than a generation. Empires, the French, German, and Italian, disintegrated; and even the British, greatest of all, has gone far toward liquidation. It is quite obvious that the age of European supremacy and exploitation of the earth's teeming populations has come to an end. The right of self-determination has been recognized and it embraces not only nations but individuals.

Not only has the revolt against authority swept away imperialistic rule, but it has likewise invalidated the imperatives of beauty, morality, and religion, as upheld by the best men. Democracy, or the rule of the common man or the majority, signifies government by the ordinary, the mediocre. Life has levelled off; art, intelligence, and spirit no longer aspire to the sublime, but are content with the commonplace. The superlative degree has become an unnecessary refinement, the good is the motivation of action, the best is a starry-eyed illusion. The very suggestion of the universal, conceptual, perfect, or the infinite induces a shudder of revulsion down the spine of the sophisticated.

Morality has been divested of its imperative. Anthropology has disclosed no virtues which are universally respected and practiced; philosophy has found no principles of ethics absolutely binding. All morals are held to be relative and man-made. Moreover there is no fixed reality behind or within them. Nothing commands absolute respect, much less obedience at all times and all places and for all men under all circumstances. In consequence, all authority is looked upon as external and foreign to action, an imposition interposed between interest and the goal it seeks to achieve. Imperialistic government, moral principles, and religion are fetishes which medicine men and the priestly hierarchy have employed in the past to perpetuate their paternalistic power over the offspring generations.

The increase of crime. Never have sex perversions; unscrupulous disregard of the evil effect of liquor, narcotics, and tobacco upon children; divorce; rape; murder; political chicanery; debauchery; gambling; corrupt athletics; and contempt for law and order been so rampant and unblushing as they are today. The revolting sexual perversion extending from multiple divorce to criminal assault upon women and even little girls, frequently ending with the brutal murder of the victim; the increase in sexual relations of high school students; the heartless killings by youth of high IQ out of sheer moral idiocy; all such behavior testifies to the deterioration of public and private morality and sanity. The gangsterism of the underworld in the large cities, the corruption of the police and control over local and national politicians sworn to uphold the law; the gambling mania and its support of the underworld; the defiance of law and order by black-marketeers and public officials; the toleration and the granting of paroles and pardons to hardened criminals by high officials; the employment of gangsters by corporations to break strikes; the prevalent sale of narcotics to teen-age children; and, capping all, the systematic slaughter of millions of men, women, and children by Nazi Germany mark western civilization as the most scientific and efficient exhibition of the demoniac. There have always been bestial men, but never have they had the instruments of science at hand so abundantly.

Since World World II J. Edgar Hoover, Director of the Federal Bureau of Investigation (FBI), has continually warned against the increase of crime, especially among teen-age youth. But nothing awakened the nation to the moral deterioration so much as the Kefauver Congressional investigation in 1951, the basketball scandals in the universities, and the widespread cheating at examinations. That such evils are common even in high schools is well known. Amid the charges and countercharges, one conclusion is certain: the strong claims of a century ago that a system of public schools would do away with crime now look absurd.

The exaltation of immorality and crime. The newspapers, magazines, comics, radio, television, and the movies have entered into rivalry to debauch the finer sensibilities of the young and to exalt the criminal. The tendency to exalt the reprobate and hardened criminal into a brave and heroic creature has had its inevitable harvest. The criminal who walks to the electric chair with jaunty air and a poker face or who boasts that he will never be taken alive has been played up to our youth as an example of sublime heroism.

Widespread cynicism. The public conscience has been drugged into insensibility while selfish sophisticates have taken refuge in blatant cynicism. Unwilling to face the facts of moral deterioration, many leaders sneer at all reformers and at faith in human betterment. They quote pessimistic warnings of despair from Jeremiahs in every era, and declaim that there have always been murders, sexual perversions, and all these other evils, and there is no possibility of getting rid of them. It is this complacent sense of futility and cynicism which forms the chief index that faith and idealism are decadent. The knowledge of moral principles and religious faith is no longer considered essential for the educated man. Ethical principles are regarded as relative, and in consequence a revolt against all moral imposition has become common.

Not only has public education failed to eliminate crime but it is in some measure responsible for the increase of these various evils. Discipline has been practically abandoned in many schools or watered down into a wishy-washy so-called democratic process. The youth receive insufficient positive guidance as to what is right or wrong in conduct. Down to the end of the last century, educational leaders were college graduates who had studied ethics and the Evidences of Christianity, and the teachers were the products of an education which respected law and reverenced moral principles and religious sanction. All this was changed at about the end of the century, and today practically none of the teachers of America have studied ethics, much less the principles of moral education. A sampling poll of 1,500,000 students in higher institutions showed that less than 5 per cent have studied ethics.

The situation in moral education. Moral education has undergone a major alteration. In the schools generally moral conceptions have been replaced by social interaction, and gradually discipline was dissolved into the so-called "democratic process." Cheating on examinations has become common, much stealing goes on, and teachers and school officers rarely make an issue of the matter because of the unpleasantness it causes with the parents. While individuals here and there lift their voices in protest, general apathy to the situation has prevailed.

Making moral civilization concrete. The general trend of modern education from verbalism and abstraction to the employment of the concrete was accomplished on the intellectual side by Pestalozzi in his object lesson teaching. A similar transition is taking place in regard to moral cultivation.

The prevailing theory of moral education is that the development of character arises from the interaction of the individual with his fellows in the social environment; it comes by experiencing human relations in the various situations of active living. Intelligent participation in the realization of social ends brings a knowledge of fair play, cooperation, and subordination of individual to group interests; this is the democratic process. Self-discipline, it is contended, is not learned by obedience to injunctions or directives imposed by external authority, but by playing a role in group activity. Imposition by the teacher, parent, or government stands against the command which arises out of the end to be achieved and the means of realizing it. The end dictates the means, and because there is no ultimate goal of character, proximate ends come to justify the means. "To get by" is the principle of conduct.

Meanwhile, a profound alteration has taken place in the former method of bringing up children by participation in the work of the world. The industrial revolution transferred the arts and crafts from the home to the factory, and children no longer come into direct contact with them, much less are they engaged in them. Child labor laws still further removed children from processes of production. Agriculture also declined, and fewer children received the training that comes from engaging in meaningful occupations.

The passing of humanistic education and of religious inculcation as a basis of moral action, combined with the increased leisure time in towns and cities, has greatly weakened the moral training of the past two or three generations.

Froebel and Dewey began the transition from the old method of teaching moral behavior by means of proverbs, moral codes, ethical injunctions, and religious prescriptions to the teaching of conduct by living situations. Children learn the nature of approved personal relations, or what is the right thing to do by actual doing in interrelation with one another. Froebel utilized play, games, the orderly conduct of school, and cooperation in activities. Dewey, Hart, and the other pragmatists made use of the practical activities of life, and Burnham designated it "the task."

Socialization through institutional life. On the recreational front much progress has been made during the past decade. Interest in the philosophy of play led to the discovery of the gang spirit and its function in the unfolding of the social nature of the child. The first effort to satisfy this need, apart from the spontaneous games and play of youth, was the George Junior Republic.

Since that organization showed the way, various organizations have been formed. The most popular of these is the Boy Scouts, organized on both the national and international levels. Millions of boys have been given experience of social life and action through this organization. The Sea Scouts is organized along the same line, and the Cub Scouts extend the movement to younger boys. For the girls the Girl Scouts and Brownies have been organized.

Of similar character are the work of Boy's Town, boy's ranches, and similar groups. Innumerable less permanent organizations such as music clubs, civic clubs, athletic clubs, and summer camps, have grown up to meet the recreational and social needs of the youth. In towns and cities playgrounds, swimming pools, and other facilities have been furnished. All of these movements are highly educational and an evaluation shows their effectiveness in the social, moral, and civic, as well as the physical life, to be very great.

These movements must be formally recognized as an indispensable factor in education. The fact that some of them are organized apart from the school is an evidence that people generally have no unified concept of what constitutes a philosophy of education. The need for integration of all the forces that make an impact upon the child in the organizing of his personality has not yet been recognized. It must likewise be realized that if such experience is valuable for the children of the privileged classes, it is even more essential for the less fortunate. It is, among other things, the social poverty of the underprivileged that drives many of them into delinquency.

Several investigations in regard to character, and many books have been written on the subject but so far no consensus has been reached.[29]

THE DILEMMA OF RELIGIOUS EDUCATION

Its crucial character. The teaching of religion has always been beset by peculiar difficulties because of differences in doctrines and conflicts between the roles of family, state, and church. The prodigious changes in human affairs during the past half-century have still further increased this confusion. The secularization of the public schools of the United States and of France has been followed by unremitting discussion and agitation, because of the failure to inculcate moral principles. The Catholic Church generally, and many Protestants individually, have denounced the system. The alarming increase in crime, delinquency, sex perversion, and other forms of immorality, such as the use of narcotics by minors, are cited as reasons for its condemnation.

Failure to solve the problem. But the teaching of religion in regular state schools can hardly be held more successful in solving the problem. German educational practice placed religion first on every course

---

[29] Hartshorne, Hugh, May, Mark A., and others, *Studies in the Nature of Character: I Studies in Deceit; II Studies in Service and Self-Control; III Studies in the Organization of Character.* New York: The Macmillan Company, 1930.

Havighurst, Robert J., Taba, Hilda and others, *Adolescent Character and Personality.* New York: John Wiley and Sons, Inc., 1949.

of study and employed Protestant, Catholic, and Jewish clergymen to teach it. This method was effectual in inculcating the historic and literary facts of the Scriptures and the various religious doctrines. But who would claim that it quickened the ethical life or instilled the Christian spirit in these people even as successfully as has the American plan of secular schools?

The English have been more stubborn than any other Protestant people in adhering to church schools and a religious syllabus; but more than any other thing this very conservatism has retarded the education of the masses in England. It is a demonstrated fact that the formalized teaching of religion in the schools is not followed by an increase in church attendance or membership, or even by a high moral standard of life. To teach religion in the schools along with other subjects has invariably reduced it to the status of a formal study to be put aside and forgotten along with arithmetic, grammar, and history. Nothing but a thin and cheap veneer of Christianity has ever been imparted by this conventional approach.

In recent years the most popular method of adjusting religious instruction to the secular schools in America has been that of "released time" instruction. By this plan pupils have been excused from a class period in the school to attend religious instruction in some church or other building, the instruction being given by teachers provided by the various denominations. Children whose parents object to such instruction remain in the school. This plan of providing religious teaching was ruled unconstitutional by the Federal Supreme Court in the famous McCollum decision, in April 1948. But in that case the instruction was given in the public school building. In a more recent case from the state of New York where the teaching was not done in the school, the Supreme Court held that the constitutional amendment for the separation of church and state has not been violated. During the year 1951-52 some 1,850,000 children have been taught religion on the released time plan in the United States.

Another popular method and the only one to receive the approval of the courts is the reading of the Scriptures in the class room or school assembly. The objection to this is that Catholics and Protestants do not agree on the translation to be used, and that Jews oppose the use of the New Testament; as a consequence of the objections pupils are not required to attend this exercise.

After centuries of experiences, discussion, and effort to solve the problem of religious education, a number of conclusions are warranted: (1) Christian churches had proved so delinquent in enlightening the rational capacity of the people that their long monopoly of teaching was taken over by the states. (2) Modern states have taught Christianity in order to inculcate reverence for public morals and authority, and to perpetuate political and economic control rather than to evangelize individuals. (3) Public school religion has usually turned out to be just another curricular subject and a specious substitute for spiritual realization. It devitalizes the faith that submits to, or promotes it; and under it churches become formal and complacent, and lose their power. (4) No statement, formula, or syllabus of religious truth has been devised that is satisfactory to all Christian bodies, much less to other faiths, which all agree should be taught as a common denominator and a basis for morality. (5) In the nature of the case, state-employed teachers cannot teach Christian doctrine in a way that is acceptable to all Christian bodies. (6) No plan has yet been devised by which all church groups can teach their views in connection with the secular public schools without violating the constitutional provision of the separation of church and state. (7) The Canadian system of providing both Protestant and Catholic schools at public expense is now breaking down. (8) The European system of teaching the several creeds in the state schools is equally a violation of the rights of individual conscience. In consequence of these difficulties, the problem of religious instruction remains unsolved.

Progress in the philosophy of religious education. Colossal effort has been put forth by various Christian bodies to advance religious instruction. At the beginning of the century (1903) William Rainey Harper, President of the University of Chicago, formed the Religious Education Association which performed notable service in promoting a new and scientific interest in religious education. International organizations have more recently been formed and frequent meetings and councils have been held.

One of the most promising movements has been the establishment of departments of religious education in the Protestant seminaries for the training of ministers. Not only are candidates for the ministry required to become acquainted with religious education but a new profession of directors of religious education has been formed. Many large churches now employ these directors to promote the teaching of the Bible in the Sunday Schools and other church organizations and to direct young people's societies and daily vacation Bible schools. Many Protestant bodies have taken a deeper interest in the religious training of children and have added a department of Christian education to their regional organizations.

The Sunday school. The Sunday or Bible school movement, despite sharp criticism and contempt from many professional educators, still remains the chief means of religious inculcation in America. Evaluations of its results have varied greatly. Its effectiveness in inculcating moral principles and knowledge of Scriptures has been doubted. Nevertheless, the smaller and more evangelical bodies have employed this agency most effectively for the promotion of their work. From 80 per cent to 95 per cent of the new members of these churches are recruited from this source. The training in singing, cooperation efforts, Christian stewardship, and goodwill must be considered in any just evaluation of the school.

The daily vacation Bible school. This is a product of the 20th century. In 1901 Dr. R. G. Boville, Secretary of the New York City Baptist Ministerial Association, noticed some boys playing on the street during vacation. The thought of gathering them into the churches for instruction in Bible and also in handiwork, which had just gained some popularity, arose in his mind. The movement made an instant hit. It enrolled 1,000 students the first summer, and two years later spread to 140 cities. In 1949 over 4 million children were enrolled. In 1951 (the golden anniversary) 62,000 churches held such schools with an attendance of over 5 million children.

Uninstructed masses. Millions are being instructed by the churches but the great majority of American children are not receiving any religious teaching of any kind. This is due to the lethargy of the religious bodies.

The psychology and pedagogy of religion. Around the beginning of the century, G. Stanley Hall, Edwin Starbuck, William H. Burnham, and William James discussed the psychology of religion. Nothing much, however, has been done to provide a scientific knowledge of the origin and development of the religious emotions from the genetic viewpoint. Religious teachers have been slow to understand the various processes and experiences by which the spiritual life evolves in individuals. The sharpest diversity of views still divides the Christian world as to how the individual child becomes a Christian.

Considerable advancement has been made in the training of religious teachers, and methods of teaching have borrowed greatly from the new procedures of general education. Lesson systems have been graded to fit the mental capacity of children at different stages; visual apparatus, illustrated textbooks, pictures, drama and, to some extent, moving pictures have been utilized.

Youth movements. The past half-century has seen many efforts to meet the religious need of young people through special youth organizations such as the Young Peoples Society of Christian Endeavor (YPSCE), which was the parent of many denominational bodies. The results have varied from time to time and among the different church bodies. The universities and colleges also have recognized the need for fostering the religious spirit by special methods. But how to develop the religious nature, how to adjust religious feelings to the growing intellectual life, and what to teach in religion remains the most consequential and difficult problem of education.

Increase in church-related day schools. The increase of attendance in church and private day-schools is one of the most noteworthy phenomena during the past quarter-century, and can only be interpreted as a growing lack of confidence in public education. In 1926, 9.1 per cent of all children enrolled in schools in the United States were in church and denominational schools; in 1950 the proportion was 12 per cent. The churches enrolled 2,754,000 in the kindergarten and elementary schools and 655,000 in secondary schools. A new development is the increase in the attendance at segregated secondary schools. The great majority of these are in Catholic, Episcopal, and nonsectarian schools.

The new fact in the situation is the rapid increase in the number of elementary day-schools in the past decade conducted by Presbyterian, Baptist, and Methodist churches. Various reasons for this trend may be given: (1) the growing dissatisfaction with the lack of religious and moral training in public schools; (2) the fact that many cities do not provide kindergartens and adequate elementary school facilities; (3) the fact that churches in some parts of the country have erected and equipped large buildings for the accommodation of their Bible schools, which are not in use throughout the week. Day-schools have in many instances been organized to employ these facilities. How far this movement will go is not apparent.

The relation of the school to social progress. Aristotle took the position that education operated to sustain and perpetuate the existing government. In the 18th century, Prussian autocracy adopted the principle that the best way to control the people is by training them to be efficient farmers and producers of industrial goods. At the beginning of the 19th century, Fichte and Hegel persuaded the Prussian king to utilize the school to make obedient and intelligent subjects, and at the end of the century Emperor Wilhelm completed the movement by compelling all German schools to promote his ambitions for world conquest. There is evidence that prior to World War I the German Reich took measures to promote American neutrality by influencing public schools in all states where German residents were numerous.

Finally, the employment of the schools to promote social progress was made one of the prime functions of the pragmatic philosophy. In a series of addresses to the Progressive Education Association in 1932, George S. Counts threw down the most ringing challenge ever voiced to the teachers of America to seize the schools and use them to build "A New Social Order." It is well known that during the depression some of the universities became hotbeds of radicalism.

Even before this effort of the pragmatic philosophy to make the public school the instrument of political and economic reform, the friends of conservation had organized to wage an all-state war against high taxes for public schools. Secretly, but with utmost determination, these forces of reaction moved to secure control of education, both state and private, on all levels. Today American education, so far as its control is concerned, is apparently geared to conservatism; so far as the curriculum, methods, and aims are concerned, it is bewildered and confused.

COSMOPOLITAN EDUCATION

Nationalism versus cosmopolitanism. Education for loyalty to a particular government or ideology has always clashed with education for ecumenical citizenship. The prophet Isaiah had in view a religious fellowship that should cover the whole earth; but the priests and pharisees were rabid sectarians. Aristotle's belief that schools should train to perpetuate the existing government and his faith in the superiority of small city-states were not shared by his pupil, Alexander the Great; he preferred the view of Isocrates that Athenian culture should be made the possession of all people in the world. Jesus and Paul undertook to evangelize the whole earth to universalize the Kingdom of God. The Roman Catholic and the Greek Catholic Churches both aim at universality. Comenius' plan of Pansophism aimed "to teach all men, all things." Kant and Schiller favored cosmopolitanism, Marc Antoine Jullien, a Frenchman, and K. Chr. Fr. Krause, German philosopher in the early 19th century, strongly urged cosmopolitanism, but their messages fell on deaf ears. Pestalozzi and Froebel emphasized the "education of man" and not young Germans or Frenchmen. Unfortunately Prussian bureaucracy preferred Hegelian nationalism to universal humanitarianism. After World War I, President Woodrow Wilson promoted the formation of the League of Nations; and after World War II, the United Nations was established. Meanwhile, in 1925 a group of educators formed the International Bureau of Education with headquarters at Geneva, and later it was reorganized by the League of Nations.

Rousseau and Bertrand Russell contended that education for national patriotism and education for manhood are irreconcilable. Not only does this clash exist but what form universalism shall take is a matter of bitter dispute. Marxian Communism, the Greek and Roman Catholic Churches, and many Protestant bodies, the free enterprise economic system, world federal government, and world social democracy now contend for control of human destiny. Unfortunately for the school, it must play a leading role in preparing for the pattern which is to follow, although it cannot know which it may be.

The United Nations Educational Scientific and Cultural Organization (UNESCO). This is one of the specialized agencies of the United Nations. It arose from a feeling in England and France that some world organization is needed for the promulgation of western culture throughout the world. A conference of 44 countries was held in London in 1945 and a constitution adopted. The following year the organization was approved by the United Nations and participated in its budget. Its precise field of operation cannot be rigidly defined, but it has to do with the "life of the mind." "Since wars begin in the minds of men, it is in the minds of men that the defenses of peace must be constructed." UNESCO looks to the free sharing of cultural, scientific, and educational ideas so as to build the intellectual and moral solidarity of mankind.[30] So far it has benefited over 42,000,000 children.

Other agencies promoting cosmopolitanism. An immense number of agencies, associations, and societies have been at work during the

[30] For Constitution see *Yearbook of the United Nations,* 1946-47, pp. 712-721. Huxley, Julian, *Unesco, Its Purpose and Its Philosophy.* Washington: Public Affairs Press, 1947.

past half-century to promote cultural relations among the peoples of the earth. In 1896 the Olympic Games were revived to do for all nations what they were intended to do for Panhellenism in ancient times. The Rhodes Scholarships, Latin American Scholarships, International travelling fellowships, pupil exchange, teacher exchange at all levels, and interchange by correspondence at all school levels have gone forward at a great rate. Organizations such as the International Religious Association and Christian Missions aid in broadening the horizon and the sympathies of the Christian and non-Christian worlds.

The problem of promoting cosmopolitan democracy. The world today stands between two possible destinies, Democracy and Communism. But the task of promoting international, interracial, interclass, and interreligious good will and accord is now the supreme concern of education. Modern technology and commerce have largely eliminated all geographical lines of separation and the people inhabiting the earth are now compelled by circumstances to live and interact in closest contact. They are dependent upon each other for the things they eat, drink, wear, and use daily. Competition to control the raw materials and sources of supply is keener than ever. The problem of eliminating racial, religious, and class prejudice and hatred must be faced with every atom of astuteness and resolution that human intelligence and art can muster. Schools, homes, churches, societies, commercial interests, and every other agency must unite to meet that most gruesome of apocryphal beasts, scientific warfare.

The nature and evolution of Benevolence or Altruism. Sociologist Sorokin of Harvard has recently conducted a symposium on "altruistic love" as an antidote to war. The study of charity as an organized movement for the relief and rehabilitation of the indigent and afflicted has been going on for a long time. But little inquiry has been instituted into charitableness as a quality in the human constitution and as to its psychological nature. This inquiry is highly important and must have far-reaching consequences, provided its genetic aspect is made clear, and a method of developing it is followed in home and school.

The relation of world revolution to education. Looking at the welter of human events since the 18th century Enlightenment and the launching of the common school movement by Pestalozzi, the world has undergone the greatest transformation in all the history of man. The outstanding social phenomenon has been the awakening of the retarded masses. Literacy, contact with advanced civilization, and scientific knowledge have aroused a sense of inferiority and a desire to live the kind of life and possess the privileges enjoyed by the peoples of wealth and leisure. This has been one of the causes of the upsurging of independence the world over. It has been, moreover, at the bottom of the universal disorder of the present century. The chief point of tension has been the exploitation of the masses by the industrial and economic adventurers of free enterprise. A modicum of culture has awakened the underprivileged, but it has inculcated neither self-control nor self-help. Totalitarian governments and Communism have utilized education as a tool of ideological policy, in order to produce subservient, tractable, docile servants. After all, the obscurantist policy of the economic royalists, that is to say, the failure to educate the backward peoples of the world, was not very astute. Research has clearly shown that the more enlightened the masses become, the more goods they will consume and the greater the increase of wealth. World democracy can no longer tolerate imperialistic exploitation of the undeveloped masses.

The view has been widely accepted that human destiny is a race between education and destruction. It is now clear that the aristocratic education which began with knighthood in the Middle Ages and was reemphasized by Humanism at the Renaissance has run its course. It was nationalistic in spirit and aimed to produce a ruling class. This led to exploitation of the lower classes of people because of the superior knowledge, prestige, and power of the educated class.

About 1800 Prussia conceived the idea that the education of the masses for efficient production of goods would enhance its power. Within a century Germany became the most highly trained and industrialized country in the history of man. It lost its design for world control, however, not because of its superior education, but because of its selfishness. Germany had its chance to serve humanity, but it preferred to force humanity to serve it. Had the Germans refrained from the use of military power, they would probably have been able to lead the world. As conditions now stand, the responsibility for the future of civilization rests upon the American people. To meet that responsibility it must be recognized that moral, social, and spiritual superiority alone, not knowledge, resources, production or, military power will bring success.

Literacy at the beginning of the century. Literacy is so far the best test yet found to measure the spread of the advantages of elementary education among the masses of people. The ability to read is the beginning of the integration of world symbols and meanings which elevates the mind of the individual beyond the confines of his own narrow circle of experience. It opens a door which enables the individual to participate, if he cares to do so, in the thought of others from the earliest times to the present, and thus to enrich his experience by incalculable treasures of knowledge and wisdom. To write enables the individual to communicate with others without limitation.

The highest rate of literacy at the beginning of the century (as given by Dr. E. P. Cubberley, in Monroe, Cyclopaedia of Education) was found in Denmark (99.98 per cent), Switzerland (99.95 per cent), Sweden (97 per cent), and the German Empire, where illiteracy had been practically eliminated, except for imbeciles.

In southern European countries which did not adopt state education, the rate of illiteracy remained high in Spain (58.7 per cent), Portugal (73.4 per cent), and Italy (48.2 per cent). The same was true in eastern European countries, in Serbia (78 per cent), Roumania (64 per cent), Bulgaria (65.5 per cent), Greece (57.2 per cent), Poland (50.3 per cent), and Russia (70 per cent).

In other portions of the earth illiteracy ran still higher, in Egypt (92.7 per cent) and in India (92.5 per cent). In Latin America it varied from 54.4 per cent in Argentina to 75.3 per cent in Mexico, which was the median, to 92.7 per cent in Guatemala.

The one country which stood out conspicuously above others in the reduction of illiteracy was Japan, where it was less than 1 per cent.

Wherever the forces of conservatism prevailed the bastions of ignorance remained unbroken regardless of religion, race, or nationality. The colonies of Great Britain, Holland, Belgium, and France, so far as the native populations were concerned, remained almost totally illiterate.

The Soviet movement. At the beginning of the century Russia was a backward people retarded by a corrupt and ruthless bureaucracy and supported by a church which employed Christianity for its own ends. Less than one-third of the people had learned to read, and ignorance, superstition, and blind dependence were rife everywhere. The imperialistic regime, we are informed "did everything in its power to hamper the work of enlightenment."

After the Revolution of 1905 the progress of education along all lines, elementary, secondary, higher, and technical advanced with great rapidity. The Communists took over after 1917 and they adopted a positive and aggressive attitude toward education. It included: (1) the liquidation of illiteracy, and (2) the free and compulsory schooling of all children, beginning with the kindergarten, from three to eight years of age, and (3) the primary school from eight to 12 years of age.

The worldwide literacy movement. Frank C. Laubach, who became an American missionary to the Philippine Islands in 1915, undertook to Christianize the fierce and primitive Moro tribe, which had no written language. In attempting to give them a knowledge of how to read he hit upon a new and speedy method. So successful were his efforts that after a few years he was urged by many nations to initiate the movement among their people. Although he speaks only five or six languages, he has assisted in preparing reading charts for more than 200 peoples using different languages, and on every continent except Europe. It is held that 60 million people have learned to read because of this movement.[31]

SUMMARY OF OUTSTANDING UNSOLVED EDUCATIONAL PROBLEMS

1. **Religious instruction and development.** How the religious emotions, attitudes, and ideas, indispensable for the organization of ethical personality, may be nurtured in all children, coordinate with a system of secular public schools, constitutes the supreme problem of contemporary civilization.

2. **Wholesome sex life.** How to bring the powerful and all-important sex instinct under the control of rational ideas and hygienic practices so as to insure its most beneficent and lasting contribution to the success and happiness of the individual and society has not yet been discovered.

3. **Character cultivation.** How to sidetrack evil and criminal tendencies and to cultivate moral habits and ethical principles in children and youth still remain major problems of pedagogical science.

4. **Education for good will.** The development of democratic spirit and attitude in all human relationships has become the chief desideratum of the 20th century. This not only involves respect for other personalities, but requires the suppression of racial and class hatred and

---

[31] Laubach, Frank C., *Teaching the World to Read.* New York: Friendship Press, 1947.

———, *The Silent Million Speak.* New York: Friendship Press, 1943.

of all religious intolerance, and the positive cultivation of good will toward all people.

5. **Adequate financing of an efficient educational program.** In order that public education may make its processes effective and realize its objectives, adequate finances must be available. The amount now expendable for the education of children is wholly inadequate; to insure a system commensurate with the need will require from two to three times the present portion of the annual income allocated for the schools.

6. **The teaching staff and administrators.** The recruiting, training, and maintaining of professional instructors and administrators is obviously imperative. The program of teacher training is increasing in difficulty because of the unprecedented growth of pedagogical science and the increased complexity of the educative art. The aversion on the part of young people who possess the talent for the task of the school has become more acute as other fields that do not have the handicaps of the teaching profession multiply.

7. **Education of minority groups.** The two sorest points in this area are the segregation of Negro children and youth, and the inequality of education given Latin Americans in the Southwest.

The facilities for Negro education in the Southern States, despite legal provisions guaranteeing equal provision, have never been more than a sorry makeshift to satisfy temporary conditions. Public funds for schools have never been distributed equitably, nor have facilities and teachers been at all adequate. The recent demand for the abolition of segregation has been based on three unanswerable considerations: 1. Negroes are full-fledged citizens and the Federal Constitution as well as the principles of democracy require the right of equality of educational opportunity. 2. The very idea of segregation connotes inferiority or disqualification. The rulings recently handed down by the Federal Supreme Court so far have favored the abolition of segregation but they have all had reference to particular cases. These rulings have led to the admission of Negroes to graduate and professional study at a number of southern state universities. The main issue of segregation lies in public elementary and high schools and state colleges, and this has just been placed before the Federal Supreme Court in a case brought against the school authorities of Clarendon County, South Carolina. 3. World-wide criticism, especially from Communists and Asiatic peoples points up the inconsistency of the American theory and practice.

The problem of race discrimination is even more acute in South Africa, where the small proportion of non-native whites is opposed to the native Negroes, and the Negroes are opposed to large colonies of Hindus.

8. **The reorganization of the schools.** From the standpoint of a system of schools commensurate with the needs of contemporary civilization, a number of reorganizations are required. In cities and towns, nurseries and kindergartens must be made available for those children both of whose parents are engaged in labor. Moreover schools must keep children employed through the working day unless they are looked after by parents. Schools must be in operation twelve months of the year. Whenever children can be cared for by a parent they can be released from school earlier in the day and for a prolonged vacation. The unsupervised time of children after school hours and during the summer months is a serious weakness in the present organization of education.

American civilization is now confronted by a situation where the great industrial machine and the other vocations will not employ youth before 18 or 20 years of age. This condition requires that the schools keep them occupied with educational tasks up to maturity. The completion point of education for the vast majority of the young people must be advanced two years beyond the high school.

The reorganization of the schools for adolescents is the point of greatest consequence. The 6-3-3-2 program is seriously in need of revision. To be effective in the organization of personality and the forming of habits the program must have more time. The 6-4-4 or a 5-5-4 program offers much more likelihood of success, but it requires that the curriculum be broadened and general and vocational education be coordinated.

It is an unfortunate circumstance that the movements for recreation and for camping have been divorced from regular education. Recreation should be made an integral part of the schedule of children and youth.

9. **Physical and health education.** Whether the physical stamina of western peoples is increasing or decreasing is not known; there is reason to suspect that the western world is becoming more and more neurotic and psychotic. The number of mental patients has increased alarmingly. It would seem that a correct system of education ought to make the human body the perfect vehicle of the mind and personality, but such is far from the case. Medical science is more intent upon curing diseases than upon preventing them, except in the case of the great pestilences.

Concern for the physical development of children and youth has been lagging behind our interest in their mental development.

10. **Education for leisure.** The preparation of the individual for the most profitable use of leisure has not occupied attention to the extent it deserves. As the life-span increases more need arises for preparation to spend the years of leisure in a satisfactory way.

11. **Citizenship.** Preparation for the discharge of civic responsibilities has always been the primary argument for public education. So far the program of the schools has not succeeded to a high degree in producing the functional citizen.

12. **Education for parenthood.** The power of the home for the upgrading of the ethical life of the child must be made paramount. The competence of the home to influence the minds and hearts of the children against the downward pull of the environment must be reinforced by the help of science. To make sure that the home influences are sound and efficient, young people must be definitely trained to discharge the parental function.

13. **Education for social progress.** The school must condition children so that in adult life they will bring about normal social progress. For the teacher to utilize the school either to maintain the *status quo* or to propagandize children in favor of radical measures to build a new social order is to be recreant to the trust imposed in him.

14. **Individual differences.** The arranging of the schedule of school subjects to fit the rate of progress or the capacities of each child has been attempted but remains unsolved. Again, all capabilities of the child do not develop uniformly, that is, at the same rate. He may need to be in a number of different grades according to his advancement in each subject.

15. **A philosophy of education.** As the people of all parts of the world become aware of the power of education to control the forces of nature for their own ends, and also to make human society what it ought to be, the necessity increases to base the philosophy of education on principles that are common to all humanity, and that will build an ecumenical world order. The trend toward democracy in government during the past 50 years has been phenomenal. Since the beginning of the century some 70 countries have recognized suffrage in their constitutions. This recognition that government must be grounded on the consent of the governed has become the pillar of fire to guide backward humanity from darkness to light.

The recognition of the power of education on the one hand led autocratic governments to employ the school to perpetuate totalitarian control of the masses, but on the other it has led to the enlightenment of the voters regarding their rights and how to govern with intelligence. In planning for the future, it is essential to keep in mind that technology has unified the world; now it is imperative by means of education to unify the hearts and wills of humankind.[32]

---

[32] Monroe, Walter S., Editor, *Encyclopaedia of Educational Research,* Revised Edition. New York: The Macmillan Company, 1950.

Meyer, Adolph E., *The Development of Education in the Twentieth Century,* Second Edition. New York: Prentice-Hall, Inc., 1949.

Edwards, Newton, and Richey, Herman G., *The School in the American Social Order, The Dynamics of American Education.* Boston: Houghton Mifflin Company, 1947.

INDEX